Guide to College Reading

W9-AZL-644

Guide to College Reading

TENTH EDITION

Kathleen T. McWhorter
Niagara County Community College

PEARSON

Boston Columbus Indianapolis New York San Francisco Upper Saddle River
Amsterdam Cape Town Dubai London Madrid Milan Munich Paris Montréal Toronto
Delhi Mexico City São Paulo Sydney Hong Kong Seoul Singapore Taipei Tokyo

Editor-in-Chief: Eric Stano
Senior Development Editor: Gillian Cook
Freelance Editor: Phoebe Mathews
Senior Supplements Editor: Donna Campion
Executive Digital Producer: Stefanie Snajder
Digital Editor: Sara Gordus
Executive Marketing Manager: Roxanne McCarley
Production Manager: Denise Phillip Grant
Project Coordination, Text Design, and Electronic Page Makeup: PreMediaGlobal
Cover Design Manager/Cover Designer: John Callahan
Cover Image: Corey Rich/Getty Images
Text Permissions: Aptara
Photo Researcher: Integra
Senior Manufacturing Buyer: Dennis Para
Printer and Binder: R. R. Donnelley/Crawfordsville
Cover Printer: Lehigh-Phoenix Color/Hagerstown

Credits and acknowledgments borrowed from other sources and reproduced, with permission, in this textbook appear on the appropriate page within text [or on pages 503–515].

Library of Congress Cataloging-in-Publication Data

McWhorter, Kathleen T.
Guide to college reading / Kathleen T. McWhorter, Niagara County Community College.—Tenth edition.
pages cm.
Includes index.
ISBN-13: 978-0-321-92145-1 (alk. paper)
ISBN-10: 0-321-92145-3 (alk. paper)
1. Reading (Higher education) 2. Study skills. 3. Reading (Higher education)—Problems, exercises, etc. I. Title.
LB2395.3.M39 2013
428.4071'1—dc23
2013038814

Copyright © 2015, 2012, 2009, 2007 by Pearson Education, Inc. All rights reserved. Manufactured in the United States of America. This publication is protected by Copyright, and permission should be obtained from the publisher prior to any prohibited reproduction, storage in a retrieval system, or transmission in any form or by any means, electronic, mechanical, photocopying, recording, or likewise. To obtain permission(s) to use material from this work, please submit a written request to Pearson Education, Inc., Permissions Department, One Lake Street, Upper Saddle River, New Jersey 07458, or you may fax your request to 201-236-3290.

10 9 8 7 6 5 4 3 2 1—DOC—15 14 13

PEARSON

Student Edition ISBN 13: 978-0-321-92145-1
Student Edition ISBN 10: 0-321-92145-3
A la Carte Edition ISBN-13: 978-0-321-96001-6
A la Carte Edition ISBN-10: 0-321-96001-7

Brief Contents

Detailed Contents

Part V: Critical Reading Skills 352

Part VI: A Fiction Minireader 430

Preface

Guide to College Reading, Tenth Edition, is written to equip students of widely different backgrounds with the basic textbook reading and critical-thinking skills they need to cope with the demands of academic work.

NEW TO THE TENTH EDITION

Numerous changes and additions have been made in this tenth edition in response to changing student needs.

1. **Revised Chapter 1 "Reading and Learning: Getting Started."** This chapter has been refocused to emphasize skills students need to get started in college. Topics new to this chapter include reading and thinking visually, using writing to learn, and learning from and with other students.
2. **Revised Chapter 2 "The Basics of College Textbook Reading."** This chapter now offers a stronger emphasis on textbook reading. It begins by discussing textbook aids to learning and then focuses on previewing, developing guide questions, reading for meaning, testing recall, and reviewing. The chapter unifies the reading and learning strategies presented in the chapter by showing students how these skills, when used in sequence, form the SQ3R reading/study system.
3. **Numerous passages, reading selections, and examples.** More than fifty reading passages, sample paragraphs, and examples have been replaced throughout the book to provide relevant and current reading material. Seven full-length reading selections (Mastery Test 3) have been replaced. New topics include the allure of disaster, dating, the value of darkness, the reasons for declining marriage rates, and reality television.
4. **Issues in the Contemporary Issues Reader.** The Contemporary Issues Minireader contains three new selections on the topics of football violence, discrimination against women, and teachers texting students.

5. **Pro-Con Readings in the Contemporary Issues Minireader.** Two pairs of pro–con readings offer students the opportunity to compare and synthesize ideas on each of two topics. The first pair of readings examines the issue of gun ownership, and the second pair considers the issue of reviving extinct species. Each pair of readings culminates with questions that encourage students to discuss, respond to, and react to the issues, drawing ideas from both readings.

MyReadingLab

6. **Mastery Tests can now be completed in MyReadingLab.** All of the exercises in the three mastery tests at the end of each chapter can now be completed online through MyReadingLab, allowing students to complete and submit them online with the results flowing into the Instructor Gradebook.

THE PURPOSE OF THIS TEXT

Guide to College Reading, Tenth Edition, addresses the learning characteristics, attitudes, and motivational levels of college students. It is intended to equip them with the skills they need to handle the diverse reading demands of college coursework. Specifically, the book guides students in becoming active learners and critical thinkers. Using an encouraging, supportive, nonthreatening voice, the text provides clear instruction and a variety of everyday examples and extensive exercises that encourage students to become involved and apply the skills presented.

The chapters are divided into numerous sections; exercises are frequent but brief and explicit. The language and style are simple and direct; explanations are clear and often presented in step-by-step form. Reading topics and materials have been chosen carefully to relate to students' interests and background, while broadening their range of experience. Many students have compensated for poor reading skills with alternative learning styles; they have become visual and auditory learners. To capitalize on this adaptation, a visual approach to learning is used throughout. The importance of visual literacy in today's world is emphasized by numerous photographs—many with bubble captions designed to provoke thought about how the visuals are used to enhance and add meaning to text—drawings, diagrams, and other visual aids used to illustrate concepts.

CONTENT OVERVIEW

The text is organized into seven major sections, following the logical progression of skill development from vocabulary development to reading paragraphs, articles, essays, and chapters. It also proceeds logically from literal comprehension to critical interpretation and response. An opening chapter focuses on student success strategies, including such topics as attitudes toward college, concentration, learning styles, and comprehension monitoring.

- **Part One presents the basics for success in college reading.**
- **Part Two teaches students basic approaches to vocabulary development.** It includes contextual aids, analysis of word parts, pronunciation, and the use of a dictionary and other reference sources.
- **Part Three helps students develop literal comprehension skills.** It emphasizes prereading techniques that prepare and enable the student to comprehend and to recall content. Previewing, activating background knowledge, and using guide questions are emphasized. The unit provides extensive instruction and practice with paragraph comprehension and recognition of thought patterns. An entire chapter is devoted to stated and implied main ideas; another entire chapter focuses on supporting details and transitions.
- **Part Four teaches students textbook reading skills.** Topics include ways to read graphics and technical material, reading and evaluating Internet sources, and methods of organizing and retaining course content.
- **Part Five introduces critical reading and thinking skills.** It presents skills that enable students to interact with and evaluate written material, including material on the Internet. Topics include making inferences, identifying the author's purpose, recognizing assumptions, and distinguishing between fact and opinion.
- **Part Six, "A Fiction Minireader," offers a brief introduction to reading fiction.** An introductory section discusses the essential elements of a short story, using Chopin's "The Story of an Hour" as an example. Two additional short stories with accompanying apparatus are also included, as well as an introduction to reading novels.
- **Part Seven, "A Contemporary Issues Minireader," contains four articles on single contemporary issues and two pro–con paired readings.** Each reading is prefaced by an interest-catching introduction, prereading questions, and a vocabulary preview. Literal and critical-thinking questions as well as a words-in-context exercise, vocabulary review, summary exercise, and writing exercises follow each selection. The pro–con pairs culminate with an activity that encourages students to integrate and synthesize ideas from both readings.

SPECIAL FEATURES

The following features enhance the text's effectiveness and directly contribute to students' success:

- **Integration of reading and writing.** The text integrates reading and writing skills. Students respond to exercises by writing sentences and paragraphs.

Each reading selection is followed by "Thinking Critically about the Reading" questions, which encourage composition. Writing exercises accompany each reading selection in Part Seven.

- **Reading as thinking.** Reading is approached as a thinking process—a process in which the student interacts with textual material and sorts, evaluates, and reacts to its organization and content. For example, students are shown how to define their purpose for reading, ask questions, identify and use organization and structure as a guide to understanding, make inferences, and interpret and evaluate what they read.
- **Comprehension monitoring.** Comprehension monitoring is also addressed within the text. Through a variety of techniques, students are encouraged to be aware of and to evaluate and control their level of comprehension of the material they read.
- **Skill application.** Chapters 2 through 11 conclude with three mastery tests that enable students to apply the skills taught in each chapter and to evaluate their learning.
- **Lexile Levels for All Readings** Lexile® measure—the most widely used reading metric in U.S. schools—provides valuable information about a student's reading ability and the complexity of text. It helps match students with reading resources and activities that are targeted to their ability level. Lexile measures indicate the reading levels of content in MyReadingLab and the longer selections in the Annotated Instructor's Editions of all Pearson's reading books. See the Annotated Instructor's Edition of *Guide to College Reading* and the Instructor's Manual for more details.

BOOK-SPECIFIC ANCILLARY MATERIALS

- **Annotated Instructor's Edition** The Annotated Instructor's Edition is identical to the student text but includes all answers printed directly on the pages where questions, exercises, or activities occur. (ISBN: 0-321-95984-1)
- **Downloadable Instructor's Manual/Test Bank** An Instructor's Manual, including an Answer Key, accompanies the text. The manual describes in detail the basic features of the text and offers suggestions for structuring the course, for teaching nontraditional students, and for approaching each section of the text. The test bank section features two sets of chapter quizzes and a mastery test for each chapter. (ISBN: 0-321-96006-8)
- **PowerPoint Presentations** For the lab or electronic classroom, a PowerPoint presentation is available for each chapter of *Guide to College Reading*. Each chapter's presentation consists of slides highlighting key concepts from the text, as well as additional activities. They are available for download from the Instructor Resource Center.

MyReadingLab

- **MyReadingLab Where better practice makes better readers!**
  - Built on ease of use, a wealth of practice opportunity, and extensive progress tracking, MyReadingLab offers skill remediation across four levels of difficulty. MyReadingLab is the only product that improves students' reading via two practice engines: Reading Skills, mastery based skill practice offering Practice and Test exercises sets across 26 skill topics, and Reading Level, the Lexile® framework (www.Lexile.com) that measures both reader ability and text difficulty on the same scale to match students with readings within their Lexile range and monitor their progress.
  - Over the better part of a decade, MyReadingLab has been the most widely used online learning application for reading improvement, with almost 1 million student registrations across two- and four-year institutions. We have published case studies and multiple surveys demonstrating how MyReadingLab consistently benefits students' mastery of key reading skills, reading comprehension, and critical thinking.
- *Expanding Your Vocabulary*. Instructors may choose to shrink-wrap *Guide to College Reading* with a copy of *Expanding Your Vocabulary.* This book, written by Kathleen McWhorter, works well as a supplemental text by providing additional instruction and practice in vocabulary. Students can work through the book independently, or units may be incorporated into weekly lesson plans. Topics covered include methods of vocabulary learning, contextual aids, word parts, connotative meanings, idioms, euphemisms, and many more fun and interesting topics. The book concludes with vocabulary lists and exercises representative of 11 academic disciplines. To preview the book, contact your Pearson sales representative for an examination copy.

ACKNOWLEDGMENTS

I wish to express my gratitude to my reviewers for their excellent ideas, suggestions, and advice on this and previous editions of this text: Alfradene Armstrong, Tougaloo College; Carla Bell, Henry Ford Community College; Michelle Biferie, Palm Beach Community College; Dorothy Booher, Florida Community College at Jacksonville, Kent Campus; Diane Bosco, Suffolk County Community College; Sheila Bunker, State Fair Community College; Sharon Cellemme, South Piedmont Community College; Beth Childress, Armstrong Atlantic University; Pam Drell, Oakton Community College, Des Plaines Campus; Mindy Flowers, Midland College; Marty Frailey, Pima Community College Downtown Campus; Deborah Paul Fuller, Bunker Hill Community College; Shirley Hall, Middle Georgia College; Pam Hallene, Community College of Rhode Island; Kevin Hayes, Essex County College; Peggy Hopper, Walters State Community College; Danica Hubbard, College of DuPage; Suzanne

E. Hughes, Florida Community College at Jacksonville; Jacqueline Jackson, Art Institute of Philadelphia; Sharon Jackson, Lone Star College; Arlene Jellinek, Palm Beach Community College; Mahalia H. Johnson, Greenville Technical College; O. Brian Kaufman, Quinebaug Valley Community College; Jeanne Keefe, Belleville Area College; Patti Levine-Brown, Florida Community College at Jacksonville; Beulah W. Lowder, Fort Valley State University; Wendy McBride, Kishwaukee Community College; Anne Mueller, Kishwaukee Community College; Sharyn Neuwirth, Montgomery College, Tacoma Park Campus; Bernard L. Ngovo, Pima Community College; Alice Nitta, Leeward Community College; Pauline Noznick, Oakton Community College; Jean Olsen, Oakton Community College; Catherine Packard, Southeastern Illinois College; Elizabeth Parks, Kishwaukee College; Kathy Purswell, Frank Phillips College; Regina Rochford, Queensborough Community College, CUNY; Diane Schellack, Burlington County College; Marilyn Schenk, San Diego Mesa College; Jackie Stahlecker, St. Phillips College; Cynthia Taber, Schenectady County Community College, SUNY; Marie Ulmen, Harrisburg Area Community College; Pam Walsh, Schenectady County Community College, SUNY; Mary Wolting, Indiana University–Purdue University at Indianapolis; and Nora Yaeger, Cedar Valley College.

I am particularly indebted to Gillian Cook, Senior Development Editor, for overseeing this project, to Phoebe Mathews for her valuable assistance in developing and producing the manuscript, and to Eric Stano, Editor-in-Chief, Developmental Reading and Writing, for his enthusiastic support of this project.

KATHLEEN T. MCWHORTER

CHAPTER 1

Reading and Learning: Getting Started

Focusing on... College Success

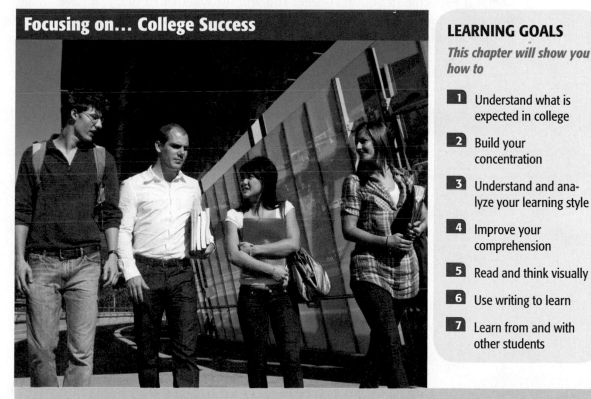

LEARNING GOALS

This chapter will show you how to

1. Understand what is expected in college
2. Build your concentration
3. Understand and analyze your learning style
4. Improve your comprehension
5. Read and think visually
6. Use writing to learn
7. Learn from and with other students

Your first semester of college is often the most difficult because you don't know what to expect. The classes you have selected are challenging and your instructors are demanding. This chapter will help you discover how to learn most effectively and help you approach the reading and study demands of your courses successfully.

College is very different from any other type of educational experience. It is different from high school, job training programs, adult education, and technical training programs. New and different types of learning are demanded, and you need new skills and techniques to meet these demands.

UNDERSTAND WHAT IS EXPECTED IN COLLEGE

1 LEARNING GOAL Understand what is expected in college

Following is a list of statements about college. Treat them like a quiz, if you wish. Decide whether each statement is true or false, and write *T* for true or *F* for false in the space provided. Each statement will make you think about the reading and study demands of college. Check your answers by reading the paragraph following each item. As you work through this quiz, you will find out a little about what is expected of you in college. You will see whether or not you have an accurate picture of what college work involves. You will also see how this text will help you to become a better, more successful student.

______ 1. For every hour I spend in class, I should spend one hour studying outside of class.

Many students feel that even one hour for each class (or 15 hours per week for students carrying a 15 credit-hour load) is a lot. Actually, the rule of thumb used by many instructors is two hours of study for each class hour. So you can see that you are expected to do a great deal of reading, studying, and learning on your own time. The purpose of this text is to help you read and learn in the easiest and best way for you.

______ 2. I should expect to read about 80 textbook pages per week in each of my courses.

A survey of freshman courses at one college indicated that the average course assignment was roughly 80 pages per week. This may seem like a lot of reading—and it is. You will need to build your reading skills to handle this task. To help you do this, techniques for understanding and remembering what you read, improving your concentration, and handling difficult reading assignments will be suggested throughout this book.

______ 3. There are a lot of words I do not know, but my vocabulary is about as good as it needs to be.

For each college course you take, there will be new words to learn. Some will be everyday words; others will be specialized or technical. Part Two of this book will show you how to develop your vocabulary by learning new words, figuring out words you do not know, and using reference sources.

_______ 4. College instructors will tell me exactly what to learn for each exam.

College instructors seldom tell you exactly what to learn or review. They expect you to decide what is important and to learn that information. In Part Three of this text you will learn how to identify what is important in sentences and paragraphs and how to follow authors' thought patterns.

_______ 5. The more facts I memorize, the higher my exam grades will be.

Learning a large number of facts is no guarantee of a high grade in a course. Some instructors and the exams they give are concerned with your ability to see how facts and ideas fit together, or to evaluate ideas, make comparisons, and recognize trends. Parts Three and Four of this text will help you to do this by showing you how to read textbook chapters, use graphic aids, and organize and remember information.

_______ 6. The only assignments that instructors give are readings in the textbook.

Instructors often assign readings in a variety of sources including periodicals, newspapers, reference and library books, and online sources. These readings are intended to add to the information presented in your text and by your instructor. The six reading selections contained in Part Seven will give you the opportunity to practice and apply your skills to readings taken from a variety of sources. These selections are similar to the outside readings your instructors will assign.

_______ 7. Rereading a textbook chapter is the best way to prepare for an exam on that chapter.

Rereading is actually one of the poorest ways to review. Besides, it is often dull and time-consuming. In Chapter 9, you will learn about four more-effective alternatives: *highlighting and marking, outlining, mapping,* and *summarizing*.

_______ 8. College instructors expect me to react to, evaluate, and criticize what I read.

Beyond understanding the content of textbooks, articles, and essays, students need to be able to criticize and evaluate ideas.

To help you read and think critically, Part Five of this text will show you how to interpret what you read, find the author's purpose, and ask critical questions.

______ 9. The best way to read a textbook assignment is to turn to the correct page, start reading, and continue until you reach the end of the assignment.

There are numerous things you can do before you read, while you read, and after you read that can improve your comprehension and retention. These techniques for improving your comprehension and recall are presented throughout this text. For example, later in this chapter you will learn techniques for building your concentration. In Chapter 2 you will be shown how to preview, think about what you will read, and use questions to guide your reading. Chapter 9 focuses on techniques to use after you read to strengthen comprehension and recall.

______ 10. You can never know whether you have understood a textbook reading assignment until you take an exam on the chapter.

As you read, it is possible and important to keep track of and evaluate your level of understanding. You will learn how to keep track of your comprehension, recognize comprehension signals, and strengthen your comprehension.

By analyzing the above statements and the correct responses, you can see that college is a lot of work, much of which you must do on your own. However, college is also a new, exciting experience that will acquaint you with new ideas and opportunities.

This text will help you to get the most out of college and to take advantage of the opportunities it offers. Its purpose is to equip you with the reading and learning skills necessary for academic success.

The opportunity of college lies ahead of you. The skills you are about to learn, along with plenty of hard work, will make your college experience a meaningful and valuable one.

BUILD YOUR CONCENTRATION

2 LEARNING GOAL
Build your concentration

Do you have difficulty concentrating? If so, you are like many other college students who say that lack of concentration is the main reason they cannot read or study effectively. Building concentration involves two steps: (1) controlling your surroundings, and (2) focusing your attention.

Controlling Your Surroundings

Poor concentration is often the result of distractions caused by the time and place you have chosen to study. Here are a few ideas to help you overcome poor concentration:

Controlling Distractions

1. **Choose a place to read where you will not be interrupted.** If people interrupt you at home or in the dormitory, try the campus library.
2. **Find a place that is relatively free of distractions and temptations.** Avoid places with outside noise, friends, a television set, or an interesting project close at hand.
3. **Silence your cell phone and ignore texts.** If left on, these will break your concentration and cost you time.
4. **Read in the same place each day.** Eventually you will get in the habit of reading there, and concentration will become easier, almost automatic.
5. **Do not read where you are too comfortable.** It is easy to lose concentration, become drowsy, or fall asleep when you are too relaxed.
6. **Choose a time of day when you are mentally alert.** Concentration is easier if you are not tired, hungry, or drowsy.

Focusing Your Attention

Even if you follow these suggestions, you may still find it difficult to become organized and stick with your reading. This takes self-discipline, but the following suggestions may help:

Strengthening Your Concentration

1. **Set goals and time limits for yourself.** Before you begin a reading assignment, decide how long it should take, and check to see that you stay on schedule. Before you start an evening of homework, write down what you plan to do and how long each assignment should take. Sample goals for an evening are shown in Figure 1-1 on the following page.

10/20	
Eng. paper–revise	$\frac{1}{2}$ hr.
Math probs. 1–10	1 hr.
Sociology read pp. 70–82	1 hr.

Figure 1-1 Goals and time limits

2. **Choose and reserve blocks of time each day for reading and study.** Write down what you will study in each time block each day or evening. Working at the same time each day establishes a routine and makes concentration a bit easier.
3. **Vary your reading.** For instance, instead of spending an entire evening on one subject, work for one hour on each of three subjects.
4. **Reward yourself for accomplishing things as planned.** Delay entertainment until after you have finished studying. Use such things as ordering a pizza, texting a friend, or watching a favorite TV program as rewards after you have completed several assignments.
5. **Plan frequent breaks.** Do this at sensible points in your reading—between chapters or after major chapter divisions.
6. **Keep physically as well as mentally active.** Try highlighting, underlining, or making summary notes as you read (see Chapter 9). These activities will focus your attention on the assignment.

EXERCISE 1-1 Analyzing Your Level of Concentration

Directions: Answer each of the following questions as honestly as you can. They will help you analyze problems with concentration. Discuss your answers with others in your class.

1. Where do you read and study? ______________________

   What interruptions, if any, occur there? Do you need to find a better place? If so, list a few alternatives.

   ____

   ____

2. How frequently do you respond to text messages? Do you ever turn your phone off while studying? ______________________

   ____

3. What is the best time of day for you to read? (If you do not know, experiment with different times until you begin to see a pattern.)

4. How long do you normally read without a break?

5. What type of distraction bothers you the most?

6. On average, how many different assignments do you work on in one evening?

7. What types of rewards might work for you?

EXERCISE 1-2 Identifying Distractions

Directions: As you read your next textbook assignment, either for this course or for another, be alert for distractions. Each time your mind wanders, try to identify the source of the distraction. List in the space provided the cause of each break in your concentration and a way to eliminate each, if possible.

EXERCISE 1-3 Setting Goals

Directions: Before you begin your next study session, make a list in the space provided of what you intend to accomplish and how long you should spend on each task.

	Assignment	Time
1.		
2.		
3.		

ANALYZE YOUR LEARNING STYLE

3 LEARNING GOAL Understand and analyze your learning style

Reading assignments are the primary focus of many college classes. Instructors give daily or weekly textbook assignments. You are expected to read the material, learn it, and pass tests on it. Class lectures and discussions are often based on textbook assignments. An important part of many college classes, then, is completing reading assignments.

Reading and understanding an assignment, however, does not mean you have learned it. In fact, if you have read an assignment once, you probably have *not* learned it. You need to do more than read to learn an assignment. Your question, then, is "What else should I do?" The answer is not a simple one.

Not everyone learns in the same way. In fact, everyone has his or her own individual way of learning, which is called *learning style*. The following section contains a brief Learning Style Questionnaire that will help you analyze how you learn and prepare an action plan for learning what you read.

Learning Style Questionnaire

Directions: Each item presents two choices. Select the alternative that best describes you. In cases in which neither choice suits you, select the one that is closer to your preference. Write the letter of your choice in the space provided.

Part One

______ 1. I would prefer to follow a set of
a. oral directions.
b. print directions.

______ 2. I would prefer to
a. attend a lecture given by a famous psychologist.
b. read an online article written by the psychologist.

______ 3. When I am introduced to someone, it is easier for me to remember the person's
a. name.
b. face.

______ 4. I find it easier to learn new information using
a. language (words).
b. images (pictures).

______ 5. I prefer classes in which the instructor
a. lectures and answers questions.
b. uses PowerPoint illustrations and videos.

______ 6. To follow current events, I would prefer to
 a. listen to the news on the radio.
 b. read the newspaper.

______ 7. To learn how to repair a flat tire, I would prefer to
 a. listen to a friend's explanation.
 b. watch a demonstration.

Part Two

______ 8. I prefer to
 a. work with facts and details.
 b. construct theories and ideas.

______ 9. I would prefer a job involving
 a. following specific instructions.
 b. reading, writing, and analyzing.

______ 10. I prefer to
 a. solve math problems using a formula.
 b. discover why the formula works.

______ 11. I would prefer to write a term paper explaining
 a. how a process works.
 b. a theory.

______ 12. I prefer tasks that require me to
 a. follow careful, detailed instructions.
 b. use reasoning and critical analysis.

______ 13. For a criminal justice course, I would prefer to
 a. discover how and when a law can be used.
 b. learn how and why it became law.

______ 14. To learn more about the operation of a robot, I would prefer to
 a. work with several robots.
 b. understand the principles on which they operate.

Part Three

______ 15. To solve a math problem, I would prefer to
 a. draw or visualize the problem.
 b. study a sample problem and use it as a model.

______ 16. To best remember something, I
 a. create a mental picture.
 b. write it down.

_______ 17. Assembling a bicycle from a diagram would be
a. easy.
b. challenging.

_______ 18. I prefer classes in which I
a. handle equipment or work with models.
b. participate in a class discussion.

_______ 19. To understand and remember how a machine works, I would
a. draw a diagram.
b. write notes.

_______ 20. I enjoy
a. drawing or working with my hands.
b. speaking, writing, and listening.

_______ 21. If I were trying to locate an office on an unfamiliar campus, I would prefer
a. a map.
b. print directions.

Part Four

_______ 22. For a grade in biology lab, I would prefer to
a. work with a lab partner.
b. work alone.

_______ 23. When faced with a difficult personal problem, I prefer to
a. discuss it with others.
b. resolve it myself.

_______ 24. Many instructors could improve their classes by
a. including more discussion and group activities.
b. allowing students to work on their own more frequently.

_______ 25. When listening to a lecturer or speaker, I respond more to the
a. person presenting the idea.
b. ideas themselves.

_______ 26. When on a team project, I prefer to
a. work with several team members.
b. divide the tasks and complete those assigned to me.

_______ 27. I prefer to shop and do errands
a. with friends.
b. by myself.

_______ 28. A job in a busy office is
a. more appealing than working alone.
b. less appealing than working alone.

Part Five

_______ 29. To make decisions, I rely on
a. my experiences and gut feelings.
b. facts and objective data.

_______ 30. To complete a task, I
a. can use whatever is available to get the job done.
b. must have everything I need at hand.

_______ 31. I prefer to express my ideas and feelings through
a. music, song, or poetry.
b. direct, concise language.

_______ 32. I prefer instructors who
a. allow students to be guided by their own interests.
b. make their expectations clear and explicit.

_______ 33. I tend to
a. challenge and question what I hear and read.
b. accept what I hear and read.

_______ 34. I prefer
a. essay exams.
b. objective exams.

_______ 35. In completing an assignment, I prefer to
a. figure out my own approach.
b. be told exactly what to do.

To score your questionnaire, record the total number of *a*'s you selected and the total number of *b*'s for each part of the questionnaire. Record your totals in the scoring grid provided at the top of the next page.

Now, circle your higher score for each part of the questionnaire. The word below the score you circled indicates a strength of your learning style. The next section explains how to interpret your scores.

Interpreting Your Scores

The questionnaire was divided into five parts; each part identifies one aspect of your learning style. Each of these five aspects is explained below.

Part One: Auditory or Visual Learners This score indicates whether you learn better by listening (auditory) or by seeing (visual). If you have a higher auditory than visual score, you tend to be an auditory learner. That is, you tend to learn more easily by hearing than by reading. A higher visual score

Scoring Grid

Parts	Choice A Total	Choice B Total
Part One	____________ Auditory	____________ Visual
Part Two	____________ Applied	____________ Conceptual
Part Three	____________ Spatial	____________ Verbal
Part Four	____________ Social	____________ Independent
Part Five	____________ Creative	____________ Pragmatic

suggests strengths with visual modes of learning—reading, studying pictures, reading diagrams, and so forth.

Part Two: Applied or Conceptual Learners This score describes the types of learning tasks and learning situations you prefer and find easiest to handle. If you are an applied learner, you prefer tasks that involve real objects and situations. Practical, real-life examples are ideal for you. If you are a conceptual learner, you prefer to work with language and ideas; you do not need practical applications for understanding.

Part Three: Spatial or Verbal (Nonspatial) Learners This score reveals your ability to work with spatial relationships. Spatial learners are able to visualize or mentally see how things work or how they are positioned in space. Their strengths may include drawing, assembling, or repairing things. Verbal learners lack skills in positioning things in space. Instead they rely on verbal or language skills.

Part Four: Social or Independent Learners This score reveals whether you like to work alone or with others. If you are a social learner, you prefer to work with others—both classmates and instructors—closely and directly. You tend to be people oriented and enjoy personal interaction. If you are an independent learner, you prefer to work alone and study alone. You tend to be self-directed or self-motivated and are often goal oriented.

Part Five: Creative or Pragmatic Learners This score describes the approach you prefer to take toward learning tasks. Creative learners are imaginative and innovative. They prefer to learn through discovery or experimentation. They are comfortable taking risks and following hunches. Pragmatic learners are practical, logical, and systematic. They seek order and are comfortable following rules.

Evaluating Your Scores

If you disagree with any part of the Learning Style Questionnaire, go with your own instincts rather than the questionnaire results. The questionnaire is just a quick assessment; trust your knowledge of yourself in areas of dispute.

Developing a Learning Action Plan

Now that you know more about *how* you learn, you are ready to develop an action plan for learning what you read. Suppose you discovered that you are an auditory learner. You still have to read your assignments, which is a visual task. However, to learn the assignment you should translate the material into an auditory form. For example, you could repeat aloud, using your own words, information that you want to remember, or you could record key information and play it back. If you also are a social learner, you could work with a classmate, testing each other out loud.

Table 1-1 lists each aspect of learning style and offers suggestions for how to learn from a reading assignment.

TABLE 1-1 Learning Styles and Reading/Learning Strategies

If your learning style is ...	Then the reading/learning strategies to use are ...
Auditory	• discuss/study with friends • talk aloud when studying • record self-testing questions and answers
Visual	• draw diagrams, charts, tables (Chapter 9) • try to visualize events • use films and videos, when available • use computer-assisted instruction, if available
Applied	• think of practical situations to which learning applies • associate ideas with their application • use case studies, examples, and applications to cue your learning

(Continued)

TABLE 1-1 Learning Styles and Reading/Learning Strategies

If your learning style is ...	Then the reading/learning strategies to use are ...
Conceptual	• organize materials that lack order • use outlining (Chapter 9) • focus on organizational patterns (Chapter 7)
Spatial	• use mapping (Chapter 9) • use outlining (Chapter 9) • draw diagrams, make charts and sketches • use visualization
Verbal (Nonspatial)	• translate diagrams and drawings into language • record steps, processes, procedures in words • write summaries (Chapter 9) • write your interpretation next to textbook drawings, maps, graphics
Social	• form study groups • find a study partner • interact with your instructor • work with a tutor
Independent	• use computer-assisted instruction, if available • purchase review workbooks or study guides, if available
Creative	• ask and answer questions • record your own ideas in margins of textbooks
Pragmatic	• study in an organized environment • write lists of steps, procedures, and processes

To use the table

1. **Circle the five aspects of your learning style in which you received the highest scores.** Disregard the others.
2. **Read through the suggestions that apply to you.**
3. **Place a check mark in front of suggestions that you think will work for you.** Choose at least one from each category.
4. **List the suggestions that you chose in the box labeled Action Plan for Learning on the facing page.**

In the Action Plan for Learning box you listed five or more suggestions to help you learn what you read. The next step is to experiment with these techniques, one at a time. (You may need to refer to chapters listed in parentheses in Table 1-1 to learn or review how a certain technique works.) Use one

Action Plan for Learning

Learning Strategy 1 ____________________

____

Learning Strategy 2 ____________________

____

Learning Strategy 3 ____________________

____

Learning Strategy 4 ____________________

____

Learning Strategy 5 ____________________

____

Learning Strategy 6 ____________________

____

technique for a while, and then move to the next. Continue using the techniques that seem to work; work on revising or modifying those that do not. Do not hesitate to experiment with other techniques listed in the table as well. You may find other techniques that work well for you.

Developing Strategies to Overcome Limitations

You should also work on developing styles in which you are weak. Your learning style is not fixed or unchanging. You can improve areas in which you scored lower. Although you may be weak in auditory learning, for example, many of your professors will lecture and expect you to take notes. If you work on improving your listening and note-taking skills, you can learn to handle lectures effectively. Make a conscious effort to work on improving areas of weakness as well as taking advantage of your strengths.

EXERCISE 1-4 Evaluating Learning Strategies

Directions: Write a brief evaluation of each learning strategy you listed in your Action Plan for Learning. Explain which worked; which, if any, did not; and what changes you have noticed in your ability to learn from reading.

EXERCISE 1-5
Learning Styles I

Directions: Form several small groups (three to five students), each of which consists of people who are either predominantly visual learners or predominantly auditory learners. Each group should discuss and outline strategies for completing each of the following tasks:

- Task 1: reading a poem for a literature class
- Task 2: revising an essay for a writing class
- Task 3: reviewing an economics textbook chapter that contains numerous tables, charts, and graphs

Groups should report their findings to the class and discuss how visual and auditory learners' strategies differ.

EXERCISE 1-6
Learning Styles II

Directions: Form several small groups (three to five students), each of which consists of people who are either predominantly social learners or predominantly independent learners. Each group should discuss and outline strategies for completing each of the following tasks:

- Task 1: reading a sociology textbook chapter that contains end-of-chapter study and review questions
- Task 2: working on sample problems for a math class
- Task 3: reading a case study (a detailed description of a criminal case) for a criminal justice class

Groups should report their findings to the class and discuss how social and independent learners' strategies differ.

IMPROVE YOUR COMPREHENSION

4 LEARNING GOAL
Improve your comprehension

Understanding what you read is the key to success in most college courses. Use the following sections to assess when you are and are not understanding what you read and to take action when you find your comprehension is weak or incomplete.

Paying Attention to Comprehension Signals

Think for a moment about how you feel when you read material you can easily understand. Now compare that with what happens when you read something difficult and complicated. When you read easy material, does it seem that everything "clicks"? That is, do ideas seem to fit together and make sense? Is that "click" noticeably absent in difficult reading?

Read each of the following paragraphs. As you read, be aware of how well you understand each of them.

Paragraph 1

"Hooking up" is a term used to describe casual sexual activity with no strings attached between heterosexual college students who are strangers or brief acquaintances. When did people start to hook up? Although the term became common in the 1990s, its use with its modern meaning has been documented as early as the mid-1980s. Studies from the early 2000s show that hooking up was already a fairly common practice on U.S. campuses, practiced by as much as 40 percent of female college students. More recent studies have shed some light on the demographic and psychological correlatives of hooking up. In a 2007 study involving 832 college students, it emerged that hooking up is practiced less by African-American than Caucasian students. Hooking up is also associated with the use of alcohol and, interestingly, with higher parental income. Increased financial resources may give teens and young adults more opportunities to socialize and hook up.

—Kunz, *THINK Marriages and Families*, p. 83

Paragraph 2

Diluted earnings per share (EPS) are calculated under the assumption that all contingent securities that would have dilutive effects are converted and exercised and are therefore common stock. They are found by adjusting basic EPS for the impact of converting all convertibles and exercising all warrants and options that would have dilutive effects on the firm's earnings. This approach treats as common stock all contingent securities. It is calculated by dividing earnings available for common stockholders (adjusted for interest and preferred stock dividends that would not be paid, given assumed conversion of all outstanding contingent securities that would have dilutive effects) by the number of shares of common stock that would be outstanding if all contingent securities that would have dilutive effects were converted and exercised.

—Gitman, *Principles of Managerial Finance*, p. 733

Did you feel comfortable and confident as you read Paragraph 1? Did ideas seem to lead from one to another and make sense? How did you feel while reading Paragraph 2? Most likely you sensed its difficulty and felt confused. Some words were unfamiliar, and you could not follow the flow of ideas.

As you read Paragraph 2, did you know that you were not understanding it? Did you feel lost and confused? Table 1-2 (page 18) lists and compares some common signals that are useful in monitoring your comprehension. Not all signals appear at the same time, and not all signals work for everyone. As you study the list, identify those positive signals you sensed as you read Paragraph 1 on hooking up. Then identify those negative signals that you sensed when reading about diluted earnings per share.

TABLE 1-2 Comprehension Signals

Positive Signals	Negative Signals
Everything seems to fit and make sense; ideas flow logically from one to another.	Some pieces do not seem to belong; the ideas do not fit together or make sense.
You are able to understand what the author is saying.	You feel as if you are struggling to stay with the author.
You can see where the author is leading.	You cannot think ahead or predict what will come next.
You are able to make connections among ideas.	You are unable to see how ideas connect.
You read at a regular, comfortable pace.	You often slow down or lose your place.
You understand why the material was assigned.	You do not know why the material was assigned and cannot explain why it is important.
You can understand the material after reading it once.	You need to reread sentences or paragraphs frequently.
You recognize most words or can figure them out from context.	Many words are unfamiliar.
You can express the key ideas in your own words.	You must reread and use the author's language to explain an idea.
You feel comfortable with the topic; you have some background knowledge.	The topic is unfamiliar; you know nothing about it.

Once you are able to recognize negative signals while reading, the next step is to take action to correct the problem. Specific techniques are given in below in the section "Working on Strengthening Your Comprehension."

EXERCISE 1-7 Monitoring Your Comprehension

Directions: Read the following excerpt from a geography textbook about environmental disturbance and disease. It is intended to be difficult, so do not be discouraged. As you read, monitor your comprehension. After reading, answer the questions that follow.

Human alteration of the environment can create breeding grounds for new viruses and increase the number of pathways viruses can take to new populations.

As new human settlements put pressure on surrounding habitats, humans come into contact with unfamiliar species that may carry disease capable of jumping to human hosts. Settlers who clear forests often reduce the natural food sources used by forest mammals, which invade the new houses looking to eat. An outbreak of hantavirus occurred in the United States in 1993, when hungry rodents, driven into human settlements by rising waters, left droppings in Arizona kitchens. “Manmade malaria” occurs frequently around irrigation systems that contain large pools of standing water in open fields—ideal mosquito breeding grounds. Even simple deforestation at the edge of a city removes the canopy that normally reduces mosquito activity while leaving behind pockmarked land that fills with water. Dengue fever and Japanese encephalitis also spread through irrigation practices in mosquito habitats. Confined animal breeding, such as pig farms and poultry pens, is under intense scrutiny as the possible cauldron of recent viral outbreaks, including SARS and H1N1. Travel, of course, effectively introduces viruses and fresh hosts who may lack the locals' resistance, shuttling disease around the world. One of the worst scenarios for public health is a highly contagious infection entering the global air transportation network. Humans no longer benefit from relative isolation and the disease barrier of distance.

Large-scale environmental alteration is likely to change the opportunities for old and new diseases to appear. Climate change is increasing the portion of Earth that is hospitable to disease-carrying insects. Mosquitoes are already appearing at previously cooler higher latitudes and higher elevations. These changes may produce more infectious disease such as diarrhea. Climate change may also affect crop production leading to malnutrition, a health problem by itself, which also limits humans' ability to fight off infections. Heart and respiratory diseases may increase due to increased ground-level ozone. Human environmental alteration may, on the other hand, eliminate a pathogen's habitat, eradicate the pathogen, and prevent future epidemics. For example, the completion of Egypt's Aswan Dam in 1971 destroyed the floodwater habitat of the *Aedes aegypti* mosquitoes, carriers of Rift Valley fever virus. By 1980, Rift Valley fever had virtually disappeared from Egypt, although the dam provided an aquatic environment that spread Schistosomiasis.

Because environmental changes are highly localized in their effects, it is impossible to make accurate predictions about what will happen where. Some regions may experience relative relief from some disease burdens but many regions will experience a shift to new, unfamiliar, disease. Vulnerable populations, especially those with weak health systems, will have a difficult time coping with these unanticipated changes.

—Dahlman, Renwick, and Bergman, *Introduction to Geography*, p. 175

1. How would you rate your overall comprehension? What positive signals did you sense? Did you feel any negative signals? ______________________

2. Test the accuracy of your rating in Question 1 by answering the following questions based on the material read.

   a Explain how changing human settlements can cause disease. ______________________

   b How does travel increase disease? ______________________

   c In what ways does climate affect disease? ______________________

   d Describe how changes to the environment caused by humans can reduce disease. ______________________

3. In which sections was your comprehension strongest? ______________________

4. Did you feel at any time that you had lost, or were about to lose, comprehension? If so, go back to that paragraph now. What made that paragraph difficult to read? ______________________

5. Underline any difficult words that interfered with your comprehension. ______________________

Working on Strengthening Your Comprehension

When you realize your comprehension is not as strong as needed, be sure to approach the reading task positively and take action right away.

Positive Approaches to Reading

1. **Stick with a reading assignment.** If an assignment is troublesome, experiment with different methods of completing it. Consider highlighting, outlining, testing yourself, preparing vocabulary cards, or drawing diagrams, for example. You will learn these methods in later chapters.
2. **Plan on spending time.** Reading is not something you can rush through. The time you invest will pay off in increased comprehension.
3. **Actively search for key ideas as you read.** Try to connect these ideas with what your instructor is discussing in class. Think of reading as a way of sifting and sorting out what you need to learn from the less important information.

4. **Think of reading as a way of unlocking the writer's message to you, the reader.** Look for clues about the writer's personality, attitudes, opinions, and beliefs. This will put you in touch with the writer as a person and help you understand his or her message. Part Five of this book offers valuable suggestions.

Overcoming Weak Comprehension At times, you will realize that your comprehension is poor or incomplete. When this occurs, take immediate action. Identify as specifically as possible the cause of the problem. Do this by answering the following question: "Why is this not making sense?" Determine whether it is difficult words, complex ideas, organization, or your lack of concentration that is bothering you. Next, make changes in your reading to correct or compensate for the problem. Table 1-3 below lists common problems and offers strategies to correct them.

TABLE 1-3 How to Improve Your Comprehension

Problems	Strategies
Your concentration is poor.	1. Take limited breaks. 2. Tackle difficult material when your mind is fresh and alert. 3. Choose an appropriate place to study. 4. Focus your attention.
Words are difficult or unfamiliar.	1. Use context and analyze word parts. 2. Skim through material before reading. Mark and look up meanings of difficult words. Jot meanings in the margin. 3. Refer to the vocabulary preview list, footnotes, or glossary.
Sentences are long or confusing.	1. Read aloud. 2. Locate the key idea(s). 3. Check difficult words. 4. Express each sentence in your own words.
Ideas are hard to understand, complicated.	1. Rephrase or explain each in your own words. 2. Make notes. 3. Locate a more basic text that explains ideas in simpler form. 4. Study with a classmate; discuss difficult ideas.
Ideas are new and unfamiliar; you have little or no knowledge about the topic, and the writer assumes you do.	1. Make sure you didn't miss or skip introductory information. 2. Get background information by referring to a. an earlier section or chapter in the book. b. an encyclopedia. c. a more basic text.
The material seems disorganized or poorly organized.	1. Pay more attention to headings. 2. Read the summary, if available. 3. Try to discover organization by writing an outline or drawing a map as you read (see Chapter 9).
You do not know what is and is not important.	1. Preview. 2. Ask and answer guide questions. 3. Locate and underline topic sentences (see Chapter 5).

EXERCISE 1-8 Monitoring Your Comprehension

Directions: Read each of the following difficult paragraphs, monitoring your comprehension as you do so. After reading each passage, identify and describe any problems you experienced. Then indicate what strategies you would use to correct them.

A. How are motives identified? How are they measured? How do researchers know which motives are responsible for certain kinds of behavior? These are difficult questions to answer because motives are hypothetical constructs—that is, they cannot be seen or touched, handled, smelled, or otherwise tangibly observed. For this reason, no single measurement method can be considered a reliable index. Instead, researchers usually rely on a combination of research techniques to try to establish the presence and/or the strength of various motives. By combining a variety of research methods—including responses to questionnaires or surveys' data (i.e., self-reports of opinions and behaviors), and insights from focus group sessions and depth interviews (i.e., to discover underlying motives)—consumer researchers achieve more valid insights into consumer motivations than they would by using any one technique alone.

—Schiffman, Kanuk, and Wisenblit, *Consumer Behavior*, p. 106

Problem: ____

Strategies: ____

B. According to the **biological species concept**, a species is defined as a group of individuals that, in nature, can interbreed and produce fertile offspring but cannot reproduce with members of other species. In practice, this definition can be difficult to apply. For example, species that reproduce asexually (such as most bacteria) and species known only via fossils do not easily fit into this species concept. However, the biological species concept does help us understand why species are distinct from each other.

—Belk and Maier, *Biology*, p. 277

Problem: ____

Strategies: ____

C. A surprising use for elastomers is in paints and other coatings. The substance in a paint that hardens to form a continuous surface coating, often called the *binder*, or resin, is a polymer, usually an elastomer. Paint made with elastomers is resistant to cracking. Various kinds of polymers can be used as binders, depending on the specific qualities desired in the paint. Latex paints, which have polymer particles dispersed in water, and thus avoiding the use of organic solvents, are most common. Brushes and rollers are easily cleaned in soap and water. This replacement of the hazardous organic solvents historically used in paints with water is a good example of green chemistry.

—Hill, McCreary, and Kolb, *Chemistry for Changing Times*, p. 278

Problem: ____________________

Strategies: ____________________

LEARNING STYLE TIPS

If you are a(n) . . .	Then improve your comprehension by . . .
Auditory learner	Reading aloud
Visual learner	Visualizing paragraph organization
Applied learner	Thinking of real-life situations that illustrate ideas in the passage
Conceptual learner	Asking questions

EXERCISE 1-9 **Analyzing Difficult Readings**

Directions: Bring to class a difficult paragraph or brief excerpt. Working in groups, each student should read each piece, and then, together, members should (1) discuss why each piece was difficult and (2) compare the negative and positive signals they received while reading them (refer to Table 1-2). Each student should then select strategies to overcome the difficulties he or she experienced.

READ AND THINK VISUALLY

5 LEARNING GOAL Read and think visually

Visuals are important in today's world, since Web sites, textbooks, television, and even academic journals contain more graphics than ever before. Visuals include graphics (such as charts, maps, and graphs) and photographs, as well as text that is made more visually appealing by using color, symbols, and design. You will see visuals in every chapter of this book and in most full-length readings. You will learn much about visuals in detail in Chapter 8.

The Importance of Visuals

Authors use visuals because they can convey a lot of information in a small amount of space. Visuals are important for you because they are time-savers, allowing you to grasp main ideas, implied main ideas, and details very quickly. Because your brain stores visuals differently, they may be easier to retrieve, as well.

Reading and Analyzing Visuals

When reading any type of visual, be sure to do the following:

- **Read the title or caption.** Often the caption or title identifies its subject.
- **Read any accompanying text.** The corresponding text often explains what the author wants the reader to notice.
- **Identify its main point.** What is the visual trying to explain, show, or illustrate?
- **Identify its purpose.** Determine why it was included.

EXERCISE 1-10 Examining a Visual

Directions: Look at the following graphic from a sociology book, and answer the following questions:

1. What is the first thing you notice when you see this visual?
2. Without reading a single word in the graphic, what do you think it is going to be about?
3. By looking at the graphic, what do you think the textbook chapter in which it was included is about?
4. Carefully examine the graphic. About how many facts do you think are contained in this graphic? Is it more effective to see all of this information in a visual form that to read a long paragraph or textbook section listing all of these facts? Why or why not?
5. This graphic allows you to make numerous comparisons. List as many as you can find.

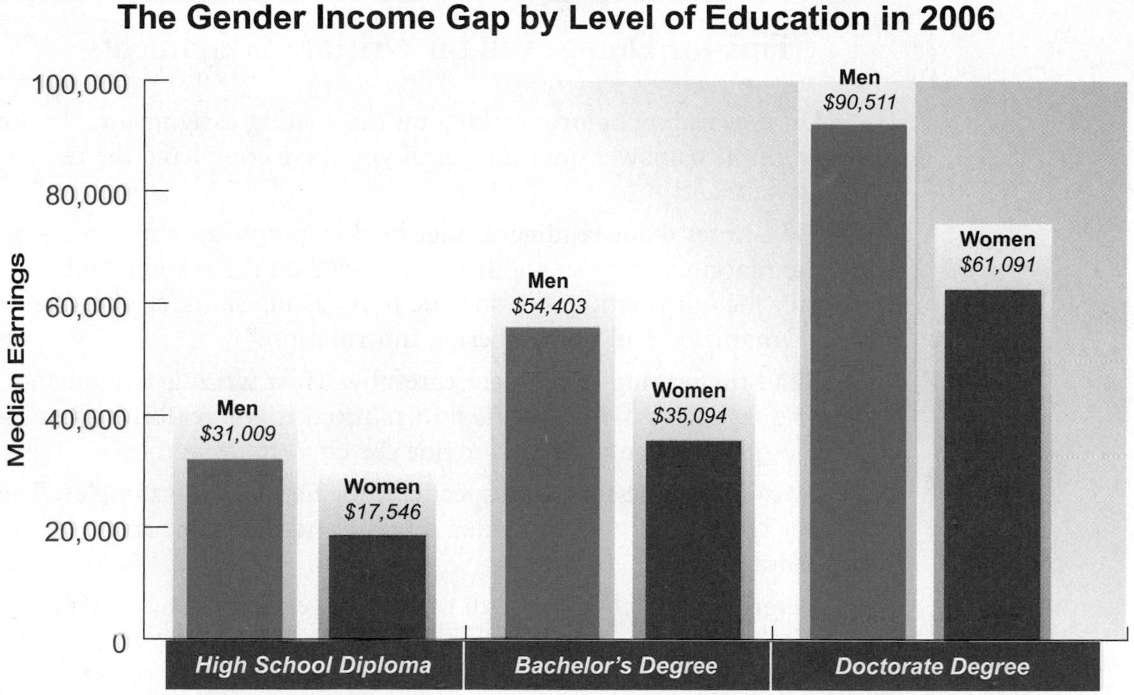

Source: Carl, *THINK Sociology*, p. 197.

USE WRITING TO LEARN

6 LEARNING GOAL
Use writing to learn

Do you read with a pen or pencil in hand? Do you write notes in the margin of your textbook and take notes while your instructors lecture? If so, you have already discovered that writing is one of the best ways to learn. Taking notes as you read makes the process more active. The act of writing out key points and important vocabulary helps cement the information in your brain. It also develops your writing skills, which are valuable in all careers.

Working with Writing Exercises and Assignments

Some students don't like to write because they feel their command of grammar and spelling is not perfect. But grammar is easily learned, and reference tools (such as dictionaries) can help you check your spelling. If you are using a computer program such as Word to write, you can use the program's spell-check and grammar-check features to help you analyze your mistakes and correct them.

Remember that good writing is as much about *ideas* as it is about grammar. Writing exercises and assignments are designed to help you work with information and think deeply about the material.

The tips on the following page can help you approach writing exercises and assignments in the right frame of mind.

Tips for Doing Well on Writing Assignments

1. **Do the reading before working on the writing assignment.** Do not attempt to answer questions until you have completed the reading assignment!
2. **Take notes while reading.** Underline key points and take notes in the margin. Doing so will help you focus on the reading and retain the information. For specific note-taking skills, see Chapter 9, "Organizing and Remembering Information."
3. **Read the writing assignment carefully.** Most writing assignments or questions ask for specific information. If you read the question too quickly, you may not provide the correct answer.
4. **Answer the question with specific information and examples.** The key to good writing is making a point and then supporting it with examples.
5. **Determine the correct length of the answer/response.** Students sometimes write everything they know instead of just the answer to the question. Not all answers require a paragraph or essay; sometimes one sentence is enough.
6. **In writing assignments, "Yes" or "No" is not a complete answer.** Some writing exercises will ask you a "yes or no" or "agree or disagree" question. It is important to include the *reasons* for your answer because the assignment is really asking you how you arrived at your opinion.
7. **Write complete sentences.** On most writing assignments and essay exams, it is important to write in complete sentences. Examine the question to determine when it is acceptable to provide a briefer answer. For example, fill-in-the-blank questions usually requirc you to write only key words or phrases, not whole sentences.

EXERCISE 1-11 Analyzing Exam Questions

Directions: For each of the essay exam/writing questions that follow, determine whether the best answer would be a single sentence, a paragraph, or a complete essay.

1. Define the term *monopoly* as it is used by economists. ____________

2. Compare and contrast the work of William Thackeray and Charles Dickens, making specific reference to at least two books by each novelist. ____________

3. Do you agree with the idea of decriminalizing marijuana use in the United States? Why or why not? ____________

4. List four of Freud's defense mechanisms, providing a definition of each. ____________

5. Provide a brief summary of the public reception to Pablo Picasso's famous painting *Guernica*. ____________

6. What is the difference between fiction and nonfiction? ____________

An Introduction to Summarizing

A **summary** is a brief review of the major idea(s) of something you have read. Its purpose is to record the reading's most important ideas in a condensed form.

Summarizing is an extremely valuable skill because it forces you to identify a reading's key points. It is quite helpful in many college writing situations, such as

- Answering essay questions on exams
- Reviewing a film
- Recording the results of a lab experiment
- Summarizing the plot (main events) of a short story

Understanding how to write a good summary requires an understanding of main ideas (Chapter 5) and details (Chapter 6). Complete directions for summary writing are provided in Chapter 9, "Organizing and Remembering Information."

Every chapter in this book includes a summary writing exercise. In early chapters, the summaries are provided in a fill-in-the-blank format that asks you to fill in missing words. In later chapters, you'll be writing complete sentences and more complete summaries.

Here is a reading passage, followed by a sample summary.

On Visiting an Art Museum

It is a mistake to enter a museum with the belief that you should like everything you see—or even that you should see everything that is there. Without selective viewing, the visitor to a large museum is likely to come down with a severe case of museum exhaustion.

It makes sense to approach an art museum the way a seasoned traveler approaches a city for a first visit: Find out what there is to see. In the museum, inquire about the schedule of special shows, then see those exhibitions and outstanding works that interest you.

If you are visiting without a specific exhibition in mind, follow your interests and instincts. Browsing can be highly rewarding. Zero in on what you feel are the highlights, savoring favorite works and unexpected discoveries.

Don't stay too long. Take breaks. Perhaps there is a garden or café in which you can pause for a rest. The quality of your experience is not measured by the amount of time you spend in the galleries or how many works you see. The most rewarding experiences can come from finding something that "speaks" to you, then sitting and enjoying it in leisurely contemplation.

—adapted from Frank, *Prebles' Artforms*, p. 100

Summary

When you are visiting an art museum, you should practice selective viewing. Find out what the museum has to offer. Decide what special exhibitions and outstanding works appeal to you. Follow your instincts and focus on the highlights. Don't stay too long, and take breaks. Find art that speaks to you and take time to enjoy it.

Note that the summary goes one step beyond recording what the writers say. It pulls together the writers' ideas by condensing and grouping them together.

EXERCISE 1-12 Writing a Summary

Directions: Read the passage, and then complete the summary that follows.

What can you do if you have trouble sleeping? Several techniques may help. Restrict your sleeping hours to the same nightly pattern. Avoid sleeping late in the morning, napping longer than an hour, or going to bed earlier than usual, all of which will throw off your schedule, creating even more sleep difficulties. Use your bed only for sleep (don't read or watch TV in bed). Avoid ingesting substances with stimulant properties. Don't smoke cigarettes or drink beverages with alcohol or caffeine in the evening. Alcohol may cause initial drowsiness, but it has a "rebound effect" that leaves many people wide awake in the middle of the night. Don't drink water close to bedtime; getting up to use the bathroom can lead to poor sleep. Consider meditation or progressive muscle relaxation. Either technique can be helpful, if used regularly.

—adapted from Kosslyn and Rosenberg, *Fundamentals of Psychology*, pp. 368–369

Summary

To get a good night's sleep, go to bed at the same ____________ every night and get up at the same time every ____________. Don't do anything in your bed except

__________. Don't smoke or drink beverages with __________ or __________ in the evening, and don't drink __________ before bedtime. Try __________ or progressive muscle relaxation.

LEARN FROM AND WITH OTHER STUDENTS

7 LEARNING GOAL Learn from and with other students

Many college assignments and activities involve working with a partner or small group of classmates. For example, a sociology professor might divide the class into groups and ask each group to brainstorm solutions to the economic or social problems of recent immigrants. Group presentations may be required in a business course, or groups in your American history class might be asked to research and present a topic.

The Value of Working with Classmates

Group, or *collaborative*, projects are designed to help students learn from one another. Consider the benefits of group projects:

- They help you meet other students.
- They allow you to develop your thinking processes by evaluating the contributions of the group's members.
- They take advantage of your strengths while helping you compensate for your weaknesses. For example, if you are not good with numbers, you can ask one of your group members for help.
- They bring a variety of perspectives to the task. Multiple perspectives provide a deeper, richer understanding of the course content.
- They encourage you to develop interpersonal communication skills that will be valuable in your chosen career.
- They can motivate you to study and stay focused.
- They can lower your workload on a given project.
- They can help you prepare for exams.

In short, group projects are excellent learning opportunities. Throughout this text you will notice that some exercises are labeled "Working Together." These are intended to give you experience working with classmates. Look for this icon:

Tips for Working with Classmates

Some students are reluctant to work in groups. They are shy, or they dislike having their grade depend on the performance of others. Use the following suggestions to help your group function effectively.

How to Work Effectively as a Group

1. **Select alert, energetic classmates** if you are permitted to choose group members.
2. **Create a roster of group members with all contact information** (phone, e-mail, and so forth). Get to know your group members. It is always easier to work together when you know something about your collaborators.
3. **Approach each activity seriously.** Save joking and socializing until the group work has been completed.
4. **Be an active, responsible participant.** Accept your share of the work and ask others to do the same.
5. **Choose a leader who will keep the group focused.** The leader should direct the group in analyzing the assignment, organizing a plan of action, distributing the assignments, and establishing deadlines.
6. **Take advantage of individual strengths.** For instance, a person who has strong organizational skills might be assigned the task of recording the group's findings. A person with strong communication skills might be chosen to present group results to the class.
7. **Treat others as you would like to be treated.** Offer praise when it is deserved. Listen to others, but be willing to disagree with them if doing so is in the group's best interests.
8. **If the group is not functioning effectively or if one or more members are not doing their share, take action quickly.** Table 1-4, on the next page, lists a few common complaints about working with others in groups and possible solutions for each.

TABLE 1-4 Improving Group Dynamics

If a Group Member . . .	You Might Want to Say . . .
Hasn't begun the work he or she has been assigned	"You've been given a difficult part of the project. How can we help you get started?"
Complains about the workload	"We all seem to have the same amount of work to do. Is there some way we might lessen your workload?"
Seems confused about the assignment	"This is an especially complicated assignment. Would it be useful to summarize each member's job?"
Is uncommunicative and doesn't share information	"Since we are all working from different angles, let's each make an outline of what we've done so far, so we can plan how to proceed from here."
Misses meetings	"To ensure that we all meet regularly, would it be helpful if I called everyone the night before to confirm the day and time?"
Seems to be making you or other members do all the work	Make up a chart before the meeting with each member's responsibilities. Give each member a copy and ask, "Is there any part of your assignment that you have questions or concerns about? Would anyone like to change his or her completion date?" Be sure to get an answer from each member.

EXERCISE 1-13 Analyzing a Group Project

Directions: Imagine that your psychology instructor has assigned a group project on the elderly in America. You must choose two classmates to be part of your group. The project has three components: (1) Read a chapter from the textbook and prepare a brief written overview of the problems facing the elderly. (2) Interview three people over age 80 and provide transcripts of those interviews. (3) Prepare a multimedia presentation of photographs, music, and video to accompany your presentation.

1. Which of these three tasks best suits you? Which task suits you least?

2. Take a show of hands. Ask students who are interested in component (1) to raise their hands: then do the same for components (2) and (3). Based on the results, everyone in class should choose two teammates.

3. With your teammates, discuss why you have chosen your specific activity. Did your choice have anything to do with your learning style(s)? Why did you *not* choose the other two activities?

SELF-TEST SUMMARY

1 What is expected of you in college?	You are expected to take control of your learning by reading and studying effectively and efficiently.
2 What can you do to control your concentration?	Building concentration involves two steps: 1. Control your surroundings by wisely choosing your time and place of study and avoiding distractions. 2. Focus your attention on the assignment by setting goals and rewarding yourself for achieving them by working in planned, small time blocks with frequent breaks, and by getting actively involved in the assignment.
3 What is learning style and how can knowing your learning style make you a better student?	Learning style refers to your profile of relative strengths as a learner. Its five components are: 1. Auditory or visual learner 2. Applied or conceptual learner 3. Spatial or verbal learner 4. Social or independent learner 5. Creative or pragmatic learner Discovering what type of learner you are can help you find out what strategies work best for you in reading and studying. It will also help you to recognize your limitations so that you can work on overcoming them.
4 How can you monitor and strengthen your comprehension?	Pay attention to whether you sense positive or negative signals while reading. If you sense poor or incomplete comprehension, take immediate action to identify the source of the problem. Determine whether lack of concentration, difficult words, complex ideas, or confusing organization is causing the problem.
5 What steps should you take when reading a visual?	First read the title. Next, read any text that accompanies it, which may explain it. Identify the main point of the visual and identify its purpose.

6 What is the purpose of writing a summary when learning new material?	Writing a summary allows you to record the reading's most important ideas in a condensed form, so you will be able to remember them.
7 What are the benefits of working in groups?	Working in groups can • help you meet fellow students • develop your thinking processes by evaluating contributions from the group • bolster your strengths and compensate for your weaknesses. • offer multiple perspectives • develop interpersonal skills • keep you focused • reduce your workload

GOING ONLINE

1. **Learning Styles Questionnaires**

   Do an Internet search to locate several other learning style questionnaires. Choose one and complete it. Compare your results with those from the assessment in this book. How do online tests differ from those on paper? Which do you prefer? Is this a result of your learning style?

2. **Exploring Campus Resources**

   Visit your college's Web site and look for the page titled "Student Life" or "Student Resources." What types of services does your college offer to students? Which of these might help you with your studies and with juggling the demands of school, work, and family?

3. **Managing Your Time**

   Some students like to keep track of their schedules in a paper notebook, while others prefer electronic apps. Conduct a Web search for "time management apps" and download one of your choice. Use it for a week and prepare a report listing its features and benefits. How might it be improved? Would you recommend this app or not? Why? Share your thoughts with the class.

4. **Using Collaborative Online Tools**

   The Web offers many free applications that allow online collaboration. (Some collaboration applications may also be found on the home page of online courses.) Conduct a Web search for applications that can help you collaborate with your classmates. Which of these seem to be the most useful? Share your recommendations with the class.

CHAPTER 1

MASTERY TEST 1 Reading Selection

This **Mastery Test** can be completed in **MyReadingLab**.

Name ______________________ Section __________

Date __________ Number right ________ × 10 points = Score ________

ASSESSMENT READING SELECTION

This reading and the questions that follow are intended to help you assess your current level of skill. Read the article and then answer the questions that measure your comprehension. You may refer back to the reading in order to answer them. Compute your score by filling in the score grid above.

The Allure of Disaster

Eric G. Wilson

In this article, which originally appeared in *Psychology Today*, the author discusses why we are drawn to disasters.

Vocabulary Preview

unbridgeable (par. 1) impossible to cross or span
unaccountably (par. 2) without explanation
morbid (par. 6) gruesome
sordid (par. 6) distasteful
macabre (par. 7) suggesting death and decay
propensity (par. 7) tendency, inclination
foments (par. 9) promotes
coalesced (par. 14) began to form

1 STOP STARING. I bet you heard this more than once growing up. This command, after all, marks the unbridgeable gap between the impulsiveness of the child, who gawks at whatever seizes his attention, and the adult's social awareness, based on a fear of giving offense.

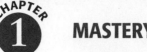

2 The auto mechanic has a huge mole on his nose. There's a woman crying unaccountably in the supermarket aisle. The little boy looks and looks, while the mother pulls him away, scolding all the while.

3 Most children eventually get the point and quit their gaping. For good reason: Although we're tempted to gaze at the car wreck on the side of the highway, suffering is involved.

4 But let's be honest. We're running late for work. We hit a traffic jam. We creep angrily ahead, inch by inch, until we finally see the source of the slowdown: an accident. As we near the scene, we realize that the highway's been cleared. The dented cars are on the shoulder. This is just an onlooker delay, rubberneckers braking to stare.

5 We silently judge all those seekers of sick thrills—for making us late, for exploiting the misfortune of others. Surely we won't look, we tell ourselves as we pull beside the crash. Then it comes: the need to stare, like a tickle in the throat before a cough or the awful urge to sneeze. We hold it back until the last minute, then gawk for all we're worth, enjoying the experience all the more because it's frowned upon.

6 Why do we do this? Our list of morbid fascinations is longer than we'd like to admit, including disaster footage on the TV news, documentaries featuring animal attacks, sordid reality shows, funny falls on YouTube, celebrity scandals, violent movies and television shows, gruesome video games, mixed martial arts, *TMZ, Gawker*, and the lives of serial killers.

7 Everyone loves a good train wreck. We are enamored of ruin. Our secret and ecstatic wish: Let it all fall down. Why? Does this macabre propensity merely reflect humanity's most lurid tendencies? Or might this grimmer side produce unexpected virtues?

8 In *Killing Monsters: Why Children Need Fantasy, Superheroes and Make-Believe Violence,* Gerard Jones argues that children can benefit from exposure to fictional violence because it makes them feel powerful in a "scary, uncontrollable world." The child's fascination with mayhem has less to do with the fighting and more to do with how the action makes her feel. Children like to feel strong. Those committing violence are strong. By pretending to be these violent figures, children take on their strength and with it negotiate daily dangers.

9 Carl Jung made a similar argument for adults. He maintained that our mental health depends on our shadow, that part of our psyche that harbors our darkest energies, such as murderousness. The more we repress the morbid, the more it foments neuroses or psychoses. To achieve wholeness, we must acknowledge our most demonic inclinations.

10 Yes, I took pleasure in my enemy's tumble from grace. No, I couldn't stop watching 9/11 footage. Once we welcome these unseemly admissions as integral portions of our being, the devils turn into angels. Luke owns the Vader within, offers affection to the actual villain; off comes the scary mask, and there stands a father, loving and in need of love.

11 The gruesome brings out the generous: a strange notion. But think of the empathy that can arise from witnessing death or destruction. This emotion—possibly the grounding of all morals—is rare, but it frequently arises when we are genuinely curious about dreadful occurrences.

12 Renaissance scholars kept skulls on their desks to remind them how precious this life is. John Keats believed that the real rose, because it is dying, exudes more beauty than the porcelain one.

13 In the summer of 2010, I visited the National September 11th Memorial Museum in New York City. Photographs of the tragedy and its aftermath covered the walls. On a portable audio player, I listened to commentaries on each. After an hour of taking in the devastation, raw with sadness and wanting nothing more than to return to my wife and daughter, I stood before a picture of a clergyman praying in an eerie gray haze.

14 The man in the photo was blessing the rescue workers before their day's hellish efforts. They kneeled amidst the fog-covered wreckage, heads bowed. I hit the play button. The commentator spoke. As the search for bodies lengthened and grief and fatigue worsened; as hopes coalesced only to be immediately crushed; as firemen, bonded by their labor, grew close; as those who had lost their children and their parents, their wives and their husbands, realized the depth of their affection—as all of this was transpiring—this horrific terrain had turned into "holy ground."

15 At that moment, I understood the terrible logic of suffering: When we agonize over what has cruelly been taken from us, we love it more, and know it better, than when we were near it. Affliction can reveal what is most sacred in our lives, essential to our joy. Water, Emily Dickinson writes, is "taught by thirst."

16 Staring at macabre occurrences can lead to mere insensitivity—gawking for a cheap thrill—or it can result in stunned trauma, muteness before the horror. But in between these two extremes, morbid curiosity can sometimes inspire us to imagine ways to transform life's necessary darkness into luminous vision. Go ahead. Stare. Take a picture. It will last longer.

MASTERY TEST SKILLS CHECK

Directions: Select the choice that best completes each of the following statements.

Checking Your Comprehension

_____ 1. The main point of this selection is that
   a. terrible events can help make us better people.
   b. children control their emotions better than adults.
   c. clergy can explain disasters to people.
   d. people should not look at car wrecks.

_____ 2. According to the author, adults enjoying gawking because they know
   a. it sets a bad example for children.
   b. they shouldn't.
   c. they will have nightmares.
   d. it distracts the police.

_____ 3. When we come upon a car accident, the author says we
   a. fear for our safety.
   b. look away.
   c. can't help but look.
   d. worry about the people in the crash.

_____ 4. The word *enamored* (par. 7) means
a. compared
b. fascinated
c. puzzled
d. comforted

_____ 5. Gerard Jones says children benefit from exposure to fictional violence because it
a. helps them feel powerful in an uncontrollable world.
b. teaches them what not to do.
c. allows them to break the rules.
d. shows them there are good people nearby.

_____ 6. Carl Jung believed that to achieve wholeness we must
a. spend years praying.
b. reject our morbid thoughts.
c. pretend there is no evil.
d. acknowledge our dark side.

_____ 7. Renaissance scholars keep skulls on their desks to remind themselves
a. that the brain is the most important organ.
b. of how precious life is.
c. that we are all alike.
d. of the past.

_____ 8. The photo the author saw at the 9/11 memorial depicted
a. a clergyman praying.
b. medics helping people.
c. what the towers looked like before they fell.
d. plans for the new tower.

_____ 9. The word *portable* in paragraph 13 means
a. numbered carefully.
b. repaired quickly.
c. carried by hand.
d. invented long ago.

_____10. The main point of paragraph 14 is that
a. a horrific event changed how people thought and felt.
b. the rescue workers were successful.
c. the clergyman had given up hope.
d. disasters make us lose faith.

For more practice, ask your instructor for an opportunity to work on the mastery tests that appear in the Test Bank.

CHAPTER 2

The Basics of College Textbook Reading

LEARNING GOALS

This chapter will show you how to

1. Use textbooks as a learning tool
2. Preview before reading
3. Develop questions to guide your reading
4. Read for meaning
5. Test your recall as you read
6. Review after reading
7. Use the SQ3R system

Focusing on ... College Textbooks

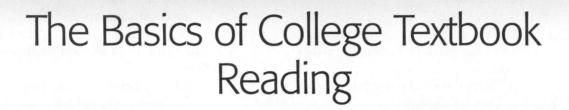

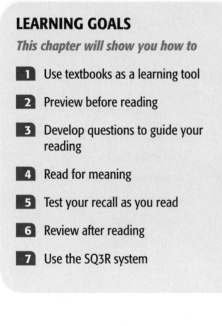

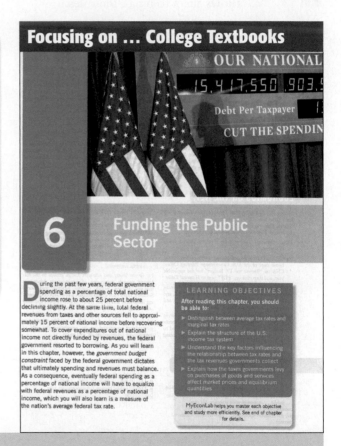

During the past few years, federal government spending as a percentage of total national income rose to about 25 percent before declining slightly. At the same time, total federal revenues from taxes and other sources fell to approximately 15 percent of national income before recovering somewhat. To cover expenditures out of national income not directly funded by revenues, the federal government resorted to borrowing. As you will learn in this chapter, however, the *government budget constraint* faced by the federal government dictates that ultimately spending and revenues must balance. As a consequence, eventually federal spending as a percentage of national income will have to equalize with federal revenues as a percentage of national income, which you will also learn is a measure of the nation's average federal tax rate.

LEARNING OBJECTIVES

After reading this chapter, you should be able to:

- Distinguish between average tax rates and marginal tax rates
- Explain the structure of the U.S. income tax system
- Understand the key factors influencing the relationship between tax rates and the tax revenues governments collect
- Explain how the taxes governments levy on purchases of goods and services affect market prices and equilibrium quantities

MyEconLab helps you master each objective and study more efficiently. See end of chapter for details.

The visual shows the opening page of an introductory economics textbook chapter. This opener is designed to stimulate your interest in the topics covered in the chapter. It includes a list of learning objectives, a photograph, an introduction to what you will learn in the chapter, and a link to an online study lab.

The entire economics chapter is 17 pages long; it is filled with detailed information on the federal tax system. If this were your textbook for your economics course, how would you read this chapter? How would you know what to learn? How would you go about learning it all?

This chapter is designed to help you answer these questions. It will show you what features textbook chapters commonly contain to help you learn. It will also show you five strategies that, when combined, lead to a tested and proven method of reading—the SQ3R system.

TEXTBOOKS AS LEARNING TOOLS

1 LEARNING GOAL
Use textbooks as a learning tool

While textbooks may seem to be long and impersonal, they are actually carefully crafted teaching and learning systems. They are designed to work with your instructor's lecture to provide you with reliable and accurate information and to help you practice your skills.

Why Buy and Study Textbooks?

Did you know the following?

- **Nearly all textbook authors are college teachers.** They work with students daily and understand students' needs.
- **Along with your instructor, your textbook is the single best source of information for the subject you are studying.**
- **The average textbook costs only about $10-15 a week.** For the price of a movie ticket, you are getting a complete learning system that includes not only a textbook but also a companion Web site and other study materials.
- **Your textbook can be a valuable reference tool in your profession.** For example, many nursing majors keep their textbooks and refer to them often when they begin their career.

Textbooks are an investment in your education and in your future. A textbook is your ally—your partner in learning.

Using Textbook Organization to Your Advantage

Have you ever walked into an unfamiliar supermarket and felt lost? How did you finally find what you needed? Most likely, you looked for the signs hanging over the aisles indicating the types of products shelved in each section. Walking along the aisle, you no doubt found that similar products were grouped together.

For example, all the cereal was in one place, all the meat was in another, and so forth.

You can easily feel lost or intimidated when beginning to read a textbook chapter, too. It may seem like a huge collection of unrelated facts, ideas, and numbers that have to be memorized. Actually, a textbook chapter is much like a supermarket. It, too, has signs that identify what is located in each section. These signs are the major **headings** that divide the chapter into topics. Underneath each heading, similar ideas are grouped together, just as similar products are grouped together in a supermarket aisle. In most cases, several paragraphs come under each heading.

Sometimes headings are further divided into **subheadings** (usually set in smaller type than the main heading or indented or set in a different color). Using headings and subheadings, chapters take a major idea, break it into its important parts, and then break those parts into smaller parts, so you can learn it one step a time.

A typical textbook chapter might have an organization that looks like the diagram on the left.

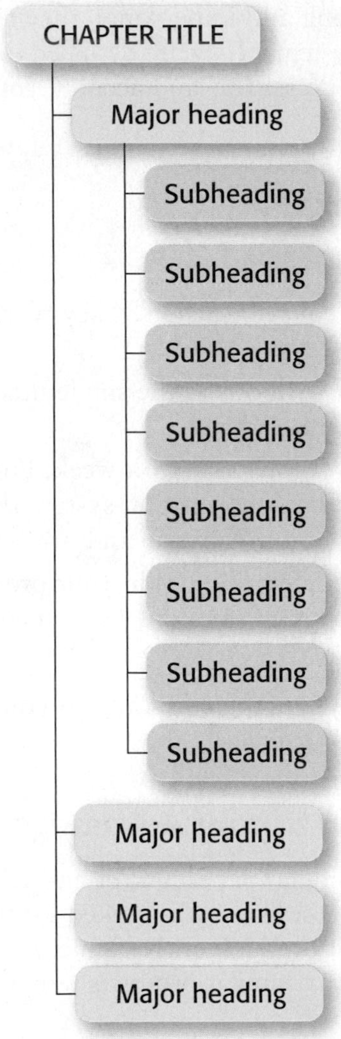

Notice that this diagram shows a chapter divided into four major headings, and the first major heading is divided into eight subheadings. The number of major headings and subheadings and the number of paragraphs under each will vary from chapter to chapter in a book.

Once you know how a chapter is organized, you can use this knowledge to guide your reading. Once you are familiar with the organization, you will also begin to see how ideas are connected. The chapter will then seem orderly, moving from one idea to the next in a logical fashion.

Look at the following partial list of headings and subheadings from a chapter of a sociology textbook.

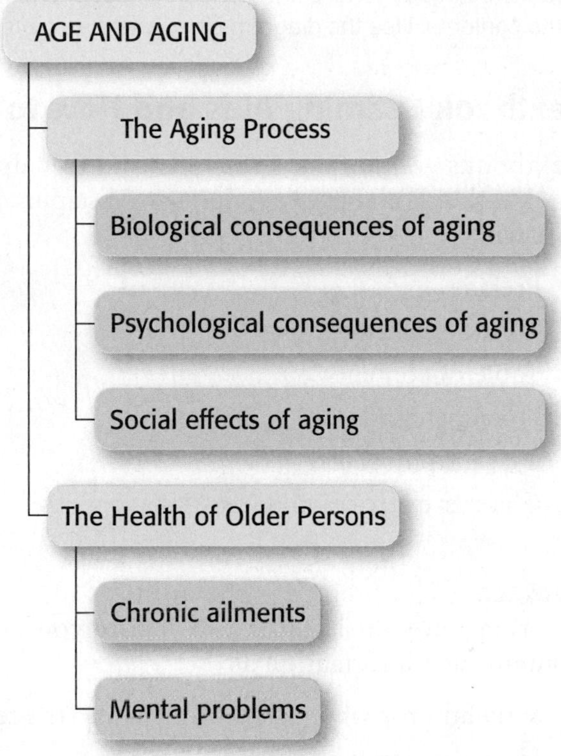

In this chapter on age and aging, "The Aging Process" and "The Health of Older Persons" are the first two major topics. The topic "The Aging Process" is broken into three parts: biological consequences, psychological consequences, and social effects. "Health of Older Persons" is divided into two parts: chronic ailments and mental problems.

The titles and headings, taken together, form a brief outline of a chapter. Later, in Chapter 9, you will see how these headings can help you make a more complete outline of a chapter. For now, think of headings as guides that direct you through a chapter one step at a time.

EXERCISE 2-1 Analyzing Chapter Organization

Directions: Draw a diagram of headings and subheadings for this chapter of *Guide to College Reading*.

EXERCISE 2-2 **Drawing an Organizational Diagram**

Directions: Choose a textbook that you are using for another course. Select a chapter you have already read. On a separate sheet of paper, draw an organizational diagram of its contents. Use the diagram on page 40 as a guide.

Textbook Learning Aids and How to Use Them

Textbooks contain numerous features to help you learn. Features vary from book to book and from discipline to discipline, but most textbooks contain the following:

- Preface
- To the Student
- Table of contents
- Opening chapter
- Typographical aids
- Chapter exercises and questions
- Boxes and case studies
- Vocabulary lists
- Chapter summary
- Glossary
- Index

Preface The preface is the author's introduction to the text. It presents information you should know before you begin reading Chapter 1. It may contain such information as

- Why and for whom the author wrote the text
- How the text is organized
- The purpose of the text
- References and authorities consulted
- Major points of emphasis
- Learning aids included and how to use them
- Special features of the text
- New materials included since the book's last update

The last point is particularly important. Knowledge is not static; it is ever-changing. Textbooks must include this new information, as well as new *perspectives*, or ways of looking at the subject. As an example, for many years most of the art shown in art history textbooks was created by male artists. In the last decade, however, art history textbooks have included more works by female artists.

To the Student Some textbooks contain a section titled "To the Student." This section is written specifically for you. It contains practical information about the text. It may, for example, explain textbook features and how to use them, or it may offer suggestions for learning and studying the text. Often, a "To the Instructor" section precedes or follows "To the Student" and contains information useful to your instructor.

EXERCISE 2-3 Analyzing a Preface

Directions: Use the Preface to *Guide to College Reading* to answer the following questions.

1. Look at the book's content overview (pp. xiv–xv). In what part of the book are vocabulary skills discussed? ______________ Which part of the book is devoted to developing your critical reading skills? ______________
2. Name three special features of *Guide to College Reading* that are designed to enhance the text's effectiveness. (*Hint*: Look for the heading titled "Special Features.")

   ____

   ____

EXERCISE 2-4 Analyzing "To the Student"

Directions: Read the "To the Student" section in a textbook from one of your other courses and answer the following questions.

1. What is the purpose of the text?

   ____

   ____

2. How is the textbook organized?

   ____

   ____

3. What learning aids does the book contain? How useful have you found them?

   ____

   ____

Table of Contents The **table of contents** is an outline of a text found at the beginning of the book. It lists all the important topics and subtopics covered. Glancing through a table of contents will give you an overview of a text and suggest its organization.

Before beginning to read a chapter, refer to the table of contents. Although chapters are intended to be separate parts of a book, it is important to see how they fit together as parts of the whole—the textbook itself.

A table of contents can be a useful study aid when preparing for exams. To review the material on which you will be tested, read through the table of contents listings for chapters covered on the exam. This review will give you a sense of which topics you are already familiar with and which topics you have yet to learn about.

EXERCISE 2-5 Analyzing the Table of Contents

Directions: Use the table of contents for this book to answer the following questions.

1. This textbook includes not only a *detailed* table of contents (pp. vii–xi) but also a *brief* table of contents (p. v). What is the difference between the two?

____

____

2. What value do you see in the brief table of contents?

____

____

3. In which chapter will you learn about stated and implied main ideas?

____

4. Name two of the writers whose work is represented in the Contemporary Issues Minireader.

____

Opening Chapter The first chapter of a textbook is one of the most important and deserves close attention. Here the author sets the stage for what is to follow. More important, it defines the discipline, explains basic principles, and introduces terminology that will be used throughout the text.

Typically, you can expect to find as many as 20 to 50 new words introduced and defined in the first chapter. These words are the language of the course, so to speak. To be successful in any new subject area, you must learn to read and speak its language. (Chapters 3 and 4 of this text will help you develop your vocabulary skills.)

EXERCISE 2-6 Analyzing Chapter 1

Directions: Refer to Chapter 1 of *Guide to College Reading.* List at least two techniques or features the author uses to get students involved with and interested in the material.

Typographical Aids Textbooks contain various **typographical aids** (arrangements or types of print) that make it easy to pick out what is important to learn and remember. These include the following:

1. **Different types of font.** Italic type (*slanted print*) and boldfaced type (**dark print**) are often used to call attention to a particular word or phrase. Often new terms are printed in italics or boldface in the sentence in which they are defined. For example:

   > The term *drive* is used to refer to internal conditions that force an individual to work toward some goal.

   > **Animism** is the belief that inanimate objects, such as trees, rocks, and rivers, possess souls.

   Note: Colored print is sometimes used to emphasize important ideas or definitions.
2. **Enumeration. Enumeration** refers to the numbering or lettering of facts and ideas within a paragraph. It is used to emphasize key ideas and make them easy to locate.

   > Consumer behavior and the buying process involve five mental states: (1) awareness of the product, (2) interest in acquiring it, (3) desire or perceived need, (4) action, and (5) reaction or evaluation of the product.

3. **Listing. Bulleted lists** and **numbered lists** provide important information in a list format. (A bullet looks like this: •).These lists are typically indented, which makes them easy to find as you read and review the chapter.

   > Sigmund Freud defined three parts of the human psyche:
   > 1. Id
   > 2. Ego
   > 3. Superego

North America is sometimes divided into eight distinctive regions:

- New England and the Atlantic Provinces
- Quebec
- The Old Economic Core
- The American South (The Southeast)
- The Great Plains Breadbasket
- The Continental Interior
- The Pacific Northwest
- Southern California and the Southwest

EXERCISE 2-7 Evaluating Typographical Aids

Directions: Bring a textbook from one of your other courses to class. With a partner or in a small group, point out the typographical aids used in the book. Discuss how each can help you learn.

Chapter Exercises and Questions Exercises and questions fall into several categories.

1. ***Review questions* cover the factual content of the chapter.**
   - **In-chapter review questions appear at the end of a major section.** They allow you to test your mastery of the material before you move on to the next section.
   - **End-of-chapter review questions appear at the end of the chapter. They test your comprehension of the entire chapter.**

   Here are some examples of review questions from a marketing textbook:

   - List some product characteristics that are of concern to marketers.
   - Distinguish between a trademark and a brand name.
   - What are two characteristics of a good brand name?

2. ***Discussion questions* deal with interpretations of content.** These are often meant to be jumping-off points for discussion in the classroom or with other students. Here are some examples of discussion questions from the marketing textbook:

   - What do you think is the future of generic products?
   - How has the downturn in the economy affected American consumers' buying habits?

3. ***Application questions* ask you to apply your knowledge to the world around you or to a real-life situation.** Many students like these questions because they help prepare them for their chosen career. Here are some sample application questions:

   - Go to your local grocery store and look at the ways the products are packaged. Find three examples of packages that have value in themselves. Find three examples of packages that promote the products' effectiveness.
   - How would you go about developing a brand name for a new type of soft drink?

4. ***Critical-thinking questions* ask you to think deeply about a topic or issue.** These questions require close attention and are often asked on exams. Here are two sample critical-thinking questions:

   - There is much controversy about the issue of warning labels on products. Outline the pros and cons of putting warning labels on products.
   - How is advertising good for society? How is it bad for society?

5. ***Problem questions* are usually mathematical in nature.** You are given an equation to solve, or you are given a problem in words and asked to use mathematical concepts to find the solution. Working with problems is one of the most important parts of any math, science, or technical course. Here are two sample problems:

   - If $x = 6$, $4x + 5 = ?$
   - If a microwave oven costs the retailer $325 and the markup is 35%, find the selling price of the microwave.

Boxes and Case Studies Many textbooks include boxed inserts or case studies that are set off from the text. Generally, these "boxes" contain interesting information or extended examples to illustrate text concepts. Boxes are sometimes a key to what the author considers important. For example, a business textbook may contain boxes in each chapter about green business practices. From the presence of these boxes, you can assume that the author is interested in how business practices can be changed to help preserve the environment. (Note that the word *green* here refers to the movement to preserve Planet Earth.)

Case studies usually follow the life history of a person, or the business practices of a particular company. These are valuable applications of the textbook concepts to the real world.

Vocabulary Lists Textbooks usually contain a list of new terms introduced in each chapter. This list may appear at the beginning or end of the chapter. Sometimes they include page numbers that identify where the term is defined.

Regardless of where they appear, vocabulary lists are a valuable study aid. Here is a sample vocabulary list (sometimes called a **key terms list**) from a financial management textbook:

Key Terms

assets
budget
cash flow statement
fixed disbursements
liabilities
money market fund
net worth

Notice that the author identifies the terms but does not define them. In such cases, mark the new terms as you come across them in the chapter. (The key terms are often printed in boldfaced type, so pay close attention whenever you see boldface.) After you have finished the chapter, review each marked item and its definition. To learn the terms, use the index card system suggested in Chapter 4 ("A System for Learning New Words," p. 135).

EXERCISE 2-8 Creating a List of Key Terms

Directions: If a textbook does not contain a key terms list, you should make one of your own for each chapter. Using boldfaced terms as your guide, create a key terms list for this chapter of *Guide to College Reading*.

Chapter Summary In most textbooks, each chapter ends with a **chapter summary** that reviews all the chapter's key points. While the summary is sometimes in paragraph form, it is more often formatted as a numbered list. If you are having difficulty extracting the main points from the chapter, the summary is an excellent resource.

This text features a "Self-Test Summary" at the end of each chapter. For an example, see page 67. Note how the summary is provided in a question-and-answer format to help you quiz yourself on the concepts.

Glossary Usually found at the end of the book, a **glossary** is a mini-dictionary that lists alphabetically the important vocabulary used in the book. Because it is built into the textbook, a glossary is faster and more convenient to use than a dictionary. It does not list all the common meanings of a word, as a dictionary does, but instead gives only the meaning used in the text.

Glossary entries are usually focused and specific. Sometimes the glossary includes the page numbers on which the vocabulary words are defined. Here is an excerpt from the glossary of a health textbook:

> **latent functions** unintended beneficial consequences of people's actions
>
> **leader** someone who influences other people
>
> **leadership styles** ways in which people express their leadership
>
> **leisure** time not taken up by work or necessary activities
>
> —Henslin, *Sociology*, p. G4

In some textbooks, a key term is defined in the text, and the term and its definition are repeated in the margin. Many students say that a **marginal glossary** is one of the most useful textbook features.

Index Suppose you are studying for a final exam and want to review a vocabulary term, but you can't remember where it's located in your textbook. The book's **index**, found at the end of the book, is an alphabetical listing of all the topics in the book. It includes not only key terms, but also topics, names of authors, and titles of texts or readings. Next to each entry you will find the page number(s) on which the topic is discussed.

EXERCISE 2-9 Evaluating Textbook Learning Aids

Directions: With a partner or in a small group, choose a textbook from one of your other courses. Each person in the group should take turns answering the following questions and showing examples.

1. What learning aids does the book contain? Does it contain any special features not listed in this section? If so, what are they and what is their function? Which of these features do you expect to use most often?

2. Explain how you will use each learning aid to study.

3. How is the information given in the preface important?

____

____

4. Look at the opening chapter. What is its function?

____

____

5. Review the table of contents. What are its major parts?

____

____

PREVIEW

2 LEARNING GOAL
Preview before reading

Would you cross a city street without checking for traffic first? Would you pay to see a movie you had never heard of and knew nothing about? Would you buy a car without test-driving it or checking its mechanical condition?

Most likely you answered "no" to each of these questions. Now answer a related question, one that applies to reading: Should you read an article or textbook chapter without knowing what it is about or how it is organized? You can probably guess that the answer is "no." This section explains a technique called previewing.

Previewing is a way of quickly familiarizing yourself with the organization and content of written material *before* beginning to read it. It is an easy method to use and will make a dramatic difference in how effectively you read.

How to Preview

When you preview, try to (1) find only the most important ideas in the material, and (2) note how they are organized. To do this, look only at the parts that state these important ideas and skip the rest. Previewing is a fairly rapid technique. You should take only a few minutes to preview a 15- to 20-page textbook chapter. The parts to look at in previewing a textbook chapter are listed here:

How to Preview Textbook Chapters

1. **The title and subtitle** The title is a label that tells what the chapter is about. The subtitle, if there is one, suggests how the author approaches the subject. For example, an article titled "Brazil" might be subtitled "The World's Next Superpower." In this instance, the subtitle tells which aspects of Brazil the article discusses.

2. **Chapter introduction** Read the entire chapter introduction if it is brief. If it is lengthy, read only the first few paragraphs.
3. **The first paragraph** The first paragraph, or introduction, of each section of the chapter may provide an overview of the section and/or offer clues about its organization.
4. **Boldfaced headings** Headings, like titles, serve as labels and identify the topic of the material. By reading each heading, you will be reading a list of the important topics the chapter covers. Together, the headings form a mini-outline of the chapter.
5. **The first sentence under each heading** The first sentence following the heading often further explains the heading. It may also state the central thought of the entire selection. If the first sentence is purely introductory, read the second as well.
6. **Typographical aids** Typographical aids are those features of a page that help to highlight and organize information. These include *italics*, **boldfaced type**, marginal notes, colored ink, underlining, and enumeration (listing). A writer frequently uses typographical aids to call attention to important key words, definitions, and facts.
7. **Graphs, charts, and pictures** Graphs, charts, and pictures will point you toward the most important information. Glance at these to determine quickly what information is being emphasized or clarified.
8. **The final paragraph or summary** The final paragraph or summary will give a condensed view of the chapter and help you identify key ideas. Often, a summary outlines the key points of the chapter.
9. **End-of-chapter material** Glance through any study or discussion questions, vocabulary lists, or outlines that appear at the end of the chapter. These will help you decide what in the chapter is important.

Demonstration of Previewing

The article on pp. 52–53 was taken from a chapter of a nutrition textbook on fats. It discusses the six reasons fats are an important part of your diet and has been included to demonstrate previewing. Everything that you should look at or read has been shaded. Preview this excerpt now, reading only the shaded portions.

Why Do We Need to Eat Fats?

Dietary fat provides energy and helps our body perform some essential internal functions.

Fats Provide Energy

Dietary fat is a primary source of energy. Fat provides 9 kcal per gram, while carbohydrate and protein provide only 4 kcal per gram. This means that fat is much more energy-dense. For example, just 1 tablespoon of butter or oil contains about 100 kcal, whereas it takes 2.5 cups of steamed broccoli or 1 slice of whole-wheat bread to provide 100 kcal.

When we are at rest, approximately 30% to 70% of the energy used by our muscles and organs comes from fat. The exact amount of fat you burn when you are at rest depends on how much fat you eat in your diet, how physically active you are, and whether you are gaining or losing weight.

Fat is also a major energy source during physical activity. In fact, one of the best ways of losing body fat is through regular aerobic exercise. During exercise, the body begins to break down fat stores to fuel the working muscles. The amount and source of the fat used depend on your level of fitness; the type, intensity, and duration of the exercise; and what and how much you've eaten, before you exercise. Because the body has only a limited supply of stored carbohydrate (as glycogen) in muscle tissue, the longer you exercise, the more fat you use for energy.

Fats Store Energy for Later Use

Our bodies store extra energy as fat in our adipose tissue, which then can be used for energy at rest, during exercise, or during periods of low energy intake. Adipose tissue provides the body with an energy source even when we choose not to eat (or are unable to eat), when we are exercising, and while we are sleeping. Our body has relatively little stored carbohydrate—only enough to last about 1 to 2 days—and there is no place that our body can store extra protein. We cannot consider our muscles and organs as a place where "extra" protein is stored! For these reasons, although we don't want too much stored adipose tissue, some is essential to keep the body going.

Fats Enable the Transport of Fat-Soluble Vitamins

Dietary fat enables the transport of the fat-soluble vitamins A, D, E, and K. Vitamin A is important for vision, vitamin D helps maintain bone health, vitamin E prevents and repairs damage to cells, and vitamin K is important for blood clotting and bone health. Without an appropriate intake of dietary fat, our body can become deficient in these important vitamins.

Fats Help Maintain Cell Function and Provide Protection to the Body

Fats are a critical part of every cell membrane. There, they help determine what substances are transported into and out of the cell and regulate what substances can bind to the cell; thus, fats strongly influence the function of the cell. In addition, fats help maintain cell fluidity and other physical properties of the cell membrane. Fats enable our red blood cells, for example, to be flexible enough to bend and move through the smallest capillaries in our body, delivering oxygen to all our cells.

Stored body fat pads the body and protects our organs, such as the kidneys and liver, when we fall or are bruised. The fat under our skin acts as insulation to help us retain body heat. Although we often think of all body fat as "bad," it does play an important role in keeping our body healthy and functioning properly.

Fats Contribute to the Flavor and Texture of Foods

Dietary fat adds texture and flavor to foods. Fat makes salad dressings smooth and ice cream "creamy," and it gives cakes and cookies their moist, tender texture. Frying foods in fat, as with doughnuts or french fries, gives them a crisp, flavorful coating. On the other hand, foods containing fats, such as cookies, crackers, chips, and breads, become rancid quickly if they are not stored properly. Manufacturers add preservatives to increase the shelf life of foods with fats.

Fats Help Us Feel Satiated

Fats in foods help us feel satiated—satisfied—after a meal. Two factors probably contribute to this effect: first, as noted earlier, fat has a much higher energy density than carbohydrate or protein. An amount of butter weighing the same number of grams as a medium apple would contain 840 kcal! Second, fat takes longer to digest than protein or carbohydrate because more steps are involved in the digestion process. This may help you feel satisfied for a longer period of time because energy is slowly being released into your body.

—Thompson and Manore, *Nutrition for Life*, pp. 106–107

Although you may not realize it, you have gained a substantial amount of information from the minute or so that you spent previewing. You have become familiar with the key ideas in this section. To demonstrate, read each of the following statements and mark them *T* for true or *F* for false based on what you learned by previewing.

______ 1. Fat is the most important source of energy in our diet.

______ 2. Fat is stored in the adipose tissue.

_______ 3. Too much fat prevents the body from using vitamins A, D, E, and K.

_______ 4. Fat makes food taste better.

_______ 5. Eating fat helps you feel fuller after a meal.

This quiz tested your recall of some of the more important ideas in the article. Check your answers by referring back to the article. Did you get most or all of the above items correct? You can see, then, that previewing acquaints you with the major ideas contained in the material before you read it.

EXERCISE 2-10 Practicing Previewing

Directions: Preview Chapter 5 in this book. After you have previewed it, complete the items below.

1. What is the subject of Chapter 5? _______________

2. List the three major topics Chapter 5 covers.

   a. _______________

   b. _______________

   c. _______________

EXERCISE 2-11 Previewing Your Textbooks

Directions: Preview a chapter from one of your other textbooks. After you have previewed it, complete the items below.

1. What is the chapter title?

   ____

   ____

2. What subject does the chapter cover?

   ____

   ____

3. List some of the major topics covered.

   ____

   ____

Previewing Articles and Essays

Previewing works on articles and essays, as well as textbook chapters. However, you may have to make a few changes in the steps listed on pages 50–51. Here are some guidelines:

How to Preview Articles and Essays

1. **Check the author's name.** If you recognize the author's name, you may have an idea of what to expect in the article or essay. For example, you would expect humor from an article by Dave Barry but more serious material from an article written by the governor of your state.
2. **Check the source of the article.** Where was it originally published? The source may suggest something about the content or slant of the article. (For more about sources, see Chapter 11.)
3. **If there are no headings, read the first sentence of a few paragraphs throughout the essay.** These sentences will usually give you a sense of what each paragraph is about.

EXERCISE 2-12 Previewing a Reading Selection

Directions: Preview the reading selection that appears at the end of this chapter, "Looking for Love." Then answer the following questions.

1. What is the purpose of the article?

____

2. Which types of dating can you recall?

____

Discovering What You Already Know

After you have previewed an assignment, take a moment to discover what you already know about the topic. Regardless of the topic, you probably know *something* about it. We will call this your **background knowledge.** Here is an example.

A student was about to read an article titled "Growing Urban Problems" for a sociology class. At first she thought she knew very little about urban problems, since she lived in a small town. Then she began thinking about her recent trip to a nearby city. She remembered seeing homeless people and overcrowded housing. Then she recalled reading about drug problems, drive-by shootings, and muggings.

Now let us take a sample chapter from a business textbook titled *Small Business Management*. The headings are listed below. Spend a moment thinking about each one; then make a list of things you already know about each.

- Characteristics of Small Businesses
- Small-Business Administration
- Advantages and Disadvantages of Small Businesses
- Problems of Small Businesses

Discovering what you already know is useful for three important reasons. First, it makes reading easier because you have already thought about the topic. Second, the material is easier to remember because you can connect the new information with what you already know. Third, topics become more interesting if you can link them to your own experiences. You can discover what you know by using one or more of the following techniques:

How to Activate Your Background Knowledge

1. **Ask questions and try to answer them.** For the above business textbook headings, you might ask and try to answer questions such as: Would I want to own a small business or not? What problems could I expect?
2. **Draw upon your own experience.** For example, if a chapter in your business textbook is titled "Advertising: Its Purpose and Design," you might think of several ads you have seen on television, in magazines, and in newspapers and analyze the purpose of each and how it was constructed.
3. **Brainstorm.** On a scratch sheet of paper, jot down everything that comes to mind about the topic. For example, suppose you are about to read a chapter on domestic violence in your sociology textbook. You might list types of violence—child abuse, rape, and so on. You could write questions such as: "What causes child abuse?" or "How can it be prevented?" Or you might list incidents of domestic violence you have heard or read about. Any of these approaches will help to make the topic interesting.

EXERCISE 2-13 Discovering What You Already Know

Directions: Assume you have just previewed a chapter in your American government text on freedom of speech. Discover what you already know about freedom of speech by using each of the techniques suggested above. Then answer the questions below.

1. Did you discover you knew more about freedom of speech than you initially thought?

   ____

2. Which technique worked best? Why?

   ____

   ____

EXERCISE 2-14 Discovering What You Already Know

Directions: Preview the essay "Looking for Love" at the end of the chapter, and discover what you already know about types of dating by using one of three techniques described in this section.

LEARNING STYLE TIPS

If you tend to be a(n) …	Then strengthen your previewing skills by …
Auditory learner	Asking and answering guide questions aloud or recording them
Visual learner	Writing guide questions and their answers

DEVELOP QUESTIONS TO GUIDE YOUR READING

3 LEARNING GOAL Develop questions to guide your reading

Did you ever read an entire page or more and not remember anything you read? Have you found yourself going from paragraph to paragraph without really thinking about what the writer is saying? Most likely you are not looking for anything in particular as you read. As a result, you do not notice or remember anything specific, either. The solution is a relatively simple technique that takes just a few seconds: develop questions that will guide your reading and hold your attention.

How to Ask Guide Questions

Here are a few useful suggestions to help you form questions to guide your reading:

How to Ask Guide Questions

1. **Preview before you try to ask questions.** Previewing will give you an idea of what is important and indicate which questions you should ask.
2. **Turn each major heading into a series of questions.** The questions should ask something that you feel is important to know.
3. **As you read the section, look for the answers to your questions.** Highlight the answers as you find them.
4. **When you finish reading a section, stop and check to see whether you can recall the answers.** Place check marks by those you cannot recall.
5. **Avoid asking questions that have one-word answers.** Questions that begin with *what*, *why*, or *how* are more useful.

Here are a few headings and some examples of questions you could ask:

Heading	Questions
1. Reducing Prejudice	1. How can prejudice be reduced? What type of prejudice is discussed?
2. The Deepening Recession	2. What is a recession? Why is it deepening?
3. Newton's First Law of Motion	3. Who is or was Newton? What is his First Law of Motion?

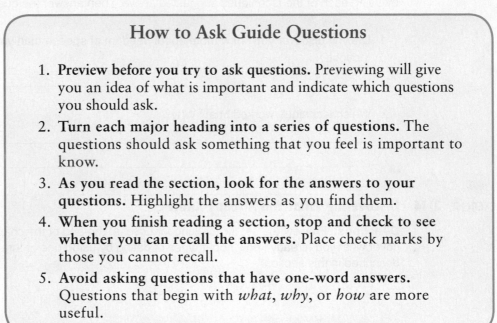

EXERCISE 2-15 Writing Guide Questions

Directions: Write at least one question for each of the following headings.

Heading	Questions
1. World War II and Black Protest	1. ______
2. Foreign Policy Under Reagan	2. ______
3. The Increase of Single-Parent Families	3. ______
4. Changes in Optical Telescopes	4. ______
5. Causes of Violent Behavior	5. ______

EXERCISE 2-16 Writing Guide Questions

Directions: Preview Chapter 7 of this book. Then write a question for each major heading.

1. ______
2. ______
3. ______
4. ______
5. ______
6. ______

EXERCISE 2-17 Writing and Answering Guide Questions

Directions: Turn back to the textbook excerpt on pages 52–53. You have already previewed it. Without reading the article, write four important questions to be answered after finishing it. Then read the article and answer your questions.

1. ______________________________

2. ______________________________

3. ______________________________

4. ______________________________

EXERCISE 2-18 Previewing and Writing Guide Questions

Directions: Select a textbook from one of your other courses. Preview a five-page portion of a chapter that you have not yet read. Then write questions for each heading.

____

____

____

EXERCISE 2-19 Previewing and Writing Guide Questions

Directions: Bring two brief magazine or newspaper articles or two 2-page textbook excerpts on interesting subjects to class. You should preview and then read both articles before class. Working with another student, exchange and preview each other's articles. Take turns predicting each article's content and organization. The student who has read the article verifies or rejects the predictions. Alternatively, the "reader" may ask the "previewer" about the article's content or organization. Then work together to generate a list of guide questions that could be used when reading the material.

READ FOR MEANING

4 LEARNING GOAL
Read for meaning

Once you have previewed an assignment and written guide questions to focus your attention, you are ready to begin reading. Read to answer your guide questions. Each time you find an answer to one of your guide questions, highlight it. Also, highlight what is important in each paragraph. In Chapter 5 you will learn more about how to discover what is important in a paragraph; in Chapter 9 you will learn specific strategies for highlighting.

TEST YOUR RECALL AS YOU READ

5 LEARNING GOAL
Test your recall as you read

Many students read an assignment from beginning to end without stopping. Usually, this is a mistake. Instead, it is best to stop frequently to test yourself to see if you are remembering what you are reading. You can do this easily by using your guide questions. If you write guide questions in the textbook margin next to the section to which they correspond, you can easily use them as test questions after you have read the section. Cover the textbook section and try to recall the answer. If you cannot, reread the section. You have not yet learned the material. Depending on your learning style, you might either repeat the answer aloud (auditory style) or write it (verbal style).

REVIEW AFTER YOU READ

6 LEARNING GOAL
Review after reading

Once you have finished reading, it is tempting to close the book, take a break, and move on to your next assignment. If you want to be sure that you remember what you have just read, take a few moments to go back through the material, looking things over one more time.

You can review using some or all of the same steps you followed to preview (see pages 50–51). Instead of viewing the assignment *before* reading, you are viewing it again *after* reading. Think of it as a "re-view." Review will help you pull ideas together as well as help you retain them for later use on a quiz or exam.

EXERCISE 2-20 Practicing Reviewing

Directions: Work with a partner to choose a chapter in this book that you have already read. Review the chapter, previewing for the important information listed in the box on pages 50–51. Next, each student should write five questions on the chapter content. Test each other's recall of the chapter content by taking turns asking and answering your questions.

BUILD A SYSTEM: SQ3R

7 LEARNING GOAL
Use the SQ3R system

Each of techniques presented in this chapter, (1) previewing, (2) asking guide questions, (3) reading for meaning, (4) testing yourself, and (5) reviewing will make a difference in how well you comprehend and remember what you read. While each of these makes a difference by itself, when you use all five together you will discover a much bigger difference. Because these five techniques do work together, numerous researchers and psychologists have put them together into a reading–learning system. One of the most popular systems is called SQ3R.

The steps in the system are listed below. You will see that the steps are just other names for what you have already learned in this chapter.

SQ3R

S	Survey	(Preview)
Q	Question	(Ask Guide Questions)
R	Read	(Read for Meaning)
R	Recite	(Test Your Recall)
R	Review	(Review After You Read)

Be sure to use SQ3R on all your textbook assignments. You will find that it makes an important difference in the amount of information you can learn and remember.

EXERCISE 2-21 Using SQ3R

Directions: Read the following excerpt from a chapter on digestion in a nutrition textbook (pp. 62–65), following the steps listed above.

1. Preview the excerpt. Write a sentence describing what the excerpt will be about.

   ____

   ____

2. Form several questions that you want to answer as you read. Write them in the space provided.

   ____

   ____

3. Read the excerpt, and on a separate sheet of paper, answer your guide questions.
4. Review the excerpt immediately after you finish reading.

What Happens to the Fats We Eat?

Because fats are not soluble in water, they cannot enter our bloodstream easily from the digestive tract. Thus, fats must be digested, absorbed, and transported within the body differently from carbohydrates and proteins, which are water **soluble**.

The digestion and absorption of fat is shown in Figure A. Dietary fats usually come mixed with other foods in our diet, which we chew and then swallow. Salivary enzymes have a limited role in the breakdown of fats, and so they reach the stomach intact (Figure A, step 1). The primary role of the stomach in fat digestion is to mix and break up the fat into droplets. Because they are not soluble in water, these fat droplets typically float on top of the watery digestive juices in the stomach until they are passed into the small intestine (Figure A, step 2).

Foods containing fats, such as bread, can spoil quickly.

The Gallbladder, Liver, and Pancreas Assist in Fat Breakdown

Because fat is not soluble in water, its digestion requires the help of digestive enzymes from the pancreas and mixing compounds from the gallbladder. Recall that the gallbladder is a sac attached to the underside of the liver, and the pancreas is an oblong-shaped organ sitting below the stomach. Both have a duct connecting them to the small intestine. As fat enters the small intestine from the stomach, the gallbladder contracts and releases a substance called bile (Figure A, step 3). Bile is produced in the liver from cholesterol and is stored in the gallbladder until needed. You can think of bile acting much like soap, breaking up the fat into smaller and smaller droplets. At the same time,

How could you use this diagram to test your recall of chapter content?

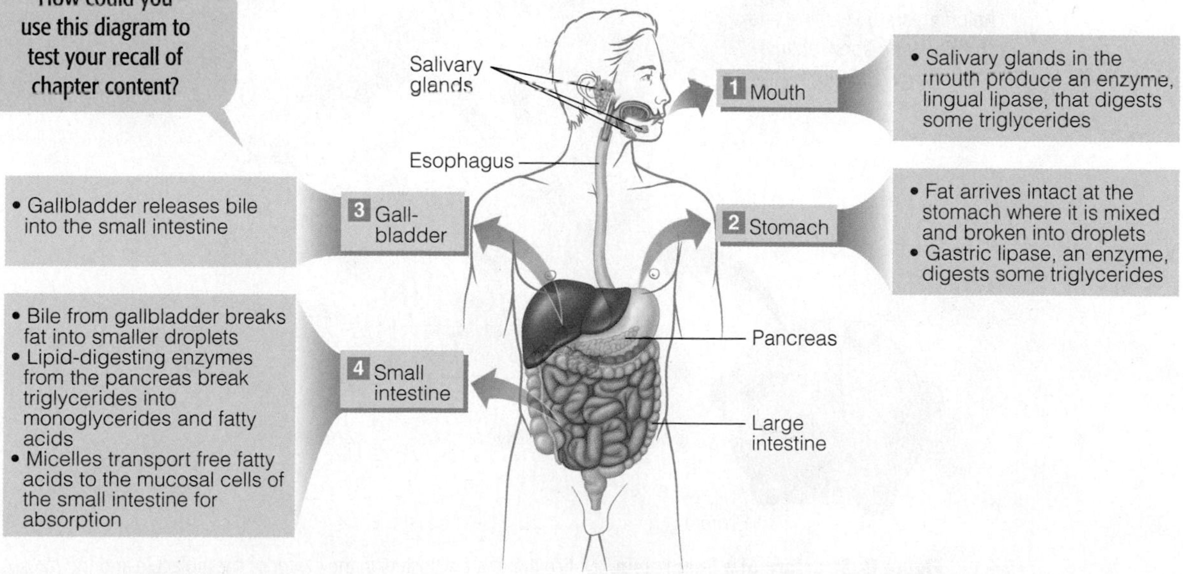

Salivary glands
Esophagus
Pancreas
Large intestine
1 Mouth
• Salivary glands in the mouth produce an enzyme, lingual lipase, that digests some triglycerides
2 Stomach
• Fat arrives intact at the stomach where it is mixed and broken into droplets
• Gastric lipase, an enzyme, digests some triglycerides
3 Gall-bladder
• Gallbladder releases bile into the small intestine
4 Small intestine
• Bile from gallbladder breaks fat into smaller droplets
• Lipid-digesting enzymes from the pancreas break triglycerides into monoglycerides and fatty acids
• Micelles transport free fatty acids to the mucosal cells of the small intestine for absorption

Figure A The process of fat digestion.

lipid-digesting enzymes produced in the pancreas travel through the pancreatic duct into the small intestine. Once bile has broken the fat into small droplets, these pancreatic enzymes take over, breaking some of the fatty acids away from the glycerol backbone. Each triglyceride molecule is thus broken down into two free fatty acids and one *monoglyceride,* which is the glycerol backbone with one fatty acid still attached.

Most Fat Is Absorbed in the Small Intestine

The free fatty acids and monoglycerides next need to be transported to the cells that make up the wall of the small intestine (Figure A, step 4), so that they can be absorbed into the body. This trip requires the help *of micelles,* spheres of bile and phospholipids that surround the free fatty acids and monoglycerides and transport them to the intestinal cell wall. Once there, shorter fatty acids can pass directly across the intestinal cell membrane. Longer fatty acids first bind to a special carrier protein and then are absorbed.

After absorption into the small intestine, the shortest fatty acids cross unassisted into the bloodstream and are then transported throughout the body. In contrast, the longer fatty acids and monoglycerides are reformulated back into triglycerides. As you know, triglyceride molecules don't mix with water, so they can't cross independently into the bloodstream. Once again, their movement requires special packaging, this time in the form of lipoproteins. A **lipoprotein** is a spherical compound in which triglycerides cluster deep in the center and phospholipids and proteins, which are water soluble, form the surface of the sphere (Figure B).

How useful is this diagram in helping you to visualize and understand lipoproteins?

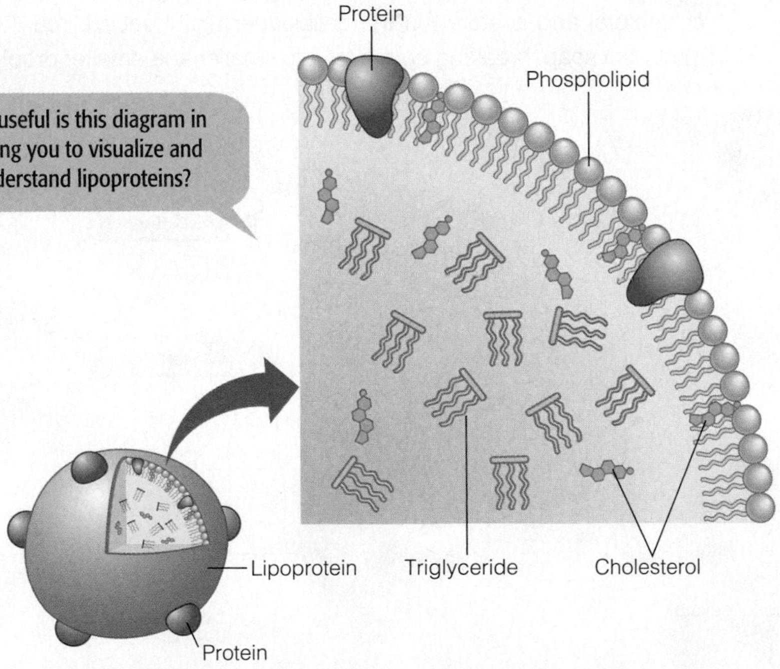

Figure B Structure of a lipoprotein. Notice that the fat clusters in the center of the molecule and the phospholipids and proteins, which are water soluble, form the outside of the sphere. This enables lipoproteins to transport fats in the bloodstream.

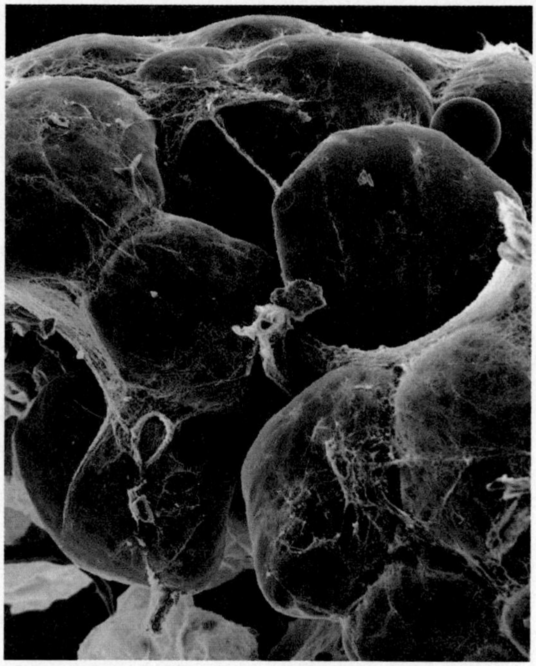

During times of weight gain, excess fat consumed in the diet is stored in adipose tissue.

The specific lipoprotein that transports fat from a meal is called a **chylomicron**. Packaged as chylomicrons, dietary fat finally arrives in your blood.

Fat Is Stored in Adipose Tissues for Later Use

The chylomicrons, which are filled with the fat you just ate, now begin to circulate through the blood looking for a place to unload. There are three primary fates of this dietary fat: (1) If your body needs the fat for energy, it will be quickly transported into your cells and used as fuel. (2) If the fat is not needed for immediate energy, it can be used to make lipid-containing compounds such as certain hormones and bile. (3) Alternatively, it can be stored in your muscles or adipose tissue for later use. If you are physically active, your body will preferentially store this extra fat in the muscle tissue first, so the next time you go out for a run, the fat is readily available for energy. That is why people who engage in regular physical activity are more likely to have extra fat stored in the muscle tissue and to have less adipose tissue—something many of us would prefer. Of course, fat stored in the adipose tissue can also be used for energy during exercise, but it must be broken down first and then transported to the muscle cells.

Recap: Fat digestion begins when fats are broken into droplets by bile. Enzymes from the pancreas subsequently digest the triglycerides into two free fatty acids and one monoglyceride. These end products of digestion are then transported to the intestinal cells with the help of micelles. Once inside the intestinal cells, triglycerides are re-formed and packaged into lipoproteins called chylomicrons. Their outer layer is made up of proteins and phospholipids, which allows them to dissolve in the blood. Dietary fat is transported by the chylomicrons to cells within the body that need energy. Fat stored in the muscle tissue is used as a source of energy during physical activity. Excess fat is stored in the adipose tissue and can be used whenever the body needs energy.

—Thompson and Manore, *Nutrition for Life*, pp. 109–111

EXERCISE 2-22 Using SQ3R

Directions: Choose a chapter from one of your textbooks, or use a later chapter in this book. Complete each of the following steps.

1. Preview the chapter. Write a sentence describing what the chapter will be about.

   ____

   ____

2. Form several questions that you want to answer as you read. Write them in the space provided.

   ____

   ____

3. Read the first section (major heading) of the chapter, and highlight the important information.
4. Review the section immediately after you finish reading and highlighting.
5. On a separate sheet, write a brief outline or draw a map of the major ideas in the section of the chapter that you read.
6. Evaluate how effectively SQ3R worked for you. Explain how it helped you or what you would change to make it work better for you.

SELF-TEST SUMMARY

1 How can I use textbooks as learning tools?	Use headings and subheadings to understand chapter organization. Use the preface, to the student, table of contents, opening chapter, typographical aids, chapter exercises and questions, boxes and case studies, vocabulary lists, chapter summary, glossary, and index.

2 What is previewing?	Previewing is a method of becoming familiar with the content and organization of written material before reading.
3 What are guide questions?	Guide questions focus your attention on what you need to learn and remember.
4 How can you read for meaning?	Highlight answers to your guide questions. Also, highlight important information in each paragraph.
5 How can you test your recall as you read?	Cover the text and try to recall answers to each of your guide questions.
6 How can you review after you read?	Use the steps you followed to preview the assignment.
7 What is the SQ3R system?	SQ3R is a system that enables you to learn as you read (Survey, Question, Read, Recite, and Review).

GOING ONLINE

1. **Exploring Online Textbook Learning Aids**
   Most of your college textbooks offer a companion Web site. These sites often offer a variety of helpful study resources. Choose a textbook from one of your other courses and visit its Web site. Make a list of the resources provided. Which of these would you find most helpful and useful? Why?

This **Mastery Test** can be completed in **MyReadingLab**.

CHAPTER 2

MASTERY TEST 1 Working with Textbook Features

Name ______________________________ Section ______________

Date ________________ Number right ________ × 20 points = Score __________

Directions: Read the following excerpt from a communication textbook. Then answer the questions that follow.

Under-the-Radar Advertising

Inundated with advertisements, 6,000 a week on network television, double since 1983, many people tune out. The problem is ad clutter. Advertisers are trying to address the clutter in numerous ways, including stealth ads. Although not hidden or subliminal, stealth ads are subtle—even covert. You might not know you're being pitched unless you're really attentive.

- **Stealth ads.** So neatly can ***stealth ads*** fit into the landscape that people may not recognize they're being pitched. Consider the Bamboo lingerie company, which stenciled messages on a Manhattan sidewalk: "From here it looks like you could use new underwear." Sports stadiums like FedEx Field outside of Washington, D.C., work their way into everyday dialogue, subtly reinforcing product identity.
- **Product placement.** In the 1980s advertisers began wiggling brand-name placements into movie scripts, creating an additional minor revenue stream for filmmakers. The practice, ***product placement***, stirred criticism about artistic integrity, but it gained momentum. For the 2005 release of *The Green Hornet*, Miramax was seeking an automaker willing to pay at least $35 million for its products to be written into the script.
- **Infomercials.** Less subtle is the ***infomercial***, a program-length television commercial dolled up to look like a newscast, a live-audience participation show, or a chatty talk show. With the proliferation of 24-hour television service and of cable channels, airtime is so cheap at certain hours that advertisers of even offbeat products can afford it.

—adapted from Vivian, *The Media of Mass Communication*, pp. 336–338

_____ 1. The reading selection uses all of the following typographical aids *except*

a. boldfaced type.
b. numbered list.
c. bulleted list.
d. italic type.

_____ 2. The key terms list for this selection would most likely include which set of terms?

a. radar, stealth, product placement
b. advertising, filmmakers, cable channels
c. Bamboo, FedEx, Miramax
d. stealth ad, product placement, infomercial

_____ 3. What does the heading "Under-the-Radar Advertising" mean?

a. sneaky advertising
b. television advertising
c. creative advertising
d. movie advertising

_____ 4. Which is the best example of a critical-thinking question based on the reading?
   a. What is stealth advertising?
   b. What are the three types of under-the-radar advertising?
   c. What are two examples of stealth advertising at work?
   d. What ethical issues are involved with stealth advertising?

_____ 5. Which of the following would be the best glossary entry for **infomercial**?
   a. **infomercial:** a form of stealth advertising
   b. **infomercial:** a common and inexpensive type of cable TV advertising
   c. **infomercial:** a program-length TV commercial made to look like a newscast, audience participation show, or talk show
   d. **infomercial:** stealth advertising used by companies to sell products

CHAPTER 2

MASTERY TEST 2 Thinking Skills

This **Mastery Test** can be completed in **MyReadingLab**.

Name ______________________ Section ____________

Date ____________ Number right ________ × 10 points = Score ________

Directions: Preview the following selection by reading only the title, first paragraph, headings, first sentence of each paragraph, and last paragraph. *Do not read* the entire selection. Then select the choice that best completes each of the statements that follow.

What negative effect of technology does this photograph illustrate?

Health Today

Taming Technostress

1 Are you "twittered out"? Is all that texting causing your thumbs to seize up in protest? If so, you're not alone. Like millions of others, you may find that all of the pressure for contact is more than enough stress for you! Known as *technostress*, this bombardment is defined as stress created by a dependence on technology and the constant state of being plugged in or wirelessly connected.

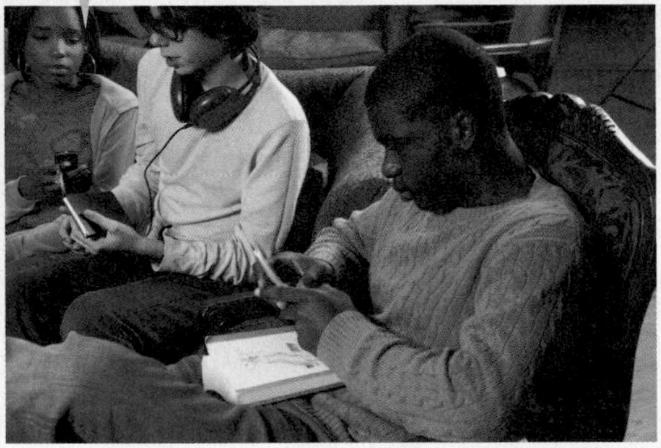

Technology may keep you in touch, but it can also add to your stress.

2 There is much good that comes from all that technological wizardry; however, for some, technomania can become obsessive—a situation in which people would rather hang out online, talking to strangers, than study, talk to friends, socialize in person, or generally connect in the real world. Although technology can allow us to multitask, work on the go, and communicate in new and different ways, there are some clear downsides to all of that "virtual" interaction.

3 • **Distracted driving.** Exact numbers are hard to come by, but some sources estimate that as much as 25 percent of distracted driving is the result of people either talking or texting on their cell phones or manipulating music devices. About 90 percent of the U.S. population, more than 270 million people, have cell phones and at any given moment, 11 percent of them are using those phones while driving. Because research indicates that doing so puts people at risk, more than 250 cities and several states have passed laws or are considering legislation that would either prohibit or restrict the use of cell phones by drivers.

4 • **Practice Safe Text!** This catchy website title emerged in 2008 and brought international attention to the repetitive stress injury (RSI) known as *Blackberry thumb*. If you are one of a growing number of persons who have this malady,

you already know that it refers to a problem experienced by too much thumb use on today's personal digital assistant (PDA) devices. It causes pain, swelling, or numbness of the thumb. The best advice is to avoid the malady by stretching thumb muscles before texting and keeping messaging to a minimum.

5 • **Other repetitive stress injuries.** Sitting in front of a computer screen set at the wrong height, or working hunched over a laptop for hours can result in stressed muscles, ligaments, and tendons, often with painful consequences. Back pain, neck cramps, and carpal tunnel syndrome are all possible outcomes. Keeping sessions short, stretching muscles frequently, and getting an ergonomic check of your work station can all help prevent future problems.

6 • **Social distress.** Authors Michell Weil and Larry Rosen describe *technosis*, a very real syndrome in which people become so immersed in technology that they risk losing their own identity. Worrying about checking your voice mails, constantly switching to e-mail or Facebook to see who has left a message or is online, perpetually posting to Twitter, and so on can keep you distracted and take important minutes or hours from your day.

7 To avoid technosis and to prevent technostress, set time limits on your technology usage, and make sure that you devote at least as much time to face-to-face interactions with people you care about as a means of nurturing your relationships. Screen your contacts, especially when you are in public or engaged in face-to-face communication with someone. You don't always need to answer your phone or respond to a text or e-mail immediately. Leave your devices at home or turn them off when you are out with others or on vacation. *Tune in* to your surroundings, your loved ones and friends, your job, and your classes by shutting off your devices.

Sources: AAA Foundation for Traffic Safety, "Safety Culture: Cell Phones and Driving: Research Update," 2008, www.aaafoundation.org/pdf/CellPhonesandDrivingFS.pdf; M. Weil and L Rosen, "Technostress: Are You a Victim?" 2007, www.technostress.com.

—Donatelle, *Health,* p. 66

_____ 1. The title of this selection is
- a. "Stress and Technology."
- b. "Stress-Related Injuries."
- c. "Taming Technostress."
- d. "Technomania."

_____ 2. The selection focuses mainly on stress related to
- a. technology.
- b. social networking.
- c. driving.
- d. relationships.

_____ 3. Which sentence in the first paragraph best describes what the rest of the selection will be about?
- a. Sentence 1
- b. Sentence 2
- c. Sentence 4
- d. Sentence 5

_____ 4. Technostress is defined in the selection as stress created primarily by
- a. a repetitive injury.
- b. a dependence on technology.
- c. an obsession with online relationships.
- d. real-world interactions.

_____ 5. According to the selection, what percentage of distracted driving is the result of people using cell phones or manipulating music devices?
a. 1 percent
b. 5 percent
c. 10 percent
d. 25 percent

_____ 6. The heading "Practice Safe Text!" refers to
a. driving while texting.
b. avoiding a repetitive stress injury.
c. calling instead of texting.
d. multitasking at work.

_____ 7. The best guide question for the heading before paragraph 5 is
a. How can repetitive stress injuries be avoided?
b. Is technology related to repetitive stress?
c. Can anyone get a repetitive stress injury?
d. Is repetitive stress a physical malady?

_____ 8. The best guide question for the heading before paragraph 6 is
a. Does technology cause social distress?
b. Is social distress a serious problem?
c. How can technology lead to social distress?
d. What should be done about social distress?

_____ 9. At the end of the selection, the author makes all of the following recommendations *except*
a. set time limits on your technology usage.
b. always respond to texts and e-mails immediately.
c. spend time engaging in face-to-face interactions.
d. turn off your devices when you are on vacation.

_____ 10. The author's purpose in writing this selection is to
a. complain and criticize.
b. entertain and amuse.
c. inform and advise.
d. persuade and promote.

CHAPTER 2

MASTERY TEST 3 Reading Selection

This **Mastery Test** can be completed in **MyReadingLab**.

Name ______________________________ Section ______________

Date ________________ Number right* ________ × 10 points = Score ________

Looking for Love

Jenifer Kunz

This selection, taken from the sociology textbook *Think Marriages and Families*, explores the dating ritual.

Vocabulary Preview

primping (par. 1) carefully grooming
intimacy (par. 2) closeness
conformity (par. 4) fitting in with others
compatibility (par. 8) ability to get along with each other
accelerated (par. 13) faster

1 Dating has changed, but many aspects of it remain the same. Visit the home of a single man or woman on a typical Saturday night and you will likely witness a familiar routine: the primping and preening in front of the mirror, the nervous glancing at the watch, the hopeful conversations with friends and family members about tonights date. But apart from the excitement of a night out, what do people get out of dating?

Reasons for Dating

2 Dating fulfills a number of important functions in people's lives. It is a form of recreation that enables couples to socialize together and have fun. It provides companionship and intimacy. Dating also helps individuals learn social skills, gain self-confidence, and develop one-on-one communication skills. Through their relationships with other people, adolescents in particular develop a sense of their own identity, increasing their feelings of self-worth. Finally, dating is a possible opportunity to meet a future martial partner through the process of mate selection.

3 Researchers describe the dating process as a **marriage market**. Just as employers in a labor market attempt to hire the best possible employees for the lowest possible wage, potential spouses in the marriage market look for a partner with the highest number of desired characteristics and the fewest flaws. The three components to the marriage market include the *supply* of man and women who are looking for partners, the *preferences* of these men and women for particular

*To calculate the number right, use items 1–10 under "Mastery Test Skills Check".

Relationship Escalation Model

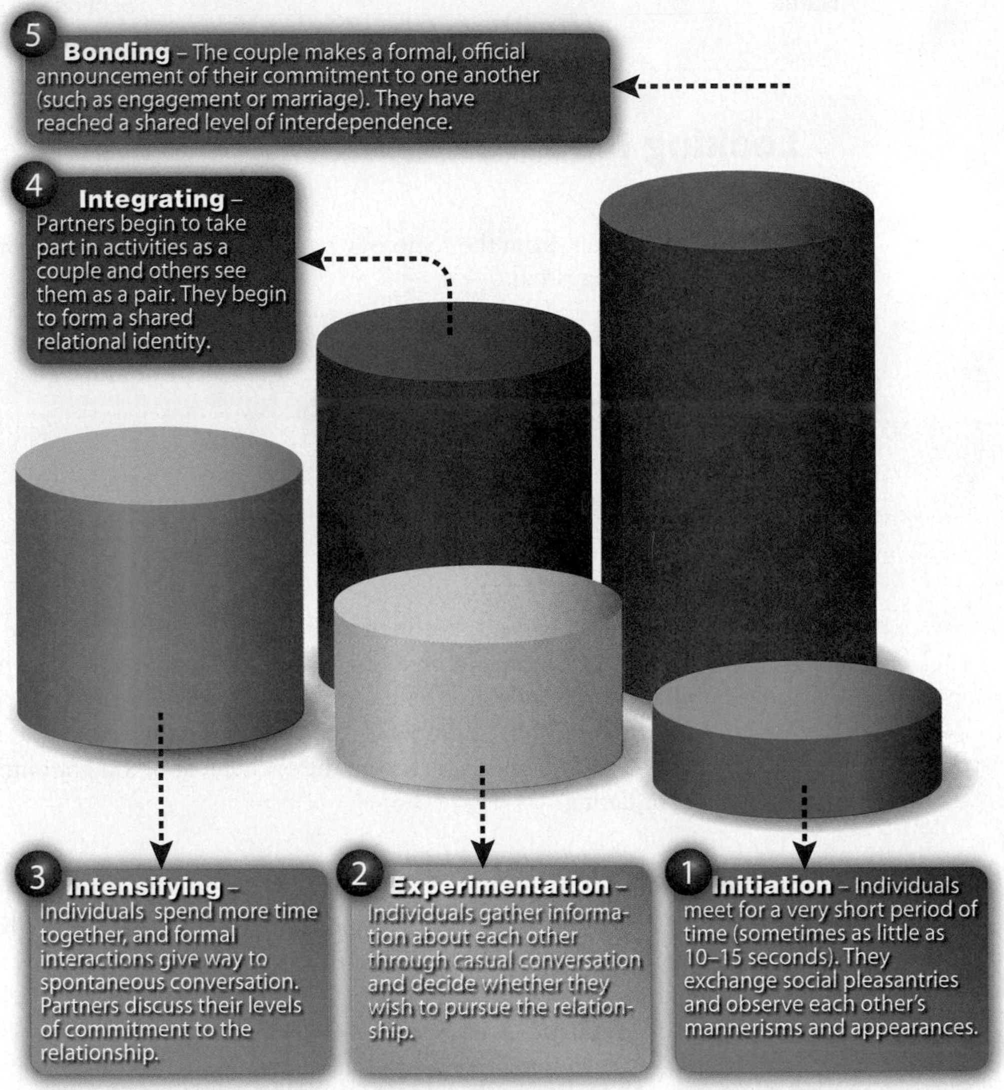

5 Bonding – The couple makes a formal, official announcement of their commitment to one another (such as engagement or marriage). They have reached a shared level of interdependence.
4 Integrating – Partners begin to take part in activities as a couple and others see them as a pair. They begin to form a shared relational identity.
3 Intensifying – Individuals spend more time together, and formal interactions give way to spontaneous conversation. Partners discuss their levels of commitment to the relationship.
2 Experimentation – Individuals gather information about each other through casual conversation and decide whether they wish to pursue the relationship.
1 Initiation – Individuals meet for a very short period of time (sometimes as little as 10–15 seconds). They exchange social pleasantries and observe each other's mannerisms and appearances.

Relationship Escalation Model

Source: Knapp, Mark, *Interpersonal Communication and Human Relationships*. (Boston: Allyn & Bacon, 1984).

physical characteristics and personal attributes in their partners, and the *resources* that the men and women can offer potential partners themselves (attributes that other people are likely to find attractive). Unlike the labor market, which tends to value the same characteristics in all potential employees—for example, punctuality, reliability, and efficiency—the marriage market is extremely varied. Although most people value qualities such as honesty and integrity in a partner, few would agree on any one description of the perfect woman or perfect man.

Types of Dating

Going Steady

4 A term that became common in the 1930s, **going steady** meant that two people were dating exclusively. Going steady sometimes led to engagement, although it was often a short-lived experience, lasting anywhere from a few days to a few years. In the 1950s, going steady became the dominant form of dating, and a 1958 study found that 68 percent of college coeds had gone steady at least once. The practice of going steady was less about true love and more about status and peer pressure, representing the teenage desire for security and conformity.

Pack Dating

5 Popular among undergraduates, **pack dating** is a less pressurized form of dating, in which small groups of students go to dinner, watch movies, or go out dancing together. The packs (usually consisting of about five or six individuals) provide students with a sense of identity and self-assurance, but enable them to avoid long-term committed relationships. This may appeal to people who do not plan on settling down until their 30s or who have little free time to commit to a relationship between work and study responsibilities.

Serious Dating

6 When a couple begins to date seriously, they see each other exclusively and usually spend most of their leisure time together. They may discuss marriage or the possibility of living together and begin to talk about the future as a couple, rather than as two individuals with independent life goals. Many couples are sexually intimate by this point, although the practice of premarital sex often depends on whether one or both partners have strong religious beliefs opposing premarital sex. Studies have found that religious commitment is inversely related to the age at first sexual intercourse and the number of lifetime sexual partners.

Engagement

7 **Engagement** is a public commitment made by a couple when they announce their intention to marry. During the engagement period, couples plan their wedding and discuss issues such as where they will live, whether they will have children, and what they hope to accomplish together in the future.

8 An engagement is also a chance for couples to test their compatibility and may be a time of high stress and conflict. If one partner is considerably wealthier than the other, he or she may wish to draw up a **prenuptial agreement**, which stipulates what should happen financially in the event of a divorce. Researchers have discovered that prenuptial agreements are almost always sought by the economically stronger party in a relationship, usually masking underlying issues of power, trust, and sharing. When prenuptial agreements are used to legally reinforce unequal power in a relationship, they may negatively affect the couple's chance of a healthy marriage.

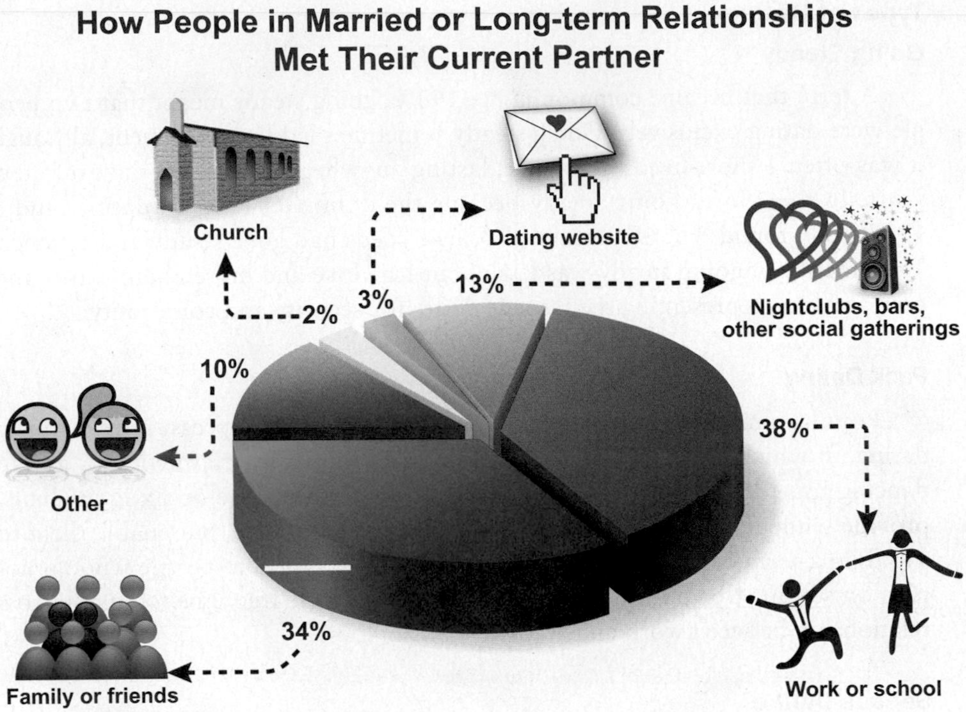

9 The trend toward longer periods of engagement provides couples with more than enough time to question whether the relationship is truly right. This, coupled with high levels of stress, has led to an increasing number of **disengagements**—calling off the engagement to avoid a later divorce. Authors Rachel Safier and Wendy Roberts estimate that about 15 percent of all engagements are called off each year. Some couples realize that they are incompatible before the big day, others are unable to work through the stresses that accompany marriage preparation, and many fear that the issues raised during the stressful planning period may soon escalate into divorce if they proceed with the wedding.

Meeting Potential Partners

10 "How did you two meet?" is a common question asked of new couples. Although traditional responses such as "through a friend" or "at work" are still the most popular answers, matchmaking is becoming an increasingly creative business. In addition, people can now meet potential partners on a singles cruise, during singles nights at their local supermarket, or even by placing a flirtatious bumper sticker on their car to let other drivers know that they are available. Other avenues include online dating and speed dating.

Online Dating

11 Once dismissed as the last resort, **online dating**—the use of specialist dating Web sites—has become an acceptable way to meet a potential partner. In a 2006 Pew survey of Internet users, 31 percent of American adults said that they knew someone

who had used a dating Web site, and 15 percent said that they knew someone who was in a long-term relationship with a person that he or she had met online.

12 Although online dating has proven to be highly successful, members of dating Web sites need to be wary of certain risk factors. Internet users do not necessarily portray themselves accurately—in one study, 81 percent of daters lied at least once or their online profile, most frequently about their weight, height, or age. Others lie about their marital status or even their gender. Researchers also point to the use of the Internet as a forum for casual sexual encounters, increasing the potential risk of sexually transmitted diseases.

Speed Dating

13 No time to socialize? Surely you can spare six minutes. That's how long potential couples usually spend getting acquainted while **speed dating**—an accelerated form of dating in which men and women choose whether to see each other again based on a very short interaction. Originally created for young Jewish singles in 1999, speed dating now provides homosexuals, heterosexuals, and a number of religious and ethnic groups with an opportunity to participate in quick, one-on-one dates with like-minded singles. Individuals spend six minutes talking to each date. If both individuals are interested, they are provided with each other's e-mail addresses.

14 Although a fun dating strategy, speed dating is superficial by nature. Researchers have noted that speed-daters usually focus on physical attractiveness and rarely ask pertinent questions about charactaristics such as education and religion. Whan it comes to speed dating, social scientists Michéle Belot and Marco Francesconi note that women prefer men who are young and tall, and men prefer women who ara young and thin. Both sexes prefer partners of a similar age, height, and education, and select partners according to physical attributes that might predict soeioeconomic status (such as age, height and weight).

—Kunz, *Think Marriages and Families*, pp. 118–120

MASTERY TEST SKILLS CHECK

Directions: Select the choice that best completes each of the following statements.

Checking Your Comprehension

_____ 1. The purpose of this selection is to
  a. offer dating advice.
  b. discuss why and how people date.
  c. explore cultural differences in dating.
  d. compare old and new dating styles.

_____ 2. According to the author, dating fulfills all of the following functions *except*
  a. it helps people improve their social status.
  b. it helps people learn social skills.
  c. it creates opportunities to meet a future spouse.
  d. it allows people to socialize and have fun.

_____ 3. The type of dating in which small groups of people go out together is called
  a. going steady.
  b. initiation.
  c. disengagement.
  d. pack dating.

_____ 4. The marriage market includes all of the following components *except*
a. the supply of men and women who are looking for partners.
b. people's preferences for certain attributes in their partners.
c. financial arrangements agreed upon by prospective partners.
d. the resources that people can offer potential partners themselves.

_____ 5. The main point of paragraph 11 is that online dating
a. is more effective than speed dating.
b. offers the most potential mates.
c. will most likely lead to a long-term relationship.
d. has become popular and accepted.

Applying Your Skills

_____ 6. All of the following terms would most likely be included on a key terms list for this selection *except*
a. marriage market.
b. disengagement.
c. labor market.
d. speed dating.

_____ 7. The purpose of the Relationship Escalation Model on page 74 is to
a. demonstrate how dating has changed over time.
b. explain the stages relationships go through.
c. illustrate the various ways to meet potential partners.
d. describe how the Internet has influenced dating.

_____ 8. According to the pie chart on page 76, the most common way to meet a partner is
a. through work or school.
b. at nightclubs, bars, or other social gatherings.
c. through family or friends.
d. on a dating website.

_____ 9. The best glossary entry for the term **prenuptial agreement** is
a. a public announcement of a couple's decision to marry.
b. a system in which prospective partners evaluate potential spouses.
c. the breakdown of a relationship or engagement.
d. a legal document stipulating financial arrangements in the event of divorce.

_____ 10. The explanation of speed dating is found under the heading
a. Reasons for Dating.
b. Types of Dating.
c. Pack Dating.
d. Meeting Potential Partners.

Studying Words

_____ 11. The word *punctuality* (par. 3) means
a. exclusivity.
b. cooperation.
c. promptness.
d. uncertainty.

_____ 12. The word *inversely* (par. 6) means
a. having the opposite effect.
b. making a comparison.
c. at the same time.
d. having no effect.

_____ 13. The word *escalates* (par. 9) means
a. increases.
b. improves.
c. removes.
d. hides.

_____ 14. The word *wary* (par. 12) means
a. angry.
b. joyful.
c. accepting.
d. guarded.

_____ 15. The word *superficial* (par. 14) means
a. expensive.
b. shallow.
c. spontaneous.
d. lengthy.

Summarizing the Reading

Directions: Complete the following summary of the reading by filling in the blanks.

Dating fulfills ____________________ in people's lives. The dating process is described as a _______________, which includes the components of supply, _______________, and resources. Types of _______________ include going steady, pack dating, serious dating, and _______________. People meet potential partners in many ways, but online dating and _______________ have recently become popular methods.

Reading Visually

1. According to the Relationship Escalation Model (p. 74), how do relationships begin?

____

____

2. How are the stages in the Relationship Escalation Model (p. 74) similar to the types of dating discussed in the selection?

____

____

____

3. What is the purpose of the pie chart on page 76?

____

____

Thinking Critically about the Reading

1. Make a connection between your own dating life and the Relationship Escalation Model graphic on page 74. How many stages have you experienced? Why is it important for a relationship to progress through these stages?
2. What do you think is the most effective way to meet people to date? What has worked for you in the past? What might you be willing to try?

CHAPTER 3

Using Context Clues

LEARNING GOALS

This chapter will show you how to:

1. Understand context clues
2. Use five types of context clues
3. Understand the limitations of context clues

Focusing on ... Context Clues

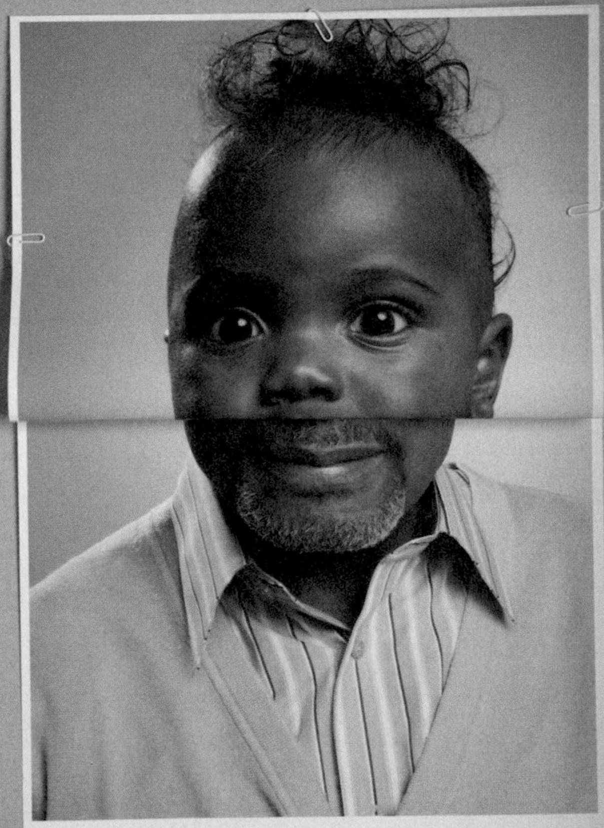

Suppose you saw this photograph in a psychology textbook. Why is the photo confusing? The top half of the photo does not fit with the bottom half. No doubt you would have trouble understanding and explaining the photograph. What is missing is its context—the information surrounding the image shown in the photo. However, if you read the chapter opener and learned that the chapter is about the aging process, then you would be able to grasp its meaning and purpose.

WHAT IS CONTEXT?

1 LEARNING GOAL
Understand context clues

Try to figure out what is missing in the following brief paragraph. Write the missing words in the blanks.

> Most Americans can speak only one ____________. Europeans, however, ____________ several. As a result, Europeans think ____________ are unfriendly and unwilling to communicate with them.

Did you insert the word *language* in the first blank, *speak* or *know* in the second blank, and *Americans* in the third blank? Most likely, you correctly identified all three missing words. You could tell from the sentence which word to put in. The words around the missing words—the sentence context—gave you clues as to which word would fit and make sense. Such clues are called **context clues.**

While you probably will not find missing words on a printed page, you will often find words that you do not know. Context clues can help you figure out the meanings of unfamiliar words.

> **Example**
>
> **Phobias,** such as fear of heights, water, or confined spaces, are difficult to eliminate.

From the sentence, you can tell that *phobia* means "fear of specific objects or situations."

Here is another example:

> The couple finally **secured** a table at the popular, crowded restaurant.

You can figure out that *secured* means "got" or "took ownership of" the table.

TYPES OF CONTEXT CLUES

2 LEARNING GOAL
Use five types of context clues

There are five types of context clues to look for: (1) definition, (2) synonym, (3) example, (4) contrast, and (5) inference.

Definition Clues

Many times a writer defines a word immediately following its use. The writer may directly define a word by giving a brief definition or a synonym (a word that has the same meaning). Such words and phrases as *means, is, refers to,* and *can be defined as* are often used. Here are some examples:

Corona refers to the outermost part of the sun's atmosphere.

A **soliloquy** is a speech made by a character in a play that reveals his or her thoughts to the audience.

At other times, rather than formally define the word, a writer may provide clues or synonyms. Punctuation is often used to signal that a definition clue to a word's meaning is to follow. Punctuation also separates the meaning clue from the rest of the sentence. Three types of punctuation are used in this way. In the examples below, notice that the meaning clue is separated from the rest of the sentence by punctuation.

1. Commas

An **oligopoly,** *control of a product by a small number of companies,* exists in the long-distance phone market.

Equity, *general principles of fairness and justice,* is used in law when existing laws do not apply or are inadequate.

2. Parentheses

A leading cause of heart disease is a diet with too much **cholesterol** (*a fatty substance made of carbon, hydrogen, and oxygen*).

3. Dashes

Ancient Egyptians wrote in **hieroglyphics**—*pictures used to represent words.*

Facets—*small flat surfaces at different angles*—bring out the beauty of a diamond.

EXERCISE 3-1 Using Definition Context Clues

Directions: Read each sentence and write a definition or synonym for each boldfaced word or phrase. Use the definition context clue to help you determine word meaning.

1. **Glog,** a Swedish hot punch, is often served at holiday parties.

____

2. The judge's **candor**—his sharp, open frankness—shocked the jury.

____

3. A **chemical bond** is a strong attractive force that holds two or more atoms together.

____

4. **Lithium** (an alkali metal) is so soft it can be cut with a knife.

____

5. Hearing, technically known as **audition,** begins when a sound wave reaches the outer ear.

____

6. Five-line rhyming poems, or **limericks,** are among the simplest forms of poetry.

____

7. Our country's **gross national product**—the total market value of its national output of goods and services—is increasing steadily.

____

8. A **species** is a group of animals or plants that share similar characteristics and are able to interbreed.

____

9. Broad, flat noodles that are served covered with sauce or butter are called **fettuccine.**

____

10. Many diseases have **latent periods,** periods of time between the infection and the first appearance of a symptom.

____

Synonym Clues

At other times, rather than formally define the word, a writer may provide a synonym—a word or brief phrase that is close in meaning. The synonym may appear in the same sentence as the unknown word.

The author purposely left the ending of his novel **ambiguous,** or *unclear,* so readers would have to decide for themselves what happened.

Other times, it may appear anywhere in the passage, in an earlier or later sentence.

After the soccer match, a **melee** broke out in the parking lot. Three people were injured in the *brawl,* and several others were arrested.

EXERCISE 3-2 Using Synonym Context Clues

Directions: Read each sentence and write a definition or synonym for each boldfaced word or phrase. Use the synonym context clue to help you determine word meaning.

1. The mayor's assistant was accused of **malfeasance,** although he denied any wrongdoing. ______________________

2. The words of the president seemed to excite and **galvanize** the American troops, who cheered enthusiastically throughout the speech. ______________________

3. Venus and Serena Williams's superior ability and **prowess** on the tennis court have inspired many girls to become athletes. ______________________

4. Many gardeners improve the quality of their soil by **amending** it with organic compost. ______________________

5. Eliminating salt from the diet is a **prudent,** sensible decision for people with high blood pressure. ______________________

6. The **cadence,** or rhythm, of the Dixieland band had many people tapping their feet along with the music. ______________________

7. Edgar Allan Poe is best known for his **macabre** short stories and poems. His eerie tale "The Fall of the House of Usher" was later made into a horror movie starring Vincent Price. ______________________

8. While she was out of the country, Greta authorized me to act as her **proxy,** or agent, in matters having to do with her business and her personal bank accounts.

   ____

9. The **arsenal** of a baseball pitcher ideally includes several different kinds of pitches. From this supply of pitches, he or she needs to have at least one that can fool the batter. ______________________

10. A **coalition** of neighborhood representatives formed to fight a proposed highway through the area. The group also had the support of several local businesses.

____

Example Clues

Writers often include examples that help to explain or clarify a word. Suppose you do not know the meaning of the word *toxic,* and you find it used in the following sentence:

> **Toxic** materials, such as arsenic, asbestos, pesticides, and lead, can cause bodily damage.

This sentence gives four examples of toxic materials. From the examples given, which are all poisonous substances, you could conclude that *toxic* means "poisonous."

Examples

Forest floors are frequently covered with **fungi**—molds, mushrooms, and mildews.

Legumes, such as peas and beans, produce pods.

Arachnids, including tarantulas, black widow spiders, and ticks, often have segmented bodies.

Newsmagazines, like *Time* or *Newsweek,* provide more details about news events than newspapers because they focus on only a few stories.

EXERCISE 3-3 Using Example Context Clues

Directions: Read each sentence and write a definition or synonym for each boldfaced word or phrase. Use the example context clue to help you determine meaning.

1. Many **pharmaceuticals,** including morphine and penicillin, are not readily available in some countries. ______________________

2. The child was **reticent** in every respect; she would not speak, refused to answer questions, and avoided looking at anyone. ______________________

3. Most **condiments,** such as pepper, mustard, and catsup, are used to improve the flavor of foods. ______________________

4. Instructors provide their students with **feedback** through test grades and comments on papers. ______________________

5. **Physiological needs**—hunger, thirst, and sex—promote survival of the human species. ______________________

6. Clothing is available in a variety of **fabrics,** including cotton, wool, polyester, and linen.

____

7. In the past month, we have had almost every type of **precipitation**—rain, snow, sleet, and hail. ______________________

8. **Involuntary reflexes,** like breathing and beating of the heart, are easily measured. ______________________

9. The student had a difficult time distinguishing between **homonyms**—words such as *see* and *sea, wore* and *war,* and *deer* and *dear.*

____

10. Abstract paintings often include such **geometrics** as squares, cubes, and triangles.

____

Contrast Clues

It is sometimes possible to determine the meaning of an unknown word from a word or phrase in the context that has an opposite meaning. If a single word provides a clue, it is often an **antonym**—a word opposite in meaning to the unknown word. Notice, in the following sentence, how a word opposite in meaning to the boldfaced word provides a clue to its meaning:

> One of the dinner guests **succumbed** to the temptation to have a second piece of cake, but the others resisted.

Although you may not know the meaning of *succumbed,* you know that the one guest who succumbed was different from the others who resisted. The word *but* suggests this. Since the others resisted a second dessert, you can tell that one guest gave in and had a piece. Thus, *succumbed* means the opposite of *resist*; that is, "to give in to."

Examples

The professor **advocates** testing on animals, *but* many of her students feel it is cruel.

Most of the graduates were **elated,** *though* a few felt sad and depressed.

The old man acted **morosely,** *whereas* his grandson was very lively.

The gentleman was quite **portly,** *but* his wife was thin.

EXERCISE 3-4 Using Contrast Context Clues

Directions: Read each sentence and write a definition or synonym for each boldfaced word. Use the contrast clue to help you determine meaning.

1. Some city dwellers are **affluent;** others live in or near poverty.

 ____

2. I am certain that the hotel will hold our reservation; however, if you are **dubious,** call to make sure. ______________________________

3. Although most experts **concurred** with the research findings, several strongly disagreed. ______________________________

4. The speaker **denounced** certain legal changes while praising other reforms.

 ____

5. The woman's parents **thwarted** her marriage plans though they liked her fiancé.

 ____

6. In medieval Europe, **peasants** led difficult lives, whereas the wealthy landowners lived in luxury. ______________________________

7. When the couple moved into their new home they **revamped** the kitchen and bathroom but did not change the rest of the rooms. ______________________________

8. The young nurse was **bewildered** by the patient's symptoms, but the doctor realized she was suffering from a rare form of leukemia. ______________________________

9. Despite my husband's **pessimism** about my chances of winning the lottery, I was certain I would win. ______________________________

____

10. The mayoral candidate praised the town council, while the mayor **deprecated** it.

____

Inference Clues

Many times you can figure out the meaning of an unknown word by using logic and reasoning skills. For instance, look at the following sentence:

> Bob is quite **versatile;** he is a good student, a top athlete, an excellent car mechanic, and a gourmet cook.

You can see that Bob is successful at many different types of activities, and you could reason that *versatile* means "capable of doing many things competently."

Examples

When the customer tried to pay with Mexican **pesos,** the clerk explained that the store accepted only U.S. dollars.

The potato salad looked so plain that I decided to **garnish** it with parsley and paprika to give it some color.

We had to leave the car and walk up because the **incline** was too steep to drive.

Since Reginald was nervous, he brought his rabbit's foot **talisman** with him to the exam.

EXERCISE 3-5 Using Inference Context Clues

Directions: Read each sentence and write a definition or synonym for each boldfaced word. Try to reason out the meaning of each word using information provided in the context.

1. The **wallabies** at the zoo looked like kangaroos. ______________________________

2. The foreign students quickly **assimilated** many aspects of American culture.

____

3. On hot, humid summer afternoons, I often feel **languid.** ______

4. Some physical fitness experts recommend jogging or weight lifting to overcome the effects of a **sedentary** job. ______

5. The legal aid clinic was **subsidized** by city and county funds. ______

6. When the bank robber reached his **haven,** he breathed a sigh of relief and began to count his money. ______

7. The teenager was **intimidated** by the presence of a police officer walking the beat and decided not to spray-paint the school wall. ______

8. The vase must have been **jostled** in shipment because it arrived with several chips in it. ______

9. Although she had visited the fortune-teller several times, she was not sure she believed in the **occult.** ______

10. If the plan did not work, the colonel had a **contingency** plan ready. ______

EXERCISE 3-6 Using Context Clues

Directions: Read each sentence and write a definition or synonym for each boldfaced word. Use the context clue to help you determine meaning.

1. The economy was in a state of continual **flux;** inflation increased one month and decreased the next. ______

2. The grand jury **exonerated** the police officer of any possible misconduct or involvement in illegal activity. ______

3. Art is always talkative, but Ed is usually **taciturn.** ______

4. Many **debilities** of old age, including poor eyesight and loss of hearing, can be treated medically. ______

5. Police **interrogation,** or questioning, can be a frightening experience.

____

6. The soap opera contained numerous **morbid** events: the death of a young child, the suicide of her father, and the murder of his older brother.

____

7. After long hours of practice, Xavier finally learned to type; Riley's efforts, however, were **futile.** ______________________________

8. Although the farm appeared **derelict,** we discovered that an elderly man lived there.

____

9. The newspaper's error was **inadvertent;** the editor did not intend to include the victim's name. ______________________________

10. To save money, we have decided to **curtail** the number of DVDs we buy each month. ______________________________

11. Steam from the hot radiator **scalded** the mechanic's hand.

____

12. The businesswoman's **itinerary** outlined her trip and listed Cleveland as her next stop. ______________________________

13. **Theologies,** such as Catholicism, Buddhism, and Hinduism, are discussed at great length in the class. ______________________________

14. Sven had a very good **rapport** with his father but was unable to get along well with his mother. ______________________________

15. The duchess had a way of **flaunting** her jewels so that everyone could see and envy them. ______________________________

EXERCISE 3-7 Using Context Clues

Directions: Read each of the following passages and use context clues to figure out the meaning of each boldfaced word or phrase. Write a synonym or brief definition for each in the space provided.

A. Some **visionaries** say that we can **transform** nursing homes into warm, inviting places. They started with a clean piece of paper and asked how we could redesign nursing homes so they **enhance** or maintain people's quality of life. The model they came up with doesn't look or even feel like a nursing home. In Green Houses, as they are called, elderly people live in a homelike setting. Instead of a **sterile** hallway lined with rooms, 10 to 12 residents live in a carpeted ranch-style house. They receive medical care suited to their personal needs, share meals at a **communal** dining table, and, if they want to, they can cook together in an open kitchen. They can even play **virtual** sports on plasma televisions. This home-like setting **fosters** a sense of community among residents and staff.

—adapted from Henslin, *Sociology*, p. 386

This photograph is a visual context clue for one of the terms used in the paragraph. Find the term and circle it.

1. visionaries ______________________
2. transform ______________________
3. enhance ______________________
4. sterile ______________________
5. communal ______________________
6. virtual ______________________
7. fosters ______________________

B. Marketers and consumers **coexist** in a complicated, two-way relationship. It's often hard to tell where marketing efforts leave off and "the real world" begins. One result of these **blurred** boundaries is that we are no longer sure (and perhaps we don't care) where the line separating this **fabricated** world from reality begins and ends. Sometimes, we **gleefully** join in the illusion. A story line in a Wonder Woman comic book featured the usual out-of-this-world **exploits** of a **vivacious** superhero. But it also included the real-world proposal of the owner of a chain of comic book stores, who persuaded DC Comics to let him **woo** his beloved in the issue.

—Solomon, *Consumer Behavior*, p. 19

8. coexist ______________________
9. blurred ______________________
10. fabricated ______________________
11. gleefully ______________________
12. exploits ______________________
13. vivacious ______________________
14. woo ______________________

C. Rising tuition; roommates who bug you; social life drama; too much noise; no privacy; long lines at the bookstore; pressure to get good grades; never enough money; worries about the economy, terrorism, and natural disaster all add up to: STRESS! You can't run from it, you can't hide from it, and it can affect you in **insidious** ways that you aren't even aware of. When we try to sleep, it **encroaches** on our **psyche** through outside noise or internal worries over all the things that need to be done. While we work at the computer, stress may interfere in the form of noise from next door, strain on our eyes, and **tension** in our back. Even when we are out socializing with friends, we feel guilty, because there is just not enough time to do what needs to be accomplished. The **precise** toll that stress exacts from us over a lifetime is unknown, but increasingly, stress is recognized as a major threat to our health.

—Donatelle, *Health*, p. 57

15. insidious ______________________________

16. encroaches ______________ 18. tension ______________

17. psyche ______________ 19. precision ______________

EXERCISE 3-8 Working with Context Clues

Directions: Bring a brief textbook excerpt, editorial, or magazine article that contains difficult vocabulary to class. Working with another student, locate and underline at least three words in the article that your partner can define by using context clues. Work together in reasoning out each word, checking a dictionary to verify meanings.

EXERCISE 3-9 Using Context Clues

Directions: Bring to class three sentences, each containing a word whose meaning is suggested by the context of the sentence. The sentences can come from textbooks or other sources, or you can write them yourself. Write each sentence on a separate index card, underlining the word to be figured out.

Form groups of three to five students. Each student should create a definition sheet to record meanings.

Pass the index cards around the group. For each card, each student should list the underlined word and write its meaning on the definition sheet. When everyone has read each card, compare meanings.

EXERCISE 3-10 A Nonsense Words Activity

Directions: Each student should write five sentences, each containing a nonsense word whose meaning is suggested by the context of the sentence. Here is an example:

> Before I went out to pick up a pizza, I put on my purplut. I buttoned up my purplut and went outside, glad that it was filled with down.
>
> (Can you figure out the meaning of a purplut?)

Form groups of three to five students. Students should take turns reading aloud their sentences as group members guess the meanings of the nonsense words.

THE LIMITATIONS OF CONTEXT CLUES

3 LEARNING GOAL
Understand the limitations of context clues

There are two limitations to the use of context clues. First, context clues seldom lead to a complete definition. Second, sometimes a sentence does not contain clues to a word's meaning. In these cases you will need to draw on other vocabulary skills. Chapter 4 will help you with these skills.

LEARNING STYLE TIPS

If you tend to be a(n) . . .	Then use context by . . .
Auditory learner	Reading the context aloud
Visual learner	Visualizing the context

SELF-TEST SUMMARY

1 What are context clues used for?	They are used to figure out the meaning of an unknown word used in a sentence or paragraph.
2 What are the five types of context clues?	The five types of context clues are: • Definition—a brief definition of or synonym for a word • Synonym—a word or phrase that is similar in meaning to the unknown word • Example—specific instances or examples that clarify a word's meaning • Contrast—a word or phrase of opposite meaning • Inference—the use of reasoning skills to figure out word meanings
3 What are the limitations of context clues?	Context clues usually do not offer a complete definition. Context clues are not always provided.

GOING ONLINE

1. **Synonyms**
   The Web is home to many free dictionaries and thesauruses, most of which offer a synonym search function. Using an online dictionary, thesaurus, or synonym finder, list five synonyms for each of the following words: *apathetic*, *belligerent*, *eschew*, *vice*, *wrest*.
2. **Antonyms (Contrast Clues)**
   Using an online dictionary or thesaurus, list five antonyms for each of the following words: *meager*, *overt*, *futile*, *ennui*, *torrid*. Compile a list of all student responses and discuss some of the most popular antonyms for each word. What other shades of meaning (called *connotations*) does each of these words have?

CHAPTER 3

MASTERY TEST 1 Vocabulary Skills

This **Mastery Test** can be completed in **MyReadingLab**.

Name ______________________ Section ____________

Date ____________ Number right ________ × 20 points = Score ________

Directions: For each of the following statements, select the answer that correctly defines the boldfaced word.

_____ 1. In the past two hundred years, many species of whales have been hunted almost to the point of extinction. In response to worldwide concern over whales, the International Whaling Commission (IWC) declared a **moratorium** on commercial whaling in 1986.

a. promotion
b. proposition
c. stopping of activity
d. competition

_____ 2. After months of declining profits, the company president declared that he would cut his salary to $1 until business improved. His announcement was intended to restore trust in the company and **avert** panic in its stockholders.

a. repair
b. prevent
c. inspire
d. ignore

_____ 3. Although Lillian was 94 years old, she was healthy and mentally sharp. As she had done for most of her life, she insisted on living in her own apartment, buying her own groceries and paying her own bills, taking care of herself and making her own decisions—it was clear that she valued her **autonomy** above all else.

a. social life
b. family support
c. loneliness
d. independence

_____ 4. Our idea of the perfect vacation includes first-class airline tickets, a deluxe hotel room, and 24-hour room service, whereas Anne and Neil prefer something much more **rustic.** The last place they stayed didn't even have indoor plumbing!

a. elegant
b. simple
c. comfortable
d. active

_____ 5. The third-grade teacher marveled at the physical **disparities** among her students. Some were the size of kindergartners while others were almost as tall as she was.

a. dislikes
b. attitudes
c. differences
d. appearances

CHAPTER 3

MASTERY TEST 2 Vocabulary Skills

This **Mastery Test** can be completed in **MyReadingLab**.

Name ______________________________ Section ____________

Date ________________ Number right ________ × 20 points = Score ________

What information do this photograph and caption provide that the passage does not?

Schools are one of the primary agents of socialization. One of their chief functions is to sort young people into the adult roles thought appropriate for them, and to teach them attitudes and skills that match these roles. What sorts of attitudes, motivations, goals, and adult roles do you think this student is learning?

Directions: Read the following passage and choose the answer that best defines each boldfaced word from the passage.

At home, children learn attitudes and values that match their family's situation in life. At school, they learn a broader **perspective** that helps prepare them to take a role in the world beyond the family. At home, a child may have been the almost **exclusive** focus of **doting** parents, but in school, the child learns *universality*—that the same rules apply to everyone, regardless of who their parents are or how special they may be at home. These new values and ways of looking at the world sometimes even replace those the child learns at home.

Sociologists have also identified a hidden **curriculum** in our schools. This term refers to values that, although not **explicitly** taught, are part of a school's "cultural message." For example, the stories and examples that are used to teach math and English may bring with them lessons in patriotism, democracy, justice, and honesty.

—adapted from Henslin, *Sociology*, p. 83

_____ 1. perspective
- a. education
- b. skill
- c. system
- d. point of view

_____ 2. exclusive
- a. unfriendly
- b. sole
- c. restricted
- d. selective

_____ 3. doting
- a. harmless
- b. elderly
- c. devoted
- d. uncomfortable

_____ 4. curriculum
- a. program
- b. appearance
- c. replacement
- d. classroom

_____ 5. explicitly
- a. importantly
- b. openly
- c. rudely
- d. typically

CHAPTER 3

MASTERY TEST 3 Reading Selection

This **Mastery Test** can be completed in **MyReadingLab**.

Name ______________________ Section ____________

Date ____________ Number right* ________ × 20 points = Score ________

Compulsive or Pathological Gambling

Rebecca J. Donatelle

This selection from the health textbook *Access to Health, Green Edition,* describes the characteristics and consequences of the disorder known as compulsive gambling.

Vocabulary Preview

pathological (par. 2) caused by or related to a disease

1 Gambling is a form of recreation and entertainment for millions of Americans. Most people who gamble do so casually and moderately to experience the excitement of anticipating a win.

2 However, over 2 million Americans are **compulsive (pathological) gamblers**, and 6 million more are considered at risk for developing a gambling addiction. The American Psychiatric Association (APA) recognizes pathological gambling as a mental disorder and lists ten characteristic behaviors, including preoccupation with gambling, unsuccessful efforts to cut back or quit, using gambling to escape problems, and lying to family members to conceal the extent of involvement.

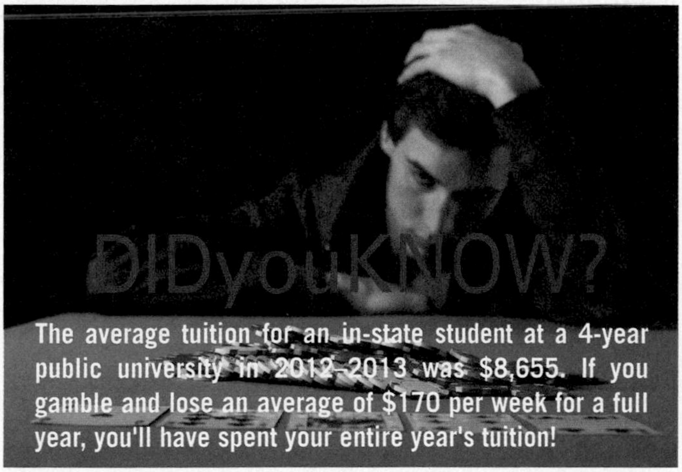

DIDyouKNOW?
The average tuition for an in-state student at a 4-year public university in 2012–2013 was $8,655. If you gamble and lose an average of $170 per week for a full year, you'll have spent your entire year's tuition!

Source: Trends in College Pricing 2012. The College Board.

3 Gamblers and drug addicts describe many similar cravings and highs. A recent study supports what many experts believe to be true: that compulsive gambling is like drug addiction. Compulsive gamblers in this study were found to have decreased blood flow to a key section of the brain's reward system. Much as with people who abuse drugs, it is thought that compulsive gamblers compensate for this deficiency in their brain's reward system by overdoing it and getting hooked. Most compulsive gamblers state that they seek excitement even more than money. They place progressively larger bets to obtain the desired level of exhilaration.

*To calculate the number right, use items 1–10 under "Mastery Test Skills Check."

4 Gambling problems are more prevalent among men than among women. Gambling prevalence is also higher among lower-income individuals, those who are divorced, African Americans, older adults, and people residing within 50 miles of a casino. Residents in Southern states, where opportunities to gamble have increased significantly over the past 20 years, also have higher gambling rates.

5 Among students, gambling is on the rise on college campuses across the nation. Since 2002, the University of Pennsylvania's Annenburg Public Policy Center has been conducting a tracking survey of gambling among young people aged 14 to 22. Their survey reported that in 2005, 15.5 percent of college students reported gambling once a week, up from 8.3 percent in 2002, an 87 percent increase. Men dominated the gambling scene, with 26 percent reportedly doing it each week, whereas 5.5 percent of women reported gambling weekly.

6 What accounts for this trend? College students have easier access to gambling opportunities than ever before, with the advent of online gambling, a growing number of casinos, scratch tickets, lotteries, and sports-betting networks. In particular, the largest boost has been from the increasing popularity of poker. Access to poker on the Internet and poker tournaments that are frequently televised have revived the game, causing many young people to spend an unhealthy amount of time and money participating in online poker tournaments.

7 Other characteristics associated with gambling among college students include spending more time watching TV and using computers for nonacademic purposes, spending less time studying, earning lower grades, participating in intercollegiate athletics, engaging in heavy episodic drinking, and using illicit drugs in the past year. See the Health Headlines box on page 99 for more on college students and gambling.

8 Whereas casual gamblers can stop anytime they wish and are capable of understanding why they need to stop, compulsive gamblers are unable to control the urge to gamble even in the face of devastating consequences: high debt, legal problems, and the loss of everything meaningful, including homes, families, jobs, health, and even their lives. Gambling can also have a detrimental effect on health: cardiovascular problems affect 38 percent of compulsive gamblers, and their suicide rate is 20 times higher than that of the general population.

Health Headlines

Gambling and College Students

9 Although many people gamble occasionally without it ever becoming a problem, many otherwise "model" students can find themselves caught up in the rush of making big bets and winning even bigger money. Consider the story of John,* a Lehigh University sophomore, who is the son of a Baptist minister, a fraternity member, a cellist in the university orchestra, and the sophomore class president—the epitome of a responsible student active in the community and serving as a role model to the student body. When John was arrested for allegedly robbing the Wachovia Bank branch in Allentown, Pennsylvania, making off with $2,781, many wondered why such a good kid would be driven to such an act. According to the Associated Press, his lawyer stated that his client had run up about $5,000 in debt playing online poker. In a desperate move to feed his compulsive gambling addiction, John turned to bank robbery.

10 Compulsive gambling on college campuses has become a big concern for college administrators as gambling grows ever more popular among students. The National Collegiate Athletic Association (NCAA) estimates that each year during March Madness (the men's college basketball tournament), there are over 1.2 million active gambling pools, with over 2.5 billion dollars gambled. More and more of these dollars come from the pockets of college students. There is growing evidence, in fact, that betting on college campuses is interfering with students' financial and academic futures. In a recent survey, approximately 60 percent of students reported they had gambled, and almost 13 percent reported a significant loss of time and 12 percent a significant loss of money. Consider the following:

- Almost 53 percent of college students have participated in most forms of gambling, including casino gambling, lottery tickets, racing, and sports betting in the past month.
- At least 78 percent of youths have placed a bet by the age of 18.
- An estimated 18 percent of men and 4 percent of women on college campuses could be classified as problem gamblers.
- The three most common reasons college students give for gambling are risk, excitement, and the chance to make money.

---

*Not his real name

11 Although most college students who gamble are able to do so without developing a problem, warning signs of problem gambling include the following:

- Frequent talk about gambling
- Spending more time or money on gambling than can be afforded
- Borrowing money to gamble
- Encouraging or challenging others to gamble
- Selling sports-betting cards or organizing sports pools
- Possession of gambling paraphernalia such as lottery tickets or poker items
- Missing or being late for school, work, or family activities due to gambling
- Feeling sad, anxious, fearful, or angry about gambling losses

—Donatelle, *Access to Health*, pp. 355–356

MASTERY TEST SKILLS CHECK

Directions: Select the choice that best completes each of the following statements.

Checking Your Comprehension

_____ 1. The purpose of this selection is to
   a. compare different forms of recreation and entertainment.
   b. identify treatment options for people with addictions.
   c. describe compulsive gambling and its effects.
   d. discuss popular trends on college campuses.

_____ 2. The main point of paragraph 3 is that
   a. compulsive gambling is similar to drug addiction.
   b. compulsive gamblers often become addicted to drugs.
   c. drug addicts have decreased blood flow to the brain's reward system.
   d. gamblers and drug addicts crave excitement.

_____ 3. The largest boost to college gambling has come from the increasing popularity of
   a. lotteries.
   b. sports-betting networks.
   c. scratch tickets.
   d. poker.

_____ 4. Gambling rates are higher among all of the following groups *except*
   a. divorced people.
   b. women.
   c. residents in Southern states.
   d. people living within 50 miles of a casino.

_____ 5. Paragraph 8 is primarily about
   a. casual gamblers' legal problems.
   b. the causes of addictive behavior.
   c. health problems among gamblers.
   d. the negative consequences of compulsive gambling.

Applying Your Skills

_____ 6. In paragraph 2, the word that is given as a synonym clue for *compulsive* is
a. pathological.
b. psychiatric.
c. mental.
d. unsuccessful.

_____ 7. In paragraph 3, the synonym for the word *exhilaration* is
a. addiction.
b. compulsive.
c. excitement.
d. cravings.

_____ 8. In paragraph 4, inference clues indicate that the word *prevalent* means
a. unusual or rare.
b. widespread or common.
c. decreasing in popularity.
d. expensive.

_____ 9. In paragraph 8, the examples of "high debt, legal problems, and the loss of everything meaningful" indicate that the word *devastating* means
a. unimportant.
b. rewarding.
c. pleasant.
d. crushing.

_____ 10. In paragraph 8, the meaning of the word *detrimental* is indicated by which of the following types of context clues?
a. contrast
b. example
c. definition
d. inference

Studying Words

_____ 11. The word *deficiency* (par. 3) means
a. similarity.
b. shortage.
c. creation.
d. approach.

_____ 12. In the sentence "Men dominated the gambling scene" (par. 5), the word *dominated* means
a. took command.
b. were powerful.
c. were larger in number.
d. looked down on.

_____ 13. The word *advent* (par. 6) means
a. arrival.
b. average.
c. ending.
d. advertisement.

_____ 14. The word *nonacademic* (par. 7) means
a. published.
b. studious.
c. not harmful.
d. not educational.

_____ 15. The word *epitome* (par. 9 in the Health Headlines box) means
a. opponent.
b. model.
c. message.
d. delivery.

For more practice, ask your instructor for an opportunity to work on the mastery tests that appear in the Test Bank.

Summarizing the Reading

Directions: Complete the following summary of the reading by filling in the blanks.

Over 2 million Americans are ________________ or pathological gamblers, and 6 million more may develop a gambling ________________. The American ________________ Association recognizes pathological gambling as a ________________ with ten characteristic behaviors. Compulsive gambling is similar to ________________. Gambling problems are more ________________ among men, and gambling rates are higher among several groups. Gambling is increasing among ________________, a trend related to students' easy access to gambling opportunities and especially to the revival of ________________. In contrast to ________________ gamblers, compulsive gamblers cannot ________________ the urge to gamble despite facing harmful ________________ for their financial, emotional, and physical health.

Reading Visually

1. What concept does the "Did You Know?" box on page 97 illustrate or correspond to in the reading?

   ____

2. What is your overall impression of the photograph in the Health Headlines box on page 99? How does the photograph contrast with the information that is discussed in the box?

   ____

   ____

   ____

Thinking Critically about the Reading

1. How big a problem do you think gambling is at your school or among the people you know? Were the statistics in the selection surprising to you?
2. Reread the warning signs of problem gambling in the Health Headlines box. Could those warning signs apply to any of your own habits or behaviors? Try replacing the word *gambling* with another word or phrase such as *shopping*, *texting*, or *video gaming*.
3. Why did the author include the story about John (par. 9 in the Health Headlines box)? What does his story contribute to the selection?

CHAPTER 4

Using Word Parts and Learning New Words

Focusing on … Word Parts

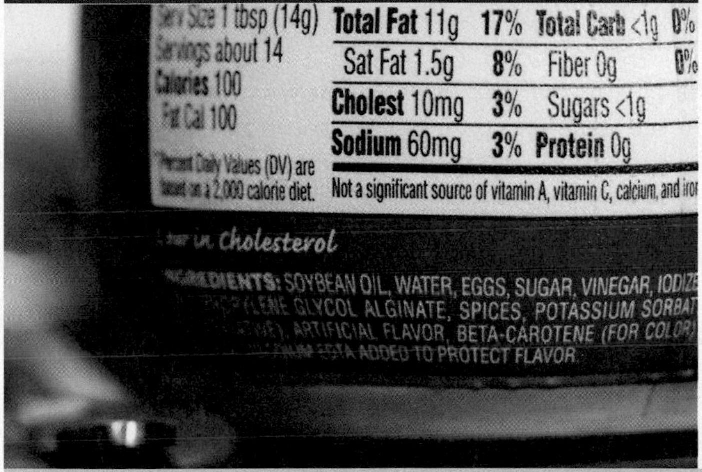

Total Fat 11g 17% Total Carb <1g 0%
Sat Fat 1.5g 8% Fiber 0g
Cholest 10mg 3% Sugars <1g
Sodium 60mg 3% Protein 0g
Servings about 14
Calories 100
Not a significant source of vitamin A, vitamin C, calcium, and
Cholesterol
SOYBEAN OIL, WATER, EGGS, SUGAR, VINEGAR,
ALGINATE, SPICES, POTASSIUM
ARTIFICIAL FLAVOR, BETA-CAROTENE (FOR
ADDED TO PROTECT FLAVOR

LEARNING GOALS

This chapter will show you how to

1. Use prefixes, roots, and suffixes
2. Learn new words
3. Use a dictionary and thesaurus
4. Pronounce unfamiliar words
5. Develop a system for learning new words

This ingredients label is taken from a jar of mayonnaise. How many of the ingredients and terms are familiar? Do you know what propylene glycol alginate and beta-carotene are? If not, how could you figure out the meanings?

This chapter shows you how to use your knowledge of word parts to figure out the meanings of words you do not know, how to use a dictionary and thesaurus, and how to use an index card system to learn and remember new words.

LEARN PREFIXES, ROOTS, AND SUFFIXES

1 LEARNING GOAL
Use prefixes, roots, and suffixes

Many students build their vocabulary word by word: if they study ten new words, then they have learned ten new words. If they study 30 words, they can recall 30 meanings. Would you like a better and faster way to build your vocabulary?

By learning the meanings of the parts that make up a word, you will be able to figure out the meanings of many more words. For example, if you learn that *pre-* means "before," then you can begin to figure out hundreds of words that begin with *pre-* (*premarital, premix, preemployment*).

In this chapter you will learn about compound words and about the beginnings, middles, and endings of words called prefixes, roots, and suffixes.

Suppose that you came across the following sentence in a human anatomy textbook:

> Trichromatic plates are used frequently in the text to illustrate the position of body organs.

If you did not know the meaning of *trichromatic,* how could you determine it? There are no clues in the sentence context. One solution is to look up the word in a dictionary. An easier and faster way is to break the word into parts and analyze the meaning of each part. Many words in the English language are made up of word parts called **prefixes, roots,** and **suffixes.** These word parts have specific meanings that, when added together, can help you determine the meaning of the word as a whole.

The word *trichromatic* can be divided into three parts: its *prefix, root*, and *suffix.*

	Prefix	+	Root	+	Suffix	=	**New word**
	tri	+	chrom	+	atic	=	**trichromatic**
Meaning ⟶	three	+	color	+	characteristic of	=	having three colors

You can see from this analysis that *trichromatic* means "having three colors."

Here are a few other examples of words that you can figure out by using prefixes, roots, and suffixes:

The parents thought the child was **unteachable.**

un- = not

teach = help someone learn

-able = able to do something

unteachable = not able to be taught

The student was a **nonconformist.**

non- = not

conform = go along with others

-ist = one who does something

nonconformist = someone who does not go along with others

The first step in using the prefix-root-suffix method is to become familiar with the most commonly used word parts. The prefixes and roots listed in Tables 4-1 (p. 107) and 4-2 (p. 111) will give you a good start in determining the meanings of thousands of words without looking them up in the dictionary. For instance, more than ten thousand words can begin with the prefix *non-*. Not all these words are listed in a collegiate dictionary, but they would appear in an unabridged dictionary. Another common prefix, *pseudo-*, is used in more than four hundred words. A small amount of time spent learning word parts can yield a large payoff in new words learned.

Before you begin to use word parts to figure out new words, there are a few things you need to know:

1. **In most cases, a word is built upon at least one root.**
2. **Words can have more than one prefix, root, or suffix.**
   a. Words can be made up of two or more roots (geo/logy).
   b. Some words have two prefixes (in/sub/ordination).
   c. Some words have two suffixes (beauti/ful/ly).
3. **Words do not always have a prefix and a suffix.**
   a. Some words have neither a prefix nor a suffix (read).
   b. Others have a suffix but no prefix (read/ing).
   c. Others have a prefix but no suffix (pre/read).
4. **The spelling of roots may change as they are combined with suffixes.** Some common variations are included in Table 4-2.
5. **Different prefixes, roots, or suffixes may have the same meaning.** For example, the prefixes *bi-*, *di-*, and *duo-* all mean "two."

6. **Sometimes you may identify a group of letters as a prefix or root but find that it does not carry the meaning of that prefix or root.** For example, the letters *mis* in the word *missile* are part of the root and are not the prefix *mis-*, which means "wrong, bad."

Prefixes

Prefixes appear at the beginning of many English words: they alter the meaning of the root to which they are connected. For example, if you add the prefix *re-* to the word *read*, the word *reread* is formed, meaning "to read again." If *pre-* is added to the word *reading*, the word *prereading* is formed, meaning "before reading." If the prefix *post-* is added, the word *postreading* is formed, meaning "after reading." In Table 4-1 (p. 107), more than 40 common prefixes are grouped according to meaning.

EXERCISE 4-1 Using Prefixes

Directions: Using the list of common prefixes in Table 4-1, match each word in Column A with its meaning in Column B. Write the letter of your choice in the space provided.

	Column A	Column B
______	1. misplaced	a. half of a circle
______	2. postgraduate	b. build again
______	3. dehumidify	c. tiny duplicate of printed material
______	4. semicircle	d. continuing studies past graduation
______	5. nonprofit	e. not fully developed
______	6. reconstruct	f. put in the wrong position
______	7. triathlete	g. build up electrical power again
______	8. microcopy	h. not for making money
______	9. recharge	i. to remove moisture from
______	10. immature	j. one who participates in three-part sporting events

TABLE 4-1 Common Prefixes

Prefix	Meaning	Sample Word
Prefixes referring to amount or number		
mono/uni	one	monocle/unicycle
bi/di/du	two	bimonthly/divorce/duet
tri	three	triangle
quad	four	quadrant
quint/pent	five	quintet/pentagon
deci	ten	decimal
centi	hundred	centigrade
milli	thousand	milligram
micro	small	microscope
multi/poly	many	multipurpose/polygon
semi	half	semicircle
equi	equal	equidistant
Prefixes meaning "not" (negative)		
a	not	asymmetrical
anti	against	antiwar
contra	against, opposite	contradict
dis	apart, away, not	disagree
in/il/ir/im	not	incorrect/illogical/irreversible/impossible
mis	wrongly	misunderstand
non	not	nonfiction
pseudo	false	pseudoscientific
un	not	unpopular
Prefixes giving direction, location, or placement		
ab	away	absent
ad	toward	adhesive
ante/pre	before	antecedent/premarital
circum/peri	around	circumference/perimeter
com/col/con	with, together	compile/collide/convene
de	away, from	depart
dia	through	diameter
ex/extra	from, out of, former	ex-wife/extramarital
hyper	over, excessive	hyperactive
inter	between	interpersonal
intro/intra	within, into, in	introduction/intramural
post	after	posttest
re	back, again	review
retro	backward	retrospect
sub	under, below	submarine
super	above, extra	supercharge
tele	far	telescope
trans	across, over	transcontinental

EXERCISE 4-2 Using Prefixes

Directions: Use the list of common prefixes in Table 4-1 (p. 107) to determine the meaning of each of the following words. Write a brief definition or synonym for each. If you are unfamiliar with the root, you may need to check a dictionary.

1. interoffice: ______
2. supernatural: ______
3. nonsense: ______
4. introspection: ______
5. prearrange: ______
6. reset: ______
7. subtopic: ______
8. transmit: ______
9. multidimensional: ______
10. imperfect: ______

EXERCISE 4-3 Using Prefixes to Write Brief Definitions

Directions: Write a brief definition for each word in boldfaced type.

1. an **atypical** child: ______
2. to **hyperventilate**: ______
3. an **extraordinary** request: ______
4. **semisoft** cheese: ______
5. **antisocial** behavior: ______
6. to **circumnavigate** the globe: ______
7. a **triweekly** publication: ______
8. an **uneventful** weekend: ______

9. a **disfigured** face: ______________________________

10. to **exhale** smoke: ______________________________

EXERCISE 4-4 Using Prefixes

Directions: Read each of the following sentences. Use your knowledge of prefixes to fill in the blank to complete the word.

1. A person who speaks two languages is _______**lingual.**
2. A letter or number written beneath a line of print is called a _______**script.**
3. The new sweater had a snag, and I returned it to the store because it was _______**perfect.**
4. The flood damage was permanent and _______**reversible.**
5. I was not given the correct date and time; I was _______**informed.**
6. People who speak several different languages are _______**lingual.**
7. A musical _______**lude** was played between the events in the ceremony.
8. I decided the magazine was uninteresting, so I _______**continued** my subscription.
9. Merchandise that does not pass factory inspection is considered _______**standard** and sold at a discount.
10. The tuition refund policy approved this week will apply to last year's tuition as well; the policy will be __ina__**active** to January 1 of last year.
11. The elements were _______**acting** with each other when they began to bubble and their temperature rose.
12. _______**ceptives** are widely used to prevent unwanted pregnancies.
13. All of the waitresses were required to wear the restaurant's _______**form.**
14. The _______**viewer** asked the presidential candidates unexpected questions about important issues.
15. The draperies were _______**colored** from long exposure to the sun.

EXERCISE 4-5 Using Prefixes

Directions: Use your knowledge of prefixes to supply the missing word in each sentence. Write the word in the space provided.

1. Our house is a duplex. The one next door with three apartments is a ________________.
2. A preparation applied to the skin to reduce or prevent perspiration is called an ________________.
3. A person who cannot read or write is ________________.
4. I did not use my real name; instead I gave a ________________.
5. If someone seems to have greater powers than do normal humans, he or she might be called ________________.
6. If you plan to continue to take college courses after you graduate, you will be taking ________________ courses.
7. Substances that fight bacteria are known as ________________ drugs.
8. The branch of biology that deals with very small living organisms is ________________.
9. In the metric system a ________________ is one one-hundredth of a meter.
10. One one-thousandth of a second is called a ________________.

EXERCISE 4-6 Using Prefixes

Directions: Working in teams of two, list as many words as you can think of for two of the following prefixes: *multi-, mis-, trans-, com-, inter-*. Then share your lists with the class.

Roots

Roots carry the basic or core meaning of a word. Hundreds of root words are used to build words in the English language. More than thirty of the most common and most useful are listed in Table 4-2. Knowledge of the meanings of these roots will enable you to unlock the meanings of many words. For example, if you know that the root *dic/dict* means "tell or say," then you would have a clue

TABLE 4-2 Common Roots

Common Root	Meaning	Sample Word
aster/astro	star	astronaut
aud/audit	hear	audible
bene	good, well	benefit
bio	life	biology
cap	take, seize	captive
chron/chrono	time	chronology
cog	to learn	cognitive
corp	body	corpse
cred	believe	incredible
dict/dic	tell, say	predict
duc/duct	lead	introduce
fact/fac	make, do	factory
geo	earth	geophysics
graph	write	telegraph
log/logo/logy	study, thought	psychology
mit/miss	send	permit/dismiss
mort/mor	die, death	immortal
path	feeling	sympathy
phono	sound, voice	telephone
photo	light	photosensitive
port	carry	transport
scop	seeing	microscope
scrib/script	write	inscription
sen/sent	feel	insensitive
spec/spic/spect	look, see	retrospect
tend/tens/tent	stretch or strain	tension
terr/terre	land, earth	territory
theo	god	theology
ven/vent	come	convention
vert/vers	turn	invert
vis/vid	see	invisible/video
voc	call	vocation

to the meanings of such words as *dictate* (to speak for someone to write down), *diction* (wording or manner of speaking), or *dictionary* (book that "tells" what words mean).

EXERCISE 4-7 Using Roots

Directions: Using the list of common roots in Table 4-2 (p. 111), match each word in Column A with its meaning in Column B. Write the letter of your choice in the space provided.

Column A	Column B
____ 1. benediction	a. undertaker
____ 2. audible	b. went back to
____ 3. missive	c. able to respond to light
____ 4. telemarketing	d. come between two things
____ 5. mortician	e. channel or pipe that brings water from a distance
____ 6. intervene	f. use the voice
____ 7. reverted	g. blessing
____ 8. aqueduct	h. letter or message
____ 9. photoactive	i. can be heard
____ 10. vocalize	j. selling a product by phone

EXERCISE 4-8 Using Roots

Directions: Use the list of common roots in Table 4-2 to determine the meanings of the following words. Write a brief definition or synonym for each, checking a dictionary if necessary.

1. dictum: ____________________
2. biomedicine: ____________________
3. photocopy: ____________________

4. porter: ______________________________

5. visibility: ______________________________

6. credentials: ______________________________

7. speculate: ______________________________

8. terrain: ______________________________

9. audition: ______________________________

10. sentiment: ______________________________

11. astrophysics: ______________________________

12. capacity: ______________________________

13. chronicle: ______________________________

14. corporation: ______________________________

15. facile: ______________________________

16. autograph: ______________________________

17. sociology: ______________________________

18. phonometer: ______________________________

19. sensation: ______________________________

20. vocal: ______________________________

EXERCISE 4-9 Completing Sentences

Directions: Complete each of the following sentences with one of the words listed below.

apathetic	dictated	graphic	scriptures	tendon
captivated	extensive	phonics	spectators	verdict
deduce	extraterrestrial	prescribed	synchronized	visualize

1. The jury brought in its ____________________ after one hour of deliberation.

2. Religious or holy writings are called ____________________.

3. She closed her eyes and tried to ____________________ the license plate number.

4. The ____________________ watching the football game were tense.

5. The doctor ____________________ two types of medication.

6. The list of toys the child wanted for his birthday was ____________________.

7. The criminal appeared ____________________ when the judge pronounced the sentence.

8. The runners ____________________ their watches before beginning the race.

9. The textbook contained numerous ____________________ aids, including maps, charts, and diagrams.

10. The study of the way different parts of words sound is called ____________________.

11. The athlete strained a(n) ____________________ and was unable to continue training.

12. The movie was about a(n) ____________________, a creature not from earth.

13. The district manager ____________________ a letter to her secretary, who then typed it.

14. Through his attention-grabbing performance, he ____________________ the audience.

15. By putting together the clues, the detective was finally able to ____________________ who committed the crime.

EXERCISE 4-10 Using Roots

Directions: List two words for each of the following roots: *dict/dic, spec/spic/spect, fact/fac, phono, scrib/script*.

Suffixes

Suffixes are word endings that often change the part of speech of a word. For example, adding the suffix *-y* to the noun *cloud* forms the adjective *cloudy.* Accompanying the change in part of speech is a shift in meaning (*cloudy* means "resembling clouds; overcast with clouds; dimmed or dulled as if by clouds").

Often, several different words can be formed from a single root word by adding different suffixes.

Root	+	Suffix	=	New word
class	+	ify	=	**classify**
class	+	ification	=	**classification**
class	+	ic	=	**classic**
right	+	ly	=	**rightly**
right	+	ful	=	**rightful**
right	+	eous	=	**righteous**

If you know the meaning of the root word and the ways in which different suffixes affect the meaning of the root word, you will be able to figure out a word's meaning when a suffix is added. A list of common suffixes and their meanings appears in Table 4-3 (p. 116).

You can expand your vocabulary by learning the variations in meaning that occur when suffixes are added to words you already know. When you find a word that you do not know, look for the root. Then, using the sentence the word is in (its context; see Chapter 3), figure out what the word means with the suffix added. Occasionally you may find that the spelling of the root word has been changed. For instance, a final *e* may be dropped, a final consonant may be doubled, or a final *y* may be changed to *i.* Consider the possibility of such changes when trying to identify the root word.

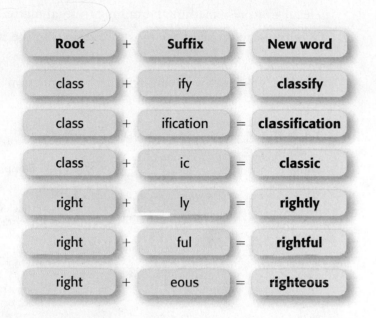

The article was a **compilation** of facts.

root + suffix

compil(e) + -ation = something that has been compiled, or put together into an orderly form

We were concerned with the **legality** of our decision to change addresses.

root + suffix

legal + -ity = something pertaining to legal matters

Our college is one of the most **prestigious** in the state.

root + suffix

prestig(e) + -ious = having prestige or distinction

TABLE 4-3 Common Suffixes

Suffix	Sample Word
Suffixes that refer to a state, condition, or quality	
able	touchable
ance	assistance
ation	confrontation
ence	reference
ible	tangible
ion	discussion
ity	superiority
ive	permissive
ment	amazement
ness	kindness
ous	jealous
ty	loyalty
y	crcamy
Suffixes that mean "one who"	
an	Italian
ant	participant
ee	referee
eer	engineer
ent	resident
er	teacher
ist	activist
or	advisor
Suffixes that mean "pertaining to or referring to"	
al	autumnal
ship	friendship
hood	brotherhood
ward	homeward

EXERCISE 4-11 Using Suffixes

Directions: For each suffix shown in Table 4-3, write another example of a word you know that has that suffix.

EXERCISE 4-12 Creating New Words by Adding Suffixes

Directions: For each of the words listed, add a suffix so that the word will complete the sentence. Write the new word in the space provided. Check a dictionary if you are unsure of the spelling.

1. converse

   Our phone ____________________ lasted ten minutes.

2. assist

   The medical ____________________ labeled the patient's blood samples.

3. qualify

   The job applicant outlined his ____________________ to the interviewer.

4. intern

   The doctor completed her ____________________ at Memorial Medical Center.

5. eat

   We did not realize that the blossoms of the plant could be ____________________.

6. audio

   She spoke so softly that her voice was not ____________________.

7. season

   It is usually very dry in July, but this year it has rained constantly. The weather is not very ____________________.

8. permit

   The professor granted her ____________________ to miss class.

9. instruct

   The lecture on Freud was very ____________________.

10. remember

    The wealthy businessman donated the building in ____________________ of his deceased father.

11. mortal

    The ____________________ rate in Ethiopia is very high.

12. president

    The ____________________ race held many surprises.

13. feminine

    She called herself a ____________________, although she never actively supported the movement for equal rights for women.

14. hazard

    The presence of toxic waste in the lake is ____________________ to health.

15. destine

    The young man felt it was his ____________________ to become a priest.

EXERCISE 4-13 Adding Suffixes

Directions: Working with a classmate, for each word listed below, write as many new words as you can create by adding suffixes. Share your findings with the class.

1. compare: ____________________
2. adapt: ____________________
3. right: ____________________
4. identify: ____________________
5. will: ____________________
6. prefer: ____________________
7. notice: ____________________
8. like: ____________________
9. pay: ____________________
10. promote: ____________________

How to Use Word Parts

Think of roots as being at the root or core of a word's meaning. There are many more roots than are listed in Table 4-2. You already know many of these because they are used in everyday speech. Think of prefixes as word parts that are added before the root to qualify or change its meaning. Think of suffixes as add-ons that make the word fit grammatically into the sentence in which it is used.

When you come upon a word you do not know, keep the following pointers in mind:

Using Word Parts

1. **First, look for the root.** Think of this as looking for a word inside a larger word. Often a letter or two will be missing.

un/utter/able	defens/ible
inter/colleg/iate	re/popular/ize
post/operat/ive	non/adapt/able
im/measur/ability	non/commit/tal

2. **If you do not recognize the root, then you will probably not be able to figure out the word.** The next step is to check its meaning in a dictionary. For tips on locating words in a dictionary rapidly and easily, see "Using a Dictionary" page 128.
3. **If you did recognize the root word, look for a prefix.** If there is one, determine how it changes the meaning of the word.

un/utterable	un- = not
post/operative	post- = after

4. **Locate the suffix.** Determine how it further adds to or changes the meaning of the root word.

unutter/able	-able = able to
postoperat/ive	-ive = state or condition

5. **Next, try out the meaning in the sentence in which the word was used.** Substitute your meaning for the word, and see whether the sentence makes sense.

Some of the victim's thoughts were **unutterable** at the time of the crime.

unutterable = cannot be spoken

My sister was worried about the cost of **postoperative** care.

postoperative = describing state or condition after an operation

EXERCISE 4-14 Identifying Roots and Writing Definitions

Directions: Use the steps listed previously to determine the meaning of each bold-faced word. Underline the root in each word, and then write a brief definition of the word that fits its use in the sentence.

1. The doctor felt the results of the X-rays were **indisputable**

____

2. The **dissimilarity** among the three brothers was surprising.

____

3. The **extortionist** demanded two payments of $10,000 each, threatening physical harm if it was not paid on time.

____

4. It is **permissible** to camp in most state parks.

____

5. The student had an unusually **retentive** memory.

____

6. The **traumatic** event changed the child's attitude toward animals.

____

7. We were surprised by her **insincerity**.

____

8. The child's **hypersensitivity** worried his parents.

____

9. The English instructor told Peter that he had written a **creditable** paper.

____

10. The rock group's agent hoped to **repopularize** their first hit song.

____

11. The gambler was filled with **uncertainty** about the horse race.

____

12. The **nonenforcement** of the speed limit led to many deaths.

____

13. The effects of the disease were **irreversible**.

____

14. The mysterious music seemed to **foretell** the murder of the movie's heroine.

____

15. The **polyphony** filled the concert hall.

____

16. Sailors used to think the North Sea **unnavigable**.

____

17. She received a **dishonorable** discharge from the Marines.

____

18. The criminal was **unapologetic** to the judge about the crimes he had committed.

____

19. A systems analysis revealed that the factory was **underproductive**.

____

20. He rotated the dial **counterclockwise**.

____

EXERCISE 4-15 Using Word Parts

Directions: Read each of the following paragraphs and determine the meaning of each boldfaced word. Write a brief definition for each in the space provided.

A. The values and norms of most **subcultures** blend in with mainstream society. In some cases, however, some of the group's values and norms place it at odds with the dominant culture. **Sociologists** use the term **counterculture** to refer to such groups. To better see this distinction, consider motorcycle enthusiasts and motorcycle gangs. Motorcycle **enthusiasts**—who emphasize personal freedom and speed and **affirm** cultural values of success through work or education—are members of a subculture. In contrast, the Hell's Angels, Pagans, and Bandidos not only stress freedom and speed but also value dirtiness and contempt toward women, work, and education. This makes them a counterculture. Countercultures do not have to be negative, however. Back in the 1800s, the Mormons were a counterculture that challenged the dominant culture's core value of **monogamy**.

—Henslin, *Sociology*, p. 52

What is the purpose of this photo and caption?

Why is professional dancing a subculture and not a counterculture?
Source: Bonnie Kamin/Photo Edit, Inc.

1. subcultures ______________________________

2. sociologists ______________________________

3. counterculture ______________________________

4. enthusiasts ______________________________

5. affirm ______________________________

6. monogamy ______________________________

B. Our **perception** of the richness or quality of the material in clothing, bedding, or upholstery is linked to its "feel," whether rough or smooth, flexible or **inflexible**. We **equate** a smooth fabric, such as silk, with luxury, whereas we consider denim to be practical and **durable**. Fabrics composed of **scarce** materials or that require a high degree of processing to achieve their smoothness or fineness tend to be more expensive and thus we assume they are of a higher class.

—adapted from Solomon, *Consumer Behavior*, pp. 62–63

7. perception

____

8. inflexible

____

9. equate

____

10. durable

____

11. scarce

____

C. The college years mark a critical **transition** period for young adults as they move away from families and establish themselves as **independent** adults. The transition to independence will be easier for those who have successfully accomplished earlier developmental tasks, such as learning how to solve problems, make and evaluate decisions, define and **adhere** to personal values, and establish both casual and **intimate** relationships. People who have not fulfilled these earlier tasks may find their lives interrupted by **recurrent** "crises" left over from earlier stages. For example, if they did not learn to trust others in childhood, they may have difficulty establishing intimate relationships as adults.

—Donatelle, *Health*, p. 34

12. transition

____

13. independent

____

14. adhere

____

15. intimate

____

16. recurrent

____

D. An ecosystem is a group of living organisms and the **abiotic** spheres with which they interact. **Ecology** is the scientific study of ecosystems. Ecologists study **interrelationships** between living organisms and their environments within particular ecosystems, as well as interrelationships among various ecosystems in the **biosphere**.

—Rubenstein, *Contemporary Human Geography*, p. 25

17. abiotic

____

18. ecology

____

19. interrelationships

____

20. biosphere

____

EXERCISE 4-16 Using Prefixes to Change Meaning

Directions: Write a sentence using each of the key words listed below. Exchange your sentences with a partner. Read each sentence and change the meaning of the key word by adding a prefix and/or suffix, and then rewrite the sentence to reflect the change in meaning. Exchange sentences to check each other's work.

Key Words: allow interest regular agree direct

LEARN NEW WORDS

2 LEARNING GOAL Learn new words

Most people think they have just one level of vocabulary and that this can be characterized as large or small, strong or weak. Actually, everyone has at least four levels of vocabulary, and each varies in strength:

1. Words you use in everyday speech or writing

   Examples: decide, death, daughter, damp, date

2. Words you know but seldom or never use in your own speech or writing

   Examples: rebuke, bleak, literate, originality, orient

3. Words you have heard or seen before but cannot fully define

Examples: denounce, deficit, decadent, deductive, decisive

4. Words you have never heard or seen before

Examples: doggerel, dogma, denigrate, deleterious, diatropism

In the spaces provided, list five words that fall under each of these four categories. It will be easy to think of words for Category 1. Words for Categories 2–4 may be taken from the following list:

contort	garbanzo	voluntary	impertinent
continuous	logic	resistance	delicacy
credible	connive	alien	impartial
activate	congruent	meditate	delve
deletion	demean	fraught	attentive
focus	liberate	gastronome	osmosis
manual	heroic	havoc	

Category 1	Category 2	Category 3	Category 4
________	________	________	________
________	________	________	________
________	________	________	________
________	________	________	________
________	________	________	________

To build your vocabulary, try to shift as many words as possible from a less familiar to a more familiar category. Use the following steps:

1. Start by noticing words.
2. Question, check, and remember their meanings.
3. Record new words and their meanings in a log, notebook, or computer file.
4. Use these new words often in your speech and writing.

SELECT AND USE A DICTIONARY

3 LEARNING GOAL Use a dictionary and thesaurus

Every writer needs to use a dictionary, not only to check spellings, but also to check meanings and the appropriate usage of words.

Print Dictionaries

You should have a desk or collegiate dictionary plus a pocket dictionary that you can carry with you to classes. Widely used dictionaries include:

The American Heritage Dictionary of the English Language
Merriam-Webster's Collegiate Dictionary
Webster's New World Dictionary of the American Language

If you have difficulty with spelling, a misspeller's dictionary is another valuable reference tool. It can help you locate correct spellings easily. Two commonly used sources are *Webster's New World Misspeller's Dictionary* and *How to Spell It: A Handbook of Commonly Misspelled Words.*

Online Dictionaries

Several dictionaries are available online. Some of the most widely used are *Merriam-Webster Online* (http://www.m-w.com), *The American Heritage Dictionary* (http://www.ahdictionary.com/), and Dictionary.com (http://www.dictionary.com).

Online dictionaries have several important advantages over print dictionaries:

- **Audio component.** Most online dictionaries feature an audio component that allows you to hear how the word is pronounced.
- **Multiple dictionary entries.** Some sites, such as Dictionary.com, display entries from several dictionaries at once for a particular word. They may also include definitions from specialized subject area dictionaries as well.
- **Misspellings.** If you aren't sure of how a word is spelled or you mistype it, several suggested words will be returned.
- **Links.** Most online dictionaries will allow you to click links to see listings for some of the key words used in the definition you reading.
- **Related Questions.** Many online dictionaries have a section with questions related to the word you are looking up, Clicking on them allows you to read text descriptions that may help you understand the word more clearly.
- **Citations.** The dictionary entry may include a link to an automatically generated citation for the definition you are reading.

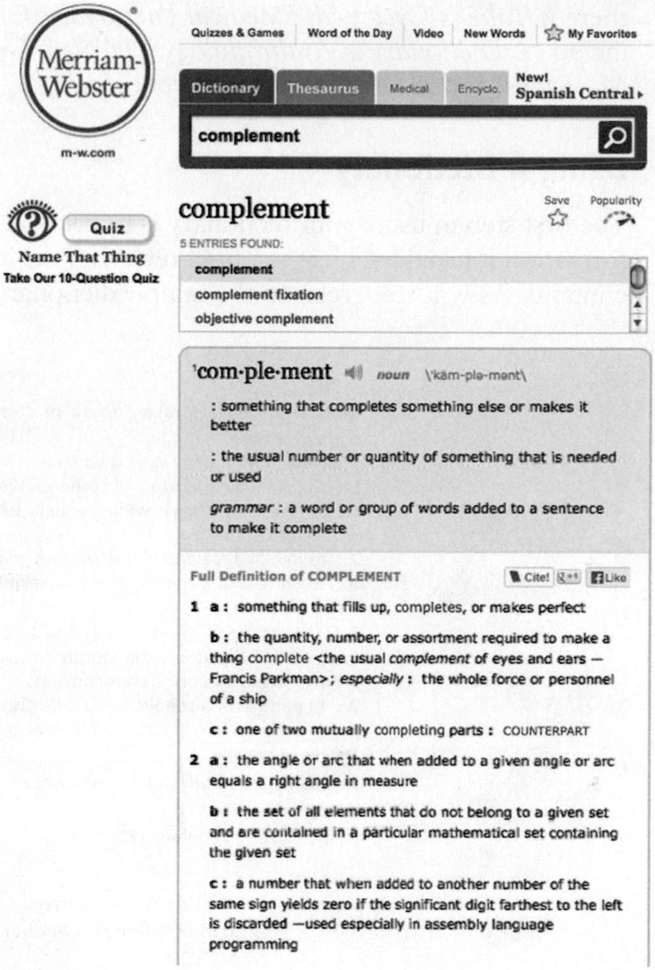

By permission. From *Merriam-Webster's Collegiate® Dictionary,* 11th Edition, © 2013 by Merriam-Webster, Inc. (www.Merriam-Webster.com).

ESL Dictionaries

If you are an ESL student, be sure to purchase an ESL dictionary. Numerous ones are available in paperback editions, including *The Longman Advanced American Dictionary.*

Subject Area Dictionaries

Many subject areas have specialized dictionaries that list most of the important words used in that field. These dictionaries give specialized meanings for words and suggest how and when to use them. For the field of nursing, for instance, there is *Taber's Cyclopedic Medical Dictionary.* Other subject area dictionaries include *A Dictionary of Anthropology, The New Grove Dictionary of Music and Musicians,* and *A Dictionary of Economics.*

Using a Dictionary

The first step in using your dictionary is to become familiar with the kinds of information it provides. Here is a brief review of the information a dictionary entry contains. As you read, refer to the sample dictionary entry below.

drink ***verb*** \ˈdriŋk\ **drank drunk** *or* **drank drink·ing**
transitive verb
1 a : swallow, imbibe <*drink water*>
b : to take in or suck up : absorb <*drinking* air into his lungs>
c : to take in or receive avidly —usually used with *in* <*drank* in every word of the lecture>
2 : to join in a toast to <I'll *drink* your good health>
3 : to bring to a specified state by drinking alcoholic beverages<*drank* himself into oblivion>
intransitive verb
1 a : to take liquid into the mouth for swallowing
b : to receive into one's consciousness
2 : to partake of alcoholic beverages <has quit *drinking*>
3 : to make or join in a toast <I'll *drink* to that!>
Origin of DRINK
Middle English, from Old English *drincan*; akin to Old High German *trinkan* to drink
First Known Use: before 12th century

—By permission. From *Merriam-Webster's Collegiate® Dictionary, 11th Edition*
© 2013 by Merriam-Webster, Inc. (www.Merriam-Webster.com).

1. **Pronunciation** The pronunciation of the word is given in backslashes or parentheses. Symbols are used to indicate the sounds letters make within specific words. Refer to the pronunciation key printed on each page or on alternate pages of your print dictionary.
2. **Grammatical information** The part of speech is indicated, as well as information about different forms the word may take. Most dictionaries include
   - Spelling of word variations
   - Principal forms of verbs (both regular and irregular)
   - Plural forms of irregular nouns
   - Comparative and superlative forms of adjectives and adverbs
3. **Meanings** Meanings are numbered and are usually grouped by the part of speech they represent.

4. **Restrictive meanings** Meanings that are limited to special situations are labeled. Some examples are:
   - *Slang*—casual language used only in conversation.
   - *Biol.*—words used in specialized fields, in this case biology.
   - *Regional*—words used only in certain parts of the United States.
5. **Synonyms** Words with similar meanings may be listed.
6. **Word history** The origin of the word (its etymology) is described. (Not all dictionaries include this feature.)

Beyond definitions, a dictionary contains a wealth of other information as well. For example, in the *American Heritage Dictionary*, Fifth Edition, you can find the history of the world *vampire*, the population of Vancouver, and an explanation of the New England expression "Vum!" Consider your dictionary a helpful and valuable resource that can assist you in expressing your ideas more clearly and correctly.

7. **Usage Notes** Some collegiate dictionaries contain a usage note or synonym section of the entry for words that are close in meaning to others. For example, a usage note for the word *indifferent* may explain how it differs in meaning from *unconcerned*, *detached*, and *uninterested*.
8. **Idioms** An idiom is a phrase that has a meaning other than what the common definitions of the words in the phrase indicate. For example, the phrase *wipe the slate clean* is not about slates. It means "to start over." Most idiomatic expressions are not used in academic writing because they are considered trite or overused.

EXERCISE 4-17 Using a Dictionary

Directions: Use a dictionary to answer the following questions:

1. How many meanings are listed for the word *fall*?

   ____

2. How is the word *phylloxera* pronounced? (Record the phonetic spelling.)

   ____

3. Can the word *protest* be used other than as a verb? If so, how?

   ____

4. The word *prime* can mean first or original. List some of its other meanings.

____

5. What does the French expression *savoir faire* mean?

____

6. List three meanings for the word *fault*.

____

7. List several words that are formed using the word *dream*.

____

8. What is the plural spelling of *addendum*?

____

9. Explain the meaning of the idiom *turn over a new leaf.*

____

10. Define the word *reconstituted* and write a sentence using the word.

____

____

Finding the Right Meaning

Most words have more than one meaning. When you look up the meaning of a new word, you must choose the meaning that fits the way the word is used in the sentence context. The meanings are often grouped by part of speech and are numbered consecutively in each group. Generally, the most common meanings of the word are listed first, with more specialized, less-common meanings appearing toward the end of the entry.

Here are a few suggestions for choosing the correct meaning from among those listed in an entry:

Finding Correct Meanings

1. **If you are familiar with the parts of speech, try to use these to locate the correct meaning.** For instance, if you are looking up the meaning of a word that names a person, place, or thing, you can save time by reading only those entries given after *n* (noun).

2. **For most types of college reading, you can skip definitions that give slang and colloquial (abbreviated *colloq.*) meanings.** Colloquial meanings refer to informal or spoken language.
3. **If you are not sure of the part of speech, read each meaning until you find a definition that seems correct.** Skip over restrictive meanings that are inappropriate.
4. **Test your choice by substituting the meaning in the sentence with which you are working.** Substitute the definition for the word and see whether it makes sense in the context (see Chapter 3).

Suppose you are looking up the word *oblique* to find its meaning in this sentence:

My sister's oblique answers to my questions made me suspicious.

Oblique is used in the above sentence as an adjective. Looking at the entries listed after *adj.* (adjective) below, definition 2a (not straightforward, indirect) best fits the way *oblique* is used in the sentence.

oblique *adjective* \ō-'blēk, ə-, -'blīk; *military usually* ī\
1 a : neither perpendicular nor parallel : inclined
b : having the axis not perpendicular to the base <an *oblique*cone>
c : having no right angle <an *oblique* triangle>
2 a : not straightforward : indirect; *also* : obscure
b : devious, underhanded
3 : situated at an angle and having one end not inserted on bone <*oblique* muscles>
4 : taken from an airplane with the camera directed horizontally or diagonally downward <an *oblique* photograph>
– **oblique·ly** *adverb*
– **oblique·ness** *noun*
Origin of OBLIQUE
Middle English *oblike*, from Latin *obliquus*
First Known Use: 15th century
oblique
noun \ō-'blēk, ə-, -'blīk; *military usually* ī\
1 : something (as a line) that is oblique
2 : any of several oblique muscles; *especially* : any of the thin flat muscles forming the middle and outer layers of the lateral walls of the abdomen

—By permission. From *Merriam-Webster's Collegiate® Dictionary, 11th Edition*
© 2013 by Merriam-Webster, Inc. (www.Merriam-Webster.com).

EXERCISE 4-18 Finding Multiple Meanings

Directions: The following words have two or more meanings. Look them up in your dictionary, and write two sentences with different meanings for each word.

1. culture: ______________________________

   ____

2. perch: ______________________________

   ____

3. surge: ______________________________

   ____

4. apron: ______________________________

   ____

5. irregular: ______________________________

   ____

EXERCISE 4-19 Finding the Right Meaning

Directions: Use a dictionary to help you write an appropriate meaning for the bold-faced word in each of the following sentences.

1. The last contestant did not have a **ghost** of a chance. ______________

2. The race car driver won the first **heat**. ______________

3. The police took all possible **measures** to protect the witness.

   ____

4. The orchestra played the first **movement** of the symphony.

   ____

5. She tried to **couch** her criticism in polite language.

   ____

Using a Thesaurus

A thesaurus is a dictionary of synonyms. It groups words with similar meanings together. A thesaurus is particularly useful when you want to do the following:

- Locate the precise term to fit a particular situation
- Find an appropriate descriptive word
- Replace an overused or unclear word
- Convey a more specific shade of meaning

Suppose you are looking for a more precise word for the expression *tell us about* in the following sentence:

> In class today, our chemistry instructor will **tell us about** our next assignment.

Among the choices a thesaurus may list are *explain, spell out, comment on, annotate, restate, unravel, transcribe*, and so forth.

Some choices fit well, such as *explain* fit well. Others such as *unravel* or *transcribe* do not. Be sure to choose a word that fits the context in which you will use it. The most widely used thesaurus is *Roget's Thesaurus*. Inexpensive paperback editions are available in most bookstores; you can also access thesauruses online.

EXERCISE 4-20 Using a Thesaurus

Directions: Using a print or online thesaurus, replace the boldfaced word or phrase in each sentence with a more precise or descriptive word. Write the word in the space provided. Rephrase the sentence, if necessary.

1. Although the movie was **good,** it lasted only an hour.

   ____

2. The judge **looked at** the criminal as she pronounced the sentence.

   ____

3. The accident victim was awarded a **big** cash settlement.

   ____

4. The lottery winner was **happy** to win the $100,000 prize, but he was surprised to learn that a sizable portion had already been deducted for taxes.

   ____

5. On the first day of class, the instructor **talked to** the class about course requirements.

   ____

PRONOUNCE UNFAMILIAR WORDS

4 LEARNING GOAL
Pronounce unfamiliar words

At one time or another, we come across words that we are unable to pronounce. To pronounce an unfamiliar word, sound it out syllable by syllable. Here are a few simple guidelines for dividing words into syllables:

1. **Divide compound words between the individual words that form the compound word.**

house/broken	house/hold	space/craft
green/house	news/paper	sword/fish

2. **Divide words between prefixes (word beginnings) and roots (base words) and/or between roots and suffixes (word endings).**

Prefix + Root		
pre/read	post/pone	anti/war
Root + Suffix		
sex/ist	agree/ment	list/ing

3. **Each syllable is a separate, distinct speech sound.** Pronounce the following words and try to hear the number of syllables in each.

expensive	ex/pen/sive = 3 syllables
recognize	rec/og/nize = 3 syllables
punctuate	punc/tu/ate = 3 syllables
complicated	com/pli/cat/ed = 4 syllables

4. **Each syllable has at least one vowel and usually one or more consonants.** (The letters *a, e, i, o, u,* and sometimes *y* are vowels. All other letters are consonants.)

as/sign	re/act	cou/pon	gen/er/al

5. **Divide words before a single consonant, unless the consonant is the letter *r*.**

hu/mid	re/tail	fa/vor	mor/on

6. **Divide words between two consonants appearing together.**

pen/cil   lit/ter   lum/ber   sur/vive

7. **Divide words between two vowel sounds that appear together.**

te/di/ous   ex/tra/ne/ous

These rules will prove helpful but, as you no doubt already know, there will always be exceptions.

EXERCISE 4-21 Syllabication

Directions: Use vertical marks (|) to divide each of the following words into syllables.

1. polka
2. pollute
3. ordinal
4. hallow
5. judicature
6. innovative
7. obtuse
8. germicide
9. futile
10. extol
11. tangelo
12. symmetry
13. telepathy
14. organic
15. hideous
16. tenacity
17. mesmerize
18. intrusive
19. infallible
20. fanaticism

EXERCISE 4-22 Pronouncing Words

Directions: Locate ten words that you find difficult to pronounce. Sources may be a dictionary, a textbook, or one of the reading selections in Part Seven of this book. Write each of the ten words on a separate index card, and then create a list of the words and how they are pronounced. Your instructor will form groups. Pass the cards around the group. Each student should attempt a pronunciation. The student who pronounces the word correctly keeps the card. Make a note of words that you were unable to pronounce; check their pronunciation in your dictionary.

A SYSTEM FOR LEARNING NEW WORDS

5 LEARNING GOAL
Develop a system for learning new words

As you read textbook assignments and reference sources and while listening to your instructors' class presentations, you are constantly exposed to new words. Unless you make a deliberate effort to remember and use these words, many of them will probably fade from your memory. One of the most practical and easy-to-use systems for expanding your vocabulary is the index card system. It works like this:

1. **Whenever you hear or read a new word that you intend to learn, jot it down in the margin of your notes or mark it some way in the material you are reading.**
2. **Later, write the word on the front of an index card.** Then look up its meaning and write it on the back of the card. Also, record a phonetic key for the word's pronunciation, its part of speech, other forms the word may take, and a sample sentence or example of how the word is used. Your cards should look like the one in Figure 4-1.

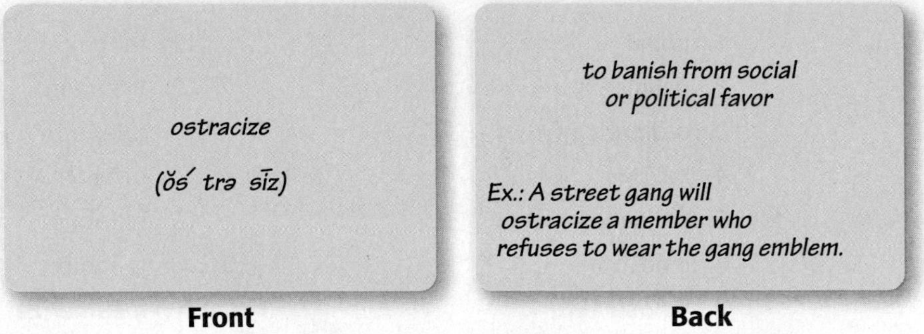
ostracize
(ŏs′ trə sīz)
to banish from social
or political favor
Ex.: A street gang will
ostracize a member who
refuses to wear the gang emblem.
Front
Back

Figure 4-1 Sample index card.

3. **Once a day, take a few minutes to go through your pack of index cards.** For each card, look at the word on the front and try to recall its meaning on the back. Then check the back of the card to see whether you were correct. If you were unable to recall the meaning or if you confused the word with another word, retest yourself. Shuffle the cards after each use.
4. **After you have gone through your pack of cards several times, sort the cards into two piles—words you know and words you have not learned.** Then, putting the known words aside, concentrate on the words still to be learned.
5. **Once you have learned the entire pack of words, review them often to refresh your memory.**

This index card system is effective for several reasons. First, you can review the cards in the spare time that is often wasted waiting for a class to begin, riding a bus, and so on. Second, the system enables you to spend time learning what you do *not* know rather than wasting time studying what you already know. Finally, the system overcomes a major problem that exists in learning information that appears in list form. If the material to be learned is presented in a fixed order, you tend to learn it in that order and may be unable to recall individual items when they appear alone or out of order. By shuffling the cards, you scramble the order of the words and thus avoid this problem.

EXERCISE 4-23 Using the Index Card System

Directions: Make a set of at least 20 word cards, choosing words from one of your textbooks or from one of the reading selections in Part Six of this book. Then study the cards using the method described in this chapter.

LEARNING STYLE TIPS

If you tend to be a(n) . . .	Then strengthen your vocabulary by . . .
Social learner	Studying with a group of classmates
Independent learner	Making up review tests, or asking a friend to do so, and practice taking the tests
Creative learner	Experimenting with new words in both speech and writing
Pragmatic learner	Creating lists or computer files of words you need to learn and use

SELF-TEST SUMMARY

1 What are prefixes, roots, and suffixes and why are they useful?	Prefixes are beginnings of words, roots are middles of words, and suffixes are endings of words. They unlock the meanings of thousands of English words.
2 How many levels of vocabulary does a person have?	Everyone has at least four levels of vocabulary: everyday words, words you know but seldom use, words you have heard before but cannot define, and words you have never heard.

3 What reference sources are useful in building a strong vocabulary?	Collegiate and unabridged dictionaries, online dictionaries, ESL dictionaries, subject area dictionaries, and the thesaurus are all useful in building a strong vocabulary.
4 How do you pronounce unfamiliar words?	To pronounce unfamiliar words, use the pronunciation key in your dictionary and apply the seven rules listed in this chapter.
5 Explain the index card system.	The index card system is a method of learning vocabulary. Write a word on the front of an index card and its meaning on the back. Study the cards by sorting them into two piles—known and unknown words.

GOING ONLINE

1. **Pronunciation**

   Many online reference works (encyclopedias, wikis, dictionaries, and so on) offer an audio feature. Look for the audio icon and click on it to hear the word pronounced. Find an online reference work with an audio feature and listen to the pronunciations of these words: *Kyrgyzstan*, *queue*, *aporia*, *munificent*, *logorrhea*.

2. **Slang**

   Many idiomatic words and phrases fall into the category of *slang*, which is composed of informal words and phrases that are used much more often in speech than in writing. The Web offers many sites that help define slang words. Find a site and list five common (or uncommon) slang words/phrases and their meanings. Share these with a small group or the class. Can any classmates define these idioms?

3. **Word Meanings**

   Quiz yourself on word meanings with the online game called Free Rice (freerice .com). The difficulty of the multiple-choice questions adjusts to your level. For every answer that you get right, the nonprofit site donates ten grains of rice to help end world hunger. Watch bowls fill up with rice as you learn new vocabulary words.

CHAPTER 4 MASTERY TEST 1 Vocabulary Skills

This **Mastery Test** can be completed in **MyReadingLab**.

Name ______________________ Section ______________

Date ______________ Number right ________ × 10 points = Score ________

Part A

Directions: For each of the following statements, select the answer that provides the correct prefix, root, or suffix that makes sense in the blank next to the boldfaced word.

_____ 1. Students who attend ethnically diverse schools are often exposed to a variety of foreign languages. One suburban Atlanta elementary school, for instance, has students whose native languages are Spanish, Vietnamese, Romanian, and Sudanese. Parents and administrators in this school speak in glowing terms about their ____________**lingual** student population.

a. mono
b. tri
c. multi
d. semi

_____ 2. Samuel L. Clemens was born in 1835 in Hannibal, Missouri. Using the ____________**nym** Mark Twain, he drew upon his childhood experiences along the Mississippi River to write *Tom Sawyer* and *The Adventures of Huckleberry Finn.*

a. anti
b. pseudo
c. poly
d. retro

_____ 3. Melanie's father and grandfather are both police officers, so it was not surprising that she decided to pursue a career in law enforcement. She has already enrolled at the community college where she plans to major in criminal justice and take classes in **crimino**____________ in order to learn more about crime, criminals, and criminal behavior.

a. graphy
b. scopy
c. pathy
d. logy

_____ 4. The portion of the earth that is inhabited by living things is known as the earth's ____________**sphere**. It includes the atmosphere and the oceans to specified heights and depths, as well as lakes and rivers.

a. bio
b. astro
c. geo
d. chrono

_____ 5. Our composition instructor always asked us to exchange our essays with each other in class in order to get another person's feedback on our work. He allowed us to give only **construct**____________ criticism, encouraging us to keep in mind how we would want our own work to be reviewed.

a. ent
b. ible
c. ive
d. or

Part B

Directions: Using your knowledge of roots, prefixes, and suffixes, choose the correct definition for each of the boldfaced words from the following passage.

What additional information does this graphic contribute to the passage?

1 In the U.S. legal system, the family has traditionally been defined as a unit consisting of a heterosexual married couple and their child or children. Many scholars have a more flexible definition of "family," taking into account the **extended** family of grandparents, aunts and uncles, and cousins, and sometimes even people who are not related by blood at all.

2 Class, race, and ethnicity are important factors to consider as we define what makes a family. The traditional, middle-class Caucasian family with lots of cheerful children depicted in many classic movies has always been a **projection** of the class that produced it rather than a reality. Not only is U.S. society a **composite** of many different economic statuses, but it is also made up of different races and an increasing variety of ethnicities that are in turn mixing to create **interracial** and **multi-ethnic** families.

—adapted from Kunz, *Think Marriages and Families*, pp. 278–279

Percentage of Americans Approving of Marriage Between African-Americans and Whites

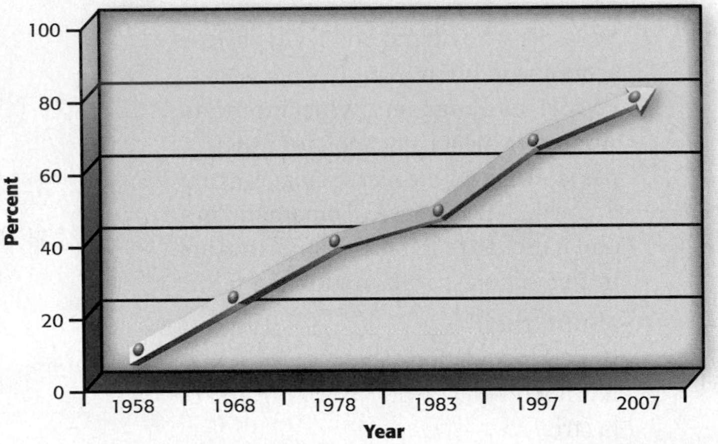

Percentage of Americans Approving of Marriage Between African Americans and Whites

_____ 6. extended
  a. limited
  b. larger
  c. artificial
  d. unrelated

_____ 7. projection
  a. difference
  b. advertisement
  c. vision
  d. mistake

_____ 8. composite
  a. property
  b. complex
  c. division
  d. mixture

_____ 9. interracial
  a. away from races
  b. between races
  c. against races
  d. equal races

_____ 10. multiethnic
  a. not ethnic
  b. one ethnicity
  c. many ethnicities
  d. beyond ethnicity

CHAPTER 4

MASTERY TEST 2 Dictionary Skills

This **Mastery Test** can be completed in **MyReadingLab**.

Name ______________________________ Section ______________

Date ______________ Number right ________ × 10 points = Score __________

Part A

Directions: Each numbered sentence below is followed by a dictionary entry for the boldfaced word. Use this entry to select the choice that best fits the meaning of the word as it is used in the sentence.

_____ 1. At the entrance to the international exhibition hall, visitors are greeted by a **panoply** of flags representing every nation in the world.

> **pan•o•ply** *noun* \'pa-nə-plē\ : a group or collection that is impressive because it is so big or because it includes so many different kinds of people or things
> *plural* **pan•o•plies**
>
> **Full Definition of PANOPLY**
> 1. **a :** a full suit of armor
>   **b :** ceremonial attire
> 2. **:** something forming a protective covering
> 3. **a :** a magnificent or impressive array <the full *panoply* of a military funeral>
>   **b :** a display of all appropriate appurtenances <no need for the *panoply* of power>
>
> **Origin of PANOPLY**
> Greek *panoplia,* from *pan-* + *hopla* arms, armor, plural of *hoplon* tool, weapon — more at HOPLITE
> First Known Use: 1632
>
> —By permission. From *Merriam-Webster's Collegiate® Dictionary, 11th Edition* © 2013 by Merriam-Webster, Inc. (www.Merriam-Webster.com).

a. a full suit of armor
b. ceremonial attire
c. something forming a protective covering
d. a magnificent or impressive array

_____ 2. At the town meeting, several citizens **ventilated** their concerns about the proposed increase in property taxes.

> **ven•ti•late transitive verb** \'ven-tə-ˌlāt\
> **ven•ti•lat•ed ven•ti•lat•ing**
> 1. **a :** to examine, discuss, or investigate freely and openly : EXPOSE <*ventilating* family quarrels in public>
>   **b :** to make public : UTTER <*ventilated* their objections at length>
> 2. *archaic* **:** to free from chaff by winnowing
> 3. **a :** to expose to air and especially to a current of fresh air for purifying, curing, or refreshing <*ventilate* stored grain>; *also* : OXYGENATE, AERATE <*ventilate* blood in the lungs>
>   **b :** to subject the lungs to <u>ventilation</u> <artificially *ventilate* a patient in respiratory distress>
> 4. **a :** *of a current of air* **:** to pass or circulate through so as to freshen
>   **b :** to cause fresh air to circulate through (as a room or mine)
> 5. **:** to provide an opening in (a burning structure) to permit escape of smoke and heat
>
> **Origin of VENTILATE**
> Middle English, discussed, aired, from Late Latin *ventilatus,* past participle of *ventilare,* from Latin, to fan, winnow, from *ventus* wind— more at WIND
> First Known Use: 15th century
>
> —By permission. From *Merriam-Webster's Collegiate® Dictionary, 11th Edition* © 2013 by Merriam-Webster, Inc. (www.Merriam-Webster.com).

a. to examine, discuss; to make public
b. to expose to air

c. to cause fresh air to circulate through
d. to provide an opening in to permit escape of smoke and heat

_____ 3. Many people with coronary artery disease do not **manifest** symptoms until they have their first heart attack.

[1]**man•i•fest** *adjective* \'ma-nə-ˌfest\

1. : readily perceived by the senses and especially by the sense of sight
2. : easily understood or recognized by the mind : OBVIOUS
—**man•i•fest·ly** *adverb*

Origin of MANIFEST
Middle English, from Anglo-French or Latin; Anglo-French*manifeste,* from Latin *manifestus* caught in the act, flagrant, obvious, perhaps from *manus* + *-festus* (akin to Latin in*festus* hostile)
First Known Use: 14th century
[2]**man•i•fest** *transitive verb* \'ma-nə-ˌfest\
: to show (something) clearly
: to make evident or certain by showing or displaying
—**man•i•fest•er** *noun*
[3]**man•i•fest** *noun* \'ma-nə-ˌfest\
1. : MANIFESTATION, INDICATION
2. : MANIFESTO
3. : a list of passengers or an invoice of cargo for a vehicle (as a ship or plane)

—By permission. From *Merriam-Webster's Collegiate® Dictionary, 11th Edition* © 2013 by Merriam-Webster, Inc. (www.Merriam-Webster.com).

a. readily perceived by the senses
b. easily understood or recognized by the mind
c. to make evident or certain by showing or displaying
d. a list of passengers or an invoice of cargo for a vehicle

_____ 4. After moving halfway across the country for his new job, Kerry was **besieged** by rumors that the company was going out of business.

be•siege *transitive verb* \bi-'sēj, bē-\
: to surround a city, building, etc., with soldiers and try to take control of it
: to gather around (someone) in a way that is aggressive, annoying, etc.
: to overwhelm (someone) *with* too many questions or requests for things
be•sieged be•sieg•ing

Full Definition of BESIEGE
1. : to surround with armed forces
2. a : to press with requests : IMPORTUNE
b : to cause worry or distress to : BESET <doubts *besieged* him>
—**be•sieg•er** *noun*

First Known Use of BESIEGE
14th century

—By permission. From *Merriam-Webster's Collegiate® Dictionary, 11th Edition* © 2013 by Merriam-Webster, Inc. (www.Merriam-Webster.com).

***Synonyms** besiege, beleaguer, blockade, invest, siege.* These verbs mean to surround with hostile forces: *besiege a walled city; the enemy beleaguered the enclave; blockaded the harbor; investing a fortress; a castle sieged by invaders.*

a. to gather around in a way that is aggressive, annoying
b. to surround with armed forces
c. to press with requests
d. to cause worry or distress to

_____ 5. The student task force obviously did not spend much time considering the problem of the limited number of parking spaces on campus; its **facile** solution to the problem disappointed all of us.

fac•ile *adjective* \'fa-səl\
: too simple : not showing enough thought or effort
: done or achieved in a way that is too easy
: working, moving, or performing well and very easily

Full Definition of FACILE

1. a (1) : easily accomplished or attained <a *facile* victory> (2): SHALLOW, SIMPLISTIC <I am not concerned . . . with offering any *facile* solution for so complex a problem—T. S. Eliot>
b : used or comprehended with ease
c. readily manifested and often lacking sincerity or depth<*facile* tears>
2. *archaic* : mild or pleasing in manner or disposition
3. a : READY, FLUENT <*facile* prose>
b : POISED, ASSURED
—**fac•ile•ly** *adverb*
— **fac•ile•ness** *noun*

Origin of FACILE
Middle French, from Latin *facilis,* from *facere* to do— more at DO First Known Use: 15th century

—By permission. From *Merriam-Webster's Collegiate® Dictionary, 11th Edition* © 2013 by Merriam-Webster, Inc. (www.Merriam-Webster.com).

a. easily accomplished or attained
b. shallow, simplistic
c. mild or pleasing in manner or disposition
d. poised, assured

Part B

Directions: Use a dictionary to select the best answer for each of the following questions.

_____ 6. The definition of the word *ligature* is
a. legal suit
b. relief
c. coal
d. bond

_____ 7. The most accurate phonetic spelling for the word *neuropathy* is
a. nyu ro path e
b. nyur o path e
c. nyu rop a the
d. nyu rop a te

_____ 8. What part of speech is the word *tole*?
a. noun
b. verb
c. adjective
d. adverb

_____ 9. What is the origin of the word *hirsute*?
a. French
b. German
c. Latin
d. Middle English

_____ 10. The correct syllabication of the word *marsupial* is
a. mar sup i al
b. mar su pi al
c. mars up ial
d. mar su pial

CHAPTER 4

MASTERY TEST 3 Reading Selection

This **Mastery Test** can be completed in **MyReadingLab**.

Name ______________________________ Section ______________

Date ________________ Number right* ________ 10 points = Score ____________

The "McDonaldization" of Society

John J. Macionis

This selection appeared in a sociology textbook, *Society: The Basics*, by John Macionis. Read the selection to find out how the concept behind McDonald's has had an effect on American society.

Vocabulary Preview

rationalization (par. 13) replacing traditional beliefs and emotions with those that are planned and calculated

1 McDonald's has enjoyed enormous success, now operating more than 33,000 restaurants in the United States and around the world. Japan has more than 3,300 Golden Arches, and the world's largest McDonald's, which seats more than 1,500 customers, is found in London.

2 McDonald's is far more than a restaurant chain; it is a symbol of U.S. culture. Not only do people around the world associate McDonald's with the United States, but also here at home, one poll found that 98 percent of schoolchildren could identify Ronald McDonald, making him as well known as Santa Claus.

3 Even more important, the organizational principles that underlie McDonald's are coming to dominate our entire society. Our culture is becoming "McDonaldized," an awkward way of saying that we model many aspects of life on the approach taken by this restaurant chain: Parents buy toys at worldwide chain stores all

*To calculate the number right, use items 1–10 under "Mastery Test Skills Check."

carrying identical merchandise; we drop in at a convenient shop for a ten-minute drive-through oil change; face-to-face communication is being replaced more and more with electronic methods such as voice mail, e-mail, and instant messaging; more vacations take the form of resorts and tour packages; television packages the news in the form of ten-second sound bites; college admissions officers size up applicants they have never met by glancing at their GPA and SAT scores.

4 Can you tell what all these developments have in common?

Four Principles

5 According to George Ritzer who wrote a book about the McDonaldization of society, four basic organizational principles are involved.

6 1. **Efficiency**. Ray Kroc, the marketing genius behind the expansion of McDonald's, set out to serve a hamburger, French fries, and a milkshake to a customer in fifty seconds. Today, one of the company's most popular items is the Egg McMuffin, an entire breakfast packaged into a single sandwich. In the restaurant, customers pick up their meals at a counter, dispose of their own trash, and stack their own trays as they walk out the door or, better still, drive away from the pickup window taking whatever mess they make with them. Such efficiency is now central to our way of life. We tend to think that anything done quickly is, for that reason alone, good.

7 2. **Predictability**. An efficient organization wants to make everything it does as predictable as possible. McDonald's prepares all food using set formulas. Company policies guide the performance of every job.

8 3. **Uniformity**. The first McDonald's operating manual declared the weight of a regular raw hamburger to be 1.6 ounces, its size to be 3.875 inches across, and its fat content to be 19 percent. A slice of cheese weighs exactly half an ounce, and French fries are cut precisely 9/32 inch thick.

9 Think about how many of the objects we see every day around the home, the workplace, and the campus are designed and mass-produced uniformly according to a standard plan. Not just our environment but our everyday life experiences—from traveling the nation's interstates to sitting at home viewing national TV shows—are more standardized than ever before.

10 Almost anywhere in the world, a person can walk into a McDonald's restaurant and buy the same sandwiches, drinks, and desserts prepared in the same way. Uniformity results from a highly rational system that specifies every action and leaves nothing to chance.

11 4. **Control.** The most unreliable element in the McDonald's system is human beings. After all, people have good and bad days, and they sometimes let their minds wander or decide to do something a different way. To minimize the unpredictable human element, McDonald's has automated its equipment to cook food at a fixed temperature for a set length of time. Even the cash registers at McDonald's are keyed to pictures of the menu items so that ringing up a customer's order is as simple as possible.

12 Similarly, automatic teller machines are replacing bank tellers, highly automated bakeries produce bread while people stand back and watch, and chickens and eggs (or is it eggs and chickens?) emerge from automated hatcheries. In supermarkets, laser scanners at self-checkouts are phasing out human checkers. Much of our shopping now occurs in malls, where everything from temperature and humidity to the kinds of stores and products sold are subject to continuous control and supervision.

Can Rationality Be Irrational?

13 There is no doubt about the popularity or efficiency of McDonald's. But there is another side to the story. Max Weber* was alarmed at the increasing rationalization of the world, fearing that formal organizations would cage our imaginations and crush the human spirit. As he saw it, rational systems are efficient but dehumanizing. McDonaldization bears him out. Each of the principles we have just discussed limits human creativity, choice, and freedom. Echoing Weber, Ritzer states that "the ultimate irrationality of McDonaldization is that people could lose control over the system and it would come to control us." Perhaps even McDonald's understands the limits of rationalization—the company has now expanded its offerings of more upscale foods, such as premium roasted coffee and salad selections that are more sophisticated, fresh, and healthful.

—Macionis, *Society*, pp. 121–122

*Max Weber, an influential sociologist, is often considered to be one of the founding fathers of sociology.

MASTERY TEST SKILLS CHECK

Directions: Select the choice that best completes each of the following statements.

Checking Your Comprehension

_____ 1. The main point of the article is that our society

a. is becoming similar to McDonald's, with everything the same.
b. has too much fast food in our diet because of McDonald's.
c. does not allow children to have good role models.
d. emphasizes commercial success more than any other type of success.

_____ 2. According to this article, people have come to believe that if something is done speedily that it is done

a. poorly
b. incompletely
c. cheaply
d. well

_____ 3. When products become standardized it means

a. employees work less.
b. there is a loss of efficiency.
c. items are produced identically.
d. nothing can be automated.

_____ 4. The most unreliable part of McDonald's system is its
a. food quality.
b. employees.
c. packaging.
d. profits.

_____ 5. Max Weber believed that systems like McDonald's work well but have the effect of being
a. expensive.
b. unproductive.
c. dehumanizing.
d. polluting.

Applying Your Skills

_____ 6. The root word of *uniformity* (par. 8) means
a. unattractive.
b. hidden.
c. valuable.
d. the same.

_____ 7. The root of the word *standardized* (par. 9) means
a. heatedly discussed.
b. the same or very similar.
c. used by different people for different purposes.
d. easily changed or altered.

_____ 8. The prefix of the word *unpredictable* (par. 11) means
a. not
b. for
c. after
d. away

_____ 9. The prefix of the word *automated* (par. 11) means
a. against
b. false
c. self-acting
d. out of

Studying Words

_____ 10. The word *applicant* (par. 3) means a
a. person who is praying.
b. person seeking admission.
c. relative you don't know.
d. stranger asking for a favor.

_____ 11. The word *expansion* (par. 6) means
a. study.
b. idea.
c. expense.
d. growth.

_____ 12. The word *formulas* as used in paragraph 7 means
a. clear methods.
b. infant beverages.
c. mathematical equations.
d. chemical representations.

_____ 13. The word *manual* as used in paragraph 8 means
a. done by hand.
b. a book or guide.
c. a type of transmission.
d. method for holding a rifle.

_____ 14. The word *minimize* (par. 11) means to make
a. larger.
b. smaller.
c. different.
d. the same.

For more practice, ask your instructor for an opportunity to work on the mastery tests that appear in the Test Bank.

Summarizing the Reading

Directions: Complete the following summary of the reading by filling in the blanks.

McDonald's is a company known across many _______________ and is also a symbol of _______________. Many parts of _____________ follow the approach taken by _______________, using its four ________________________: Efficiency, _______________, _____________, and _____________. We value efficiency, thinking that ______________________________. _______________ and _______________ are important so that we can expect many things to be the same. Control often means reducing _______________________ in work since machines can be ___________________________. These principles reduce _______________________ _____________ and result in the __________________ of our world.

Reading Visually

1. What does the photograph contribute to the reading?
2. Does the photograph demonstrate any the four principles of McDonaldization? If so, which ones, and how?

Thinking Critically about the Reading

1. Why does the author mention the statistic about children and Ronald McDonald? How would you describe the author's feelings about this?
2. In paragraph 3, the author discusses examples of McDonaldization in our society. What is the author's attitude about these changes?

CHAPTER 5

Understanding Paragraphs: Topics and Main Ideas

Focusing on ... Topics and Main Ideas

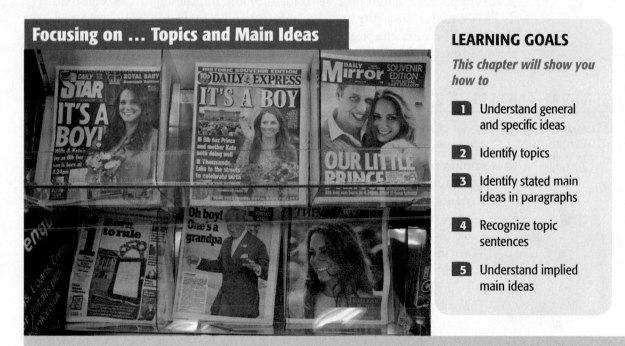

LEARNING GOALS

This chapter will show you how to

1. Understand general and specific ideas
2. Identify topics
3. Identify stated main ideas in paragraphs
4. Recognize topic sentences
5. Understand implied main ideas

The newspaper headlines above announce what the articles are about. Each suggests the main point the author wants to make about the topic. Paragraphs work the same way. Each is built around a topic—the one thing the paragraph is about—and each paragraph presents a main point—or main idea—about the topic. This chapter will show you how to identify topics and main ideas.

Understanding a paragraph is a step-by-step process. The first thing you need to know is what the paragraph is about. Then you have to understand what each sentence is saying. Next, you have to see how the sentences relate to one another. Finally, to understand the main point of the paragraph, you have to consider what all the sentences, taken together, mean.

The one subject the whole paragraph is about is called the **topic**. The point that the whole paragraph makes is called the **main idea**. The sentences that explain the main idea are called **details**. To connect their ideas, writers use words and phrases known as **transitions**.

A paragraph, then, is a group of related sentences about a single topic. It has four essential parts: (1) topic, (2) main idea, (3) details, and (4) transitions. To read paragraphs most efficiently, you will need to become familiar with each part of a paragraph and be able to identify and use these parts as you read.

This chapter concentrates on understanding main ideas, both stated and implied. The next chapter, Chapter 7, focuses on supporting details, transitions, and expressing paragraph ideas in your own words.

GENERAL AND SPECIFIC IDEAS

1 LEARNING GOAL
Understand general and specific ideas

To identify topics and main ideas in paragraphs, it will help you to understand the difference between **general** and **specific**. A general idea is a broad idea that applies to a large number of individual items. The term *clothing* is general because it refers to a large collection of individual items—pants, suits, blouses, shirts, scarves, and so on. A specific idea or term is more detailed or particular. It refers to an individual item. The word *scarf*, for example, is a specific term. The phrase *red plaid scarf* is even more specific.

General:	pies	**General:**	countries
Specific:	chocolate cream	**Specific:**	Great Britain
	apple		Finland
	cherry		Brazil
General:	types of context clues	**General:**	word parts
Specific:	definition	**Specific:**	prefix
	example		root
	contrast		suffix

EXERCISE 5-1 Analyzing General and Specific Ideas

Directions: Read each of the following items and decide what term(s) will complete the group. Write the word(s) in the spaces provided.

1. General: college courses
   Specific: math
   ____

2. General: ______________________________
   Specific: roses
   tulips
   narcissus

3. General: musical groups
   Specific: ______________________________
   ____

4. General: art
   Specific: sculpture
   ____
   ____

5. General: types of movies
   Specific: comedies
   ____
   ____

EXERCISE 5-2 Identifying General Ideas

Directions: For each set of specifics, select the general idea that best describes it.

_____ 1. Specific ideas: Michelle Obama, Laura Bush, Nancy Reagan
   a. famous twentieth-century women
   b. famous American parents
   c. famous wives
   d. wives of American presidents

_____ 2. Specific ideas: touchdown, home run, 3-pointer, 5 under par
- a. types of errors in sports
- b. types of activities
- c. types of scoring in sports
- d. types of sports

c 3. Specific ideas: for companionship, to play with, because you love animals
- a. reasons to visit the zoo
- b. reasons to feed your cat
- c. reasons to get a pet
- d. ways to solve problems

_____ 4. Specific ideas: taking a hot bath, going for a walk, watching a video, listening to music
- a. ways to relax
- b. ways to help others
- c. ways to listen
- d. ways to solve problems

_____ 5. Specific ideas: listen, be helpful, be generous, be forgiving
- a. ways to get a job
- b. ways to keep a friend
- c. ways to learn
- d. ways to appreciate a movie

EXERCISE 5-3 Identifying General Terms

Directions: Underline the most general term in each group of words.

1. pounds, ounces, kilograms, weights
2. soda, coffee, beverage, wine
3. soap operas, news, TV programs, sports specials
4. home furnishings, carpeting, drapes, wall hangings
5. sociology, social sciences, anthropology, psychology

Applying General and Specific to Paragraphs

Now we will apply the idea of general and specific to paragraphs. The main idea is the most general statement the writer makes about the topic. Pick out the most general statement among the following sentences:

1. People differ according to height.
2. Hair color distinguishes some people from others.
3. People differ in a number of ways.
4. Each person has his or her own personality.

Did you choose item 3 as the most general statement? Now we will change this list into a paragraph by rearranging the sentences and adding a few facts.

> People differ in a number of ways. They differ according to physical characteristics, such as height, weight, and hair color. They also differ in personality. Some people are friendly and easygoing. Others are more reserved and formal.

In this brief paragraph, the main idea is expressed in the first sentence. This sentence is the most general statement expressed in the paragraph. All the other statements are specific details that explain this main idea.

EXERCISE 5-4 Identifying General Statements

Directions: For each of the following groups of sentences, select the most general statement the writer makes about the topic.

_____ 1. a. Brightly colored annuals, such as pansies and petunias, are often used as seasonal accents in a garden.
b. Most gardens feature a mix of perennials and annuals.
c. Some perennials prefer shade, while others thrive in full sun.
d. Butterfly bushes are a popular perennial.

_____ 2. a. Hiring a housepainter is not as simple as it sounds.
b. You should try to obtain a cost estimate from at least three painters.
c. Each painter should be able to provide reliable references from past painting jobs.
d. The painter must be able to work within the time frame you desire.

_____ 3. a. Flaxseed is an herbal treatment for constipation.
b. Some people use Kava to treat depression.
c. Gingko biloba is a popular remedy for memory loss.
d. A growing number of consumers are turning to herbal remedies to treat certain ailments.

_____ 4. a. Many students choose to live off-campus in apartments or rental houses.
b. Most colleges and universities offer a variety of student housing options.
c. Sororities and fraternities typically allow members to live in their organization's house.
d. On-campus dormitories provide a convenient place for students to live.

_____ 5. a. Try to set exercise goals that are challenging but realistic.
b. Increase the difficulty of your workout gradually.
c. Several techniques contribute to success when beginning an exercise program.
d. Reduce soreness by gently stretching your muscles before you exercise.

IDENTIFY THE TOPIC

2 LEARNING GOAL Identify topics

The **topic** is the subject of the entire paragraph. Every sentence in a paragraph in some way discusses or explains this topic. If you had to choose a title for a paragraph, the one or two words you would choose are the topic.

To find the topic of a paragraph, ask yourself: What is the one thing the author is discussing throughout the paragraph?

Now read the following paragraph with that question in mind:

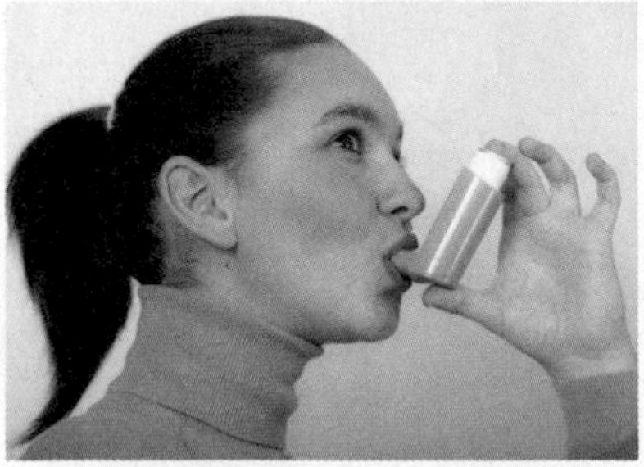

What causes asthma?

Asthma is caused by inflammation of the airways in the lungs, leading to wheezing, chest tightness, shortness of breath, and coughing. In most people, asthma is brought on by allergens or irritants in the air; some people also have exercise-induced asthma. People with asthma can generally control their symptoms through the use of inhaled medications, and most asthmatics keep a "rescue" inhaler of medication on hand to use in case of a flare-up.

—adapted from Donatelle, *Health*, p. 424

In this example, the author is discussing one topic—asthma—throughout the paragraph. Notice that the word *asthma* is used several times. Often the repeated use of a word can serve as a clue to the topic.

EXERCISE 5-5 Identifying the Topic

Directions: Read each of the following paragraphs and then select the topic of the paragraph from the choices given.

_____ 1. People have been making glass in roughly the same way for at least 2,000 years. The process involves melting certain Earth materials and cooling the liquid quickly before the atoms have time to form an orderly crystalline structure. This is the same way that natural glass, called obsidian, is generated from lava. It is possible to produce glass from a variety of materials, but most commercial glass is produced from quartz sand and lesser amounts of carbonate minerals.

—Lutgens et al., *Essentials of Geology*, p. 62

a. Earth
b. glass
c. atoms
d. lava

_____ 2. The large majority of shoplifting is not done by professional thieves or by people who genuinely need the stolen items. About 2 million Americans are charged with shoplifting each year, but analysts estimate that for every arrest, 18 unreported incidents occur. About three-quarters of those caught are middle- or high-income people who shoplift for the thrill of it or as a substitute for affection. Shoplifting is also common among adolescents. Research evidence indicates that teen shoplifting is influenced by factors such as having friends who also shoplift.

—Solomon, *Consumer Behavior*, p. 35

a. shoplifting
b. shopping
c. professional thieves
d. adolescents

_____ 3. Kidney transplants are performed when the kidneys fail due to kidney disease. The kidneys are a pair of bean-shaped organs located under the rib cage by the small of the back. Each kidney is a little smaller than a fist and functions as a filter to remove toxins and wastes from the blood. When kidneys fail, waste products build up in the blood, which can be toxic.

—adapted from Belk and Maier, *Biology*, p. 438

a. organ transplants
b. organ disease
c. kidneys
d. toxins

_____ 4. In order to survive, hunting and gathering societies depend on hunting animals and gathering plants. In some groups, the men do the hunting, and the women the gathering. In others, both men and women (and children) gather plants, the men hunt large animals, and both men and women hunt small animals. Hunting and gathering societies are small, usually consisting of only 25 to 40 people. These groups are nomadic. As their food supply dwindles in one area, they move to another location. They place high value on sharing food, which is essential to their survival.

—adapted from Henslin, *Sociology*, p. 148

a. hunters
b. food supplies
c. survival
d. hunting and gathering societies

_____ 5. People who call themselves **freegans** are modern-day scavengers who live off discards as a political statement against corporations and consumerism. They forage through supermarket trash and eat the slightly bruised produce or just-expired canned goods that we routinely throw out, and obtain surplus food from sympathetic stores and restaurants. Freegans dress in castoff clothes and furnish their homes with items they find on the street. They get the word on locations where people are throwing out a lot of stuff by checking out postings at freecycle.org and at so-called *freemeets* (flea markets where no one exchanges money),

—adapted from Solomon, *Consumer Behavior*, pp. 392–393

a. scavengers
b. freegans
c. recycling
d. freemeets

Notice that the photograph helps you identify the topic of the paragraph.

EXERCISE 5-6 Identifying the Topic

Directions: Read each of the following paragraphs and then write the topic of the paragraph in the space provided.

A. The word **locavore** has been coined to describe people who eat only food grown or produced locally, usually within close proximity to their homes. Locavores rely on farmers' markets, homegrown foods, or foods grown by independent farmers. Locavores prefer these foods because they are thought to be fresher, more environmentally friendly, and require far fewer resources to get them to market and keep them fresh for longer periods of time. Locavores believe that locally grown organic food is preferable to large corporation- or supermarket-based organic foods, as local foods have a smaller impact on the environment.

—adapted from Donatelle, *Health*, p. 282

Topic: ____

B. A monopoly exists when an industry or market has only one producer (or else is so dominated by one producer that other firms cannot compete with it). A sole supplier enjoys nearly complete control over the prices of its products. Its only constraint is a decrease in consumer demand due to increased prices or government regulation. In the United States, laws forbid many monopolies and regulate prices charged by natural monopolies—industries in which one company can most efficiently supply all needed goods or services. Many electric companies are natural monopolies because they can supply all the power needed in a local area.

—adapted from Ebert and Griffin, *Business Essentials*, p. 12

Topic: ____

C. Values represent cultural standards by which we determine what is good, bad, right, or wrong. Sometimes these values are expressed as proverbs or sayings that teach us how to live. Do you recognize the phrase, "Life is like a box of chocolates—you never know what you're going to get"? This modern-day saying is popular among those who embrace life's unpredictability. Cultures are capable of growth and change, so it's possible for a culture's values to change over time.

—Carl, *Think Sociology*, p. 51

Topic: ____

D. They go by many different names—capsule hotels, modular hotels, and pod hotels—but they all have one thing in common: very efficient use of space in a small footprint. The concept of modular hotels was pioneered by the Japanese, but the idea is sweeping across the world. Priced well below most competitors, these small, 75- to 100-square-foot rooms don't waste any space. Most modular units include the basics: private bathrooms, beds that are designed for two, flat-screen televisions, and a small work space. Weary travelers looking for nothing more than a place to sleep are finding that modular hotels "fit the bill."

—adapted from Cook et al., *Tourism*, p. 347

Topic: ______________________________

E. Television commercials provide a rich source of material to analyze. Begin by asking, "What reasons am I being given to lead me to want to buy this product?" Often, commercials do not overtly state the reasons; instead, they use music, staging, gestures, and visual cues to suggest the ideas they want us to have. We probably will not find a commercial that comes right out and says that buying someone a bottle of perfume or piece of jewelry will lead to a fulfilling love life, but several holiday commercials certainly imply as much.

—adapted from Facione, *Think Critically*, p. 90

Topic: ______________________________

FIND THE STATED MAIN IDEA

3 LEARNING GOAL
Identify stated main ideas in paragraphs

The **main idea** of a paragraph is the most important idea; it is the idea that the whole paragraph explains or supports. Usually it is expressed in one sentence called the **topic sentence.** To find the main idea, use the following suggestions.

Locating the Topic

You have learned that the topic is the subject of a paragraph. The main idea is the most important thing the author wants you to know about the topic. To find the main idea, ask yourself, "What is the one most important thing to know about the topic?" Read the following paragraph and then answer this question.

Rather than traveling for rest and relaxation, more and more of the world's population is traveling for sport-related reasons. Sport tourism has exploded in the last ten years and is now seen as a major form of special-interest tourism. Sport tourism is travel away from home to play sport, watch sport, or to visit a sport attraction including both competitive and noncompetitive activities. Think of the vast array of travel that is included in this definition. Sport team members traveling to out-of-town tournaments are included; booster and alumni clubs trekking to "bowl" games are included; golf fans traveling to the British Open are included; a snowboard/ski club traveling to the Rockies for spring break is included!

—Cook et al., *Tourism*, p. 52

In this example, the topic is sport tourism. The most important point the author is making is that sport tourism has become a popular form of travel.

Locating the Most General Sentence

The most general sentence in the paragraph expresses the main idea. This sentence is called the topic sentence. This sentence must be broad enough to include or cover all the other ideas (details) in the paragraph. In the paragraph on the preceding page, the second sentence makes a general statement about sport tourism—that it is becoming more and more popular. The rest of the sentences provide specifics.

Studying the Rest of the Paragraph

The main idea must connect, draw together, and make meaningful the rest of the paragraph. You might think of the main idea as the one that all the details, taken together, add up to, explain, or support. In the paragraph on the preceding page, sentence one serves as an introductory sentence. Sentence three offers a definition of sports tourism. Sentences four and five provide examples.

EXERCISE 5-7 Writing Main Ideas

Directions: Bring to class a list of bumper sticker or T-shirt messages you have recently seen. Form groups of three or four students. Each group should select three messages. For each, identify the topic and write a sentence that states its main idea. Groups should share their work with the class. The class may choose to select the most fun, innovative, or effective message and corresponding main idea.

IDENTIFY TOPIC SENTENCES

4 LEARNING GOAL Recognize topic sentences

The topic sentence can be located anywhere in the paragraph. However, there are several positions where it is most likely to be found.

Topic Sentence First

Most often the topic sentence is placed first in the paragraph. In this type of paragraph, the author first states his or her main point and then explains it.

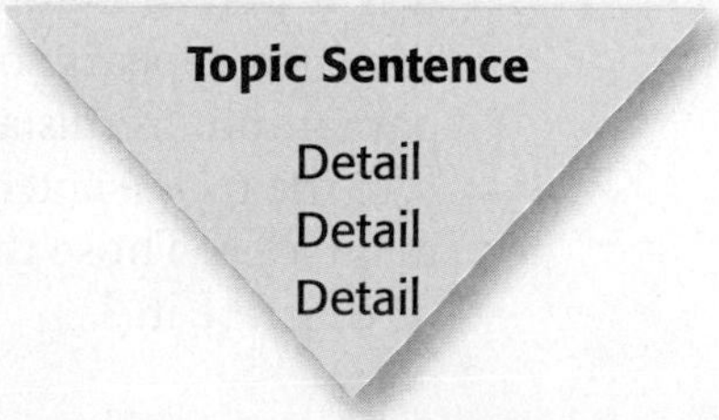

The extended family consists of *two or more closely related families who share a household and are economically bound to others in the group*. For example, among the Navajo, relationships among sisters and other female kin often take precedence over the husband-wife relationships, not only because these relationships are defined as more satisfying but because women—not husbands and wives—live and work together and own property in common. Extended families take two major forms: *vertical extended families*, which include three or more generations—parents, their married children, grandchildren, and so on—and *joint families*, consisting of siblings and their spouses and their children.

—Thompson and Hickey, *Society in Focus*, p. 360

Here the writer first defines an extended family. The rest of the paragraph offers more details about specific types of extended families.

Topic Sentence Last

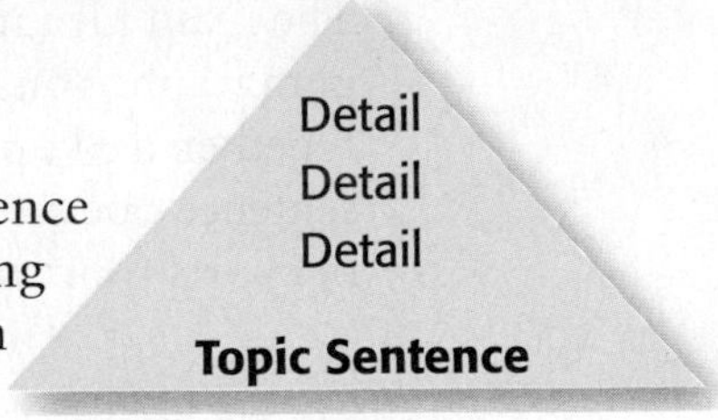

The second most likely place for a topic sentence to appear is last in the paragraph. When using this arrangement, a writer leads up to the main point and then directly states it at the end.

Art can inform, embellish, inspire, arouse, awaken, and delight us. Art can challenge us to think and see in new ways, and help each of us to develop a personal sense of beauty and truth. It can also deceive, humiliate, and anger us. A given work of art may serve several functions all at once.

—Frank, *Prebles' Artforms*, p. 5

This paragraph first describes the positive effects that art can have on us, then describes other effects that are more negative. The paragraph ends with a general statement about the many functions of art.

Topic Sentence in the Middle

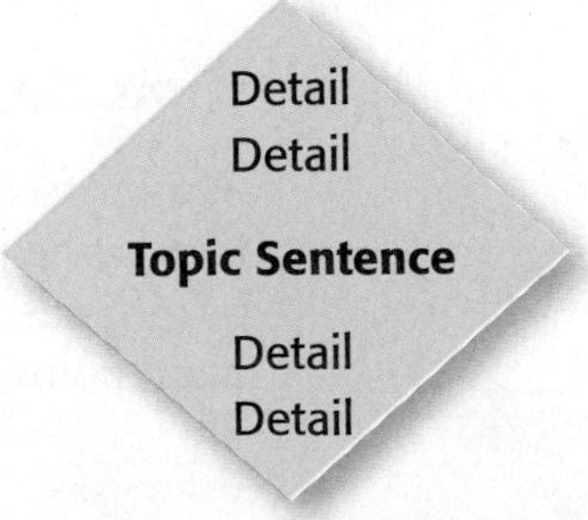

If it is placed neither first nor last, then the topic sentence appears somewhere in the middle of the paragraph. In this arrangement, the sentences before the topic sentence lead up to or introduce the main idea. Those that follow the main idea explain or describe it.

> If a person won the lottery or invested in the right stocks, his or her social class could change in an upward direction in an instant. Likewise, the mortgage crisis and corporate downsizing have sent many middle-class families plummeting into poverty. Social mobility is a term that describes social class change, either upward or downward. Wherever we are in life, then, there's always the chance that something could happen to us that would change our status. If social class is a ladder, social mobility occurs when we are moved either up or down it.
>
> —adapted from Carl, *Think Sociology*, p. 128

In this paragraph, the author begins with examples of upward as well as downward mobility. He then states his main point and follows it with a general statement about status.

Topic Sentence First and Last

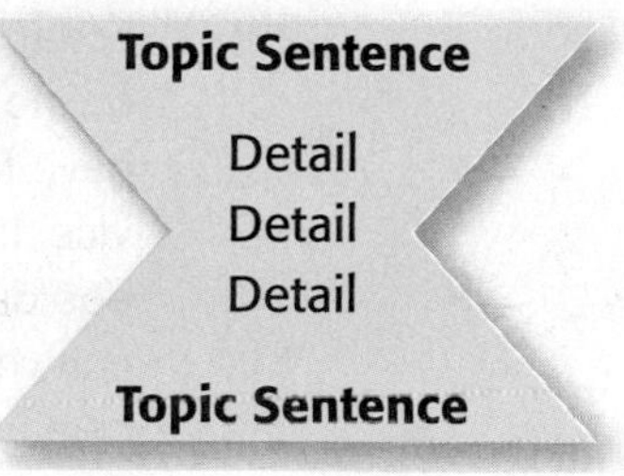

Occasionally the main idea will appear at the beginning of a paragraph and again at the end. Writers may use this organization to emphasize an important idea or to explain an idea that needs clarification.

> Modeling, or learning behaviors by watching others perform them, is one of the most effective strategies for changing behavior. For example, suppose that you have trouble talking to people you don't know very well. One of the easiest ways to improve your communication skills is to select friends whose social skills you envy. Observe them. Do they talk more or listen more? How do people respond to them? Why are they such good communicators? If you observe behaviors you admire, you can model the steps of your behavior-change technique on a proven success.
>
> —adapted from Donatelle, *Health*, p. 18

The first and last sentences both state, in slightly different ways, that modeling can be an effective way to change behavior.

EXERCISE 5-8 Identifying Topic Sentences

Directions: Underline the topic sentence(s) in each of the following paragraphs.

A. Sociologists have several different ways of defining poverty. *Transitional poverty* is a temporary state that occurs when someone loses a job for a short time. *Marginal poverty* occurs when a person lacks stable employment (for example, if your job is lifeguarding at a pool during the summer season, you might experience marginal poverty when the season ends). The next, more serious level, *residual poverty*, is chronic and multigenerational. A person who experiences *absolute poverty* is so poor that he or she doesn't have resources to survive. *Relative poverty* is a state that occurs when we compare ourselves with those around us.

—adapted from Carl, *Think Sociology*, p. 122

B. With so many people participating in social networking sites and keeping personal blogs, it's increasingly common for a single disgruntled customer to wage war online against a company for poor service or faulty products. Unhappy customers have taken to the Web to complain about broken computers or poor customer service. Individuals may post negative reviews of products on blogs, upload angry videos outlining complaints on YouTube, or join public discussion forums where they can voice their opinion about the good and the bad. In the same way that companies celebrate the viral spread of good news, they must also be on guard for online backlash that can damage a reputation.

—adapted from Ebert and Griffin, *Business Essentials*, p. 161

C. Elections serve a critical function in American society. They make it possible for most political participation to be channeled through the electoral process rather than bubbling up through demonstrations, riots, or revolutions. Elections provide regular access to political power, so that leaders can be replaced without being overthrown. This is possible because elections are almost universally accepted as a fair and free method of selecting political leaders. Furthermore, by choosing who is to lead the country, the people—if they make their choices carefully—can also guide the policy direction of the government.

—adapted from Edwards et al., *Government in America*, p. 306

D. Whether you realize it or not, you have probably been eating genetically modified foods for your entire life. Some genetic modifications involve moving genes between organisms in labs. Other modifications have occurred over the last several thousand years due to farmers' use of selective breeding techniques—breeding those cattle that produce the most milk or crossing crop plants that are easiest to harvest. While this artificial selection does not involve moving a gene from one organism to another, it does change the overall frequency of certain alleles for a gene in the population. Unless you eat only certified organic foods, you have been eating food that has been modified.

— adapted from Belk and Maier, *Biology*, p. 208

E. People have not limited themselves to investigating nature. To try to understand life, they have also developed fields of science that focus on the social world. The social sciences examine human relationships. Just as the natural sciences attempt to understand the world of nature, the social sciences attempt to understand the social world. Just as the world of nature contains relationships that are not obvious but must be discovered through controlled observations, so the relationships of the human or social world are not obvious and must be revealed by means of repeated observations.

—adapted from Henslin, *Sociology*, p. 6

F. Darwin hypothesized sexual selection as an explanation for differences between males and females within a species. For instance, the enormous tail on a male peacock results from female peahens that choose mates with showier tails. Because large tails require so much energy to display and are more conspicuous to their predators, peacocks with the largest tails must be both physically strong and smart to survive. Peahens can use the size of the tail, therefore, as a measure of the "quality" of the male. When a peahen chooses a male with a large tail, she is making sure that her offspring will receive high-quality genes. Sexual selection explains the differences between males and females in many species.

—adapted from Belk and Maier, *Biology*, p. 305

G. In Japan, it's called *kuroi kiri* (black mist); in Germany, it's *schmiergeld* (grease money), whereas Mexicans refer to *la mordida* (the bite), the French say *pot-de-vin* (jug of wine), and Italians speak of the *bustarella* (little envelope). They're all talking about *baksheesh,* the Middle Eastern term for a "tip" to grease the wheels of a transaction. Giving "gifts" in exchange for getting business is common and acceptable in many countries, even though this may be frowned on elsewhere.

—adapted from Solomon, *Consumer Behavior*, p. 21

H. When you hear the word *bird*, what mental image comes to mind? Does it resemble an ostrich? Or is your image closer to a robin, sparrow, or blue jay? The likely image that comes to mind at the suggestion to imagine a bird is what psychologists call a prototype. **Prototypes** are mental representations of an average category member. If you took an average of the three most familiar birds, you would get a prototypical bird. Prototypes allow for classification by resemblance. When you encounter a little creature you have never seen before, its basic shape—maybe just its silhouette—can be compared to your prototype of a bird. A match will then be made and you can classify the creature as a bird.

—Krause and Corts, *Psychological Science*, pp. 273–274

What aspect of geology does this photograph illustrate?

I. The standards of our peer groups tend to dominate our lives. If your peers, for example, listen to rap, rock and roll, country, or gospel, it is almost inevitable that you also prefer that kind of music. In high school, if your friends take math courses, you probably do too. It is the same for clothing styles and dating standards. Peer influences also extend to behaviors that violate social norms. If your peers are college-bound and upwardly striving, that is most likely what you will be; but if they use drugs, cheat, and steal, you are likely to do so too.

—adapted from Henslin, *Sociology*, p. 85

J. In the western and southwestern United States, sedimentary rocks often exhibit a brilliant array of colors. In the walls of Arizona's Grand Canyon we can see layers that are red, orange, purple, gray, brown, and buff. Some of the sedimentary rocks in Utah's Bryce Canyon are a delicate pink color. Sedimentary rocks in more humid places are also colorful but they are usually covered by soil and vegetation.

—Lutgens et al., *Essentials of Geology*, p. 144

LEARNING STYLE TIPS

If you tend to be a . . .	Then find topic sentences by . . .
Creative learner	Looking away from the paragraph and stating its main point in your own words. Find a sentence that matches your statement.
Pragmatic learner	Reading through the paragraph, sentence by sentence, evaluating each sentence.

EXERCISE 5-9 Writing Main Ideas

Working Together

Directions: Form groups of three students. Each group writes a topic at the top of a sheet of paper. Groups exchange papers and each group then writes a topic sentence based on the topic. Groups continue to exchange papers and write topic sentences until every group has written a topic sentence for each topic, and then papers are returned to the groups that wrote the original topic. Groups then read aloud the topic and suggested topic sentences. The class evaluates the topic sentences and selects the most effective ones for each topic.

IMPLIED MAIN IDEAS

5 LEARNING GOAL
Understand implied main ideas

When you **imply** something, you suggest an idea, but you do not state it outright. Study the cartoon below. The point the cartoonist is making is clear—relationships change quickly. Notice, however, that this point is not stated directly. To get the cartoonist's point, you had to study the details and read the signs in the cartoon, and then reason out what the cartoonist is trying to say. You need to use the same reasoning process when reading paragraphs that lack a topic sentence. You have to study the details and figure out what all the details mean when considered together. This chapter will show you how to figure out main ideas that are suggested (implied) but not directly stated in a paragraph.

© The New Yorker Collection 1979 Mischa Richter from cartoonbank.com. All rights reserved.

What Does *Implied* Mean?

Suppose your favorite shirt is missing from your closet and you know that your roommate often borrows your clothes. You say to your roommate, "If that blue plaid shirt is back in my closet by noon, I'll forget that it was missing." Now, you did not directly accuse your roommate of borrowing your shirt, but your message was clear—return my shirt! Your statement implied, or suggested, that your roommate had borrowed it and should return it. Your roommate, if he understood your message, inferred (reasoned out) that you suspected that he had borrowed your shirt and that you want it back.

Speakers and writers imply ideas. Listeners and readers must make inferences in order to understand them. Here are two important terms you need to know:

Imply means **to suggest an idea but not state it directly.**

Infer means **to reason out something based on what has been said.**

Here is another statement; what is the writer implying?

I wouldn't feed that cake to my dog.

No doubt you inferred that the writer dislikes the cake and considers it inedible, but notice that the writer did not say that.

EXERCISE 5-10 Identifying Implications

Directions: For each of the following statements, select the choice that best explains what the writer is implying but has not directly stated.

_____ 1. Jane's hair looks as if she just came out of a wind tunnel.
   a. Jane's hair needs rearranging.
   b. Jane's hair needs coloring.
   c. Jane's hair needs styling.
   d. Jane's hair is messy.

_____ 2. I would not recommend Professor Wright's class to my worst enemy.
   a. The writer likes Professor Wright's class.
   b. The writer dislikes Professor Wright's class.
   c. Professor Wright's class is popular.
   d. Professor Wright's class is unpopular.

_____ 3. The steak was overcooked and tough; the mashed potatoes were cold; the green beans were withered; and the chocolate pie was mushy.
   a. The dinner was tasty.
   b. The dinner was prepared poorly.
   c. The dinner was nutritious.
   d. The dinner was served carelessly.

_____ 4. Professor Rodriguez assigns three 5-page papers, gives weekly quizzes, and requires both a midterm and final exam. In addition to weekly assigned chapters in the text, we must read three to four journal articles each week. It is difficult to keep up.
a. Professor Rodriguez's course is demanding.
b. Professor Rodriguez is not a good teacher.
c. Professor Rodriguez likes to give homework.
d. Professor Rodriguez's course is unpopular.

_____ 5. It was my favorite time of year. The lilacs were blooming—finally!—and even though we still wore sweaters, the breeze held the promise of warm days to come.
a. It was autumn.
b. It was springtime.
c. It was summertime.
d. There was a storm coming.

_____ 6. When Alton got the estimate for repairing his car, he knew he had a tough decision to make.
a. Alton was going to repair his own car.
b. Alton would have to find another car repair shop.
c. Alton's car repairs were going to be inexpensive.
d. Alton would have to decide whether to repair the car or buy a different one.

_____ 7. Charlie limped over to the couch and lay down. He put his foot up on a pillow and carefully placed the ice pack on his ankle.
a. Charlie is getting ready to take a nap.
b. Charlie has the flu.
c. Charlie has an injured ankle.
d. Charlie has been running.

_____ 8. After the girls' sleepover party last Saturday, it looked like a bomb had gone off in the basement.
a. The girls made a mess in the basement.
b. The electricity went out during the sleepover party.
c. There was an explosion in the basement after the sleepover party.
d. The sleepover party was too loud.

_____ 9. When it was Kei's turn to give her speech, her stomach did a flip, and her face felt as if it were on fire.
a. Kei looked forward to giving her speech.
b. Kei was experienced at giving speeches.
c. Kei was nervous about giving her speech.
d. Kei enjoyed giving speeches.

_____ 10. People filed out of the movie theater slowly and quietly; many of them wiped their eyes and noses with tissues as they walked to their cars.
a. The movie was sad.
b. The movie was funny.
c. The theater was cold.
d. The moviegoers were disappointed.

Figuring Out Implied Main Ideas

Implied main ideas, when they appear in paragraphs, are usually larger, more important ideas than the details. You might think of **implied ideas** as general ideas that are suggested by specifics.

What larger, more important idea do these details point to?

> The wind was blowing at 35 mph.
>
> The windchill was 5 degrees below zero.
>
> Snow was falling at the rate of 3 inches per hour.

Together these three details suggests that a snowstorm or blizzard was occurring. You might visualize this as follows:

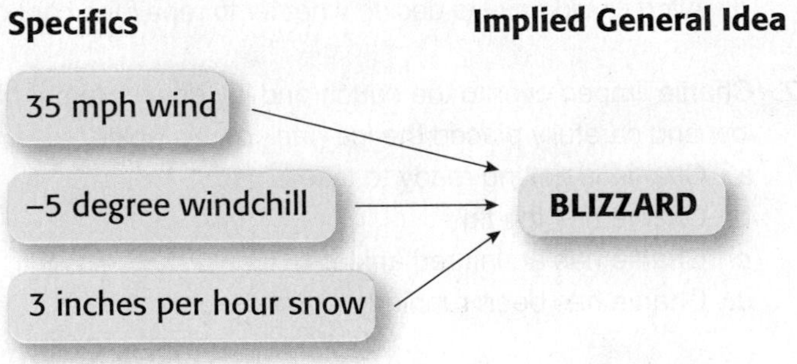

Now what idea does the following set of specifics suggest?

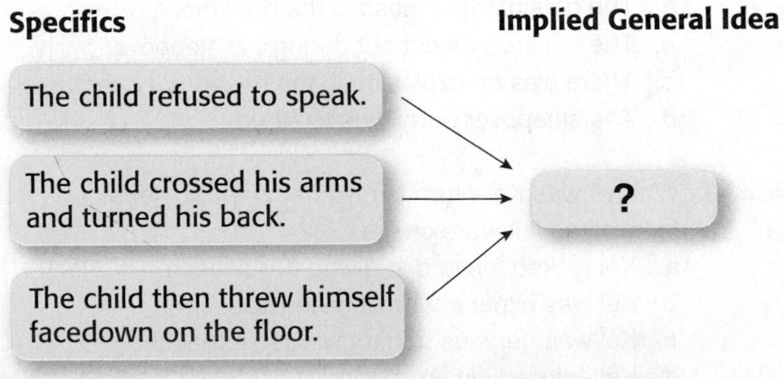

You probably determined that the child was angry or having a temper tantrum.

EXERCISE 5-11 Inferring General Ideas

Directions: Find a word from the list below that describes the larger idea or situation each set of specifics suggests. Each will require you to infer a general idea.

tonsillitis	closed	dying	flu
power outage	accident	burglary	going too fast

1. The child has a headache.

   The child has a queasy stomach.

   The child has a mild fever.

   General idea: The child has the ____________________

2. The plant's leaves were withered.

   The blossoms had dropped.

   Its stem was drooping.

   General idea: The plant was ____________________

3. The windshield of the car was shattered.

   The door panel was dented.

   The bumper was crumpled.

   General idea: The car had been in a(n) ____________________

4. The lights went out.

   The television shut off.

   The refrigerator stopped running.

   General idea: There was a(n) ____________________

5. The supermarket door was locked.

   The parking lot was nearly empty.

   A few remaining customers were checking out.

   General idea: The supermarket was ____________________

Implied Ideas in Paragraphs

In paragraphs, writers sometimes leave their main idea unstated. The paragraph contains only details. It is up to you, the reader, to infer the writer's main point. You can visualize this type of paragraph as follows:

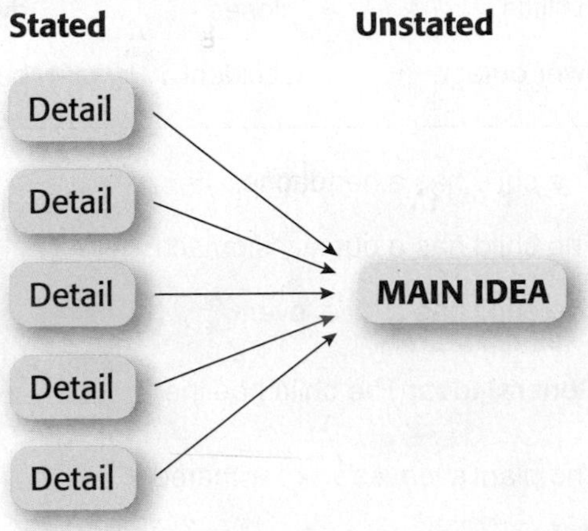

The details, when taken together, all point to a larger, more important idea. Think of the paragraph as a list of facts that you must add up or put together to determine the meaning of the paragraph as a whole. Use the following steps as a guide to find implied main ideas:

1. **Find the topic.** Ask yourself, "What is the one thing the author is discussing throughout the paragraph?"
2. **Decide what the writer wants you to know about that topic.** Look at each detail and decide what larger general idea each explains.
3. **Express this idea in your own words.** Make sure the main idea is a reasonable one. Ask yourself, "Does it apply to all the details in the paragraph?"

Read the following paragraph; then follow the three steps listed above.

> Some advertisers rely on star power. Commercials may use celebrities to encourage consumers to purchase a product. Other commercials may use an "everyone's buying it" approach that argues that thousands of consumers could not possibly be wrong in their choice, so the product must be worthwhile. Still other commercials may use visual appeal to catch the consumers' interest and persuade them to make purchases.

The topic of this paragraph is commercials. More specifically it is about devices advertisers use to build commercials. Three details are given: use of star power, an everyone's-buying-it approach, and visual appeal. Each of the three details is a different persuasive device. The main point the writer is trying to make, then, is that commercials use various persuasive devices to appeal to consumers. Notice that no single sentence states this idea clearly.

You can visualize this paragraph as follows:

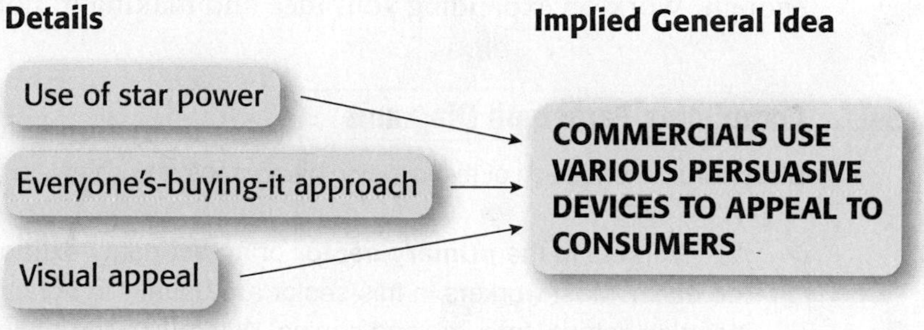

Here is another paragraph. Read it and then fill in the diagram that follows:

> Yellow is a bright, cheery color; it is often associated with spring and hopefulness. Green, since it is a color that appears frequently in nature (trees, grass, plants), has come to suggest growth and rebirth. Blue, the color of the sky, may suggest eternity or endless beauty. Red, the color of both blood and fire, is often connected with strong feelings such as courage, lust, and rage.

Topic: Colors

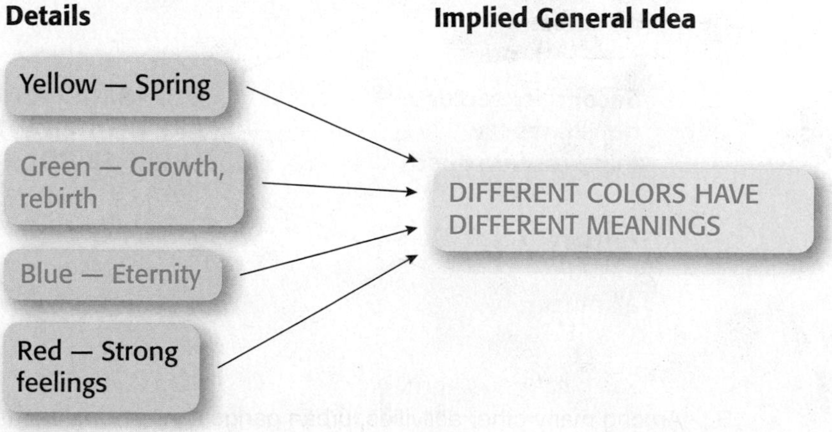

How to Know if You Have Made a Reasonable Inference

There is a test you can perform to discover whether you inferred a reasonable main idea. The idea you infer to be the main idea should be broad enough so that every sentence in the paragraph explains the idea you have chosen. Work through the paragraph, sentence by sentence. Check to see that each sentence explains or gives more information about the idea you have chosen. If some sentences do not explain your chosen idea, your main idea probably is not broad enough. Work on expanding your idea and making it more general.

EXERCISE 5-12 Completing Paragraph Diagrams

Directions: Read each of the following paragraphs and complete the diagram that follows.

A. Workers in the **primary sector** of an economy extract resources directly from the earth. Most workers in this sector are usually in agriculture, but the sector also includes fishing, forestry, and mining. Workers in the **secondary sector** transform raw materials produced by the primary sector into manufactured goods. Construction is included in this sector. All other jobs in an economy are within the **tertiary sector,** sometimes called the **service sector**. The tertiary sector includes a great range of occupations, from a store clerk to a surgeon, from a movie ticket seller to a nuclear physicist, from a dancer to a political leader.

—Bergman and Renwick, *Introduction to Geography,* p. 365

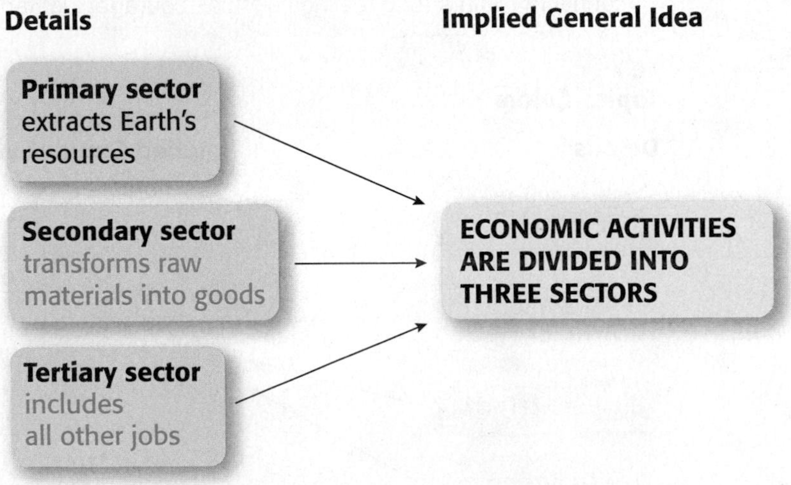

B. Among many other activities, urban gangs fight among themselves and prey on the weak and vulnerable. They delight in demonstrating ownership and control of their "turf," and they sometimes turn neighborhoods into war zones in defense of it. Once gangs form, their graffiti soon adorn buildings and alleyways, and membership is displayed through hand signs, clothing, and special colors. As a newly formed gang grows in reputation and confidence, it soon finds itself attracting those who would like to be members in order to reap the benefits: safety, or girlfriends, or a reputation for toughness.

—Barlow, *Criminal Justice in America,* p. 271

Details **Implied Main Idea**

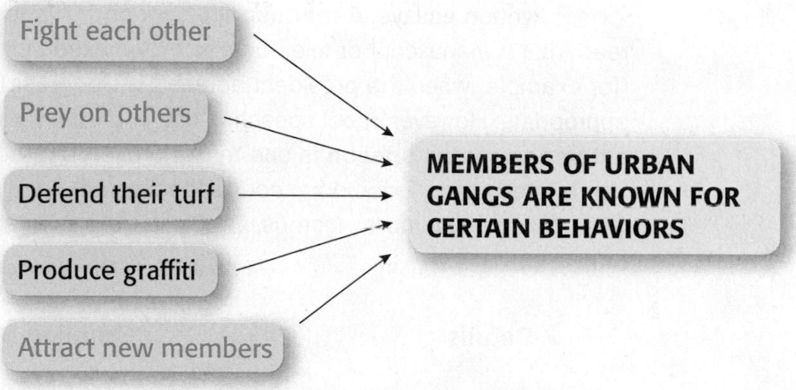

C. More than 30 percent of all foodborne illnesses result from unsafe handling of food at home. What can you do to prevent such illnesses? Among the most basic of precautions are to wash your hands and to wash all produce before eating it. Avoid cross-contamination in the kitchen by using separate cutting boards and utensils for meats and produce. Temperature control is also important; hot foods must be kept hot and cold foods kept cold in order to avoid unchecked bacterial growth. Leftovers need to be eaten within 3 days, and if you're unsure how long something has been sitting in the fridge, don't take chances. When in doubt, throw it out.

—adapted from Donatelle, *Health*, p. 280

Details **Implied Main Idea**

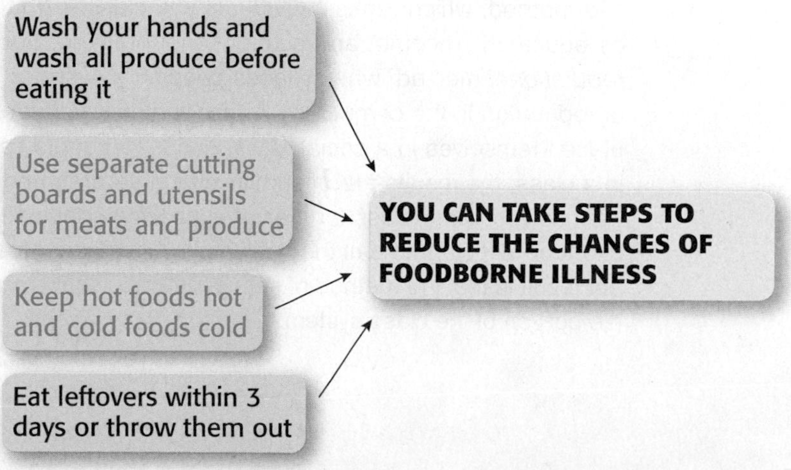

D. How should you present your speech? Let's consider your options. An **impromptu speech** is delivered on the spur of the moment, without preparation. The ability to speak off the cuff is useful in an emergency, but impromptu speeches produce unpredictable outcomes. It's certainly not a good idea to rely on impromptu speaking in place of solid preparation. Another option is a **memorized speech.** Speakers who use memorized presentations are usually most effective when they write their speeches to sound like informal and conversational speech rather than formal, written essays. A **manuscript speech** is written out beforehand and then read from a manuscript or teleprompter. When extremely careful wording is required (for example, when the president addresses Congress), the manuscript speech is appropriate. However, most speeches that you'll deliver will be extemporaneous. An **extemporaneous speech** is one that is prepared in advance and presented from abbreviated notes. Extemporaneous speeches are nearly as polished as memorized ones, but they are more vigorous, flexible, and spontaneous.

—German et al., *Principles of Public Speaking,* pp. 190–191

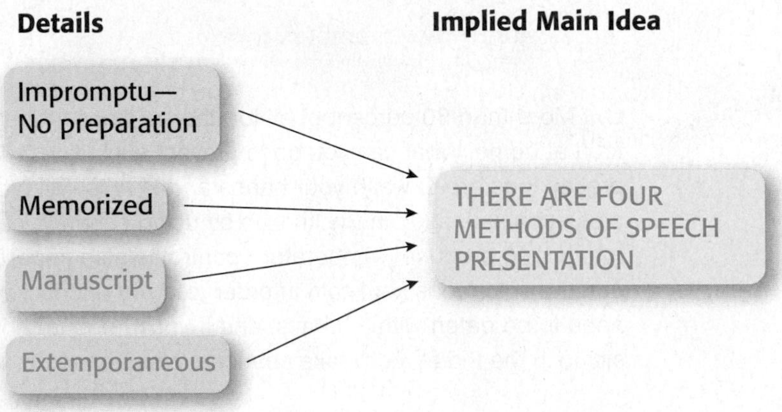

E. In order to measure social class standing, sociologists may use the *objective* method, which ranks individuals into classes on the basis of measures such as education, income, and occupational prestige. Sociologists may also use the *reputational* method, which places people into various social classes on the basis of reputation in the community. A third method, *self-identification,* allows people to place themselves in a social class. Although people can readily place themselves in a class, the results are often difficult to interpret. People might be hesitant to call themselves upper-class for fear of appearing snobbish, but at the same time they might be reluctant to call themselves lower-class for fear of being stigmatized. The net result is that the method of self-identification substantially overestimates the middle portion of the class system.

—Curry et al., *Sociology for the 21st Century,* p. 138

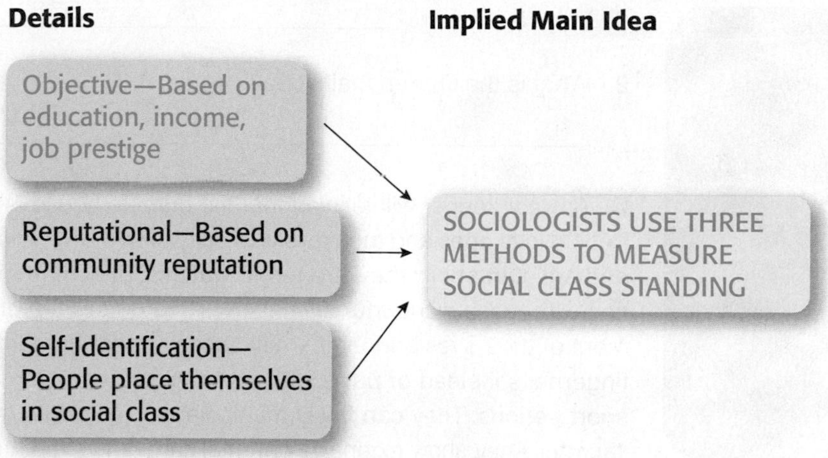

EXERCISE 5-13 Analyzing Paragraphs

Directions: Read each of the following paragraphs and answer the questions that follow.

A. Thanks to the Internet, you can shop 24 hours a day without leaving home, you can read today's newspaper without getting drenched picking up a hard copy in a rainstorm, and you don't have to wait for the 6:00 news to find out what the weather will be like tomorrow—at home or around the globe. And, with the increasing use of handheld devices and wireless communications, you can get that same information—from stock quotes to the weather—even when you're away from your computer.

—Solomon and Stuart, *The Brave New World of E-Commerce,* p. 13

1. What is the topic? ______________________________.

2. What is the implied main idea? ______________________________

______________________________.

B. Research suggests that women who are considered attractive are more effective in changing attitudes than are women thought to be less attractive. In addition, more attractive individuals are often considered to be more credible than less attractive people. They are also perceived to be happier, more popular, more sociable, and more successful than are those rated as being less attractive. With respect to shape and body size, people with fat, round silhouettes are consistently rated as older, more old-fashioned, less good-looking, more talkative, and more good-natured. Athletic, muscular people are rated as more mature, better looking, taller, and more adventurous. Tall and thin people are rated as more ambitious, more suspicious of others, more tense and nervous, more pessimistic, and quieter.

—Beebe and Masterson, *Communicating in Small Groups,* p. 150

1. What is the topic? ______________________________

2. What is the implied main idea? ______________________________

____

C. Any zookeeper will tell you that the primate house is their most popular exhibit. People love apes and monkeys. It is easy to see why—primates are curious, playful, and agile. In short, they are fun to watch. But something else drives our fascination with these wonderful animals: We see ourselves reflected in them. The placement of their eyes and their small noses appear humanlike. They have hands with fingernails instead of paws with claws. Some can stand and walk on two legs for short periods. They can finely manipulate objects with their fingers and opposable thumbs. They show extensive parental care, and even their social relations are similar to ours—they tickle, caress, kiss, and pout.

—adapted from Belk and Maier, *Biology*, p. 236

How do these photographs suggest the implied main idea?

1. What is the topic? ______________________________

2. What is the implied main idea? ______________________________

____

D. The Web has enabled people to work, "talk" to friends across town and across the ocean, and buy goods from online retailers without leaving their houses. It has also made some criminal enterprises and unethical behavior easier to accomplish and harder to trace—for example, people can scam others out of large sums of money, buy college term papers, and learn how to build a bomb.

—adapted from Divine et al., *America Past and Present*, p. 449

1. What is the topic? ______________________________

2. What is the implied main idea? ______________________________

E. Sleep conserves body energy so that we are rested and ready to perform during high-performance daylight hours. Sleep also restores the neurotransmitters that have been depleted during the waking hours. This process clears the brain of unimportant details as a means of preparing for a new day. Getting enough sleep to feel ready to meet daily challenges is a key factor in maintaining optimal physical and psychological status.

—adapted from Donatelle and Davis, *Access to Health,* p. 42

1. What is the topic? ______________________________

2. What is the implied main idea? ______________________________

____

EXERCISE 5-14 Writing Implied Main Ideas

Directions: None of the following paragraphs has a topic sentence. Read each paragraph and, in the space provided, write a sentence that expresses the main idea.

A. When registering for online services under a screen name, it can be tempting to think your identity is a secret to other users. Many people will say or do things on the Internet that they would never do in real life because they believe that they are acting anonymously. However, most blogs, e-mail and instant messenger services, and social networking sites are tied to your real identity in some way. While your identity may be superficially concealed by a screen name, it often takes little more than a quick Google search to uncover your name, address, and other personal and possibly sensitive information.

—Ebert and Griffin, *Business Essentials*, p. 188

Implied main idea: ______________________________

B. Governments in this country spend billions of dollars on schools, libraries, hospitals, and dozens of other public institutions. Some of these services, like highways and public parks, can be shared by everyone and cannot be denied to anyone. These kinds of services are called public goods. Other services, such as a college education or medical care, can be restricted to individuals who meet certain criteria and may be provided by the private sector as well. Governments typically provide these services to make them accessible to people who may not be able to afford privately available services.

—Edwards et al., *Government in America*, p. 9

Implied main idea: ______________________________

C. Sociologists use the term **norms** to describe the rules of behavior that develop out of a group's values. The term **sanctions** refers to the reactions people receive for following or breaking norms. A positive sanction expresses approval for following a norm, and a negative sanction reflects disapproval for breaking a norm. Positive sanctions can be material, such as a prize, a trophy, or money, but in everyday life they usually consist of hugs, smiles, a pat on the back, or even handshakes and "high fives." Negative sanctions can also be material—being fined in court is one example—but negative sanctions, too, are more likely to be symbolic: harsh words, or gestures such as frowns, stares, clenched jaws, or raised fists.

—adapted from Henslin, *Sociology*, p. 46

Implied main idea: ______________________________

D. The amount of air forced past the vocal cords determines the volume of our speech, while muscles that control the length of the vocal cords help to determine the pitch of our speech. The shape of our mouths, lips, and tongue and the position of our teeth determine the actual sound that is produced. Sustained exposure to tobacco smoke can cause parts of the larynx to become covered with scar tissue, often making long-time smokers sound quite hoarse.

—Belk and Maier, *Biology*, p. 447

Implied main idea: ______________________________

E. Most sporting goods manufacturers have long sold products for women, but this often meant simply creating an inferior version of the male product and slapping a pink label on it. Then the companies discovered that many women were buying products intended for boys because they wanted better quality, so some of them figured out that they needed to take this market segment seriously. Burton Snowboard Company was one of the early learners. When the company started to offer high-quality clothing and gear made specifically for women, female boarders snapped them up. Burton also changed the way it promotes these products and redesigned its Web site after getting feedback from female riders.

—adapted from Solomon, *Consumer Behavior*, p. 189

Implied main idea: ______________________________

____

F. If you've ever noticed that you feel better after a belly laugh or a good cry, you aren't alone. Old adages such as "laughter is the best medicine" and "smile and the world smiles with you" didn't just evolve out of the blue. Scientists have long recognized that smiling, laughing, singing, dancing, and other actions can elevate our moods, help us live longer, and help us improve our relationships. Crying can have similar positive physiological effects. Recent research has shown that laughter and joy can increase endorphin levels, increase oxygen levels in the blood, increase immune system functioning, decrease stress levels, relieve pain, enhance productivity, reduce risks of heart disease, and help fight cancer.

—Donatelle, *Health*, p. 71

Implied main idea: ______________________________

____

G. As the effects of caffeine begin to wear off, users may feel let down, mentally or physically depressed, exhausted, and weak. To counteract these effects, people commonly choose to drink another cup of coffee. But before you say yes to another cup of coffee, consider this. Although you would have to drink between 66 and 100 cups of coffee in a day to produce a fatal overdose of caffeine, you may experience sensory disturbances after consuming only 10 cups of coffee within a 24-hour period. These symptoms include tinnitus (ringing in the ears), spots before the eyes, numbness in arms and legs, poor circulation, and visual hallucinations. Because 10 cups of coffee is not an extraordinary amount for many people to drink within a 24-hour period, caffeine use is clearly something to think about.

—Donatelle and Davis, *Access to Health,* pp. 289–290

Implied main idea: ______________________________

H. In 1946, the Levitt Company was finishing up Levittown. Practically overnight, what was formerly a Long Island potato field 25 miles east of Manhattan became one of America's newest suburbs, changing the way homes were built. The land was bulldozed and the trees removed, and then trucks dropped building materials at precise 60-foot intervals. Construction was divided into 26 distinct steps. At the peak of production, the company constructed 30 new single-family homes each day.

—Bergman and Renwick, *Introduction to Geography,* p. 422

Implied main idea: ____

____

I. Children who exercise are more likely to continue exercising in adulthood than children who do not exercise. In a country where most adults do not get the recommended 30 to 60 minutes of exercise most days of the week, it makes sense to encourage everyone to become more athletic. When good exercise habits are carried into adulthood, there is a decreased risk of heart disease, obesity, diabetes, and many cancers. Additional benefits include lowered cholesterol, and studies suggest that exercise may decrease anxiety and depression.

—Belk and Maier, *Biology*, p. 509

Implied main idea: ____

J. *Turn-requesting cues* tell the speaker that you, as a listener, would like to take a turn as speaker; you might transmit these cues by using some vocalized "er" or "um" that tells the speaker that you would now like to speak, by opening your eyes and mouth as if to say something, by beginning to gesture with a hand, or by leaning forward.

Through *turn-denying cues* you indicate your reluctance to assume the role of speaker by, for example, intoning a slurred "I don't know"; giving the speaker some brief grunt that signals you have nothing to say; avoiding eye contact with the speaker who wishes you now to take on the role of speaker; or engaging in some behavior that is incompatible with speaking—for example, coughing or blowing your nose.

Through *backchanneling cues* you communicate various meanings back to the speaker—but without assuming the role of the speaker. For example, you can indicate your *agreement* or *disagreement* with the speaker through smiles or frowns, nods of approval or disapproval; brief comments such as "right," "exactly," or "never"; or vocalizations such as "uh-huh" or "uh-uh."

—DeVito, *Messages*, pp. 224–225

Implied main idea: ____

____

EXERCISE 5-15 Identifying Main Ideas

Directions: Separate into groups. Using a reading selection from Part Seven of this book, work with your group to identify and underline the topic sentence of each paragraph. If any of the main ideas are unstated, write a sentence that states the main idea. When all the groups have completed the task, the class should compare the findings of the various groups.

SELF-TEST SUMMARY

1 What are general and specific ideas?	A general idea is broad and can apply to many things. A specific idea is detailed and refers to a smaller group, or an individual item.
2 How can you identify the topic of a paragraph?	Look for the one idea the author is discussing throughout the entire paragraph.
3 How can you find the stated main idea of a paragraph?	Find the topic and then locate the one sentence in the paragraph that is the most general. Check to be sure that this one sentence relates to all the details in the paragraph.
4 What is a topic sentence?	The topic sentence states the main idea of a paragraph. The topic sentence can be located anywhere in the paragraph. The most common positions are first or last, but the topic sentence can also appear in the middle, or first and last.
5 How can one figure out implied main ideas?	Implied main ideas are suggested but not directly stated in a paragraph. To find implied main ideas, • find the topic • figure out what general idea the paragraph explains • express the idea in your own words

GOING ONLINE

1. **Main Ideas in Electronic Communications**
   Imagine the following situation: You need to communicate with a group of friends or classmates about several important matters. For this reason, you need to compose an e-mail rather than send a text message. What can you do to make sure the main ideas or topic sentences of your email "pop off the screen" (that is, get your readers' attention)?

2. **Implied Ideas and Emoticons**
   You have seen *emoticons* – small symbols like ☺ used in electronic communications. Many people believe emoticons have become popular because they help readers better understand the writer's emotions and intentions. For example, on a text message, a writer may use the ☺ emoticon to suggest "I am kidding." Abbreviations such as LOL ("laughing out loud") are also common. With a group of classmates, brainstorm a list of five common emoticons or abbreviations, and provide a definition of each. Write a sentence that uses each. Does including an emoticon or abbreviation help you better express yourself?

CHAPTER 5 MASTERY TEST 1 Paragraph Skills

This **Mastery Test** can be completed in **MyReadingLab.**

Name ______________________ Section ____________

Date ____________ Number right ________ × 20 points = Score ________

Directions: Read each of the following paragraphs, and select the choice that correctly identifies the paragraph's main idea.

_____ 1. Many "everyday" consumers have become entrepreneurs by participating in **virtual auctions.** Millions of consumers log on to eBay.com and other auction sites to bid on an enormous variety of new and used items offered by both businesses and individuals. From an economic standpoint, auctions offer savvy consumers the opportunity to buy overruns or excess inventories of new items at discounted prices much as they would in bricks-and-mortar discount stores. For many, however, the auctions also have become a form of entertainment. Players in the auction game spend hours a day on the auction sites, buying and selling collectibles or other items of (assumed?) value.

—Solomon and Stuart, *The Brave New World of E-Commerce,* p. 16

a. Millions of consumers use eBay.com to buy and sell a wide variety of items.
b. Virtual auctions offer consumers the chance to buy and sell items and to be entertained.
c. Virtual auctions provide the same service as traditional discount stores.
d. Most consumers view virtual auctions as a form of entertainment.

_____ 2. Pollutants have diverse sources. Some come from a *point source*—they enter a stream at a specific location, such as a wastewater discharge pipe. Others may come from a *nonpoint source*—they come from a large diffuse area, as happens when organic matter or fertilizer washes from a field during a storm. Point-source pollutants are usually smaller in quantity and much easier to control. Nonpoint sources usually pollute in greater quantities and are much harder to control.

—Bergman and Renwick, *Introduction to Geography*, p. 386

How does the inclusion of this visual help you understand the main idea of the paragraph?

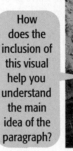

a. Point sources of pollution include wastewater discharge pipes.
b. Nonpoint sources of pollution are worse for the environment than point sources.
c. Nonpoint-source pollutants come from a widespread area, whereas point-source pollutants come from a specific location.
d. Pollutants can come from point or nonpoint sources.

_____ 3. How does friendship change during one's life? Children are mostly interested in having someone to play with, and their friendships are more centered on personal needs. In middle school, friendships become more exclusive and based on mutual interests. College students often have to find new friendships if they leave town to attend school. After graduation, young adults tend to focus on few meaningful friendships and "weed out" more superficial acquaintances. This tendency becomes more pronounced as people enter important romantic relationships, in a pattern referred to as **dyadic withdrawal.** By midlife, friendship with members of the opposite sex diminishes considerably, as couples tend to spend more time with common friends and family. In old age, research shows that people tend to focus more and more on a few, selected friends rather than acquaintances.

—Kunz, *THINK Marriages and Families*, p. 83

a. Children have more intense friendships than adults.
b. Elderly people need fewer friendships.
c. The type and nature of friendships change throughout life.
d. Friendship is more important than romantic relationships.

_____ 4. Support groups are an important part of stress management. Friends, family members, and co-workers can provide us with emotional and physical support. Although the ideal support group differs for each of us, you should have one or two close friends in whom you are able to confide and neighbors with whom you can trade favors. You should take the opportunity to participate in community activities at least once a week. A healthy, committed relationship can also provide vital support.

—adapted from Donatelle and Davis, *Access to Health*, p. 78

a. Support groups are important in managing stress.
b. Support groups consist of friends and family.
c. Participation in community activities is one way of managing stress.
d. The ideal support group is different for each person.

_____ 5. In politics, as in many other aspects of life, the squeaky wheel gets the grease. The way citizens "squeak" in politics is to participate. Americans have many avenues of political participation open to them, and political scientists generally distinguish between two broad types: conventional and unconventional. Conventional participation includes many widely accepted modes of influencing government—voting, trying to persuade others, ringing doorbells for a petition, running for office, and so on. In contrast, unconventional participation includes activities that are often dramatic, such as protesting, civil disobedience, and even violence.

—adapted from Edwards et al., *Government in America*, pp. 205–206

a. Politics are like many other aspects of life.
b. Political participation can generally be classified as conventional or unconventional.
c. Influencing government primarily consists of voting and running for office.
d. Unconventional political participation may involve violent activities.

CHAPTER 5

MASTERY TEST 2 Paragraph Skills

This **Mastery Test** can be completed in **MyReadingLab**.

Name ______________________________ Section ____________

Date ______________ Number right ________ × 10 points = Score ________

Directions: Read the following selection from a nutrition textbook, and select the choice that best completes each of the statements that follow.

Nutrition Myth or Fact?

Is Bottled Water Safer than Tap Water?

1 Bottled water has become increasingly popular during the past 20 years. Many people prefer the taste of bottled water to that of tap water. They also feel that bottled water is safer than tap water. Is this true?

2 The water we drink in the United States generally comes from two sources: surface water and groundwater.

- *Surface water* comes from lakes, rivers, and reservoirs. Common contaminants of surface water include runoff from highways, pesticides, animal wastes, and industrial wastes. Many of the cities across the United States obtain their water from surface-water sources.
- *Groundwater* comes from spaces between underground rock formations called *aquifers*. People who live in rural areas generally pump groundwater from a well as their water source. Hazardous substances leaking from waste sites, dumps, landfills, and oil and gas pipelines can contaminate groundwater. Groundwater can also be contaminated by naturally occurring substances such as arsenic or high levels of iron.

3 The most common chemical used to treat and purify our water is *chlorine*. Chlorine is effective in killing many contaminants in our water supply. Ozone is also commonly used. Water treatment plants also routinely check our water supplies for hazardous chemicals, minerals, and other contaminants. Because of these efforts, the United States has one of the safest water systems in the world.

What idea does this photograph suggest?

4 The Environmental Protection Agency (EPA) sets and monitors the standards for our municipal water systems. The EPA does not monitor water from private

wells, but it publishes recommendations for well owners to help them maintain a safe water supply. Local water regulatory agencies must provide an annual report on specific water contaminants to all households served by that agency.

5 In contrast, the Food and Drug Administration (FDA) regulates bottled water. It does not require that bottled water meet higher quality standards than public water. As with tap water, bottled water is taken from either surface water or groundwater sources. Bottled water is often treated and filtered differently than tap water, which changes its taste and appearance.

6 Although bottled water may taste better than tap water, there is no evidence that it is safer to drink. Look closely at the label of your favorite bottled water. If the label states "From a public water source," it has come directly from the tap! Some types of bottled water may contain more minerals than tap water, but there are no other additional nutritional benefits of drinking bottled water.

—adapted from Thompson and Manore, *Nutrition for Life*, p. 240

_____ 1. The main point of this selection is to
- a. recommend the use of bottled water.
- b. discuss the safety of bottled water versus tap water.
- c. describe the effects of water pollution.
- d. promote stricter water regulations.

_____ 2. The main idea of paragraph 2 is expressed in the
- a. first sentence.
- b. second sentence.
- c. third sentence.
- d. last sentence.

_____ 3. The topic of paragraph 2 is
- a. bottled water.
- b. sources of water.
- c. water pollution.
- d. pesticides.

_____ 4. According to the selection, groundwater comes from
- a. lakes.
- b. rivers.
- c. reservoirs.
- d. aquifers.

_____ 5. The topic of paragraph 3 is
- a. chlorine treatment.
- b. ozone treatment.
- c. treatment of the water supply.
- d. hazardous chemicals.

_____ 6. The main idea of paragraph 3 is that
- a. chlorine kills contaminants in our water.
- b. ozone is used to treat and purify water.
- c. water treatment plants routinely check our water supplies.
- d. our water system is one of the safest in the world.

_____ 7. The implied main idea of paragraph 4 is that
- a. the EPA does not monitor well water.
- b. water safety is regulated locally and by the EPA.
- c. local agencies report on water contaminants.
- d. many households are served by local agencies.

_____ 8. The topic of paragraph 5 is
a. tap water.
b. public water.
c. bottled water.
d. water standards.

_____ 9. The main idea of paragraph 6 is expressed in the
a. first sentence.
b. second sentence.
c. third sentence.
d. last sentence.

_____ 10. The conclusion reached in this selection is that
a. tap water tastes better than bottled water.
b. bottled water is much safer than tap water.
c. bottled water is no safer than tap water.
d. tap water has more nutritional value than bottled water.

CHAPTER 5

MASTERY TEST 3 Reading Selection

This **Mastery Test** can be completed in **MyReadingLab**.

Name ______________________________ Section ____________

Date ____________________ Number right* ________ × 10 points = Score __________

War Torn

Joshua Kors

This selection, which first appeared in a November 2008 issue of *Current Science* magazine, discusses the traumatic effects of war on veterans and their families.

Vocabulary Preview

insurgents (par. 1) armed rebels; guerillas

Veterans and their families are coping with the lingering trauma of Iraq and Afghanistan

1 Chuck Luther woke up in a cold sweat. Nightmares again. The former Army sergeant was home in Killeen, Texas. But in his dreams, he was still in Iraq, where he had led an elite unit that battled insurgents. Two years earlier, Luther had been stationed in a combat outpost north of Baghdad when a mortar blast exploded nearby and knocked him to the floor. Luther survived the attack. However, the jolt to his head damaged his hearing and left him with severe headaches.

2 Luther was also plagued by visions of the mortar attack and haunted by the blood and pain he had seen. The memories made functioning as a husband and father difficult when he returned home to Texas. He began experiencing panic attacks and uncharacteristic bursts of rage.

3 "Before Iraq, my wife and I never fought at all," says Luther. "But when I got back, I was so angry. We started fighting all the time. I'd tear up the house and break things. My kids became scared of me. It was awful."

4 Luther suffers from a psychological illness common among soldiers returning from war. During World War I, it was called shell shock; during World War II, battle fatigue. Today the condition is known as post-traumatic stress disorder (PTSD). The illness has become epidemic (widespread) in the United States. A recent RAND Corporation study found that 300,000 soldiers returning from Iraq and Afghanistan suffer from it.

*To calculate the number right, use items 1–10 under "Mastery Test Skills Check."

Never-Ending Crisis

5 During war, the demands on the human brain are relentless. Soldiers on the battlefield are in constant crisis. Staying alert and focused is more than a necessity; it's a matter of life and death.

6 The brain can become locked into that state of hypervigilance and remain that way, even when the threat of war is gone and the soldier has returned home. That's when PTSD can develop. Keith Armstrong is a professor of psychiatry at the University of California, San Francisco. He says that soldiers with PTSD are "always scanning the environment for threats. During battle, that vigilance might help save another soldier's life." Back home, however, that focus makes the soldiers overprotective of their children and more critical of their kids' mistakes. "Their reaction to everything becomes much more dramatic. That can strain relations in families," Armstrong says.

7 Many veterans try to cope with PTSD on their own, often in inappropriate ways, says Michelle Sherman, a psychologist who treats soldiers at a veterans hospital in Oklahoma City. They might refuse to leave the house. Or they might avoid everything that triggers memories of war—the screaming crowds at their daughters' basketball games or the loud bangs of a Fourth of July parade.

8 A large number of vets also try to numb themselves with drugs and alcohol, according to Sherman. "The thing is, when you numb the pain, you numb the pleasure," says Sherman. "My goal is to show soldiers that they don't need to emotionally withdraw or create a wall between themselves and their families. With help, they can learn to turn that page and move on to the next chapter of their lives."

Page Turners

9 There are many emerging ways to treat PTSD. Some vets get regular massages to ease the tension left over from war. Others enroll in group therapy, where they can discuss their situations in safe settings with other soldiers who have experienced the traumas of war. Armstrong has pioneered a family counseling program in which vets bring their wives and children and talk as families about the challenges they're facing. "When a soldier talks with family, his family has the ability to be supportive," says Armstrong. "Family can be part of the healing process."

10 Sherman is coauthor of *Finding My Way: A Teen's Guide to Living with a Parent Who Has Experienced Trauma.* In it, she speaks directly to young readers, offering them guidance about how to help their parents—and how to care for themselves.

11 She encourages soldiers' children to recognize that changes in parental behavior are due to struggles with PTSD. The changes have nothing to do with the kids or their parents' love for them. She asks readers to understand the new limitations on their mother's or father's abilities. A parent may not be able to attend band concerts because the bang of the drums is too loud, too much like the gunfire of

war. "Teens need to ask themselves, Is there someone else who can come to my recital, someone else I can turn to when I need a laugh or feel like crying?'" says Sherman.

12 Luther recently purchased Sherman's book for his 14-year-old daughter, Alexa. She and her siblings have struggled with the change in their father's temperament and tried their best to be patient and sympathetic. "Things are hard now; there's no denying that" says Luther. "But with time, I do believe things will get better for me and my family."

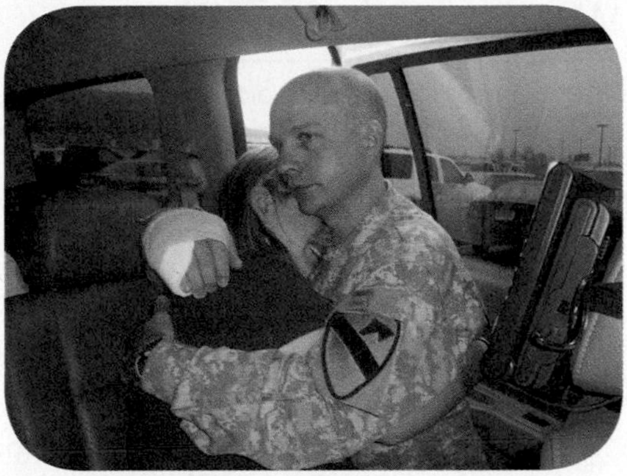

Under Fire

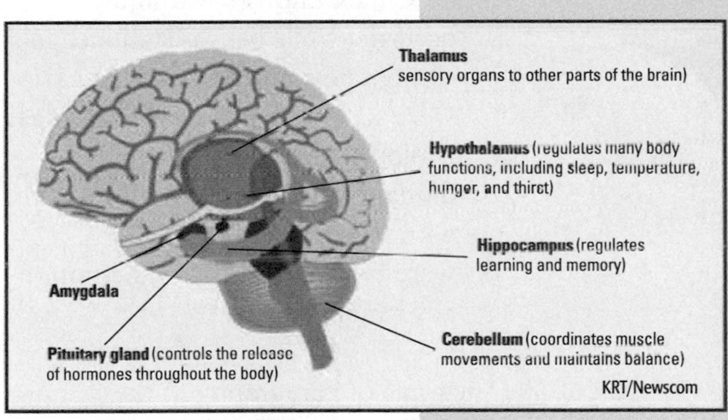

KRT/Newscom

13 The human brain is organized into many regions, some of which are shown here. Each one has a separate function. Neurologists studying post-traumatic stress disorder (PTSD) have zeroed in on the amygdala, the part of the brain that processes emotions. A recent study found that soldiers with PTSD have a hyperactive amygdala; the neurons (nerve cells) in that region fire at a faster-than-normal rate. With the emotion center of the brain working overtime, soldiers who were even-tempered before war may be quicker to anger and more easily frightened when they return.

—Kors, *Current Science*

MASTERY TEST SKILLS CHECK

Directions: Select the choice that best completes each of the following statements.

Checking Your Comprehension

_____ 1. The purpose of this selection is to
a. describe how PTSD affects war veterans and their families.
b. explore different causes of post-traumatic stress disorder (PTSD).
c. compare the experiences of soldiers in different wars.
d. argue for better treatment programs for war veterans.

_____ 2. Chuck Luther can best be described as
a. a psychologist who treats veterans with PTSD.
b. an author who has written a book about PTSD.
c. an Iraq war veteran suffering from PTSD.
d. a professor who has established PTSD counseling programs.

_____ 3. All of the following statements about PTSD are true *except*
a. A recent study found that 300,000 soldiers returning from Iraq and Afghanistan suffer from PTSD.
b. In soldiers with PTSD, the nerve cells in the emotion center of the brain fire at a slower-than-normal rate.
c. Many soldiers with PTSD are sensitive to loud noises that trigger memories of war and gunfire.
d. Chuck Luther's PTSD symptoms included panic attacks and uncharacteristic bursts of rage.

_____ 4. Based on the box "Under Fire," the part of the brain that processes emotions and is hyperactive in soldiers with PTSD is the
a. thalamus.
b. amygdala.
c. cerebellum.
d. pituitary gland.

_____ 5. According to the selection, emerging treatments for PTSD include
a. regular massages.
b. group therapy.
c. family counseling.
d. all of the above.

Applying Your Skills

_____ 6. The implied main idea of paragraph 2 is that Chuck Luther's war injuries
a. occurred while he was stationed in a combat post north of Baghdad.
b. were caused when a mortar blast exploded nearby.
c. damaged his hearing and left him with severe headaches.
d. were both physically and emotionally traumatic.

_____ 7. The topic of paragraph 4 is the
a. shell shock of World War I veterans.
b. battle fatigue of World War II veterans.
c. PTSD of Iraq and Afghanistan veterans.
d. stress-related psychological illness among war veterans.

_____ 8. The implied main idea of paragraph 6 is that
   a. soldiers' brains become locked into a state of hypervigilance.
   b. soldiers with PTSD are always on the lookout for threats.
   c. hypervigilance is essential in war but causes problems at home.
   d. being vigilant can help save another soldier's life.

_____ 9. The topic sentence of paragraph 9 is the
   a. first sentence.
   b. second sentence.
   c. third sentence.
   d. last sentence.

_____ 10. The main idea of paragraph 11 is that Michelle Sherman's book encourages soldiers' children to
   a. ignore the signs of PTSD in their parents.
   b. realize that changes in parental behavior are due to PTSD.
   c. cope with the effects of PTSD on their own.
   d. take part in family counseling programs.

Studying Words

_____ 11. The word *elite* (par. 1) means
   a. large.
   b. top quality.
   c. typical.
   d. remote.

_____ 12. The word *plagued* (par. 2) means
   a. disappointed.
   b. interested.
   c. tormented.
   d. wondered.

_____ 13. The synonym clue for the word *epidemic* (par. 4) is
   a. fatigue.
   b. condition.
   c. shock.
   d. widespread.

_____ 14. The prefix in the word *hypervigilance* (par. 6) means
   a. excessive.
   b. against.
   c. before.
   d. under.

_____ 15. The word *temperament* (par. 12) means
   a. anger.
   b. speech.
   c. personality.
   d. ability.

For more practice, ask your instructor for an opportunity to work on the mastery tests that appear in the Test Bank.

Summarizing the Reading

Directions: Complete the following summary of the reading by filling in the blanks.

Chuck Luther is an ______________ suffering from __________________________. Referred to in previous wars as ______________________, the ______________ illness is common to ______________. The extreme ______________ that soldiers must have ______________ can create ______________________. Veterans with ______________ may try to ______________________ or try to ______________________________. Emerging ways to treat ______________ include ______________________________________ ______________ and author Michelle Sherman offers guidance to ______________ about how to ______________________________. Children are encouraged to recognize that ______________________________________.

Reading Visually

1. What do the photographs that accompany this article tell you about soldiers in general and Chuck Luther in particular? What details do you notice about the two close-ups of Luther?
2. How does the diagram contribute to your understanding of the concepts discussed in the article? What aspects of the illustration made it helpful?
3. Explain how the title of this selection reflects the subject matter. How do the headings add to the readability of this selection?

Thinking Critically about the Reading

1. Why did the author begin by telling Chuck Luther's story? Explain how his personal experience contributes to your overall understanding of PTSD.
2. How would you describe the author's attitude toward this subject? What feelings are you left with at the end of the article?
3. Connect the information in this article with what you already know about PTSD. What other traumatic events can bring about this condition?

CHAPTER 6

Understanding Paragraphs: Supporting Details and Transitions

Focusing on ... Supporting Details and Transitions

Parent Teacher Yellow Cake

2 cups of flour
2 teaspoons of double-acting baking powder
1/2 teaspoon of salt
1 stick of unsalted butter, room temperature
1 cup of sugar
3 egg yolks
1 cup milk
2 teaspoons of pure vanilla extract
Preheat oven to 375 degrees.
Mix all of your dry ingredients except sugar in a bowl. Put aside. With an electric mixer, cream your butter and sugar until light and fluffy, add the egg yolks, and mix thoroughly. Add the dry ingredients to the butter mixture, alternating with milk until thoroughly blended. Stir in the vanilla.
Bake in 2 greased and floured 8-inch cake pans for 25 minutes.

LEARNING GOALS

This chapter will show you how to

1. Recognize supporting details
2. Identify types of supporting details
3. Use transitions to guide your reading
4. Paraphrase paragraphs

In order to produce the cake shown in the photo at left, the baker had to follow the recipe closely, paying attention to each detailed step. The baker also had to complete each step in the order presented. Reading a paragraph involves a similar process. The reader must pay attention to all the details that support the main idea. Also, the reader must pay attention to the order of details and their relationship to one another, often signaled by the use of connecting words called transitions.

Suppose you read the following sentence in a business communication textbook. It appears as the opening sentence of a paragraph.

> Distractions are a major problem in business communication, but everyone in an organization can help minimize them.

After reading this sentence you are probably wondering how distractions can be minimized.

Only poor writers make statements without supporting them. So you expect, then, that in the remainder of the paragraph the author will support the statement about eliminating distractions. Here is the full paragraph.

> Distractions are a major problem in business communication, but everyone in an organization can help minimize them. A small dose of common sense and courtesy goes a long way. Turn off that mobile phone before you step into a meeting. Don't talk across the tops of other people's cubicles. Be sensitive to personal differences, too; for instance, some people enjoy working with music on, but music is an enormous distraction for others.
>
> —Thill and Bovée, *Excellence in Business Communication*, p. 14

In this paragraph, the authors explained their statement by giving examples of how distractions can be minimized. The first sentence expresses the main idea; the remaining sentences are supporting details. You will recall from Chapter 5 that a paragraph has four essential elements:

- **Topic**—the one thing the whole paragraph is about
- **Main idea**—the broad, general idea the whole paragraph is concerned with
- **Supporting details**—the ideas that explain or support the main idea
- **Transitions**—the words or phrases that link ideas together

This chapter will focus on how to recognize supporting details and how to use transitions to guide your reading. You will also learn how to paraphrase paragraphs and longer pieces of writing.

RECOGNIZE SUPPORTING DETAILS

1 LEARNING GOAL Recognize supporting details

Supporting details are those facts and ideas that prove or explain the main idea of a paragraph. While all the details in a paragraph support the main idea, not all details are equally important. As you read, try to identify and pay attention to the most important details. Pay less attention to details of lesser importance.

The **key details** directly explain the main idea. Other **minor details** may provide additional information, offer an example, or further explain one of the key details.

The diagram in Figure 6-1 shows how details relate to the main idea and how details range in degree of importance. In the diagram, less important details appear below the important details they explain.

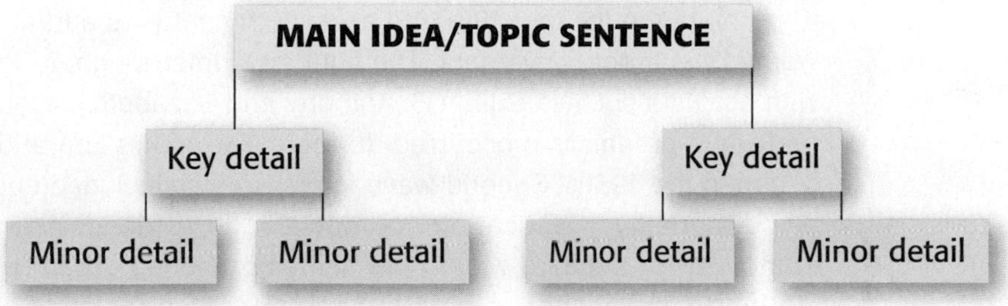

Figure 6-1

Read the following paragraph and study the diagram that follows.

> <u>The skin of the human body has several functions.</u> First, it serves as a protective covering. In doing so, it accounts for 17 percent of the body weight. Skin also protects the organs within the body from damage or harm. The skin serves as a regulator of body functions. It controls body temperature and water loss. Finally, the skin serves as a receiver. It is sensitive to touch and temperature.

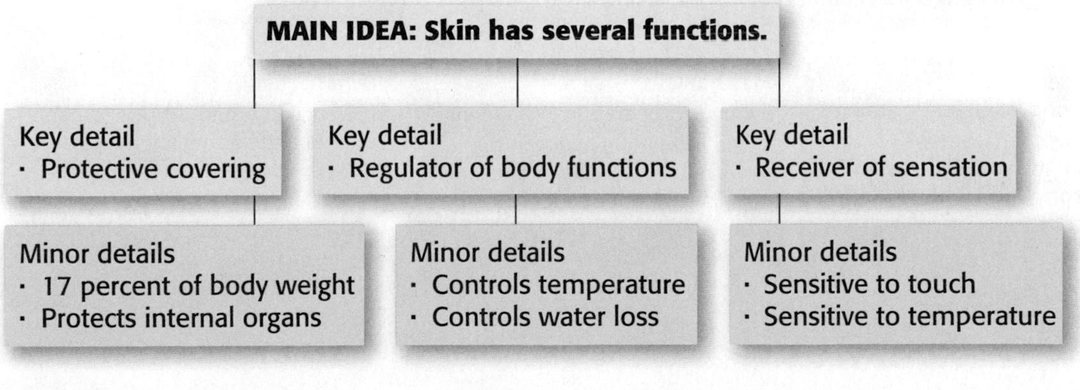

Figure 6-2

From the diagram in Figure 6-2 you can see that the details that state the three functions of skin are the key details. Other details, such as "protects internal organs," provide further information and are at a lower level of importance.

Read the following paragraph and try to pick out the more important details.

> The history of the feminist movement goes back to the eighteenth century. Mary Wollstonecraft's famous essay "A Vindication of the Rights of Woman" is one of the earliest examples of western feminist thought. It predates modern feminism which can be divided into three "waves." What is considered the first wave began in the late 19th and early 20th centuries and revolved around the women's suffrage movement. The fight for women's right to vote began in 1848 with activists such as Susan B. Anthony and Elizabeth Cady Stanton. The second wave of feminism occurred during the women's liberation movement that began in the 1960s. Second-wave feminism also included equality in the workplace, equality in education and social independence from men. Beginning in the 1990s, the third wave of feminism branched out to include multiple racial and socioeconomic groups and connected topics like race, capitalism and gender.
>
> —adapted from Carl, *Think Sociology*, p. 200

This paragraph could be diagrammed as follows:

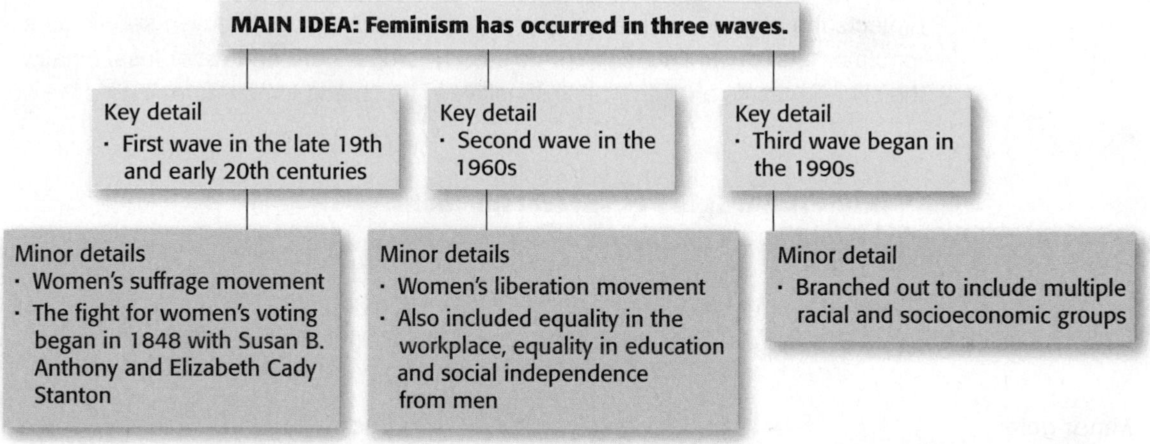

Figure 6-3

EXERCISE 6-1 Identifying Key and Minor Details

Directions: Read each of the following paragraphs, and then answer the multiple-choice questions about the diagram that follows.

Paragraph 1

What does it mean to be a vegetarian? For some, it's an eating style, for others a lifestyle. In its broadest description, vegetarian means avoiding foods from animal sources: red meat, poultry, seafood, eggs, and dairy products. But the term has many subcategories:

- The strictest vegetarians are *vegans*. They consume no animal products—no red meat, poultry, seafood, eggs, milk, cheese, or other dairy products.
- More moderate vegetarians are *lacto-ovo-vegetarians*. They avoid red meat, poultry, and seafood but will consume dairy products and eggs.
- *Pesco-vegetarians* avoid red meat and chickens but will eat seafood (*pesce* means fish), dairy products, and eggs.
- *Semivegetarians* (also called *flexitarians*) may avoid only red meat, or may eat animal-based foods only once or twice a week.

—Lynch et al., *Choosing Health*, p. 83

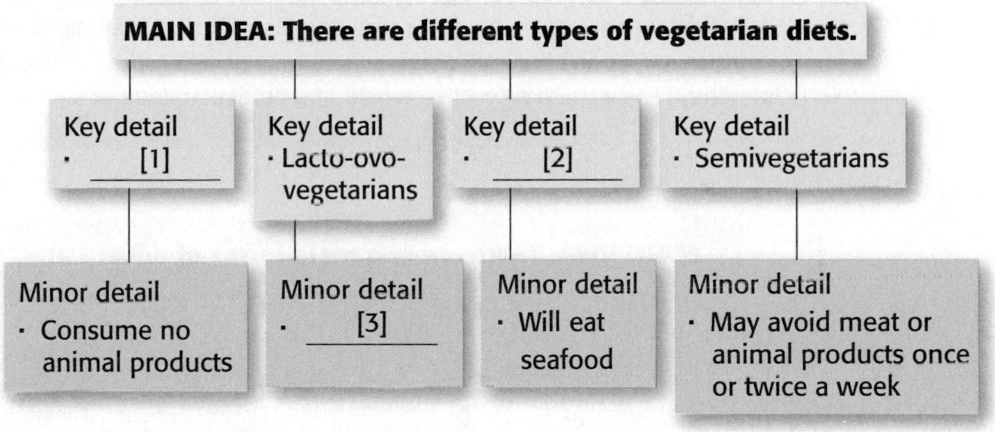

Figure 6-4

_____ 1. The correct word to fill in the blank labeled [1] is
   a. Flexitarians.
   b. Vegans.
   c. Eggs.
   d. Moderate.

_____ 2. The correct word or phrase to fill in the blank labeled [2] is
   a. Vegans.
   b. Dairy products.
   c. Pesco-vegetarians.
   d. Poultry.

_____ 3. The correct phrase to fill in the blank labeled [3] is
   a. Will eat seafood.
   b. Will not eat eggs.
   c. Consume red meat.
   d. Consume dairy products and eggs.

Paragraph 2

Advertising is not a one-size-fits-all proposition; rather, it comes in so many forms and options that the types of advertising seem to be limitless. However, there continue to be two primary kinds: institutional advertising and product advertising. **Institutional advertising** provides information about an organization rather than a specific product, and is intended to create awareness about the firm and enhance its image. This advertising is exemplified by the Bank of America ads that focus on the company as the "bank of opportunity" rather than promoting particular financial products. Such advertising is designed to build general credibility and recognition for specific products or services. **Product advertising** is designed to create awareness, interest, purchasing behavior, and post-purchase satisfaction for specific products and services. Typically, small, entrepreneurial companies expend their advertising resources on product advertising. For example, they may want to promote the sale of a particular item, or a store-wide sale.

—Mariotti and Glackin, *Entrepreneurship & Small Business Management*, p. 216

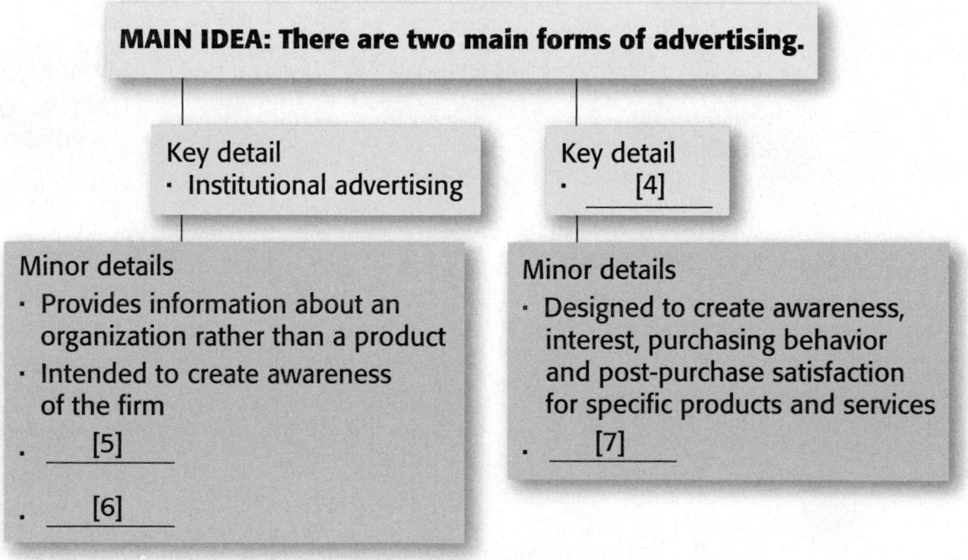
MAIN IDEA: There are two main forms of advertising.
Key detail
· Institutional advertising
Key detail
· [4]
Minor details
· Provides information about an organization rather than a product
· Intended to create awareness of the firm
· [5]
· [6]
Minor details
· Designed to create awareness, interest, purchasing behavior and post-purchase satisfaction for specific products and services
· [7]

Figure 6-5

_____ 4. The correct phrase to fill in the blank labeled [4] is
a. Satisfaction.
b. Purchasing behavior.
c. Product advertising.
d. Financial products.

_____ 5. The correct phrase to fill in the blank labeled [5] is
a. Bank of opportunity.
b. Financial products.
c. The most popular form of advertising.
d. Bank of America is an example.

_____ 6. The correct phrase to fill in the blank labeled [6] is
a. Image enhancement.
b. Designed to build general credibility and recognition.
c. Cost-prohibitive.
d. Works best with social media.

_____ 7. The correct phrase to fill in the blank labeled [7] is
a. Used most by small entrepreneurial companies.
b. Advertising resources.
c. Recognition of purchase satisfaction.
d. Requires the most outreach.

Paragraph 3

There are four different dimensions of an arrest: legal, behavioral, subjective, and official. In **legal** terms, an arrest is made when someone lawfully deprives another person of liberty; in other words, that person is not free to go. The actual word *arrest* need not be uttered, but the other person must be brought under the control of the arresting individual. The **behavioral** element in arrests is often nothing more than the phrase "You're under arrest." However, that statement is usually backed up by a tight grip on the arm or collar, or the drawing of an officer's handgun, or the use of handcuffs. The **subjective** dimension of arrest refers to whenever people believe they are not free to leave; to all intents and purposes, they are under arrest. In any case, the arrest lasts only as long as the person is in custody, which might be a matter of a few minutes or many hours. Many people are briefly detained on the street and then released. **Official** arrests are those detentions that the police record in an administrative record. When a suspect is "booked" at the police station, a record is made of the arrest.

—adapted from Barlow, *Criminal Justice in America,* p. 238

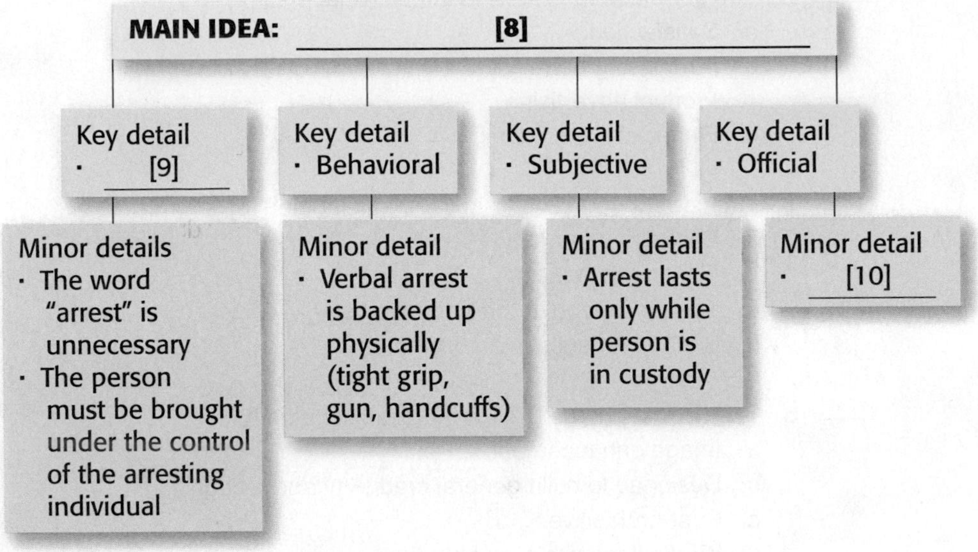

Figure 6-6

_____ 8. The correct sentence to fill in the blank labeled [8] is
   a. When a person is lawfully deprived of freedom, it is not necessary to use the word *arrest.*
   b. The four different dimensions of an arrest are legal, behavioral, subjective, and official.
   c. People can be subjectively under arrest even when they are not officially under arrest.
   d. The only official arrests are those that are recorded at the police station.

_____ 9. The correct word or phrase to fill in the blank labeled [9] is
   a. Dimensions.
   b. Liberty.
   c. Not free to go.
   d. Legal.

_____ 10. The correct word or phrase to fill in the blank labeled [10] is
   a. Arrest is recorded at police station.
   b. Detentions.
   c. Briefly detained.
   d. Booked.

EXERCISE 6-2 Identifying Key Details

Directions: Each of the following topic sentences states the main idea of a paragraph. After each topic sentence are sentences containing details that may or may not support the topic sentence. Read each sentence and write a *K* beside those that contain **key details** that support the topic sentence.

1. *Topic sentence:* Many dramatic physical changes occur during adolescence between the ages of 13 and 15.

   Details:

   K a. Voice changes in boys begin to occur at age 13 or 14.

   K b. Facial proportions may change during adolescence.

   K c. Adolescents, especially boys, gain several inches in height.

   ____ d. Many teenagers do not know how to react to these changes.

   K e. Primary sex characteristics begin to develop for both boys and girls.

2. *Topic sentence:* The development of speech in infants follows a definite sequence or pattern of development.

   Details:

   K a. By the time an infant is six months old, he or she can make 12 different speech sounds.

   ____ b. Mindy, who is only three months old, is unable to produce any recognizable syllables.

   K c. During the first year, the number of vowel sounds a child can produce is greater than the number of consonant sounds he or she can make.

   K d. Between 6 and 12 months, the number of consonant sounds a child can produce continues to increase.

   ____ e. Parents often reward the first recognizable word a child produces by smiling or speaking to the child.

3. *Topic sentence:* The main motives for attending a play are the desire for recreation, the need for relaxation, and the desire for intellectual stimulation.

   Details:

   ____ a. By becoming involved with the actors and their problems, members of the audience temporarily forget about their personal cares and concerns and are able to relax.

   ____ b. In America today, the success of a play is judged by its ability to attract a large audience.

   ____ c. Almost everyone who attends a play expects to be entertained.

   ____ d. Even theater critics are often able to relax and enjoy a good play.

   ____ e. There is a smaller audience that looks to theater for intellectual stimulation.

4. *Topic sentence:* Licorice is used in tobacco products because it has specific characteristics that cannot be found in any other single ingredient.

   Details:

   _____ a. McAdams & Co. is the largest importer and processor of licorice root.

   _____ b. Licorice blends with tobacco and provides added mildness.

   _____ c. Licorice provides a unique flavor and sweetens many types of tobacco.

   _____ d. The extract of licorice is present in relatively small amounts in most types of pipe tobacco.

   _____ a. Licorice helps tobacco retain the correct amount of moisture during storage.

5. *Topic sentence:* An oligopoly is a market structure in which only a few companies sell a certain product.

   Details:

   _____ a. The automobile industry is a good example of an oligopoly, even though it gives the appearance of being highly competitive.

   _____ b. The breakfast cereal, soap, and cigarette industries, although basic to our economy, operate as oligopolies.

   _____ c. Monopolies refer to market structures in which only one industry produces a particular product.

   _____ d. Monopolies are able to exert more control and price fixing than oligopolies.

   _____ e. In the oil industry there are only a few producers, so each producer has a fairly large share of the sales.

EXERCISE 6-3 Identifying Key Details

Directions: Read each of the following paragraphs and write the numbers of the sentences that contain only the most important key details.

Paragraph 1

[1]There are four main characteristics of a tourism product. [2]The first is service, which is intangible because it cannot be inspected physically. [3]For example, a tourist cannot sample a Caribbean cruise or a European tour before purchasing one. [4]The second characteristic is that the tourism product is largely psychological in its attraction. [5]It is more than airline seats or car rentals; it is the temporary use of a different environment, its culture, heritage, and experiences. [6]A third characteristic is that the product frequently varies in quality and standards. [7]A tourist's hotel experience may be excellent one time and not so good at the next visit. [8]A fourth characteristic of the tourism product is that the supply of the product is fixed. [9]For example, more hotel rooms cannot be instantly created to meet increased demand.

—adapted from Walker and Walker, *Tourism*, p. 11

Key details: ____

Paragraph 2

[1]Political activists depend heavily on the media to get their ideas placed high on the governmental agenda. [2]Their arsenal of weapons includes press releases, press conferences, and letter writing; convincing reporters and columnists to tell their side; trading on personal contacts; and, in cases of desperation, resorting to staging dramatic events. [3]The media are not always monopolized by political elites; the poor and downtrodden have access to them too. [4]Civil rights groups in the 1960s relied heavily on the media to tell their stories of unjust treatment. [5]Many believe that the introduction of television helped to accelerate the movement by showing Americans just what the situation was. [6]Protest groups have learned that if they can stage an interesting event that attracts the media's attention, at least their point of view will be heard. [7]Radical activist Saul Alinsky once dramatized the plight of one neighborhood by having its residents collect rats and dump them on the mayor's front lawn. [8]The story was one that local reporters could hardly resist.

—adapted from Edwards et al., *Government in America*, p. 239

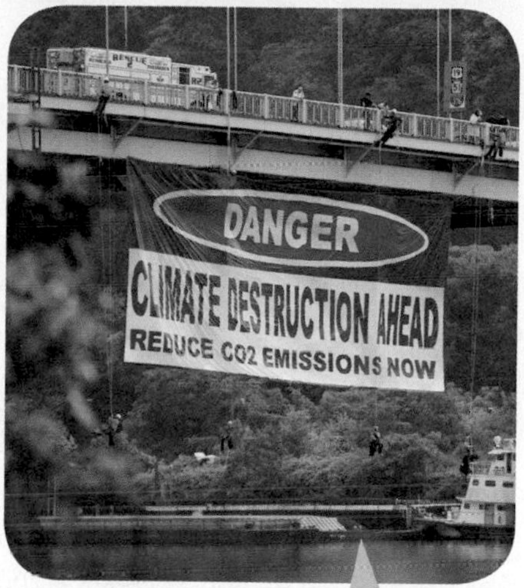

These photographs depict examples of activism. Which example is more effective?

Key details: ____

Paragraph 3

[1]To be patented, an invention must be novel, useful, and nonobvious. [2]An invention is *novel* if it is new and has not been invented and used in the past. [3]If the invention has been used before, it is not novel and cannot be patented. [4]An invention is *useful* if it has some practical purpose. [5]For example, an inventor received a patent for "forkchops," which are a set of chopsticks with a spoon at one handle-end and a fork on the other handle-end. [6]This invention is useful. [7]If the invention is *nonobvious*, it qualifies for a patent; if the invention is obvious, then it does not qualify for a patent. [8]For example, inventors received a patent for a cardboard sleeve that can be placed over a paper coffee cup so that the cup will not be as hot as if there were no sleeve. [9]This invention is novel, useful, and nonobvious.

—adapted from Goldman and Cheeseman, *The Paralegal Professional*, pp. 736–737

Key details: ____

Paragraph 4

[1]People who exercise their mental abilities have been found to be far less likely to develop memory problems and even senile dementias such as Alzheimer's in old age. [2]"Use it or lose it" is the phrase to remember. [3]Working challenging crossword puzzles, for example, can be a major factor in maintaining a healthy level of cognitive functioning. [4]Reading, having an active social life, going to plays, taking classes, and staying physically active can all have a positive impact on the continued well-being of the brain.

—adapted from Ciccarelli and White, *Psychology*, p. 249

Key details: ____

Paragraph 5

[1]A general law practice is one that handles all types of cases. [2]This is what people usually think of as the small-town lawyer, the generalist to whom everyone in town comes for advice. [3]The reality is that the same generalists practice in cities as well as small towns throughout the country. [4]Their practices are as diverse as the law itself, handling everything from adoptions to zoning appeals. [5]As general practitioners, they serve the same function in the law as the general family practice doctor does in medicine. [6]Lawyers in this type of practice often work in several areas of law within the same day. [7]Their day may include attending a hearing in small-claims court in the morning, preparing a will before lunch, meeting with an opposing attorney to discuss settlement of an accident case, then helping someone who is forming a corporation, and finally appearing at a municipal government meeting in the evening to seek a zoning approval.

—adapted from Goldman and Cheeseman, *The Paralegal Professional*, p. 81

Key details: ____

TYPES OF SUPPORTING DETAILS

2 LEARNING GOAL
Identify types of supporting details

There are many types of details that a writer can use to explain or support a main idea. As you read, be sure you know *how* a writer supports his or her main idea—or what types of detail he or she uses. As you will see in later chapters, the way a writer explains and supports an idea may influence how readily you accept or agree with it. The most common types of supporting details are (1) examples, (2) facts or statistics, (3) reasons, (4) descriptions, and (5) steps or procedures. Each will be briefly discussed here.

Examples

One way a writer may support an idea is by using examples. Examples make ideas and concepts real and understandable. In the following paragraph, an example is used to explain heat and temperature.

Heat and temperature are measures of energy. **Heat** is the total amount of energy associated with the movements of atoms and molecules in a substance. **Temperature** is a measure of the intensity of heat—for example, how fast the molecules in the substance are moving. When you are swimming in a cool lake, your body has a higher temperature than the water; however, the lake contains more heat than your body because even though its molecules are moving more slowly, the sum total of molecular movement in its large volume is much greater than the sum total of molecular movements in your much smaller body.

—Belk and Maier, *Biology*, pp. 95–96

In this paragraph the author uses a person swimming in a lake to explain heat and temperature. As you read illustrations and examples, try to see the relationship between the examples and the concepts or ideas they illustrate.

Facts or Statistics

Another way a writer supports an idea is by including facts and/or statistics. The facts and statistics may provide evidence that the main idea is correct. Or the facts may further explain the main idea. For example, to prove that the divorce rate is high, the author may give statistics about the divorce rate and percentage of the population that is divorced. Notice how, in the following paragraph, the main idea stated in the first sentence is explained using statistics.

The term **graying of America** refers to the increasing percentage of older people in the U.S. population. In 1900 only 4 percent of Americans were age 65 and older. Today almost 13 percent are. The average 65-year-old can expect to live another eighteen years. U.S. society has become so "gray" that the median age has doubled since 1850, and today there are seven million *more* elderly Americans than teenagers. Despite this change, on a global scale Americans rank fifteenth in life expectancy.

—Henslin, *Sociology*, p. 383

In this paragraph, the main idea that the number of older Americans is increasing is supported using statistics.

Reasons

A writer may support an idea by giving reasons *why* a main idea is correct. A writer might explain *why* nuclear power is dangerous or give reasons *why* a new speed limit law should be passed by Congress. In the following paragraph, the author explains why record stores are disappearing.

Record stores are fast disappearing. Small independent record stores struggle to stay open, but most cannot. Four in five national chain stores, such as Tower Records, have closed since 1991. Yet music remains a lynchpin of American popular and youth culture. So who killed the record store? Some blame mass marketers, like Best Buy, and discount marketers, like Target, who certainly took sales from record stores. The same cultural preferences for selection, convenience, and portability that increased sales and diversified musical genres have more recently shifted demand toward digital downloads. Instead of paying for whole albums, consumers can buy just a few tracks and carry them everywhere. Virtual stores, such as iTunes, eliminate the need for physical stores. But the shift to digital didn't stop there. Digital technology makes it easy to "share" songs, and an estimated 40 billion tracks were illegally downloaded in 2008. That's 95 percent of all music downloads. Not all those tracks would translate to legal sales, but "sharing" does explain why fewer and fewer young people go to music stores anymore.

—adapted from Dahlman et al., *Introduction to Geography*, p. 215

Descriptions

When the topic of a paragraph is a person, object, place, or process, the writer may develop the paragraph by describing the object. Descriptions are details that help you create a mental picture of the object. In the following paragraph, the author describes a sacred book of the Islamic religion by telling what it contains.

The Koran is the sacred book of the Islamic religion. It was written during the lifetime of Mohammed (570–632) during the years in which he recorded divine revelations. The Koran includes rules for family relationships, including marriage and divorce. Rules for inheritance of wealth and property are specified. The status of women as subordinate to men is well defined.

Steps or Procedures

When a paragraph explains how to do something, the paragraph details are often lists of steps or procedures to be followed. For example, if the main idea of a paragraph is how to prepare an outline for a speech, then the details would list or explain the steps in preparing an outline. In the following paragraph the author explains how to do an examination of a patient's abdomen.

To palpate the abdomen, use the fingertips of several fingers and gently press into the abdomen in each quadrant. While palpating, feel for rigidity or hardening and ask or observe whether this causes pain for the patient. If the initial gentle palpation does not cause pain or discomfort, you may palpate a bit deeper. Once you have found pain, discomfort, or abnormality, there is no need to palpate further in that area.

—Limmer and O'Keefe, *Emergency Care*, p. 581

EXERCISE 6-4 Identifying Types of Details

Directions: Each topic sentence is followed by a list of details that could be used to support it. Label each detail as example, fact or statistic, reason, description, or step or procedure.

1. *Topic sentence:* People make inferences about you by the way you dress.

   ________ First, they size you up from head to toe.

   example ________ College students assume casually dressed instructors are friendly and flexible.

   fact ________ Robert Molloy wrote a book called *Dress for Success* in which he discusses appropriate business attire.

2. *Topic sentence*: Probably the most spectacular and best known of all optical phenomena in our atmosphere is the rainbow.

   reason ________ Rainbows are generated because water droplets act like prisms, dispersing sunlight into the spectrum of colors.

   description ________ Although the clarity of the colors varies with each rainbow, the observer can usually discern six rather distinct bands of color.

   Statistic ________ The angle between the incoming (incident) rays and the dispersed colors that constitute the rainbow is 42° for red light and 40° for violet.

— Lutgens and Tarbuck, *The Atmosphere*, pp. 455–456

3. *Topic sentence:* Every April 15th, millions of Americans make their way to the post office to mail their income tax forms.

   ~~example~~ fact ________ Corporate taxes account for about 10 cents of every federal revenue dollar, compared with 47 cents from individual income taxes.

   ~~fact~~ example ________ This year, the Burnette family filed a return that entitles them to a substantial refund on their state income taxes.

   process ________ In order to submit an income tax return, you must first obtain the proper forms.

—Edwards et al., *Government in America*, pp. 458–459

4. *Topic sentence:* Schizophrenia is one of the most difficult psychological disorders to understand.

_______________ Diagnosis is difficult due to the lack of physical tests for schizophrenia; researchers do not know if schizophrenia results from a single process or several processes.

_______________ Although the rate of schizophrenia is approximately equal in men and women, it strikes men earlier and with greater severity.

_______________ After spending time in mental hospitals and homeless shelters, Greg was finally diagnosed with schizophrenia; he has responded well to medication and now lives in a group home.

_______________ Schizophrenia involves a range of symptoms, including disturbances in perception, language, thinking, and emotional expression.

—Davis and Palladino, *Psychology,* pp. 563, 564, 566

5. *Topic sentence:* Many Americans are obsessed with losing weight.

_______________ Weight loss obsession is often triggered by major events looming in the near future, such as a high school reunion or a "milestone" birthday.

_______________ The two ways to lose weight are to lower caloric intake (through improved eating habits) and to increase exercise (expending more calories).

_______________ Studies show that on any given day in America, nearly 40 percent of women and 24 percent of men over the age of 20 are trying to lose weight.

_______________ Orlando, a college freshman from Raleigh, admits that he has been struggling with a weight problem since he reached puberty.

—Donatelle and Davis, *Access to Health,* pp. 358, 371

6. *Topic sentence:* In the 1920s, many young American writers and artists left their country behind and became expatriates.

_______________ One of the most talented of the expatriates was Ernest Hemingway.

_______________ The expatriates flocked to Rome, Berlin, and Paris, in order to live cheaply and escape what seemed to them the "conspiracy against the individual" in America.

_______________ Some earned a living as journalists, translators, and editors, or made a few dollars by selling a poem to an American magazine or a painting to a tourist.

—Garraty and Carnes, *The American Nation,* p. 706

7. *Topic sentence:* Historical and cultural attractions can be found in a variety of shapes, sizes, and locations throughout the world.

_______________ In Europe, for every museum that existed in 1950, there are now more than four.

_______________ Living History Farms, located near Des Moines, Iowa, is an attraction that offers a "hands-on" experience for visitors.

_______________ More and more communities and countries are taking action to preserve historical sites because they attract visitors and generate income for local residents.

—Cook et al., *Tourism*, p. 209

8. *Topic sentence:* Knitting has become a popular hobby for many young career women.

_______________ Typically, aspiring knitters begin by visiting a yarn shop and then enrolling in a knitting class.

_______________ Knitting is popular because it provides a relaxing outlet and an opportunity to create something beautiful as well as useful.

_______________ Far from the image of the grandmotherly knitter, today's devoted knitters include a wide range of women, from Wall Street stockbrokers to movie stars like Julia Roberts.

9. *Topic sentence:* Search engines have become one of the most popular ways for people to access information.

_______________ The first few results from an Internet search may provide basic information. Continue reading through several pages of results to get in-depth information.

_______________ In 2012, Google performed 70 percent of all Internet searches.

_______________ Search engines are primarily used for research, shopping, and entertainment.

10. *Topic sentence:* The Anasazi Indians are best known for their artistic, architectural, and technological achievements.

_______________ The Anasazi used all of the available materials to build their settlements; with wood, mud, and stone, they erected cliff dwellings and the equivalent of terraced apartment houses.

_______________ The Anasazi built one structure with 500 living units; it was the largest residential building in North America until the completion of an apartment house in New York in 1772.

_______________ One example of their technological genius was their use of irrigation: they constructed sand dunes at the base of hills to hold the runoff from the sometimes torrential rains.

_______________ The Anasazi produced pottery that could rank in beauty with any in the world.

—Brummet et al., *Civilization,* p. 348

EXERCISE 6-5 Identifying Types of Details

Directions: For each paragraph in Exercise 6-3 on pages 202–204, identify the type or types of details used to support the main idea. Write your answers below.

1. Type(s) of details: _______________
2. Type(s) of details: _______________
3. Type(s) of details: _______________
4. Type(s) of details: _______________
5. Type(s) of details: _______________

EXERCISE 6-6 Writing Supporting Details

Directions: Write a topic sentence on one of following topics:

1. one value or danger of social networking
2. driving and the use of cell phones or texting
3. a currently popular movie

Working in groups of three, choose one topic sentence for each topic and generate a list of details that support the chosen topic sentence. Share results with the class. As a class, identify the types of supporting details used.

EXERCISE 6-7 Identifying Topic Sentences and Supporting Details

Directions: Form small groups. Using a reading selection from Part Seven of this book, work with your group to identify and underline the topic sentence of each paragraph. Try to identify key supporting details and/or the type of supporting details. When all the groups have completed the task, the class should compare the findings of the various groups.

LEARNING STYLE TIPS

If you tend to be a . . .	Then understand supporting details by . . .
Spatial learner	Drawing diagrams that show the relationship among details
Creative learner	Making notes Evaluating the appropriateness, accuracy, and sufficiency of details provided

TRANSITIONS

3 LEARNING GOAL Use transitions to guide your reading

Transitions are linking words or phrases used to lead the reader from one idea to another. If you get in the habit of recognizing transitions, you will see that they often guide you through a paragraph, helping you to read it more easily.

In the following paragraph, notice how the circled transitions lead you from one important detail to the next.

> The principle of rhythm and line also contributes to the overall unity of the landscape design. This principle is responsible for the sense of continuity between different areas of the landscape. One way in which this continuity can be developed is by extending planting beds from one area to another. For example, shrub beds developed around the entrance to the house can be continued around the sides and into the backyard. Such an arrangement helps to tie the front and rear areas of the property together. Another means by which rhythm is given to a design is to repeat shapes, angles, or lines between various areas and elements of the design.
>
> —Reiley and Shry, *Introductory Horticulture,* p. 114

Not all paragraphs contain such obvious transitions, and not all transitions serve as such clear markers of major details. Transitions may be used to alert you to what will come next in the paragraph. If you see the phrase *for instance* at the beginning of a sentence, then you know that an example will follow. When you see the phrase *on the other hand,* you can predict that a different, opposing idea will follow. Table 6-1 (p. 212) lists some of the most common transitions used within a paragraph and indicates what they tell you.

TABLE 6-1 Common Transitions

Type of Transition	Examples	What They Tell the Reader
Time/Sequence	first, later, next, finally	The author is arranging ideas in the order in which they happened.
Example	for example, for instance, to illustrate, such as	An example will follow.
Enumeration	first, second, third, last, one, another, next	The author is marking or identifying each major point (sometimes these may be used to suggest order of importance).
Continuation	also, in addition, and, further, another	The author is continuing with the same idea and is going to provide additional information.
Contrast	on the other hand, in contrast, however	The author is switching to a different, opposite, or contrasting idea from that previously discussed.
Comparison	like, likewise, similarly	The writer will show how the previous idea is similar to what follows.
Cause/Effect	because, thus, therefore, since, consequently	The writer will show a connection between two or more things, how one thing caused another, or how something happened as a result of something else.
Summation	to sum up, in conclusion	The writer will draw his or her ideas together.

EXERCISE 6-8 Understanding Transitions

Directions: Match each transition in Column A with a transition of similar meaning in Column B. Write the letter of your choice in the space provided.

	Column A	Column B
e	1. because	a. therefore
g	2. in contrast	b. also
j	3. for instance	c. likewise
a	4. thus	d. after that
i	5. first	e. since
h	6. one way	f. in conclusion
c	7. similarly	g. on the other hand
d	8. next	h. one approach
b	9. in addition	i. in the beginning
f	10. to sum up	j. for example

you would expect to find next in the paragraph. Summarize your findings in the space provided.

1. Price is not the only factor to consider in choosing a pharmacy. Many provide valuable services that should be considered. For instance, . . .

   ____

2. There are a number of things you can do to prevent a home burglary. First, . . .

   ____

3. Most mail order businesses are reliable and honest. However, . . .

   ____

4. One advantage of a compact stereo system is that all the components are built into the unit. Another . . .

   ____

5. Taking medication can have an effect on your hormonal balance. Therefore, . . .

   ____

6. To select the presidential candidate you will vote for, you should examine his or her philosophy of government. Next . . .

   ____

7. Eating solely vegetables drastically reduces caloric and fat intake, two things on which most people overindulge. On the other hand, . . .

   ____

8. Asbestos, a common material found in many older buildings in which people have worked for decades, has been shown to cause cancer. Consequently, . . .

   ____

9. Cars and trucks are not designed randomly. They are designed individually for specific purposes. For instance, . . .

   ____

10. Jupiter is a planet surrounded by several moons. Likewise, . . .

   ____

EXERCISE 6-12 Identifying Transitions

Directions: Reread each paragraph in Exercise 6-3 on pages 202–204. Underline any transitions that you find.

PARAPHRASE PARAGRAPHS

4 LEARNING GOAL
Paraphrase paragraphs

Paraphrasing paragraphs is a useful technique for both building and checking your comprehension. By taking a paragraph apart sentence by sentence, you are forced to understand the meaning of each sentence and see how ideas relate to one another. Paraphrasing paragraphs is similar to paraphrasing sentences. It involves the same two steps:

1. Substituting synonyms
2. Rearranging sentence parts

Here are some guidelines for paraphrasing paragraphs.

1. Concentrate on maintaining the author's focus and emphasis. Ideas that seem most important in the paragraph should appear as most important in your paraphrase.
2. Work sentence by sentence, paraphrasing the ideas in the order in which they appear in the paragraph.

Here are two sample paraphrases of a paragraph. One is a good paraphrase; the other is poor and unacceptable.

Paragraph

Even if you're not among the 6 million Americans currently practicing yoga, you probably have a friend or relative who is. Virtually unknown in the United States 50 years ago, yoga has grown steadily in popularity. Although many styles of yoga are practiced in the United States today, all teach students basic postures called *asanas*. In a yoga session of 60 to 90 minutes, the full body is stretched. In addition, several postures can be linked together in one seamless sequence of dynamic stretching, such as the Sun Salutation. Throughout the yoga session, students practice controlled breathing, coordinating their inhalations and exhalations with their movements.

—Adapted from Blake, *Nutrition & You*, p. 24/7

Good Paraphrase

Yoga has become more popular over the last 50 years and now 6 million Americans practice it. Many styles are practiced but all include asanas, basic postures. The entire body is stretched in a yoga session. Postures can be linked together into dynamic stretching sequences, like Sun Salutations. Controlled breathing is used to coordinate breath with movement.

Poor and Unacceptable Paraphrase

Americans are getting crazy about yoga. All types of yoga require you to contort yourself into all sorts of positions called asanas. A yoga session takes at least an hour. One of the nuttiest things in yoga is the Sun Salutation, that stretches the whole body. People who practice yoga also have to hold their breath.

The second paraphrase is unacceptable because it is inaccurate and incomplete.

EXERCISE 6-13 Writing a Paraphrase

Directions: Write paraphrases of Paragraphs 1, 2, and 3 in Exercise 6-3 (pp. 202–203) on a separate sheet of paper.

SELF-TEST SUMMARY

1 What are supporting details?	Supporting details explain or add support to a paragraph's main idea.
2 What are the five types of details used to support the main idea?	The types of details are examples, facts or statistics, reasons, descriptions, and steps or procedures.
3 What are transitions, and what information do they give the reader?	Transitions are linking words and phrases that lead the reader from one idea to another. They suggest time/sequence, example, enumeration, continuation, contrast, comparison, cause/effect, and summation.
4 What two steps are involved in paraphrasing paragraphs?	Paraphrasing paragraphs involves 1. substituting synonyms 2. rearranging sentence parts

GOING ONLINE

1. **Paraphrasing Online Sources**
   Given the amount of online research you will likely conduct during your college studies, it can be helpful to paraphrase online sources. Select a Web site and paraphrase the contents of its home page.

2. **Finding Reliable Online Sources of Statistics**
   Facts and statistics are important types of supporting details. In your college courses, you will often need to use statistics in your writing assignments. Conduct a Web search for U.S. government–sponsored sources of facts and statistics. (*Hint*: These Web sites will usually end with .gov.) List at least five reliable online data sources, and work with a group of classmates to present a table summarizing the types of data provided by each source and the types of college courses in which this information might be useful.

CHAPTER 6

MASTERY TEST 1 Paragraph Skills

This Mastery Test can be completed in MyReadingLab.

Name ______________________ Section ______________

Date ______________ Number right ________ × 20 points = Score

Directions: Read each of the following paragraphs; then select the choice that correctly identifies the type of details used in the paragraph.

_____ 1. Many people do not know what to look for when considering the type of skin cancer called melanoma. A simple *ABCD* rule outlines the warning signals of melanoma: *A* is for asymmetry. One half of the mole does not match the other half. *B* is for border irregularity. The edges are ragged, notched, or blurred. *C* is for color. The pigmentation is not uniform. *D* is for diameter greater than 6 millimeters. Any or all of these symptoms should cause you to visit a physician.

—Donatelle and Davis, *Access to Health*, pp. 446–447

a. statistics
b. reasons
c. descriptions
d. procedures

_____ 2. In the second week of May 1940, the German armies overran neutral Holland, Belgium, and Luxembourg. The next week they went into northern France and to the English Channel. Designated as an open city by the French in order to spare its destruction, Paris fell on June 14. As the German advance continued, the members of the French government who wanted to continue resistance were voted down. Marshall Philippe Pétain, a 74-year-old World War I hero, became premier. He immediately asked Hitler for an armistice. On June 22, 1940, in the same dining car in which the French had imposed armistice terms on the Germans in 1917, the Nazis and French signed another peace agreement. The Germans had gained revenge for their shame in 1917.

—Brummet et al., *Civilization*, p. 919

a. facts
b. reasons
c. descriptions
d. examples

_____ 3. Ethnic minority group members in the United States have a much higher dropout rate for psychotherapy than do white clients. Among the reasons ethnic clients terminate treatment so early are a lack of bilingual therapists and therapists' stereotypes about ethnic clients. The single most important reason may be that therapists do not provide culturally responsive forms of therapy. They may be unaware of values and customs within a culture that would help in understanding and treating certain behaviors. Therapy should be undertaken with an understanding of cultural values.

—Davis and Palladino, *Psychology*, p. 609

a. steps
b. procedures
c. facts
d. reasons

_____ 4. Festivals celebrate a variety of special occasions and holidays. Some are derived from religious observances, such as New Orleans' or Rio de Janeiro's huge Mardi Gras festivals. Other festivals focus on activities as peaceful as ballooning (the Albuquerque Balloon Festival) or as terrifying as the running of the bulls in Pamplona, Spain. Often, festivals center on the cultural heritage of an area, such as the clan festivals that are prominent in the North Atlantic province of Nova Scotia. More recently, food has become the center of attention at locations such as the National Cherry Festival in Traverse City, Michigan, or the Garlic Festival in Gilroy, California.

—Cook et al., *Tourism,* p. 214

a. statistics
b. examples
c. facts
d. procedures

What type of celebration does this festival illustrate?

_____ 5. The **dissolution** stage, in both friendship and romance, is the cutting of the bonds tying you together. At first it usually takes the form of *interpersonal separation,* in which you may not see each other anymore. If you live together, you move into separate apartments and begin to lead lives apart from each other. If this relationship is a marriage, you may seek a legal separation. If this separation period proves workable and if the original relationship is not repaired, you may enter the phase of *social* or *public separation.* If this is a marriage, this phase corresponds to divorce. Avoidance of each other and a return to being "single" are among the primary identifiable features of dissolution. In some cases, however, the former partners change the definition of their relationship; for example, ex-lovers become friends, or ex-friends become "just" business partners. This final, "goodbye," phase of dissolution is the point at which you become an ex-lover or ex-friend. In some cases this is a stage of relief and relaxation; finally it's over. In other cases this is a stage of anxiety and frustration, of guilt and regret, of resentment over time ill spent and now lost. In more materialistic terms, the goodbye phase is the stage when property is divided and when legal battles may ensue over who should get what.

—DeVito, *Messages,* p. 284

a. examples
b. reasons
c. descriptions
d. steps

CHAPTER 6

MASTERY TEST 2 Paragraph Skills

This **Mastery Test** can be completed in **MyReadingLab**.

Name ____________________ Section ____________

Date ____________ Number right ________ × 10 points = Score ________

Directions: Read the passage below, and select the choice that best completes each of the statements that follow.

1 A **punishment** is an unpleasant experience that occurs as a result of an undesirable behavior. Punishment is most effective if it has these three characteristics. First, punishment should be swift, occurring immediately after the undesired behavior. The old threat "Wait till you get home!" undermines the effectiveness of the punishment. Second, punishment must be consistent. The undesired behavior must be punished each and every time it occurs. Finally, the punishment should be sufficiently unpleasant without being overly unpleasant. For instance, if a child doesn't mind being alone in her room, then being sent there for pushing her brother won't be a very effective punishment.

2 Although punishment may decrease the frequency of a behavior, it doesn't eliminate the ability to perform that behavior. For example, your little sister may learn not to push you because your mother will punish her, but she may continue to push her classmates at school because the behavior has not been punished in that context. She may also figure out that if she hits you, but then apologizes, she will not get punished.

3 Furthermore, physical punishment, such as spanking, should be avoided. It may actually increase aggressive behavior in the person on the receiving end. In addition, the one being punished may come to live in fear of the one doing the punishing, even if the punishment is infrequent.

4 Overall, punishment alone hasn't been found to be an effective way of controlling behavior. This is because punishment doesn't convey information about what behavior should be exhibited in place of the undesired, punished behavior. That is, the person being punished knows what they should not do, but the person does not know what he or she should do.

—Kosslyn and Rosenberg, *Psychology*, pp. 180–181

_____ 1. The primary purpose of the selection is to
   a. describe the concept of punishment.
   b. discourage the use of physical punishment.
   c. identify behaviors that require punishment.
   d. discuss alternative methods of discipline.

_____ 2. The main type of transition used in paragraph 1 is
   a. time/sequence.
   b. enumeration.
   c. continuation.
   d. summation.

_____ 3. The transition word or phrase in paragraph 1 that indicates an example will follow is
   a. first.
   b. second.
   c. finally.
   d. for instance.

_____ 4. The main idea of paragraph 1 is that
- a. punishment must be consistent.
- b. punishment must be unpleasant.
- c. punishment has three qualities.
- d. punishment is targeted toward undesired behavior.

_____ 5. The main idea of paragraph 2 is supported by
- a. examples.
- b. facts.
- c. reasons.
- d. descriptions.

_____ 6. The main idea of paragraph 2 is that
- a. punishment decreases the frequency of a behavior.
- b. a behavior that is punished at home may not be punished elsewhere.
- c. punishment does not eliminate a person's ability to engage in a behavior.
- d. a child may learn to avoid punishment by apologizing for a behavior.

_____ 7. The transition words in paragraph 3 that indicate a continuation of the same idea are
- a. may actually.
- b. such as.
- c. even if.
- d. in addition.

_____ 8. A key detail in paragraph 3 that directly supports the main idea is
- a. spanking harms children.
- b. physical punishment may increase aggression in the person giving the punishment.
- c. physical punishment may increase aggression in the person receiving the punishment.
- d. physical punishment may become addictive.

_____ 9. The word or phrase that indicates a cause/effect transition in paragraph 4 is
- a. because.
- b. alone.
- c. overall.
- d. in place of.

_____ 10. The best paraphrase of paragraph 4 is
- a. Punishment alone is not an effective means of controlling behavior. Punishment does not convey information about what behavior should take the place of the undesired, punished behavior.
- b. Combining punishment and reinforcement is more effective than using punishment by itself. Punishment quickly lets people know what behaviors are not desirable.
- c. Punishment should never be used because it does not demonstrate desirable behavior.
- d. Punishment does not give information about what behavior should replace the undesired, punished behavior.

CHAPTER 6

MASTERY TEST 3 Reading Selection

This Mastery Test can be completed in MyReadingLab.

Name ______________________ Section ____________

Date ____________ Number right* ________ × 10 points = Score ________

Let There Be Dark

Paul Bogard

This selection appeared in *The Los Angeles Times* opinion section in late fall. Read the selection to learn the author's opinion about darkness in our environment.

Vocabulary Preview

solstice (par. 2) two times in a year when the sun is farthest from the equator
carcinogen (par. 4) something that causes cancer
crepuscular (par. 5) active at twilight

1 When I was a child, I knew real darkness.

2 At my family's cabin on a Minnesota lake, I knew woods so dark that my hands disappeared before my eyes. I knew night skies in which meteors left smoky trails across sugary spreads of stars. But now, when 8 of 10 children born in the United States will never know a sky dark enough for the Milky Way, I worry we are rapidly losing night's natural darkness before realizing its worth. This winter solstice, as we cheer the days' gradual movement back toward light, let us also remember the irreplaceable value of darkness.

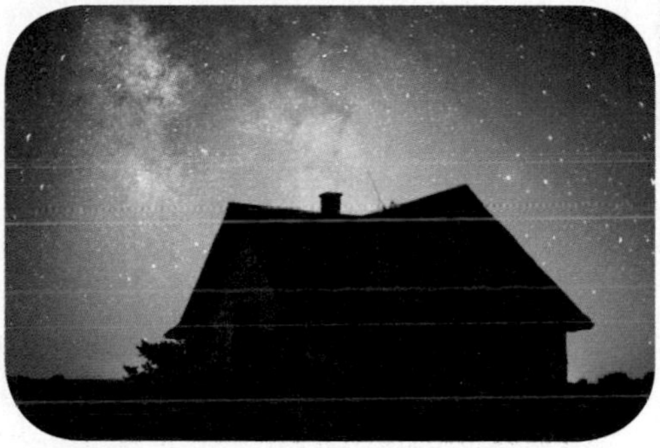

3 All life evolved to the steady rhythm of bright days and dark nights. Today, though, when we feel the closeness of nightfall, we reach quickly for a light switch. And too little darkness, meaning too much artificial light at night, spells trouble for all.

4 Already the World Health Organization classifies working the night shift as a probable human carcinogen, and the American Medical Assn. has voiced its unanimous support for "light pollution reduction efforts and glare reduction efforts at both the national and state levels." Our bodies need darkness to produce the hormone melatonin, which keeps certain cancers from developing, and our bodies need darkness for sleep. Sleep disorders have been linked to diabetes, obesity, cardiovascular disease and depression, and recent research suggests one main cause of "short sleep" is "long light." Whether we work at night or simply take our

*To Calculate the number right, use numbers 1–10 under "Masters Test Skills Check."

tablets, notebooks and smartphones to bed, there isn't a place for this much artificial light in our lives.

5 The rest of the world depends on darkness as well, including nocturnal and crepuscular species of birds, insects, mammals, fish and reptiles. Some examples are well known—the 400 species of birds that migrate at night in North America, the sea turtles that come ashore to lay their eggs—and some are not, such as the bats that save American farmers billions in pest control and the moths that pollinate 80% of the world's flora. Ecological light pollution is like the bulldozer of the night, wrecking habitat and disrupting ecosystems several billion years in the making. Simply put, without darkness, Earth's ecology would collapse.

6 Darkness shapes our lives in less dramatic ways as well. Consider how it brings us together with those we love, how we illuminate our most intimate experiences with flame or moonlight, with subtlety. What would a winter evening's stroll through the park be without it? Or a candlelight dinner? Or a New Year's bonfire with friends? It's only with night's natural darkness that we appreciate the lights of the city, and of the season. No one thinks much of these lights at noon.

7 In today's crowded, louder, more fast-paced world, night's darkness can provide solitude, quiet and stillness, qualities increasingly in short supply. Every religious tradition has considered darkness invaluable for a soulful life, and the chance to witness the universe has inspired artists, philosophers and everyday stargazers since time began. In a world awash with electric light, St. John of the Cross could not have offered us the wisdom from his "dark night of the soul." And how would Van Gogh have given the world his "Starry Night"? Who knows what this vision of the night sky might inspire in each of us, in our children or grandchildren?

8 Yet all over the world, our nights are growing brighter. In the United States and Western Europe, the amount of light in the sky increases an average of about 6% every year. Computer images of the United States at night, based on NASA photographs, show that what was a very dark country as recently as the 1950s is now nearly covered with a blanket of light. Much of this light is wasted energy, which means wasted dollars. Those of us over 35 are perhaps among the last generation to have known truly dark nights. Even the northern lake where I was lucky to spend my summers has seen its darkness diminish.

9 It doesn't have to be this way. Light pollution is readily within our ability to solve, using new lighting technologies and shielding existing lights. Already, many cities and towns across North America and Europe are changing to LED streetlights, which offer dramatic possibilities for controlling wasted light. Other communities are finding success with simply turning off portions of their public lighting after midnight. Even Paris, the famed "city of light," which already turns off its monument lighting after 1 A.M., will this summer start to require its shops, offices and public buildings to turn off lights after 2 A.M. Though primarily designed to save energy, such reductions in light will also go far in addressing light pollution. But we will never truly address the problem of light pollution until we become aware of the irreplaceable value and beauty of the darkness we are losing.

10 This winter solstice, this longest night of the year, let us begin.

MASTERY TEST SKILLS CHECK

Directions: Select the choice that best completes each of the following statements.

Checking Your Comprehension

_____ 1. The purpose of this selection is to
a. offer suggestions for reducing light pollution at home.
b. explain how darkness can be dangerous.
c. explain the importance of restoring darker nights to our world.
d. discuss how expensive light pollution is.

_____ 2. The main idea of paragraph 4 is that
a. working the night shift may cause cancer.
b. both national and local governments should reduce light pollution.
c. sleep disorders have been linked to serious health problems.
d. too much artificial light is unhealthy for us.

_____ 3. According to the author, solutions to light pollution include
a. changing to LED streetlights.
b. shielding existing lights.
c. turning off public lighting after midnight.
d. all of the above.

_____ 4. The amount of light in the sky in the United States and Western Europe is
a. impossible to measure.
b. increasing every year.
c. caused entirely by technology.
d. less than it was in the 1950s.

_____ 5. The main point of paragraph 6 is that
a. we use light to celebrate holidays.
b. candlelight is not light pollution.
c. darkness allows us to appreciate special kinds of light.
d. it is easier to share things in the dark.

Applying Your Skills

_____ 6. The supporting details that the author uses in this selection include
a. statistics.
b. examples.
c. facts.
d. all of the above.

_____ 7. The second sentence in paragraph 5 is an example of a
a. main idea.
b. key detail.
c. minor detail.
d. topic sentence.

_____ 8. The author indicates a transition in paragraph 8 with the word
a. recently.
b. perhaps.
c. based.
d. yet.

_____ 9. In paragraph 3, the transition *though* indicates that the author is
a. arranging ideas in order of importance.
b. continuing with the same idea.
c. switching to a contrasting idea.
d. showing how one thing caused another.

_____ 10. The topic of paragraph 7 is the
a. decreasing darkness.
b. benefits of darkness.
c. ecological effects of darkness.
d. health benefits of darkness.

Studying Words

_____ 11. The word *irreplaceable* (par. 2) means
a. related to weather.
b. gradual.
c. having no substitute.
d. overrated.

_____ 12. From context, you can tell that the word *melatonin* (par. 4) refers to
a. a hormone.
b. a disease.
c. short sleep.
d. a type of technology.

_____ 13. The word *disrupting* (par. 5) means
a. removing.
b. calming.
c. interrupting.
d. lifting.

_____ 14. The word *illuminate* (par. 6) means
a. brighten.
b. discourage.
c. contact.
d. allow.

_____ 15. The word *diminish* (par. 8) means
a. expand.
b. digitize.
c. frustrate.
d. decrease.

For more practice, ask your instructor for an opportunity to work on the mastery tests that appear in the Test Bank.

Summarizing the Reading

Directions: Complete the following summary of the reading by filling in the blanks.

The ________________ has important memories of ________________ from his childhood. Today there is less darkness due to ________________, which negatively affects our ________________. The lack of darkness also impacts other living creatures, negatively affecting Earth's ________________. Darkness is a valuable part of our lives, allowing us to enjoy candles and ________________. Darkness is also important in religion and ________________. The amount of light is ________________ in the United States and ________________ yearly. Light ________________ can be controlled by reducing ________________ at night. We need to understand the importance of ________________.

Reading Visually

1. What is the purpose of the photo included with this article? How does it illustrate the main point of the article?
2. What other types of photos might help emphasize the author's point?
3. Explain how the title of this article relates to the subject. Can you think of another title that would also work for this selection?

Thinking Critically about the Reading

1. How important is darkness in your life? What does it allow you to do? Describe some activities that would not be the same without darkness.
2. What do you think is beautiful about darkness? How did this article help you appreciate that? Why do you think humans work so hard to eliminate darkness?
3. What could you do in your own life to decrease light pollution? What changes could happen in your own town or city that would reduce light pollution?

CHAPTER 7

Following the Author's Thought Patterns

LEARNING GOALS

This chapter will show you how to

1. Recognize six commonly used thought patterns
2. Recognize other useful thought patterns

Focusing On … Thought Patterns

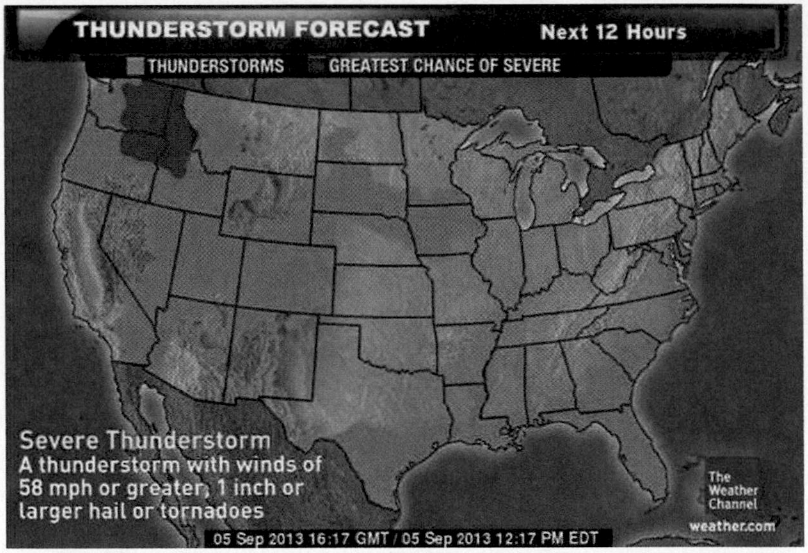

This map shows a pattern of weather. You can see that while there is a significant chance of severe thunderstorms in the Northwest and strong thunderstorms in along the Gulf coast and in a band reaching from Nevada to Iowa, the Northeast will have calm weather. Just as weather map patterns are useful in helping you understand the weather that is coming your way, patterns in paragraphs are useful in helping you work your way through paragraphs. In this chapter you will see how writers organize their ideas using patterns.

As a way to begin thinking about authors' thought patterns, complete each of the following steps:

1. Study each of the drawings below for a few seconds (count to ten as you look at each one).
2. Cover up the drawings and try to draw each from memory.
3. Check to see how many you had exactly correct.

Most likely you drew all but the fourth correctly. Why did you get that one wrong? How does it differ from the others?

Drawings 1, 2, 3, and 5 have patterns. Drawing 4, however, has no pattern; it is just a randomly jagged line.

From this experiment you can see that it is easier to remember drawings that have a pattern, some understandable form of organization. The same is true of written material. If you can see how a paragraph is organized, it will be easier to understand and remember. Writers often present their ideas in a recognizable order. Once you can recognize the organizational pattern, you will remember more of what you read.

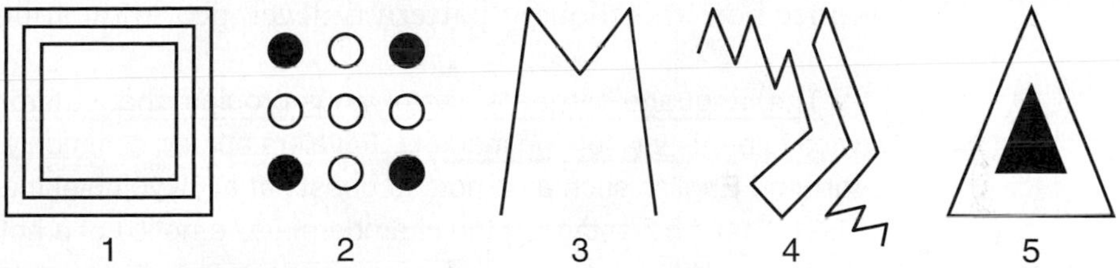

SIX COMMON THOUGHT PATTERNS

1 LEARNING GOAL
Recognize six commonly used thought patterns

This chapter discusses six of the more common thought patterns that writers use and shows how to recognize them: (1) illustration/example, (2) definition, (3) comparison/contrast, (4) cause/effect, (5) classification, and (6) chronological order/process. A brief overview of other useful patterns is provided in the section that follows.

Illustration/Example

One of the clearest, most practical, and most obvious ways to explain something is to give an **example** to illustrate what you are saying. Suppose you had to explain what anthropology is. You might give examples of the topics you study. By using examples, such as the study of apes and early humans, and the development of modern humans, you would give a fairly good idea of what anthropology is all about. When a subject is unfamiliar, an example often makes it easier to understand.

Usually a writer will state an idea first and then follow with examples. Several examples may be given in one paragraph, or a separate paragraph may be used for each example. It may help to visualize the illustration/example pattern this way:

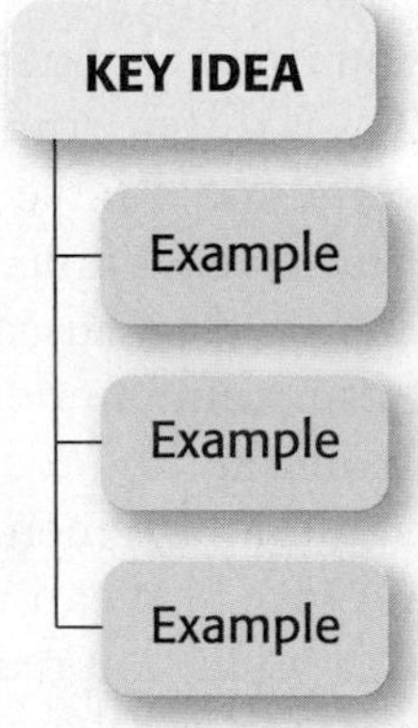

Notice how this thought pattern is developed in the following passage.

> The language barrier is one obvious problem that confronts marketers who wish to break into foreign markets. Travelers abroad commonly encounter signs in tortured English such as a note to guests at a Tokyo hotel that said, "You are invited to take advantage of the chambermaid," a notice at a hotel in Acapulco that proclaimed "The manager has personally passed all the water served here," or a dry cleaner in Majorca that urged passing customers to "drop your pants here for best results."
>
> —Solomon et al., *Marketing,* p. 85

In the preceding passage, the concept of miscommunication due to language barriers is explained through examples. You could visualize the selection as follows:

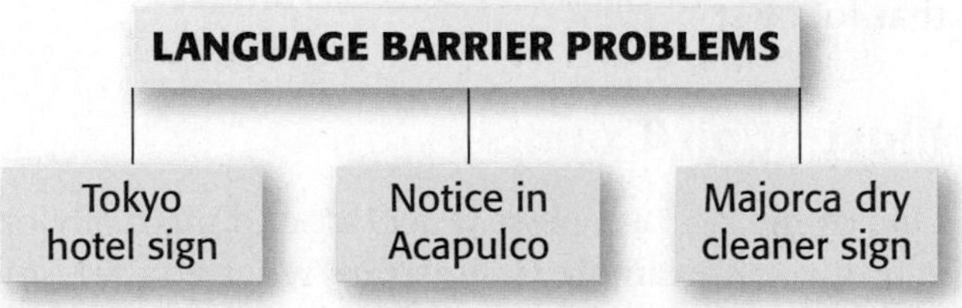

Here is another passage in which the main idea is explained through example:

> Many companies today are localizing their products, advertising, promotion, and sales efforts to fit the needs of individual regions, cities, and neighborhoods. For example, Walmart operates virtually everywhere but has developed special formats tailored to specific types of geographic locations. In strongly Hispanic neighborhoods, Walmart operates Supermercado de Walmart stores, which feature signage, product assortments, and bilingual staff that are more relevant to local Hispanic customers. In markets where full-size superstores are impractical, Walmart has opened smaller Walmart Market supermarkets and even smaller Walmart Express and Walmart on Campus stores. Similarly, Macy's, the nation's second-largest department store chain, lets its 1,600 district managers around the country customize merchandise in their local stores.
>
> —Armstrong and Kotler, *Marketing*, pp. 165–166

The author explains the way companies localize by offering examples from Walmart and Macy's.

Paragraphs and passages organized using illustration/example often use transitional words and phrases to connect ideas. Examples of such words and phrases include:

for example	for instance	to illustrate

EXERCISE 7-1 Analyzing Illustration/Example Paragraphs

Directions: For each of the following paragraphs, underline the topic sentence and list the examples used to explain it.

1. Networking is the process of making informal connections with mutually beneficial business contacts. Networking takes place wherever and whenever people talk: at industry functions, at social gatherings, at sports events and recreational activities, at alumni reunions and so on. Social networks, including Facebook, and business-oriented websites such as LinkedIn, Ryze, and Spoke have become powerful networking resources.

   —adapted from Thill and Bovée, *Excellence in Business Communication,* p. 473

   Examples: ______________________________

2. As part of your day-to-day body functioning, a variety of chemical reactions called *oxidation reactions* continually occur. Although normal, oxidation reactions sometimes produce harmful chemicals called *free radicals*, which can start chain reactions that can damage cells. It is impossible for you to avoid damage by

free radicals; however, certain components of foods can help neutralize them. These substances are generally referred to as *antioxidants* because they work against oxidation. Some antioxidants are nutrients. These include vitamins C and E, beta-carotene (a form of vitamin A), and the mineral selenium. Many other antioxidants are non-nutrients; these include phytochemicals and certain other substances in food.

—adapted from Lynch et al., *Choosing Health*, pp. 75–76

Examples: ______________________________

____

3. Problems arise when the marketing of adult products spills over into the children's segment—intentionally or unintentionally. For example, Victoria's Secret targets its highly successful Pink line of young, hip, and sexy clothing to young women from 18 to 30 years old. However, critics charge that Pink is now all the rage among girls as young as 11 years old. Responding to Victoria's Secret's designs and marketing messages, tweens are flocking into stores and buying Pink, with or without their mothers. Critics worry that marketers of everything from lingerie and cosmetics to Barbie dolls are directly or indirectly targeting young girls with provocative products, promoting a premature focus on sex and appearance.

—adapted from Armstrong and Kotler, *Marketing,* p. 181

Examples: ______________________________

EXERCISE 7-2 Writing an Illustration/Example Paragraph

Directions: Choose one of the following topics. On a separate sheet of paper, write a paragraph in which you use illustration/example to organize and express your ideas on the topic. Then draw a diagram showing the organization of your paragraph.

1. Parents or friends are helpful (or not helpful) in making decisions.

2. Attending college has (has not) made a major change in my life.

Definition

Another way to provide an explanation is to offer a definition. A **definition** should have two parts: (1) tell what general group or class an item belongs to and (2) explain how that item is different or distinguishable from other items in the group. Let us say that you see an opossum while driving in the country. You mention this to a friend. Since your friend does not know what an opossum is, you have to give a definition. Your definition should include the fact that an opossum is an animal (the general group it belongs to) and a description of the features of an opossum that would help someone tell the difference between it and other animals, such as dogs, raccoons, and squirrels. Thus, you could define an opossum as follows:

> An opossum is an animal with a ratlike tail that lives in trees. It carries its young in a pouch. It is active at night and pretends to be dead when trapped.

This definition can be diagrammed as follows:

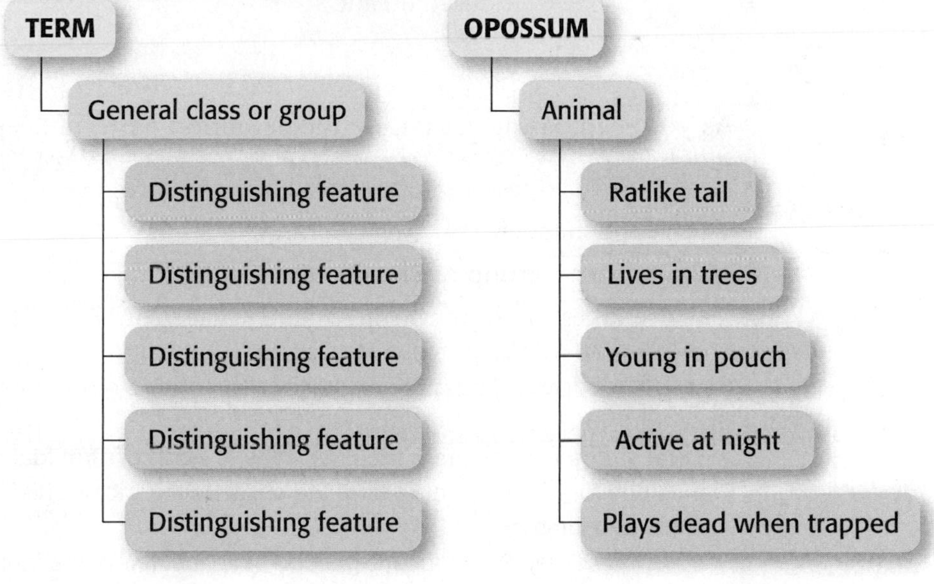

The following passage was written to define the term *ragtime music.*

> Ragtime music is a piano style that developed at the turn of the twentieth century. Ragtime music usually has four themes. The themes are divided into four musical sections of equal length. In playing ragtime music, the left hand plays chords and the right hand plays the melody. There is an uneven accenting between the two hands.

The thought pattern of this passage might be diagrammed as follows:

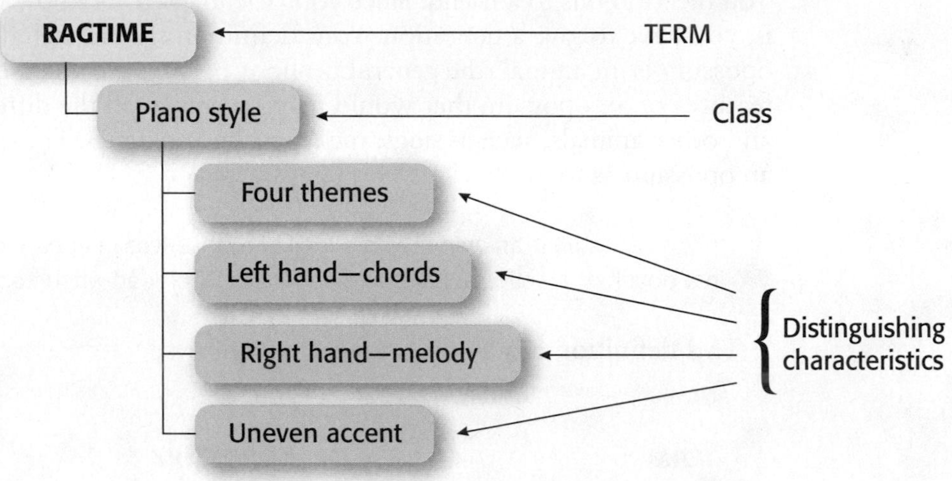

As you read passages that use the definition pattern, keep these questions in mind:

1. What is being defined?
2. What general group or class does it belong to?
3. What makes it different from others in the group?

Read the following passage and apply the above questions.

Nez Perce Indians are a tribe that lives in north-central Idaho. The rich farmlands and forests in the area form the basis for the tribe's chief industries—agriculture and lumber.

The name *Nez Perce* means *pierced nose,* but few of the Indians ever pierced their noses. In 1805, a French interpreter gave the name to the tribe after seeing some members wearing shells in their noses as decorations.

The Nez Perce originally lived in the region where the borders of Idaho, Oregon, and Washington meet. Prospectors overran the Nez Perce reservation after discovering gold there in the 1860s.

Part of the tribe resisted the efforts of the government to move them to a smaller reservation. In 1877, fighting broke out between the Nez Perce and U.S. troops. Joseph, a Nez Perce chief, tried to lead a band of the Indians into Canada. But he surrendered near the United States–Canadian border.

—World Book Online Reference Center

This passage was written to define the Nez Perce. The general group or category is "Indian tribe." The distinguishing characteristics include the source of their name, their original location, and their fight against relocation.

EXERCISE 7-3 Analyzing Definition Paragraphs

Directions: Read each of the following paragraphs. Then identify the term being defined, its general class, and its distinguishing features.

1. The Sun's most conspicuous features are large sunspots, caused by magnetic storms on the Sun. Individual sunspots may range in diameter from 10,000 to 50,000 km (6,200 to 31,000 mi), with some growing as large as 160,000 km (100,000 mi), more than 12 times the Earth's diameter. These surface disturbances produce flares and prominences.

—Christopherson, *Elemental Geosystems*, p. 40

Term: ____________________

General class: ____________________

Distinguishing features: ____________________

____

2. A special case of an emotionally charged memory is a flashbulb memory, an unusually vivid and detailed memory of a dramatic event. It is as if a flashbulb in the mind goes off at key moments, creating instant records of the events. Perhaps you have such a memory for the moment you heard about the planes crashing into the World Trade Center towers on September 11, 2001. Researchers have found that people's ratings of how vivid their flashbulb memories are—and of how strongly they believe that the memories are accurate—do not diminish over time. Nevertheless, when these memories are objectively tested, researchers find that they often become distorted over time (Neisser & Harsch, 1992). And this distortion becomes progressively worse with the passage of time (Schmolck et al., 2000).

—Kosslyn and Rosenberg, *Introducing Psychology*, p. 166

Term: ____________________

General class: ____________________

Distinguishing features: ____________________

____

____

3. The Baby Boomer age cohort consists of people whose parents established families following the end of World War II and during the 1950s when the peacetime

economy was strong and stable. As teenagers in the 1960s and 1970s, the "Woodstock generation" created a revolution in style, politics, and consumer attitudes. As they aged, they fueled cultural events as diverse as the Free Speech movement and hippies in the 1960s to Reaganomics and yuppies in the 1980s. Now that they are older, they continue to influence popular culture.

—Solomon, *Consumer Behavior*, p. 508

Term: ______________________________

General class: ______________________________

Distinguishing features: ______________________________

____

____

Paragraphs and passages that are organized using definition often use transitional words and phrases to connect ideas. Examples of theses transitional words and phrases include:

can be defined as	consists of	involves
is	is called	is characterized by
means	refers to	

EXERCISE 7-4 **Writing a Definition Paragraph**

Directions: Choose one of the topics listed below. On a separate sheet of paper, write a paragraph in which you define the topic. Be sure to include both the general group and what makes the item different from other items in the same group. Then draw a diagram showing the organization of your paragraph.

1. A type of music
2. Social networks
3. Junk food

Comparison/Contrast

Often a writer will explain something by using **comparison** or **contrast**—that is, by showing how it is similar to or different from a familiar object or idea. Comparison treats similarities, while contrast emphasizes differences. For example, an article comparing two car models might mention these common, overlapping features: radial tires, clock, radio, power steering, and power brakes. The cars may differ in gas mileage, body shape, engine power, braking distance, and so forth. When comparing the two models, the writer would focus on shared features. When contrasting the two cars the writer would focus on individual differences. Such an article might be diagrammed as follows:

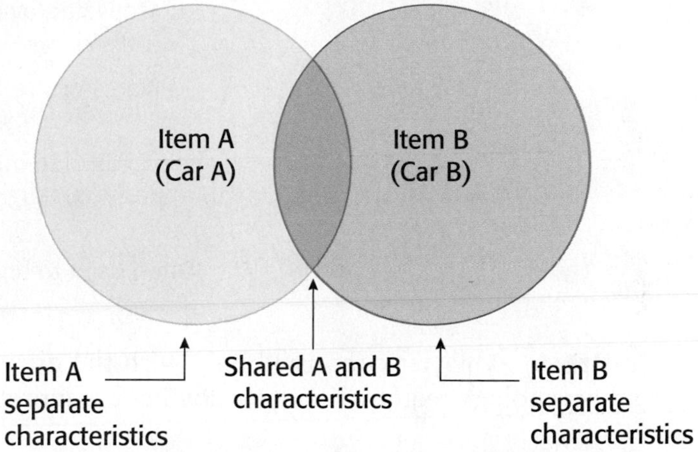

In this diagram, Items A and B are different except where they overlap and share the same characteristics.

In most articles that use the comparison/contrast method, you will find some passages that only compare, some that only contrast, and others that both compare and contrast. To read each type of passage effectively, you must follow the pattern of ideas. Passages that show comparison and/or contrast can be organized in a number of different ways. The organization depends on the author's purpose.

Comparison If a writer is concerned only with similarities, he or she may identify the items to be compared and then list the ways in which they are alike. The following paragraph shows how permanent and temporary body adornment are similar.

> Every culture has some kind of body adornment. Some are permanent, including tattoos and piercings. Others are temporary, and include clothing, paint or makeup, and jewelry. Both types of adornment are motivated by specific cultural beliefs and vary from culture to culture. The adornment is often used to indicate social position, rank, religion, or ethnic identity. Adornment of both types is also often used to highlight certain areas of the body that are culturally significant.

Such a pattern can be diagrammed as follows:

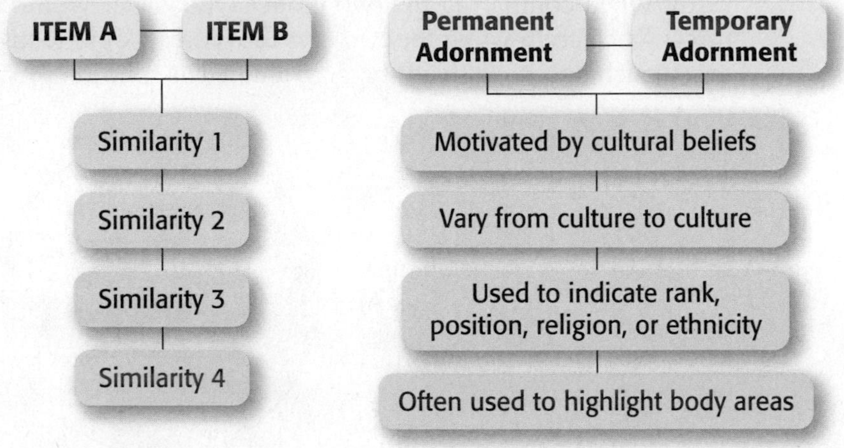

Contrast A writer concerned only with the differences between sociology and psychology might write the following paragraph:

> Sociology and psychology, although both social sciences, are very different fields of study. Sociology is concerned with the structure, organization, and behavior of groups. Psychology, on the other hand, focuses on individual behavior. While a sociologist would study characteristics of groups of people, a psychologist would study the individual motivation and behavior of each group member. Psychology and sociology also differ in the manner in which research is conducted. Sociologists obtain data and information through observation and survey. Psychologists obtain data through carefully designed experimentation.

Such a pattern can be diagrammed as follows:

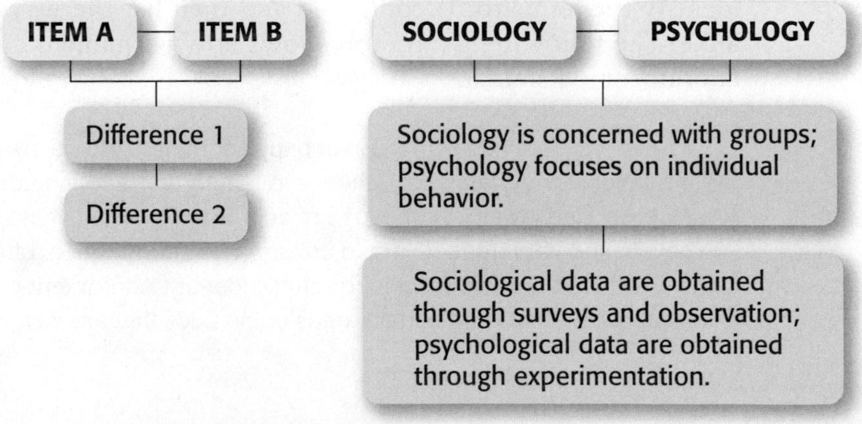

Comparison and Contrast In many passages, writers discuss both similarities and differences. Suppose you wanted to write a paragraph discussing the similarities and differences between sociology and psychology. You could organize the paragraph in different ways.

1. You could list all the similarities and then all the differences, as shown in this diagram:

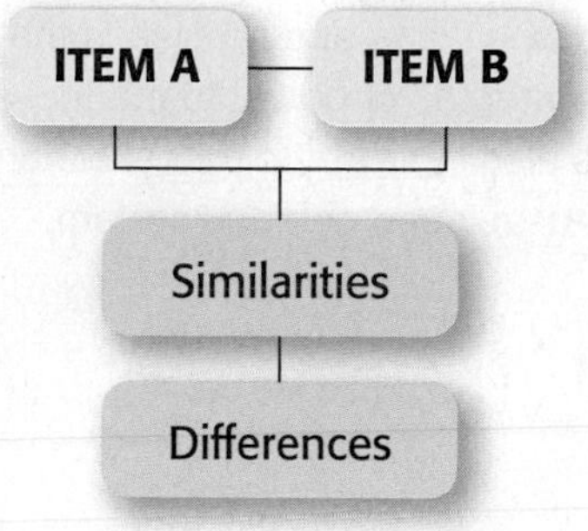

2. You could discuss Item A first, presenting both similarities and differences, and then do the same for Item B. Such a pattern would look like this:

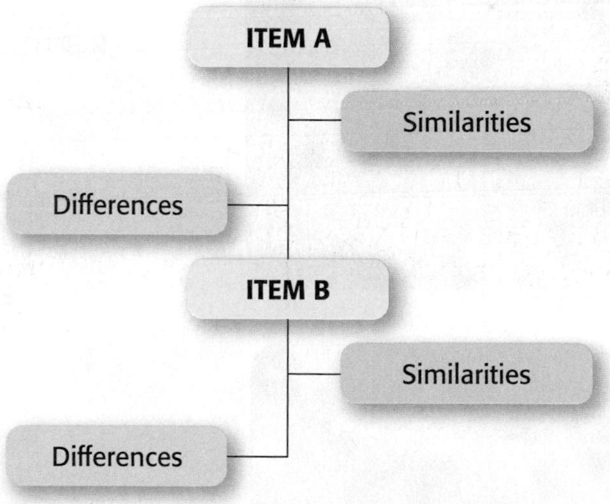

The following paragraph discusses amphibians and reptiles. As you read it, try to visualize its pattern.

Although reptiles evolved from amphibians, several things distinguish the two kinds of animals. Amphibians (such as frogs, salamanders, and newts) must live where it is moist. In contrast, reptiles (which include turtles, lizards and snakes, and crocodiles and alligators) can live away from the water. Amphibians employ external fertilization, as when the female frog lays her eggs on the water and the male spreads his sperm on top of them. By contrast, all reptiles employ internal fertilization—eggs are fertilized inside the female's body. Another difference between amphibians and reptiles is that reptiles have a tough, scaly skin that conserves water, as opposed to the thin amphibian skin that allows water to escape. Reptiles also have a stronger skeleton than amphibians, more efficient lungs, and a better-developed nervous system.

—adapted from Krogh, *Biology*, pp. 466–467, 474

Which contrast between reptiles and amphibians is illustrated by these photos?

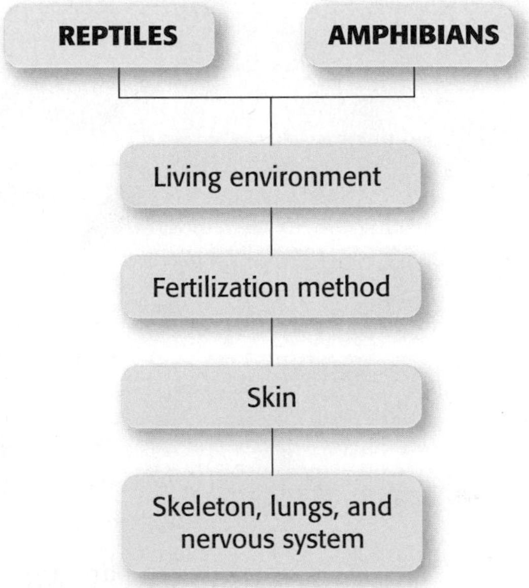

Now read the following passage and decide whether it discusses similarities, differences, or both.

> Groups have two types of leaders. The first is easy to recognize. This person, called an **instrumental leader**, tries to keep the group moving toward its goals. These leaders try to keep group members from getting sidetracked, reminding them of what they are trying to accomplish. The **expressive leader**, in contrast, usually is not recognized as a leader, but he or she certainly is one. This person is likely to crack jokes, to offer sympathy or to do other things that help to lift the group's morale. Both types of leadership are essential: the one to keep the group on track, the other to increase harmony and minimize conflicts.
>
> It is difficult for the same person to be both an instrumental and an expressive leader, for these roles tend to contradict one another. Because instrumental leaders are task oriented, they sometimes create friction as they prod the group to get on with the job. Their actions often cost them popularity. Expressive leaders, in contrast, who stimulate personal bonds and reduce friction, are usually more popular.
>
> —adapted from Henslin, *Sociology*, p. 164

This passage *contrasts* two types of group leaders, focusing on differences between the two types.

Paragraphs and passages that use comparison/contrast often contain transitional words and phrases that guide readers through the material. These include:

Comparison	Contrast
both, in comparison, in the same way, likewise, similarly, to compare	as opposed to, differs from, however, in contrast, instead, on the other hand, unlike

EXERCISE 7-5 Analyzing Comparison/Contrast Paragraphs

Directions: Read each of the following passages and identify the items being compared or contrasted. Then describe the author's approach to the items. Does the author compare, contrast, or both compare and contrast?

1. Congress is bicameral, meaning that it is made up of two houses, the Senate and the House of Representatives. According to the Constitution, all members of Congress must be residents of the states that they have been elected to represent. The Constitution also specifies that representatives must be at least 25 years old and American citizens for 7 years, whereas senators must be at least 30 and American citizens for 9 years. The roles of majority and minority leaders are similar in both houses, and both use committees to review bills and to set their legislative agenda. Despite these similarities, there are many important differences between the two houses. First, the term of office is two years for representative but six years for senators. Further,

each state is guaranteed two senators but its number of representatives is determined by the state's population; thus, the House of Representatives has 435 members and the Senate has 100. Another difference involves procedure: the House places limits on debate, whereas the Senate allows unlimited debate, which sometimes leads to a filibuster.

Items compared or contrasted: ______________________________

Approach: ______________________________

2. Whenever direct comparisons are made, the Neanderthals do indeed look primitive in comparison with ancient *Homo sapiens*. Neanderthals thrust spears at prey, but humans developed the valuable technique of *throwing* spears from a distance. The Neanderthals used nothing but stone for their relatively primitive tools, while *H. sapiens* used bone and antler as well as stone in constructing their much finer implements. And the Neanderthals were "foragers," while ancient humans were "collectors." What's the difference? Humans monitored their environments and used "forward planning" by, for example, placing their campsites near animal migration paths. By contrast, Neanderthals do not appear to have timed their migrations in this way. Such differences may have been important to the fate of the Neanderthals, as you'll see.

—Krogh, *Biology*, p. 370

Items compared or contrasted: ______________________________

Approach: ______________________________

3. The first step in evaluating your computer system needs is determining whether you want a desktop or a laptop. The main distinction between desktops and laptops is portability. If you need to take your computer with you to work or school, or even want the flexibility to move from room to room in your house, a laptop is the best choice. If portability is not an absolute factor, you should consider a desktop. Desktop systems are invariably a better value than laptops in terms of computing power gained for your dollar. Because of the laptop's small size, you pay more for each component. In addition, a desktop system offers more expandability options. It's easier to add new ports and devices because of the amount of room available in the desktop computer's design. Desktop systems are also more reliable. Because of the amount of vibration that a laptop experiences and the added exposure to dust, water, and temperature fluctuations that portability provides, laptops do not last as long as desktop computers.

—adapted from Evans et al., *Technology in Action*, p. 271

Items compared or contrasted: ______________________________

Approach: ______________________________

EXERCISE 7-6 **Writing a Comparison/Contrast Paragraph**

Directions: Choose one of the topics listed below. On a separate sheet of paper, write a paragraph in which you compare and/or contrast the two items. Then draw a diagram showing the organization of your paragraph.

1. Two restaurants

2. Two friends

3. Two musical groups

Cause/Effect

The **cause/effect** pattern is used to describe an event or action that is caused by another event or action. A cause/effect passage explains why or how something happened. For example, a description of an automobile accident would probably follow a cause/effect pattern. You would tell what caused the accident and what happened as a result. Basically, this pattern describes four types of relationships:

1. Single cause/single effect

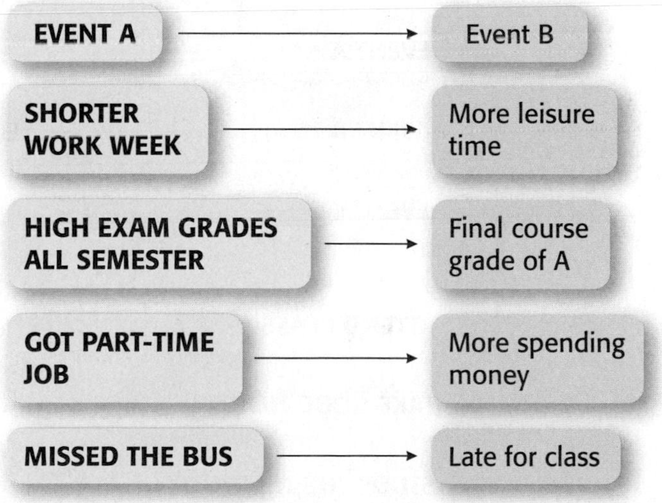

2. Single cause/multiple effects

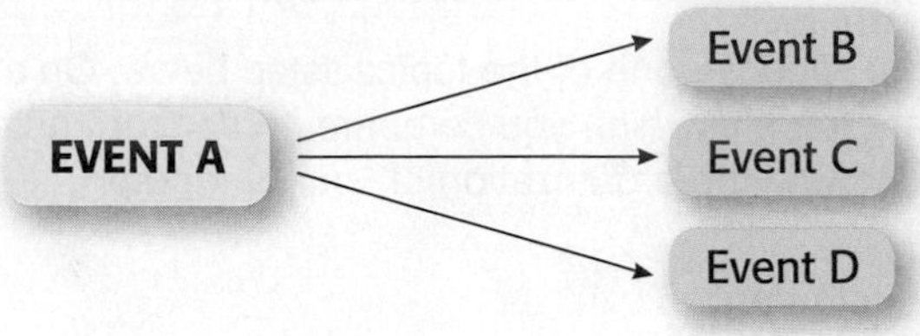

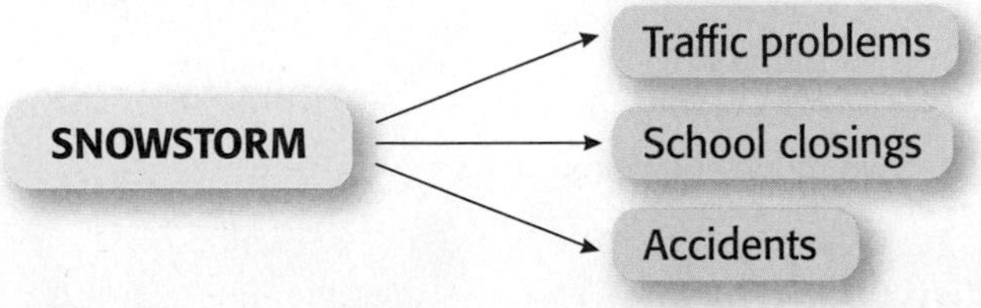

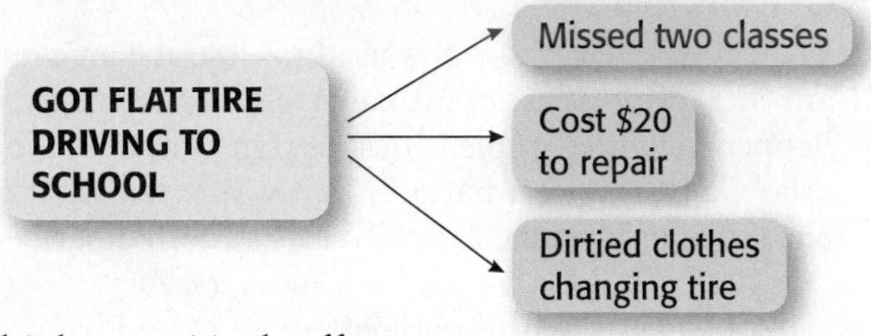

3. Multiple cause/single effect

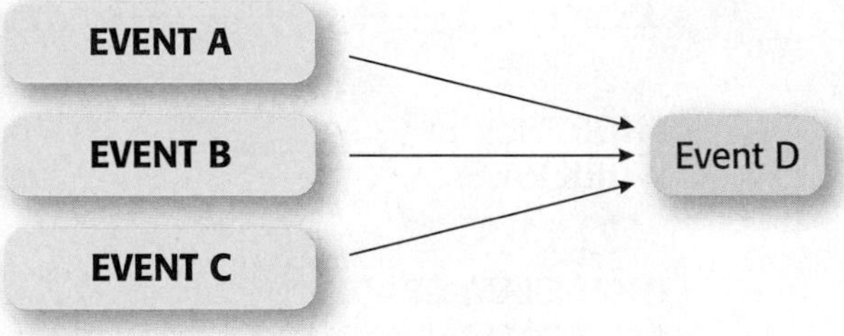

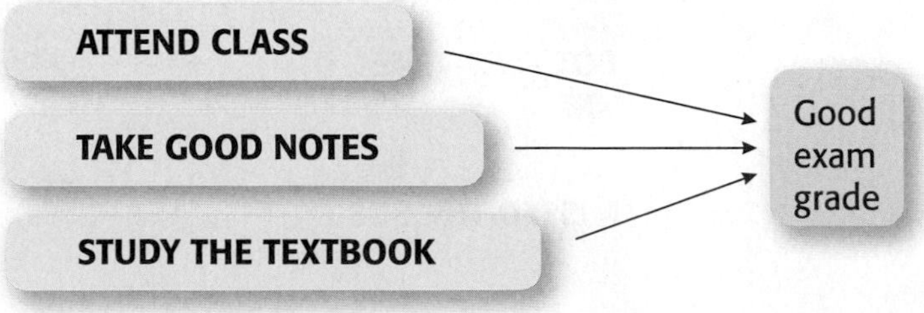

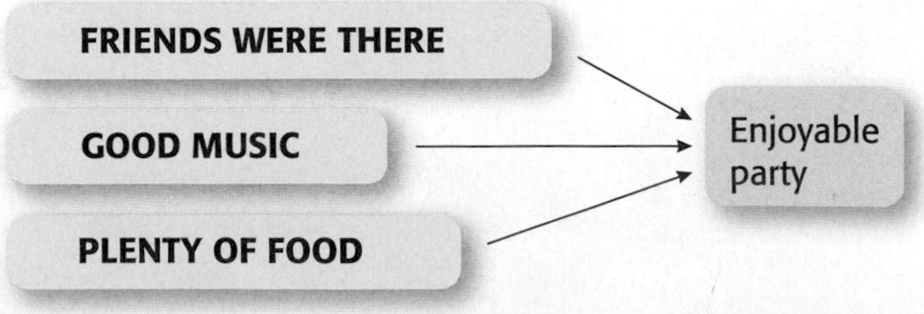

4. Multiple causes/multiple effects

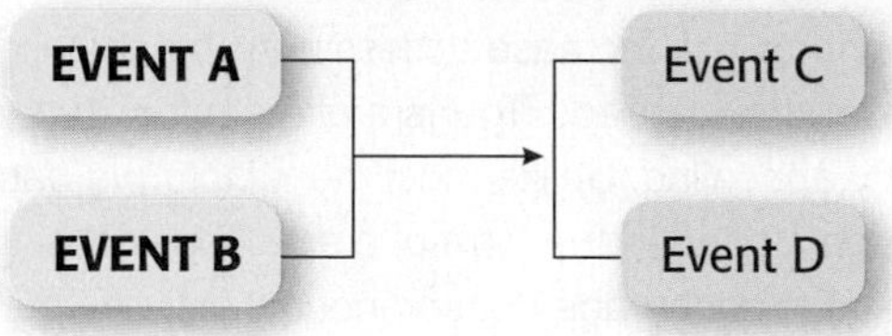

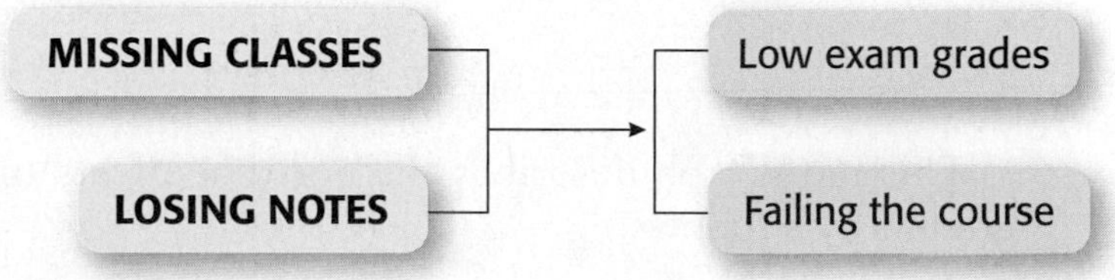

Read the following paragraph and determine which of the four relationships it describes.

> Research has shown that mental illnesses have various causes, but the causes are not fully understood. Some mental disorders are due to physical changes in the brain resulting from illness or injury. Chemical imbalances in the brain may cause other mental illnesses. Still other disorders are mainly due to conditions in the environment that affect a person's mental state. These conditions include unpleasant childhood experiences and severe emotional stress. In addition, many cases of mental illness probably result from a combination of two or more of these causes.

In this paragraph a single effect (mental illness) is stated as having multiple causes (chemical and metabolic changes, psychological problems).

To read paragraphs that explain cause/effect relationships, pay close attention to the topic sentence. It usually states the cause/effect relationship that is detailed in the remainder of the paragraph. Then look for connections between causes and effects. What event happened as the result of a previous action? How did one event cause the other to happen?

Look for the development of the cause/effect relationship in the following paragraph about tourism.

> Tourism offers several positive economic benefits. First, tourism can provide stability in an economy. Business travel remains relatively constant during changes in economic cycles; and even though people may cut back on the amount they spend on travel during harder economic times, citizens of most industrial nations have come to view vacationing as a necessity of life. Second, tourism provides economic diversity. A stable economy is one that provides jobs and revenues from a variety of industries; tourism can be added as another economic engine to the industry mix. Third, tourism

often provides the economic incentive to improve infrastructure that can be enjoyed by residents as well as tourists. For example, state-of-the-art airports are built by communities primarily to increase accessibility, but the airport can also be used by locals to meet their travel needs. Tourism offers a fourth positive impact that you may find particularly appealing. Unlike most manufacturing-based enterprises, a tourism business can be started in the form of a small business. In this way, the tourism industry can be used to encourage entrepreneurial activity. Tourism provides plenty of chances for creative, motivated individuals to start their own businesses.

—adapted from Cook et al., *Tourism*, p. 282

This paragraph describes the positive effects of tourism. It can be diagrammed as follows:

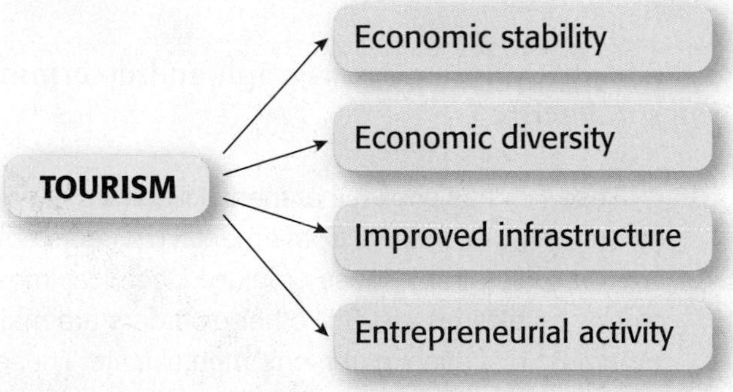

Paragraphs and passages that are organized using cause/effect often use transitional words and phrases to guide the reader. These include:

Cause	Effect
because, because of, for, since, stems from, one cause is, one reason is, for this reason, due to	consequently, one result is, as a result, therefore, thus, hence, results in

EXERCISE 7-7 Analyzing Cause/Effect Paragraphs

Directions: Read each of the following paragraphs and describe the cause/effect relationship in each.

1. The effects of marijuana are relatively mild compared to the other hallucinogens. Most people do report a feeling of mild euphoria and relaxation, along with an altered time sense and mild visual distortions. Higher doses can lead to hallucinations, delusions, and the all-too-common paranoia. Most studies of marijuana's effects have concluded that while marijuana can create a powerful psychological dependency, it does not produce physical dependency or physical withdrawal symptoms. Newer studies, however, suggest that long-term marijuana use can produce signs of withdrawal such

as irritability, memory difficulties, sleep difficulties, and increased aggression. A recent study of the long-term effects of marijuana use has also correlated smoking marijuana with an increased risk of psychotic behavior, with a greater risk for heavier users.

—adapted from Ciccarelli and White, *Psychology*, p. 280

Cause(s): ______________________________

Effect(s): ______________________________

____

____

What does this photograph suggest about the importance of bees?

2. Bees have suffered dramatic declines in recent years. Steady declines in wild and domesticated bee populations occurred from the 1970s through 2005; however, in 2006 and 2007, the declines reached crisis proportions. The exact causes of these dramatic declines are not known but are believed to result from an increased level of bee parasites, competition with the invading Africanized honeybees ("killer bees"), and habitat destruction.

—adapted from Belk and Maier, *Biology*, p. 372

Cause(s): ______________________________

Effect(s): ______________________________

3. An important consequence of culture within us is ethnocentrism, a tendency to use our own group's ways of doing things as a yardstick for judging others. All of us learn that the ways of our own group are good, right, and even superior to other ways of life. Ethnocentrism has both positive and negative consequences. On the positive side, it creates in-group loyalties. On the negative side, ethnocentrism can lead to discrimination against people whose ways differ from ours.

—adapted from Henslin, *Sociology*, p. 37

Cause(s): ______________________________

Effect(s): ______________________________

EXERCISE 7-8 Writing a Cause/Effect Paragraph

Directions: Choose one of the topics listed below. On a separate sheet of paper, write a paragraph using one of the four cause/effect patterns described above to explain the topic. Then draw a diagram showing the organization of your paragraph.

1. Why you are attending college
2. Why you chose the college you are attending
3. How a particularly frightening or tragic event happened

Classification

A common way to explain something is **classification**, dividing a topic into parts and explaining each part. For example, you might explain how a home computer works by describing what each major component does. You would explain the functions of the monitor (screen), the disc drive, and the central processing unit. Or you might explain the kinds of courses taken in college by dividing the courses into such categories as electives, required basic courses, courses required for a specific major, and so on, and then describing each category.

Textbook writers use the classification pattern to explain a topic that can easily be divided into parts. These parts are selected on the basis of common characteristics. For example, a psychology textbook writer might explain human needs by classifying them into two categories, primary and secondary. Or in a chemistry textbook, various compounds may be grouped or classified according to common characteristics, such as the presence of hydrogen or oxygen.

The following paragraph explains horticulture. As you read, try to identify the categories into which the topic of horticulture is divided.

> Horticulture, the study and cultivation of garden plants, is a large industry. Recently it has become a popular area of study. The horticulture field consists of four major divisions. First, there is pomology, the science and practice of growing and handling fruit trees. Then there is olericulture, which is concerned with growing and storing vegetables. A third field, floriculture, is the science of growing, storing, and designing flowering plants. The last category, ornamental and landscape horticulture, is concerned with using grasses, plants, and shrubs in landscaping.

This paragraph approaches the topic of horticulture by describing its four areas or fields of study. You could diagram the paragraph as follows:

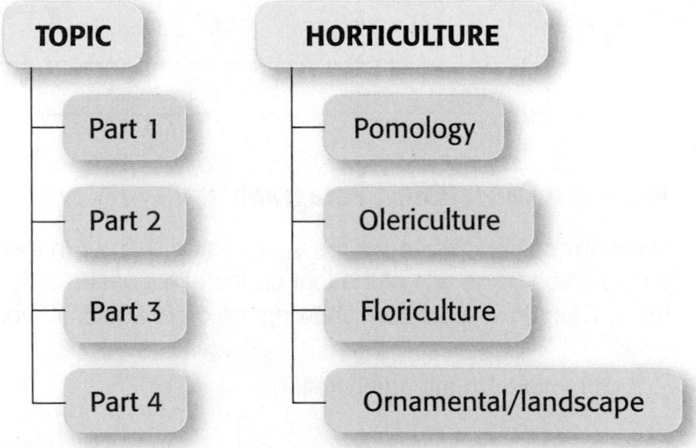

When reading textbook material that uses the classification pattern, be sure you understand *how* and *why* the topic was divided as it was. This technique will help you remember the most important parts of the topic.

Here is another example of the classification pattern:

A newspaper is published primarily to present current news and information. For large city newspapers, more than 2,000 people may be involved in the distribution of this information. The staff of large city papers, headed by a publisher, is organized into departments: editorial, business, and mechanical. The editorial department, headed by an editor-in-chief, is responsible for the collection of news and preparation of written copy. The business department, headed by a business manager, handles circulation, sales, and advertising. The mechanical department is run by a production manager. This department deals with the actual production of the paper, including typesetting, layout, and printing.

You could diagram this paragraph as follows:

Paragraphs and passages that are organized using classification frequently use transitional words and phrases to guide the reader. These include:

another	another kind	classified as	include	is composed of	one	types of

EXERCISE 7-9 Analyzing Classification Paragraphs

Directions: Read each of the following passages. Then identify the topic and the parts into which each passage is divided.

1. We can separate the members of the plant kingdom into a mere four types. These are the *bryophytes*, which include mosses; the *seedless vascular plants*, which include ferns; the *gymnosperms*, which include coniferous ("cone-bearing")

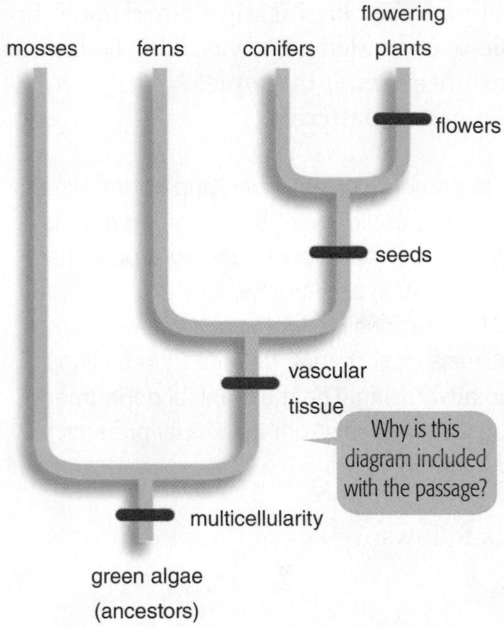

trees; and the *angiosperms*, a vast division of flowering plants—by far the most dominant on Earth today—that includes not only flowers such as orchids, but also oak trees, rice, and cactus.

—adapted from Krogh, *Biology*, p. 429

Topic: ______________________________

Parts: ______________________________

____

2. People are born with a need for certain elements necessary to maintain life, such as food, water, air, and shelter. We also can be motivated to satisfy either utilitarian or hedonic needs. When we focus on a *utilitarian need* we emphasize the objective, tangible attributes of products, such as miles per gallon in a car; the amount of fat, calories, and protein in a cheeseburger; or the durability of a pair of blue jeans. *Hedonic needs* are subjective and experiential; here we might look to a product to meet our needs for excitement, self-confidence, or fantasy—perhaps to escape the mundane or routine aspects of life. Of course, we can also be motivated to purchase a product because it provides *both* types of benefits. For example, a woman (perhaps a politically incorrect one) might buy a mink coat because of the luxurious image it portrays and because it also happens to keep her warm through the long, cold winter.

—adapted from Solomon, *Consumer Behavior*, pp. 132–133

What needs does this photograph illustrate?

Topic: ______________________________

Parts: ______________________________

3. The amount of space that people prefer varies from one culture to another. North Americans use four different "distance zones." *Intimate distance* extends to about 18 inches from our bodies. We reserve this space for comforting, protecting, hugging, intimate touching, and lovemaking. *Personal distance* extends from 18 inches to 4 feet. We reserve it for friends and acquaintances and ordinary conversations. *Social distance*, extending out from us about 4 to 12 feet, marks impersonal or formal relationships. We use this zone for such things as job interviews. *Public distance*, extending beyond 12 feet,

marks even more formal relationships. It is used to separate dignitaries and public speakers from the general public.

—adapted from Henslin, *Sociology*, pp. 109, 111

Topic: ____________________

Parts: ____________________

EXERCISE 7-10 Writing a Classification Paragraph

Directions: Choose one of the topics listed below. On a separate sheet of paper, write a paragraph explaining the topic, using the classification pattern. Then draw a diagram showing the organization of your paragraph.

1. Advertising
2. Colleges
3. Entertainment

Chronological Order/Process

The terms **chronological order** and **process** both refer to the order in which something is done. Chronological order, also called sequence of events, is one of the most obvious patterns. In a paragraph organized by chronology, the details are presented in the order in which they occur. That is, the event that happened first, or earliest in time, appears first in the paragraph, and so on. Process refers to the steps or stages in which something is done. You might expect to read a description of the events in a World War II battle presented in the order in which they happened—in chronological order. Similarly, in a computer programming manual, the steps to follow to locate an error in a computer program would be described in the order in which you should do them.

Both chronological order and process patterns can be diagrammed as follows:

Read the following paragraph, paying particular attention to the order of the actions or steps.

> In the early 1830s, the newly established Federal Bureau of Narcotics took on a crucial role in the fight against marijuana. Under the directorship of Harry J. Anslinger, a rigorous campaign was waged against the drug and those using it. By 1837 many states had adopted a standard bill making marijuana illegal. In that same year, the federal government stepped in with the Marijuana Tax Act, a bill modeled after the Harrison "Narcotics" Act. Repressive legislation continued, and by the 1850s severe penalties were imposed on those convicted of possessing, buying, selling, or cultivating the drug.
>
> —Barlow, *Criminal Justice in America*, p. 332

This paragraph traces the history of actions taken to limit the use of marijuana. These actions are described in chronological order, beginning with the earliest event and concluding with the most recent.

When reading text material that uses the chronological order/process pattern, pay particular attention to the order of the information presented. Both chronological order and process are concerned with the sequence of events in time.

Paragraphs and passages that use chronological order/process to organize ideas often contain transitional words and phrases to guide the reader. They include:

after	before	by the time	during	finally	first	later
meanwhile	on	second	then	until	when	while

EXERCISE 7-11 Analyzing Chronological Order/Process Paragraphs

Directions: Read each of the following paragraphs. Identify the topic and write a list of the actions, steps, or events described in each paragraph.

1. Two important traditions are typically performed when new lodging properties are constructed. First, when the final floor is completed, an evergreen tree is placed on the top of the building. This act signifies that the building will rise no higher. It also symbolically ties the building safely to the ground through the "roots of the tree." The second important tradition is performed when the ceremonial ribbon is cut on opening day. At that time, the key to the front door is symbolically thrown onto the roof because it will never be used again. This is a symbol signifying that the building is more than just a building. It has become a place that will always be open

to those who are seeking a home for the night or more appropriately a "home away from home."

—adapted from Cook et al., *Tourism*, p. 170

Topic: ____________________

Steps: ____________________

2. In jury selection, the pool of potential jurors usually is selected from voter or automobile registration lists. Potential jurors are asked to fill out a questionnaire. Lawyers for each party and the judge can ask questions of prospective jurors to determine if they would be biased in their decision. Jurors can be "stricken for cause" if the court believes that the potential juror is too biased to render a fair verdict. Lawyers may also exclude a juror from sitting on a particular case without giving any reason for the dismissal. Once the appropriate number of jurors is selected (usually six to twelve jurors), they are impaneled to hear the case and are sworn in. The trial is ready to begin.

—adapted from Goldman and Cheeseman, *The Paralegal Professional*, p. 266

Topic: ____________________

Steps: ____________________

____

3. At 12:30 on the afternoon of May 1, 1915, the British steamship *Lusitania* set sail from New York to Liverpool. The passenger list of 1,257 was the largest since the outbreak of war in Europe in 1914. Six days later, the *Lusitania* reached the coast of Ireland. The passengers lounged on the deck. As if it were peacetime, the ship sailed straight ahead, with no zigzag maneuvers to throw off pursuit. But the submarine U-20 was there, and its commander, seeing a large ship, fired a single torpedo. Seconds after it hit, a boiler exploded and blew a hole in the *Lusitania's* side. The ship listed immediately, hindering the launching of lifeboats, and in eighteen minutes it sank. Nearly 1,200 people died, including 128 Americans. As the ship's bow lifted and went under, the U-20 commander for the first time read the name: *Lusitania*.

—adapted from Divine et al., *America Past and Present*, p. 596

Topic: ____________________

Steps: ____________________

____

EXERCISE 7-12 Writing a Process Paragraph

Directions: On a separate sheet of paper, write a paragraph explaining how to do something that you do well or often, such as cross-country ski or change a tire, for example. Use the chronological order/process pattern. Then draw a diagram showing the organization of your paragraph.

EXERCISE 7-13 Identifying Thought Patterns

Directions: Working in pairs of groups of three, read each of the following passages and identify the thought pattern used. Write the name of the pattern in the space provided. Choose from among these patterns: *illustration/example*, *definition*, *comparison/contrast*, *cause/effect*, *classification*, and *chronological order/process*. Next, write a sentence explaining your choice. Identify any transitions. Then, on a separate sheet of paper, draw a diagram that shows the organization of each selection.

1. **Optimists** are people who always tend to look for positive outcomes. For an optimist, a glass is half full, whereas for a pessimist, the glass is half empty. **Pessimists** seem to expect the worst to happen. Researchers have found that optimism is associated with longer life and increased immune system functioning. Mayo Clinic researchers conducted a study of optimists and pessimists over a period of 30 years. The results for pessimists were not good: They had a much higher death rate than did the optimists, and those that were still living in 1994 had more problems with physical and emotional health, more pain, less ability to take part in social activities, and less energy than optimists. The optimists had a 50 percent lower risk of premature death and were more calm, peaceful, and happy than the pessimists.

—adapted from Ciccarelli and White, *Psychology*, p. 321

Pattern: ____________________

Reason: ____________________

2. Along with polar ice, **tundra** is the biome of the far north, stretching in a vast, mostly frozen, ring around the northern rim of the world. So inaccessible is tundra that the average person may never have heard of it, yet it occupies about a fourth of Earth's land surface. The word *tundra* comes from a Finnish word that means "treeless plain," and the description is apt. Its flat terrain stretches out for mile after mile with little change in the vegetational pattern of low shrubs, mosses, lichens, grasses, and the grass-like sedge.

—adapted from Krogh, *Biology*, p. 750

Pattern: ____________________

Reason: ____________________

3. In 1000 B.C., the Cherokee Indians took up residence in the Smoky Mountains. They were virtually isolated until the Spanish conquistadors arrived in 1540, and, more than two hundred years later, other immigrants from the Old World began to settle, first in small groups, and then increasingly in overwhelming numbers. The two groups of people, indigenous and immigrants, lived side by side with only occasional quarreling. In 1838, however, more than 13,000 Cherokee were forced to leave their native lands. Only a few rebellious natives remained along with their Caucasian counterparts.

—adapted from Walker and Walker, *Tourism*, pp. 53–54

Pattern: ______________________________

Reason: ______________________________

4. Several types of strikes have been held to be illegal and are not protected by federal labor laws. Illegal strikes take the form of violent strikes, sit-down strikes, and partial or intermittent strikes. In **violent strikes**, striking employees cause substantial damage to property of the employer or a third party. Courts usually tolerate a certain amount of isolated violence before finding that the entire strike is illegal. In **sit-down** strikes, striking employees continue to occupy the employer's premises. Such strikes are illegal because they deny the employer's statutory right to continue its operations during the strike. In **partial** or **intermittent strikes**, employees strike part of the day or workweek and work the other part. This type of strike is illegal because it interferes with the employer's right to operate its facilities at full operation.

—adapted from Goldman and Cheeseman, *The Paralegal Professional*, p. 641

Pattern: ______________________________

Reason: ______________________________

5. Because many natural poisons are alkaloids that occur in plants, it is not surprising that poisons are found in gardens and on farms or ranches. In addition to the toxic pesticides that might be found on a shelf, some of the plants themselves are toxic. For example, oleander (*Nerium oleander*), a beautiful shrub, contains several types of poison, including the potent cardiac glycosides *oleandrin* and *neriine*. (Cardiac glycosides are compounds that have a steroid part and a sugar part and that increase the heart's force of contraction.) Oleander's poisons are so strong that one can be poisoned by eating the honey made by bees that have fed on oleander nectar. Iris, azaleas, and hydrangeas all are poisonous. So are holly berries, wisteria seeds, and the leaves and berries of privet hedges.

—Hill et al., *Chemistry for Changing Times*, p. 682

Pattern: ______________________________

Reason: ______________________________

6. Behaviors, thoughts, and feelings always occur in a context, that is, in a situation. Situations can be divided into two components: the events that come before and those that come after. *Antecedents* are the setting events for a behavior; they stimulate a person to act in certain ways. Antecedents can be physical events, thoughts, emotions, or the actions of other people. *Consequences*—the results of behavior—affect whether a person will repeat that action. Consequences also can consist of physical events, thoughts, emotions, or the actions of other people.

—Donatelle, *Health*, p. 20

Pattern: ______________________________

Reason: ______________________________

Preserving beauty: Following a few simple rules can prolong the life of cut flowers.

7. Xylem is the plant tissue through which water moves *up*, from roots through leaves. The flowers we put in vases in our homes have lost their roots, of course, but they haven't lost their xylem, which continues to function long after the flower has been picked. Given this, many flowers can last a long time indoors if we follow a few simple rules. First, realize that the liquid in the xylem is under negative pressure—its natural tendency is to move up *into* the stem, not to flow out of it. As such, if the stems are cut when they are out of water, *air* gets sucked up into the cut ends, creating air bubbles that can then get trapped in the xylem and keep water from rising up through it. When this happens, flowers can wilt, even when their stems are submerged in clean water. Recutting the stem under water can remove this blockage.

—adapted from Krogh, *Biology*, p. 488

Pattern: ______________________________

Reason: ______________________________

8. The risks of active smoking, in addition to lung and airway damage, include increased rates of throat, bladder, and pancreatic cancer; higher rates of heart attack, stroke, and high blood pressure; and premature aging of the skin. All of these effects occur because many of the components of tobacco smoke can cross into the bloodstream and move throughout the body.

—adapted from Belk and Maier, *Biology*, p. 451

Pattern: ______________________________

Reason: ______________________________

9. Surveys or questionnaires can be broken down into several types. They may be based on opinion; interpretative; or based on facts. **Opinion surveys** ask respondents questions regarding what they think about particular topics. Answers are based

on personal opinion. Therefore, the answers are not necessarily right or wrong. An opinion survey may ask respondents to evaluate a certain topic or express their attitudes and beliefs. **Interpretative surveys** ask respondents to answer why they chose a particular course. For example, a hotel may ask its guests why they chose to stay at the hotel; an airline may ask why passengers chose to fly with them. **Factual surveys** can be thought of as being more concrete in the questions they ask. For example, they may ask travelers what recreational activities they participated in while they were traveling. The answers are based on fact alone, no interpretation or opinion is expressed.

—adapted from Walker and Walker, *Tourism*, p. 241

Pattern: ______________________________

Reason: ______________________________

10. People who live long, healthy lives may change careers frequently during their lifetimes, and their most satisfying and perhaps most financially rewarding career may come later in life. Novelist James Michener was first published after the age of 40; Colonel Sanders started Kentucky Fried Chicken (now called KFC) after he was 50 years old; Dr. Ruth became a celebrity talk-show sex therapist when she was age 48; Sam Walton opened his first Wal-Mart at age 44; and Ted Turner started Cable News Network (CNN) at age 42. Don't forget Margaret Mitchell, who won her first Pulitzer Prize, for *Gone with the Wind*, when she was 37 years old; Shirley Temple Black, who was named ambassador to Ghana at age 47; and Jerry Brown, elected as Governor of California at age 72.

—Sukiennik et al., *The Career Fitness Program*, p. 111

Pattern: ______________________________

Reason: ______________________________

OTHER USEFUL PATTERNS OF ORGANIZATION

2 LEARNING GOAL
Recognize other useful thought patterns

The patterns presented in the preceding section are the most common. Table 7-1 (page 258) presents a brief review of those patterns and their corresponding transitional words. However, writers do not limit themselves to these six patterns. Especially in academic writing, you may find one or more of the patterns listed in Table 7-2 (page 259), as well.

Statement and Clarification

Many writers make a statement of fact and then proceed to clarify or explain that statement. For instance, a writer may open a paragraph by stating that

TABLE 7-1 A Review of Patterns and Transitional Words

Pattern	Characteristics	Transitional Words
Illustration/ Example	Organizes examples that illustrate an idea or concept	*for example, for instance, such as, to illustrate*
Definition	Explains the meaning of a word or phrase	*are those that, can be defined as, consists of, corresponds to, entails, involves, is, is a term that, is called, is characterized by, is literally, means, occurs when, refers to*
Comparison/ Contrast	Discusses similarities and/or differences among ideas, theories, concepts, objects, or persons	Similarities: *also, as well as, both, correspondingly, in comparison, in the same way, like, likewise, resembles, share, similarly, to compare, too*
		Differences: *as opposed to, despite, differs from, however, in contrast, in spite of, instead, nevertheless, on the other hand, unlike, whereas*
Cause/Effect	Describes how one or more things cause or are related to another	Causes: *because, because of, cause is, due to, for, for this reason, one cause is, one reason is, since, stems from*
		Effects: *as a result, consequently, hence, one result is, results in, therefore, thus*
Classification	Divides a topic into parts based on shared characteristics	*another, another kind, classified as, comprises, different groups that, different stages of, finally, first, include, is composed of, last, one, second, types of, varieties of*
Chronological Order/Process	Describes events, processes, procedures	*after, as soon as, by the time, during, finally, first, following, in, last, later, meanwhile, next, on, second, then, until, when, while*

"The best education for you may not be the best education for someone else." The remainder of the paragraph would then discuss that statement and make its meaning clear by explaining how educational needs are individual and based on one's talents, skills, and goals. Here is another example:

> The Constitution of the United States of America is the *supreme law of the land*. This means that any law—federal, state, or local—that conflicts with the U.S. Constitution is unconstitutional and, therefore, unenforceable. The principles enumerated in the Constitution are extremely broad, because the founding fathers intended them to be applied to evolving social, technological, and economic conditions. The U.S. Constitution often is referred to as a "living document" because it is so adaptable. States also have their own constitutions, often patterned after the U.S. Constitution. Provisions of state constitutions are valid unless they conflict with the U.S. Constitution or any valid federal law.
>
> —adapted from Goldman and Cheeseman, *The Paralegal Professional*, p. 183

Transitional words associated with this pattern are listed in Table 7-2.

TABLE 7-2 A Review of Additional Patterns and Transitional Words

Pattern	Characteristics	Transitional Words
Statement and Clarification	Gives information explaining an idea or concept	*clearly, evidently, in fact, in other words, obviously*
Summary	Provides a condensed review of an idea or piece of writing	*in brief, in conclusion, in short, in summary, on the whole, to sum up, to summarize*
Addition	Provides additional information	*additionally, again, also, besides, further, furthermore, in addition, moreover*
Spatial Order	Describes physical location or position in space	*above, behind, below, beside, in front of, inside, nearby, next to, opposite, outside, within*

Summary

A summary is a condensed statement that recaps the key points of a larger idea or piece of writing. The summaries at the end of each chapter of this text provide a quick review of the chapter's contents. Often writers summarize what they have already said or what someone else has said. For example, in a psychology textbook you will find many summaries of research. Instead of asking you to read an entire research study, the textbook author will summarize the study's findings. Other times a writer may repeat in condensed form what he or she has already said as a means of emphasis or clarification. Here is a sample paragraph:

> To sum up, the minimax strategy is a general principle of human behavior that suggests that humans try to minimize costs and maximize rewards. The fewer costs and the more rewards we anticipate from something, the more likely we are to do it. If we believe that others will approve an act, the likelihood increases that we will do it. In short, whether people are playing cards with a few friends or are part of a mob, the principles of human behavior remain the same.
>
> —adapted from Henslin, *Sociology*, p. 637

Transitional words associated with this pattern are listed in Table 7-2.

Addition

Writers often introduce an idea or make a statement and then supply additional information about that idea or statement. For instance, an education textbook may introduce the concept of homeschooling and then provide in-depth information about its benefits. This pattern is often used to expand, elaborate, or discuss an idea in greater detail. Here is an example:

> Millions of people work at home on computers connected to an office, an arrangement known as telecommuting. Telecommuting eases the pressure on transport facilities, saves fuel, and reduces air pollution. Moreover, it has been shown to increase workers' productivity and reduce absenteeism. It also allows employers to accommodate employees who want flexible work arrangements, thus opening employment opportunity to more people, such as women who are still homemakers.
>
> —Bergman and Renwick, *Introduction to Geography*, p. 430

Transitional words associated with this pattern are listed in Table 7-2 (p. 259).

Spatial Order

Spatial order is concerned with the physical location or position in space. Spatial order is used in disciplines in which physical descriptions are important. A photography textbook may use spatial order to describe the parts of a camera. An automotive technology textbook may use spatial order to describe disk brake operation. Here is a sample paragraph:

> We can taste food because chemoreceptors in the mouth respond to certain chemicals in food. The chemoreceptors for taste are located in structures called **taste buds**, each of which contains 50–150 receptor cells and numerous support cells. At the top of each bud is a pore that allows receptor cells to be exposed to saliva and dissolved food molecules. Each person has over 10,000 taste buds, located primarily on the tongue and the roof of the mouth, but also located in the pharynx.
>
> —Germann and Stanfield, *Principles of Human Physiology*, pp. 303–304

Transitional words associated with this pattern are listed in Table 7-2 (p. 259).

EXERCISE 7-14 Identifying Thought Patterns

Directions: For each of the following statements, identify the pattern that is evident and indicate it in the space provided. Choose from among the following patterns:

a. statement and clarification
b. summary
c. addition
d. spatial order

_____ 1. Short fibers, dendrites, branch out around the cell body and a single long fiber, the axon, extends from the cell body.

_____ 2. Aspirin is not as harmless as people think. It may cause allergic reactions and stomach irritation. In addition, aspirin has been linked to an often fatal condition known as Reye's syndrome.

_____ 3. If our criminal justice system works, the recidivism rate—the percentage of people released from prison who return—should decrease. In other words, in a successful system, there should be a decrease in the number of criminals who are released from prison and then become repeat offenders.

_____ 4. Students who are informed about drugs tend to use them in greater moderation. Furthermore, they tend to help educate others.

_____ 5. To sum up, a successful drug addiction treatment program would offer free or very cheap drugs to addicts.

_____ 6. In conclusion, it is safe to say that crime by women is likely to increase as greater numbers of women assume roles traditionally held by men.

_____ 7. The pollutants we have just discussed all involve chemicals; we can conclude that they threaten our environment and our well-being.

_____ 8. A residual check valve that maintains slight pressure on the hydraulic system is located in the master cylinder at the outlet for the drum brakes.

_____ 9. Sociologists study how we are socialized into sex roles—the attitudes expected of males and females. Sex roles, in fact, identify some activities and behaviors as clearly male and others as clearly female.

_____ 10. The meninges are three membranes that lie just outside the organs of the central nervous system.

EXERCISE 7-15 Predicting

Directions: Locate and mark five paragraphs in one of your textbooks or in Part Seven of this text that are clear examples of the thought patterns discussed in this chapter. Write the topic sentence of each paragraph on a separate index card. Once your instructor has formed small groups, choose a group "reader" who will collect all the cards and read each sentence aloud. Groups should discuss each and predict the pattern of the paragraph from which the sentence was taken. The "finder" of the topic sentence then confirms or rejects the choice, quoting sections of the paragraph if necessary.

Using Transitional Words

As you learned earlier in the chapter, transitional words can help you identify organizational patterns. These words are called **transitional words** because they help you make the transition or connection between ideas. They may also be called *clue words* or *directional words* because they provide readers with clues about what is to follow.

Transitional words are also helpful in discovering or clarifying relationships between and among ideas in any piece of writing. Specifically, transitional words help you grasp connections between and within sentences. Transitional words can help you predict what is to come next within a paragraph. For instance, if you are reading along and come upon the phrase *in conclusion,* you know that the writer will soon present a summary. If you encounter the word *furthermore,* you know that the writer is about to present additional information about the subject at hand. If you encounter the word *consequently* in the middle of a sentence (The law was repealed; consequently, ...), you know that the writer is about to explain what happened as a result of the repeal. Tables 7-1 and 7-2 on pages 258 and 259 list the transitional words that correspond to the patterns discussed in this chapter.

EXERCISE 7-16 Predicting

Directions: Each of the following beginnings of paragraphs uses a transitional word or phrase to tell the reader what will follow in the paragraph. Read each, paying particular attention to the underlined transitional word or phrase. Working with a partner, discuss what you expect to follow. Then, in the space provided, summarize your findings.

1. Many Web sites on the Internet are reliable and trustworthy. However, . . .

   ____

2. One advantage of using a computer to take notes is that you can rearrange information easily. Another . . .

   ____

3. There are a number of ways to avoid catching the cold virus. First of all, . . .

____

4. Some pet owners care for their animals responsibly. However, others . . .

____

5. When planning a speech, you should choose a topic that is familiar or that you are knowledgeable about. Next, . . .

____

6. Following a high protein diet may be rewarding because it often produces quick weight loss. On the other hand, . . .

____

7. The iris is a doughnut-shaped portion of the eyeball. In the center . . .

____

8. Price is not the only factor consumers consider when making a major purchase. They also . . .

____

9. Cholesterol, commonly found in many fast foods, is associated with heart disease. Consequently, . . .

____

10. Many Web sites provide valuable links to related sites. To illustrate, visit . . .

____

LEARNING STYLE TIPS

If you tend to be a ...	Then identify thought patterns by ...
Spatial learner	Drawing a diagram of the ideas in the passage
Verbal learner	Outlining the passage

SELF-TEST SUMMARY

1 What are the six common thought patterns?	A thought pattern is the way in which an author organizes ideas. The six common thought patterns are: 1. **Illustration/example**—An idea is explained by providing specific instances or experiences that illustrate it. 2. **Definition**—An object or idea is explained by describing the general class or group to which it belongs and how the item differs from others in the same group (distinguishing features). 3. **Comparison/contrast**—A new or unfamiliar idea is explained by showing how it is similar to or different from a more familiar idea. 4. **Cause/effect**—Connections between events are explained by showing what caused an event or what happened as a result of a particular event. 5. **Classification**—An object or idea is explained by dividing it into parts and describing or explaining each. 6. **Chronological order/process**—Events or procedures are described in the order in which they occur in time.
2 What other thought patterns are used in academic writing?	1. **Statement and clarification**—An explanation will follow. 2. **Summary**—A condensed view of the subject will be presented. 3. **Addition**—Additional information will follow. 4. **Spatial order**—Physical location or position will be described.

GOING ONLINE

1. **Patterns of Organization and Online Images**
Many photos suggest a pattern of organization. Do a Google Image search for a topic of interest to you, and print out three photos that you find interesting. Then write a sentence (caption) to accompany each photo. Each sentence should use one of the following patterns of organization: illustration/example, definition, comparison/contrast, cause/effect, classification, or chronological order/process. For example, you might use a photo of a maple tree to write a definition or example sentence, such as "The maple is one example of a deciduous tree, which is a type of tree that loses its leaves in the fall."

2. **Comparing and Contrasting Books**
Go to an online book review Web site and look up reviews of the following two books: *One for the Money* by Janet Evanovich and *An Unsuitable Job for a Woman* by P.D. James. Browse the reviews and, if possible, any sample chapters that may be available for the books. Then, working with a group of classmates, prepare a comparison/contrast of these two books. How are the two books similar? How are they different?

CHAPTER 7

MASTERY TEST 1 Identifying Patterns

This **Mastery Test** can be completed in **MyReadingLab**.

Name ______________________ Section ____________

Date ______________ Number right* ________ × 10 points = Score ________

Directions: Read the passage below, and select the choice that best completes each of the statements that follow.

1 "Marry afar" is advice given by the pygmy men of Africa, by which they mean, "marry a woman who lives far from your home." The pygmies point to the hunting rights a man acquires by marrying a woman from a remote region, but there is another benefit to this practice: It helps ensure genetic diversity. When pygmies from remote locations marry, it cuts down on the chances of *inbreeding*, meaning mating in which close relatives produce offspring. Inbreeding can have harmful effects not only on humans, but in any species.

2 Consider what has happened in the United States with "purebred" dogs, which is to say dogs that over many generations have been bred solely with members of their own breed (cocker spaniels mating only with cocker spaniels, and so forth). In the mid-1990s it was estimated that up to one-fourth of all U.S. purebred dogs had some sort of serious genetic defect—ranging from improper joint formation, to heart defects, to deafness.

What concept does this photograph illustrate?

3 You might think that there are no uses for genetic similarity, but consider what humans have been doing for centuries with dog breeding. Cocker spaniels did not come about by accident. Dogs with cocker spaniel features were bred together for many generations, ultimately giving us today's dog. While the breeding done to produce American cocker spaniels has resulted in dogs with cute, floppy ears, the unintended effect of this practice is a breed that is also prone to ear infections and a "rage syndrome" that can result in unprovoked aggression. Inbreeding produces a range of unique features, some desirable but others more aptly referred to as genetic defects.

—adapted from Krogh, *Biology*, pp. 318–319

_____ 1. The purpose of this passage is to
   a. describe the pygmy men of Africa.
   b. compare and contrast marriage rituals.
   c. classify types of purebred dogs.
   d. discuss the effects of inbreeding.

_____ 2. The pattern that the author uses to organize his ideas in the first paragraph is
a. classification.
b. comparison/contrast.
c. chronological order.
d. definition.

_____ 3. The pattern that the author uses to organize his ideas in the second paragraph is
a. illustration/example.
b. classification.
c. chronological order.
d. process.

_____ 4. The type of cause/effect relationship that the author describes throughout this passage is
a. single cause/single effect.
b. single cause/multiple effects.
c. multiple causes/single effect.
d. multiple causes/multiple effects.

_____ 5. The pattern that the author uses to organize his ideas in the third paragraph is
a. comparison/contrast.
b. definition.
c. cause/effect.
d. classification.

CHAPTER 7

MASTERY TEST 2 Identifying Patterns

This **Mastery Test** can be completed in **MyReadingLab**.

Name ______________________ Section ____________

Date ____________ Number right* ________ × 10 points = Score ________

Directions: Read each of the following paragraphs. In the space provided, write the letter of the main thought pattern used.

a. definition
b. comparison/contrast
c. illustration/example
d. cause/effect
e. classification
f. chronological order/process

_____ 1. Soon after its inception, advertising through the mass media came under heavy scrutiny. As early as the 1920s, consumer groups attacked deceptive advertising and attempted to force the Federal Communications Commission (FCC) and the Federal Trade Commission (FTC) to enact stricter regulations governing commercial advertisements. Consumer groups received little assistance from theses agencies, however, and even through the 1960s and 1970s, when an organized consumer movement was under way, most of the rules that applied to media advertising relied on voluntary compliance and industry self-regulation. In 1978, the FTC attempted to ban television advertising geared to vulnerable, prepubescent children, but the issue became protection of the marketplace versus protection of children, and the marketplace won.

—Thompson and Hickey, *Society in Focus*, p. 493

_____ 2. The experimental roots of chemistry are in alchemy, a mixture of chemistry and magic that flourished in Europe during the Middle Ages, from about C.E. 500 to 1500. Alchemists searched for a "philosophers' stone" that would turn cheaper metals into gold and for an elixir that would bring eternal life. Although alchemists never achieved these goals, they discovered many new chemical substances and perfected techniques such as distillation and extraction that are still used today. Modern chemists inherited from the alchemists an abiding interest in human health and the quality of life.

—Hill et al., *Chemistry for Changing Times*, p. 3

_____ 3. Colors surely influence our perceptions and our behaviors. People's acceptance of a product, for example, is largely determined by its package. The very same coffee taken from a yellow can was described as weak, from a dark brown can too strong, from a red can rich, and from a blue can mild. Even our acceptance of a person may depend on the colors worn. Consider, for example, the comments of one color expert: "If you have to pick the wardrobe for your defense lawyer in court and choose anything but blue, you deserve to lose the case. . . ." Black is so powerful it could work against a lawyer with the jury. Brown lacks sufficient authority. Green would probably elicit a negative response.

—DeVito, *The Interpersonal Communication Book*, pp. 219–220

_____ 4. Hospice care is built around the idea that the people who are dying and their families should control the process of dying. Whereas hospitals are dedicated to prolonging life, hospice care is dedicated to providing dignity in death and making people comfortable during the living-dying interval. In the hospital, the focus is on the patient; in hospice care, the focus switches to both the dying person and his or her friends and family. In the hospital, the goal is to make the patient well; in hospice care, it is to relieve pain and suffering and make death easier to bear. In the hospital, the primary concern is the individual's physical welfare; in hospice care, although medical needs are met, the primary concern is the individual's social—and in some instances, spiritual—well-being.

—adapted from Henslin, *Sociology*, pp. 389–390

_____ 5. It was at the 1893 World's Columbian Exposition in Chicago that Milton Hershey first became fascinated with the art of chocolate. Hershey, a small-time candy manufacturer, decided he wanted to make chocolate to coat his caramels. He opened his new establishment in Lancaster, Pennsylvania, and named it Hershey Chocolate Company. In the 1900s, the company started to produce mass quantities of milk chocolate, which resulted in immediate success. Soon after, Hershey decided to increase his production facilities so he built a new factory on the farmland of south-central Pennsylvania. The following decades brought many product-line expansions and, in 1968, the company was renamed Hershey Foods Corporation. Today, the company is the leading manufacturer of chocolate, non-chocolate confectionery, and grocery products in North America.

—adapted from Walker, *Introduction to Hospitality Management*, p. 361

_____ 6. Five environmental systems influence the family: microsystems, mesosystems, exosystems, macrosystems, and chronosystems. The **microsystem** is the child's immediate environment, including any immediate relationships or organizations that the child interacts with, such as family members or teachers at school. The **mesosystem** describes how different parts of the child's microsystem interact. For example, children whose parents play an active role in their education often do better in school than children with poorer home–school connections. The **exosystem** includes outside influences that the child may not interact with personally, but that have a large impact on the child, such as parents' workplaces or members of the extended family. The **macrosystem** describes the culture in which an individual lives, including the relative freedoms permitted by the national government, cultural values, and the economy—all of which may affect a child positively or negatively. Finally, **chronosystems** examine the impact of life transitions, which may include puberty, changing schools, marriage, and retirement as well as unexpected events within a family, such as death or divorce.

—adapted from Kunz, *Think Marriages and Families*, p. 16

Diego Rivera.
Detail from *Detroit Industry.* 1932–1933.
Fresco.
Detroit Institute of Arts, MI. Gift of Edsel B. Ford. Bridgeman Art Library.

Why was this image included in the text?

_____ 7. True fresco, or *buon fresco*, is an ancient wallpainting technique in which finely ground pigments suspended in water are applied to a damp lime-plaster surface. Generally, a full-size drawing called a cartoon is completed first, then transferred to the freshly laid plaster wall before painting. Because the plaster dries quickly, only the portion of the wall that can be painted in one day is prepared. The painter works quickly in a rapid staining process similar to watercolor. The lime in the plaster becomes the binder, creating a smooth, extremely durable surface. Once the surface has dried, the painting is part of the wall.

—adapted from Frank, *Prebles' Artforms*, p. 127

_____ 8. Glaciers erode the land primarily in two ways—plucking and abrasion. First, as a glacier flows over a fractured bedrock surface, it loosens and lifts blocks of rock and incorporates them into the ice. This process, known as **plucking,** occurs when meltwater penetrates the cracks and joints of bedrock beneath a glacier and freezes. When water freezes it expands, exerting tremendous leverage that pries the rock loose. The second major erosional process is **abrasion.** As the ice and its load of rock fragments slide over bedrock, they function like sandpaper to smooth and polish the surface below. The pulverized rock is appropriately called *rock flour*. So much rock flour may be produced that meltwater streams flowing out of a glacier often have the grayish appearance of skim milk and offer visible evidence of the grinding power of ice.

—adapted from Lutgens et al., *Essentials of Geology*, pp. 252–253

_____ 9. **Marsupials** are mammals in which the young develop within the mother to a limited extent, inside an egg that has a membranous shell. Marsupials are represented by several Australian animals, including the kangaroo, and by several animals in the Western Hemisphere, including the North American opossum. Early in development, the egg's membrane disappears, and in a few days time, a developmentally immature but active marsupial is delivered from the mother. In the case of a kangaroo, the tiny youngster has just enough capacity to climb up its mother's body, into her "pouch," and begin suckling there.

—adapted from Krogh, *Biology*, p. 471

_____ 10. **Database marketing** involves tracking specific consumers' buying habits very closely and crafting products and messages tailored precisely to people's wants and needs based on this information. Wal-Mart stores massive amounts of information on the 100 million people who visit its stores each week, and the company uses these data to fine-tune its offerings. When the company analyzed how shoppers' buying patterns react when forecasters predict a major hurricane, for example, it discovered that people do a lot more than simply stock up on flashlights. Sales of strawberry Pop-Tarts increase by about 700 percent and the top-selling product of all is—beer. Based on these insights, Wal-Mart loads its trucks with toaster pastries and six-packs to stock local stores when a big storm approaches.

—adapted from Solomon, *Consumer Behavior*, p. 13

CHAPTER 7

MASTERY TEST 3 Reading Selection

This Mastery Test can be completed in MyReadingLab.

Name ______________________________ Section ____________

Date ____________________ Number right* __________ × 10 points = Score ____________

Right Place, Wrong Face

Alton Fitzgerald White

In this selection, the author describes what it was like to be treated as a criminal on the basis of nothing more than having the "wrong face."

Vocabulary Preview

ovation (par. 3) enthusiastic, prolonged applause

overt (par. 4) not secret, obvious

splurged (par. 5) indulged in a luxury

vestibule (par. 5) a small entrance hall or passage into the interior of a building

residue (par. 9) something that remains after a substance is taken away

violation (par. 14) the condition of being treated unfairly or disrespectfully

1 As the youngest of five girls and two boys growing up in Cincinnati, I was raised to believe that if I worked hard, was a good person, and always told the truth, the world would be my oyster. I was raised to be a gentleman and learned that these qualities would bring me respect.

2 While one has to earn respect, consideration is something owed to every human being. On Friday, June 16, 1999, when I was wrongfully arrested at my Harlem apartment building, my perception of everything I had learned as a young man was forever changed—not only because I wasn't given even a second to use the manners my parents taught me, but mostly because the police, whom I'd always naively thought were supposed to serve and protect me, were actually hunting me.

3 I had planned a pleasant day. The night before was payday, plus I had received a standing ovation after portraying the starring role of Coalhouse Walker Jr. in the Broadway musical *Ragtime*. It is a role that requires not only talent but also an honest emotional investment of the morals and lessons I learned as a child.

4 Coalhouse Walker Jr. is a victim (an often misused word, but in this case true) of overt racism. His story is every black man's nightmare. He is hardworking, successful, talented, charismatic, friendly, and polite. Perfect prey for someone with authority and not even a fraction of those qualities. On that Friday afternoon, I became a real-life Coalhouse Walker. Nothing could have prepared me for it. Not even stories told to me by other black men who had suffered similar injustices.

*To calculate the number right, use items 1—10 under "Mastery Test Skills Check."

Alton Fitzgerald White

5 Friday for me usually means a trip to the bank, errands, the gym, dinner, and then off to the theater. On this particular day, I decided to break my pattern of getting up and running right out of the house. Instead, I took my time, slowed my pace, and splurged by making strawberry pancakes. Before I knew it, it was 2:45; my bank closes at 3:30, leaving me less than 45 minutes to get to midtown Manhattan on the train. I was pressed for time but in a relaxed, blessed state of mind. When I walked through the lobby of my building, I noticed two light-skinned Hispanic men I'd never seen before. Not thinking much of it, I continued on to the vestibule, which is separated from the lobby by a locked door.

6 As I approached the exit, I saw people in uniforms rushing toward the door. I sped up to open it for them. I thought they might be paramedics, since many of the building's occupants are elderly. It wasn't until I had opened the door and greeted them that I recognized that they were police officers. Within seconds, I was told to "hold it"; they had received a call about young Hispanics with guns. I was told to get against the wall. I was searched, stripped of my backpack, put on my knees, handcuffed, and told to be quiet when I tried to ask questions.

7 With me were three other innocent black men who had been on their way to their U-Haul. They were moving into the apartment beneath mine, and I had just bragged to them about how safe the building was. One of these gentlemen got off his knees, still handcuffed, and unlocked the door for the officers to get into the lobby where the two strangers were standing. Instead of thanking or even acknowledging us, they led us out the door past our neighbors, who were all but begging the police in our defense.

8 The four of us were put into cars with the two strangers and taken to the precinct station at 165th and Amsterdam. The police automatically linked us, with no questions and no regard for our character or our lives. No consideration was given to where we were going or why. Suppose an ailing relative was waiting upstairs, while I ran out for her medication? Or young children, who'd been told that Daddy was running to the corner store for milk and would be right back? My new neighbors weren't even allowed to lock their apartment or check on the U-Haul.

9 After we were lined up in the station, the younger of the two Hispanic men was identified as an experienced criminal, and drug residue was found in a pocket of the other. I now realize how naive I was to think that the police would then uncuff me, apologize for their mistake, and let me go. Instead, they continued to search my backpack, questioned me, and put me in jail with the criminals.

10 The rest of the nearly five-hour ordeal was like a horrible dream. I was handcuffed, strip-searched, taken in and out for questioning. The officers told me that they knew exactly who I was, knew I was in *Ragtime,* and that in fact they already had the men they wanted.

11 How then could they keep me there, or have brought me there in the first place? I was told it was standard procedure. As if the average law-abiding citizen knows what that is and can dispute it. From what I now know, "standard procedure" is something that every citizen, black and white, needs to learn, and fast.

12 I felt completely powerless. Why, do you think? Here I was, young, pleasant, and successful, in good physical shape, dressed in clean athletic attire. I was carrying a backpack containing a substantial paycheck and a deposit slip, on my way to the bank. Yet after hours and hours I was sitting at a desk with two officers who not only couldn't tell me why I was there but seemed determined to find something on me, to the point of making me miss my performance.

13 It was because I am a black man!

14 I sat in that cell crying silent tears of disappointment and injustice with the realization of how many innocent black men are convicted for no reason. When I was handcuffed, my first instinct had been to pull away out of pure insult and violation as a human being. Thank God I was calm enough to do what they said. When I was thrown in jail with the criminals and strip-searched, I somehow knew to put my pride aside, be quiet, and do exactly what I was told, hating it but coming to terms with the fact that in this situation I was a victim. They had guns!

15 Before I was finally let go, exhausted, humiliated, embarrassed, and still in shock, I was led to a room and given a pseudo-apology. I was told that I was at the wrong place at the wrong time. My reply? "I was where I live."

16 Everything I learned growing up in Cincinnati has been shattered. Life will never be the same.

—White, The Nation

MASTERY TEST SKILLS CHECK

Directions: Select the choice that best completes each of the following statements.

Checking Your Comprehension

_____ 1. The author's main purpose in this selection is to
a. describe his recent experience with racism.
b. discuss the effects of racism on young people.
c. criticize the New York police department.
d. contrast Cincinnati with New York.

_____ 2. Coalhouse Walker Jr. is the name of
a. the author of the article.
b. a black actor in New York.
c. the main character in a Broadway play.
d. a racist police officer.

_____ 3. The main idea of paragraph 5 is that the author
a. had errands to take care of.
b. was making strawberry pancakes.
c. lives 45 minutes from midtown Manhattan.
d. changed his routine and was enjoying a leisurely day.

_____ 4. The two strangers in the lobby of the building were
a. friends of the author.
b. new residents of the building.
c. undercover police officers.
d. suspected criminals.

_____ 5. After opening the door for the police, the author was
a. thanked by the police and released to go.
b. assaulted by criminals.
c. handcuffed and taken away by the police.
d. harassed by his neighbors.

_____ 6. "Life will never be the same" for the author because he
a. can no longer trust in what he was raised to believe about manners and respect.
b. was injured by the police.
c. does not understand the criminal justice system.
d. cannot face his neighbors.

Applying Your Skills

_____ 7. The main thought pattern used in this selection is
a. definition.
b. chronological order.
c. enumeration.
d. classification.

_____ 8. In paragraph 2, the transitional word or phrase that indicates the chronological order thought pattern is
a. while.
b. on Friday.
c. because.
d. but.

_____ 9. In paragraph 9, all of the following transitional words indicate the chronological order thought pattern *except*
a. after.
b. now.
c. instead.
d. then.

_____ 10. The main thought pattern used in paragraphs 12 and 13 is
a. cause/effect.
b. summary.
c. enumeration.
d. definition.

Studying Words

_____ 11. In paragraph 2, the word *naively* means
a. innocently.
b. negatively.
c. purposely.
d. unfortunately.

_____ 12. What is the correct pronunciation of the word *charismatic* (par. 4)?
a. KARE iz mat ik
b. kar IZ ma tick
c. kar iz MAT ik
d. kare IZ ma tick

_____ 13. The word *vestibule* (par. 5) originated from which of the following languages?
a. Latin
b. French
c. German
d. Greek

_____ 14. What is the best definition of the word *dispute* as it is used in paragraph 11?
a. strive to win
b. question the truth of
c. quarrel angrily
d. engage in discussion

_____ 15. The prefix of the word *pseudo-apology* (par. 15) indicates that the apology was
a. excessive.
b. false.
c. written.
d. small.

For more practice, ask your instructor for an opportunity to work on the mastery tests that appear in the Test Bank.

Summarizing the Reading

Directions: Complete the following summary of the reading by filling in the blanks.

On ____________________, Alton Fitzgerald White was starring in ____________________ ____________________. On his way out that day, White saw ____________________ ____________________. Soon after, ____________________ arrived, responding to ____________________. After White let the police in the building, he was ____________________ along with ____________________.

Even though the police knew ____________________ and had ____________________, White was ____________________, where police ____________________ ____________________. When he was finally released, the police ____________________ and told him ____________________. The experience was ____________________; he knew it happened because ____________________.

Reading Visually

1. What does the photograph on page 273 contribute to this reading? What details do you notice about it that help you understand the author's story?
2. What does the title of this selection mean? What made the author's face "wrong"?
3. How is White's profession as an actor important to his story? (See p. 272.) Did being a well-known actor seem to help his situation with the police?

Thinking Critically about the Reading

1. Why was it significant that the strangers in the lobby were Hispanic?
2. How do you think you would react in a similar situation?
3. Have you ever been misjudged based on your outward appearance? What was your response? How was it similar to or different from the author's?

CHAPTER 8

Reading Visuals and Electronic Sources

Focusing On ... Visuals and Electronic Sources

LEARNING GOALS

This chapter will show you how to

1. Read and analyze photographs
2. Read and interpret graphics
3. Understand the types of graphics
4. Evaluate Internet sources

These signs are everyday visuals. They carry meaning with few or no words, yet they are easy to understand. In your textbooks you will also encounter a variety of visuals, including tables, graphs, charts, diagrams, maps, and photographs. This chapter focuses on reading and interpreting photographs and graphics. It also discusses evaluating another often highly visual type of information—online sources.

Students sometimes complain that reading graphics (tables, charts, diagrams, and photographs) is time-consuming. Others complain about assignments that require Internet research. These students do not realize that graphic aids are designed to make the chapter itself easier to read and that they summarize and condense information and actually save you time. In addition, Web sites and other electronic sources provide access to current, up-to-date information.

Try reading the following paragraph without looking at the diagram shown in Figure 8-1.

> Skeletal muscle fibers, like most living cells, are soft and surprisingly fragile. Yet skeletal muscles can exert tremendous power—how so? The reason they are not ripped apart as they exert force is that thousands of their fibers are bundled together by connective tissue, which provides strength and support to the muscle as a whole. Each muscle fiber is enclosed in a delicate connective tissue called an **endomysium**. Several sheathed muscle fibers are then wrapped by a coarser fibrous membrane called a **perimysium** to form a bundle of fibers called a **fascicle**. Many fascicles are bound together by an even tougher "overcoat" of connective tissue called an **epimysium**, which covers the entire muscle. The epimysia blend into strong cordlike **tendons**, or sheetlike **aponeuroses**, which attach muscles indirectly to bones, cartilages, or connective tissue coverings of each other.
>
> —Marieb, *Essentials of Human Anatomy & Physiology*, pp. 162, 164

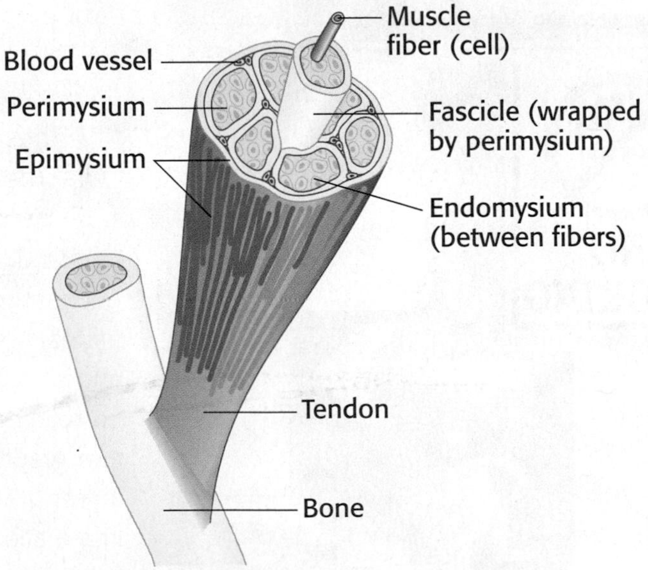

Figure 8-1 Diagram of connective tissue wrappings of skeletal muscles.
—Marieb, *Essentials of Human Anatomy & Physiology*, p. 164

Did you find the paragraph difficult and confusing? Study Figure 8-1 and then reread the paragraph.

Now the paragraph should be easier to understand. So you can see that graphics are a valuable aid, not a hindrance. This chapter will describe the various types of graphics commonly included in college textbooks. You will learn how to approach and interpret each kind. You will also learn about various types of electronic learning aids.

READ AND ANALYZE PHOTOGRAPHS

1 LEARNING GOAL Read and analyze photographs

An old saying goes, "A picture is worth a thousand words." In some cases, a photograph will substitute for words, but photos in textbooks are typically used *in addition to* words. Photographs are used to

- Spark interest
- Provide perspective
- Draw out an emotional response
- Introduce new ideas
- Offer examples
- Give students an opportunity to write, either formally or in writing journals

Use these suggestions when studying the photographs in your textbooks:

TIPS FOR STUDYING PHOTOGRAPHS

1. **Read the caption and title.** The **caption** is the text that accompanies the photo. It is usually placed above, below, or to the side of the photo. The caption will usually explain how the photo fits into the textbook discussion. When a title is provided, read it before examining the photo.
2. **Ask: What is my first overall impression?** Because photos can be so powerful, they are often chosen to elicit a strong reaction. Analyze your response to the photo, which can help you discover why the author chose to include it.
3. **Examine the details.** Look closely at the picture, examining both the foreground and the background. Details can provide clues regarding the date the photograph was taken and its location. For example, people's hairstyles and clothing often give hints as to the year or decade. Landmarks help point to location. If you saw a photo of a smiling couple with the Eiffel Tower in the background, you would know that the photo was taken in Paris, France.

4. **Look for connections to the textbook, society, or your life.** As you view the photograph and read the caption, ask yourself how the photo works with the textbook concepts. Putting the image in context will help you learn the textbook material *and* help you prepare for exams.

Here's an example of how to apply the above suggestions using the photograph from a geography textbook shown in Figure 8-2. Sample student responses are provided for each question.

Figure 8-2 A favela in Rio de Janeiro. Shantytowns are very common in South American countries, where they often develop in close proximity to wealthy neighborhoods in big cities with large populations. These shantytowns are called *favelas, barrios, colonias,* or *barriadas.* The people who live in favelas sometimes organize themselves to press the government for social services.

1. What did you learn from reading the caption? The photo was taken in Rio de Janeiro, Brazil. key vocabulary terms like *favelas, barrios, colonias,* and barriadas.

2. What are your first impressions? This is clearly a densely settled area. There are many houses built very close together on a steep hill. There are a few trees.

3. What does the photograph tell you about the income level of the people who live in this favela? It suggests the people who live here are probably poor, perhaps with limited access to electricity or other utilities like running water.

4. Compare the way poor people live in South America with the way poor people live in the United States. How is this favela similar to low-income neighborhoods in U.S. cities? It is similar as many people who live in low-income neighborhoods in the United States live in crowded conditions and receive poor services and experience social problems.

EXERCISE 8-1 Analyzing Photographs

Directions: Analyze the photos below and answer the accompanying questions.

Photograph from a Sociology book.

1. Describe what may be happening in the picture.

2. What does this picture reveal that words alone cannot?

3. Why might this photograph be included in a section of a sociology textbook chapter titled "The Costs of War"?

In a society as culturally diverse as the United States, companies try to ensure that their advertising is appealing to as many people as possible.

4. What does the term *culturally diverse society* mean?

5. Which culturally diverse groups are represented in this photo?

6. What do the hairstyles and clothing of the people in the photo tell you about their income level? (Also notice the type of car being driven.)

7. What audience do you think the advertiser is trying to reach with this photo? For example, is this ad trying to appeal to senior citizens? To college students? To recent college graduates?

EXERCISE 8-2 Analyzing Photographs

Working Together

Directions: Form groups of four students. Each student should look through various magazines and choose three photos to bring to class. Discuss each photo and caption as a group. What concept is the photo trying to illustrate? What is your reaction to each one?

READ AND INTERPRET GRAPHICS

2 LEARNING GOAL
Read and interpret graphics

In addition to photographs, you will encounter many other types of graphics in college textbooks. These include

- Tables
- Pictograms
- Cartoons
- Diagrams
- Flowcharts
- Maps
- Graphs

Read the Step-by-Step Guide to Reading Graphics on page 284, and as you read it, apply each step to the graph shown below in Figure 8-3.

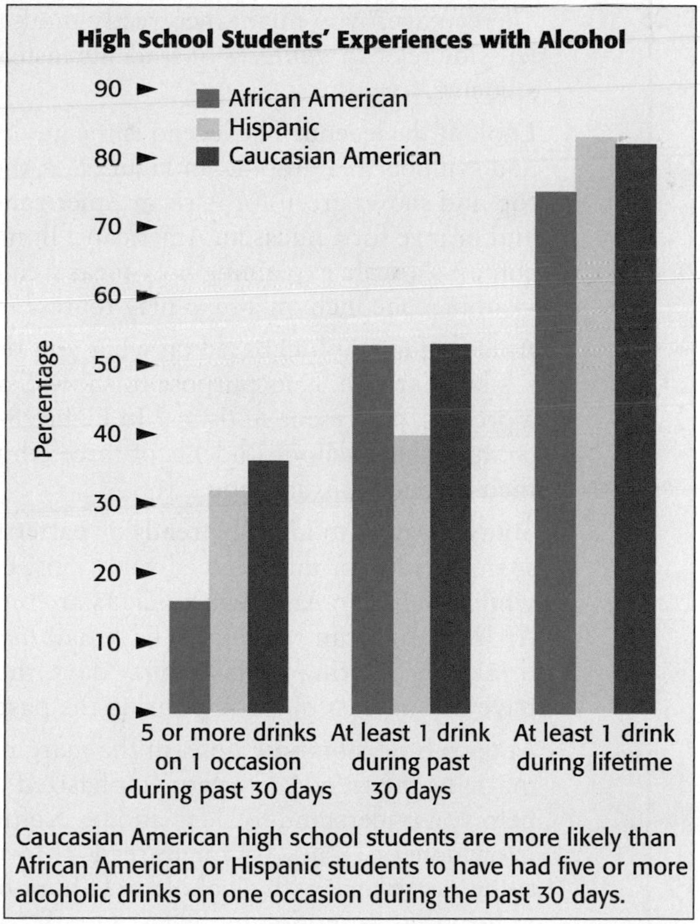

Figure 8-3 A sample graph.

—Fabes and Martin, *Exploring Child Development*, p. 454

STEP-BY-STEP GUIDE TO READING GRAPHICS

1. **Look for the references in the text.** The textbook authors will refer you to specific graphics. When you see a reference in a text, finish reading the sentence, then look at the graphic.
2. **Read the title and caption.** The title identifies the subject, and the caption provides important information about what appears in the graphic, sometimes specifying the key take-away point.
3. **Examine how the graphic is organized.** Read column headings and labels, which are sometimes turned sideways as in Figure 8-3. Labels tell you what topics or categories are being discussed, and they are important. For example, if Figure 8-3 did not specify "Percentage," you might incorrectly think the numbers along the left side refer to *numbers* of students instead of *percentage* of students.
4. **Look at the legend.** The **legend** is the guide to the colors, terms, and symbols in a graphic. In Figure 8-3, the legend appears at the top and shows green for African Americans, yellow for Hispanics, and orange for Caucasian Americans. In maps, the legend usually contains a **scale** explaining how measurements should be read, for example, one inch on a map may represent one mile.
5. **Analyze the graphic.** Based on what you see, determine the graphic's key purpose. Is its purpose to show change over time, describe a process, or present statistics? In Figure 8-3 the purpose is to compare high school students of three ethnic groups in terms of their alcohol consumption.
6. **Study the data to identify trends or patterns.** Note changes, unusual statistics, or unexplained variations. For instance, note that while Caucasian American students are much more likely than African American students to have had *five or more* alcoholic drinks once during the past thirty days, they are equally likely to have had at least *one* drink during the past thirty days.
7. **Make a brief summary note.** In the margin, jot a brief note summarizing the trend or pattern emphasized by the graphic. It will help you understand the idea and be useful for reviewing. A summary note of Figure 8-3 might read, "Most adolescents have had some experience with alcohol, and about one-third have engaged in heavy consumption in the last month."

TYPES OF GRAPHICS

3 LEARNING GOAL
Understand the types of graphics

This section will describe six types of graphics: *tables*, *graphs*, *charts*, *diagrams*, *maps*, and *infographics*.

Tables

A **table** is an organized arrangement of facts, usually numbers or statistics. A table condenses large amounts of data to allow you to read and interpret it easily. Use the steps listed below to read the table in Figure 8-4.

1. **Determine how the information is divided and arranged.** The table in Figure 8-4 is divided into four columns: moderate exercise and calories, and vigorous exercise and calories.
2. **Make comparisons and look for trends.** Do this by surveying rows and columns, noting how each compares with the others. Look for similarities, differences, or sudden or unexpected variations. Underline or highlight unusual or outstanding figures. For Figure 8-4, note that golf, light gardening, and dancing burn the same number of calories.

Calories Used During Activities

Moderate Physical Activity	Approximate Calories/Hour for a 154-lb Person*	Vigorous Physical Activity	Approximate Calories/Hour for a 154 lb Person*
Hiking	370	Running/jogging (5 mph)	590
Light gardening/yard work	330	Bicycling (>10 mph)	590
Dancing	330	Swimming (slow freestyle laps)	510
Golf (walking and carrying clubs)	330	Aerobics	480
Bicycling (<10 mph)	290	Walking (4.5 mph)	460
Walking (3.5 mph)	280	Heavy yard work (chopping wood)	440
Weight lifting (general light workout)	220	Weight lifting (vigorous effort)	440
Stretching	180	Basketball (vigorous)	440

*Calories burned per hour will be higher for persons who weigh more than 154 lbs (70 kg) and lower for persons who weigh less. Data adapted from: Centers for Disease Control and Prevention, at: cdc.gov/healthyweight/physicalactivity/index.html.

Figure 8-4 A sample table.

—Blake, *Nutrition & You*, p. 21/13

3. **Draw conclusions.** Decide what the numbers mean and what they suggest about the subject. This table appeared in a section of a nutrition textbook dealing with overweight and obesity. You can conclude that the more rigorous the activity, the more calories you will burn.

4. **Look for clues in corresponding text.** The textbook paragraph that corresponds to the table in Figure 8-4 is reprinted below.

> Research shows that regular physical activity is associated with a healthier body weight. Devoting up to 60 minutes daily to moderate-intensity activities can help prevent people at a healthy weight from becoming overweight and can aid in weight loss for those who need to lose weight. Moderately intense physical activity is the equivalent of walking 3.5 miles per hour.
>
> —Blake, Nutrition & You, p. 21/13

Notice the author explains the importance of the data presented in the table. She connects the data to the amount of activity needed to remain healthy.

EXERCISE 8-3 Analyzing a Table

Directions: Study the table in Figure 8-4 (p. 285) and answer the following questions.

1. How is the table arranged?

____

2. Several activities appear in both the Moderate Physical Activity and the Vigorous Physical Activity columns. For which activity is there the greatest difference between moderate and vigorous activity?

____

3. For what activity did the amount of calories burned surprise you?

____

Graphs

There are four types of graphs: *bar, multiple bar, stacked bar*, and *linear*. Each plots a set of points on a set of axes.

Bar Graphs A **bar graph** is often used to make comparisons between quantities or amounts, and is particularly useful in showing changes that occur with passing time. Bar graphs usually are constructed to emphasize differences. The graphs shown in Figure 8-5 compare lottery players with the general population according to age and education.

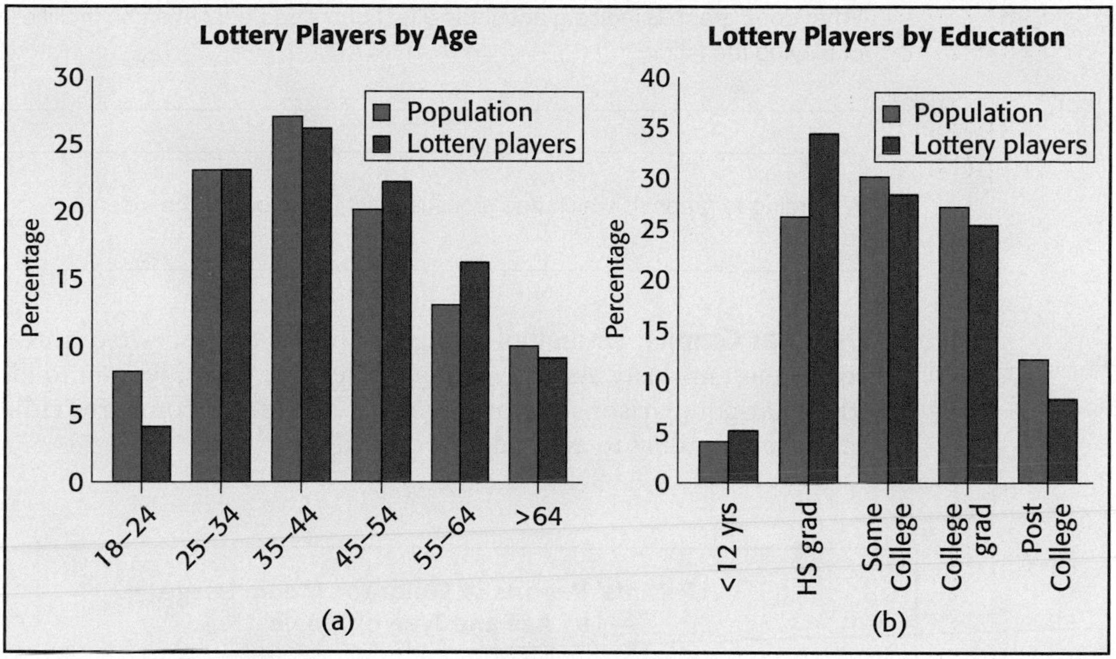

Figure 8-5 A sample bar graph

Two figures showing (a) age and (b) education of Colorado lottery players compared to the general population.

—Bennett et al., *Statistical Reasoning for Everyday Life*, p. 233

EXERCISE 8-4 Analyzing a Bar Graph

Directions: Study the graphs shown in Figure 8-5 and answer the following questions.

1. How are both graphs organized?

____

____

2. In graph A, how does the percentage of lottery players compare with the percentage of the general population in each age group?

____

____

3. In graph A, which age groups play the lottery at a higher rate than their population level?

____

4. What does graph B indicate about the effect of college education on the likelihood of playing the lottery?

____

____

5. According to graph A, which age group is least likely to play the lottery?

____

Multiple Bar Graphs A **multiple bar graph** makes at least two or three comparisons simultaneously. As you read multiple bar graphs, be sure to identify exactly what comparisons are being made. Figure 8-6 compares children's media usage according to age and type of media.

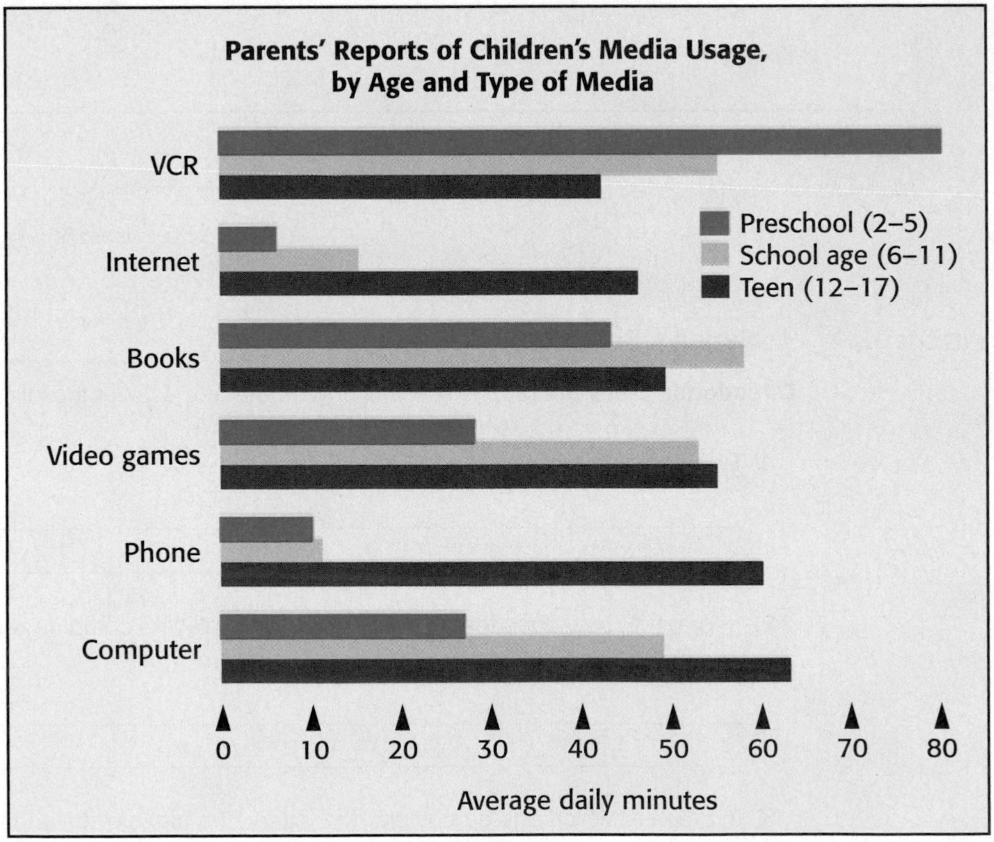

Figure 8-6 A sample multiple bar graph.

—Fabes and Martin, *Exploring Child Development,* p. 281

EXERCISE 8-5 Analyzing a Multiple Bar Graph

Directions: Study the graph shown in Figure 8-6 and answer the following questions.

1. How is this graph organized?

____

____

2. For which type of media is there the greatest difference between preschool usage and teen usage?

____

3. What patterns are evident?

____

____

____

____

Stacked Bar Graphs A **stacked bar graph** is an arrangement of data in which bars are placed one on top of another rather than side by side. This variation is often used to emphasize whole/part relationships. Stacked bar graphs show the relationship of a part to an entire group or class. The graph in Figure 8-7 (p. 290) shows day care arrangements by three ethnic groups: Caucasian American, African American, and Hispanic. Stacked bar graphs also allow numerous comparisons. The graph in Figure 8-7 compares five different day care arrangements for the three ethnic groups: parent, relative, nanny, family child care, and center-based care.

Linear Graphs A **linear, or line, graph** plots and connects points along a vertical and a horizontal axis. A linear graph allows more data points than a bar graph. Consequently, it is used to present more detailed and/or larger quantities of information. A linear graph may compare two variables; if so, then it consists of a single line. Often, however, linear graphs are used to compare relationships among several sets of variables, and multiple lines are included. The graph shown in Figure 8-8 (p. 290) examines the number of Americans with diabetes.

Linear graphs are usually used to display continuous data—data connected in time or events occurring in sequence. The data in Figure 8-8 are continuous as they move from 1980 to 2007.

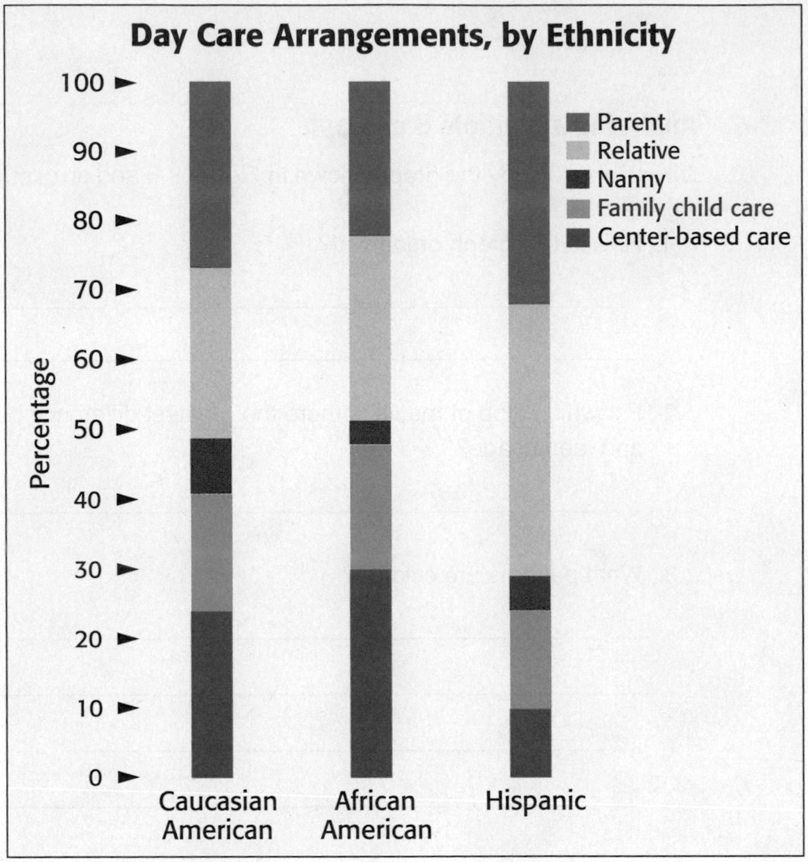

Figure 8-7 A sample stacked bar graph.

—Fabes and Martin, *Exploring Child Development,* p. 196

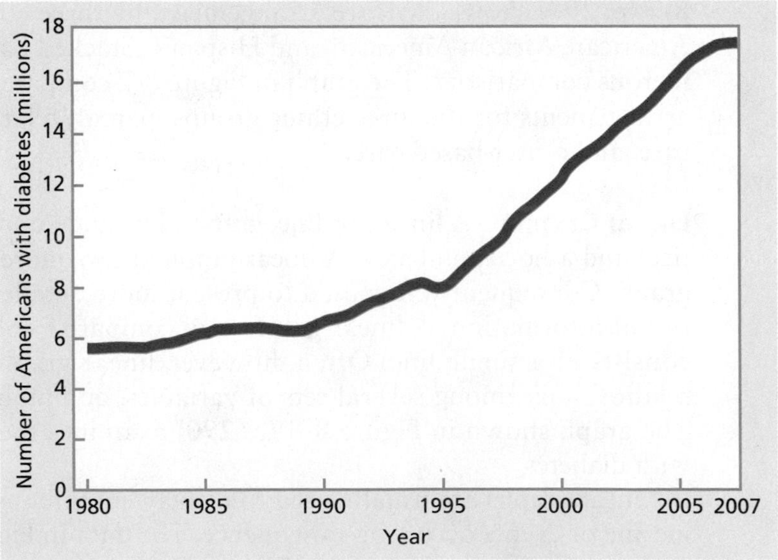

Figure 8-8 A sample linear graph.

—Lynch et al., *Choosing Health,* p. 273

EXERCISE 8-6 Analyzing a Linear Graph

Directions: Study the graph shown in Figure 8-8 and answer the following questions.

1. Describe the purpose of the graph.

____

2. What trend is evident?

____

3. Think of some reasons the rate of diabetes has increased so dramatically.

____

Charts

Three types of charts are commonly used in college textbooks: *pie charts, organizational charts*, and *flowcharts.*

Pie Charts **Pie charts,** sometimes called circle graphs, are used to show whole/part relationships or to depict how given parts of a unit have been divided or classified. They enable the reader to compare the parts with each other as well as to compare each part with the whole. The chart in Figure 8-9 on the following page compares the living arrangements of children in the United States according to race/ethnic origin and compares each with the national average.

EXERCISE 8-7 Analyzing Charts

Directions: Study the charts shown in Figure 8-9 (p. 292) and answer the following questions.

1. What three categories of living arrangements are compared?

____

2. What living arrangement changes least from group to group?

____

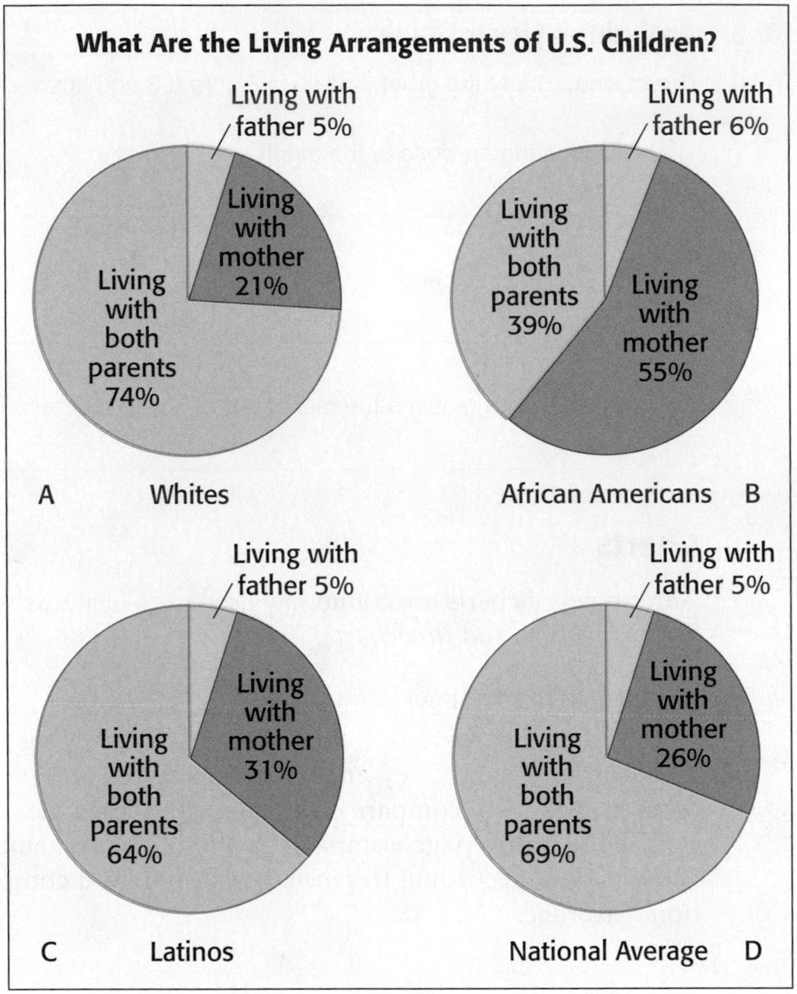

Figure 8-9 Sample pie charts.

—Henslin, *Social Problems,* p. 368

3. What other patterns are evident?

____

____

____

____

Organizational Charts An **organizational chart** divides an organization, such as a corporation, a hospital, or a university, into its administrative parts, staff positions, or lines of authority. Figure 8-10 shows the organization of an American political party. It reveals that party members belong to precinct and ward organizations. From these organizations, county committees are formed. County committee members are represented on state committees, and state delegates are chosen for national positions.

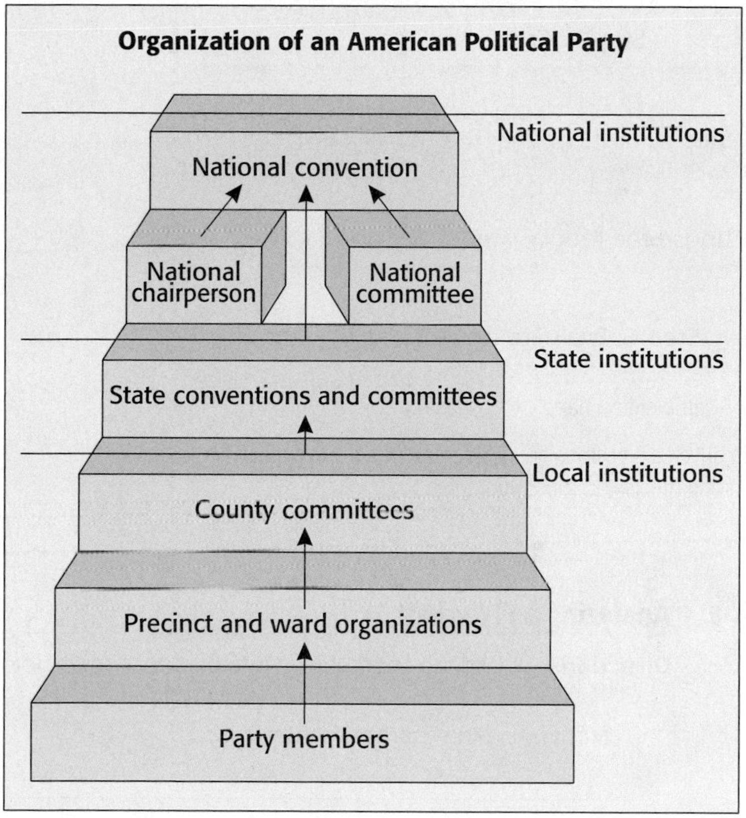

Figure 8-10 A sample organizational chart.

—Lineberry and Edwards, *Government in America,* p. 253

Flowcharts A **flowchart** is a specialized type of chart that shows how a process or procedure works. Lines or arrows are used to indicate the direction (route or routes) through the procedure. Various shapes (boxes, circles, rectangles) enclose what is done at each stage or step. You could draw, for example, a flowchart to describe how to apply for and obtain a student loan or how to locate a malfunction in your car's electrical system. Refer to the flowchart shown in Figure 8-11 (p. 294), taken from a business marketing textbook. It describes the steps in the development of an advertising campaign.

Steps to Develop an Advertising Campaign
Step 1: Understand the Target Audience
Step 2: Establish Message and Budget Objectives
Step 3: Create the Ads
Step 4: Pretest What the Ads Will Say
Step 5: Choose the Media Type(s) and Media Schedule
Step 6: Evaluate the Advertising

Figure 8-11 A sample flowchart.

Developing an advertising campaign includes a series of steps that will ensure that the advertising meets communication objectives.

—Solomon et al., *Marketing*, p. 406

To read flowcharts effectively, use the following suggestions:

1. **Identify what process the flowchart shows.**
2. **Next, follow the chart, using the arrows and reading each step.** Start at the top or far left of the chart.
3. **When you have finished, summarize the process in your own words.** Try to draw the chart from memory without referring to the text. Compare your drawing with the chart and note discrepancies.

EXERCISE 8-8 Analyzing a Flowchart

Directions: Using the chart shown in Figure 8-11, complete the following tasks.

1. Summarize the chart's organization.

____

2. Explain the steps in the process in your own words.

____

____.

Diagrams

Diagrams are often included in technical and scientific as well as many other college texts to explain processes. Diagrams are intended to help you visualize relationships between parts and understand sequences. They may also be used to illustrate ideas or concepts. Reading diagrams differs from reading other types of graphics in that diagrams often correspond to fairly large segments of text, requiring you to switch back and forth frequently between the text and the diagram to determine which part of the process each paragraph refers to. Figure 8-12, taken from a biology textbook, shows the structure of a nail. It accompanies the following text:

> A **nail** is a scalelike modification of the epidermis that corresponds to the hoof or claw of other animals. Each nail has a *free edge*, a *body*, (visible attached portion), and a *root* (embedded in the skin). The borders of the nail are overlapped by skin folds, called *nail folds*. The thick proximal nail is commonly called the *cuticle*. The stratus basale of the epidermis extends beneath the nail as the *nail bed*. Its thickened proximal area, called the *nail matrix*, is responsible for nail growth. The region over the thickened nail matrix that appears as a white crescent is called the *lunula*.
>
> —Marieb, *Essentials of Human Anatomy & Physiology,* p. 106

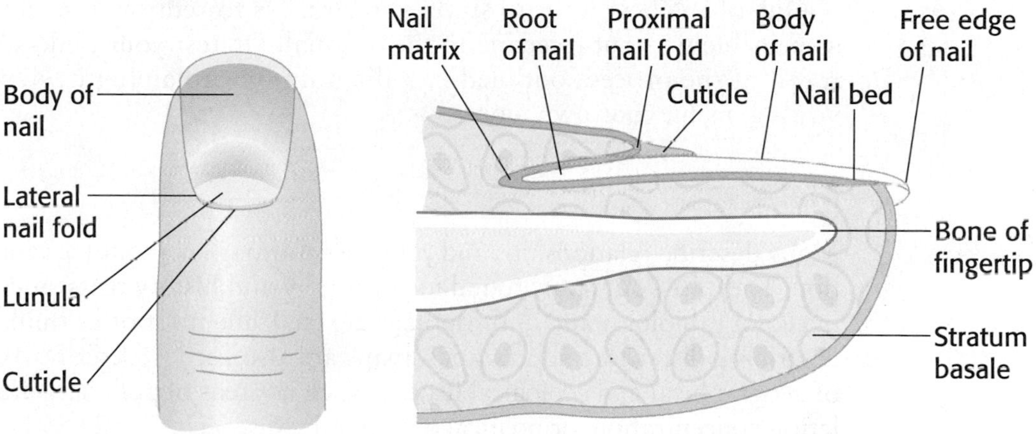

Structure of a nail. Surface view (left) and longitudinal section of the distal part of a finger (right), showing nail parts and the nail matrix that forms the nail.

Figure 8-12 Text and diagram showing the structure of the nail.

—Marieb, *Essentials of Human Anatomy & Physiology,* p. 106

EXERCISE 8-9 Analyzing a Diagram

Directions: Study the diagram and text in Figure 8-12 and answer the following questions.

1. What is the purpose of the diagram?

____

2. Define the term *cuticle.*

___

3. What part of the nail is responsible for nail growth?

___

4. Could you accurately draw a diagram of the nail by referring only to the text, without referring to the diagram?

___

Because diagrams of processes and their corresponding text are often difficult, complicated, or highly technical, plan on reading these sections more than once. Read first to grasp the overall process. In subsequent readings, focus on the details of the process, examining each step and understanding its progression.

One of the best ways to study a diagram is to redraw it in as much detail as possible without referring to the original. Or, test your understanding and recall of the process outlined in a diagram by explaining it, step by step in writing, using your own words.

Maps

Maps describe relationships and provide information about location and direction. They are commonly found in geography and history texts, and also appear in ecology, biology, and anthropology texts. While most of us think of maps as describing distances and locations, maps are also used to describe the placement of geographical and ecological features such as areas of pollution, areas of population concentration, or political data (voting districts).

When reading maps, use the following steps:

1. **Read the caption.** This identifies the subject of the map.
2. **Use the legend or key to identify the symbols or codes used.**
3. **Note distance scales.**
4. **Study the map, looking for trends or key points.** Often the text that accompanies the map states the key points the map illustrates.
5. **Try to visualize, or create a mental picture of, the map.**
6. **As a learning and study aid, write, in your own words, a statement of what the map shows.**

The map in Figure 8-13 shows the degree of risk for tornadoes in the United States.

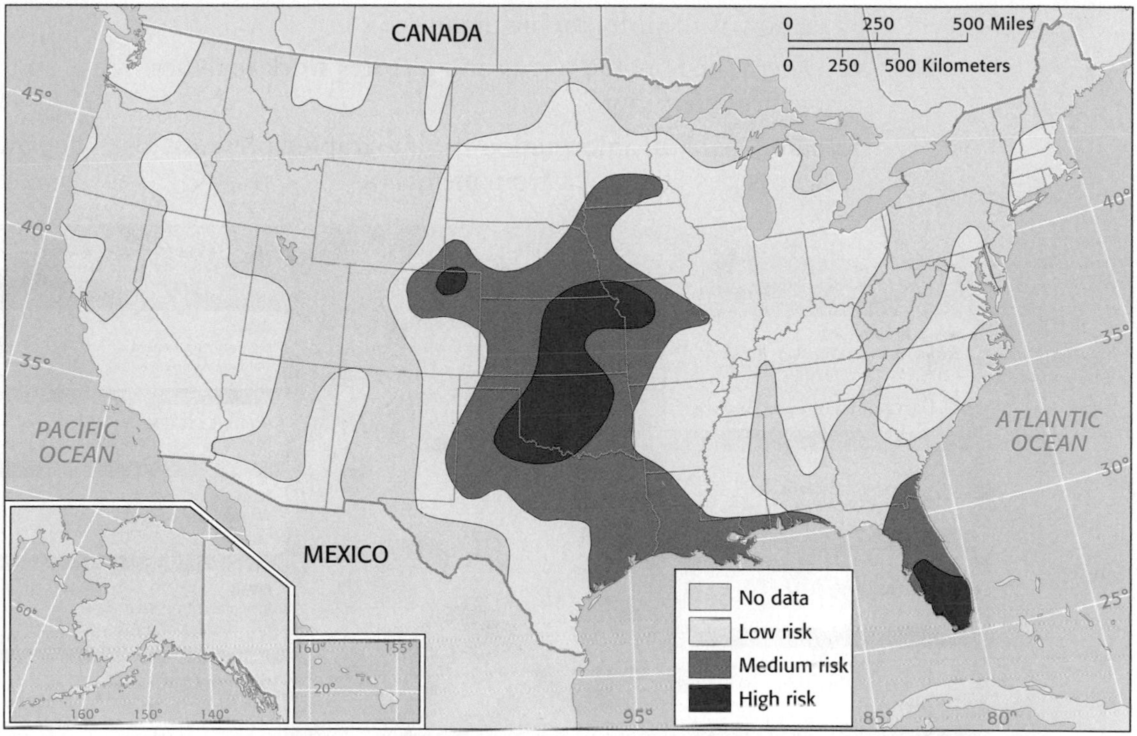

Tornado risk in the United States is greatest in the southern plains, the Southeast (especially central Florida), and the Midwest. (Alaska and Hawaii not to scale.)

Figure 8-13 A sample map.

–Bergman and Renwick, *Introduction to Geography*, p. 69

Infographics

Graphic designers are often looking for new, visually interesting ways to present information. A relatively new type of graphic is the infographic. **Infographics** usually combine several types of visual aids into one, often merging photographs with text, diagrams or tables. Unlike other graphics, infographics are sometimes designed to stand on their own; they do not necessarily repeat or summarize what is in the text. Figure 8-14 (p. 298) shows an example from a health book.

To read an infographic, use the following guidelines:

1. **Identify the subject.** What is the purpose of the graphic?
2. **Identify how you should follow the flow of the infographic.** Should you read it top to bottom, left to right, or clockwise or

counterclockwise? Look for visual clues, such as arrows or headings, to determine where to start.

3. **Examine how the artist has chosen to present the information.** That is, how is the infographic organized?
4. **Determine how the words and pictures work together.** What do the pictures contribute?
5. **Summarize the information the infographic presents.** Use your own words. Try to draw it from memory.

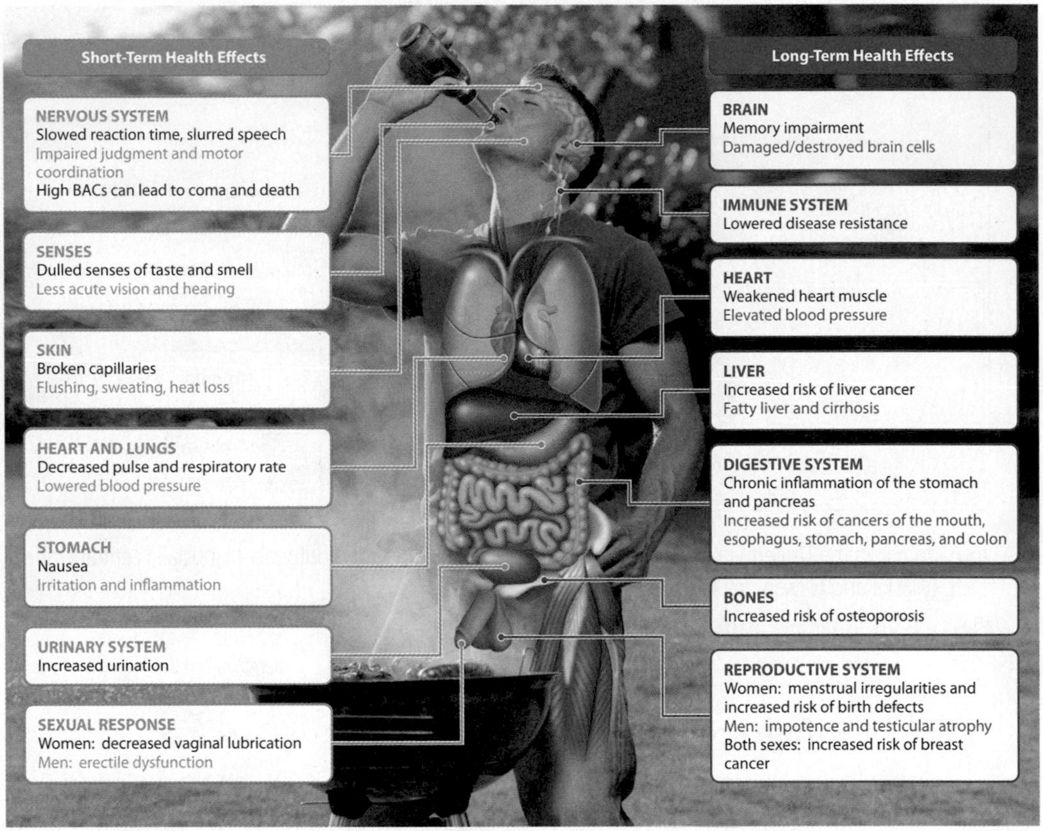

Figure 8-14 A sample infographic.

–Donatelle, *Health*, p. 229

EXERCISE 8-10 Evaluating Graphics

Directions: Bring a copy of your local newspaper or *USA Today* to class. After your instructor forms groups, each group should select and tear out four or five graphics. For each graphic, the group should identify the type of graphic, analyze its purpose, and identify the trend or pattern it reveals. Groups should then discuss what other types of graphics could be used to accomplish the author's purpose. Each group should submit one graphic to the instructor along with a brief summary of the members' analysis.

EXERCISE 8-11 Planning Graphics

Working Together

Directions: Working in pairs, discuss what type(s) of graphic(s) would be most useful in presenting each of the following sets of information. Share and compare your findings with other teams.

1. Damage done to ancient carved figures by sulfur dioxide in the air
2. A comparison of the types of products the United States imports with those it exports
3. Changes in worker productivity each year from 1970 through 2010 in Japan, France, Germany, and the United States
4. The probabilities of being murdered, broken down by various racial and ethnic groups in the United States
5. Foreign revenue, total revenue, foreign operating profit, foreign assets, and total assets for the ten largest American multinational corporations
6. Living arrangements (one parent, two parents, neither parent) for white, black, and Hispanic-origin children under 18 years of age in 1970, 1980, 1990, 2000, and 2010.
7. The basic components of a robot's manipulator arm
8. A description of how the AIDS virus affects the immune system
9. Sites of the earliest Neanderthal discoveries in Western Europe
10. Number of receipts of, and profits for, three types of businesses: sole proprietorships, partnerships, and corporations

LEARNING STYLE TIPS

If you tend to be a …	Then study graphics by …
Spatial learner	Examining the graphic so that you can visualize it
Verbal learner	Writing sentences that summarize what the graphic shows

EVALUATE INTERNET SOURCES

4 LEARNING GOAL
Evaluate Internet sources

Although the Internet contains a great deal of valuable information and a great many resources, it also contains rumor, gossip, and misinformation. In other words, not all Internet sources are trustworthy. You must evaluate each source before accepting it.

Discovering the Purpose of a Web Site

There are thousands of Web sites, and they vary widely in purpose. Table 8-1 summarizes five primary types of Web sites.

TABLE 8-1 Types of Web Sites

Type	Purpose	Description	URL Suffix
Informational	To present facts, information, and research data	May contain reports, statistical data, results of research studies, and reference materials	.edu or .gov
News	To provide current information on local, national, and international news	Often supplements print newspapers, periodicals, and television news programs	.com
Advocacy	To promote a particular cause or point of view	May be concerned with a controversial issue; often sponsored by nonprofit groups	.org
Personal	To provide information about an individual and his or her interests and accomplishments	May list publications or include the individual's résumé	URL will vary. May contain .com or .org or may contain a tilde (˜)
Commercial	To promote goods or services	May provide news and information related to a company's products	.com

Evaluating the Content of a Web Site

When evaluating the content of a Web site, evaluate its appropriateness, its source, its level of technical detail, its presentation, its completeness, and its links.

Evaluate a Site's Appropriateness To be worthwhile, a Web site should contain the information you need. It should answer one or more of your search questions. If the site only touches upon answers to your questions but does not address them in detail, check the links on the site to see if they will lead you to more detailed information. If they do not, search for a more useful site.

Evaluate the Source Another important step in evaluating a Web site is to determine its source. Ask yourself, "Who is the sponsor?" and "Why was this site put up on the Web?" The sponsor of a Web site is the person or organization who paid for it to be created and placed on the Web. The sponsor will often suggest the purpose of a Web site. For example, a Web site sponsored by Nike is designed to promote its products, while a site sponsored by a university library is designed to help students learn to use its resources more effectively.

If you are not sure who sponsors a Web site, check its URL, its copyright, and the links it offers. The ending of the URL often suggests the type of sponsorship. The copyright indicates the owner of the site. Links may also reveal the sponsor. Some links may lead to commercial advertising, while others may lead to sites sponsored by nonprofit groups.

Evaluate the Level of Technical Detail Some sites may provide information that is too sketchy for your search purposes; others assume a level of background knowledge or technical sophistication that you lack. For example, if you are writing a short, introductory-level paper on threats to the survival of marine animals, the Web site of the Scripps Institution of Oceanography may be too technical and contain more information than you need. Unless you have some previous knowledge in that field, you may want to search for a different Web site.

Evaluate the Presentation Information on a Web site should be presented clearly and should be well written. If you find a site that is not clear and well written, you should be suspicious of it. If the author did not take time to present ideas clearly and correctly, he or she may not have taken time to collect accurate information either.

Evaluate the Completeness Determine whether the site provides complete information on its topic. Does it address all aspects of the topic that you feel it should? For example, if a Web site on Important Twentieth-Century American Poets does not mention Robert Frost, then the site is incomplete. If you discover that a site is incomplete, search for sites that provide a more thorough treatment of the topic.

Evaluate the Links Many reputable sites supply links to other related sites. Make sure that the links work and are current. Also check to see if the sites to which you were sent are reliable sources of information. If the links do not work or the sources appear unreliable, you should question the reliability of the site itself. Also determine whether the links provided are comprehensive or only present a representative sample. Either is acceptable, but the site should make clear the nature of the links it is providing.

EXERCISE 8-12 Evaluating the Content of Web Sites

Directions: Suppose you are writing a research paper on species extinction and you need to find out which species are currently in danger of becoming extinct. Use a search engine to locate at least three Web sites that address the topic. Evaluate the content of the sites. Explain why you would either trust or distrust the content on each site.

Evaluating the Accuracy of a Web Site

When using information on a Web site for an academic paper, it is important to be sure that you have found accurate information. One way to determine the accuracy of a Web site is to compare it with print sources (periodicals and books) on the same topic. If you find a wide discrepancy between the Web site and the printed sources, do not trust the Web site. Another way to determine accuracy of the information on a site is to compare it with other Web sites that address the same topic. If discrepancies exist, further research is needed to determine which site is more accurate.

The site itself will also provide clues about the accuracy of its information. Ask yourself the following questions:

EVALUATING A WEB SITE'S ACCURACY

1. **Are the author's name and credentials provided?** A well-known writer with established credentials is likely to author only reliable, accurate information. If no author is given, you should question whether the information is accurate.
2. **Is contact information for the author included on the site?** Often, a site provides an e-mail address where the author may be contacted.
3. **Is the information complete, or in summary form?** If it is a summary, use the site to find the original source. Original information has less chance of containing errors and is usually preferred in academic papers.

4. **If opinions are offered, are they clearly presented as opinions?** Authors who disguise their opinions as facts are not trustworthy.
5. **Does the site provide a list of works cited?** As with any form of research, sources used to put information up on a Web site must be documented. If sources are not credited, you should question the accuracy of the Web site.

It may be helpful to determine whether the information is available in print form. If it is, try to obtain the print version. Errors may occur when the article or essay is put up on the Web. Web sites move, change, and delete information, so it may be difficult for a reader of an academic paper to locate the Web site that you used in writing it. Also, page numbers are easier to cite in print sources than in electronic ones.

EXERCISE 8-13 Evaluating the Accuracy of Web Sites

Directions: Suppose you are preparing for a class discussion on surveillance cameras and the right to privacy. Use a search engine to locate at least three Web sites that address the topic. Evaluate the accuracy of the sites. Explain why you would either trust or distrust the content on each site.

Evaluating the Timeliness of a Web Site

Although the Web is well known for providing up-to-the-minute information, not all Web sites are current. Evaluate the timeliness by checking

- the date on which the Web site was posted (put on the Web)
- the date when the document you are using was added
- the date when the site was last revised
- the date when the links were last checked

This information is usually provided at the end of the site's home page or at the end of the document you are using.

EXERCISE 8-14 Evaluate the Timeliness of Web Sites

Directions: Suppose you are writing an essay on the use of cell phones as a teaching tool in classrooms. Use a search engine to locate at least three Web sites that address the topic. Evaluate the timeliness of the sites. Explain why you would either trust or distrust the content on each site.

SELF-TEST SUMMARY

1 How do you analyze photographs?	When looking at a photo, read its caption, read its title, from a general impression, then examine its details. Understand how the photo illustrates text concepts.
2 How should you read and analyze graphics?	To analyze graphics, read the title and caption, look at the legend, study the graph's organization and data, and make a brief summary note.
3 How many types of graphics are there, what are they, and how are they used?	There are six major types of graphics: 1. **Tables** are used to arrange and organize facts. 2. **Graphs**—including bar, multiple bar, stacked bar, and linear graphs—are used to make comparisons between or among sets of information. 3. **Charts**—including pie charts, organizational charts, and flowcharts—present visual displays of information. 4. **Diagrams** demonstrate physical relationships between parts and display sequences. 5. **Maps** describe information about location and direction. 6. **Infographics** usually combine several types of visuals and can often stand alone.
4 What factors should you consider when evaluating a Web site?	Consider the site's purpose to determine its type and usefulness. Evaluate the content: analyze the site's appropriateness, source, level of technical detail, presentation, completeness, and links. Judge the accuracy of a site by considering the author credentials and contact information, completeness of information, opinionated content, and availability of works cited list. Check the timeliness of the site by checking the posting and revision dates.

GOING ONLINE

1. **Evaluating an Internet Source**
   The extension .org at the end of a Web site signals a nonprofit organization. The materials provided on a nonprofit organization's Web site may or may not be reliable. Choose a nonprofit Web site and evaluate it on the basis of the criteria discussed in this chapter: purpose, content, accuracy, and timeliness.

2. **Tips for Creating Effective Graphics**
   This chapter focused on reading graphics effectively. However, in your college assignments you may wish to create graphics to include with your writing. Conduct an Internet search on the topic of how to create effective graphics. Working with a small group, compile a list of ten tips for creating effective graphics. Share your list with the class.

CHAPTER 8

MASTERY TEST 1 Graphic Skills

This Mastery Test can be completed in MyReadingLab.

Name ______________________ Section ____________

Date ____________ Number right ________ × 10 points = Score ________

Directions: Use the text and table below to select the choice that best completes each of the statements that follow.

TABLE A What Cohabitation Means: Does It Make a Difference?

		After 5 to 7 years			
				Of Those Still Together	
What Cohabitation Means	**Percent of Couples**	**Split Up**	**Still Together**	**Married**	**Cohabitating**
Substitute for Marriage	10%	35%	65%	37%	63%
Step toward Marriage	46%	31%	69%	73%	27%
Trial Marriage	15%	51%	49%	66%	34%
Coresidential Dating	29%	46%	54%	61%	39%

Source: Recomputed from Bianchi and Casper 2000.

From the outside, all cohabitation may look the same, but not to the people who are living together. As you can see from Table A, for about 10 percent of couples, cohabitation is a substitute for marriage. These couples consider themselves married but for some reason don't want a marriage certificate. Some object to marriage on philosophical grounds ("What difference does a piece of paper make?"); others do not yet have a legal divorce from a spouse. Almost half of cohabitants (46 percent) view cohabitation as a step on the path to marriage. For them, cohabitation is more than "going steady" but less than engagement. Another 15 percent of couples are simply "giving it a try." They want to see what marriage to one another might be like. For the least committed, about 29 percent, cohabitation is a form of dating. It provides a dependable source of sex and emotional support.

—Henslin, *Sociology*, p. 483

_____ 1. One purpose of the table is to compare
   a. marital success of those who cohabitate (live together) with those who marry.
   b. the meaning of cohabitation with the status of the relationship after 5 to 7 years.
   c. couples who cohabitate and couples who end up getting a divorce.
   d. characteristics of couples who split up with those of couples that stay together.

_____ 2. According to the table, the meaning of cohabitation that is most common is
a. substitute for marriage.
b. step toward marriage.
c. trial marriage.
d. coresidential dating.

_____ 3. After 5 to 7 years, which meaning of cohabitation shows the largest percentage of couples still cohabitating?
a. substitute for marriage
b. step toward marriage
c. trial marriage
d. coresidential dating

_____ 4. Couples in the coresidential dating category regard cohabitation as
a. a source of sex and emotional support.
b. a means of going steady.
c. a way to give marriage a try without thc legal issues.
d. a step toward marriage.

_____ 5. Of the following facts, the only one that appears *both* in the text and in the graphic is
a. 65 percent of couples who regard cohabitation as a substitute for marriage are still together five years later.
b. of trial marriages, only 28 percent of the couples actually marry after five years.
c. 15 percent of couples who cohabitate are doing so to give marriage a try.
d. coresidential dating results in the second largest number of split-ups.

CHAPTER 8

MASTERY TEST 2 Graphic Skills

This **Mastery Test** can be completed in **MyReadingLab**.

Name ______________________________ Section ______________

Date __________________ Number right* ________ × 10 points = Score ________

Directions: Study the graph below from a sociology text and answer the questions that follow.

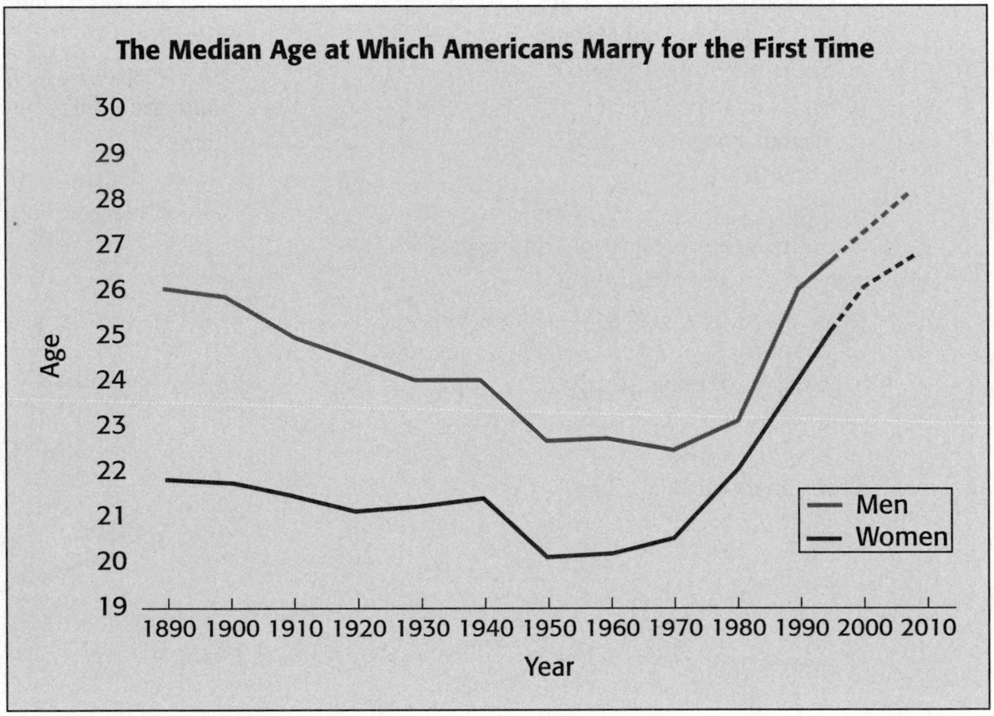

—Henslin, *Sociology,* p. 489

_____ 1. What is the purpose of the graph?
   a. to compare the ages at which men and women marry from 1890 to 2010
   b. to show that the age at which Americans marry is decreasing
   c. to show that men and women marry at similar ages
   d. to compare how men and women have changed from 1890 to 2010

_____ 2. In which of the following years was there the largest difference in ages between men and women?
   a. 1990
   b. 1930
   c. 1970
   d. 1910

_____ 3. Which of the following statements describes the trend shown between 1890 and 1990?

a. Women married at an older age than men.
b. Men married at an older age than women.
c. Men married older women.
d. Women married younger men.

_____ 4. Which marriage trend does the graph show?

a. The age gap between men and women has been gradually narrowing.
b. Women's average age has been steadily decreasing throughout history.
c. Men's average age has shown little change.
d. Women's average age has shown a steady decline.

Directions: Study the pie chart below and answer the questions that follow.

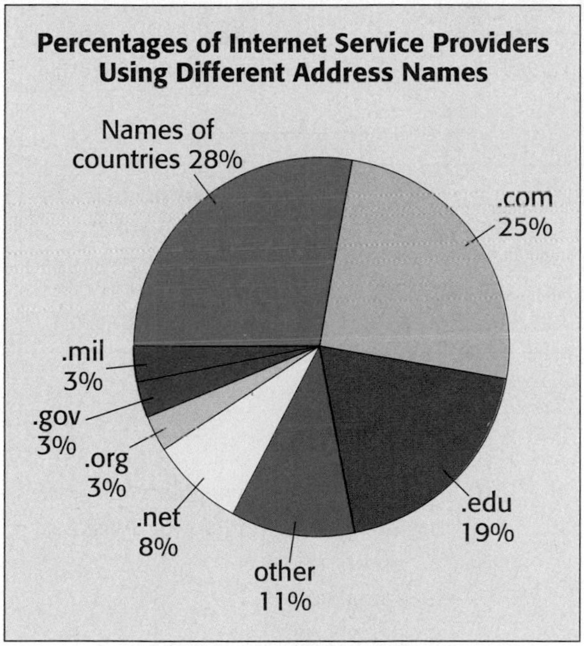

_____ 5. Which of the following address names is used by the second largest percentage of Internet service providers?

a. .edu
b. other
c. .com
d. names of countries

_____ 6. Which of the following address names contain the same percentages of Internet service providers?

a. .mil and .net
b. .edu and .com
c. .gov and .org
d. .com and names of countries

_____ 7. What percentage of Internet service providers use the name of a country in their addresses?

a. 25 percent
b. 8 percent
c. 10 percent
d. 28 percent

Directions: Study the chart below and answer the questions that follow.

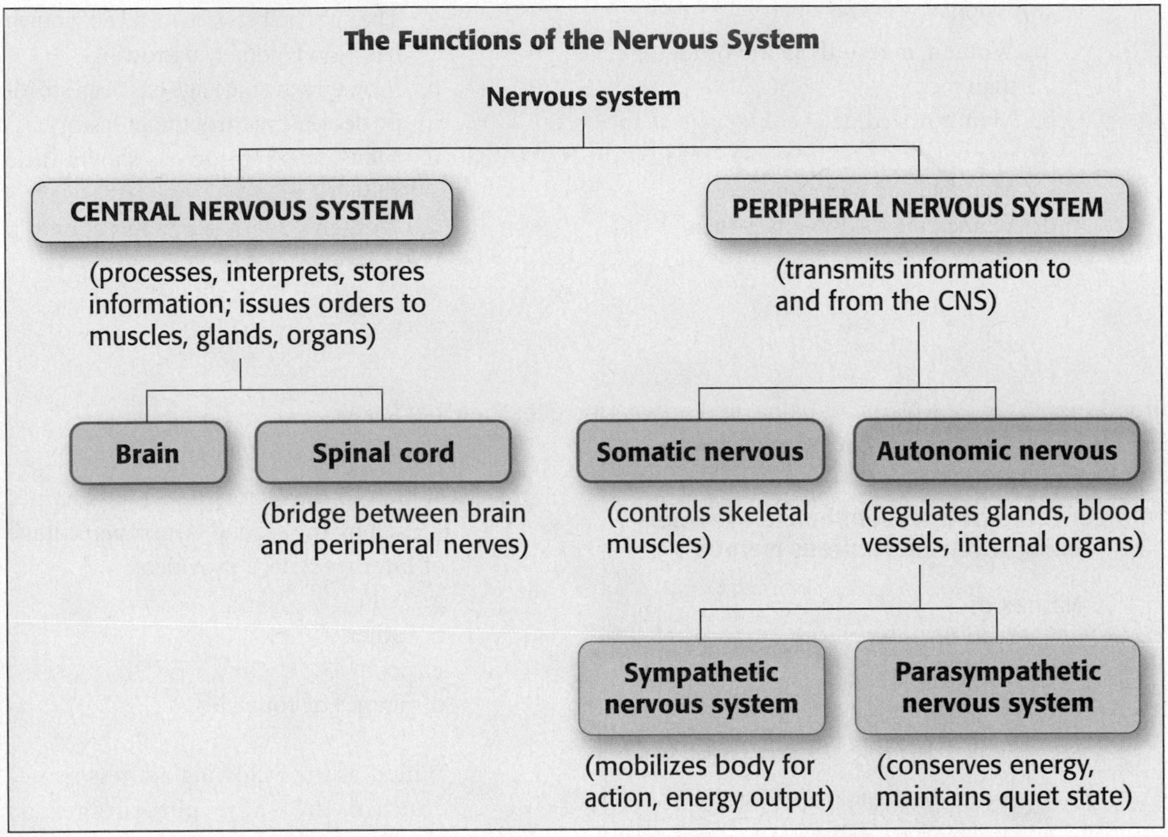

_____ 8. The brain is part of the
a. spinal cord.
b. autonomic nervous system.
c. peripheral nervous system.
d. central nervous system.

_____ 9. Which of the following nervous systems controls muscles?
a. somatic nervous system
b. autonomic nervous system
c. brain
d. central nervous system

_____ 10. Which of the following nervous systems has the greatest number of divisions?
a. autonomic
b. spinal cord
c. peripheral
d. sympathetic

CHAPTER 8

MASTERY TEST 3 Reading Selection

This Mastery Test can be completed in MyReadingLab.

Name ______________________________ Section ____________

Date ____________ Number right* ________ × 10 points = Score ________

Who Needs Marriage?

Mary Ann Schwartz and Barbara Marliene Scott

This selection, taken from a sociology textbook, examines whether marriage is relevant anymore. Before reading, try to predict what facts the author might talk about.

Vocabulary Preview

contours (par. 2) shape

socioeconomic (par. 4) social and economic

median (par. 4) middle

sociopolitical construction (par 6) something made up by society and politics

Current Trends in American Marriages and Families.

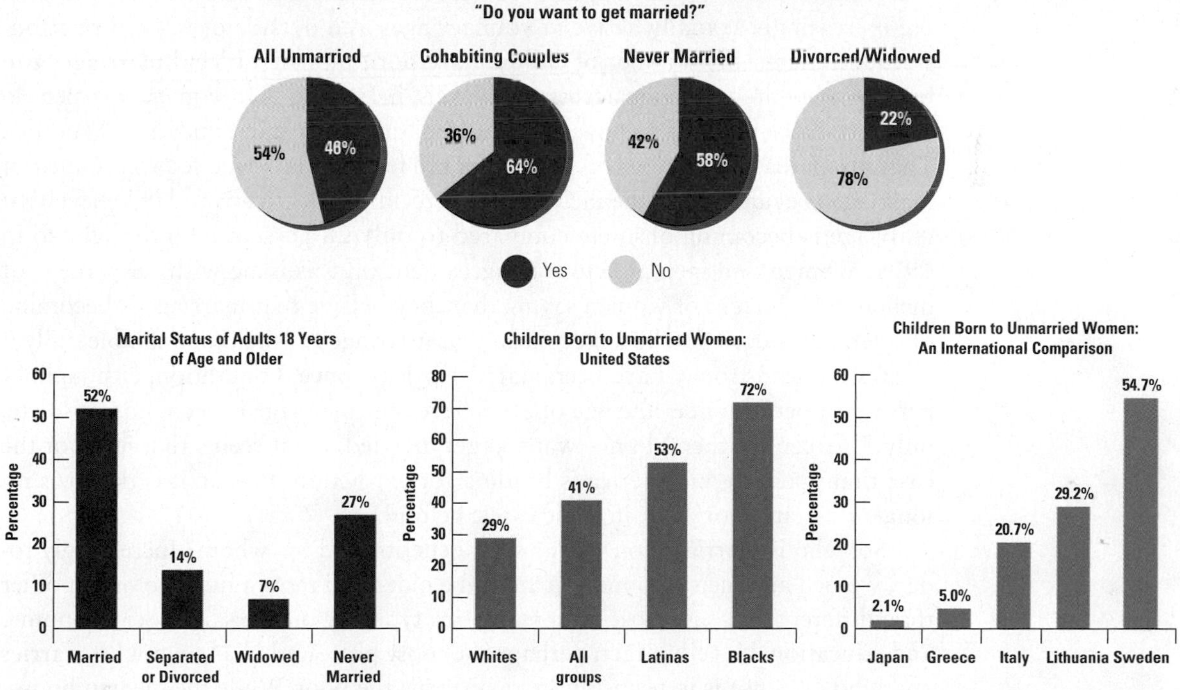

Figure A

Source: Belinda Luscombe, 2010. "Marriage: What's It Good For?" *Time* magazine. Vol. 176, No. 22, pp. 48–56.

*To calculate the number right, use items 1–10 under "Mastery Test Skills Check."

1 Why don't people marry? Consider the following: In 1960, almost 70 percent of American adults were married; today only about one-half are. Back then, two-thirds of adults in their twenties were married; in 2008 only 16 percent were. And in a reversal of past trends, college graduates are now far more likely to marry (64 percent) than those without a college education (48 percent). In addition, eight times as many children are born to unmarried mothers today than in 1960 (see Figure A, p. 311).

2 So, what is going on with America's marriages and families? According to Belinda Luscombe of the Pew Research Center, when institutions such as these that are so very vital to human experience shift and change shape in the course of a couple of generations it is noteworthy. It is so noteworthy that *Time* magazine devoted its November 29, 2010 cover to the topic under the heading: Who Needs Marriage? Inside, the results of a 2010 nationwide poll conducted by the Pew Research Center in association with *Time* magazine revealed the contours of modern American marriages and new American families.

3 What do people want and expect out of marriage and family life today? Whatever the appeal and the reasons why people married in the past, in purely practical terms, for many people, marriage is not as necessary as it used to be. In the overall population, only 52 percent of adults 18 years old and older are married; 27 percent have never married and the remaining 21 percent have been married but are now either separated, divorced or widowed. American women and men are increasingly sexually active at younger ages and outside of marital relationships, an increasing number of children are born outside of legal marriage, and both of these are occurring across class levels, indicating that women and men do not have to be married to have sex, have children or attain educational success. That an increasing number of Americans are less and less wedded to the idea of marriage is evidenced in the fact that 39 percent of Americans today believe that marriage is becoming obsolete compared to only 28 percent who thought so in 1978. Women and men are close in agreement on this issue with 36 percent of men and 41 percent of women saying that they believe that marriage is becoming obsolete. This does not, however, mean that marriage is dead. For example, fully 7 in 10 Americans today have been married at least once. In addition, although 44 percent of people under the age of 30 believe that marriage is becoming obsolete, only 5 percent of them do not want to get married. So, it seems that it is not the case that marriage in America is heading for extinction. Rather, it is that it is no longer obligatory or even, in some cases, helpful.

4 So, who is marriage for, what are its benefits, and for whom? Increasingly today, women and men who marry tend to be older and more similar to one another than different. That is, those who marry are typically on the same socioeconomic and educational level. In fact, perhaps the most profound change in who marries and who does not is in terms of the rich versus the poor. While the median household income of married adults has always been higher than that of single adults after adjusting for household size, today that gap has increased from 12 percent in 1960 to 41 percent today. Put another way, the richer and more educated one is,

TABLE A Trends That are Good or Bad for Society

What do you think of these trends?	Bad for Society	Good for Society
More women never having children	29%	11%
More unmarried couples raising children	43%	10%
More single women having children without a male partner	69%	4%
More lesbian and gay couples raising children	43%	12%
More people living together without getting married	43%	9%
More mothers of young children working outside the home	37%	21%

Source: Belinda Luscombe. 2010. "Marriage: What's it Good For?" *Time* magazine. Vol. 176, No. 22, pp. 48–56.

the more likely one is to get married or to already be married. In other words, if you are married today, you are more likely to be well off.

5 This trend is related to other broader issues and trends (see Table A). For example, almost two-thirds (62 percent) of Americans (compared to less than one-half in 1978) think that the ideal marriage is one in which both the wife and the husband work outside of the home. This should not come as a surprise given that in the early 1970s only about 40 percent of wives worked compared to 61 percent today. In the past, some researchers have suggested that when women work, they are more likely to meet eligible men, and their economic independence might be an attraction in the marriage market. In addition, this trend is related to what people look for in a marital mate. Beginning with economic support, two-thirds of all people think that a man should be a good provider while about one-third think that it is important for women to be good providers as well. This might well explain the delay in marriage especially among the 20-somethings. If people are expecting a partner who is equally educated and economically stable, then it would make sense that they are delaying marriage at least until they finish college. This fact notwithstanding, curiously, high school educated couples who, in the past, made it to the altar sooner than college graduates, are now lagging behind, marrying even later than college graduates. According to sociologist Andrew Cherlin, college-educated couples delay marriage until they have completed their education and established themselves in a career whereas less educated couples delay marriage until they feel comfortable financially.

6 Social scientists have long known that economic factors are often key considerations in decisions to marry or not. While low income and economic marginality do not appear to affect men's development and formation of intimate romantic relationships, however, they do become factors in the decision regarding marriage. A variety of studies, for example, have indicated that during depressions and periods of high unemployment, men tend to put off getting married. However, when men have relatively good access to economic opportunities and

resources; when there is economic prosperity (for example, a high availability of jobs or access to good-paying jobs) they are more likely to make the decision to marry. In this regard, race is an important sociopolitical construction that has a major impact on a person's decision of whether to marry. Several writers have suggested that the lack of employment opportunities, which hits poor people and people of color disproportionately, and the unlikeliness of a livable guaranteed minimum income often act as a deterrent to marriage. For example, the increasing economic marginality of many African American men has meant that marriage is often not a viable option. Given that men are still expected (consciously or unconsciously) to be the family "breadwinner" the disproportionately higher rates of African American male unemployment, sporadic or seasonal employment, and underemployment make marriage an unattractive proposition for many African American women and men. In this context, it appears that among low-income African American men, many men tend to postpone marriage untill they feel they can support a family (fulfill the traditional "good provider" role). On the other hand, during times of economic prosperity African American women and men are far more likely to marry and start a family and the chances of staying married increase dramatically.

7 In any event, in today's crumbling economic climate, with the increasing loss of decent paying jobs and high unemployment rates, it is increasingly more difficult for people to get and stay married. However, that does not mean that they are not coupling and committing to long-term relationships. For example, as the percentage of people marrying has decreased, there has been a dramatic increase in couples living together. This increase has been attributed to the economic recession that began in 2008; people are cohabiting because they don't have enough economic resources to go it alone and they are not marrying until they do. But it is not just those who are economically strapped that are cohabiting. Well-off couples are also increasingly choosing to cohabit before marrying, if they marry at all. Beyond educational and economic success, other qualities that Americans look for in a mate include someone who will be a good mother or father, who will put family before anything else, who is good at household chores, and who is a good sexual partner.

8 Finally, although most people believe that raising children is best done within marriage, the new face of American families increasingly includes single-parent, unmarried mother families. The number of children living in a single-parent home has almost tripled since 1950. However, contrary to the conservative view that these children are "fatherless" or without a man in their lives, most of the children born to unwed mothers (more than one-half) were the product of a loving and committed relationship where both parents were living together at the time of their birth. Another 30 percent of these children were born to parents who were romantically committed and involved though not married nor living together.

—Schwartz and Scott, Marriages and Families, pp. 237–240

MASTERY TEST SKILLS CHECK

Directions: Select the choice that best completes each of the following statements.

Checking Your Comprehension

_____ 1. The primary purpose of this selection is to describe why
  a. the divorce rate is rising.
  b. fewer people are marrying.
  c. gay marriage is necessary.
  d. more people are graduating from college.

_____ 2. According to the author, people with a college degree are more likely to
  a. divorce.
  b. not marry at all.
  c. have children before they are married.
  d. marry than those without a college degree.

_____ 3. People who are married are more likely to be
  a. rich.
  b. voters.
  c. high school dropouts.
  d. female.

_____ 4. According to this selection, people are likely to delay marriage until after college because
  a. weddings are increasingly expensive.
  b. longer engagements are now common.
  c. they want a mate who is as educated and economically stable as they are.
  d. they do not believe it is important for a mate to be a good provider.

_____ 5. According to this selection, most children born to unmarried mothers were born
  a. to two parents who were romantically involved with each other.
  b. to a woman who had no male in her life.
  c. without responsible parents.
  d. into an uneducated family.

Applying Your Skills

_____ 6. According to Figure A, the group of people least interested in getting married are those who are
  a. unmarried.
  b. cohabitating.
  c. never married.
  d. divorced or widowed.

_____ 7. Figure A indicates that most people over age 18 are
  a. never married.
  b. separated or divorced.
  c. married.
  d. widowed.

_____ 8. Based on Figure A, the group with the least children born to unmarried women in the United States is
  a. whites.
  b. all groups
  c. Latinas.
  d. blacks.

_____ 9. Figure A indicates that the country with the smallest percent of children born to unmarried women is
  a. Sweden.
  b. Italy.
  c. Greece.
  d. Japan.

_____ 10. According to Table A, the trend that is considered the worst for society is more
a. mothers of young children working outside the home.
b. lesbian and gay couples raising children.
c. single women having children without a male partner.
d. people living together without getting married.

Studying Words

_____ 11. In this context, the word *institutions* (par. 2) means
a. patterns of behavior that are part of a culture.
b. large buildings that are well known.
c. beliefs that are outside the norm.
d. mental health treatment centers.

_____ 12. The word *noteworthy* (par. 2) means
a. dangerous.
b. humorous.
c. important.
d. uncertain.

_____ 13. The word *attain* (par. 3) means
a. decline.
b. notice.
c. praise.
d. achieve.

_____ 14. The word *obsolete* (par. 3) means
a. popular.
b. out of date.
c. mentioned excitedly.
d. covered up.

_____ 15. In this context, the word *marginality* (par. 6) means
a. popularity.
b. helpfulness.
c. unimportance.
d. excitement.

For more practice, ask your instructor for an opportunity to work on the mastery tests that appear in the Test Bank.

Summarizing the Reading

Directions: Complete the following summary of the reading by filling in the blanks.

Fewer people ______________ now than they did in the ______________, but people who are more ______________ are more likely to marry now. Marriage is not as necessary as it used to be since ______________________________ ______________________________. More Americans think marriage is becoming ______________, but most Americans have been married

_______________ and most people do want to _______________. People who marry tend to be on the same _______________________________, and also tend to be rich. Most Americans think _______________ should work outside the home, and the percent of _______________ who work has increased. Many people delay marriage until _______________. _______________ are more likely to marry during good economic times, but African American men often experience difficult economic situations and are _______________ to marry because of this. More couples are now _______________________. African American families are often _______________. Most children in unmarried families are born into _______________________________.

Reading Visually

1. What is the purpose of the pie charts in Figure A?
2. How do the graphs in Figure A contribute to your understanding of the material? Why are graphs more effective in illustrating this material than text would be?
3. Why did the author include Table A? How does it enhance your understanding of the material?

Thinking Critically about the Reading

1. Did the trends identified in the selection surprise you? Why or why not?
2. Consider the reasons why the author says marriage is no longer as necessary as it used to be. Do you agree with these? Are there other reasons marriage might not be as necessary?
3. The author discusses the percent of people who wait until after college to marry and the percent of women who have children while unmarried, which have both increased in recent years, but does not discuss these statistics in relationship to each other. Do you think there is a link? How might these two facts impact each other?

CHAPTER 9

Organizing and Remembering Information

LEARNING GOALS

This chapter will show you how to

1. Highlight and mark important information in textbook chapters
2. Outline information to show its organization
3. Draw maps to organize information
4. Summarize ideas for review purposes
5. Review for maximum retention

Focusing On ... Organizing and Remembering Information

The blueprint above, created by an architect, is used by the contractor to build the house to specifications. The blueprint organizes all the details about the house, such as the size of rooms and the location of windows, electrical outlets, and appliances. Can you imagine how difficult it would be to keep track of all the details involved in building a house without a blueprint? Textbook chapters are also filled with details, and you need a system to keep track of them all. This chapter shows you four ways to create a "blueprint" or learning guide of a textbook chapter.

Suppose you are planning a cross-country trip next summer. To get ready you begin to collect all kinds of information: maps, newspaper articles on various cities, places to visit, names of friends' friends, and so forth. After a while, you find that you have a great deal of information and that it is difficult to locate any one item. You begin to realize that the information you have collected will be of little or no use unless you organize it in some way. You decide to buy large envelopes and put different kinds of information into separate envelopes, such as information on individual states.

In this case, you found a practical, commonsensical solution to a problem. The rule or principle that you applied was this: When something gets confusing, organize it.

This rule also works well when applied to college textbooks. Each text contains thousands of pieces of information—facts, names, dates, theories, principles. This information quickly becomes confusing unless it is organized. Once you have organized it, you will be able to find and remember what you need more easily than if your text were still an unsorted heap of facts.

Organizing information requires sifting, sorting, and in some cases rearranging important facts and ideas. There are five common methods of organizing textbook materials:

- Highlighting
- Marking
- Outlining
- Mapping
- Summarizing

In this chapter you will learn techniques for doing each. You will also see how to study and review more effectively.

HIGHLIGHTING AND MARKING

1 LEARNING GOAL
Highlight and mark important information in textbook chapters

Highlighting and **marking** important facts and ideas as you read are effective methods of identifying and organizing information. They are also the biggest time-savers known to college students. Suppose it took you four hours to read an assigned chapter in sociology. One month later you need to review that chapter to prepare for an exam. If you did not highlight or mark as you read the first time, then, in order to review the chapter once, you would have to spend another four hours rereading it. However, if you had highlighted and marked as you read, you could review the chapter in an hour or less—a savings of 300 percent. This means you can save many hours each semester. More important, the less time you spend identifying what to learn, the more thoroughly you can learn the necessary information. This strategy can help improve your grades.

Highlighting Effectively

Here are a few basic suggestions for highlighting effectively:

HOW TO HIGHLIGHT

1. **Read a paragraph or section first.** Then go back and highlight what is important.
2. **Highlight important portions of the topic sentence.** Also highlight any supporting details you want to remember (see Chapter 6).
3. **Be accurate.** Make sure your highlighting reflects the content of the passage. Incomplete or hasty highlighting can mislead you as you review the passage and may cause you to miss the main point.
4. **Use a system for highlighting.** There are several from which to choose: for instance, using two or more different colors of highlighters to distinguish between main ideas and details, or placing a bracket around the main idea and using a highlighter to mark important details. No one system is more effective than another. Try to develop a system that works well for you.
5. **Highlight as few words as possible in a sentence.** Seldom should you highlight an entire sentence. Usually highlighting the key idea along with an additional phrase or two is sufficient. Read the following paragraph. Notice that you can understand its meaning from the highlighted parts alone.

   Police are primarily a reactive force. In the vast majority of cases, police are informed of an incident *after* it occurs by a complaining victim, a witness, or an alarm. (A study of police response time found that only about 6 percent of callers reported crimes while they were in progress.) In addition, the National Crime Victimization Survey (NCVS) reveals that only about a third of serious crime is reported to police. It is difficult to hold police responsible for increases in the crime rate when they are not called for most crimes or are called after the incident has ended. Several other factors may cause the crime rate to rise, such as an increase in the proportion of young people in the population, higher rates of long-term unemployment, and the criminalization of drug use. Police have no control over these conditions. Thus, the crime rate is really not a useful indictor of police effectiveness.

6. **Use headings to guide your highlighting.** Use the headings to form questions that you expect to be answered in the section (see Chapter 2). Then highlight the answer to each question.

Highlighting the Right Amount

If you highlight either too much or too little, you defeat the purpose. By highlighting too little, you miss valuable information, and your review and study of the material will be incomplete. On the other hand, if you highlight too much, you are not identifying the most important ideas and eliminating less important facts. The more you highlight, the more you will have to reread when studying and the less of a time-saver the procedure will prove to be. As a general rule of thumb, highlight no more than 20 to 30 percent of the material.

Here is a paragraph highlighted in three different ways. First read the paragraph that has not been highlighted; then look at each highlighted version. Try to decide which version would be most useful if you were rereading it for study purposes.

> The Maglevs are coming. Not aliens from outer space, but superfast trains suspended in the air and propelled by magnetic force. Maglevs can travel at speeds of more than 300 miles per hour, lifted off the ground on a cushion formed by magnetic forces and pulled forward by magnets. They run more quietly and smoothly and can climb steeper grades than conventional trains can. Maglevs are more energy efficient, have lower maintenance costs, and require fewer staff than does comparable transportation. However, given the high cost of construction, the concept may not prove viable.
>
> —adapted from Walker, *Introduction to Hospitality Management*, p. 45

Example 1

The Maglevs are coming. Not aliens from outer space, but superfast trains suspended in the air and propelled by magnetic force. Maglevs can travel at speeds of more than 300 miles per hour, lifted off the ground on a cushion formed by magnetic forces and pulled forward by magnets. They run more quietly and smoothly and can climb steeper grades than conventional trains can. Maglevs are more energy efficient, have lower maintenance costs, and require fewer staff than does comparable transportation. However, given the high cost of construction, the concept may not prove viable.

Example 2

The Maglevs are coming. Not aliens from outer space, but superfast trains suspended in the air and propelled by magnetic force. Maglevs can travel at speeds of more than 300 miles per hour, lifted off the ground on a cushion formed by magnetic forces and pulled forward by magnets. They run more quietly and smoothly and can climb steeper grades than conventional trains can. Maglevs are more energy efficient, have lower maintenance costs, and require fewer staff than does comparable transportation. However, given the high cost of construction, the concept may not prove viable.

Example 3

The Maglevs are coming. Not aliens from outer space, but superfast trains suspended in the air and propelled by magnetic force. Maglevs can travel at speeds of more than 300 miles per hour, lifted off the ground on a cushion formed by magnetic forces and pulled forward by magnets. They run more quietly and smoothly and can climb steeper grades than conventional trains can. Maglevs are more energy efficient, have lower maintenance costs, and require fewer staff than does comparable transportation. However, given the high cost of construction, the concept may not prove viable.

The last example is the best example of effective highlighting. Only the most important information has been highlighted. In the first example, too little of the important information has been highlighted, while what *has* been highlighted is either unnecessary or incomplete. The second example, on the other hand, has too much highlighting to be useful for review.

EXERCISE 9-1 Practicing Highlighting

Directions: Read and highlight the following passage using the guidelines presented in this section.

Generic Names

When filing for a trademark, if a word, name, or slogan is too generic, it cannot be registered as a trademark. If it is not generic, it can be trademarked. For example, the word "apple" cannot be trademarked because it is a generic name. However, the brand name "Apple Computer" is permitted to be trademarked because it is not a generic name. Similarly, the word "secret" cannot be trademarked because it is a generic name, but the brand name "Victoria's Secret" is permitted to be trademarked because it is not a generic name.

Once a company has been granted a trademark, the company usually uses the mark as a brand name to promote its goods or services. However, sometimes a company may be *too* successful in promoting a mark and at some point the public begins to use the brand name as a common name for the product or service being sold, rather than as the trademark of the individual seller. A trademark that becomes a common term for a product line or type of service is called **a generic name**. Once a trademark becomes a generic name, the term loses its protection under federal trademark law. To illustrate, sailboards are surfboards that have sails mounted on them and are used by one person to glide on oceans and lakes. There were many manufacturers and sellers of sailboards. The most successful brand was "Windsurfer." However, the word "windsurfing" was used so often by the public for all brands of sailboards that the trademarked name "Windsurfer" was found to be a generic name and its trademark was canceled.

—adapted from Goldman and Cheeseman, *The Paralegal Professional*, p. 745

EXERCISE 9-2 Highlighting Chapter 5

Directions: Read or reread and highlight Chapter 5 in this book. Follow the guidelines suggested in this chapter.

Testing Your Highlighting

As you highlight, check to be certain your highlighting is effective and will be helpful for review purposes. To test the effectiveness of your highlighting, take any passage and reread only the highlighted portions. Then ask yourself the following questions:

TESTING YOUR HIGHLIGHTING

- Does the highlighting tell what the passage is about?
- Does it make sense?
- Does it indicate the most important idea in the passage?

EXERCISE 9-3 Evaluating Your Highlighting

Directions: Test the effectiveness of your highlighting for the material you highlighted in Exercises 9-1 and 9-2. Make changes, if necessary.

Marking

Highlighting alone will not clearly identify and organize information in many types of textbooks. Also, highlighting does not allow you to react to or sort ideas. Try making notes in the margin in addition to highlighting. Notice how the marginal notes in the passage on the following page organize the information in a way that highlighting cannot.

Seasonal Affective Disorder (SAD)

Some people only get depressed at certain times of the year. In particular, depression seems to set in during the winter months and goes away with the coming of spring and summer. If this describes someone you know, it could be seasonal affective disorder (SAD). SAD is a mood disorder caused by the body's reaction to low levels of light present in the winter months.

def. of SAD

SAD can cause feelings of tiredness, lack of energy, and daytime sleepiness that the mind interprets as depression. Other symptoms include excessive eating, a craving for sugary and starchy foods, excessive sleeping, and weight gain. The worst months for SAD are January and February, and true SAD disappears in the spring and summer.

Symptoms

Treatment of SAD can include antidepressant drugs, but one of the most effective treatments is **phototherapy**, or daily exposure to bright light. Lamps are used to create an "artificial daylight" for a certain number of hours during each day, and the person with SAD sits under that light. Milder symptoms can be controlled with more time spent outdoors when the sun is shining and increasing the amount of sunlight that comes into the workplace or home.

treatment

—adapted from Ciccarelli and White, *Psychology*, p. 454

Here are a few examples of useful types of marking:

1. **Circle words you do not know.**

   Sulfur is a yellow, solid substance that has several (allotropic) forms

2. **Mark definitions with an asterisk.**

   **Chemical reactivity* is the tendency of an element to participate in chemical reactions.

3. **Write summary words or phrases in the margin.**

   reaction w/air

   Some elements, such as aluminum (Al) or Copper (Cu), tarnish just from sitting around in the air. They react with oxygen (O_2) in the air.

4. **Number lists of ideas, causes, and reasons.**

   Metallic properties include ① conductivity, ② luster, and ③ ductility.

5. **Place brackets around important passages.**

   In Group IVA, carbon (C) is a nonmetal, silicon (Si) and germanium (Ge) are metaloids, and tin (Sn) and lead (Pb) are metals.

6. Draw arrows or diagrams to show relationships or to clarify information.

graphite

> Graphite is made up of a lot of carbon layers stacked on top of one another, like sheets of paper. The layers slide over one another, which makes it a good lubricant.

7. Make notes to yourself, such as "good test question," "reread," or "ask instructor."

Test!

> Carbon is most important to us because it is a basic element in all plant and animal structures.

8. Put question marks next to confusing passages or when you want more information.

why?

> Sometimes an element reacts so violently with air, water, or other substances that an explosion occurs.

Try to develop your own code or set of abbreviations. Here are a few examples:

Types of Marking	Examples
ex	example
T	good test question
sum	good summary
def	important definition
RR	reread later

EXERCISE 9-4 Practicing Highlighting and Marking

Directions: Read each of the following passages and then highlight and mark each. Try various ways of highlighting and marking.

Passage A

National and Regional Presidential Primary Proposals

1 The idea of holding a **national primary** to select party nominees has been discussed virtually ever since state primaries were introduced. In 1913, President Woodrow Wilson proposed it in his first message to Congress. Since then, over 250 proposals for a national presidential primary have been introduced in Congress. These proposals do not lack public support; opinion polls have consistently shown that a substantial majority of Democrats, Republicans, and Independents alike favor such reform.

2 According to its proponents, a national primary would bring directness and simplicity to the process for the voters as well as the candidates. The length of the campaign would be shortened, and no longer would votes in one state have more political impact than votes in another. The concentration of media coverage on this one event, say its advocates, would increase not only political interest in the nomination decision but also public understanding of the issues involved.

3 A national primary would not be so simple, respond the critics. Because Americans would not want a candidate nominated with 25 percent of the vote from among a field of six candidates, in most primaries a runoff election between the top two finishers in each party would have to be held. So much for making the campaign simpler, national primary critics note. Each voter would have to vote three times for president—twice in the primaries and once in November.

4 Perhaps more feasible than a national primary is holding a series of **regional primaries** in which, say, states in the eastern time zone would vote one week, those in the central time zone the next, and so on. This would impose a more rational structure and cut down on candidate travel. A regional primary system would also put an end to the jockeying between states for an advantageous position in the primary season.

5 The major problem with the regional primary proposal, however, is the advantage gained by whichever region goes first. For example, if the Western states were the first to vote, any candidate from California would have a clear edge in building momentum. Although most of the proposed plans call for the order of the regions to be determined by lottery, this would not erase the fact that regional advantages would surely be created from year to year.

—adapted from Edwards et al., *Government in America*, p. 285

Passage B

Predators

1 Predation is the process by which animals capture, kill, and consume animals of another species, their prey. Predators employ two basic feeding strategies—filter feeding and hunting.

2 Filter-feeding predators use webs or netlike structures to catch their prey. Spiders use webs to "filter" organisms from their environment. As marine shrimp swim through the water, they trap small organisms in the hairlike setae on their legs and transfer them to their mouths. Blue whales, Earth's largest living animals, are filter feeders. Blue whales and their baleen whale relatives use their comblike "teeth" to filter plankton from the water.

3 Hunting predators actively stalk and capture their prey. Natural selection has favored predators with keen senses of sight and smell as well as structures such as talons, claws, and sharp teeth that allow predators to seize and kill their prey. Coevolution has played a significant role in predator-prey relationships, and prey organisms have evolved a variety of defenses against capture.

4 Populations of predators are often limited by the availability of prey. Likewise, populations of prey are often limited by their predators. Where predators are dependent on a single species of prey, interactions between the two species may result in synchronized cycles of population growth and decline.

—Christensen, *The Environment and You*, p. 153

EXERCISE 9-5 **Comparing Highlighting and Marking**

Directions: Read, highlight, and mark a reading selection from Part Six assigned by your instructor. Then, working with a partner, review each other's highlighting, discuss similarities and differences, and settle upon an acceptable version.

OUTLINING

2 LEARNING GOAL
Outline information to show its organization

Outlining is a good way to create a visual picture of what you have read. In making an **outline**, you record the writer's organization and show the relative importance of and connection between ideas.

Outlining has a number of advantages:

- It gives an overview of the topic and enables you to see how various subtopics relate to one another.
- Recording the information in your own words tests your understanding of what you read.
- It is an effective way to record needed information from reference books you do not own.

How to Outline

Generally, an outline follows a format like the one below.

I. First major idea
  A. First supporting detail
    1. Detail
    2. Detail
  B. Second supporting detail
    1. Detail
      a. Minor detail or example
      b. Minor detail or example
II. Second major idea
  A. First supporting detail

Notice that the most important ideas are closer to the left margin. Less important ideas are indented toward the middle of the page. A quick glance at an outline shows what is most important, what is less important, and how ideas support or explain one another.

USING THE OUTLINE FORMAT

1. **Do not be overly concerned with following the outline format exactly.** As long as your outline shows an organization of ideas, it will work for you.
2. **Write words and phrases rather than complete sentences.**
3. **Use your own words.** Do not lift words from the text.
4. **Do not write too much.** If you need to record numerous facts and details, underlining rather than outlining might be more effective.
5. **Pay attention to headings.** Be sure that all the information you place underneath a heading explains or supports that heading. Every heading indented the same amount on the page should be of equal importance.

What key point does this photograph illustrate?

Now read the following passage on sleep apnea and then study the outline of it.

From insomnia to sleepwalking to narcolepsy, sleep disorders are more common than you might think. There are more than 80 different clinical sleep disorders, and it is estimated that between 50 and 70 million Americans—children and adults—suffer from one. Many aren't even aware of their disorder, and many others never seek treatment.

Sleep Apnea

Sleep apnea is a disorder in which breathing is briefly and repeatedly interrupted during sleep. *Apnea* refers to a breathing pause that lasts at least 10 seconds. During that time, the chest may rise and fall, but little or no air may be exchanged, or the person may actually not breathe until the brain triggers a gasping inhalation. Sleep apnea affects more than 18 million Americans, or 1 in every 15 people.

There are two major types of sleep apnea: central and obstructive. *Central sleep apnea* occurs when the brain fails to tell the respiratory muscles to initiate breathing. Consumption of alcohol, certain illegal drugs, and certain medications can contribute to this condition. *Obstructive sleep apnea (OSA)*, which is the more common form, occurs when air cannot move in and out of a person's nose or mouth, even though the body tries to breathe.

Typically, OSA occurs when a person's throat muscles and tongue relax during sleep and block the airways. People who are overweight or obese often have more tissue that flaps or sags, which puts them at higher risk for sleep apnea. People with OSA are prone to heavy snoring, snorting, and gasping. These sounds occur because, as oxygen saturation levels in the blood fall, the body's autonomic nervous system is stimulated to trigger inhalation, often via a sudden gasp of breath. This response may wake the person, preventing deep sleep and causing the person to wake up in the morning feeling tired and unwell. More serious risks of OSA include chronic high blood pressure, irregular heartbeats, heart attack, and stroke. Apnea-associated sleeplessness may be a factor in an increased risk of type 2 diabetes, immune system deficiencies, and a host of other problems.

—Donatelle, *Health*, pp. 94 and 96

Sleep Apnea

- *I. Disorder with brief, repeated interruptions in breathing*
  - *A. Pause in breathing for at least 10 seconds*
  - *B. Over 18 million Americans (1 in 15) affected*
- *II. Two major types*
  - *A. Central sleep apnea*
    - *1. Occurs when brain fails to initiate breathing*
    - *2. Associated with alcohol, drugs, medications*
  - *B. Obstructive sleep apnea (OSA)*
    - *1. Occurs when air can't move in and out despite body's efforts*
      - *a. Throat muscles and tongue relax in sleep and block airways*
    - *2. Overweight or obese people at higher risk*
    - *3. Low levels of oxygen trigger snoring, gasping*
    - *4. Many health effects/risks*
      - *a. Feeling tired, unwell from lack of deep sleep*
      - *b. High blood pressure, irregular heartbeats, heart attack, stroke*
      - *c. Increased risk of type 2 diabetes, immune system deficiencies*

EXERCISE 9-6 Completing an Outline

Directions: Read the following passage and the incomplete outline that follows. Fill in the missing information in the outline.

The Victims' Rights Movement

Several events were key to the emergence of the **victims' rights movement.** First, the 1960s brought general concern about individual rights in many arenas, including civil rights, women's rights, inmates' rights, gay rights, and students' rights. The women's rights movement was a particularly strong supporter of victims' rights because its agenda included addressing the harms caused by the way in which the criminal justice system processed rape cases and domestic violence cases. Second, several government initiatives increased awareness and provided financial support for victim-assistance programs. Results from national surveys helped raise awareness of the harms caused by crime and documented the large number of victims who do not report their victimization to the police. The Law Enforcement Assistance Administration (LEAA) provided funds to assist in the professionalization of law enforcement. The LEAA also provided funds for the support of innovative programs to reduce crime and research to evaluate the impact of these programs. Third, the number of victims' rights organizations increased dramatically, and national coordinating bodies such as the **National Organization for Victim Assistance (NOVA)** were founded.

—Fagin, *CJ*, p. 31

I. Key events in emergence of victims' rights movement

A. 1960s general concern about individual rights

1. civil rights

2. women's rights: strong supporter of victims' rights, including rape and domestic violence

3. inmate's rights

4. ____________________

5. ____________________

B. ____________________

____

1. ____________________

2. ____________________

C. ____________________

1. ____________________

MAPPING

3 LEARNING GOAL Draw maps to organize information

Mapping is a visual method of organizing information. It involves drawing diagrams to show how ideas in an article or chapter are related. Some students prefer mapping to outlining because they feel it is freer and less tightly structured.

Maps can take numerous forms. You can draw them in any way tha the relationships of ideas. Figure 9-1 shows two sample maps. Each was drawn to show the overall organization of Chapter 5 in this book. First refer back to Chapter 5 and then study each map.

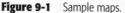

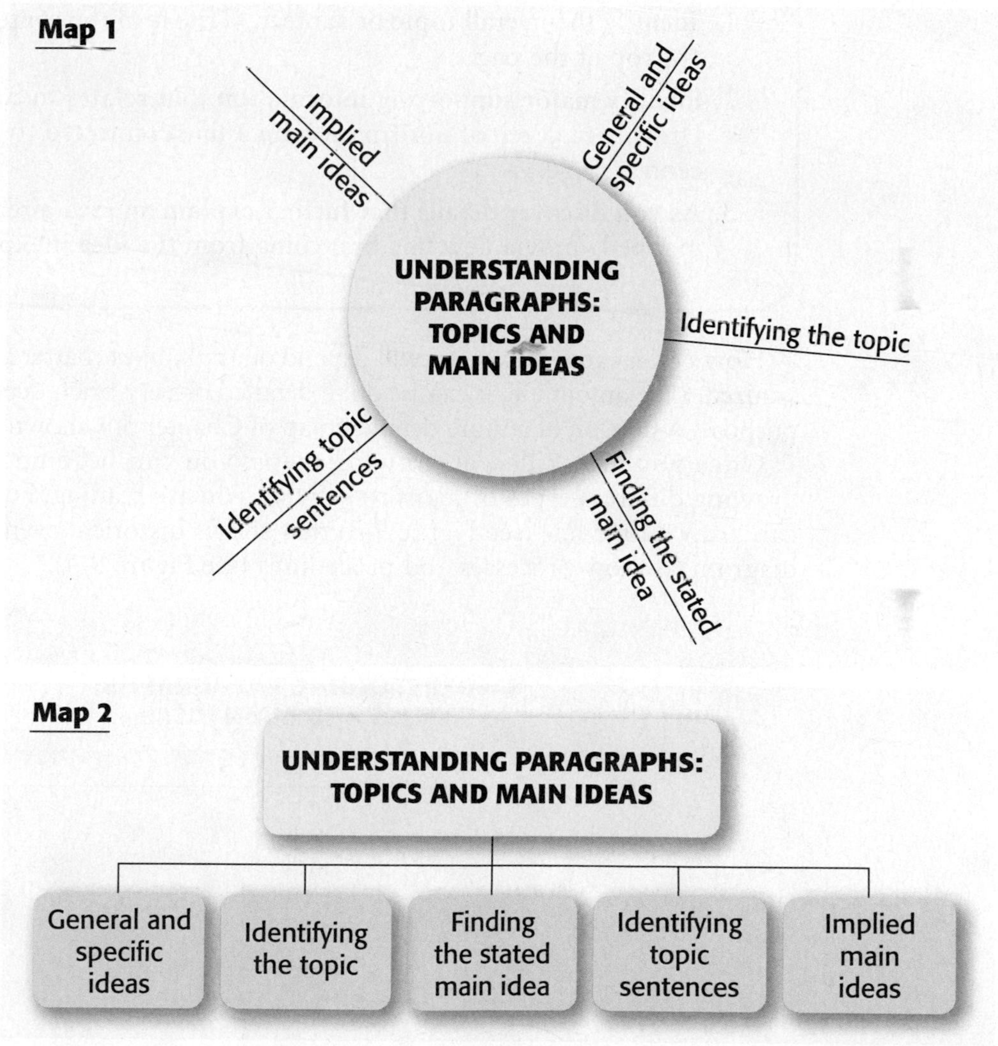

Figure 9-1 Sample maps.

How to Draw Maps

Think of a map as a picture or diagram that shows how ideas are connected.

DRAWING A MAP

1. **Identify the overall topic or subject.** Write it in the center or at the top of the page.
2. **Identify major supporting information that relates to the topic.** Draw each piece of information on a line connected to the central topic.
3. **As you discover details that further explain an idea already mapped, draw a new line branching from the idea it explains.**

How you arrange your map will depend on the subject matter and how it is organized. Like an outline, it can be quite detailed or very brief, depending on your purpose. A portion of a more detailed map of Chapter 5 is shown in Figure 9-2.

Once you are skilled at drawing maps, you can become more creative, drawing different types of maps to fit what you are reading. For example, you can draw a time line (see Figure 9-3) that shows historical events, or a process diagram to show processes and procedures (see Figure 9-4).

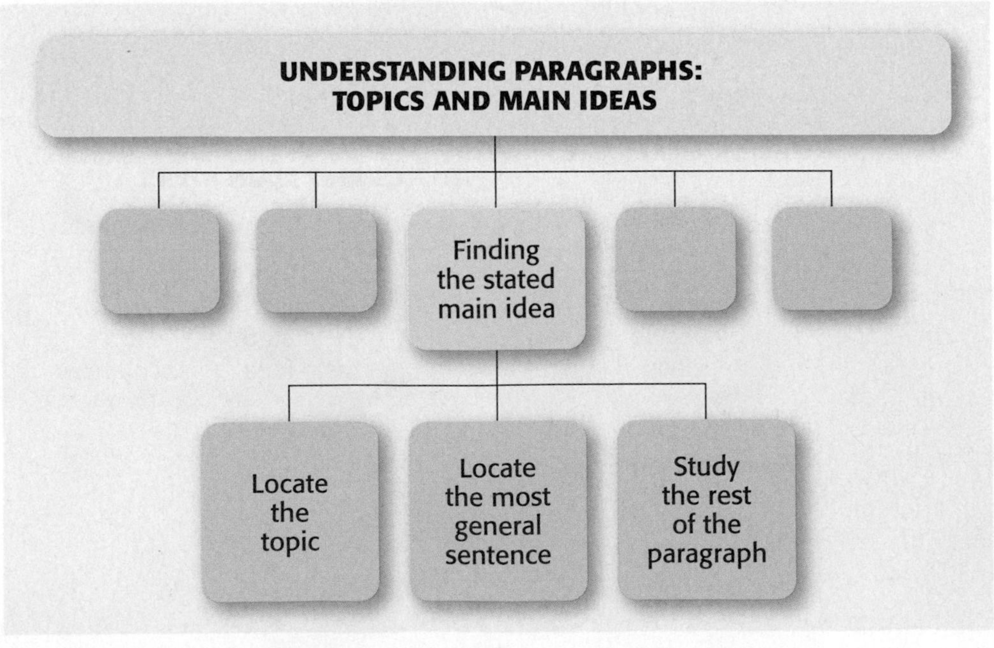

Figure 9-2 Map with greater detail.

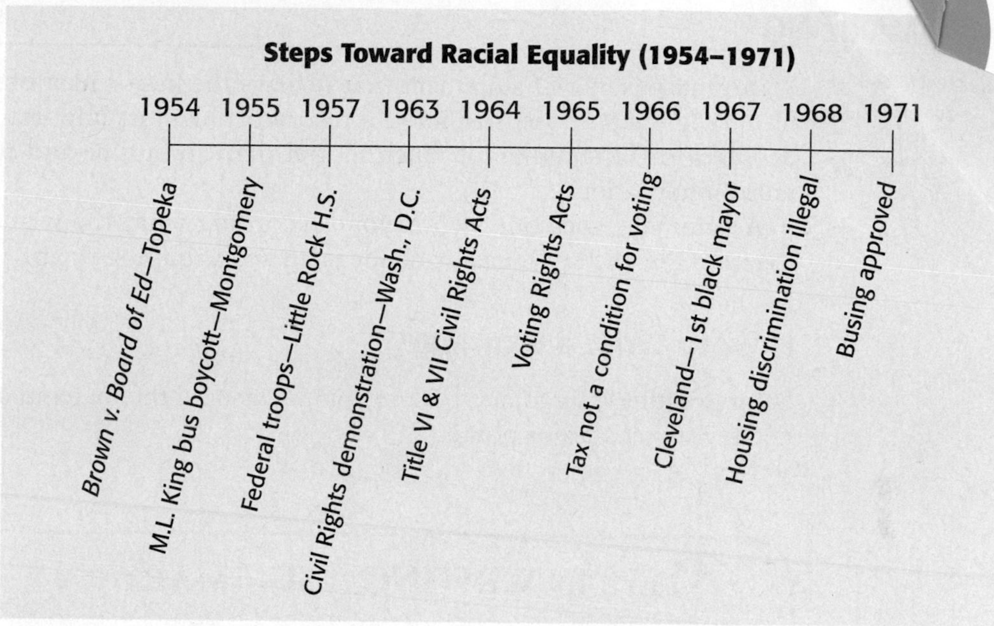

Figure 9-3 Sample time line.

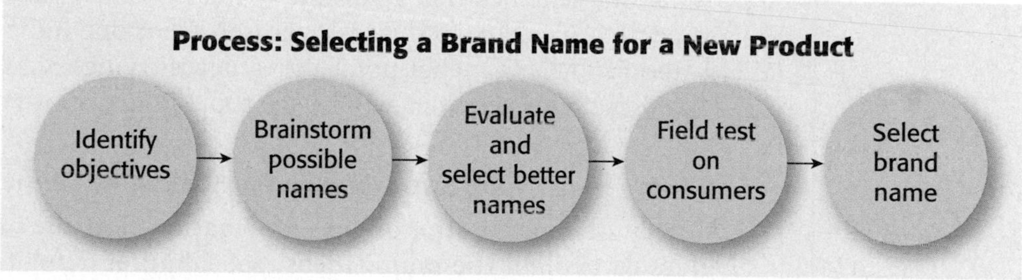

Figure 9-4 Sample process diagram.

EXERCISE 9-7

Drawing a Map

Directions: Draw a map of the excerpt "Generic Names" on pp. 322–323.

EXERCISE 9-8

Drawing a Map

Directions: Draw a map of Chapter 6 of this book.

SUMMARIZING

4 LEARNING GOAL
Summarize ideas for review purposes

A **summary** is a brief statement that reviews the major idea of something you have read. Its purpose is to make a record of the most important ideas in condensed form. A summary is much shorter than an outline and contains less detailed information.

A summary goes one step beyond recording what the writer says. It pulls together the writer's ideas by condensing and grouping them.

How to Write a Summary

Before writing a summary, be sure you understand the material and have identified the writer's major points.

STEPS IN WRITING A SUMMARY

1. **Write a brief outline of the material or underline each major idea.**
2. **Write one sentence that states the writer's overall concern or most important idea.** To do this, ask yourself what one topic the material is about. Then ask what point the writer is trying to make about that topic. This sentence will be the topic sentence of your summary.
3. **Be sure to use your own words rather than those of the author.**
4. **Review the major supporting information that the author gives to explain the major ideas.** See Chapter 7 for further information.
5. **Decide on the level of detail you need.** The amount of detail you include, if any, will depend on your purpose for writing the summary.
6. **Normally, present ideas in the summary in the same order in which they appear in the original materials.**
7. **For other than textbook material, if the writer presents a clear opinion or expresses an attitude toward the subject matter, include it in your summary.**
8. **Do not concentrate on correctness when writing summaries for your own use.** Some students prefer to write summaries using words and phrases rather than complete sentences.

Read the following summary of "The Victims' Rights Movement," which appeared on pp. 329–330.

Notice that this summary contains only the broadest, most important ideas. Details are not included.

Sample Summary

Three events were important in the growth of the victims' rights movement. In the 1960s there was concern about individual rights, including women's rights, and the women's rights movement was supportive of victims' rights because the victims were often female. Government programs and surveys raised awareness of victims' rights and created funding for victims' programs and research, as well as for training law enforcement. The number of victims' rights organizations increased and national coordinating bodies were formed.

EXERCISE 9-9 Writing a Summary

Directions: Form teams of three or four students. Each team should choose and agree to watch a particular television show that airs before the next class. During the next class meeting, collaborate to write a summary of the show. Summaries may be presented to the class for discussion and evaluation.

EXERCISE 9-10 Writing a Summary

Directions: On a separate sheet of paper, write a summary of one of the reading selections in Part Six of this text.

EXERCISE 9-11 Writing a Summary

Directions: Write a summary of the article "Sleep Apnea" on p. 328. When you have finished, compare it with the sample summary shown in Figure 9-5 on p. 336. Then answer the following questions.

1. How does your summary differ from the sample?
2. Does your summary begin with a topic sentence? How does it compare with the one in the sample?
3. Does your summary include ideas in the order in which they were given in the article?

Sleep apnea is a disorder in which breathing is repeatedly interrupted during sleep, with pauses lasting at least 10 seconds. The two major types are central sleep apnea, in which the brain fails to initiate breathing, and obstructive sleep apnea (OSA), in which air is unable to move in and out of a person's nose or mouth, typically because airways are blocked. Falling oxygen saturation levels in the blood trigger sudden inhalation, which may prevent deep sleep. People with OSA may feel tired or unwell from sleep interruptions or they may face much more serious health problems.

Figure 9-5 Sample summary: "Sleep Apnea."

EXERCISE 9-12 Comparing Methods of Organization

Directions: Your instructor will choose a reading from Part Six and will then divide the class into three groups. Members of one group should outline the material, another group should draw maps, and the third should write summaries. When the groups have completed their tasks, the class members should review each other's work. Several students can read their summaries, draw maps, and write outlines on the chalkboard. Discuss which of the three methods seemed most effective for the material and how well prepared each group feels for (a) an essay exam, (b) a multiple-choice exam, and (c) a class discussion.

IMMEDIATE AND PERIODIC REVIEW

5 LEARNING GOAL Review for maximum retention

Once you have read and organized information, the last step is to learn it. Fortunately, this is not a difficult task if you have organized the information effectively. In fact, through underlining, outlining, and/or summarizing, you have already learned a large portion of the material. **Review**, then, is a way to fix, or store, information in your memory for later recall. There are two types of review, *immediate* and *periodic*.

How Immediate Review Works

Immediate review is done right after you have finished reading an assignment or writing an outline or summary. When you finish any of these, you may feel like breathing a sigh of relief and taking a break. However, it is worth the time and effort to spend another five minutes reviewing what you just read and refreshing your memory. The best way to do this is to go back through the chapter and reread the headings, graphic material, introduction, summary, and any underlining or marginal notes.

Immediate review works because it consolidates, or draws together, the material just read. It also gives a final, lasting impression of the content. Considerable research has been done on the effectiveness of immediate review. Results indicate that review done immediately rather than delayed until a later time makes a large difference in the amount remembered.

How Periodic Review Works

Although immediate review will increase your recall of information, it will not help you retain information for long periods of time. To remember information over time, periodically refresh your memory. This is known as **periodic review.** Go back over the material on a regular basis. Do this by looking again at those sections that carry the basic meaning and reviewing your underlining, outlining, and/or summaries. Below is an example of a schedule one student set up to periodically review assigned chapters in a psychology textbook. You can see that this student reviewed each chapter the week after reading it and again two weeks later. This schedule is only an example. You will need to make a schedule for each course that fits the course requirements. For math and science courses, for example, you may need to include a review of previous homework assignments and laboratory work. In other courses, less or more frequent review of previous material may be needed.

Week 1	*Read ch. 1*
Week 2	*Review ch. 1*
	Read ch. 2
Week 3	*Review ch. 2*
	Read ch. 3
Week 4	*Review ch. 3*
	Review ch. 1
	Read ch. 4
Week 5	*Review ch. 4*
	Review ch. 2
	Read ch. 5

EXERCISE 9-13 Planning a Review Schedule

Directions: Choose one of your courses that involves regular textbook reading assignments. Plan a reading and periodic review schedule for the next three weeks. Assume that new chapters will be assigned as frequently as in previous weeks and that you want to review whatever has been covered over the past three weeks.

LEARNING STYLE TIPS

If you tend to be a . . .	Then strengthen your review strategies by . . .
Creative learner	Brainstorming before and after each assignment to discover new ways to tie the material together
Pragmatic learner	Creating, writing, and answering review questions; preparing and taking self-tests

SELF-TEST SUMMARY

1 What are highlighting and marking and how are they used?	**Highlighting** is a way of sorting important information from less important information. It eliminates the need to reread entire textbook chapters in order to review their major content. It also has the advantage of helping you stay active and involved with what you are reading. **Marking** is a system that involves using signs, symbols, and marginal notes to react to, summarize, or comment on the material.
2 What is outlining and how is it used?	**Outlining** is a method of recording the most important information and showing the organization and relative importance of ideas. It is particularly useful when you need to see how ideas relate to one another or when you want to get an overview of a subject.
3 What is mapping and how is it used?	**Mapping** is a visual method of organizing information. It involves drawing diagrams to show how ideas in an article or chapter are related.
4 What is summarizing and how is it used?	**Summarizing** is a way to pull together the most important ideas in condensed form. It provides a quick review of the material and forces you to explain the writer's ideas in your own words.

5 What are two types of review and how do they increase retention?	Immediate review is done right after finishing an assignment. It consolidates the material and makes it stick in your memory. Periodic review is done regularly, at specified intervals. It keeps information fresh in your mind.

GOING ONLINE

1. **Highlighting Text Electronically**
   Most word processing programs (including Microsoft Word) offer highlighting capabilities. Go to a Web site of your choice, and cut and paste three paragraphs into a Word document. (Be sure to provide complete source information at the end of your document.) Read the paragraphs and then highlight the document on screen. How is this process similar to highlighting a printed document? How is it different?

2. **Exploring Your Web Browser**
   While most students surf the Web every day, many are not aware of all of their Web browser's capabilities. Take 15 minutes to explore the menu options on your Web browser. Name two or three features that might be helpful as you read online. Share your findings with the class. Specify which browser you have evaluated (such as Internet Explorer, Firefox, or Safari).

This Mastery Test can be completed in MyReadingLab.

CHAPTER 9

MASTERY TEST 1 Mapping and Summarizing Skills

Name ______________________________ Section ______________

Date ______________ Number right ________ × 20 points = Score __________

Directions: Read the passage below and then complete the map and the summary by selecting the choice that best completes each of the statements that follow them.

The first thing good listeners must do is figure out why they're listening. Researchers have identified five kinds of listening that reflect purposes you may have when communicating with others: appreciative, discriminative, empathic, comprehension, and critical.

Appreciative listening focuses on something other than the primary message. Some listeners enjoy seeing a famous speaker. Others relish a good speech, a classic movie, or a brilliant performance. On these occasions, you listen primarily to entertain yourself.

Discriminative listening requires listeners to draw conclusions from the way a message is presented rather than from what is said. In discriminative listening, people seek to understand the meaning behind the message. You're interested in what the speaker really thinks, believes, or feels. You're engaging in discriminative listening when you draw conclusions about how angry your parents are with you, based not on what they say but on how they say it. You draw inferences from the presentation of the message rather than from the message itself.

Empathic or therapeutic listening is intended to provide emotional support for the speaker. Although it is more typical of interpersonal than public communication, empathic listening does occur in public speaking situations, for example, when you hear an athlete apologize for unprofessional behavior or a classmate reveal a personal problem to illustrate a speech. In each case, your role is supportive.

Listening for comprehension occurs when you want to gain additional information or insights from the speaker. You are probably most familiar with this form of listening because you've relied heavily on it for your education. When you listen to a radio newscast, to a classroom lecture on marketing strategies, or to an elections official explaining new registration procedures, you're listening to understand—to comprehend information, ideas, and processes.

Critical listening is the most difficult kind of listening because it requires you to both interpret and evaluate the message. It demands that you go beyond understanding the message to interpreting it and evaluating its strengths and weaknesses. You'll practice this sort of listening in class. A careful consumer also uses critical listening to evaluate television commercials, political campaign speeches, or arguments offered by salespeople. When you are listening critically, you decide whether to accept or reject ideas and whether to act on the message.

—German and Gronbeck, *Principles of Public Speaking,* pp. 38–39

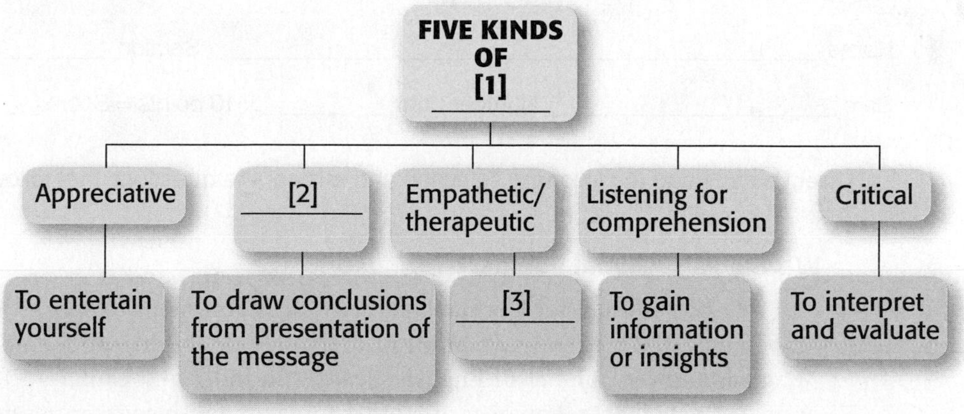

Refer to the map to answer questions 1–3.

_____ 1. The word that correctly fills in blank [1] is
- a. Purposes.
- b. Listening.
- c. Communicating.
- d. Responding.

_____ 2. The word that correctly fills in blank [2] is
- a. Conclusive.
- b. Emotional.
- c. Comprehensive.
- d. Discriminative.

_____ 3. The phrase that correctly fills in blank [3] is
- a. to apologize for behavior.
- b. to reveal a personal problem.
- c. to illustrate a speech.
- d. to provide emotional support.

Refer to the following summary of the passage to answer questions 4 and 5.

Summary: In communication, there are five types of listening. Appreciative listening is mainly for your own entertainment. Discriminative listening is when you have to figure out what the speaker means by ______ [4] ______. Empathic or therapeutic listening requires you to give emotional support to the speaker; it happens more in interpersonal communication than in public speaking situations. Listening for comprehension is when you are trying to learn information or gain understanding. Critical listening is the most difficult because you have to interpret and then ______ [5] ______ the message.

_____ 4. The phrase that correctly fills in blank [4] is
- a. how the message is presented.
- b. what the speaker says.
- c. how you feel about the speaker.
- d. what you want to hear.

_____ 5. The phrase that correctly fills in blank [5] is
- a. understand.
- b. repeat.
- c. evaluate.
- d. respond to.

CHAPTER 9

MASTERY TEST 2 Outlining Skills

This Mastery Test can be completed in MyReadingLab.

Name____ Section ________________

Date ____________________ Number right _________ × 10 points = Score ____________

Directions: Read the following selection and answer the questions that follow.

What's Your Global Perspective?

1 It's not unusual for Germans, Italians, or Indonesians to speak three or four languages. "More than half of all primary school children in China now learn English and the number of English speakers in India and China—500 million—now exceeds the total number of mother-tongue English speakers elsewhere in the world." On the other hand, most U.S. children study only English in school—only 24,000 are studying Chinese. And only 22 percent of the population in the United States speaks a language other than English. Americans tend to think of English as the only international business language and don't see a need to study other languages. This could lead to future problems as a major research report commissioned by the British Council says that the "competitiveness of both Britain and the United States is being undermined" by only speaking English.

2 Monolingualism is one sign that a nation suffers from **parochialism**—viewing the world solely through one's own eyes and perspectives. People with a parochial attitude do not recognize that others have different ways of living and working. They ignore others' values and customs and rigidly apply an attitude of "ours is better than theirs" to foreign cultures. This type of narrow, restricted attitude is one approach that managers might take, but isn't the only one. In fact, there are three possible global attitudes. Let's look at each more closely.

3 First, an **ethnocentric attitude** is the belief that the best work approaches and practices are those of the *home* country (the country in which the company's headquarters are located). Managers with an ethnocentric attitude believe that people in foreign countries don't have the needed skills, expertise, knowledge, or experience to make the best business decisions as people in the home country do. They don't trust foreign employees with key decisions or technology.

4 Next, a **polycentric attitude** is the view that employees in the *host* country (the foreign country in which the organization is doing business) know the best work approaches and practices for running their business. Managers with this attitude view every foreign operation as different and hard to understand. Thus, they're likely to let employees there figure out how best to do things.

5 The final type of global attitude managers might have is a **geocentric attitude**, a *world-oriented* view that focuses on using the best approaches and people from around the globe. Managers with this type of attitude have a global view and look for the best approaches and people regardless of origin.

—Robbins and Coulter, *Management*, pp. 71–72

_____ 1. The subject of this selection is
a. language skills.
b. foreign businesses.
c. global attitudes.
d. management styles.

_____ 2. A manager who focuses on using the best approaches and people regardless of origin is said to have
a. a parochial attitude.
b. an ethnocentric attitude.
c. a polycentric attitude.
d. a geocentric attitude.

_____ 3. The word *monolingualism* (par. 2) refers to
a. one language.
b. more than one language.
c. many languages.
d. a lack of language.

_____ 4. The most useful marginal notations for paragraph 1 are
a. Other countries = many languages.
b. Over $^1/_2$ Chinese students learn English vs. 24,000 U.S. study Chinese.
c. More English speakers in India & China than anywhere.
d. 22 percent in U.S. speak another language.

_____ 5. The most useful highlighting of the last sentence of paragraph 1 is
a. could lead / future problems / research report / British Council / competitiveness / both Britain / United States / being undermined / only speaking English.
b. future problems / British Council / competitiveness / English.
c. major research report / competitiveness of both Britain and the United States / speaking English.
d. report / British Council / competitiveness / Britain / United States / undermined / only speaking English.

_____ 6. The most useful marking of paragraph 2 is
a. marking the definition of *parochialism* with an asterisk.
b. circling the phrase "ours is better than theirs."
c. numbering each sentence.
d. placing brackets around the last sentence.

_____ 7. The map that best presents the ideas in the selection is

a.

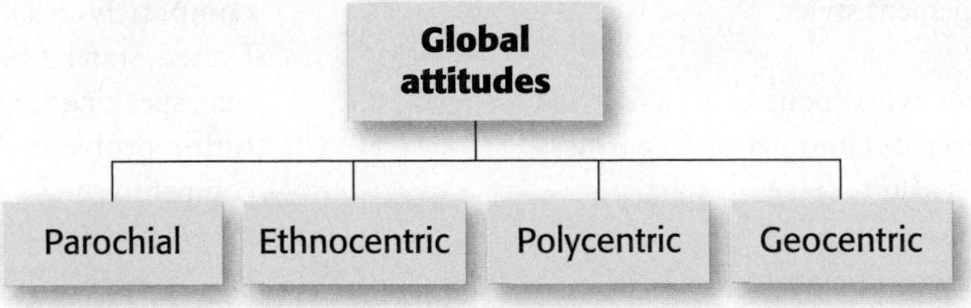

b.

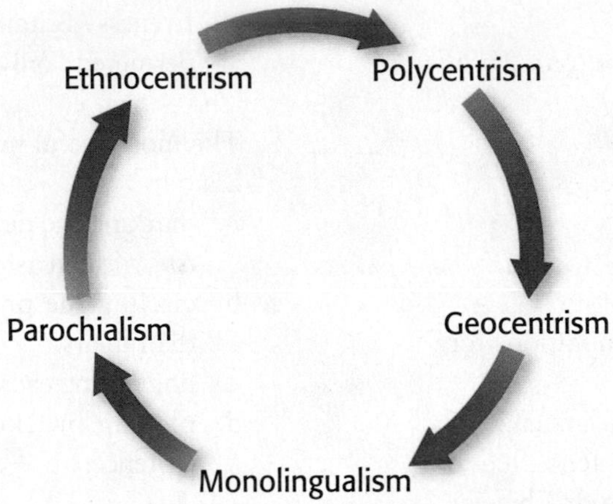

c.

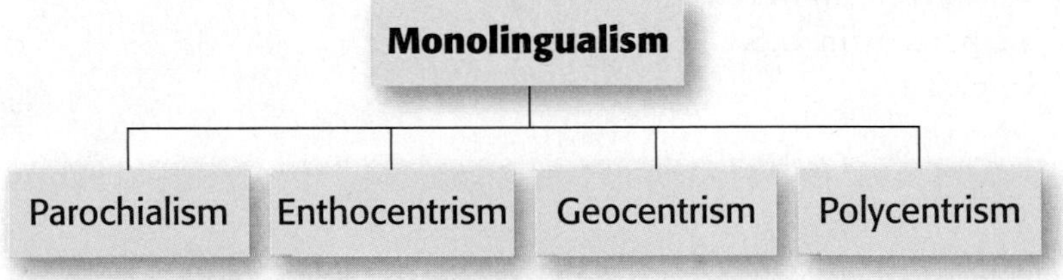

d.

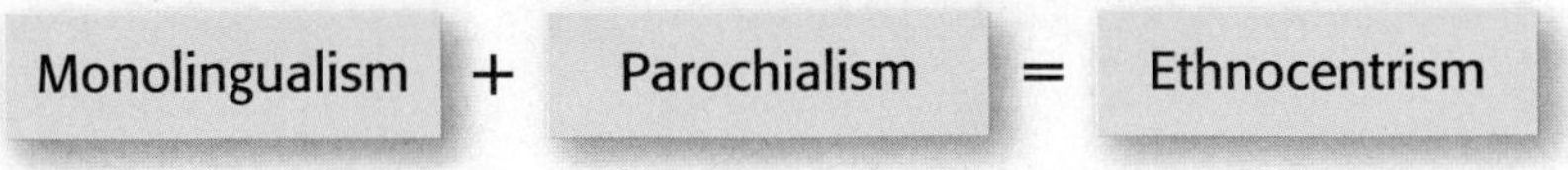

Use the following outline of paragraphs 3–5 to answer questions 8–10.

Global Attitudes

I. Ethnocentric
  A. Best work approaches/practices are from [1]
  B. Foreign employees don't have skills, expertise, knowledge, experience
  C. Foreign employees can't be trusted with key decisions/technology

II. Polycentric
  A. Best work approaches/practices are from [2]
  B. Foreign operations viewed as different and hard to understand
  C. Likely to let foreign employees figure out how best to do things

III. [3]
  A. World-oriented view
  B. Focuses on using best approaches and people regardless of origin

_____ 8. The word or phrase that correctly fills in blank [1] is
a. parochialism.
b. foreign employees.
c. the home country.
d. the host country.

_____ 9. The word or phrase that correctly fills in blank [2] is
a. the home country.
b. the host country.
c. company headquarters.
d. managers.

_____ 10. The word or phrase that correctly fills in blank [3] is
a. Global.
b. Geocentric.
c. Polycentric.
d. Foreign.

CHAPTER 9

MASTERY TEST 3 Reading Selection

This Mastery Test can be completed in MyReadingLab.

Name ______________________________ Section ______________

Date ____________________ Number right*________ 10 points = Score ____________

Applying Psychology to Everyday Life: Are You Sleep Deprived?

Saundra K. Ciccarelli and J. Noland White

This selection, taken from a psychology textbook, explores the causes and hazards of sleep deprivation. Would you consider yourself sleep deprived?

Vocabulary Preview

insomnia (par. 4) the inability to fall asleep, stay asleep, or get enough sleep

narcolepsy (par. 5) a disorder in which a person falls suddenly into a deep sleep

How serious is the problem of sleep deprivation?

1 Sleep deprivation has long been considered a fact of life for many people, especially college students. Dr. William Dement, one of the most renowned sleep experts in the field, believes that people are ignorant of the detrimental effects of sleep deprivation. Here are some of the facts he points out concerning the widespread nature of sleep deprivation:

- 55 percent of drowsy driving fatalities occur under the age of 25.
- 56 percent of the adult population reports that daytime drowsiness is a problem.
- In a study of 1,000 people who reported no daytime drowsiness, 34 percent were actually found to be dangerously sleepy.
- In samples of undergraduates, nurses, and medical students, 80 percent were dangerously sleep deprived.

2 Dr. Dement cautions that drowsiness should be considered a red alert. Contrary to many people's belief that drowsiness indicates the first step in failing asleep, he states that drowsiness is the last step—if you are drowsy, you are seconds away from sleep.

3 In an article published by CNN on its interactive Web site, the National Commission on Sleep Disorders estimates that "sleep deprivation costs $150 billion a year in higher stress and reduced workplace productivity." Sleep deprivation was one of the factors indicated in such disasters as the explosion of the *Challenger,* the Exxon *Valdez* oil spill, and the Chernobyl disaster.

---

*To calculate the number right, use items 1–10 under "Mastery Test Skills Check."

The student in the background is unable to stay awake during his class, indicating that he is seriously sleep deprived. Has this happened to you?

More disturbing facts:

- 30 to 40 percent of all heavy truck accidents can be attributed to driver fatigue.
- Drivers who are awake for 17 to 19 hours were more dangerous than drivers with a blood alcohol level of .05.
- 16 to 60 percent of road accidents involve sleep deprivation (the wide variation is due to the inability to confirm the cause of accidents, as the drivers are often killed).
- Sleep deprivation is linked to higher levels of stress, anxiety, depression, and unnecessary risk taking.

4 Clearly, sleep deprivation is a serious and all-too-common problem. In today's 24-hour-a-day society, stores are always open, services such as banking and transportation are always available, and many professionals (such as nurses, doctors, and firefighters) must work varying shifts around the clock. As stated earlier, shift work can seriously disrupt the normal sleep–wake cycle, often causing insomnia.

CAUSES OF SLEEP DEPRIVATION

5 Many of the sleep disorders that were discussed in this chapter are themselves causes of sleep deprivation. Sleep apnea, narcolepsy, sleepwalking, night terrors, and a condition called "restless leg syndrome," in which a person constantly moves his or her legs that are tingly or have crawling sensations, are all causes. Yet these problems are not the sole, or most common, cause of sleep deprivation.

6 The most obvious cause is the refusal of many people to go to sleep at a reasonable time, so that they can get the 8 hours of sleep that most adults need in order to function well. People want to watch that last bit of news or get a little more work done or party into the wee hours. Another reason for sleep loss is worry. People live in stressful times, and many people worry about a variety of concerns: debts, the stock market, relationships, war, rising crime, and so on. Finally, some medications that people take, both prescription and over-the-counter drugs, interfere with the sleep–wake cycle. For example, decongestants that some people take to relieve sinus congestion may cause a racing heartbeat, preventing them from relaxing enough to sleep.

How Can You Tell If You Are Sleep Deprived?

7 You may be sleep deprived if you:

- actually need your alarm clock to wake up.
- find getting out of bed in the morning is a struggle.
- feel tired, irritable, or stressed out for much of the day.
- have trouble concentrating or remembering.
- fall asleep watching TV, in meetings, lectures, or warm rooms.
- fall asleep after heavy meals or after a low dose of alcohol.
- fall asleep within 5 minutes of getting into bed. (A well-rested person actually takes 15 to 20 minutes to fall asleep.)

8 If you are interested in learning more about sleep deprivation and sleep disorders that can cause it, try searching the Internet. There are some excellent sites about sleep and sleep disorders, including many with online tests that can help people decide whether or not they have a sleep disorder.

—Ciccarelli and White, Psychology, pp. 169–171

MASTERY TEST SKILLS CHECK

Directions: Select the choice that best completes each of the following statements.

Checking Your Comprehension

_____ 1. The focus of this selection is on
   a. the sleep–wake cycle.
   b. brain activity during sleep.
   c. sleep deprivation.
   d. common sleep disorders.

_____ 2. The main idea of paragraph 1 is that
   a. sleep deprivation is a fact of life for college students.
   b. sleep deprivation is widespread and harmful.
   c. Dr. William Dement is an authority on sleep deprivation.
   d. drowsiness is actually a sign of being dangerously sleepy.

_____ 3. Of the following signs, the only one that does *not* indicate you may be sleep deprived is
   a. you actually need your alarm clock to wake up.
   b. you fall asleep after heavy meals.
   c. it takes you 15 to 20 minutes to fall asleep after going to bed.
   d. it is a struggle to get out of bed in the morning.

_____ 4. According to the selection, the most obvious cause of sleep deprivation is
   a. restless leg syndrome.
   b. narcolepsy.
   c. sleep apnea.
   d. the failure to go to bed at a reasonable time.

_____ 5. The authors use all of the following types of supporting details in this selection *except*
   a. examples.
   b. facts.
   c. statistics.
   d. procedures.

Applying Your Skills

_____ 6. The most important words to highlight in the last sentence of paragraph 2 are
a. drowsiness sleep.
b. drowsiness last step from sleep.
c. many people's belief drowsiness first step falling asleep last step drowsy away from sleep.
d. Contrary many people's belief drowsiness indicates first step falling asleep drowsiness is last step you are drowsy seconds away from sleep.

_____ 7. The most important words to highlight in the last sentence of paragraph 4 are
a. shift work seriously normal.
b. work can disrupt normal cycle often.
c. shift work disrupt sleep–wake cycle insomnia.
d. shift work seriously disrupt normal sleep–wake cycle often insomnia.

Use the following outline of paragraphs 5 and 6 to answer questions 8–10.

Causes of Sleep Deprivation

- I. Sleep disorders
  - A. Sleep apnea
  - B. Narcolepsy
  - C. ______________
  - D. Night terrors
  - E. ______________
    - 1. Tingly/crawling sensations cause legs to move
- II. Refusal to go to bed on time
- III. Worry
- IV. ______________
  - A. Prescription and over-the-counter
  - B. Interfere with sleep–wake cycle

_____ 8. The phrase that belongs next to [C] in the outline is
a. Sleep deprivation.
b. Sleepwalking.
c. Sleep–wake cycle.
d. Sleep disorder.

_____ 9. The phrase that belongs next to [E] in the outline is
a. Shift work.
b. Common cause.
c. Restless leg syndrome.
d. Sleepwalking.

_____ 10. The word or words that belong next to [IV] in the outline are
a. Some medications.
b. Illegal drugs.
c. Decongestants.
d. Racing heartbeat.

Studying Words

_____ 11. The word *renowned* (par. 1) means
a. unpopular.
b. famous.
c. unfamiliar.
d. local.

_____ 12. The word *detrimental* (par. 1) means
a. harmful.
b. emotional.
c. pleasant.
d. skillful.

_____ 13. The word *cautions* (par. 2) means
a. reminds.
b. guesses.
c. warns.
d. allows.

_____ 14. The prefix of the word *interactive* (par. 3) means
a. away.
b. between.
c. over.
d. without.

_____ 15. The word *disrupt* (par. 4) means
a. assist.
b. surround.
c. maintain.
d. disturb.

For more practice, ask your instructor for an opportunity to work on the mastery tests that appear in the Test Bank.

Summarizing the Reading

Directions: Complete the following summary of the reading by filling in the blanks.

Sleep deprivation is ________________________________. The National Commission on ____________________ estimates ______________________________ ____.

Sleep deprivation was a factor ____________________ and is linked to ____ ________________________________. Sleep deprivation may be caused by ____ ________________________.

Reading Visually

1. What does the photograph contribute to the reading overall? What details do you notice about it that are relevant to the reading?
2. What is the purpose of the box included with the reading? How might the information in the box be helpful to the author's audience?
3. If you can, take an online test for sleep disorders, as mentioned in paragraph 8. Did you identify a sleep problem?

Thinking Critically about the Reading

1. Do you consider yourself sleep deprived? Were you aware of any of the serious effects before you read this selection?
2. How does our "24-hour-a-day society" contribute to the problem of sleep deprivation?
3. If you knew someone suffering from sleep deprivation, what advice would you give him or her?

CHAPTER 10

Interpreting the Writer's Message and Purpose

LEARNING GOALS

This chapter will show you how to

1. Understand connotative meanings
2. Make inferences about what you read
3. Understand figurative language
4. Discover the author's purpose
5. Recognize tone
6. Examine language

Focusing on ... Interpreting What You Read

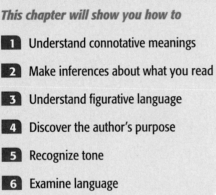

"Actually, I'm sitting here reading a book—just to see if I can still do it."

What point or message does this cartoon convey? While the point is clear, it is not directly stated. You had to use the information in the cartoon to reason out its point. This chapter concentrates on the reasoning processes readers must use to figure out ideas that are not directly stated.

Up to this point, we have been primarily concerned with building vocabulary, understanding a writer's basic organizational patterns, acquiring factual information, and organizing that information for learning and recall. So far, each chapter has been concerned with understanding what the author says, with factual content. Now our focus must change. To read well, you must go beyond what the author says and also consider what he or she means.

Many writers directly state some ideas but only hint at others. It is left to the reader to pick up the clues or suggestions and use logic and reasoning skills to figure out the writer's unstated message as you did in the cartoon on the preceding page. This chapter will explain several features of writing that suggest meaning. Once you are familiar with these, you will better understand the writer's unstated message. This chapter will also discuss how to discover the author's purpose and recognize tone.

CONNOTATIVE MEANINGS

1 LEARNING GOAL
Understand connotative meanings

Which of the following would you like to be a part of: a *crowd, mob, gang, audience, congregation,* or *class*? Each of these words has the same basic meaning: "an assembled group of people." But each has a different *shade* of meaning. *Crowd* suggests a large, disorganized group. *Audience,* on the other hand, suggests a quiet, controlled group. Try to decide what meaning each of the other words in the list suggests.

This example shows that words have two levels of meaning—a literal meaning and an additional shade of meaning. These two levels of meaning are called denotative and connotative. A word's **denotative meaning** is the meaning stated in the dictionary—its literal meaning. A word's **connotative meaning** is the additional implied meanings, or nuances, that a word may take on. Often the connotative meaning carries either a positive or negative, favorable or unfavorable impression. The words *mob* and *gang* have a negative connotation because they imply a disorderly, disorganized group. *Congregation, audience,* and *class* have a positive connotation because they suggest an orderly, organized group.

Here are a few more examples. Would you prefer to be described as "slim" or "skinny"? As "intelligent" or "brainy"? As "heavy" or "fat"? As "particular" or "picky"? Notice that each pair of words has a similar literal meaning, but that each word within the pair has a different connotation.

Depending on the words they choose, writers can suggest favorable or unfavorable impressions of the person, object, or event they are describing. For example, through the writer's choice of words, the following two sentences create two entirely different impressions. As you read them, underline words that have a positive or negative connotation.

The unruly crowd forced its way through the restraint barriers and ruthlessly attacked the rock star.

The enthusiastic group of fans burst through the fence and rushed toward the rock star.

When reading any type of informative or persuasive material, pay attention to the writer's choice of words. Often a writer may communicate subtle or hidden messages, or he or she may encourage the reader to feel positive or negative toward the subject.

Read the following paragraph on athletes' nutrition and, as you read, underline words that have a strong positive or negative connotation.

Athletes tend to eat either too much or too little protein, depending on their health consciousness, accuracy of nutrition education, or lifestyle. Some athletes fill up on too much meat. Others proclaim themselves vegetarian, yet they sometimes neglect to replace the beef with beans and are, in fact, only non-meat-eaters—and often protein deficient, at that. Although slabs of steak and huge hamburgers have no place in any athlete's diet—or anyone's diet—adequate amounts of protein are important for building muscles and repairing tissues.

—Clark, *Nancy Clark's Sports Nutrition Guidebook*, pp. 21–22

Did you mark words such as fill *up on, neglect, deficient, slabs,* and *huge*?

EXERCISE 10-1 Examining Connotative Meanings

Directions: For each of the following pairs of words, underline the word with the more positive connotation.

1. request demand
2. overlook neglect
3. ridicule tease
4. glance stare
5. display expose
6. garment gown
7. gaudy showy
8. clumsy awkward

9. artificial fake

10. token keepsake

EXERCISE 10-2 Writing Positive Connotations

Directions: For each word listed below, write a word that has a similar denotative meaning but a negative connotation. Then write a word that has a positive connotation. Use your dictionary or thesaurus, if necessary.

	Negative	Positive
Example: eat	gobble	dine
1. take	________	________
2. ask	________	________
3. look at	________	________
4. walk	________	________
5. dress	________	________
6. music	________	________
7. car	________	________
8. laugh	________	________
9. large	________	________
10. woman	________	________

IMPLIED MEANINGS

2 LEARNING GOAL
Make inferences about what you read

An **inference** is an educated guess or prediction about something unknown based on available facts and information. It is the logical connection that you draw between what you observe or know and what you do not know.

Suppose that you arrive ten minutes late for your sociology class. All the students have papers in front of them, and everyone is busily writing. Some students have worried or concerned looks on their faces. The instructor is seated and is reading a book. What is happening? From the known information you can make an inference about what you do not know. Did you figure out that the instructor had given the class a surprise quiz? If so, then you made a logical inference.

While the inference you made is probably correct, you cannot be sure until you speak with the instructor. Occasionally a logical inference can be wrong. Although it is unlikely, perhaps the instructor has laryngitis and has written notes on the board for the students to copy. Some students may look worried because they do not understand what the notes mean.

Here are more everyday situations. Make an inference for each.

- You are driving on an expressway and you notice a police car with flashing red lights behind you. You check your speedometer and notice that you are going ten miles an hour over the speed limit.
- A woman seated alone in a bar nervously glances at everyone who enters. Every few minutes she checks her watch.

In the first situation, a good inference might be that you are going to be stopped for speeding. However, it is possible that the officer only wants to pass you to get to an accident ahead or to stop someone driving faster than you. In the second situation, one inference is that the woman is waiting to meet someone who is late.

The following paragraph is taken from a book by Jenny Lawson called *Let's Pretend This Never Happened: (A Mostly True Memoir)*. First, read it for factual content.

When I was little, my father used to sell guns and ammo at a sporting goods store, but I always told everyone he was an arms dealer, because it sounded more exciting. Eventually, though, he saved up enough money to quit his job and build a taxidermy shop next to our house (which was tiny and built out of asbestos back when people still thought that was a good thing). My dad built the taxidermy shop himself out of old wood from abandoned barns and did a remarkable job, fashioning it to look exactly like a Wild West saloon, complete with swinging doors and gaslights and a hitching post for horses. Then he hired a bunch of guys to work for him, many of whom looked to me as if they were fresh from prison or just about to go back in. I can't help feeling sorry for the confused strangers who would wander into my father's taxidermy shop, expecting to find a bar and a stiff drink, and who instead found several rough-looking men my father had hired, covered in blood and elbow deep in animal carcasses. I suspect, though, that the blood-covered taxidermists probably shared their personal flasks with the baffled stranger, because although they seemed slightly dangerous, they also were invariably good-hearted, and I'm fairly certain they recognized that anyone stumbling onto that kind of scene would probably need a strong drink even more than when they'd first set out looking for a bar to begin with.

—Lawson, *Let's Pretend This Never Happened: (A Mostly True Memoir)*, p.18

The paragraph is primarily factual—it tells who did what, when, and where. However, some ideas are not directly stated and must be inferred from the information given. Here are a few examples. Some are fairly obvious inferences; others are less obvious.

- The author sometimes exaggerates.
- Asbestos is dangerous.
- The author's father had building skills.
- People mistook the taxidermy shop for a bar.
- Taxidermy involves removing the innards from animal carcasses.
- Taxidermy can be an upsetting process to watch.

Although none of the above ideas is directly stated, they can be inferred from clues provided in the passage. Some of the statements could be inferred from actions, others by adding facts together, and still others by the writer's choice of words.

Now read the following passage to find out what has happened to Katja's brother.

Due to her own hardship, Katja was not thrilled when her younger brother called her from Warsaw and said that he was going to join her in the U.K. Katja warned him that opportunities were scarce in London for a Polish immigrant. "Don't worry," he said in an effort to soothe her anxiety. "I already have a job in a factory."

An advertisement in a Warsaw paper had promised good pay for Polish workers in Birmingham. A broker's fee of $500 and airfare were required, so her brother borrowed the money from their mother. He made the trip with a dozen other young Polish men.

The "broker" picked the young men up at Heathrow and piled them in a van. They drove directly to Birmingham, and at nightfall the broker dropped the whole crew off at a ramshackle house inside the city. He ordered them to be ready to be picked up in the morning for their first day of work. A bit dazed by the pace, they stretched out on the floor to sleep.

Their rest was brief. In the wee hours of the night, the broker returned with a gang of 10 or so thugs armed with cricket bats. They beat the young Polish boys to a pulp and robbed them of all their valuables. Katja's brother took some heavy kicks to the ribs and head, then stumbled out of the house. Once outside, he saw two police cars parked across the street. The officers in the cars obviously chose to ignore the mayhem playing out in front of their eyes. Katja's brother knew better than try to convince them otherwise; the police in Poland would act no differently. Who knows, maybe they were part of the broker's scam. Or maybe they just didn't care about a bunch of poor Polish immigrants "invading" their town.

—Batstone, "Katja's Story," as appeared in *Sojourners Magazine*, June 2006

If you made the right inferences, you realized that Katja's brother became a victim of a scam. Let's look at the kinds of clues the writer gave that led to this inference.

1. **Description.** By the way the writer describes what happened to Katja's brother, you begin to understand the situation. He is promised a well-paying job, but is told that job opportunities are scarce for Polish immigrants. A broker's fee of $500 is charged. The house they are taken to on arrival is described as *ramshackle*. The young men slept on the floor.
2. **Conversation.** The brother sounded very confident, perhaps overconfident: "Don't worry. I already have a job in a factory."
3. **Action.** The actions make it clear what is happening. The brother is "piled" into a van with 12 other workers. They are robbed and brutally beaten after arriving at the house. The police do not respond.
4. **Writer's commentary/details.** As the writer describes the situation, he provides numerous clues. The trip was made with a dozen other men. The word *broker* is placed in quotation marks, suggesting the term is inaccurate or questionable. The men's rest was described as *brief*, suggesting that something is about to change. The broker returns with people the writer calls a "gang of . . . thugs." The police are described as having obviously chosen "to ignore the mayhem."

How to Make Inferences

Making an inference is a thinking process. As you read, you are following the author's thoughts. You are also alert for ideas that are suggested but not directly stated. Because inference is a logical thought process, there is no simple step-by-step procedure to follow. Each inference depends entirely on the situation, the facts provided, and the reader's knowledge and experience.

However, here are a few guidelines to keep in mind as you read. These will help you get in the habit of looking beyond the factual level to the inferential.

MAKING INFERENCES

1. **Be sure you understand the literal meaning.** You should have a clear grasp of the key idea and supporting details of each paragraph.
2. **Notice details.** Often a detail provides a clue that will help you make an inference. When you spot a striking or unusual detail, ask yourself: Why did the writer include this piece of information?

3. **Add up the facts.** Consider all the facts taken together. Ask yourself: What is the writer trying to suggest from this set of facts? What do all these facts and ideas point toward?
4. **Watch for clues.** The writer's choice of words and detail often suggest his or her attitude toward the subject. Notice, in particular, descriptive words, emotionally charged words, and words with strong positive or negative connotations.
5. **Be sure your inference is supportable.** An inference must be based on fact. Make sure there is sufficient evidence to justify any inference you make.

EXERCISE 10-3 Making Inferences

Directions: Read each of the following passages. Then answer the questions that follow. You will need to reason out, or infer, the answers.

Passage A

Schmoozing

If we want to be successful, we need to develop and enhance our conversational prowess in the face to face space. Schmooze or lose is the rule for both personal and professional success. Schmooze means relaxed, friendly, easygoing conversation. Period. End of story. There is no end result that is preplanned as a goal. Formal research from Harvard to Stanford and places in between indicates that the ability to converse and communicate is a key factor of successful leaders. Oral communication skills are consistently rated in the top three most important skill sets in surveys by universities and workplace specialists.

While we're able to communicate digitally, we must still be proficient in the face to face shared space as well as in cyberspace. As corporations continue to merge, jobs disappear and industries are offshored, we need conversation and communication more than ever before.

—RoAne, *Face to Face*, pp. 2–3

1. What is the author's attitude toward digital communication?

____

2. Not everyone loves to schmooze. Why does the author think it is essential for success?

____

3. What information sources does the author trust?

____

4. What do you think the author considers success to be?

____

Passage B

Government Surveillance

Governments have long relied on . . . spying. What is new about today's surveillance is the ease with which it can be conducted; over the past several decades, technological advances have vastly expanded the government's monitoring ability. Wiretapping and bugging have been joined by space-age eavesdropping and computer-hacking techniques that make interception of oral and written communications infinitely easier than in J. Edgar Hoover's day. Observation of physical activities, once reliant on naked eye observation and simple devices like binoculars, can now be carried out with night scopes and thermal imagers, sophisticated telescopic and magnification devices, tracking tools and "see-through" detection technology. Records of transactions with hospitals, banks, stores, schools, and other institutions, until the 1980s usually found only in file cabinets, are now much more readily obtained with the advent of computers and the Internet.

Which surveillance technique does this image illustrate?

A second difference between the surveillance of yesteryear and today is the strength of the government's resolve to use it. Especially since September 11, 2001, the United States government has been obsessed, as perhaps it should be, with ferreting out national security threats, and modern surveillance techniques—ranging from data mining to global positioning systems—have played a major role in this pursuit. But the new surveillance has also increasingly been aimed at ordinary criminals, including those who represent only a trivial threat to public safety. And more than occasionally it has also visited significant intrusion on large numbers of law-abiding citizens—sometimes inadvertently, sometimes not.

Sophisticated surveillance technology and a powerful government eager to take advantage of it make a dangerous combination—a recipe for continuous mass surveillance.

While surveillance can be a valuable law enforcement tool, it also poses a significant threat to our legitimate freedoms—to express what we believe, to do what we want to do, to be the type of person we really are. In short, it can diminish our privacy and autonomy.

—Slobogin, *Privacy at Risk*, pp. 3–4

5. What is the author's attitude toward the government?

____

6. Why should the government be more interested in monitoring the behavior of its citizens today?

____

7. How are surveillance techniques being misused?

____

8. Where do you think the author stands on the issue of right to privacy? (What rights to privacy do we or should we have?)

____

Passage C

UFOs

There should be little doubt that many claimed sightings of ghosts, UFOs, angels, and monsters by sincere witnesses are a result of the way our vision works. Contrary to what you may have assumed, we don't really "see" what we look at. What happens when you aim your eyes at something is that your brain "tells" you what you see. And your brain never tells you with 100 percent accuracy. It does this to be efficient and it really does help us function in a world with far too much detail and movement to take in. But sometimes this causes us to "see" things that were never there or at least not there in the form presented to us. It can also cause us to miss things that really are there. Sometimes things that our vision misses might have been the critical pieces of information that would have revealed to us that the UFO or ghost hovering out there is really just a bird or a patch of fog, for example.

—Harrison, *50 Popular Beliefs That People Think Are True*, p. 31

9. What do most people who see UFOs, ghosts, or angels believe about their sightings?

____

10. What relationship does the brain have to the eyes?

____

11. How is it helpful to not see everything?

____

12. How does the brain cause us to see things that are not real?

____

____

Passage D

Personal Comfort Zone

It's an uncomfortable fact of life, but there are people in this world who simply can't live in peace with their fellow human beings. You try to cultivate a love your neighbor philosophy, and then some mutant wrecks it by killing you. Regrettably, one violent encounter can cut short a lifetime of altruism. So you must make a personal decision either to be wholly trusting (and vulnerable) or ever vigilant. Vigilance doesn't mean you have to walk around angry. Indeed, if you take the emotion out of it, vigilance merely becomes a relaxed, practical exercise for fully participating in life.

For example, establish a personal comfort zone that no stranger is allowed to enter. This is not paranoia, just good practical sense. You need a trigger that allows you to stay relaxed most of the time. At a minimum, the zone is about as far as you can extend your arm or leg.

—Perkins et al., *Attack Proof*, p. 7

13. What attitude would you predict the author would have toward his co-workers?

____

14. How realistic is it to keep a stranger-proof comfort zone the distance of our outstretched arm?

____

15. Does the author anticipate that not all readers will agree with his ideas? How do you know?

____

____

16. How would the author define the term *comfort zone*?

____

EXERCISE 10-4 Making Inferences

Directions: Read each of the following passages and answer the questions that follow.

Passage A

Working Moms

Always a career woman, Sharon Allen panicked when she had her first child. "I thought, 'How can I have my career and a child?' " recalls the now-longtime law enforcement official. "The minute I held her, I knew she was the most important thing in my life."

Thus began Allen's personal and professional journey as a working mother and wife (she's been married to her husband for 28 years) that blended child care with police work. Whether she was a detective or now the assistant police chief, she had irregular hours and at one time worked a 4–10 shift giving her three days off—one day to take care of the house, one to be at the kids' school, and one for herself. During that time, she earned her BS and Masters Degree in Education at a local college, and even worked part-time as a security guard at a mall to make ends meet.

"I was doing well with my career even as a working mother before it was in style . . . and yes, sometimes I felt I had to work twice as hard. I made mistakes, too, such as when my son was in high school, and I badgered him to cut his long hair. 'Mother,' he said, 'I am a good person . . . I follow your rules and stay out of trouble . . . If I have long hair, it's not a big deal;' I learned to compromise. (He's now at West Point!)

"That 'S' on my chest can fade sometimes. I used to crash and burn and sleep on the weekends. People say I am so successful—I say if my children have grown up to be self-sufficient, good citizens, I've been a pretty good mom. Half the battle in life is choosing something you love to do. You need to have that sense of accomplishment in your heart and to serve people the way you would like to be served. That's key."

—Greenberg and Avigdor, *What Happy Working Mothers Know*, p. 97

1. What is Sharon Allen's attitude toward working mothers?

   ____

2. What does the "S" on her chest stand for?

   ____

3. Why do you think the author chose to profile Sharon Allen for a book about happy working mothers?

   ____

   ____

4. Why might Sharon have had to work twice as hard as others?

   ____

   ____

Passage B

Why Manners Matter

When we leave home, driven by the overwhelming need to earn a living or go to the January sales or eat good Italian food, our apprehension about what we might encounter in the world proves to be negatively reinforcing. We put on our dark glasses and avoid eye contact. Increasingly we plug in our iPods: less for tuning into the music than tuning out the people around us. We talk or text on our cell phones constantly, on the train or bus, in the shops and cinemas, on the street. It's as if we deprive ourselves of immediate sensory stimulation—shade our eyes, block our ears, stop our mouths—in order to experience the world through a protective mask.

What idea in the passage does this photograph illustrate?

Finally, when with reluctant resignation we do interact with a stranger—with say, a taxi driver or a coffee barista or a checkout person at the supermarket—we do it all with sign language and half sentences, often still talking on the phone to someone (anyone!) else as if to distract our attention away from the irritations inherent in any physical, material encounter with untested individuals. People we need, and upon whose goodwill we depend.

In our efforts to avoid all the latent rudeness and unpleasantness in the world, we, too, have become harder, and ruder, and less pleasant. Yet the more we distrust each other, the more we are confused and irritated by each other, the greater the risk that we abandon the task of finding a common language with which to peacefully interact.

In my block of units there's a different but connected problem. We share the same building, we see each other regularly, we pass close by each other in the foyer and on the stairs. But because we don't have manners, we have no formula for successfully relating to each other. Living in the noisy hubbub of the city, each one of us wants to protect our privacy, especially at home. Me, too. I consider myself something of an urban hermit. I don't want to be friends with people purely because we live in close proximity. On the other hand, it's rather strange to pretend you have no knowledge of someone who lives across the hall.

So when we cross paths we all shut our eyes or mumble Hi—but it's awkward. No one wants to cross that dreaded threshold into cozy familiarity or, God forbid, mutual obligation. Here is where manners would come in handy. In a more mannered world, we'd simply get the introductions over with, have a cup of tea and then return to pleasant but formal distance. Good morning Lovely day, isn't it? we would say. But instead we scuff and shuffle and we're not sure whether to smile or not and the whole process is uncomfortable. The fear of over familiarity with our neighbors has led to an inability to relate to each other in any way at all.

—Holdforth, *Why Manners Matter,* pp. 16–17

5. What assumption does the author make about anyone who ventures out in public?

____

6. Why does the author think that people want to isolate themselves?

____

7. The author infers that people feel uncomfortable around close neighbors because they scuff and shuffle. Is this a reasonable inference?

____

8. How and why would manners be helpful?

____

9. The author states we talk on phones to avoid talking to people face-to-face. Do you agree with this assumption?

____

EXERCISE 10-5 Making Inferences

Directions: Bring a magazine ad to class. Working in groups of three or four students, make as many inferences as possible about each ad. For example, answer questions such as "What is happening?" "How does each person feel?" and "How will this ad sell the product?" Group members who differ in their opinions should present evidence to support their own inferences. Each group should then state to the class, as clearly as possible, the purpose of each ad. Be specific; try to say more than "To sell the product."

FIGURATIVE LANGUAGE

3 LEARNING GOAL Understand figurative language

Read each of the following statements:

> The cake tasted like a moist sponge.
> The wilted plants begged for water.
> Jean wore her heart on her sleeve.

You know that a cake cannot really have the same taste as a sponge, that plants do not actually request water, and that a person's heart cannot really be attached to her sleeve. However, you know what message the writer is communicating in each sentence. The cake was soggy and tasteless, the plants were extremely dry, and Jean revealed her feelings to everyone around her.

Each of these sentences is an example of figurative language. **Figurative language** is a way of describing something that makes sense on an imaginative level but not on a factual or literal level. Notice that while none of the above expressions is literally true, each is meaningful. In many figurative expressions, one thing is compared with another for some quality they have in common. Take, for example, the familiar expression in the following sentence:

> Sam eats like a horse.

The diagram below shows the comparison being made in this figurative expression:

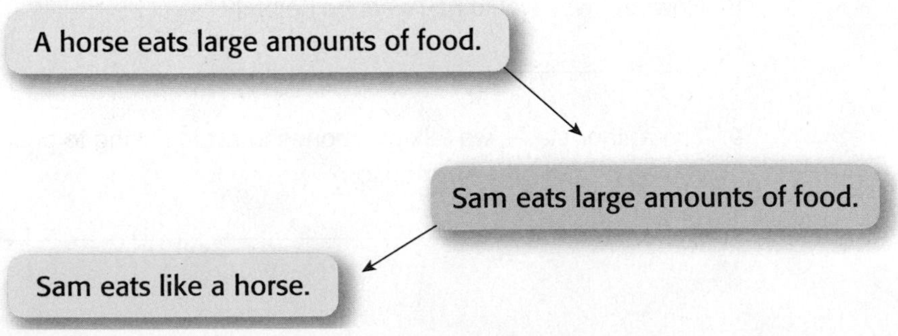

A horse eats large amounts of food.
Sam eats large amounts of food.
Sam eats like a horse.

You can see that two unlike things—Sam and a horse—are compared because they are alike in one particular way—the amount they eat.

The purpose of figurative language is to paint a word picture—to help you visualize how something looks, feels, or smells. Figurative language is a device writers use to express an idea or feeling and, at the same time, allow the reader the freedom of imagination. Since it is not factual, figurative language allows the writer to express attitudes and opinions without directly stating them. Depending on the figurative expression chosen, a writer can create a variety of impressions.

When reading an article that contains figurative language, be sure to pay close attention to the images and feelings created. Be sure you recognize that the writer is shaping your response to the topic or subject.

Figurative language is used in many types of articles and essays. It is also used in everyday speech and in slang expressions. Various types of literature, especially poetry, also use figurative language. Notice its use in the following excerpt from a play by William Shakespeare.

> All the world's a stage,
> And all the men and women merely players;
> They have their exits and entrances;
> And one man in his time plays many parts.
>
> —Shakespeare, *As You Like It*, II, vii,139

Here are a few more examples from other sources. Notice how each creates a visual image of the person, object, or quality being described.

> The red sun was pasted in the sky like a wafer.
>
> —Stephen Crane, *The Red Badge of Courage*
>
> In plucking the fruit of memory,
> one runs the risk of spoiling its bloom.
>
> —Joseph Conrad
>
> "I will speak daggers to her, but use none."
>
> —Shakespeare, *Hamlet*
>
> Life, like a dome of many-colored glass,
> Stains the white radiance of Eternity.
>
> —Shelley, "Adonais"
>
> Float like a butterfly, sting like a bee.
>
> —Muhammad Ali

EXERCISE 10-6 Analyzing Figurative Expressions

Directions: Each of the following sentences includes a figurative expression. Read each sentence and explain in your own words what the expression means.

1. My psychology quiz was a piece of cake.

   ____

2. My life is a junkyard of broken dreams.

   ____

3. "Life is as tedious as a twice-told tale." (Shakespeare, *King John III*)

   ____

4. "A sleeping child gives me the impression of a traveler in a very far country." (Ralph Waldo Emerson)

   ____

5. "I refuse to accept the cynical notion that nation after nation must spiral down a militaristic stairway into the hell of thermonuclear destruction." (Martin Luther King, Jr.)

   ____

EXERCISE 10-7 Analyzing Passages

Directions: Read each of the following passages and answer the questions that follow.

Passage A

Doing Time Together

1 Toward the end of visiting hours today, Grace, who is married to a man serving a life sentence, came out of the prison.[1] I've seen Grace visiting San Quentin since 1995. She always greets me warmly but has never really opened up to me about her personal life—so I was particularly intrigued when she said excitedly, "I have a present in the gift shop! Come on, you can come get it with me." The gift shop (or "hobby shop" as is it officially called by the San Quentin authorities) is located just outside the main gate of the prison and is staffed by one highly trusted inmate decked out

---

[1]Grace is a pseudonym, as are the names of all the participants.

What does this photograph reveal about the participants?

in a blindingly bright yellow jumpsuit (an outfit mandated after a hobby shop worker wearing the customary prison attire of a chambray shirt and blue jeans walked away from his post and into the "free" world unnoticed). This particular store consists of a dimly lit sallow room with three long display cases arranged like a horseshoe. Inside the cases and hanging on the walls are hundreds of objects crafted by prisoners, available for purchase by anyone who takes a fancy to them: paintings, drawings, earrings, note cards, clocks, and other trinkets produced by those inmates lucky enough to be permitted to engage in such "hobbies" behind the walls.

2 As we strolled the short distance to the shop, Grace explained that her wedding anniversary was this week and her husband had made a gift for her that she could now retrieve. Before I could ask any questions we reached the front of the shop and came upon the prisoner–worker standing outside the door, smoking. Visibly eager to claim her present, Grace told the worker that she had a gift to collect but added kindly, "You can finish your cigarette first." The man smiled shyly and took a few more self-conscious puffs, then stubbed out the cigarette and headed into the shop. Once inside he seemed a little uncertain of what to do, so Grace coached him through the process of giving her the correct form to fill out and of locating her gift, noting wryly, "I've done this a few times before." She signed the paperwork, and the inmate handed over a package about double the size of a shoe box, which Grace clutched to her chest. "I already know what it is," she told me, her voice quickening with anticipation. "Come on, we can go to the car and open it."

3 We walked over to the parking lot, and she set the gift on the hood of her car, unlocked the vehicle's door and threw her jacket inside, then pulled a pocket knife out of the glove compartment and began slitting open the box. Tearing away the protective packaging, Grace lifted out a wooden jewelry box, the general style of which I recognized from the others on display in the hobby shop. It was beautifully made, and Grace commented happily on the luster of the orange-colored wood and the obvious attention to detail. We both stood there admiring it, and then she opened the lid, revealing that it doubled as a music box: a tune began to tinkle, and I recognized it as a popular ballad for lovers, "Unchained Melody": "Oh, my love, my darling/I've hungered for your touch, a long lonely time/And time goes by so slowly and time can do so much."

4 While I was listening to the little chimes, I stole a glance at Grace and saw that she was teary eyed. Without saying anything, she set down the box and turned and wrapped her arms around me. We stood there hugging each other, much harder and longer than I had ever hugged her before, and the tightness of her clutch overwhelmed me with sadness. My melancholy was keenly intensified by the gray misty December weather, a fitting backdrop for the bleak scene: a lonely woman with only a graduate student conducting her fieldwork for company, opening her anniversary

gift on the hood of a car in a deserted prison parking lot, having just said goodbye to her husband before leaving him to be locked back into his cell . . . as he likely would be for a great many anniversaries to come.

—Comfort, *Doing Time Together: Love and Family in the Shadow of the Prison*, pp. 1–2

1. Answer each of the following questions by making an inference.
   a. How does wearing a yellow jumpsuit prevent the inmate from escaping?

      ____

   b. Why is it odd to call the activities the prisoners engage in "hobbies"?

      ____

   c. Why did Grace let the prisoner finish his cigarette?

      ____

      ____

   d. How does the reader know that Grace is familiar with the prison?

      ____

      ____

   e. Why is Grace's pocket knife in her car and not in her purse or on her person?

      ____

   f. What does the music say about Grace's relationship with her husband?

      ____

   g. What is unusual about the way Grace is celebrating her anniversary?

      ____

      ____

2. List several words with negative connotations that suggest how the writer feels about the prison.

   ____

3. List several words with positive connotations that suggest how the writer feels about the woman she is with.

   ____

4. What main point do you think the writer is trying to make?

   ____

Passage B

Avatar Fantasy Life: The Blurring Lines of Reality

1 Dissatisfied with your current life? Would you like to become someone else? Maybe someone rich? Maybe someone with no responsibilities? You can. Join a world populated with virtual people and live out your fantasy.

2 For some, the appeal is strong. *Second Life*, one of several Internet sites that offer an alternative virtual reality, has exploded in popularity. Of its 8 million "residents," 450,000 spend twenty to forty hours a week in their second life.

3 To start your second life, you select your avatar, a kind of digital hand puppet, to be your persona in this virtual world. Your avatar comes in just a basic form, although you can control its movements just fine. But that bare body certainly won't do. You will want to clothe it. For this, you have your choice of outfits for every occasion. Although you buy them from other avatars in virtual stores, you have to spend real dollars. You might want some hair, too. For that, too, you'll have your choice of designers. And again, you'll spend real dollars. And you might want to have a sex organ. There is even a specialty store for that.

4 All equipped the way you want to be?

5 Then it is time to meet other avatars, the virtual personas of real-life people. In this virtual world, they buy property, open businesses, and interact with one another. They share stories, talk about their desires in life, and have drinks in virtual bars.

6 Avatars flirt, too. Some even date and marry.

7 For most people, this second life is just an interesting game. They come and go. Some people, though, get so caught up in their virtual world that their real world shrinks in appeal, and they neglect friends and family. That is, they neglect their real friends and family, but remain attentive to their virtual friends and family. As the virtual replaces the real, the virtual becomes real and the real fades into nonreality.

—Henslin, *Sociology: A Down-to-Earth Approach,* p. 153

1. What is the author's attitude toward avatars?

2. Explain why the phrase "digital hand puppet" is an example of figurative language.

3. Why does the author put the word "residents" in quotation marks?

4. What kind of tone is the author using when he says "But that bare body certainly won't do"?

____

5. When the author says, "All equipped the way you want to be?" what is the author suggesting about the choices available for avatars?

____

____

____

6. What does the author think about how avatars affect people's perception of reality?

____

____

UNDERSTAND THE AUTHOR'S PURPOSE

4 LEARNING GOAL
Discover the author's purpose

Writers have many different reasons or purposes for writing. Read the statements below and try to decide why each was written:

1. About 14,000 ocean-going ships pass through the Panama Canal each year. This averages about three ships per day.
2. *New Unsalted Dry Roasted Almonds.* Finally, a snack with a natural flavor and without salt. We simply shell the nuts and dry-roast them until they're crispy and crunchy. Try a jar this week.
3. Man is the only animal that blushes or has a need to.
4. If a choking person has fallen down, first turn him or her faceup. Then knit together the fingers of both your hands and apply pressure with the heel of your bottom hand to the victim's abdomen.
5. If your boat capsizes, it is usually safer to cling to the boat than to try to swim ashore.

Statement 1 was written to give information, 2 to persuade you to buy almonds, 3 to amuse you and make a comment on human behavior, 4 to explain, and 5 to give advice.

In each of the examples, the writer's purpose was fairly clear, as it will be in most textbooks (to present information), newspaper articles (to communicate daily events), and reference books (to provide facts). However, in many other types of writing, authors have varied, sometimes less obvious, purposes. In these cases, an author's purpose must be inferred.

Often a writer's purpose is to express an opinion indirectly. Or the writer may want to encourage the reader to think about a particular issue or problem. Writers achieve their purposes by manipulating and controlling what they say and how they say it. This section will focus on techniques writers use and features of language that writers control to achieve the results they want.

Style and Intended Audience

Are you able to recognize a friend just by his or her voice? Can you identify family members by their footsteps? You are able to do so because each person's voice and footsteps are unique. Have you noticed that writers have unique characteristics as well? One author may use many examples; another may use few. One author may use relatively short sentences; another may use long, complicated ones. The characteristics that make a writer unique are known as **style**. By changing style, writers can create different effects.

Writers may vary their styles to suit their intended audiences. A writer may write for a general-interest audience (anyone who is interested in the subject but is not considered an expert). Most newspapers and periodicals, such as *Time* and *The Week*, appeal to a general-interest audience. On the other hand, a writer may have a particular interest group in mind. A writer may write for medical doctors in the *Journal of American Medicine*, for skiing enthusiasts in *Skiing Today*, or for antique collectors in *The World of Antiques*. A writer may also target his or her writing for an audience with particular political, moral, or religious attitudes. Articles in the *New Republic* often appeal to a particular political viewpoint, whereas the *Catholic Digest* appeals to a specific religious group.

Depending on the group of people for whom the author is writing, he or she will change the level of language, choice of words, and method of presentation. One step toward identifying an author's purpose, then, is to ask yourself the question: Who is the intended audience? Your response will be your first clue to determining why the author wrote the article.

EXERCISE 10-8 Analyzing Intended Audience

Directions: Read each of the following statements and decide for whom each was written. Write a sentence that describes the intended audience.

1. If you are worried about the state of your investments, meet with a broker to figure out how you can still reach your financial goals.

____

____

2. Think about all the places your drinking water has been before you drink another drop. Most likely it has been chemically treated to remove bacteria and chemical pollutants. Soon you may begin to feel the side effects of these treatments. Consider switching to filtered, distilled water today.

____

____

3. The new subwoofers from Gilberton put so much bass in your ride that they are guaranteed to keep your mother out of your car.

____

4. Bright and White laundry detergent removes dirt and stains faster than any other brand.

____

5. As a driver, you're ahead if you can learn to spot car trouble before it's too late. If you can learn the difference between drips and squeaks that occur under normal conditions and those that mean big trouble is just down the road, then you'll be ahead of expensive repair bills and won't find yourself stranded on a lonely road.

____

____

TONE

5 LEARNING GOAL Recognize tone

The **tone** of a speaker's voice helps you interpret what he or she is saying. If the following sentence were read aloud, the speaker's voice would tell you how to interpret it: "Would you mind closing the door?" In print you cannot tell whether the speaker is polite, insistent, or angry. In speech you could tell by whether the speaker emphasized the word *would, door,* or *mind.*

Just as a speaker's tone of voice tells how the speaker feels, so does a writer convey a tone, or feeling, through his or her writing. Tone refers to the attitude or feeling a writer expresses about his or her subject. A writer may adopt a sentimental tone, an angry tone, a humorous tone, a sympathetic tone, an instructive tone, a persuasive tone, and so forth. Here are a few examples of different tones. How does each make you feel?

- Instructive

> When purchasing a piece of clothing, one must be concerned with quality as well as with price. Be certain to check for the following: double-stitched seams, matched patterns, and ample linings.

- Sympathetic

> The forlorn, frightened-looking child wandered through the streets alone, searching for someone who would show an interest in helping her find her parents.

- Persuasive

> Child abuse is a tragic occurrence in our society. Strong legislation is needed to control the abuse of innocent victims and to punish those who are insensitive to the rights and feelings of others.

- Humorous

> ACQUAINTANCE, n. A person whom we know well enough to borrow from, but not well enough to lend to.
>
> CABBAGE, n. A familiar kitchen-garden vegetable about as large and wise as a man's head.
>
> CIRCUS, n. A place where horses, ponies and elephants are permitted to see men, women and children acting the fool.
>
> LOVE, n. A temporary insanity curable by marriage or by removal of the patient from the influences under which he incurred the disorder.
>
> —Ambrose Bierce

- Nostalgic

> "Framed in gold is an old inscription for my great grandmother in the living room of the Miranda house in Roswell, NM. My grandma-grandma died, but it still hangs in the very same spot her daughter, my grandmother, had placed it in her honor decades ago. Ever since my sisters and I were infants our grandmother claimed us as her own. Every weekend she would make the 3-hour trek from Roswell to Mountainair to visit us and our single parent father. Long after she had returned home, the smell of Elizabeth Taylor perfume would linger on our clothes, fried potatoes and refried beans in our kitchen. Never have we called anyone else 'mother.'"
>
> —Montoya, "A Collection for My Mother and Father," *Tribal College Journal*

In the first example, the writer offers advice in a straightforward, informative style. In the second, the writer wants you to feel sorry for the child. This is done through description. In the third example, the writer tries to convince the reader that action must be taken to prevent child abuse. The use of such words as *tragic*, *innocent*, and *insensitive* establish this tone.

The tone of an article directly affects how the reader interprets and responds to it. If, as in the fourth example, the writer's tone is humorous and you do not recognize this, you will miss the point of the entire selection. If the writer's tone is nostalgic, as in the fifth example, it is important to recognize this and the feelings it provokes in you the reader. From these examples, you can see, then, that you may not receive an objective, unbiased treatment of a subject.

The author's tone is intended to rub off on you, so to speak. If a writer's tone is humorous, the writer hopes you will be amused. If a writer's tone is persuasive, the writer hopes you will accept his or her viewpoint. You can see how tone can be important in determining an author's purpose. Therefore, a second question to ask when trying to determine an author's purpose is: What tone does the writer use? Or: How is the writer trying to make me feel about the subject?

EXERCISE 10-9 Analyzing Tone

Directions: Read each of the following statements, paying particular attention to the tone. Then write a sentence that describes the tone. Prove your point by listing some of the words that reveal the author's feelings.

1. No one says that nuclear power is risk free. There are risks involved in all methods of producing energy. However, the scientific evidence is clear and obvious. Nuclear power is at least as safe as any other means used to generate electricity.

 ____

 ____

2. The condition of our city streets is outrageous. The sidewalks are littered with paper and other garbage—you could trip while walking to the store. The streets themselves are in even worse condition. Deep potholes and crumbling curbs make it unsafe to drive. Where are our city tax dollars going if not to correct these problems?

 ____

 ____

3. I am a tired American. I am tired of watching criminals walk free while they wait for their day in court. I'm tired of hearing about victims getting as much as or more hassle than criminals. I'm tired of reading about courts of law that even accept a lawsuit in which a criminal sues his or her intended victim.

 ____

 ____

4. Cross-country skis have heel plates of different shapes and materials. They may be made of metal, plastic, or rubber. Be sure that they are tacked on the ski right where the heel of your boot will fall. They will keep snow from collecting under your foot and offer some stability.

5. A parent often must reduce her work hours to take care of a sick or disabled child, to take the child to therapy or treatments, and to handle crisis situations. With a child with significant special needs, it can be very difficult, if not impossible, for the primary caregiver parent to maintain full-time employment and provide the care the child needs. The caregiver parent often must take part-time status at work to avoid being fired completely. When the parent becomes a part-time employee, she also usually loses her health insurance, retirement and other benefits. Often part-time employees are ineligible to participate in these benefits. These restrictions present a financial loss to this parent.

—Price, *The Special Needs Child and Divorce*, p. 4

6. I fondly remember the summers I spent in Maine. The coziness of the cabin, the long summer days, and the gentleness of the ocean breezes. It was a time for our family to be together and to simply enjoy each other and our surroundings. Each day was special and slightly magical. Walks on the beach, trips to pick blueberries, and quiet moments with just the seagulls and the rushing tides filled the days and made me never want to leave.

EXERCISE 10-10 Identifying Tone

Directions: Bring to class an advertisement, photograph, newspaper headline, or paragraph that clearly expresses tone. Working in groups, students should agree on the tone each piece expresses. Then groups should exchange materials and identify the tone of each new piece. Groups should compare findings.

LANGUAGE

6 LEARNING GOAL
Examine language

One important feature that writers adjust to suit their purpose is the kind of language they use. There are two basic types of language: objective and subjective.

Objective and Subjective Language

Objective language is factual, where as **subjective language** expresses attitudes and feelings.

Read each of the following descriptions of the death penalty. As you read, decide how they differ.

The death penalty is one of the most ancient of all types of formal punishment for crime. In early criminal codes, death was the penalty for a wide range of offenses, such as kidnapping, certain types of theft, and witchcraft. Today, in the United States, the death penalty is reserved for only the most serious of crimes—murder, kidnapping, and treason.

The death penalty is a prime example of man's inhumanity to man. The death penalty violates the Eighth Amendment to the Constitution, which prohibits cruel and unusual punishment.

You probably noticed that the first paragraph gave facts about the death penalty and that the second paragraph seemed to state a case against it. These two paragraphs are examples of two different types of writing.

The first paragraph is an example of objective language. The writer reports information without showing feelings. You cannot tell whether the writer favors or is opposed to the death penalty.

The second paragraph is an example of subjective language. Here, the writer expresses freely his or her own attitudes and feelings. You know exactly how the author feels about the death penalty. Through choice of words and selection of facts, a tone of moral disapproval is evident. Such words as *inhumanity, violates,* and *cruel* have negative connotations.

EXERCISE 10-11 Writing Using Objective and Subjective Language

Directions: Choose a topic that interests you, or use one of the topics listed at the top of the next page. On a separate sheet of paper, write two brief paragraphs. In the first, use only objective, factual information. In the second, try to show your feelings about the topic by using subjective language.

1. One of your college instructors

2. Managing your time

3. Current fashion fads

Descriptive Language

Descriptive language is a particular type of subjective language. It is the use of words that appeal to one or more of the reader's senses. Descriptive words help the reader create an imaginary picture of the object, person, or event being described. Here is a paragraph that contains numerous descriptive words and phrases. As you read, underline words and phrases that help you to imagine what Yellowstone is like.

> The river edges near the mountains are prime feeding and gathering grounds for herds of elk and bison that roam the park freely. We dismount near the river and watch elk graze and sleep on the opposite river bank. They are unconcerned with us, as are bison we encounter just a mile up the river, the jagged 8,235-foot Mt. Haynes casting its shadow over the valley. The giant hairy beasts create an almost prehistoric scene as the bison bury their faces in the snow searching for food, and then wander methodically toward the river for water. Bron says bison are not unlike cattle in a field, pretty melancholy most of the time, although YouTube shows us they can get riled up and punt people who get too close. These animals routinely weigh in around 2,000 pounds, they know they are the ones in control, not us on our puny snowmobiles. We gave them a respectful amount of space.
>
> —Savage, "Inside Yellowstone," *American Snowmobiler*

Through descriptive language, a writer often makes you feel a certain way about the topic. In the preceding paragraph, the writer is trying to suggest that Yellowstone is wild and peaceful. Did you notice such words and phrases as *roam freely, jagged, hairy, wander?*

EXERCISE 10-12 Using Descriptive Language

Directions: Work with a partner to expand each of the following sentences to include as many descriptive details as possible.

1. The movie was enjoyable.

2. The restaurant serves terrible food.

3. The classmate was annoying.

EXERCISE 10-13 Analyzing Language, Tone, and Purpose

Directions: Read each of the following articles and answer the questions that follow.

Article 1

Americans and the Land

I have often wondered at the savagery and thoughtlessness with which our early settlers approached this rich continent. They came at it as though it were an enemy, which of course it was. They burned the forests and changed the rainfall; they swept the buffalo from the plains, blasted the streams, set fire to the grass, and ran a reckless scythe through the virgin and noble timber. Perhaps they felt that it was limitless and could never be exhausted and that a man could move on to new wonders endlessly. Certainly there are many examples to the contrary, but to a large extent the early people pillaged the country as though they hated it, as though they held it temporarily and might be driven off at any time.

—Steinbeck, *America and Indians*, pp. 127–128

1. Is this selection an objective or subjective account of the early settlement of America? Give examples to support your choice.

    ____

    ____

    ____

2. Describe the writer's tone. How does it make you feel?

    ____

    ____

3. Why do you think the author wrote this selection?

    ____

    ____

Article 2

Eat It Raw

Raw food is not just for hippies anymore. It is being embraced by hip-hop stars and New York restaurateurs.

The raw-food diet, once the exclusive domain of '70s food faddists, is making a comeback for the same reasons it flourished 30 years ago: health and politics. Many find it helpful in relieving a variety of maladies—including allergies, fibromyalgia, obesity, gum disease, and mood swings—while others see raw food as a way to resist the unhealthy products of an industrialized food system. No matter how you slice it, excitement about a diet of uncooked food is running high.

"Anecdotally, there's been a definite rise in interest in raw-foods diets," says nutritionist Suzanne Havala Hobbs, adjunct assistant professor at the University of North Carolina–Chapel Hill's School of Public Health. "There's been a lot of information out about celebrities that are eating raw foods, and naturally many younger people are interested in trying it out. There's also been a wave of raw-foods cookbooks and restaurants." Hobbs, who also serves as nutrition advisor to the Baltimore-based Vegetarian Resource Group, is currently conducting a research survey on the topic, called the Raw Foods Project.

A raw-food diet consists of foods that have not been processed or heated above 118 degrees Fahrenheit. These might include fresh fruits, vegetables, cold-pressed oils, sprouted grains, nuts, seeds, and even organic wine—but not meat or fish. According to June Butlin in *Positive Health* (Aug. 2001), a proper raw-food diet provides high levels of natural, essential nutrients such as fiber, essential oils, antimicrobials, plant hormones, bioflavonoids, vitamins, minerals, chlorophyll, digestive enzymes, and antioxidants. . . .

New York's raw foodists even have their own restaurant, Quintessence, a Manhattan bistro whose proprietors, Tolentin Chan and her husband, Dan Hoyt, understand the political and the personal power of the raw-food diet. "Major corporations are poisoning people with overprocessed, denatured food," says Hoyt. As for Chan, she suffered frequent colds and asthma attacks before trying a raw-food "cleanse"—the way most raw foodists get started—to see if she could get some relief. "My health improved tremendously," she says. "Now I'm 100 percent raw and my asthma is completely gone. I never get sick, and my energy is really high." Hoyt followed her lead and found relief from hay fever and food allergies. But both of them know how unappetizing raw food can seem at first.

"People think eating raw is gonna be like chewing on weeds," Hoyt says. But in the right hands, he says, it can be a refreshing culinary experience. "Raw food is very vibrant. We use lots of spices and sauces. The flavors are very strong and clean." Somebody out there must agree: Raw foods restaurants have sprung up across the United States, from Berkeley, Las Vegas, and Chicago to Minneapolis, Philadelphia, and Washington, D.C. It appears more are in the works.

—Olson, *Utne Reader,* March/April 2002, pp. 20–22

4. What is the author's purpose?

____

5. For whom is this article written?

____

6. Explain the figurative expression "People think eating raw is gonna be like chewing on weeds."

____

7. Describe the tone of the article.

____

8. List several words or phrases that have a somewhat negative connotation. List several words or phrases with positive connotations.

____

____

9. This reading is an excerpt from a larger article. What do you expect the rest of the article to contain?

____

LEARNING STYLE TIPS

If you tend to be a(n) ...	Then build your interpretive reading skills by . . .
Applied learner	Asking the questions, How can I use this information? Of what value is this information?
Conceptual learner	Studying to see how the ideas fit together, looking for connections and relationships, as well as inconsistencies

SELF-TEST SUMMARY

1 What are connotative meanings?	Connotative meanings are the shades of meaning a word may have in addition to its literal (denotative) meaning.
2 What are implied meanings?	Implied meanings are those suggested by facts and information given by the author, but not directly stated.
3 What is figurative language?	Figurative language is a way of describing things that make sense on an imaginative level but not on a factual level.
4 How can you identify the author's purpose?	Examine the writer's style: A writer will change his or her style (level of language, choice of words, and method of presentation) to suit the intended audience. Examine the intended audience: Analyzing the style and identifying the intended audience are the first steps toward identifying an author's purpose.
5 What is tone?	A writer's tone (serious, humorous, angry, sympathetic) is a clue to how the writer wants you to feel about the topic.
6 What types of language provide clues about the author's purpose?	A writer's language may be objective or subjective, depending on whether the writer is simply presenting facts or expressing an opinion or feelings. This language presents one or more clues to the writer's purpose.

GOING ONLINE

1. **Examining Political Web Sites**

   Political Web sites are often filled with rich, connotative, and sometimes biased language. Conduct a Web search for sites that focus on political matters. (You might choose a political party's Web site, for example.) Closely examine the language used on the home page and throughout the site. Identify words with strong connotations and look for implied meanings. Is the language used objective or subjective? Provide examples.

2. **Types of Figurative Language**

   This chapter provides an overview of figurative language, which comes in many types. Conduct a Web search to identify three different types of figurative language (for example, simile, metaphor, personification). Provide a definition and an example of each. Working with classmates, compile a table that lists as many different types of figurative language as possible (along with definitions and examples).

CHAPTER 10

MASTERY TEST 1 Interpretive Skills

This **Mastery Test** can be completed in **MyReadingLab**.

Name ______________________ Section ______________

Date ______________ Number right ________ × 20 points = Score __________

Directions: Read each of the following paragraphs and answer the questions that follow.

Paragraph 1

Over the past 20 years, psychologists have made a science of the joys and devastations of couples' relationships. They've come to understand, at least in part, why some relationships happily endure and what contributes to the hellhole interactions that claim over half of all first marriages, usually within the first seven years. Although these same psychologists note that most marriages start with great optimism and true love, they get into trouble for a very humbling reason: we just don't know how to handle the negative feelings that are a result of the differences between two people, the very differences that formed the basis for attraction in the first place.

—Donatelle and Davis, *Access to Health*, p. 146

_____ 1. One inference that can be made from this paragraph is that

a. the author disapproves of divorce.
b. the author is a marriage counselor.
c. more than half of all first marriages end in divorce.
d. all divorces occur within the first seven years of marriage.

Paragraph 2

Alas, all is not perfect in the virtual world. E-commerce does have its limitations. Security is one important concern. We hear horror stories of consumers whose credit cards and other identity information have been stolen. While an individual's financial liability in most theft cases is limited to $50, the damage to one's credit rating can last for years. Some shady companies are making money by prying and then selling personal information to others. Pretty scary. Almost daily we hear of hackers getting into a business or even a government Web site and causing havoc. Businesses risk the loss of trade secrets and other proprietary information. Many must spend significant amounts to maintain security and conduct regular audits to ensure the integrity of their sites.

—Solomon and Stuart, *The Brave New World of E-Commerce*, p. 17

_____ 2. In this paragraph, an example of *objective* language is

a. "horror stories."
b. "financial liability."
c. "shady companies."
d. "Pretty scary."

Paragraph 3

If we want to create safe classrooms in which teachers and students have the right to question existing knowledge and produce new knowledge, we must prepare you, who are planning to teach, for the problems you will face. One of your most frustrating problems will revolve around your discovery that power can shape and even dominate your life and your school. Power is a basic reality of human existence, present in all human relationships, including those of lovers, business partners, basketball teams, teachers and students, college faculties, courts, government bodies and so on.

—Kincheloe et al., *Contextualizing Teaching*, pp. 90–91

_____ 3. For paragraph 3, the author's intended audience is
   a. parents of school-age children.
   b. people who work in positions of power.
   c. college professors.
   d. people who are planning to become teachers.

Paragraph 4

Computer games are big business, but many of the best-sellers are filled with gore and violence that are not the best things for children to see. Is there an alternative? A company formed by five young people in Sweden thinks so, and they're succeeding by offering product alternatives that prove you don't need to be bloody to be the best. The company, called Daydream Software, got its start when one of the programmers gave a computer to his little sister for Christmas. He had a hard time finding appropriate games she could play, however. This frustrating discovery led to discussions with friends about finding methods to push players' thrill buttons other than endless blood and splatter. All of Daydream's founders have children, and they design games they would want their own kids to play. They want the player to come away with more than just the echo of machine guns and a sore trigger finger.

—Solomon and Stuart, *Marketing*, p. 59

_____ 4. One inference that can be made from this paragraph is that
   a. Daydream's computer games are nonviolent.
   b. Daydream's computer games are more expensive than other computer games.
   c. the people who produce violent computer games do not have children.
   d. violent computer games are always more exciting than nonviolent games.

Paragraph 5

Another shameful abandonment of human rights affected Native Americans. Between 1700 and 1763, thousands of white settlers poured into Indian lands west of the mountains. The result was bloody warfare, marked by barbarous atrocities on both sides. Looking to the British for protection, most of the tribes fought against Americans during the Revolution, only to have their territories put under control of their enemies in the peace of 1783. Protracted negotiations with the American government led to more surrenders and numerous treaties, all of which were broken as the flood of white land speculators and settlers moved westward. In desperation, the Indians attempted unification and a hopeless resistance. By 1800 enforced living on land set aside for Indians was already promoting the disintegration of Native American cultures.

—Brummett et al., *Civilization*, pp. 578–579

_____ 5. The authors' purpose in this paragraph is to
   a. explain the role of Native Americans in the settling of the West.
   b. describe the effect of westward expansion on Native Americans.
   c. criticize Native Americans for their treatment of whites in the eighteenth century.
   d. defend the actions of whites against Native Americans in the eighteenth century.

CHAPTER 10

MASTERY TEST 2 Interpretive Skills

This **Mastery Test** can be completed in **MyReadingLab**.

Name ______________________________ Section ____________

Date ____________ Number right ________ × 10 points = Score ________

Directions: After reading the selection, select the choice that best completes each of the statements that follow.

Scar

The mark on my face made me who I am

1 Growing up, I had a scar on my face—a perfect arrow in the center of my cheek, pointing at my left eye. I got it when I was 3, long before I knew that scars were a bad thing, especially for a girl. I knew only that my scar brought me attention and tenderness and candy.

2 As I got older I began to take pride in my scar, in part to stop bullies from taunting me, but mainly to counter the assumption that I should feel embarrassed. It's true, I was embarrassed the first couple of times someone pointed at my cheek and asked "what's that?" or called me Scarface. But the more I heard how unfortunate my scar was, the more I found myself liking it.

3 When I turned 15, my parents—on the advice of a plastic surgeon—decided it was time to operate on what was now a thick, shiny red scar.

4 "But I don't mind the scar, really," I told my father as he drove me home from the local mall, explaining that I would have the surgery during my summer vacation. "I don't need surgery." It had been years since I'd been teased, and my friends, along with my boyfriend at the time, felt as I did—that my scar was unique and almost pretty in its own way. After so many years, it was part of me.

5 "You do need surgery," my father said, his eyes on the road, his lips tight.

6 "But I like it," I told him. "I don't want to get rid of it."

7 "You need surgery," he said again, and he lowered his voice. "It's a deformity."

8 I don't know what hurt more that day: hearing my father call my scar a deformity or realizing that it didn't matter to him how I felt about it.

9 I did have plastic surgery that summer. They cut out the left side of the arrow, leaving a thinner, zigzag scar that blended into the lines of my face when I smiled. The following summer they did the same to the right side of the arrow. Finally, when I was 18, the surgeon sanded my cheek smooth.

10 In my late 20s, I took a long look at my scar, something I hadn't done in years. It was still visible in the right light, but no one asked me about it anymore. I examined the small steplike pattern and the way it made my cheek dimple when I smiled. As I leaned in awkwardly toward the mirror, I felt a sudden sadness.

11 There was something powerful about my scar and the defiant, proud person I became because of it. I have never been quite so strong since they cut it out.

—Audet, "Scar," *The Sun*, Issue 325, p. 96

_____ 1. The central thought of the reading is that
a. the author's scar contributed to her self-identity and gave her power.
b. parents should not make decisions for their children.
c. people really do not notice deformities.
d. beauty is in the eye of the beholder.

_____ 2. The writer's primary purpose is to
a. provide autobiographical information.
b. explain how she feels about her scar.
c. give a general overview of plastic surgery.
d. criticize her father.

_____ 3. What does the author mean when she says "scars were a bad thing, especially for a girl"?
a. Faces reveal the inner person.
b. Girls poke fun at other girls.
c. Beauty is important for girls, and a scar is thought to detract.
d. Boys do not care about how they look.

_____ 4. The connotation of the word *deformity* (par. 7) is
a. strong and forceful act.
b. frequently recurring problem.
c. unsightly, unpleasant disability.
d. unfortunate accident.

_____ 5. This article seems written primarily for which of the following audiences?
a. plastic surgery patients
b. audiences interested in personal stories
c. children with serious physical disabilities
d. parents who make decisions for their children

_____ 6. The meaning of the word *taunting* in paragraph 2 is
a. complimenting.
b. arguing with.
c. insulting.
d. accompanying.

_____ 7. Which word best describes the author's attitude toward her scar?
a. positive
b. negative
c. uncertain
d. hateful

_____ 8. Based on the reading, the author is likely to agree that
a. plastic surgeons should be more sensitive to their patients' needs.
b. parents seldom have their children's best interests in mind.
c. disabled people should be pitied.
d. disabilities can be a source of strength.

_____ 9. The father probably wanted his daughter to have surgery because he
a. thought she would look better without the scar.
b. thought the scar disturbed her.
c. blamed himself that she had a scar.
d. knew she would be happier in the long run.

_____ 10. The author helps readers make inferences about the father's attitude toward the scar by providing
a. examples.
b. opinions of others.
c. dialogue.
d. comparisons.

CHAPTER 10

MASTERY TEST 3 Reading Selection

This Mastery Test can be completed in MyReadingLab.

Name ______________________ Section ______________

Date ______________ Number right* ________ × 10 points = Score ________

Starbucks' Global Expansion

Warren J. Keegan and Mark C. Green

This selection is from a global marketing textbook. Read the selection to learn about the challenges Starbucks has faced as it has expanded into other countries.

Vocabulary Preview

per capita (par. 1) per person

perceptions (par. 4) awareness, understanding

1 Starbucks has been successful in United Kingdom and Ireland. This success comes despite competition from local rivals such as Ireland's Insomnia Coffee Company and Bewley's and the fact that per capita consumption of roasted coffee in the two countries is the lowest in Europe.

2 In January 2004, Starbucks opened its first outlets in Paris. CEO Howard Schultz acknowledged that the decision to target France was a gutsy move; after all, café culture has long been an entrenched part of the city's heritage and identity. The French prefer dark espresso, and the conventional wisdom is that Americans don't know what good coffee is. As one frenchman put it, "American coffee, it's only water. We call it *jus des chaussette*—'sock juice.'"

3 Not surprisingly, Greater China—including the mainland, Hong Kong, and Taiwan—represents another strategic growth market for Starbucks. Starting with one café in Beijing at the China World Trade Center that opened in 1999, Starbucks operates more than 220 Chinese Outlets. Another 525 units are licensed locations in prominent retail stores. Starbucks has faced several different types of challenges in this part of the world. First of all, government regulations forced the company to partner with local firms.

*To calculate the number right, use items 1–10 under "Mastery Test Skills Check."

4 Another challenge comes from the traditional Chinese teahouse. Indeed, one rival, Real Brewed Tea, aims to be "the Starbucks of tea." A related challenge is the perceptions and preferences of the Chinese, who do not care for coffee. Those who had tasted coffee were only familiar with the instant variety. Faced with one of global marketing's most fundamental questions—adapt offerings for local appeal or attempt to change local tastes—Starbucks hopes to educate the Chinese about coffee.

5 Chinese consumers exhibit different behavior patterns than in Starbucks' other locations. In China, most orders are consumed in the cafés; in the United States, by contrast, most patrons order drinks for carryout. (In the United States, Starbucks is opening hundreds of new outlets with drive-through service.) Also, store traffic in China is heaviest in the afternoon. This behavior is consistent with Starbucks' research findings, which suggest that the number one reason the Chinese go to cafés is to have a place to gather.

6 Meanwhile, as a result of the global economic downturn, cash-strapped consumers were cutting back on nonessential purchases. The notion of a "$4 latte" seemed out of step with the times, and some perceived Starbucks' premium brand image as a liability. Even before the economy nosedived, Schultz had circulated a memo to senior executives warning that over-aggressive market expansion was compromising the company's brand experience.

7 In part, the memo was a response to unofficial Web sites and blogs, such as starbucksgossip.com, where customer and employee complaints and company information were circulated. To better connect with its customers, Starbucks created a social media Web site known as My Starbucks Idea. Within months of MSI's launch in 2008, nearly 75,000 ideas had been submitted. Starbucks also stepped up efforts to communicate with the general public using traditional media. Starbucks launched a corporate branding campaign that was timed to coincide with a major revamping of its food offerings. Full-page print ads in *The New York Times* and *USA Today* were keyed to the tagline "It's Not Just Coffee. It's Starbucks."

8 Sensing a window of opportunity, McDonald's executives proceeded with plans to roll out McCafé, a new branded coffee concept featuring cappuccino and other coffee drinks at prices significantly lower than Starbucks'. At a Starbucks in Paris, for example, a cappuccino is €4.00 ($6.00); a comparable drink at McCafé is €2.00 or €2.50. McCafés feature sophisticated brewing equipment and special coffee blends.

9 Starbucks currently has about 1,000 outlets in Europe; that total includes company-operated stores in the United Kingdom, France, and Germany as well as licensed locations in the United Kingdom, Spain, Greece, and Switzerland. Starbucks is even considering targeting Italy, a notion that some observers dismiss as unwise. After all, Italy's coffee-house tradition dates back more than 400 years, and today more than 110,000 coffee bars are scattered the length and breadth of the peninsula. Sniffed a spokesman for one of Starbucks' European competitors. "The Italian café is a culture that the Americans have repackaged. They concentrate more on their image than the coffee."

MASTERY TEST SKILLS CHECK

Directions: Select the choice that best completes each of the following statements.

Checking Your Comprehension

_____ 1. The two European countries where Starbucks has been successful are
   a. Italy and Germany.
   b. Sweden and France.
   c. Ireland and the United Kingdom.
   d. Spain and Portugal.

_____ 2. One of the challenges facing Starbucks in China was that
   a. Chinese prefer espresso to coffee.
   b. Takeout containers are prohibited by the government.
   c. The government required that they partner with local firms.
   d. The currency exchange rate was unfavorable.

_____ 3. Starbucks found that the Chinese go to cafes to
   a. gather with other people.
   b. find less expensive food.
   c. to get out of their small apartments.
   d. conduct business.

_____ 4. The main point of paragraph 7 is that Starbucks
   a. raised its prices.
   b. increased its efforts to communicate with customers.
   c. did not try to compete with McDonald's.
   d. changed its branding policies.

_____ 5. McDonald's began to compete with Starbucks by offering branded coffee drinks
   a. with special mugs.
   b. in countries where Starbucks had not yet expanded.
   c. with social media advertising.
   d. at significantly lower prices than Starbucks.

Applying Your Skills

_____ 6. In paragraph 2, the Frenchman's attitude toward American coffee can be best described as
   a. friendly.
   b. excited.
   c. sad.
   d. contemptuous.

_____ 7. One inference that can be made from the selection is that
   a. Starbucks needs to offer more food at its locations.
   b. Americans do not drink as much coffee as other cultures.
   c. Starbucks has a pattern of expanding into places where its coffee might not be easy to sell.
   d. Social media is the only type of advertising that is effective for large companies.

_____ 8. The author of the business textbook in which this case study appeared most likely included it to
   a. define marketing.
   b. illustrate global marketing.
   c. show differences between two cultures
   d. provide an example of overexpansion.

_____ 9. Because Starbucks is choosing to try to change tastes about coffee in China (paragraph 4), you can infer that Starbucks
a. is confident that its product is something the Chinese can learn to love.
b. believes tea will be more successful in China.
c. will lower its prices.
d. is unable to respond to customer demand.

_____ 10. The connotative meaning of the word *sniffed* in paragraph 9 is
a. had trouble breathing.
b. recited something memorized.
c. believed he was lying.
d. said something in a derogatory way.

Studying Words

_____ 11. The word *consume* (see *consumption* par. 1) means
a. borrow.
b. use, use up.
c. taste.
d. hear.

_____ 12. The word *entrenched* (par. 2) means
a. misguided.
b. questioned.
c. established.
d. ignored.

_____ 13. From context you can tell that the word *patrons* (par. 5) means
a. workers.
b. customers.
c. owners.
d. suppliers.

_____ 14. The word *nonessential* (par. 6) means not
a. understood.
b. planned for.
c. expensive.
d. necessary.

_____ 15. The word *revamping* (par. 7) means
a. reusing.
b. returning.
c. revising.
d. receiving.

For more practice, ask your instructor for an opportunity to work on the mastery tests that appear in the Test Bank.

Summarizing the Reading

Directions: Write a summary of the reading using the opening and closing below as your starting and ending points.

Starbucks successfully expanded to Ireland and the United Kingdom and then

____

____

____

____

Starbucks' next attempted expansion will be in Italy.

Reading Visually

1. Study the photograph on page 369. What characteristics of the coffee business do you think it illustrates?
2. What photograph could be used to illustrate some of the challenges Starbucks faces when introducing its brand in a new country?
3. Explain how the title of this article relates to the subject. Why is the word *global* appropriate? Think of another title that would also work for this selection.

Thinking Critically about the Reading

1. Define Starbucks' image. Why is Starbucks so popular in the U.S.?
2. Why do you think Starbucks is trying to move into countries where it may have a difficult time getting customers?
3. Do you think that Starbucks presents an accurate image of America for the countries it is expanding into? Why or why not?

CHAPTER 11

Evaluating: Asking Critical Questions

LEARNING GOALS

This chapter will show you how to

1. Evaluate sources
2. Evaluate the authority of the author
3. Examine assumptions
4. Recognize bias
5. Evaluate slanted writing
6. Examine supporting ideas
7. Distinguish between fact and opinion
8. Identify value judgments

This excerpt from a movie review evaluates the movie *World War Z*. Movie reviews examine the value and worth of a movie and may consider factors such as its historical accuracy, the effectiveness of the actors/actresses and the script, as well as how it is carried out—the cinematography, the music, and so forth. Written material needs to be similarly evaluated for worth, value, accuracy, and delivery technique. This chapter will show you how to read and evaluate persuasive material.

Looking at ... Evaluating What You Read

Review: 'World War Z'

By MICHAEL SMITH World Scene Writer on Jun 22, 2013, at 1:57 AM *Updated on 6/22/13 at 6:54 AM*

'WORLD WAR Z'

Cast: Brad Pitt, Mireille Enos, Daniella Kertesz, James Badge Dale
Theaters: (3-D) AMC Southroads 20, Cinemark Tulsa, Cinemark Broken Arrow, Starworld 20, RiverWalk, Owasso, Sand Springs; (2-D) Admiral Twin Drive-in, Eton Square

Running time: 1 hour, 55 minutes

Rated: PG-13 (intense frightening zombie sequences, violence and disturbing images)

Quality: ★★★ (on a scale of zero to four stars)

A happy family organizes into their car for a drive into downtown Philadelphia, only to find traffic stalled, and then witnesses a large explosion in the distance. They see people running, panicked, in the opposite direction.

Something is not right, and the uncertainty makes moviegoers feel uncomfortable. Then there's the pure fear of seeing a man, or what used to be a man, head-butting his way through a windshield to chomp his rotting teeth into a motorist's arm.

"World War Z" gets right down to nasty business, and this is the first of many good decisions made in the production of this sobering "this is what the pandemic could look like" action-thriller starring Brad Pitt and based on the apocalyptic novel by Max Brooks.

That collection of oral histories about a zombie war made for fascinating reading, but it would be nearly impossible to film, so instead drawing inspiration from the novel to make a "Contagion"-meets-action movie extravaganza was wise.

With fast pacing that brings the picture in at less than two hours, "World War Z" feels streamlined compared to some of the more lumbering summer blockbusters that include an extra half-hour of carnage and blowing stuff up.

The marvel of the movie comes in the depiction of the zombie outbreak. This is no lurching crew of the undead but starving sprinters who swarm together in a deranged manner, climbing on top of one another to reach human flesh as a creepy collective.

I found these images fascinating the first time I saw them in a trailer months ago, and in the context of the film, they set my leg to pumping and my mind to thinking: Hurry up, they're coming!

This manic depiction is just as intelligently countered by the decision to make their many kills muted.

If you were thinking of purchasing a used car from a private owner, you would ask questions before deciding whether to buy it. You would ask about repairs, maintenance, gas mileage, and so forth. When it comes to buying something, most of us have learned the motto "Buyer beware." We have learned to be critical, sometimes suspicious, of a product and its seller. We realize that salespeople will often tell us only what will make us want to buy the item. They will not tell what is wrong with the item or whether it compares unfavorably with a competitor's product.

Although many of us have become wise consumers, few of us have become wise, critical readers. We need to adopt a new motto: *Reader beware*. You can think of some writers as sellers and their written material as the product to be sold. Just as you would ask questions about a car before buying it, so should you ask questions about what you read before you accept what is said. You should ask questions about who wrote the material and where it came from. You need to decide whether the writer is selling you a one-sided, biased viewpoint. You should evaluate whether the writer provides sufficient support for his or her ideas to allow you to accept them. This chapter will discuss these critical issues and show you how to apply them to articles and essays.

WHAT IS THE SOURCE OF THE MATERIAL?

1 LEARNING GOAL Evaluate sources

Just as you might check the brand label on an item of clothing before you buy it, so should you check to see where an article or essay comes from before you read it. You will often be asked to read material that is not in its original form. Many textbooks, such as this one, include excerpts or entire selections borrowed from other authors. Instructors often photocopy articles or essays and distribute them or place them on reserve in the library for students to read.

A first question to ask before you even begin to read is: What is the source; from what book, magazine, or newspaper was this taken? Knowledge of the source will help you judge the accuracy and soundness of what you read. For example, in which of the following sources would you expect to find the most accurate and up-to-date information about computer software?

- An advertisement in *Time*
- An article in *Reader's Digest*
- An article in *Software Review*

The article in *Software Review* would be the best source. This is a magazine devoted to the subject of computers and computer software. *Reader's Digest,* on the other hand, does not specialize in any one topic and often reprints or condenses articles from other sources. *Time,* a weekly newsmagazine, does contain information, but a paid advertisement is likely to provide information on only one line of software.

Knowing the source of an article will give clues to the kind of information the article will contain. For instance, suppose you went to the library to locate information for a research paper on the interpretation of dreams. You found the following sources of information. What do you expect each to contain?

- An encyclopedia entry titled "Dreams"
- An article in *Psychological Review* titled "An Examination of Research on Dreams"
- An entry on a personal Web site titled "The Interpretation of Dreams"

You can predict that the encyclopedia entry will be a factual report. It will provide a general overview of the process of dreaming. The personal Web site will likely report personal experience and contain little or no research. The article from *Psychological Review,* a journal that reports research in psychology, will present a primarily factual, research-oriented discussion of dreams.

As part of evaluating a source or selecting an appropriate source, be sure to check the date of publication. For many topics, it is essential that you work with current, up-to-date information. For example, suppose you have found an article on the safety of over-the-counter (nonprescription) drugs. If the article was written four or five years ago, it is already outdated. New drugs have been approved and released; new regulations have been put into effect; packaging requirements have changed. The year a book was published can be found on the copyright page. If the book has been reprinted by another publisher or has been reissued in paperback, look to see when it was first published and check the year(s) in the copyright notice.

Review the material on evaluating Internet sources in Chapter 8 (pp. 300–303). Follow the guidelines below when evaluating Internet sources.

HOW TO EVALUATE INTERNET SOURCES

1. **Check the author.** For Web sites, look for professional credentials or affiliations. If no author is listed, you should be skeptical. For newsgroups or discussion groups, check to see if the author has given his or her name and a signature (a short biographical description included at the end of messages).
2. **Discover the purpose of the posting.** Many Web sites have an agenda such as to sell a product, promote a cause, advocate a position, and so forth. Look for bias in the reporting of information.

3. **Check the date of the posting.** Be sure you are obtaining current information. A Web site usually includes the date on which it was last updated.
4. **Check the sponsoring organization of the site.** If a site is sponsored or provided by a well-known organization, such as a reputable newspaper like the *New York Times*, the information is apt to be reliable.
5. **Check links (addresses of other sources suggested by the Web site).** If these links are no longer working, the Web site you are visiting may be outdated or not reputable.
6. **Cross-check your information.** Try to find the same information in, ideally, two other sources, especially if the information is vitally important (issues dealing with health, financial discussion, etc.) or if it is at odds with what seems logical or correct.

EXERCISE 11-1 Evaluating Sources

Directions: For each set of sources listed below, choose the one that would be most useful for finding information on the stated topic. Then, in the space provided, give a reason for your choice.

_____ 1. **Topic:** gas mileage of American-made cars

Sources

a. A research report in *Car and Driver* magazine on American car performance

b. A newspaper article titled "Gas-Eating American Cars"

c. The U.S. Department of Energy's fuel economy site: http://www.fueleconomy.gov/

Reason: ____________________

_____ 2. **Topic:** viruses as a cause of cancer

Sources

a. A textbook titled *Well-Being: An Introduction to Health*

b. An article in *Scientific American* magazine on controlling viruses

c. An issue of the *Journal of the American Medical Association* devoted to a review of current research findings on the causes of cancer

Reason: ____________________

_____ 3. **Topic:** the effects of aging on learning and memory

Sources

a. An article from *Forbes* magazine titled "Fountain of Youth"

b. A psychology textbook titled *A General Introduction to Psychology*

c. A textbook titled *Adult Development and Aging*

Reason: ____

EXERCISE 11-2 Evaluating a Web Site

Directions: Visit a Web site and become familiar with its organization and content. Evaluate it using the suggested criteria. Then write a brief paragraph explaining why the Web site is or is not a reliable source.

WHAT IS THE AUTHORITY OF THE AUTHOR?

2 LEARNING GOAL Evaluate the authority of the author

Another clue to the reliability of the information is the author's qualifications. If the author lacks expertise in or experience with a subject, the material may not be accurate or worthwhile reading.

In textbooks, the author's credentials may appear on the title page or in the preface. In nonfiction books and general market paperbacks, a summary of the author's life and credentials may be included on the book jacket or back cover. In many other cases, however, the author's credentials are not given. You are left to rely on the judgment of the editors or publishers about an author's authority.

If you are familiar with an author's work, then you can anticipate the type of material you will be reading and predict the writer's approach and attitude toward the subject. If, for example, you found an article on world banking written by former President Clinton, you could predict it will have a political point of view. If you were about to read an article on John Lennon written by Ringo Starr, one of the other Beatles, you could predict the article might possibly include details of their working relationship from Ringo's point of view.

EXERCISE 11-3 Evaluating the Authority of the Author

Directions: Read each statement and choose the individual who would seem to be the best authority on the subject.

_____ 1. Print newspapers are becoming obsolete.

a. Michael Denton, a former *New York Times* print subscriber

b. Todd Gitlin, professor, Columbia University School of Journalism

c. Bill O'Reilly, television journalist

_____ 2. The president's recent news conference was a success.
   a. Katie Couric, a well-known news commentator
   b. David Axelrod, one of the president's advisors
   c. Howard Summers, a professor of economics

_____ 3. Amy Tan is one of the most important modern American novelists.
   a. Wayne Wang, director of the film adaptation of Tan's book *The Joy Luck Club*
   b. Nancy Pearl, former librarian, author, and commentator on books
   c. David Gewanter, professor of modern literature at Georgetown University

DOES THE WRITER MAKE ASSUMPTIONS?

3 LEARNING GOAL
Examine assumptions

An assumption is an idea, theory, or principle that the writer believes to be true. The writer then develops his or her ideas based on that assumption. Of course, if the assumption is not true or is one you disagree with, then the ideas that depend on that assumption are of questionable value. For instance, an author may believe that the death penalty is immoral and, beginning with that assumption, develop an argument for the best ways to prevent crime. However, if you believe that the death penalty *is* moral, then from your viewpoint, the writer's argument is invalid.

Read the following paragraph. Identify the assumption the writer makes, and write it in the space provided.

> Everyone suffers during an economic crisis. No one can come through unscathed, let alone better off. High unemployment and the unavailability of credit hurt all members of society as their negative effects trickle through the economic system. People who are not working cut back on their spending, which causes small businesses to close, which creates more unemployment. Closed businesses contribute to urban blight, which feeds crime and weakens our cities. Everyone across all levels suffers.

Assumption: ____

Here the assumption is stated in the first sentence—the writer assumes that an economic crisis negatively affects everyone. He makes no attempt to address how those who are independently wealthy or those who have not lost their jobs might not be suffering. He also fails to mention certain industries that thrive during troubled economic times, such as thrift stores.

EXERCISE 11-4 Identifying Assumptions

Directions: For each of the following paragraphs, identify the assumption that is made by the writer and write it in the space provided.

1. In high school, course selection is simple. Once all the mandatory courses are dropped into your schedule, you get to choose between art, drama or music. Then everything is put together automatically. In the university, things get a bit more complicated. You have some control over what day of the week each class is, or whether you take a course in three one-hour lectures a week or one three-hour lecture a week. You can even take into account who the instructor is. For incoming first-year students, choosing the right courses and putting together a schedule can seem like an impossible task.

—Dobson-Mitchell, "Beat the Clock," *Maclean's*

Assumption: ______________________________

____

2. Our lifestyles are increasingly driven by technology. Phones, computers and the internet pervade our days. There is a constant, nagging need to check for texts and email, to update Facebook, MySpace and LinkedIn profiles, to acquire the latest notebook or 3G cellphone. Are we being served by these technological wonders or have we become enslaved by them? I study the psychology of technology, and it seems to me that we are sleepwalking into a world where technology is severely affecting our well-being. Technology can be hugely useful in the fast lane of modern living, but we need to stop it from taking over.

—Amichai-Hamburger, "Depression Through Technology," *New Scientist*

Assumption: ______________________________

____

IS THE AUTHOR BIASED?

4 LEARNING GOAL Recognize bias

As you evaluate any piece of writing, always try to decide whether the author is objective or one-sided (biased). Does the author present an objective view of the subject or is a particular viewpoint favored? An objective article presents all sides of an issue, while a biased one presents only one side.

You can decide whether a writer is biased by asking yourself these questions:

1. **Is the writer acting as a reporter—presenting facts—or as a salesperson—providing only favorable information?**
2. **Are there other views toward the subject that the writer does not discuss?**

Use these questions to determine whether the author of the following paragraph is biased:

> In order for children to become literate, they need to be exposed to good storytelling. Television is a great source of good storytelling. Because of the short time frame of many programs, television shows must deliver a structured, logical, interesting, visually captivating story in about 20 minutes. In fact, a study published in 2009 in the British Journal of Development Psychology showed that preschoolers from economically disadvantaged homes develop literacy skills from watching television. Since some minority children already suffer from literacy difficulties and sometimes do not have the opportunity to hear librarians or parents read to them, television can be an important tool in their education.

The subject of this passage is the development of children's literacy skills through television viewing. The passage makes a positive connection between literacy and television and reports evidence that suggests that some children should watch television as part of their education. The other side of the issue—the negative effects of television viewing—is not mentioned. There is no discussion of such negative effects as childhood obesity, the exposure to commercials and marketing to children, the emphasis on violence, and the hindrance of creative abilities. The author is biased and expresses only a positive attitude toward television.

IS THE WRITING SLANTED?

5 LEARNING GOAL
Evaluate slanted writing

Slanting refers to the inclusion of details that suit the author's purpose and the omission of those that do not. Suppose you were asked to write a description of a person you know. If you wanted a reader to respond favorably to the person, you might write something like this:

> Alex is tall, muscular, and well-built. He is a friendly person and seldom becomes angry or upset. He enjoys sharing jokes and stories with his friends.

On the other hand, if you wanted to create a less positive image of Alex, you could omit the above information and emphasize these facts instead:

> Alex has a long nose and his teeth are crooked. He talks about himself a lot and doesn't seem to listen to what others are saying. Alex wears rumpled clothes that are too big for him.

While all of these facts about Alex may be true, the writer decides which to include, and which to omit.

Much of what you read is slanted. For instance, advertisers tell only what is good about a product, not what is wrong with it. In the newspaper advice column, Dear Abby gives her opinion on how to solve a reader's problem, but she does not discuss all the possible solutions.

As you read material that is slanted, keep these questions in mind:

1. **What types of facts has the author omitted?**
2. **How would the inclusion of these facts change your reaction or impression?**

EXERCISE 11-5 Identifying Slanted Writing

Directions: Below is a list of different types of writing. Working in pairs, decide whether each item has little slant (L), is moderately slanted (M), or is very slanted (V). Write *L*, *M*, or *V* in the space provided.

______ 1. Help-wanted ads

______ 2. An encyclopedia entry

______ 3. A newspaper editorial

______ 4. A biology textbook

______ 5. A letter inviting you to apply for a Charge account

______ 6. A college admissions Web site

______ 7. An autobiography of a famous person

______ 8. An online use agreement

______ 9. *Time* magazine

______ 10. *Catholic Digest* magazine

HOW DOES THE WRITER SUPPORT HIS OR HER IDEAS?

6 LEARNING GOAL Examine supporting ideas

Suppose a friend said he thought you should quit your part-time job immediately. What would you do? Would you automatically accept his advice, or would you ask him why? No doubt you would not blindly accept the advice but would inquire why. Then, having heard his reasons, you would decide whether they made sense.

Similarly, when you read, you should not blindly accept a writer's ideas. Instead, you should ask why he or she believes them by checking to see how the writer supports or explains his or her ideas. Then, once you have examined the supporting information, decide whether you accept the idea.

Evaluating the supporting evidence a writer provides involves using your judgment. The evidence you accept as conclusive may be regarded by someone else as insufficient. The judgment you make depends on your purpose and background knowledge, among other things. In judging the quality of supporting information a writer provides, you should watch for the use of (1) generalizations, (2) personal experience, and (3) statistics as evidence.

Generalizations

What do the following statements have in common?

Dogs are vicious and nasty.
College students are more interested in having fun than in learning.
Parents want their children to grow up to be just like them.

These sentences seem to have little in common. However, although the subjects are different, the sentences do have one thing in common: each is a generalization. Each makes a broad statement about a group—dogs, college students, parents. The first statement says that dogs are vicious and nasty. Yet the writer could not be certain that this statement is true unless he or she had seen *every* existing dog. No doubt the writer felt this statement was true based on his or her observation of and experience with dogs.

A generalization is a statement that is made about an entire group or class of individuals or items based on experience with some members of that group. It necessarily involves the writer's judgment.

The question that must be asked about all generalizations is whether they are accurate. How many dogs did the writer observe and how much research did he or she do to justify the generalization? Try to think of exceptions to the generalization, in this instance, a dog that is neither vicious nor nasty.

As you evaluate the supporting evidence a writer uses, be alert for generalizations that are presented as facts. A writer may, on occasion, support a statement by offering unsupported generalizations. When this occurs, treat the writer's ideas with a critical, questioning attitude.

EXERCISE 11-6 Identifying Generalizations

Directions: Read each of the following statements and decide whether it is a generalization. Place a check mark next to the statements that are generalizations.

_____ 1. My sister wants to attend the University of Chicago.

_____ 2. Most engaged couples regard their wedding as one of the most important occasions in their lives.

_____ 3. Senior citizens are a cynical and self-interested group.

_____ 4. People do not use drugs unless they perceive them to be beneficial.

_____ 5. Warning signals of a heart attack include pain or pressure in the left side of the chest.

EXERCISE 11-7 Identifying Generalizations

Directions: Read the following passages and underline each generalization.

1. Child care workers are undereducated in relation to the importance of their jobs. A whole generation of children is being left day after day in the hands of women with little more than high-school-level education. These children will suffer in the future for our inattention to the child care employment pool.

2. For the past few years, drivers have been getting worse. Especially guilty of poor driving are the oldest and youngest drivers. There should be stricter tests and more classes for new drivers and yearly eye exams and road tests for drivers once they hit age 60. This is the only way to ensure the safety of our roads.

3. The things that attract men and women to each other have not changed a lot over the years. Throughout history and even to this day, men and women are valued for different qualities. Men are traditionally prized for their ability to hunt and gather (i.e., provide and achieve status in the group). Women, on the other hand, are valued for their youth and beauty, because this represents an ability to produce genetically desirable children.

—Papadopoulos, *What Men Say, What Women Hear*, p. 22

EXERCISE 11-8 Evaluating Generalizations

Directions: Work in groups of three or four students. For each of the following generalizations, discuss what questions you would ask and what types of information you would need to evaluate the generalization.

1. Vegetarians are pacifists and they do not own guns.
2. Most crimes are committed by high school dropouts.
3. It always rains in Seattle.
4. Private school students get a better education than public school students.
5. Scientists don't believe in any kind of higher power.

Personal Experience

Writers often support their ideas by describing their own personal experiences. Although a writer's experiences may be interesting and reveal a perspective on an issue, do not accept them as proof. Suppose you are reading an article on drug use and the writer uses his or her personal experience with particular drugs to prove a point. There are several reasons why you should not accept the writer's conclusions about the drugs' effects as fact. First, the effects of a drug may vary from person to person. The drugs' effects on the writer may be unusual. Second, unless the writer kept careful records about times, dosages, surrounding circumstances, and so on, he or she is describing events from memory. Over time, the writer may have forgotten or exaggerated some of the effects. As you read, treat ideas supported only through personal experience as *one person's experience*. Do not make the error of generalizing the experience.

Statistics

People are often impressed by **statistics**—figures, percentages, averages, and so forth. They accept these as absolute proof. Actually, statistics can be misused, misinterpreted, or used selectively to give other than the most objective, accurate picture of a situation.

Here is an example of how statistics can be misused. Suppose you read that magazine *A* increased its readership by 50 percent, while magazine *B* had only a 10 percent increase. From this statistic, some readers might assume that magazine *A* has a wider readership than magazine *B*. The missing but crucial statistic is the total readership of each magazine prior to the increase. If magazine *A* had a readership of 20,000 and this increased by 50 percent, its readership would total 30,000. If magazine *B*'s readership was already 50,000, a 10 percent increase, bringing the new total to 55,000, would still give it the larger readership despite the smaller increase. Even statistics, then, must be read with a critical, questioning mind.

Here is another example:

> Americans in the workforce are better off than ever before. The average household income is $71,000.

At first the statement may seem convincing. However, a closer look reveals that the statistic given does not really support the statement. The term *average* is the key to how the statistic is misused. An average includes all salaries, both high and low. It is possible that some Americans earn $4,000 while others earn $250,000. Although the average salary may be $71,000, this does not mean that everyone earns $71,000.

EXERCISE 11-9 Evaluating the Use of Statistics

Directions: Read each of the following statements and decide how the statistic is misused. Write your explanation in the space provided.

1. Classrooms on our campus are not overcrowded. There are ten square feet of floor space for every student, faculty member, and staff member on campus.

   ____

   ____

   ____

2. More than 14,000 people bought a Prius last year, so it is a popular car.

   ____

   ____

   ____

3. The average water pollution by our local industries is well below the hazardous level established by the Environmental Protection Agency.

   ____

   ____

   ____

IS IT FACT OR OPINION?

7 LEARNING GOAL Distinguish between fact and opinion

Facts are statements that can be verified. They can be proven true or false. **Opinions** are statements that express a writer's feelings, attitudes, or beliefs. They are neither true nor false. Here are a few examples of each:

Facts

1. My car insurance costs $1,500.
2. The theory of instinct was formulated by Konrad Lorenz.
3. Greenpeace is an organization dedicated to preserving the sea and its animals.

Opinions

1. My car insurance is too expensive.
2. The slaughter of baby seals for their pelts should be outlawed.
3. Population growth should be regulated through mandatory birth control.

The ability to distinguish between fact and opinion is an essential part of evaluating an author's supporting information. Factual statements from reliable sources can usually be accepted as correct. Opinions, however, must be considered as one person's viewpoint that you are free to accept or reject.

EXERCISE 11-10 Distinguishing Between Fact and Opinion

Directions: Mark each of the following statements as either fact or opinion.

_______ 1. Alligators provide no physical care for their young.

_______ 2. Humans should be concerned about the use of pesticides that kill insects at the bottom of the food chain.

_______ 3. There are 24 more humans living on the earth now than there were ten seconds ago.

_______ 4. We must bear greater responsibility for the environment than our ancestors did.

_______ 5. Nuclear power is the only viable solution to our dwindling natural resources.

_______ 6. Between 1850 and 1900 the death rate in Europe decreased due to industrial growth and advances in medicine.

_______ 7. Dogs make the best pets because they can be trained to obey.

_______ 8. Solar energy is available wherever sunlight reaches the earth.

_______ 9. By the year 2020, many diseases, including cancer, will be preventable.

_______ 10. Hormones are produced in one part of the body and carried by the blood to another part of the body where they influence some process or activity.

Judgment Words

When a writer or speaker expresses an opinion he or she often uses words or phrases that can tip you off that a judgment or opinion is being offered. Here are a few examples.

> Professor Rodriguez is a *better* teacher than Professor Harrigan.
> My sister's behavior at the party was *disgusting*.

Here is a list of words that often suggests that the writer is interpreting, judging or evaluating, or expressing feelings.

bad	good	worthless	amazing	frightening
worse	better	worthwhile	wonderful	
worst	best	disgusting	lovely	

EXERCISE 11-11 Identifying Opinions

Directions: For each of the following statements, underline the word or phrase that suggests the statement is an opinion.

1. Purchasing a brand new car is a terrible waste of money.
2. Many wonderful vegetarian cookbooks are available in bookstores.
3. Of all the film versions of Victor Hugo's novel *Les Miserables,* the 1935 version starring Charles Laughton is the best.
4. The introductory biology textbook comes with an amazing DVD.
5. Volunteers for Habitat for Humanity are engaged in a worthwhile activity.

Informed Opinion

The opinion of experts is known as **informed opinion.** For example, the Surgeon General is regarded as an authority on the health of Americans and his or her opinion on this subject is more trustworthy than that of casual observers or non-professionals.

Here are a few examples of expert opinions.

- Carol Dweck, Ph.D., Stanford University psychologist: *"One of the main jobs of parents is building and protecting their children's self-esteem."*
- Federal Reserve Chairman Ben S. Bernanke: *"Clearly, we still have much to learn about how best to make monetary policy and to meet threats to financial stability in this new era. Maintaining flexibility and an open mind will be essential for successful policymaking as we feel our way forward."*
- Jane Goodall, primate expert and ethologist: *"Chimps are in massive danger of extinction from dwindling habitats—forests are being cut down at an alarming rate."*

Textbook authors, too, often offer informed opinion. As experts in their fields, they may make observations and offer comments that are not strictly factual. Instead, they are based on years of study and research. Here is an example from a cultural anthropology textbook:

What induces anthropologists to choose so broad a subject for study? In part, they are motivated by the belief that any suggested generalization about human beings, any possible explanation of some characteristic of human culture or biology, should be shown to apply to many times and places of human existence. If a generalization or explanation does not prove to apply widely, anthropologists are entitled or even obliged to be skeptical about it. The skeptical attitude, in the absence of persuasive evidence, is our best protection against accepting invalid ideas about humans.

—Ember and Ember, *Cultural Anthropology*, pp. 3–4

The authors of this statement have reviewed the available evidence and are providing their expert opinion on what the evidence indicates about the approach anthropologists take. The reader, then, is free to disagree and offer evidence to support an opposing view.

Some authors are careful to signal the reader when they are presenting an opinion. Watch for words and phrases such as:

apparently	this suggests	in my view	one explanation is
presumably	possibly	it is likely that	according to
in my opinion	it is believed	seemingly	

Other authors do just the opposite; they try to make opinions sound like facts. In the following excerpt from a sociology textbook, notice how the authors carefully distinguish factual statements from opinion by using qualifying words and phrases (underlined here for easy identification).

> After studying the urban poor in the Bronx, New York, and other cities around the world, anthropologist Oscar Lewis (1959, 1966) concluded that many poor people were held back by a **culture of poverty**, *a set of norms, beliefs, values, and attitudes that trap a small number of the urban poor in a permanent cycle of poverty*. Lewis believed that some of the distinctive attitudes and values of the "hard-core poor" include immediate gratification, apathy, and distrust, which encourages people to "blow" their earnings and live for the moment, making it hard to respond to opportunity.
>
> Most sociologists disagree with Lewis' argument that the poorest of the poor have distinctive values, and most are opposed to the idea that the "culture of poverty" is structural and therefore highly resistant to change.
>
> —Thompson and Hickey, *Society in Focus*, p. 216

EXERCISE 11-12 Identifying Informed Opinion

Directions: Read each of the following statements. In each, underline the word or phrase that suggests that the author is offering an informed opinion.

1. It seems clear that parents who would bring a young child to an R-rated movie are putting their own interests ahead of what's best for the child.

2. Voters rejected the proposed rapid transit system connecting the southern and northern suburbs, possibly because of racial issues.

3. According to the city superintendent of schools, school uniforms lead to improved behavior and fewer disruptions in the classroom.

4. One explanation for low attendance at professional sporting events is the high price of tickets.

5. It is believed that most people practice some form of recycling in their daily lives.

EXERCISE 11-13 Distinguishing Between Fact and Opinion

Directions: Each of the following paragraphs contains both facts and opinions. Read each paragraph and label each sentence as fact or opinion.

Paragraph 1

[1]Flowering plants that are native to the South include purple coneflower and rose verbena. [2]In the view of many longtime gardeners, these two plants are an essential part of the Southern landscape. [3]Trees that are native to the South include a variety of oaks, as well as flowering dogwoods and redbuds. [4]Dogwoods are especially lovely, with their white, pink, or coral blossoms announcing the arrival of spring. [5]For fall color, the deep red of Virginia willow makes a spectacular show in the native Southern garden.

Sentences

1. ____________________ 4. ____________________

2. ____________________ 5. ____________________

3. ____________________

Paragraph 2

[1]Today, many companies provide child care assistance, either on- or off-site, for their employees. [2]This suggests that employers are becoming aware that their workers' family concerns can affect the company's bottom line. [3]The Eli Lilly pharmaceutical company, for example, has built two child-development centers with a total capacity of more than 400 children. [4]In addition to assistance with daily child care, Bank of America reimburses employees for child-care expenses related to business travel. [5]It seems clear that other, less progressive employers will have to follow these companies' leads in order to attract and retain the best employees.

Sentences

1. ____________________ 4. ____________________

2. ____________________ 5. ____________________

3. ____________________

Paragraph 3

[1]Preparing a will is an important task that millions of people ignore, presumably because they prefer not to think about their own death. [2]However, if you die without

What does the photo contribute to the passage?

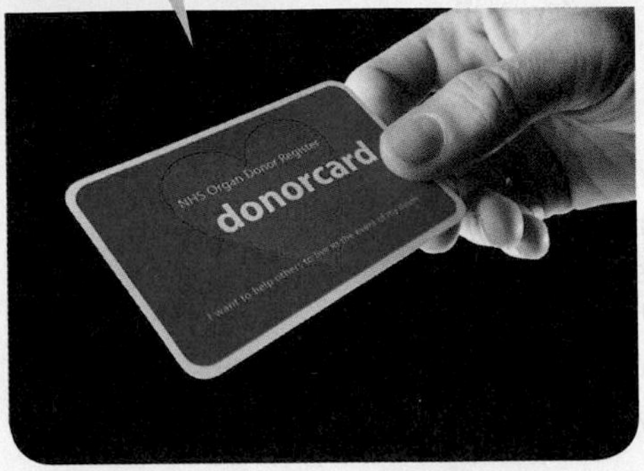

a will, the courts will determine how your assets should be distributed, as directed by state law. [3]Even more important than establishing a will, in my opinion, is expressing your willingness to be an organ donor upon your death. [4]Each year, 25,000 new patients are added to the waiting list for organ transplants. [5]The legacy of an organ donor is far more valuable than any material assets put in a will.

Sentences

1. ______________ 4. ______________

2. ______________ 5. ______________

3. ______________

DOES THE WRITER MAKE VALUE JUDGMENTS?

8 LEARNING GOAL Identify value judgments

A writer who states that an idea or action is right or wrong, good or bad, desirable or undesirable is making a **value judgment**. That is, the writer is imposing his or her own judgment on the worth of an idea or action. Here are a few examples of value judgments:

Divorces should be restricted to couples who can prove incompatibility.

Hunting animals is wrong.

Welfare applicants should be forced to apply for any job they are capable of performing.

Social drinking is acceptable.

You will notice that each statement is controversial. Each involves some type of conflict or idea over which there is disagreement:

1. Restriction versus freedom
2. Right versus wrong
3. Force versus choice
4. Acceptability versus nonacceptability

You may know of some people who would agree and others who might disagree with each statement. A writer who takes a position or side on a conflict is making a value judgment.

As you read, be alert for value judgments. They represent one person's view *only* and there are most likely many other views on the same topic. When you identify a value judgment, try to determine whether the author offers any evidence in support of the position.

EXERCISE 11-14 Answering Critical Questions

Directions: Read the following essay and answer the questions that follow.

I was at McDonald's on the West Side of Buffalo when the guy in front of me tried to order a double cheeseburger.

The cashier spoke Spanish with the workers behind the counter, who wrapped and stuffed food into white paper bags.

When the guy said, "No pickles," the cashier replied, "No understand."

The man raised his voice, as if talking to his half-deaf grandmother, and shouted: "No pickles!"

My mind jumped to a chat I once had with an old Chinese woman. I was teaching an English class at Buffalo's International Institute. The woman approached me in the lobby with a question burning on her lips. She smiled, allowing a thousand tiny wrinkles to gobble up her face.

"Teacher, I have question," she began. "Pizza in America. It have cheese and small meat on top . . . small circle meat. Very red. What is call this meat?"

"Pepperoni," I answered. She looked at me in awe, as if my ability to pronounce this word was magical. "Pep-per-o-ni," I said, sounding it out again.

She gave it a whirl, at first failing and laughing at herself. Then she tried again, insisting that she get it right. Who knows? Maybe all this was prompted by a messed-up pizza order.

That night, I found myself wondering how to say pepperoni in Chinese. I'd been studying the language for a couple of years, but hadn't come across it (the meat is not common in Chinese cuisine). I hopped on Google Translate and typed it in. Seven characters appeared, and in Chinese, each character has meaning by itself. The literal translation was: "Meaning Big Advantage Spicy Flavor Scented Intestines." Taken as a whole, it meant "pepperoni."

This was not very appetizing to me and made little sense to my Western mind. The first three characters, "Meaning Big Advantage," had no apparent connection to pork, but then I remembered that in Chinese, the characters make the sounds Yi Da Li. This is how Mandarin speakers say "Italy." I was on to something.

The remaining four characters translated into English as "Spicy Flavor Scented Intestines," a very descriptive way of getting about "sausage." So pepperoni, when uttered in Chinese, is Italian spicy sausage, roughly.

I felt just as perplexed as the old woman who had asked me about America's favorite pizza topping. Our concepts of the same food were worlds apart. She must have been wondering what small red circular meat has to do with peppers—and "oni," whatever that is.

I pondered this as I waited in line for coffee. The man in front of me continued to bark "No pickles!" in vain at the blank-faced cashier.

As an ESL instructor, I felt the need to butt in. I thought about how a seemingly simple word like pepperoni gets broken up into multiple concepts in Chinese. I tried doing the same for the word pickle in English. When you break it down, what is a pickle, really?

"A pickle is a sour green vinegar vegetable," I said, exaggerating a sour expression with my lips and drawing one of the small round McDonald's pickles in the air with my index finger.

"Ah!" exclaimed the cashier, smiling. "Thank you."

She had pieced together a pickle. The work of an off-duty Buffalo ESL instructor was done.

—Stone, "Simple Explanations Ease Communication," *The Buffalo News*

1. The subject of this essay is cross-cultural communication. How does the writer support his ideas?

   ____

   ____

2. Is the author qualified to write on the topic of cross-cultural communication? Give your reasons.

   ____

   ____

3. This essay contains both fact and opinion. Give an example of each.

   ____

   ____

   ____

4. Does the author make any value judgments? If so, explain at least one.

   ____

   ____

   ____

5. Does the author state any generalizations? If so, identify at least one.

____

____

6. Does this article express bias?

____

____

EXERCISE 11-15 Answering Critical Questions

Directions: Read the following passage and answer the questions that follow.

Consumer Privacy

1 To what extent should a consumer's personal information be available online? This is one of the most controversial ethical questions today. Scott McNealy, CEO of Sun Microsystems, said in 1999: "You already have zero privacy—get over it." Apparently many consumers don't agree: A study of 10,000 Web users found that 84 percent object to reselling of information about their online activity to other companies. One of the highest profile cases is that of DoubleClick Inc., a company that places "cookies" in your computer to let you receive targeted ads. The trouble began when DoubleClick bought Abacus Direct, a 90-million-name database, and began compiling profiles linking the two sets of data so clients would know who was receiving what kinds of ads.

2 DoubleClick's ability to track what you choose to buy and where you choose to surf is just one isolated example, though. Many companies can trace choices you make online and link them to other information about you. For example, when you register online for a product a Globally Unique Identity (GUID) is linked to your name and e-mail address. That means firms like RealJukebox, with 30 million registered users, can relay information to its parent company RealNetworks about the music each user downloads. Comet Systems, which creates customized cursors for companies featuring characters ranging from Pokemon to Energizer bunnies, reports each time a person visits any of the 60,000 Web sites that support its technology. Still other privacy violations are committed by consumers themselves: A site called disgruntledhousewife.com features a column to which women write to describe in excruciating detail the intimate secrets of former lovers. Be careful how you break off a relationship!

3 How can these thorny ethical issues be solved? One solution is an "infomediary"; an online broker who represents consumers and charges marketers for access to their data. As a Novell executive observed, "Slowly but surely consumers are going to realize that their profile is valuable. For loaning out their identity, they're

going to expect something in return." Or, perhaps the solution is to hide your identity: Zero-Knowledge Systems of Montreal sells a software package called Freedom that includes five digital pseudonyms to assign to different identities.

4 All of these precautions may be irrelevant if regulations now being considered are ever implemented. One now being discussed is an "opt in" proposal that would forbid a Web site from collecting or selling personal data unless the user checked a box letting it do so. These efforts are being resisted by the online commerce lobby, which argues these safeguards would drastically reduce ad revenues.

—Solomon, *Consumer Behavior*, p. 19

1. What is the main point of the passage?

____

2. What is the author's attitude toward women who use the disgruntled housewife site?

____

3. This passage appeared in a consumer behavior college text. Evaluate it as source for
   a. a business marketing term paper
   b. computer users who want to learn more about privacy issues on the Internet

____

____

4. Is the passage biased? Explain your answer.

____

____

5. What types of supporting evidence does the author provide? Mark several examples of each type in the passage.

____

6. What assumptions does the author make?

____

____

7. Describe the tone of the passage.

____

8. Identify the generalization that is contained in the first paragraph. How is it supported?

____

9. Identify a statement of opinion in the first paragraph.

____

10. Identify a value judgment made in the passage.

____

EXERCISE 11-16 Asking Critical Questions

Directions: Bring to class a brief (two- or three-paragraph) newspaper article, editorial, film review, etc. Working in groups of three or four students, each student should read his or her piece aloud. The group can then discuss and evaluate (1) assumptions, (2) bias, (3) slanted writing, (4) methods of support, and (5) value judgments for each article. Each group should choose one representative article and submit its findings to the class or instructor.

LEARNING STYLE TIPS

If you tend to be a . . .	Then build your critical reading skills by …
Creative learner	Asking "What if …?" and "So what?" questions to free new ideas and new ways of looking at the subject
Pragmatic learner	Writing marginal notes, recording your thoughts, reactions, and impressions

SELF-TEST SUMMARY

1 How do you evaluate sources?	Source refers to the place the material was originally published. Be sure to use trustworthy and reliable sources and check to be sure they are current.
2 How can you evaluate the authority of the author?	Evaluate the author's credentials and his or her qualifications to write about the topic. Evaluate his or her expertise with the subject matter as a further indication of the reliability of the information presented.
3 What are assumptions, and how can you identify them?	Assumptions are ideas that the author believes to be true and upon which he or she bases further ideas. If an author makes no attempt to establish the accuracy or validity of a statement, it may be an assumption.
4 What is bias, and how can you identify it?	Bias is a one-sided viewpoint; alternative viewpoints are not presented. To identify bias, look for statements that present only one side of an issue and do not present opposing or alternative ideas.
5 What is slanted writing, and how can you identify it?	Slanted writing is an author's selection of details that suit his or her purpose. To identify slanted writing, ask yourself what facts have been omitted and how might inclusion of these details change your response to the material.
6 How does the writer support his or her ideas?	Writers may support their ideas using generalizations, statements about an entire group based on experience with some members of the group. Writers may also use personal experience or statistics, as well as facts and opinions.

7 How can you distinguish between facts and opinions?	Facts are verifiable statements; opinions express beliefs, feelings, and attitudes. To distinguish facts from opinions, look for information that can be checked as true; these are facts; also look for judgment words that suggest that an author is expressing an opinion.
8 What are value judgments, and how can you identify them?	Value judgments are statements that express the author's view of what is good or bad, or right or wrong. Look for statements on a controversial issue that indicate the author's moral or religious values.

GOING ONLINE

1. **Evaluating Blogs**
   A *blog* (short for Web log) is a Web site on which a person posts his or her thoughts on a topic of interest (for example, pet care, gardening, parenting). Many blogs mix fact and opinion. Conduct a Web search for a blog that interests you, and print out a post or two. Identify the facts, opinions, and expert opinions in the posts. What types of information (if any) does the author provide to support his or her main ideas? Does the author exhibit any bias?

2. **Evaluating a Wiki**
   A *wiki* is a Web site that allows any user to post to or modify it. Wikis are very popular but often controversial. Working with a group of classmates, identify the pros and cons of wikis. Some questions to consider include: How reliable is the material provided on the wiki? How qualified are the people who post to wikis?

CHAPTER 11

MASTERY TEST 1 Critical Reading Skills

This Mastery Test can be completed in MyReadingLab.

Name ____________________ Section ____________

Date ____________ Number right ________ × 20 points = Score ________

Directions: Read each of the following paragraphs, and select the choice that best completes each of the statements that follow.

Paragraph 1

Tuition vouchers have been proposed as a way to improve the quality of public schools. Under a tuition voucher program, the government gives parents of school-age children a set amount of money to pay for school tuition. Parents can use the money at either a public or private school. In order to attract students, public schools will have to improve their meager offerings dramatically; competition from more adaptive private schools will force public schools to wake up and pay better attention to the needs of students.

—Edwards et al., *Government in America*, p. 685

_____ 1. The author's bias is revealed in the

a. first sentence.
b. second sentence.
c. third sentence.
d. last sentence.

Paragraph 2

Although the president's wife does not have an official government position, each First Lady of the past forty years has become known for her attention to a particular issue. For example, Lady Bird Johnson supported highway beautification, Rosalyn Carter was a mental health advocate, Barbara Bush promoted literacy, and Hillary Rodham Clinton was involved in health care reform during her husband's first term. During her husband's second term, however, Ms. Clinton took advantage of her position to launch her own political career as a U.S. senator. In doing so, Ms. Clinton became the first First Lady to run for political office.

—Edwards et al., *Government in America*, p. 426–427

_____ 2. The only sentence in this paragraph that contains an opinion is the

a. first sentence.
b. second sentence.
c. third sentence.
d. last sentence.

Paragraph 3

Traveling through Europe presents countless opportunities to meet people from other countries. Unfortunately, many of them don't speak English. Of course, that's part of the fun, as I discovered when I went to Europe as a senior in high school. My efforts to communicate with a Greek sailor, an Italian bus driver, and an Austrian bank teller at various times during that trip convinced me that with persistence, and a sense of humor, you can usually make yourself understood. It's not so important to be able to say the words correctly or to say them with the right accent, and it truly does not help to say the same words slowly and loudly. What works best, both abroad *and* at home, is to say them with a smile.

_____ 3. The author supports the ideas in this paragraph primarily with
a. statistics.
b. personal experience.
c. generalizations.
d. facts.

Paragraph 4

Welfare and related programs are expensive. Our country has amassed a large public debt, partially due to past spending on social services. Each year, welfare spending continues to increase. Despite the costs of welfare, it is unfair to blame welfare recipients for the past debt problems welfare programs created.

_____ 4. The statement in this paragraph that is a value judgment is the
a. first sentence.
b. second sentence.
c. third sentence.
d. last sentence.

Paragraph 5

Most of us believe that racism is a bad thing. However, when we are at a party or in another social setting where someone tells a racist joke, we often find it difficult to voice our objections. Why is that? Are we against racism only when it is convenient or easy? Our dilemma is that we see ourselves two ways: as polite people who would never purposely embarrass a friend or even an acquaintance, and as socially aware individuals who know racist comments are wrong. This moral inconsistency is even more troubling when we become parents and must serve as role models for our children. How do we explain the difference between "right" and "polite"—or is there really a difference?

_____ 5. One assumption that the author makes in this paragraph is that most people
a. would rather not embarrass another person.
b. believe children know right from wrong.
c. want their children to behave properly at parties.
d. enjoy racist jokes.

CHAPTER 11

MASTERY TEST 2 Critical Reading Skills

This **Mastery Test** can be completed in **MyReadingLab**.

Name ______________________________ Section __________

Date ________________ Number right ________ × 10 points = Score __________

Directions: Read each of the following paragraphs, and select the choice that best answers each of the questions that follow.

Paragraph 1

Having built four new elementary schools in the last five years, members of the Palmville School Board were convinced they had solved the problem with overcrowding that had plagued the public schools ever since the mid-1980s. As a result, they were disappointed when School Superintendent Marisa LaRoux made her mid-July Projected Enrollment Report. She pointed out that the town's population has expanded by several hundred more families than were projected because the good weather this year spurred home building and the low mortgage rates encouraged buyers. In addition, more families are deciding to have two or more children, bringing the average number of children per family to 1.9, much higher than the figure of 1.65 used in the past to calculate demands for school services. The superintendent also admitted that the decades-old policy of calculating a family of two as a family without children has proven to be a serious mistake because it ignored the many children growing up in single-parent families. Based on this information, the superintendent concluded that the overcrowding problem would continue this year and probably for many years in the future. Chairperson Clifton Washington summed up the school board's response this way: "The schools are overcrowded now and if more students are going to be coming to us asking for instruction, then we'd better get back into the school-building business."

____ 1. Which of the following types of evidence does the school superintendent use in her report?

a. opinions
b. personal experiences
c. facts and statistics
d. generalizations

____ 2. Which of the following is a value judgment that the school board seems to have made?

a. Public school boards should not study projected enrollments.
b. Previous enrollment studies were always wrong.
c. Overcrowding in schools helps education.
d. Education and schools are important.

____ 3. Which of the following sentences is *not* an assumption used by the school board when they studied school enrollment in the past?

a. A household of two people does not have any children.
b. The average number of children per family was 1.9.
c. Low mortgage rates encourage home buying.
d. Good weather increased new home building.

_____ 4. Which of the following, if added to the evidence, would *not* support the author's ideas?

a. Reducing overcrowding is a good idea because students usually learn better in less crowded classrooms.
b. The recent plant closing in the area has forced many people to move away from Palmville.
c. All the teachers support building new schools over expanding the school year.
d. If we build new schools, the best teachers will apply for the new jobs.

_____ 5. Which of the following is a conclusion reached by the school board?

a. They need to build more schools.
b. Schools will always be overcrowded.
c. Four new elementary schools would solve overcrowding.
d. Most families in the area have more than two children.

Paragraph 2

The latest state proposal to divert more water from agricultural to residential uses might be expected to gain support from rapidly urbanizing Palmville. Speaking through their Town Meeting, however, the citizens of the town argue that the state should not meddle with arrangements that have contributed so much to the economic and social health of the region. The report of the Town Meeting contained these arguments: (1) Farming in the Palmville area constitutes an important element in the state's food supply, which would be expensive to replace. (2) Farms and support industries provide a large proportion of the jobs of Palmville residents. (3) The farms are an important part of the social fabric of the town and the region, providing, among other things, healthful summer employment for many of the town's youth. (4) Diverting water from the farms would cause many to be sold to real estate developers, thus increasing the population *and* the demand for water. (5) The town's zoning plan will limit growth over the next decade and should slow the increasing demand for water. Whether state officials will be persuaded by these arguments remains to be seen, but Palmville residents hope to prevent changes that might threaten the community they have built so carefully.

_____ 6. Which of the following types of evidence do the town citizens rely on in their arguments?

a. statistics
b. personal experiences
c. facts
d. generalizations

_____ 7. Which of the following value judgments seems to be the reason behind the arguments by the Palmville citizens?

a. Residential areas are more important than farm areas.
b. Proposals by the state should be supported.
c. Changes will destroy the community.
d. Water is not important to Palmville.

_____ 8. Which of the following sentences is an assumption (rather than an argument) made by the citizens?

a. Farms are important to the town.
b. The town's zoning plan will limit growth over the next decade.
c. Farms and support industries provide jobs for Palmville residents.
d. Farms provide summer employment for youths from Palmville.

_____ 9. Which of the following sentences would *not* provide evidence for the Palmville citizens' ideas?

a. The state proposals should not be supported because this is a local issue.
b. Fewer farms will probably increase unemployment in the area.
c. Because farms are beautiful, they are productive.
d. Diverting the water will cause taxes to rise.

_____ 10. Which of the following is supported by the evidence presented by the citizens of Palmville?

a. State officials will be persuaded by the citizens' arguments.
b. Change will occur even if Palmville residents fight it.
c. Farming around Palmville is an important part of the economy of the region.
d. The town's zoning plan is worse than the state's latest proposal.

CHAPTER 11

MASTERY TEST 3 Reading Selection

This Mastery Test can be completed in MyReadingLab.

Name ______________________ Section __________

Date __________ Number right* ________ × 10 points = Score ________

Reality Check: Reality TV Does Not Make You Feel Better

Rosie Molinary

This selection appeared on a blog by a woman who teaches about body image and self-acceptance. Read the selection to learn about how reality TV is affecting viewers.

Vocabulary Preview

contrived (par. 1) made up
faux (par. 3) artificial or fake
predicated (par. 7) dependent upon
vulnerable (par. 7) able to be hurt
authenticity (par. 7) genuineness

1 "I watch reality television because it makes me feel better about myself, and I can just escape reality for little bit," my students often tell me. As they see young adults start a fight in a bar, women break each other down over some man they are in a contrived competition over, or see people make bad choices over and over again in their lives, my students feel vindicated.

2 "I may not be that rich, but I would never make that decision."

3 "I may not be that pretty, but I would never act so foolish." I may not have this or that or the other, but at least I've got sense, they tell themselves over and over again. And that, to many people, not just my students, is the primary gift we get from these faux-documentary-ish reality television shows: the ability to believe that while we don't have the trappings of that pretty life, we at least have these other things going for us. And those things, we tell ourselves, really are what matter most to us.

4 But, here's the thing. If you are sucked into a reality

*To calculate the number right, use items 1–10 under "Mastery Test Skills Check."

television show and what you feel while you watch it is "Oh, at least I am not that much of a train wreck," then I would argue that maybe there is a value conflict going on. Maybe it really isn't that good for your self-esteem at all.

5 When we need to compare ourselves to others—whether we see those others at the mall, at a party, in class, at the office, or on a reality television show—to determine our worth, to have it vindicated and articulated, then two things are true:

6 1. What the show has going on really does matter to us in some way because we are giving it some of our precious, finite time and our limited energy. If you give the Kardashians 30 minutes of your time, five days a week for 50 weeks a year then you have given them 7500 minutes which is 125 hours (and over 5 days of your life). I'm sorry, but you can't give away 5 days of your life accidentally without the thing that you are giving it to mattering to you in some way. So, if you are voting with your time, you are also voting with your values. You are saying, "This show and its messages matter enough to me that the trade-off is worth it. It is worth 5 whole days of my life."

7 2. You are on a slippery slope with your self-acceptance. If our ability to feel positively about ourselves is predicated by how we feel about other people and their choices, then we are always vulnerable to how we feel in a moment, what we see at any given time, who we are with at the moment of judgment, etc. And none of that is rooted in our authenticity, truth, and depth. At the end of the day, you actually do not feel better about yourself when you say, "At least, I am not that much of a train wreck." You actually feel like "all I have going for me is that I haven't done that—yet."

8 When a reality show—or anything or anyone else other than you—is your standard for your worth, then you are vulnerable, malleable, dependent on someone else's failures to articulate or even begin to recognize your own successes. Our scale, our model, our measure isn't ours and it doesn't come from an empowered place. It comes from an "at least" place and that's never a place of power.

9 We need to quit fooling ourselves. If we watch these shows and think, "well, I am better than that," then we really must quit believing that these shows have no impact on us and are just for fun and we have to face the truth. We have to come to understand that they are exploiting us by giving us low standards and slippery foundations and we can't stand on either of those.

10 I am not saying that every reality show is bad or that I never watch them. I love the talent competition shows like So You Think You Can Dance, The Voice, and Project Runway. I do know that if you are looking at some of those faux-reality shows to make yourself feel better, then you are building your esteem on a house of cards. Turn off the television and focus on who you are and how you want to be in the world. Reality TV has destroyed many a life among its stars. Don't let it take you down, too.

—Molinary, www.rosiemolinary.com

MASTERY TEST SKILLS CHECK

Directions: Select the choice that best completes each of the following statements.

Checking Your Comprehension

_____ 1. The purpose of this selection is to
   a. discuss how reality TV affects self-esteem.
   b. express admiration for reality competition TV shows.
   c. explain how reality TV harms the people in the shows.
   d. show ways in which reality TV benefits watchers.

_____ 2. The author believes people watch reality TV because they think that it
   a. sets new standards for behavior.
   b. offers a peek at wealthy lifestyles.
   c. makes them feel better about themselves.
   d. helps them analyze human behavior.

_____ 3. The main idea of paragraph 6 is that reality TV shows
   a. are too long.
   b. overemphasize celebrity fashion.
   c. are highly entertaining.
   d. use up valuable time and energy.

_____ 4. The main idea of paragraph 7 is that self-acceptance
   a. must come from yourself, not in comparison to others.
   b. never happens on reality TV shows.
   c. requires hours of work per week.
   d. helps you make better TV viewing choices.

_____ 5. The author believes reality shows are harmful because they
   a. do not have honest competitions.
   b. are uncensored.
   c. give us low standards.
   d. show people behaving badly.

Applying Your Skills

_____ 6. The author's tone throughout this selection can best be described as
   a. hopeful.
   b. objective.
   c. critical.
   d. apologetic.

_____ 7. An example of *objective* language in this selection is
   a. "If you are sucked into a reality television show and what you feel while you watch it is 'Oh, at least I am not that much of a train wreck,' then I would argue that maybe there is a value conflict going on."
   b. "If you give the Kardashians 30 minutes of your time, five days a week for 50 weeks a year, then you have given them 7500 minutes which is 125 hours (and over 5 days of your life)."
   c. "You are on a slippery slope with your self-acceptance."
   d. "We need to quit fooling ourselves."

_____ 8. Because the source of this selection is a personal blog, you can anticipate that it
   a. will contain opinion.
   b. has been fact-checked.
   c. contains research.
   d. is a paid advertisement.

_____ 9. The author's intended audience is most likely
a. reality TV stars.
b. people interested in reality TV.
c. television executives.
d. psychologists.

_____ 10. The statement that is used by the author to indicate that she is not biased is:
a. "What the show has going on really does matter to us in some way because we are giving it some of our precious, finite time and our limited energy."
b. "Maybe it really isn't that good for your self-esteem at all."
c. "I am not saying that every reality show is bad or that I never watch them."
d. "Our scale, our model, our measure isn't ours and it doesn't come from an empowered place."

Studying Words

_____ 11. The word *vindicated* (par. 1) means
a. compromised.
b. ignored.
c. affected.
d. justified.

_____ 12. The word *articulated* (par. 5) means
a. explained.
b. altered.
c. destroyed.
d. proven.

_____ 13. The word *finite* (par. 6) means
a. gradual.
b. excessive.
c. limited.
d. popular.

_____ 14. The word *malleable* (par. 8) refers to an ability to be
a. changed.
b. noticed.
c. included.
d. distracted.

_____ 15. The word *exploiting* (par. 9) means
a. encouraging expression.
b. allowing honesty from.
c. taking advantage of.
d. denying freedom to.

For more practice, ask your instructor for an opportunity to work on the mastery tests that appear in the Test Bank.

Summarizing the Reading

Directions: Write a summary of the reading using the opening below as your starting point.

Reality TV is harmful. ______________________________

____

____

____

____

Reading Visually

1. How does the photo enhance your understanding of the selection?
2. Evaluate the effectiveness of the title and the first few lines of the article in capturing your interest. Why does the author call this a reality check?
3. How might subheadings enhance the readability of this article? Try to come up with several subheadings that could be placed at different points in the reading.

Thinking Critically about the Reading

1. What types of facts has the author omitted in this article? How would these facts change your reaction or opinion?
2. What is your opinion about how reality shows affect self-acceptance? If you feel strongly one way or the other, make a case in favor of your side.
3. In its online form, this article allows readers to make comments about the content, agreeing, disagreeing, or offering another viewpoint. Do you think this aspect of online writing is helpful? Why or why not?

PART VI

A Fiction Minireader

Reading and Interpreting Short Stories

The Story of an Hour
Kate Chopin

The Tell-Tale Heart
Edgar Allan Poe

Little Brother™
Bruce Holland Rogers

Reading and Interpreting Novels

Prologue from *Water for Elephants*
Sara Gruen

READING AND INTERPRETING SHORT STORIES

A short story is a creative or imaginative work describing a series of events for the purpose of entertainment and/or communicating a serious message. It has six basic elements. The next section describes each. But first, read the following short story, "The Story of an Hour," and then refer back to it as you read about each of the six elements.

The Story of an Hour

Kate Chopin

1 Knowing that Mrs. Mallard was afflicted with heart trouble, great care was taken to break to her as gently as possible the news of her husband's death.

2 It was her sister Josephine who told her, in broken sentences; veiled hints that revealed in half concealing. Her husband's friend Richards was there, too, near her. It was he who had been in the newspaper office when intelligence of the railroad disaster was received, with Brently Mallard's name leading the list of "killed." He had only taken the time to assure himself of its truth by a second telegram, and had hastened to forestall any less careful, less tender friend in bearing the sad message.

3 She did not hear the story as many women have heard the same, with a paralyzed inability to accept its significance. She wept at once, with sudden, wild abandonment, in her sister's arms. When the storm of grief had spent itself she went away to her room alone. She would have no one follow her.

4 There stood, facing the open window, a comfortable, roomy armchair. Into this she sank, pressed down by a physical exhaustion that haunted her body and seemed to reach into her soul.

5 She could see in the open square before her house the tops of trees that were all aquiver with the new spring life. The delicious breath of rain was in the air. In the street below a peddler was crying his wares. The notes of a distant song which someone was singing reached her faintly, and countless sparrows were twittering in the eaves.

6 There were patches of blue sky showing here and there through the clouds that had met and piled one above the other in the west facing her window.

7 She sat with her head thrown back upon the cushion of the chair, quite motionless, except when a sob came up into her throat and shook her, as a child who has cried itself to sleep continues to sob in its dreams.

8 She was young, with a fair, calm face, whose lines bespoke repression and even a certain strength. But now there was a dull stare in her eyes, whose gaze was fixed away off yonder on one of those patches of blue sky. It was not a glance of reflection, but rather indicated a suspension of intelligent thought.

9 There was something coming to her and she was waiting for it, fearfully. What was it? She did not know; it was too subtle and elusive to name. But she felt it, creeping out of the sky, reaching toward her through the sounds, the scents, the color that filled the air.

10 Now her bosom rose and fell tumultuously. She was beginning to recognize this thing that was approaching to possess her, and she was striving to beat it back with her will—as powerless as her two white slender hands would have been.

11 When she abandoned herself a little whispered word escaped her slightly parted lips. She said it over and over under her breath: "free, free, free!" The vacant stare and the look of terror that had followed it went from her eyes. They stayed keen and bright. Her pulses beat fast, and the coursing blood warmed and relaxed every inch of her body.

12 She did not stop to ask if it were or were not a monstrous joy that held her. A clear and exalted perception enabled her to dismiss the suggestion as trivial.

13 She knew that she would weep again when she saw the kind, tender hands folded in death; the face that had never looked save with love upon her, fixed and gray and dead. But she saw beyond that bitter moment a long procession of years to come that would belong to her absolutely. And she opened and spread her arms out to them in welcome.

14 There would be no one to live for her during those coming years; she would live for herself. There would be no powerful will bending hers in that blind persistence with which men and women believe they have a right to impose a private will upon a fellow-creature. A kind intention or a cruel intention made the act seem no less a crime as she looked upon it in that brief moment of illumination.

15 And yet she had loved him—sometimes. Often she had not. What did it matter! What could love, the unresolved mystery, count for in face of this possession of self-assertion which she suddenly recognized as the strongest impulse of her being!

16 "Free! Body and soul free!" she kept whispering.

17 Josephine was kneeling before the closed door with her lips to the keyhole, imploring for admission. "Louise, open the door! I beg; open the door—you will make yourself ill. What are you doing, Louise? For heaven's sake open the door."

18 "Go away. I am not making myself ill." No; she was drinking in a very elixir of life through that open window.

19 Her fancy was running riot along those days ahead of her. Spring days, and summer days, and all sorts of days that would be her own. She breathed a quick prayer that life might be long. It was only yesterday she had thought with a shudder that life might be long.

20 She arose at length and opened the door to her sister's importunities. There was a feverish triumph in her eyes, and she carried herself unwittingly like a goddess of Victory. She clasped her sister's waist, and together they descended the stairs. Richards stood waiting for them at the bottom.

21 Someone was opening the front door with a latchkey. It was Brently Mallard who entered, a little travel-stained, composedly carrying his grip-sack and umbrella. He had been far from the scene of the accident, and did not even know there had been one. He stood amazed at Josephine's piercing cry; at Richards' quick motion to screen him from the view of his wife.

22 But Richards was too late.

23 When the doctors came they said she had died of heart disease—of joy that kills.

Plot

The plot is the basic story line—the sequence of events as they occur in the work. The plot focuses on conflict and often follows a predictable structure. The plot frequently begins by setting the scene, introducing the main characters, and providing the background information needed to follow the story. Next, there is often a complication or problem that arises. Suspense builds as the problem or conflict unfolds. Near the end of the story, events reach a climax—the point at which the outcome (resolution) of the conflict will be decided. A conclusion quickly follows as the story ends.

The plot of "The Story of an Hour" involves a surprise ending: Mrs. Mallard learns that her husband has been killed in a railroad disaster. She ponders his death and relishes the freedom it will bring. At the end of the story, when Mrs. Mallard discovers that her husband is not dead after all, she suffers a heart attack and dies.

Setting

The setting is the time, place, and circumstances under which the action occurs. The setting provides the mood or atmosphere in which the characters interact. The setting of "The Story of an Hour" is the Mallards' home and takes place during the course of one hour.

Characterization

Characters are the actors in a narrative story. The characters reveal themselves by what they say—the dialogue—and by their actions, appearance, thoughts, and feelings. The narrator, or person who tells the story, may also comment on or reveal information about the characters. As you read, analyze the characters' traits and motives. Also analyze their personalities and watch for character changes. Study how the characters relate to one another.

In "The Story of an Hour" the main character is Mrs. Mallard; her thoughts and actions after learning of her husband's supposed death are the crux of the story.

Point of View

The point of view refers to the way the story is presented or the person from whose perspective the story is told. Often the story is not told from the narrator's perspective. The story may be told from the perspective of one of the characters, or that of an unknown narrator. In analyzing point of view, determine the role and function of the narrator. Is the narrator reliable and knowledgeable? Sometimes the narrator is able to enter the minds of some or all of the characters, knowing their thoughts and understanding their actions and motivations. In other stories, the narrator may not understand the actions or implications of the events in the story.

"The Story of an Hour" is told by a narrator not involved in the story. The story is told by a third-person narrator who is knowledgeable and understands the characters' actions and motives. In the story's last line, the narrator tells us that doctors assumed Mrs. Mallard died of "joy that kills."

Tone

The tone or mood of a story reflects the author's attitude. Like a person's tone of voice, tone suggests feelings. Many ingredients contribute to tone, including the author's choice of detail (characters, setting, etc.) and the language that is used. The tone of a story may be, for example, humorous, ironic, or tragic. The author's feelings are not necessarily those of the characters or the narrator. Instead, it is through the narrator's description of the characters and their actions that we infer tone. In "The Story of an Hour," the tone might be described as serious. Serious events occur that dramatically affect Mrs. Mallard's life. The story also has an element of surprise and irony. We are surprised to learn that Mr. Mallard is not dead after all, and it is ironic, or the opposite of what we expect, to learn that Mrs. Mallard dies "of joy that kills."

Theme

The theme of the story is its meaning or message. The theme of a work may also be considered its main idea or main point. Themes are often large, universal ideas dealing with life and death, human values, or existence. To establish the theme, ask yourself, "What is the author trying to say about life by telling the story?" Try to explain it in a single sentence. One theme of "The Story of an Hour" is freedom. Mrs. Mallard experiences a sense of freedom upon learning of her husband's supposed death. She sees "a long procession of years to come that would belong to her absolutely." There is also a theme of rebirth, suggested by references to springtime; her life without her husband was just beginning. The author also may be commenting on the restrictive or repressive nature of marriage during the time the story was written. After Mr. Mallard's death, "There would be no powerful will bending hers. . . ." Mrs. Mallard, after all, dies not from losing her husband but from the thought of losing her newly found freedom.

If you are having difficulty stating the theme, try the following suggestions:

1. **Study the title.** Now that you have read the story, does it take on any new meanings?
2. **Analyze the main characters.** Do they change? If so, how and in reaction to what?
3. **Look for broad general statements.** What do the characters or the narrator say about life or the problems they face?
4. **Look for symbols,** figurative expressions, meaningful names (example: Mrs. Goodheart), or objects that hint at larger ideas.

The Tell-Tale Heart

Edgar Allan Poe

Edgar Allan Poe was born in Boston in 1809 and was orphaned at the age of two. He was raised by wealthy foster parents who provided him with a privileged upbringing, including education and travel. He embarked upon a successful literary career as both editor and contributor to several major journals. However, after his wife died in 1847, Poe's personal problems and heavy drinking became worse. This led to unemployment, poverty, and eventually to his death in Baltimore at the age of 40. Poe is most famous for his macabre poems and short stories, and he is considered by many to be the inventor of the modern detective story.

Vocabulary Preview

hearken (par. 1) listen, pay attention
dissimulation (par. 3) disguising one's true intentions
profound (par. 3) insightful
sagacity (par. 4) wisdom
suppositions (par. 7) assumptions or beliefs
crevice (par. 8) a narrow opening or crack
scantlings (par. 13) small pieces of lumber
suavity (par. 14) pleasantness; showing politeness and charm
deputed (par. 14) assigned or delegated
audacity (par. 15) boldness
gesticulations (par. 17) gestures or movements
derision (par. 17) ridicule or contempt

1 True!—nervous—very, very dreadfully nervous I had been and am; but why *will* you say that I am mad? The disease had sharpened my senses—not destroyed—not dulled them. Above all was the sense of hearing acute. I heard all things in the heaven and in the earth. I heard many things in hell. How, then, am I mad? Hearken! and observe how healthily—how calmly I can tell you the whole story.

2 It is impossible to say how first the idea entered my brain; but once conceived, it haunted me day and night. Object there was none. Passion there was none. I loved the old man. He had never wronged me. He had never given me insult. For his gold I had no desire. I think it was his eye! Yes, it was this! One of his eyes resembled that of a vulture—a pale blue eye, with a film over it. Whenever it fell upon me, my blood ran cold; and so by degrees—very gradually—I made up my mind to take the life of the old man, and thus rid myself of the eye for ever.

3 Now this is the point. You fancy me mad. Madmen know nothing. But you should have seen *me*. You should have seen how wisely I proceeded—with what caution—with what foresight—with what dissimulation I went to work! I was never kinder to the old man than during the whole week before I killed him. And every night, about midnight, I turned the latch of his door and opened it—oh, so gently! And then, when I had made an opening sufficient for my head, I put in a dark lantern, all closed, closed, so that no light shone out, and then I thrust in my head. Oh, you would have laughed to see how cunningly I thrust it in! I moved it slowly—very, very slowly, so that I might not disturb the old man's sleep. It took me an hour to place my whole head within the opening so far that I could see him as he lay upon his bed. Ha!—would a madman have been so wise as this? And then, when my head was well in the room, I undid the lantern cautiously—oh, so cautiously—cautiously (for the hinges creaked)—I undid it just so much that a single thin ray fell upon the vulture eye. And this I did for seven long nights—every night just at midnight—but I found the eye always closed; and so it was impossible to do the work; for it was not the old man who vexed me, but his Evil Eye. And every morning, when the day broke, I went boldly into the chamber, and spoke courageously to him, calling him by name in a hearty tone, and inquiring how he had passed the night. So you see he would have been a very profound old man, indeed, to suspect that every night, just at twelve, I looked in upon him while he slept.

4 Upon the eighth night I was more than usually cautious in opening the door. A watch's minute hand moves more quickly than did mine. Never before that night had I *felt* the extent of my own powers—of my sagacity. I could scarcely contain my feelings of triumph. To think that there I was, opening the door, little by little, and he not even to dream of my secret deeds or thoughts. I fairly chuckled at the idea; and perhaps he heard me; for he moved on the bed suddenly, as if startled. Now you may think that I drew back—but no. His room was as black as pitch with the thick darkness, (for the shutters were close fastened, through fear of robbers), and so I knew that he could not see the opening of the door, and I kept pushing it on steadily, steadily.

5 I had my head in, and was about to open the lantern, when my thumb slipped upon the tin fastening, and the old man sprang up in bed, crying out—"Who's there?"

6 I kept quite still and said nothing. For a whole hour I did not move a muscle, and in the meantime I did not hear him lie down. He was still sitting up in the bed, listening;—just as I have done, night after night, hearkening to the death watches* in the wall.

7 Presently I heard a slight groan, and I knew it was the groan of mortal terror. It was not a groan of pain or of grief—oh, no!—it was the low stifled sound that arises from the bottom of the soul when overcharged with awe. I knew the sound very well. Many a night, just at midnight, when all the world slept, it has welled up from my own bosom, deepening, with its dreadful echo, the terrors that distracted me. I say I knew it well. I knew what the old man felt, and pitied him, although I chuckled at heart. I knew that he had been lying awake ever since the first slight noise, when he had turned in the bed. His fears had been ever since growing upon him. He had been trying to fancy them causeless, but could not. He had been saying to himself—"It is nothing but the wind in the chimney—it is only a mouse crossing the floor," or "It is merely a cricket which has made a single chirp." Yes, he had been trying to comfort himself with these suppositions; but he had found all in vain. *All in vain*; because Death, in approaching him, had stalked with his black shadow before him, and enveloped the victim. And it was the mournful influence of the unperceived shadow that caused him to feel—although he neither saw nor heard—to *feel* the presence of my head within the room.

8 When I had waited a long time, very patiently, without hearing him lie down, I resolved to open a little—a very, very little crevice in the lantern. So I opened it—you cannot imagine how stealthily, stealthily—until, at length, a single dim ray, like the thread of the spider, shot from out the crevice and fell upon the vulture eye.

9 It was open—wide, wide open—and I grew furious as I gazed upon it. I saw it with perfect distinctness—all a dull blue, with a hideous veil over it that chilled the very marrow in my bones; but I could see nothing else of the old man's face or person: for I had directed the ray as if by instinct, precisely upon the damned spot.

10 And now have I not told you that what you mistake for madness is but overacuteness of the senses?—now, I say, there came to my ears a low, dull, quick sound, such as a watch makes when enveloped in cotton. I knew *that* sound well, too. It was the beating of the old man's heart. It increased my fury, as the beating of a drum stimulates the soldier into courage.

11 But even yet I refrained and kept still. I scarcely breathed. I held the lantern motionless. I tried how steadily I could maintain the ray upon the eye. Meantime the hellish tattoo of the heart increased. It grew quicker and quicker, and louder and louder every instant. The old man's terror *must* have been extreme! It grew

---

**death watches:* beetles that infest timbers. Their clicking sound was thought to be an omen of death.

louder, I say, louder every moment!—do you mark me well? I have told you that I am nervous: so I am. And now at the dead hour of the night, amid the dreadful silence of that old house, so strange a noise as this excited me to uncontrollable terror. Yet, for some minutes longer I refrained and stood still. But the beating grew louder, louder! I thought the heart must burst. And now a new anxiety seized me—the sound would be heard by a neighbor! The old man's hour had come! With a loud yell, I threw open the lantern and leaped into the room. He shrieked once—once only. In an instant I dragged him to the floor, and pulled the heavy bed over him. I then smiled gaily, to find the deed so far done. But, for many minutes, the heart beat on with a muffled sound. This, however, did not vex me; it would not be heard through the wall. At length it ceased. The old man was dead. I removed the bed and examined the corpse. Yes, he was stone, stone dead. I placed my hand upon the heart and held it there many minutes. There was no pulsation. He was stone dead. His eye would trouble me no more.

12 If still you think me mad, you will think so no longer when I describe the wise precautions I took for the concealment of the body. The night waned, and I worked hastily, but in silence. First of all I dismembered the corpse. I cut off the head and the arms and the legs.

13 I then took up three planks from the flooring of the chamber, and deposited all between the scantlings. I then replaced the boards so cleverly, so cunningly, that no human eye—not even *his*—could have detected anything wrong. There was nothing to wash out—no stain of any kind—no bloodspot whatever. I had been too wary for that. A tub had caught all—ha! ha!

14 When I had made an end of these labors, it was four o'clock—still dark as midnight. As the bell sounded the hour, there came a knocking at the street door. I went down to open it with a light heart,—for what had I *now* to fear? There entered three men, who introduced themselves, with perfect suavity, as officers of the police. A shriek had been heard by a neighbor during the night; suspicion of foul play had been aroused; information had been lodged at the police office, and they (the officers) had been deputed to search the premises.

15 I smiled,—for *what* had I to fear? I bade the gentlemen welcome. The shriek, I said, was my own in a dream. The old man, I mentioned, was absent in the country. I took my visitors all over the house. I bade them search—search *well*. I led them, at length, to *his* chamber. I showed them his treasures, secure, undisturbed. In the enthusiasm of my confidence, I brought chairs into the room, and desired them *here* to rest from their fatigues, while I myself, in the wild audacity of my perfect triumph, placed my own seat upon the very spot beneath which reposed the corpse of the victim.

16 The officers were satisfied. My *manner* had convinced them. I was singularly at ease. They sat, and while I answered cheerily, they chatted of familiar things, But, ere long, I felt myself getting pale and wished them gone. My head ached, and I fancied a ringing in my ears: but still they sat and still chatted. The ringing became more distinct:—it continued and became more distinct: I talked more

freely to get rid of the feeling: but it continued and gained definitiveness—until, at length, I found that the noise was *not* within my ears.

17 No doubt I now grew *very* pale—but I talked more fluently, and with a heightened voice. Yet the sound increased—and what could I do? It was *a low, dull, quick sound—much such a sound as a watch makes when enveloped in cotton.* I gasped for breath—and yet the officers heard it not. I talked more quickly—more vehemently; but the noise steadily increased. I arose and argued about trifles, in a high key and with violent gesticulations; but the noise steadily increased. Why *would* they not be gone? I paced the floor to and fro with heavy strides, as if excited to fury by the observations of the men—but the noise steadily increased. Oh God! what *could* I do? I foamed—I raved—I swore! I swung the chair upon which I had been sitting, and grated it upon the boards, but the noise arose over all and continually increased. It grew louder—louder—*louder!* And still the men chatted pleasantly and smiled. Was it possible they heard not? Almighty God!—no, no! They heard!—they suspected!—they *knew!*—they were making a mockery of my horror!—this I thought and this I think. But anything was better than this agony! Anything was more tolerable than this derision! I could bear those hypocritical smiles no longer! I felt that I must scream or die!—and now—again!—hark! louder! louder! louder! *louder!*—

18 "Villains!" I shrieked, "dissemble no more! I admit the deed!—tear up the planks!—here, here!—it is the beating of his hideous heart!"

Directions: Select the choice that best completes each of the following statements.

Checking Your Comprehension

_____ 1. In this story, the main character describes how
- a. an old man tried to murder him.
- b. he prevented an old man's murder.
- c. he caught and arrested a murderer.
- d. he murdered an old man.

_____ 2. The character was inspired to kill the old man because
- a. he wanted the old man's gold.
- b. the old man had wronged him.
- c. the old man had insulted him.
- d. he was disturbed by one of the old man's eyes.

_____ 3. Once the character decided to kill the old man, he
- a. killed him later that day.
- b. waited until the next day to kill him.
- c. waited a whole week before killing him.
- d. waited almost a year and then changed his mind.

_____ 4. The reason the killer waited was that he
a. wanted to find someone to help him kill the old man.
b. could not kill the old man unless the old man's eye was open.
c. needed to find a weapon.
d. was afraid of being caught.

_____ 5. When the police came to the house, they
a. immediately found the old man's body and arrested the killer.
b. searched for clues but left without making an arrest.
c. were suspicious of the man's story and took him in for questioning.
d. were satisfied with the man's story.

The Elements of a Short Story

_____ 6. The tone of the story can best be described as
a. suspenseful.
b. humorous.
c. ironic.
d. sad.

_____ 7. The setting of the story is
a. the old man's house.
b. the police station.
c. prison.
d. an insane asylum.

_____ 8. This story is told from the perspective of
a. the old man.
b. the police.
c. the killer.
d. a neighbor.

_____ 9. The title is a reference to how the
a. killer imagined the old man's heart beating so loudly that it gave him away.
b. old man knew that he was going to be murdered.
c. police officers found the old man's heart and knew he had been murdered.
d. killer gave himself away by the loud beating of his own heart.

_____ 10. Which statement best expresses the theme of the story?
a. Murder is immoral.
b. Madness is a social disease.
c. Law enforcement personnel deserve respect.
d. Guilt is powerful and self-destructive.

Discussion Questions

1. How does Poe create feelings of suspense in this story?
2. How does Poe convince us that the narrator is mad?
3. What do you think is the relationship between the old man and his killer?
4. Why do you think Poe chose to tell this story from the killer's point of view?

Little Brother™

Bruce Holland Rogers

Bruce Holland Rogers is an American writer of award-winning fiction. This story appeared in *Strange Horizons*, a weekly online magazine that features science fiction and fantasy.

1 Peter had wanted a Little Brother™ for three Christmases in a row. His favorite TV commercials were the ones that showed just how much fun he would have teaching Little Brother™ to do all the things that he could already do himself. But every year, Mommy had said that Peter wasn't ready for a Little Brother™. Until this year.

2 This year when Peter ran into the living room, there sat Little Brother™ among all the wrapped presents, babbling baby talk, smiling his happy smile, and patting one of the packages with his fat little hand. Peter was so excited that he ran up and gave Little Brother™ a big hug around the neck. That was how he found out about the button. Peter's hand pushed against something cold on Little Brother™'s neck, and suddenly Little Brother™ wasn't babbling any more, or even sitting up. Suddenly, Little Brother™ was limp on the floor, as lifeless as any ordinary doll.

3 "Peter!" Mommy said.

4 "I didn't mean to!"

5 Mommy picked up Little Brother™, sat him in her lap, and pressed the black button at the back of his neck. Little Brother™'s face came alive, and it wrinkled up as if he were about to cry, but Mommy bounced him on her knee and told him what a good boy he was. He didn't cry after all.

6 "Little Brother™ isn't like your other toys, Peter," Mommy said. "You have to be extra careful with him, as if he were a real baby." She put Little Brother™

down on the floor, and he took tottering baby steps toward Peter. "Why don't you let him help open your other presents?"

7 So that's what Peter did. He showed Little Brother™ how to tear the paper and open the boxes. The other toys were a fire engine, some talking books, a wagon, and lots and lots of wooden blocks. The fire engine was the second-best present. It had lights, a siren, and hoses that blew green gas just like the real thing. There weren't as many presents as last year, Mommy explained, because Little Brother™ was expensive. That was okay. Little Brother™ was the best present ever!

8 Well, that's what Peter thought at first. At first, everything that Little Brother™ did was funny and wonderful. Peter put all the torn wrapping paper in the wagon, and Little Brother™ took it out again and threw it on the floor. Peter started to read a talking book, and Little Brother™ came and turned the pages too fast for the book to keep up.

9 But then, while Mommy went to the kitchen to cook breakfast, Peter tried to show Little Brother™ how to build a very tall tower out of blocks. Little Brother™ wasn't interested in seeing a really tall tower. Every time Peter had a few blocks stacked up, Little Brother™ swatted the tower with his hand and laughed. Peter laughed, too, for the first time, and the second. But then he said, "Now watch this time. I'm going to make it really big."

10 But Little Brother™ didn't watch. The tower was only a few blocks tall when he knocked it down.

11 "No!" Peter said. He grabbed hold of Little Brother™'s arm. "Don't!"

12 Little Brother™'s face wrinkled. He was getting ready to cry.

13 Peter looked toward the kitchen and let go. "Don't cry," he said. "Look, I'm building another one! Watch me build it!"

14 Little Brother™ watched. Then he knocked the tower down.

15 Peter had an idea.

16 When Mommy came into the living room again, Peter had built a tower that was taller than he was, the best tower he had ever made. "Look!" he said.

17 But Mommy didn't even look at the tower. "Peter!" She picked up Little Brother™, put him on her lap, and pressed the button to turn him back on. As soon as he was on, Little Brother™ started to scream. His face turned red.

18 "I didn't mean to!"

19 "Peter, I told you! He's not like your other toys. When you turn him off, he can't move but he can still see and hear. He can still feel. And it scares him."

20 "He was knocking down my blocks."

21 "Babies do things like that," Mommy said. "That's what it's like to have a baby brother."

22 Little Brother™ howled.

23 "He's mine," Peter said too quietly for Mommy to hear. But when Little Brother™ had calmed down, Mommy put him back on the floor and Peter let him toddle over and knock down the tower.

24 Mommy told Peter to clean up the wrapping paper, and she went back into the kitchen. Peter had already picked up the wrapping paper once, and she hadn't said thank you. She hadn't even noticed.

25 Peter wadded the paper into angry balls and threw them one at a time into the wagon until it was almost full. That's when Little Brother™ broke the fire engine. Peter turned just in time to see him lift the engine up over his head and let it drop.

26 "No!" Peter shouted. The windshield cracked and popped out as the fire engine hit the floor. Broken. Peter hadn't even played with it once, and his best Christmas present was broken.

27 Later, when Mommy came into the living room, she didn't thank Peter for picking up all the wrapping paper. Instead, she scooped up Little Brother™ and turned him on again. He trembled and screeched louder than ever.

28 "My God! How long has he been off?" Mommy demanded.

29 "I don't like him!"

30 "Peter, it scares him! Listen to him!"

31 "I hate him! Take him back!"

32 "You are not to turn him off again. Ever!"

33 "He's mine!" Peter shouted. "He's mine and I can do what I want with him! He broke my fire engine!"

34 "He's a baby!"

35 "He's stupid! I hate him! Take him back!"

36 "You are going to learn to be nice with him."

37 "I'll turn him off if you don't take him back. I'll turn him off and hide him someplace where you can't find him!"

38 "Peter!" Mommy said, and she was angry. She was angrier than he'd ever seen her before. She put Little Brother™ down and took a step toward Peter. She would punish him. Peter didn't care. He was angry, too.

39 "I'll do it!" he yelled. "I'll turn him off and hide him someplace dark!"

40 "You'll do no such thing!" Mommy said. She grabbed his arm and spun him around. The spanking would come next.

41 But it didn't. Instead he felt her fingers searching for something at the back of his neck.

Directions: Select the choice that best completes each of the following statements.

Checking Your Comprehension

_____ 1. At the start of the story, Peter can best be described as

a. the oldest of several children.
b. the youngest of several children.
c. an only child.
d. a teenager.

_____ 2. Peter's initial reaction to Little Brother was
a. excitement.
b. disappointment.
c. jealousy.
d. fear.

_____ 3. When Peter hugged Little Brother, he discovered that Little Brother
a. was able to talk.
b. cried when he was held.
c. was made of plastic.
d. had a button on his neck.

_____ 4. Peter's mother became angry when
a. Little Brother broke Peter's new fire engine.
b. Peter did not pick up the wrapping paper as she had asked.
c. Peter turned off Little Brother.
d. Little Brother knocked down Peter's blocks.

_____ 5. At the end of the story, we find out that
a. Peter's mother planned to take Little Brother back.
b. Peter's father would be coming home soon.
c. Little Brother was actually a real baby.
d. Peter also had a button on his neck.

The Elements of a Short Story

_____ 6. This story is told from the perspective of
a. Peter's mother.
b. Little Brother.
c. Peter.
d. a knowledgeable narrator.

_____ 7. One possible theme of the story is
a. Technology is replacing human relationships.
b. Family is more valuable than material possessions.
c. It is important to be patient with small children.
d. Brothers should look out for each other.

_____ 8. The climax of the story occurs when
a. Peter first hugs Little Brother.
b. Peter's mother leaves the room to cook breakfast.
c. Peter's mother reaches around to switch him off.
d. Little Brother breaks the fire engine.

_____ 9. The setting of the story is
a. a store at the mall.
b. Peter's birthday party.
c. Little Brother's birthday party.
d. Christmas day at Peter's house.

_____ 10. The tone of this story can best be described as
a. serious.
b. comical.
c. ironic.
d. tragic.

Discussion Questions

1. Were you surprised by the ending of this story? Discuss what you think will happen next.
2. Why did the author include the trademark symbol (TM) in the title and throughout the story?
3. How would the story be different if it were told from the mother's point of view?
4. In addition to Little Brother, what other clues does the author give to reveal that the story is taking place in the future?
5. Evaluate the effectiveness of the story's title. Can you think of other titles that would work for this story?

READING AND INTERPRETING NOVELS

A **novel** is a full-length piece of fiction. In college, you will be expected to read novels in literature classes or for supplemental assignments in any of a wide variety of disciplines. In everyday life, you may choose to read them for fun and relaxation.

Why Read Novels?

Novels can be amusing, engaging, entertaining, and educational. But a novel is also an experience—an opportunity to get involved in a different world. Think of reading a novel as similar to watching a movie. (Many movies are actually based on novels. *The Girl with the Dragon Tattoo* movies, for example, were novels before they became movies.) In a novel, you can become lost in the lives of the characters—you sympathize with them, you feel sadness for them, you share their emotions and life problems. The experience of reading a novel can be uplifting; it can be an escape from day-to-day life worries and stress; it can be educational. Through reading novels, you can learn a great deal about the ways other people live and have relationships, discover different cultures and ways of seeing and understanding the world, and "visit" different geographic places and historical periods.

How to Read a Novel

A novel is an extended story that can tell about several generations of a family, or an entire historical period, or can take place in the space of a day. Like a short story, it contains the following elements. Refer to pages 433–435 for a review of these elements.

- Plot
- Setting
- Characterization
- Point of view
- Tone
- Theme

Here are a few tips for reading a novel.

Before Reading

1. **Study the title.** Make some guesses about what the story might be about.
2. **Preview before reading.** Spend a few minutes reading the inside front cover flap and the back cover and studying the table of contents. Discover who the author is and what he or she typically writes about. Flip through the novel, and read the first paragraph. This will give you a sense of the setting and possibly of the main characters.

While Reading

3. **Reread the first paragraph.** Many opening paragraphs immediately engage you in an event or with a critical person or people.
4. **Watch the plot evolve.** Notice the development of events. Often the story leads up to a crisis or critical point that involves suspense, and its resolution leads to changes in the life of the main character and often of the people he or she is involved with.
5. **Determine the narrator's role.** Find out if the person telling the story is functioning as a reporter, reporting facts, or as a commentator, commenting and interpreting actions and events from his or her own point of view.

6. **Study the characters.** Pay attention to physical characteristics, as well as to dialogue and actions. Notice what other characters think of the main character(s) and what the narrator tells you about him- or herself.
7. **Highlight or make notes as you read.** When a character makes a meaningful statement or the narrator makes an insightful comment, highlight it. Also highlight important or significant actions, interesting descriptions, and unique uses of language. Make note of possible developing themes.
8. **Pay attention to language.** Writers often use figurative expressions (p. 366) and descriptive language to convey meaning.
9. **Watch for clues.** Writers often give you clues about what is going to happen next. (This is called foreshadowing.)

After Reading

10. **Reread the title.** Think about what it means now that you have read the book.
11. **Analyze the themes.** Determine the author's message: what is he or she trying to convey to the reader through telling the story? Reread your highlighting or notes for clues to why the author wrote the novel.

Reading and Analyzing the Prologue from *Water for Elephants*

Water for Elephants, by Sara Gruen, is a popular novel about a critical series of events that occurred when the main character dropped out of school and joined the Benzini Brothers circus. Below is the **prologue** (the introduction) to the novel. Read it now before continuing with this section.

Prologue from *Water for Elephants*

Sara Gruen

1 Only three people were left under the red and white awning of the grease joint: Grady, me, and the fry cook. Grady and I sat at a battered wooden table, each facing a burger on a dented tin plate. The cook was behind the counter, scraping his griddle with the edge of a spatula. He had turned off the fryer some time ago, but the odor of grease lingered.

2 The rest of the midway—so recently writhing with people—was empty but for a handful of employees and a small group of men waiting to be led to the cooch tent. They glanced nervously from side to side, with hats pulled low and hands thrust deep in their pockets. They wouldn't be disappointed: somewhere in the back Barbara and her ample charms awaited.

3 The other townsfolk—rubes, as Uncle Al called them—had already made their way through their menagerie tent and into the big top, which pulsed with frenetic music. The band was whipping through its repertoire at the usual earsplitting volume. I knew the routine by heart—at this very moment, the tail end of the Grand Spectacle was exiting and Lottie, the aerialist, was ascending her rigging in the center ring.

4 I stared at Grady, trying to process what he was saying. He glanced around and leaned in closer.

5 "Besides," he said, locking eyes with me, "it seems to me you've got a lot to lose right now." He raised his eyebrows for emphasis. My heart skipped a beat.

6 Thunderous applause exploded from the big top, and the band slid seamlessly into the Gounod waltz. I turned instinctively toward the menagerie because this was the cue for the elephant act. Marlena was either preparing to mount or was already sitting on Rosie's head.

7 "I've got to go," I said.

8 "Sit," said Grady. "Eat. If you're thinking of clearing out, it may be a while before you see food again."

9 That moment, the music screeched to a halt. There was an ungodly collision of brass, reed, and percussion—trombones and piccolos skidded into cacophony, a tuba farted, and the hollow clang of a cymbal wavered out of the big top, over our heads and into oblivion.

10 Grady froze, crouched over his burger with his pinkies extended and lips spread wide.

11 I looked from side to side. No one moved a muscle—all eyes were directed at the big top. A few wisps of hay swirled lazily across the hard dirt.

12 "What is it? What's going on?" I said.

13 "*Shh,*" Grady hissed.

14 The band started up again, playing "Stars and Stripes Forever."

15 "Oh Christ. Oh shit!" Grady tossed his food onto the table and leapt up, knocking over the bench.

16 "What? What is it?" I yelled, because he was already running away from me.

17 "The Disaster March!" he screamed over his shoulder.

18 I jerked around to the fry cook, who was ripping off his apron. "What the hell's he talking about?"

19 "The Disaster March," he said, wrestling the apron over his head. "Means something's gone bad—real bad."

20 "Like what?"

21 "Could be anything—fire in the big top, stampede, whatever. Aw sweet Jesus. The poor rubes probably don't even know it yet." He ducked under the hinged door and took off.

22 Chaos—candy butchers vaulting over counters, workmen staggering out from under tent flaps, roustabouts racing headlong across the lot. Anyone and everyone

associated with the Benzini Brothers Most Spectacular Show on Earth barreled toward the big top.

23 Diamond Joe passed me at the human equivalent of a full gallop. "Jacob—it's the menagerie," he screamed. "The animals are loose. Go, go, *go!*"

24 He didn't need to tell me twice. Marlena was in that tent.

25 A rumble coursed through me as I approached, and it scared the hell out of me because it was on a register lower than noise. The ground was vibrating.

26 I staggered inside and met a wall of yak—a great expanse of curly-haired chest and churning hooves, of flared red nostrils and spinning eyes. It galloped past so close I leapt backward on tiptoe, flush with the canvas to avoid being impaled on one of its crooked horns. A terrified hyena clung to its shoulders.

27 The concession stand in the center of the tent had been flattened, and in its place was a roiling mass of spots and stripes—of haunches, heels, tails, and claws, all of it roaring, screeching, bellowing, or whinnying. A polar bear towered above it all, slashing blindly with skillet-sized paws. It made contact with a llama and knocked it flat—boom. The llama hit the ground, its neck and legs splayed like the five points of a star. Chimps screamed and chattered, swinging on ropes to stay above the cats. A wild-eyed zebra zigzagged too close to a crouching lion, who swiped, missed, and darted away, his belly close to the ground.

28 My eyes swept the tent, desperate to find Marlena. Instead I saw a cat slide through the connection leading to the big top—it was a panther, and as its lithe black body disappeared into the canvas tunnel I braced myself. If the rubes didn't know, they were about to find out. It took several seconds to come, but come it did—one prolonged shriek followed by another, and then another, and then the whole place exploded with the thunderous sound of bodies trying to shove past other bodies and off the stands. The band screeched to a halt for a second time, and this time stayed silent. I shut my eyes: *Please God let them leave by the back end. Please God don't let them try to come through here.*

29 I opened my eyes again and scanned the menagerie, frantic to find her. How hard can it be to find a girl and an elephant, for Christ's sake?

30 When I caught sight of her pink sequins. I nearly cried out in relief—maybe I did. I don't remember.

31 She was on the opposite side, standing against the sidewall, calm as a summer day. Her sequins flashed like liquid diamonds, a shimmering beacon between the multicolored hides. She saw me, too, and held my gaze for what seemed like forever. She was cool, languid. Smiling even. I started pushing my way toward her, but something about her expression stopped me cold.

32 That son of a bitch was standing with his back to her, red-faced and bellowing, flapping his arms and swinging his silver-tipped cane. His high-topped silk hat lay on the straw beside him.

33 She reached for something. A giraffe passed between us—its long neck bobbing gracefully even in panic—and when it was gone I saw that she'd picked up an iron stake. She held it loosely, resting its end on the hard dirt. She looked at me again, bemused. Then her gaze shifted to the back of his bare head.

34 "Oh Jesus," I said, suddenly understanding. I stumbled forward, screaming even though there was no hope of my voice reaching her. "Don't do it! *Don't do it!*"

35 She lifted the stake high in the air and brought it down, splitting his head like a watermelon. His pate opened, his eyes grew wide, and his mouth froze into an *O*. He fell to his knees and then toppled forward into the straw.

36 I was too stunned to move, even as a young orangutan flung its elastic arms around my legs.

37 So long ago. So long. But still it haunts me.

38 I DON'T TALK MUCH about those days. Never did. I don't know why—I worked on circuses for nearly seven years, and if that isn't fodder for conversation, I don't know what is.

39 Actually I do know why: I never trusted myself. I was afraid I'd let it slip. I knew how important it was to keep her secret, and keep it I did—for the rest of her life, and then beyond.

40 In seventy years, I've never told a blessed soul.

This prologue helps you get ready to read the novel and demonstrates many of the characteristics of a novel:

- **The setting is clearly established.** A place—the circus—is described in vivid detail.
- **The main characters are introduced.** You meet the main character of the novel, the narrator. You are also introduced to other principal characters, including Marlena (the woman the narrator falls in love with) and the evil ringmaster ("that son of a bitch").
- **Action immediately engages you.** You learn that the Disaster March is played because there is a crisis—the circus animals have escaped. You learn that someone has split someone's head open.
- **Suspense builds.** You are instantly dropped right into an action-packed story. While you learn much about the plot, there is much you do not know and you wonder about. You don't know how the animals escaped. You do not know who killed the man, who the man was, or why he was killed. You wonder what secret the narrator refers to in the last paragraph and why he has never told anyone.

- **The language is descriptive and engaging.** You can hear (the earsplitting band, the "thunderous applause" of the audience, and the screaming of the animals), smell (the odor of grease), and see (the terrified chimps, yak, polar bear, and lion) what is going on. Notice the use of figurative language—the polar bear has "skillet-sized paws," and the person's head was "split like a watermelon." Can you easily visualize the confusion and mayhem occurring as the animals escaped and the audience panicked and ran?

Based on the prologue, aren't you interested in reading the novel?

PART VII

A Contemporary Issues Minireader

Reading about Controversial Issues

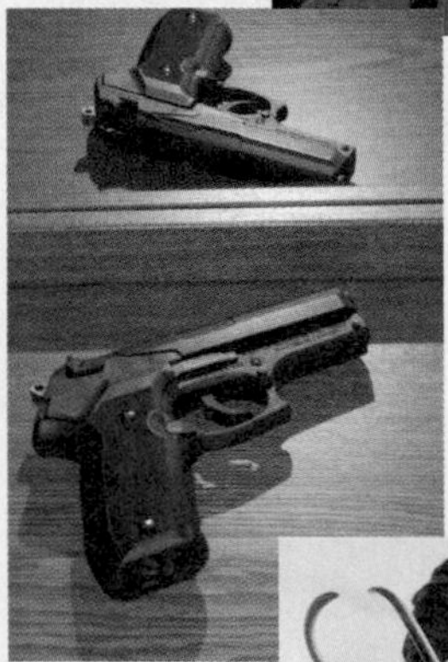

READING ABOUT CONTROVERSIAL ISSUES

A controversial issue is one about which people disagree and hold different opinions. This section offers suggestions for how to read articles about controversial issues. But first, read "The High Cost of Having Fun," below, and then refer back to it as you read the guidelines that follow it.

The High Cost of Having Fun

A majority of Americans follow at least one professional sport. Unfortunately, rising costs are making it impossible for the average fan to watch his or her favorite athlete or team in person. According to *Team Marketing Report,* the average ticket price in the NFL is $58.95, and in the NBA it's $45.28. For professional baseball, the average ticket price is $22.21, while in hockey, it's $43.13. Some argue that the high prices are justified. After all, they say, in order to please fans, teams must win more games than they lose. The best way to win is to have the top players, but teams must spend large amounts of money to get these players. These costs are passed on to the fans through ticket prices and merchandising. However, instead of raising ticket prices, team owners should raise the fees paid by corporations who sponsor stadiums and put their logo on the TV next to the score or advertise in the arena, making use of the real money in the hands of big business. The love of sports cuts across socioeconomic lines; the ability to enjoy a game in person should too.

Guidelines for Reading about Controversial Issues

Use the following suggestions when reading about controversial issues:

1. **Plan on reading the article several times.** Read the article once to get a first impression. Read it another time to closely follow the author's line of reasoning. Read it again to analyze and evaluate it.
2. **Identify the issue.** The issue is the problem or controversy that the article discusses. In "The High Cost of Having Fun," the issue is the high cost of tickets to sporting events.
3. **Identify the author's position on the issue.** In many articles, the author takes one side of the issue. In the paragraph above, the author's position is that the cost of tickets is too high. A different author could take the opposite view—that tickets are reasonably priced for the level of entertainment provided. Or another article could examine and discuss both sides of the issue, explaining why some people feel the cost is too high and why others think it is reasonable.
4. **Examine the reasons and evidence.** As you read, look closely at the reasons and types of evidence the author provides in support of the position or positions presented in the article. In "The High Cost of Having Fun,"

the author presents statistics about the cost of tickets and recognizes that running a professional sports team is expensive. The author argues that the costs are being unfairly passed on to the fans and suggests an alternative means of financing the teams—passing the costs on to sponsors. The author also argues that sports should not be only for wealthy people who can afford high ticket prices.

5. **Evaluate the evidence.** Once you have examined the evidence offered, decide whether it is of good quality and whether there is enough evidence to be convincing. In "The High Cost of Having Fun," the statistics about the cost of tickets are useful. However, the author does not present any information about how much cost sponsors already assume and what additional costs they would need to assume in order to maintain or lower ticket prices.
6. **Opposing viewpoints.** If the writer presents only one viewpoint on the issue, be sure to consider the opposing viewpoints. Sometimes the author will recognize opposing viewpoints, and sometimes even refute (present arguments against) them. In "The High Cost of Having Fun," the writer does recognize that some feel the high ticket prices are justified in order to get and keep top players.

Issue 1: Football Violence

Is Football Wrong?

Will Leitch

In this selection taken from a magazine, the author examines whether professional football has a future. As you read, identify the writer's position on the issue and evaluate the evidence offered in support of this position.

Vocabulary Preview

self-immolation (par. 2) sacrificing individuality for a group
tangential (par. 2) indirectly related to
linearly (par. 3) moving in a line
concussion (par. 6) brain injury resulting from the shake of a collision
saturation (par. 6) point of being completely full
niche (par. 6) having a small market or interest level
lucrative (par. 6) high-paying
mired (par. 6) stuck
histrionic (par. 7) overly dramatic
Faustian bargain (par. 7) trading one's future to have something now

Prereading

1. Do you expect this selection to be based on fact or opinion?

____

2. What problems might the author address about football?

____

1 One of the most quoted routines of the late George Carlin was his explication of the differences between football and baseball. "Football has hitting, clipping, spearing, piling on, personal fouls, late hitting, and unnecessary roughness. Baseball has the sacrifice." I always think about that routine when each sport is beginning to stretch its legs to prepare for the start of a new season. Baseball's spring training is all about the smell of freshly cut grass, about renewal, about being eternally young, about hope. Football's training camp is about fighting for your right to exist, about weeding out the weak, about grueling two-a-days, about a boot camp where you're expected to run until you puke and then get back up and run some more. It is about destroying yourself in order to live.

2 So much of the enjoyment of football is tied up in this notion of self-immolation: The sport doesn't really work without it. The players, outside of the glamour positions on offense, are essentially anonymous and interchangeable. Player careers are so short—and NFL franchise rules make it so easy for them to be cut with no penalty—that most franchises don't even have a signature star longer than a year or two. Fantasy football is so simple and easy to play that you can consider yourself a huge NFL fan but only know the names of about 8 percent of the players. Everyone covers their faces with masks, for crying out loud. The actual men who play the games are almost tangential to the experience: It is all about Team and Any Given Sunday and the National Football League. The NFL is about order, the organization over the individual. It is faux-military at its very essence.

3 We enjoy the NFL because we can forget what goes on behind the scenes, the brutal things these players do and put themselves through, the notion that they need to make themselves fatter and less healthy in order to better land on the quarterback with a crunch and put bounties on other teams' stars. We enjoy the NFL because it looks so good on television that you can follow it linearly—just follow the ball—without having much idea of what's actually going on. The NFL makes you believe you are an expert even though 99.999 percent of the millions who watch every Sunday couldn't say the name of a single play.

4 The NFL wants you to think about what goes on behind the curtain as little as possible. I don't blame them. There's a lot to hide back there. I'm just not sure I can do it anymore.

5 Last May, Jets linebacker Bart Scott said something curious. "I don't want my son to play football." Scott said. "I play football so he won't have to. With what is going on. I don't know if it's really worth it... I don't want to have to deal with him getting a concussion and what it would be like later in life." It is worth noting that Bart Scott is not some pearl-clutching punter sitting idly by as those big scary football players do brutal things to each other. He is one of the more powerful, violent linebackers in the NFL, famous for uttering WWE-esque screams during an ESPN interview after the Jets' upset playoff win over the New England Patriots. (He would later appear in an actual WWE event.) He is no sensitive violet. And he's talking about his job like an old coal miner with black lung who just doesn't want his children to have the same horrible life he had.

6 Football is a violent sport, and always has been, but over the past few years, the increasing evidence of widespread concussion-related brain damage (and the suicides of several high-profile players, including Hall of Famer Junior Seau) is reaching a saturation point. Earlier this summer, Terry Bradshaw—who is paid handsomely to talk about football by one of the NFL's major television partners—told Jay Leno that he believes football will be less popular than soccer in ten years because of worries about head injuries. Hall of Fame quarterback Kurt Warner, who retired in part because of his own repeated concussions, said he wouldn't allow his children to play football either. It has led some to wonder if the sport will eventually become a niche sport, like ultimate fighting (which, for what it's worth, is awfully lucrative for a "niche" sport). Ask Penn State: Institutions can crumble frighteningly quickly. Earlier this year, two economists for Grantland war-gamed a scenario in which football could be eradicated in ten to fifteen years, mired in an unstoppable downward spiral of lawsuits, universities (starting with the Ivy League and spreading to the Berkeleys of the world) dropping the sport, and corporate sponsors (the real lifeblood of the NFL) finally realizing they can't have their brand associated with what some would consider human cockfighting.

7 This still seems fantastical: The NFL is the biggest, most watched, most profitable sport in the United States, and the coverage of the 2012 season kickoff and beyond will be as massive and overwhelming as it always is. (Including in this magazine.) But as the evidence mounts and the voices become louder, every NFL observer has to, at one point, ask himself: Is it immoral to be a football fan? Can an intelligent, engaged, socially conscious person put the way he sees the world in every other context aside because he enjoys watching the Giants on Sunday? Those are legitimate questions, because you can't just pretend anymore. Every time there's a big hit on the field, I can't keep my human side—the part that wonders what that'll mean for the player when he's 45–quiet anymore. Forget your own kid playing football. The question is whether anyone's kid should. If this all seems a little histrionic, maybe it is. Maybe when the crowd gets roaring and the NFL

Films theme gets blaring and they start chanting "j-e-t-s, Jets, Jets, Jets!." I won't feel this way. Maybe I'll get back into the spirit like I always have. We've all made the bargain, the trade of entertainment for what is right and just, for a long time now. But more and more, it feels like an unfair deal. Not just for the players, but for us. Being a fan of football is being a fan of violence and self-destruction. Maybe we'll all be able to get over it and accept the game for what it is, and understand that the players have made their own Faustian bargain. But that won't change the facts. There are no big TV contracts or player salaries without fans tuning in. We're all part of the problem.

—Leitch, *New York* Magazine

Checking Your Comprehension

1. What is the main point of this reading?

   ____

2. What are two reasons so few football players are known to fans?

   ____

   ____

   ____

3. What is one reason football is easy to watch on TV?

   ____

4. Why did Bart Scott say he did not want his son to play football?

   ____

5. What sport did Terry Bradshaw say he thought would become more popular than football?

   ____

6. Give two reasons described by the Grantland economists that may lead to the downward spiral of football.

   ____

   ____

7. What is the biggest, most watched sport in the United States?

   ____

Critical Reading and Thinking

1. What is the author's purpose for writing this selection?

2. What kinds of evidence does the author present?

3. What is the tone of the reading?

4. Is the author biased or objective?

5. What kind of information is not included in this selection that might help readers evaluate the issue?

Words in Context

Directions: Locate each word in the paragraph indicated and reread that paragraph. Then, based on the way the word is used, write a synonym or brief definition. You may use a dictionary, if necessary.

1. explication (par. 1)

2. interchangeable (par. 2)

3. faux-military (par. 2)

4. war-gamed (par. 6)

5. eradicated (par. 6)

Vocabulary Review

Directions: Match each word or phrase in Column A with its meaning in Column B.

	Column A	Column B
______	1. self-immolation	a. moving in a line
______	2. tangential	b. small market or interest level
______	3. linearly	c. sacrificing individuality for the group
______	4. saturation	d. stuck
______	5. concussion	e. trading your future to have something now
______	6. niche	f. indirectly related to
______	7. lucrative	g. overly dramatic
______	8. mired	h. brain injury resulting from the shake of a collision
______	9. histrionic	i. high-paying
______	10. Faustian bargain	j. point of being completely full

Summarizing the Reading Selection

Directions: Write a summary of the reading "Is Football Wrong?" on a separate sheet of paper.

Writing Exercises

1. What would you do if your child wanted to play football? Write a paragraph describing what you would do and why.
2. Write a paragraph discussing why football players continue to play football if there is such a risk of injury.
3. Fans watch football even though the players are putting themselves at risk. Write an essay discussing whether it is right to be entertained by sports or situations that put people at risk. What other sports or activities are popular viewing yet are dangerous for the participants?
4. What is the best way to remove the dangers presented by football? Write a paragraph describing how you think this problem should be solved.

Issue 2: Discrimination Against Women

Women Are Subject to Violence and Discrimination by Both the State and Society

Nadia Shahram

This selection, which first appeared in the *Buffalo News,* discusses the way some women in other countries are treated. As you read, identify the writer's position on the issue and evaluate the evidence offered in support of this position.

Vocabulary Preview

assailants (par. 2) attackers
vulnerable (par. 2) easily harmed
extremists (par. 4) fanatics
desolate (par. 5) isolated
patriarchal (par. 8) controlled by men
exonerates (par. 8) frees from blame
adulteress (par. 11) a woman who has sex outside of marriage
excruciating (par. 19) very painful
voyeurism (par. 20) sexual pleasure from secretly watching someone
misogynistic (par. 20) hateful toward women

Prereading

1. What position do you expect the author to take on the issue of discrimination against women?

   ____

2. What kinds of discrimination against women are you familiar with?

   ____

1 For those who might have missed the news out of India, a 23-year-old medical student was viciously assaulted by a group of men while she was riding a bus with a male companion. The two had just seen a movie. Both she and the man were beaten with an iron rod, stripped, robbed and dumped on the roadside. The woman was gang-raped. She died 13 days later on Dec. 29, 2012, after suffering organ failure.

2 The assailants were strangers to the woman and her companion. All the assailants knew was that she was a woman, on the street, not accompanied by a

husband, a father or a brother, and therefore vulnerable, a fitting target for their arrogant, patriarchal rage. Protests and near-riots have broken out all over India since her death. This unnamed young woman has become the symbol of all that many Indian women have suffered for so long. Now, she is a pure and blameless rape victim because she is dead. Had she lived, there are many who would have found a way to blame her for being raped. In many countries outside the Western world, women have become the face of the family and the symbol of their male relatives' dignity. Even in cases of rape, all that matters is that the woman must be killed to save the embarrassment and shame she brought to the men. The concept is not unique to Indian women.

3 In Egypt, the ruling party is paying gangs of thugs to sexually assault women protesting in Cairo's Tahrir Square against President Mohamed Morsi.

4 In 2009, Ameneh Bahrami, a young Iranian woman, lost her sight and suffered horrific burns to her face, scalp and body in an acid attack carried out by a man who was angered that she refused his marriage proposal. Such attacks also happen in Afghanistan, Pakistan and India. In Afghanistan in November 2008, extremists subjected schoolgirls to acid attacks for attending school.

5 In Iran, Afsaneh Nowrouzi, a 34-year-old mother of two, was convicted of killing the head of security police and has spent the last six years in a desolate prison, despite her claim that she was defending herself when the man attempted to rape her.

6 A 19-year-old married man in Jordan had charges against him dropped after kidnapping a 14-year-old girl, holding her in a tent in the desert for three days and repeatedly raping her. Article 308 of Jordanian law states that if the rapist agrees to marry his victim, the charges will be dropped. A system that legally allows a man to rape any girl on the street and then get away with his crime by marrying her isn't a system. It is a crime.

7 Some would say there is no difference between these crimes happening overseas and many horrific murders, assaults and rapes that happen right here at home. The crime rates for murder and rape in the United States are among the highest in the world. So why should we treat these crimes differently? In "Les Miserables," we saw Anne Hathaway as Fantine being surrounded on the street, attacked and lured into prostitution. That was a depiction of the world in the 1800s. But it could be Afghanistan, Iraq and some other countries today.

8 The big difference is that in the United States, thanks to the hard work of many women and some men, laws and attitudes about rape have changed greatly over time. The blame is taken away from the victim. The focus is on eradicating the cause and the roots of the crime—the male's need for power and control, and the patriarchal society that exonerates the man. But make no mistake, we are far from perfect and our system of justice fails from time to time. There is much more to be done.

9 However, in many other countries, the focus has remained the same: No matter the circumstances, it is always the victim's fault. What did she do to provoke the rape? Women are subject to discrimination by both the state and society.

10 The Iranian penal code, which is based on Iranian interpretations of Islamic law, states that if a woman injures or kills a rapist in self-defense, she will not be prosecuted. But proving self-defense is equivalent to our standard of beyond a reasonable doubt, which is the highest standard of proof in our legal system. The woman must demonstrate that her defense was equal to the danger she faced. She also must prove inflicting harm was her last resort.

11 According to press reports, in the last year only one woman successfully argued self-defense while being tried for murdering an alleged rapist. In Iran, if a woman is raped, she is considered an adulteress and faces death by stoning. If she fights off a sexual predator and kills him, she can be tried for murder and face death by hanging. Women and girls who suffer rape have almost no recourse under Iranian law. It is no wonder why reports of rape and other sexual offenses are low: The victims may be executed if charges are not proven beyond a reasonable doubt.

12 Iran has no problem publicly executing, without proof, men accused of homosexual acts. Why can't the same measure of deterrence be used to stop acts of gender violence against women? A rapist can marry and escape punishment but, depending on the victim's response, she might be put to death. A man throwing acid is lightly punished because either the girl's parents cannot afford to pay the difference in blood money or the government will intervene and excuse the assailant. Suicide rates among women who have been raped or disfigured in attacks are high. Research shows the number of Afghan women committing suicide has increased to 2,300 per year.

13 Many victims, shamed into silence and callously disregarded by a male-dominated power structure, never go to the authorities to seek justice. Women are routinely blamed for inciting the violence against them.

14 In Bangladesh, acid attacks are relatively common. The Acid Survivor Foundation counted 91 attacks in 2011. The scholar Afroza Anwary points out that acid violence also occurs in Pakistan, China, Ethiopia, Cambodia and Gaza.

15 According to a Thomas Reuters Foundation survey, India is the fourth-most-dangerous place in the world for women. Regardless of class, caste, creed or religion, women are the targeted victims of this cruel form of violence and disfigurement. In India, acid attacks on women who dared to refuse a man's proposal of marriage or who asked for a divorce are a form of revenge. Acid is cheap and easily available and is the quickest way to destroy a woman's life. There have been 68 reported acid attacks in the state of Karnataka alone. Most of the victims suffer further because of police apathy in dealing with such violence.

16 In Sonali Mukherjee's well-publicized case, the perpetrators were granted bail after being sentenced to nine years of jail. Without media attention, acid attack

victims languish in pain and poverty, their families often unable to bear the medical expenses. Some of these girls end up killing themselves to take the burden away from their families.

17 According to *New York Times* reporter Nicholas Kristof, Westerners associate terrorism in Pakistan with suicide bombers, but an emerging terrorist threat for Pakistani women is acid attacks, often by their own husbands. Azar, a young mother with three small children, decided to divorce her husband, Jamsheed, and he agreed. After the divorce was final, he came to say goodbye to the children, pulled out a bottle and poured acid on his wife's face.

18 In 2002, Bangladesh introduced the death penalty for throwing acid. Under the Qisas law of Pakistan, the perpetrator may suffer the same fate as the victim, meaning the victim may choose the legal punishment of throwing acid on the perpetrator. However, this law is not binding and is rarely enforced.

19 Over the past few years, acid throwing has been recognized in many countries as one of the most excruciating forms of violence committed against women. It should be treated as a public health concern and dealt with on a national basis.

20 Recently, India's legislature passed sweeping reform laws addressing these horrific injustices. A harsher punishment for rape will, for the first time, include the death penalty in cases where the victim dies or is left in a vegetative state. The minimum sentence for gang rape, rape of a minor or rape by a person in authority has been doubled from 10 to 20 years. Trafficking of women and children will also be punished by longer jail terms. Voyeurism and stalking have been defined as new offenses. These new laws may result in a vast improvement of the treatment of women and girls, if the police and the legal culture actually give the new laws full force. However, it is going to take more than laws to change the patriarchal and misogynistic belief system that has been the cause of centuries of harsh treatment of women.

21 The popular Arab proverb, "A man's honor lies between the legs of a woman" must change to: "A man's honor is being part of his own body and soul."

22 May this young woman's death be the beginning of a serious crackdown on rape and harassment in countries around the world, and may she rest in peace.

—Shahram, *Buffalo News*

Checking Your Comprehension

1. What is the main point of this reading?

____

____

2. What are the two types of crimes against women that are described in the article?

____

3. Describe at least two ways that the laws of other countries discriminate against women, as mentioned in this selection.

4. Why was the woman who was gang-raped in India singled out for the attack?

5. How are laws about rape different in the United States according to this reading?

6. Describe one way victims of rape or disfigurement in other countries commonly react to what has happened to them.

7. Why was the woman named Azar attacked with acid?

8. How has India recently changed its laws about rape?

Critical Reading and Thinking

1. What is the author's purpose for writing this article?

2. What kinds of evidence does the author present?

3. What is the tone of the reading?

4. Does the author recognize or refute opposing viewpoints?

5. What function does the final paragraph serve?

Words in Context

Directions: Locate each word in the paragraph indicated and reread that paragraph. Then, based on the way the word is used, write a synonym or brief definition. You may use a dictionary, if necessary.

1. blameless (par. 2)

   ____

2. thugs (par. 3)

   ____

3. eradicating (par. 8)

   ____

4. recourse (par. 11)

   ____

5. perpetrators (par. 16)

   ____

Vocabulary Review

Directions: Match each word in Column A with its meaning in Column B.

	Column A	Column B
______	1. assailants	a. isolated
______	2. vulnerable	b. fanatics
______	3. excruciating	c. hateful toward women
______	4. extremists	d. easily harmed
______	5. desolate	e. very painful
______	6. exonerates	f. controlled by men
______	7. patriarchal	g. woman who has sex outside of marriage
______	8. adulteress	h. sexual pleasure from secretly watching someone
______	9. misogynistic	i. frees from blame
______	10. voyeurism	j. attackers

Summarizing the Reading Selection

Directions: Write a summary of the reading "Discrimination: Women Are Subject to Violence and Discrimination by Both the State and Society" on a separate sheet of paper.

Writing Exercises

1. How do you think the types of discrimination against women described in this article could be stopped? What kinds of changes would have to occur? Write a paragraph explaining your response.
2. Have you ever experienced or observed discrimination against women? Describe your experience and your response to it.
3. How would you feel and act if you were a woman living in one of the countries described in this selection where discrimination against women is so prevalent? How would your life be different? What would you have to do differently? Write a paragraph explaining this.
4. What evidence about this issue did you find most compelling? Write a paragraph explaining your answer.
5. Write a paragraph discussing some of the emotionally charged language used in this article. How does it affect the reader?

Issue 3: Texting between Students and Teachers

Teachers Texting Students: Should Schools Ban or Encourage?

Katherine Bindley

This article from *The Huffington Post* discusses whether is it is useful or dangerous for teachers to text with their students. As you read, consider the arguments for and against texting between teachers and students.

Vocabulary Preview

incident (par. 1) a specific event
allegedly (par. 1) supposedly
detrimental (par. 2) harmful
mandate (par. 2) a requirement to do something
engaging (par. 3) getting the attention of
compromising (par. 7) endangering
restrictive (par. 8) limiting
resistance (par. 8) opposition

Prereading

1. Do you predict that this article will be based on fact or opinion?

____

2. Do you think students and teachers should text each other?

____

1 This year has already seen a slew of controversial incidents involving teachers texting students. Earlier this month, Pennsylvania teacher Timothy Moll was accused of texting one of his students and offering good grades for naked pictures. In March, authorities discovered that Michael Zack had allegedly sent four of his students a total of 4,000 texts, including some with inappropriate pictures of him. Then there was James Hooker of California who left his wife and kids for a student; those two exchanged 8,000 texts.

2 Meanwhile, school districts and lawmakers around the country have been developing or revising policies on electronic communication and social media interaction between teachers and students. And with no shortage of scandals, many are erring on the side of caution by crafting stricter regulations. But some educators say such limitations can be detrimental to the young people they're trying to protect and could prevent teachers from taking advantage of one of the most valuable tools they have to interact with students: the text message. "There's a lot of administrators, policymakers and elected officials trying to put out these ban dates—a banning mandate," said Lisa Nielsen, who works in education in New York and authored "Teaching Generation Text: Using Cell Phones to Enhance Learning." "It makes their job easier but it's not necessarily what best for children," Nielsen added.

3 Many policymakers are placing blame on the tools used to communicate rather than the person behind the communications, Nielsen said. "What we need to be doing is making policy about behavior. It's not because of these tools that teachers are engaging this way," she said. "If a teacher has said something inappropriate to a child, are we going to ban teachers from talking to students?" Texting is far more effective as a means to engage students than email, which young people have found outdated for at least five years, Nielsen said.

4 "Teachers can send thought-provoking questions to their class for what it is they're going to be learning that day, and let students respond with their thoughts," Nielsen said. Every student gets a chance to respond and later have his or her ideas discussed, as opposed to what happens in the classroom when the teacher might not have the time to call on everyone or shyer students might be hesitant to speak. Texting is the communication mode with which young people are most comfortable: The Pew Research Center recently found that teens exchange 60 texts a day, a hike from 50 a day in 2009. And a suicide hotline in Minnesota set up a texting option in January, resulting in the receipt of more text messages in one day than phone calls in an entire month. So, while many are pushing back against the texting between teachers and students, some educators are embracing the medium as a way to more directly connect with students.

5 When former Harvard professor Mica Pollock collaborated on research for the OneVille Project with students and teachers at Massachusetts alternative school Full Circle/Next Wave, they began exploring the potential of text messages for providing students with support. "It was the most obvious way to reach young people," said Pollock, now at the University of California, San Diego. "They were saying, 'If you need to reach me, texting is the way to do it.'" While not every student has a computer or a smartphone, most have phones with texting functions, she added. As part of the continuing research project, two teachers have been texting frequently with their students—about everything from students' needs to school events. "Students started to ask questions about all sorts of school support issues," Pollock said. "We also started to see students and teachers using the channel to build relationships that were very valuable in motivating young people to come to school and to sort of feel valued by their teachers and to feel more committed."

6 Despite such touted advantages, some schools districts remain in a tough spot when it comes to encouraging the use of texting and social media, especially if the wake of a scandal: After the arrest of a teacher in Redmond, Ore., the Oregon School Boards Association last month spoke out against letting teachers send individual texts to students. The New York City Department of Education will release a new social media policy later this month. Richard J. Condon, the special commissioner of investigation for New York City schools, told *The New York Times*, just eight complaints of inappropriate communications on Facebook arrived from September 2008 to October 2009. But from October of 2010 through September 2011, that tally jumped to 85. In recent weeks, rumors have been swirling that the city's policy might ban student-teacher Facebook friendships altogether.

7 Eric Sheniger, the principal at New Milford High School in Bergen County, N.J., and a Huff Post blogger, maintained that despite these incidents, technology can be incorporated into schools without compromising the students' safety. "Many educators don't know that there are avenues out there to securely communicate with students via text messaging," Sheniger said. "It comes down to a lack of information." Some members of Sheniger's staff use Tweet text, which turns public tweets into text messages that show up on a phone. Last month one of Sheniger's teachers started using Remind 101, a texting service that blocks phone numbers so that personal information isn't exchanged. "We have the tools and we have the means. Many schools just don't have the will to move forward," he said. "We're missing a golden opportunity."

8 Mike Simpson, a general counsel for the National Education Association, said he encourages members of his organization to find a middle ground: communicate only about professional matters and use tools that can be tracked by the schools. "We encourage users not to use personal cell phones or laptops and to go though the school servers," said Simpson, whose association is the nation's largest teachers' union. "Knowing that there is an administrator looking over your shoulder is going to make a teacher think twice about saying something, even in a joking manner." At the same time, Simpson said, if states and school districts try to be too restrictive about what teachers can do, they risk being met with resistance.

9 Last fall, Missouri lawmakers overturned a pending law that banned teachers and students from interacting on social media sites. "It may be a tough area

to legislate in because believe it or not, teachers and other school employees still have some free speech rights," Simpson said.

Just last week, Scott McCleod, a professor of educational leadership at the University of Kentucky, asked readers for their opinions on a proposed Iowa social media policy. The policy proposed banning the exchange of all personal information between teachers and students. "I hate this policy, and I could never work at a school that thinks this way about managing its teachers," wrote one commenter. "It is not wrong or illegal to give personal info, so don't stop me."

—Bindley, *The Huffington Post*

Checking Your Comprehension

1. What is the main point of this reading?

____

2. How have teachers abused texting with students?

____

____

3. According to Lisa Nielson, instead of banning texting with students, what policy should school districts be concerned with?

____

4. According to Lisa Nielson, how does texting change students' class participation?

____

5. According to the Pew Research Center, how many texts do teens exchange per day?

____

6. According to Pollack what is another benefit of texting with students?

____

____

7. What are some of the services that make texting secure?

____

8. What compromise does the National Education Association suggest?

____

Critical Reading and Thinking

1. What is the author's purpose for writing this article?

____

2. What kinds of evidence does the author use to support the arguments?

____

3. Is the author biased or objective?

____

4. What kind of information is not included in this article that might be help the reader evaluate the issue?

____

____

5. What is the purpose of the first paragraph?

____

Words in Context

Directions: Locate each word in the paragraph indicated and reread that paragraph. Then, based on the way the word is used, write a synonym or brief definition. You may use a dictionary, if necessary.

1. slew (par. 1)

____

2. policies (par. 2)

____

3. crafting (par. 2)

____

4. mode (par. 4)

____

5. collaborated (par. 5)

____

6. scandal (par. 6)

____

Vocabulary Review

Directions: Match each word in Column A with its meaning in Column B.

	Column A	Column B
_______	1. incident	a. supposedly
_______	2. allegedly	b. doing something endangering
_______	3. detrimental	c. get the attention of
_______	4. mandate	d. opposition
_______	5. engage	e. harmful

_______ 6. compromising f. a requirement

_______ 7. restrictive g. a specific event

_______ 8. resistance h. limiting

Summarizing the Reading Selection

Directions: Write a summary of the reading "Teachers Texting Students: Should Schools Ban or Encourage?" on a separate sheet of paper.

Writing Exercises

1. Do you think that people's opinion about this topic varies with their age? Why or why not? Write a paragraph explaining your answer.
2. Write a paragraph arguing why teachers and students should not text with each other.
3. Write a letter to a school board explaining why texting with teachers would benefit students.
4. Write a paragraph describing a situation in which being able to text with one of your teachers would have helped you or made learning easier.

Issue 4: Cell Phones and Driving Safety

Driving While on Cell Phone Worse than Driving While Drunk

Steven Reinberg, HealthDay

Published by HealthDay, this article examines the use of cell phones while driving. As you read, identify the writer's position on the issue and evaluate the evidence offered in support of this position.

Vocabulary Preview

tolerating (par. 2) putting up with

simulator (par. 3) a device used for testing or training that models actual operational conditions

impairments (par. 3) weakened physical functions

inebriated (par. 4) intoxicated; drunk

rear-ending (par. 4) crashing into another vehicle from behind

aggressive (par. 5) acting in an assertive/hostile manner

compensating (par. 8) making up for

multi-task (par. 10) to perform two or more activities at the same time

Prereading

1. Do you expect this article to be based primarily on fact or opinion?

   ____

2. Have you ever used a cell phone while driving or observed another driver using a cell phone? Do you feel that use of the phone was distracting or potentially unsafe?

   ____

1 Thursday, June 29 (HealthDay News)—Maneuvering through traffic while talking on the phone increases the likelihood of an accident fivefold and is actually more dangerous than driving drunk, U.S. researchers report. That finding held true whether the driver was holding a cell phone or using a hands-free device, the researchers noted.

2 "As a society, we have agreed on not tolerating the risk associated with drunk driving," said researcher Frank Drews, an assistant professor of psychology at the University of Utah. "This study shows us that somebody who is conversing on a cell phone is exposing him- or herself and others to a similar risk—cell phones actually are a higher risk," he said. His team's report appears in the summer issue of the journal *Human Factors*.

3 In the study, 40 people followed a pace car along a prescribed course, using a driving simulator. Some people drove while talking on a cell phone, others navigated while drunk (meaning their blood-alcohol limit matched the legal limit of 0.08 percent), and others drove with no such distractions or impairments. "We found an increased accident rate when people were conversing on the cell phone," Drews said. Drivers on cell phones were 5.36 times more likely to get in an accident than non-distracted drivers, the researchers found.

4 The phone users fared even worse than the inebriated, the Utah team found. There were three accidents among those talking on cell phones—all of them involving a rear-ending of the pace car. In contrast, there were no accidents recorded among participants who were drunk, or the sober, cell-phone-free group. The bottom line: Cell-phone use was linked to "a significant increase in the accident rate," Drews said.

5 He said there was a difference between the behaviors of drunk drivers and those who were talking on the phone. Drunk drivers tended to be aggressive, while those talking on the phone were more sluggish, Drews said. In addition, the researchers found talking on the cell phone reduced reaction time by 9 percent in terms of braking and 19 percent in terms of picking up speed after braking. "This is significant, because it has an impact on traffic as a system," Drews said. "If we have drivers who are taking a lot of time in accelerating once having slowed down, the overall flow of traffic is dramatically reduced," he said.

6 In response to safety concerns, some states have outlawed the use of hand-held cell phones while driving. But that type of legislation may not be effective, because the Utah researchers found no difference in driver performance whether the driver was holding the phone or talking on a hands-free model. "We have seen again and again that there is no difference between hands-free and hand-held devices," Drews said. "The problem is the conversation," he added.

7 According to Drews, drivers talking on the phone are paying attention to the conversation—not their driving. "Drivers are not perceiving the driving environment," he said. "We found 50 percent of the visual information wasn't processed at all—this could be a red light. This increases the risk of getting into an accident dramatically," he said.

8 The reason that there aren't more accidents linked to cell phone use is probably due to the reactions of other—more alert—drivers, Drews said, "Currently, our system seems to be able to handle 8 percent of cell-phone drivers, because other drivers *are* paying attention," he said. "They are compensating for the errors these drivers are causing," he speculated.

9 This is a growing public health problem, Drews said. As more people are talking and driving, the accident rate will go up, he said. One expert agreed that driving and cell phone use can be a deadly mix. "We don't believe talking on a cell phone while driving is safe," said Rae Tyson, a spokesman for the U.S. National Highway Traffic Safety Administration (NHTSA). "It is a level of distraction that can affect your driving performance," he said. NHTSA has just completed a study that showed that 75 percent of all traffic accidents were preceded by some type of driver distraction, Tyson said. Tyson pointed out that talking on the phone is very different than talking to the person in the passenger seat. "If you are engaged in a conversation with a passenger, the passenger has some situational awareness, whereas a person on the phone has no idea what you are dealing with on the road," he said.

10 "Our recommendation is that you should not talk on the phone while driving, whether it's a hand-held or hand-free device," Tyson said. "We realize that a lot of people believe that they can multi-task, and in a lot of situations they probably can, but it's that moment when you need your full attention, and it's not there because you are busy talking, that you increase the likelihood that you are going to be involved in a crash," he said.

11 Tyson also sees this as a growing public health issue. "Every time we do a survey, there are more people using cell phones while driving," he said. "And the popularity of hand-held devices like Palm Pilots or Blackberries, and people using them in the car, is another problem," he added.

12 An industry spokesman said cell phones don't cause accidents, people do. "If cell phones were truly the culprit some studies make them out to be, it's only logical that we'd see a huge spike in the number of accidents [since their introduction]," said John Walls, a vice president at the industry group, the Cellular Telecommunications & Internet Association–The Wireless Association. "To the

contrary, we've experienced a decline in accidents, and an even more impressive decline in the accident rate per million miles driven," he said. "We believe educating drivers on how to best handle all of the possible distractions when you're behind the wheel is the most effective means to make better drivers, and that legislation focusing on a specific behavior falls short of that well-intended goal and creates a false sense of security," Walls said.

—Reinberg, *HealthDay*

Checking Your Comprehension

1. What is the main point of this article?

____

____

2. In the Utah study led by Frank Drews, how much did use of a cell phone while driving increase the risk of an accident?

____

____

3. In the Utah study, what kind of accidents did drivers using cell phones experience?

____

4. According to the Utah study, how were the reactions of drunk drivers different from the reactions of drivers using cell phones?

____

____

5. According to Frank Drews, why is the use of a hands-free cell phone while driving just as dangerous as the use of a handheld cell phone?

____

____

____

6. How does Frank Drews explain the fact that the number of traffic accidents has not increased since people began using cell phones while driving?

____

____

7. According to the NHTSA study, what proportion of all traffic accidents were preceded by some type of driver distraction?

____

8. According to Rae Tyson, why are driver conversations with passengers less distracting than cell phone conversations?

Critical Reading and Thinking

1. What kind of evidence does the author present?
2. How does the author organize the article?
3. Does the author recognize or refute opposing viewpoints?
4. What kind of information is not included in this selection that might help readers evaluate the issue?
5. What is the tone of the reading?

Words in Context

Directions: Locate each word or phrase in the paragraph indicated and reread that paragraph. Then, based on the way the word is used, write a synonym or brief definition. You may use a dictionary, if necessary.

1. prescribed (par. 3)
2. situational awareness (par. 9)
3. culprit (par. 12)
4. spike (par. 12)

Vocabulary Review

Directions: Match each word in Column A with its meaning in Column B.

	Column A	Column B
______	1. tolerating	a. crashing into another vehicle from behind
______	2. simulator	b. intoxicated; drunk
______	3. impairments	c. acting in an assertive/hostile manner
______	4. inebriated	d. to perform two or more activities at the same time
______	5. rear-ending	e. a device used for testing or training that models actual operational conditions
______	6. aggressive	f. making up for
______	7. compensating	g. weakened physical functions
______	8. multi-task	h. putting up with

Summarizing the Reading Selection

Directions: Write a summary of the reading "Driving While on Cell Phone Worse than Driving While Drunk" on a separate sheet of paper.

Writing Exercises

1. After reading this article, what advice would you give someone who routinely talks on a cell phone while driving? Write your advice in paragraph form.
2. Do you think there should be a law against using cell phones while driving? Write an essay explaining your answer.

Issue 5: Pro and Con: Gun Ownership

The following two readings take opposing positions on the topic of gun ownership, which has become a hotly debated issue in the United States following a string of school shootings and legislative debates.

Pro: Why I Own Guns

Sam Harris

Vocabulary Preview

zealots (par. 1) fanatics
apprehension (par. 2) uneasiness
primacy (par. 2) highest importance
psychosis (par. 2) mental illness
onerous (par. 7) difficult
plausible (par. 9) believable
stigmatized (par. 11) marked as shameful
extrapolate (par. 13) infer
atrocities (par. 14) horrible acts
protocols (par. 16) procedures

Prereading

1. Do you expect these readings to be based on fact or opinion?

____

2. What is your opinion about gun ownership?

____

1 Fantasists and zealots can be found on both sides of the debate over guns in America. Many gun-rights advocates reject even the most sensible restrictions on the sale of weapons to the public. And proponents of stricter gun laws are often unable to understand why a good person would ever want ready access to a loaded firearm. Between these two extremes, we must find grounds for a rational discussion about the problem of gun violence.

2 Unlike most Americans, I stand on both sides of this debate. I understand the apprehension that many people feel toward "gun culture," and I share their outrage over the political influence of the National Rifle Association. How is it that we live in a society in which one of the most compelling interests is gun ownership? Where is the science lobby? The safe food lobby? Where is the get-the-Chinese-lead-paint-out-of-our-kids'-toys lobby? When viewed from any other civilized society on earth, the primacy of guns in American life seems to be a symptom of collective psychosis.

3 Most of my friends do not own guns and never will. When asked to consider the possibility of keeping firearms for protection, they worry that the mere presence of them in their homes would put themselves and their families in danger. Can't a gun go off by accident? Wouldn't it be more likely to be used against them

in an altercation with a criminal? I am surrounded by otherwise intelligent people who imagine that the ability to dial 911 is all the protection against violence a sane person ever needs.

4 But, unlike my friends, I own several guns and train with them regularly. The reason for this is simple: I have always wanted to be able to protect myself and my family, and I have never had any illusions about how quickly the police can respond when called. If a person enters your home for the purpose of harming you, you cannot expect the police to arrive in time to stop him. This is not the fault of the police—it is a problem of physics.

5 In my view, only someone who doesn't understand violence could wish for a world without guns. A world without guns is one in which the most aggressive men can do more or less anything they want. It is a world in which a man with a knife can rape and murder a woman in the presence of a dozen witnesses, and none will find the courage to intervene. A world without guns is a world in which no man, not even a member of SEAL Team Six, can expect to prevail over more than one attacker at a time. A world without guns, therefore, is one in which the advantages of youth, size, strength, aggression, and sheer numbers are almost always decisive.

6 Of course, owning a gun is not a responsibility that everyone should assume. Most guns kept in the home will never be used for self-defense. They are, in fact, more likely to be used by an unstable person to threaten family members or to commit suicide. However, there is nothing irrational about judging oneself to be psychologically stable and fully committed to the safe handling and ethical use of firearms—if, indeed, one is.

7 An ethical argument against gun ownership must deal with the hard case: Where a responsible owner of a gun winds up protecting herself and her family when only a gun would avail. Such cases exist, and their importance is not canceled by the bad things that happen when the wrong people—criminals, children, and the mentally unstable—come into possession of guns. Needless to say, we should do everything we can to keep guns out of the hands of people who will use them irresponsibly, but there are already 300 million guns in the United States, and no one appears to have a plan for reducing this number. Unless we are going to institute a $150 billion buyback of existing weapons and make the penalty for possessing an illegal gun so onerous that no sane person would do it, it will remain trivially easy for career criminals to acquire guns in this country.

8 FIFTY-FIVE MILLION KIDS went to school on the day that 20 were massacred at Sandy Hook Elementary in Newtown, Conn., so the chances of a child's dying in a school shooting are remote. Seventy mass shootings have occurred in the U.S. since 1982, leaving 543 dead. These crimes were horrific, but 564,452 other homicides took place in the U.S. during the same period. Mass shootings scarcely represent 0.1 percent of all murders.

9 One problem with liberal dreams of "gun control" is that the kinds of guns used in the majority of crimes would not fall under any plausible weapons ban.

Advocates of stricter gun laws who claim to respect the rights of "sportsmen" or "hunters," and to recognize a legitimate need for "home defense," simply give the game away at the outset. The very guns that law-abiding citizens use for recreation or home defense are, in fact, the problem.

10 In the vast majority of murders committed with firearms—even most mass killings—the weapon used is a handgun. Unless we outlaw and begin confiscating handguns, the weapons best suited for being carried undetected into a classroom, movie theater, restaurant, or shopping mall for the purpose of committing mass murder will remain readily available in the U.S. No one is seriously proposing that we address the problem on this level. In fact, the Supreme Court has recently ruled, twice (in 2008 and 2010), that banning handguns would be unconstitutional. Nor is anyone advocating that we deprive hunters of their rifles. Yet any rifle suitable for killing deer will allow even an unskilled shooter to wreak havoc upon innocent men, women, and children at a range of several hundred yards.

11 The problem, therefore, is that with respect to either factor that makes a gun suitable for mass murder—ease of concealment (a handgun) or range (a rifle)—the most common and least stigmatized weapons are among the most dangerous. I support all of the reforms that gun-control advocates are calling for—universal background checks, better mental health screening, a national registry, limited-capacity magazines, a ban on "assault weapons," checks against the terrorist watch list, etc.—but they will do very little to prevent the next Newtown. We could make a gun license as difficult to get as a pilot's license, requiring dozens of hours of training. I would certainly be happy to see a policy change of this kind. But I am under no illusions that such restrictions would make it difficult for the wrong people to acquire guns illegally.

12 I see only two options with respect to keeping our schools safe: (1) We can admit that school shootings are extraordinarily rare events, hope they remain so, and then do nothing apart from implementing the above reforms; or (2) we can decide that these events, however rare, are simply intolerable to us—and we can spend the $10 billion or so it would cost each year to put a police officer in every school. There is no guarantee, of course, that option (2) would be effective. But those who think that it is *obviously* a bad idea, beyond its cost, seem to suffer from many misconceptions about guns and violence.

13 Gun-control advocates often fail to distinguish situations in which a gun in the hands of a good person would be useless (or worse) and those in which it would be likely to save dozens of innocent lives. They are eager to extrapolate from the Aurora shooting to every other possible scene of mass murder. However, a single gunman trying to force his way into a school, or roaming its hallways, or even standing in a classroom surrounded by dead and dying children, would be far easier to engage effectively—*with a gun*—than James Holmes would have been in a dark and crowded movie theater. Even in the case of the Aurora

shooting, it is not ludicrous to suppose that everyone might have been better off had a well-trained person with a gun been at the scene. The fact that bystanders do occasionally get shot, even by police officers, does not prove that putting guns in the hands of good people would be a bad idea.

14 As the parent of a daughter in preschool, I can scarcely imagine the feelings of terror, helplessness, and grief endured by the parents of Newtown. But when I contemplate atrocities of this kind, I do not think of "gun control"—because it seems extraordinarily unlikely that a deranged and/or evil person will ever find it difficult to acquire a firearm in the U.S. Rather, I think of how differently the situation might have evolved if the school had had an armed (and, I have to emphasize, *well-trained*) security guard on campus. I also think of how differently things might have gone if the shooter, who seems to have shown signs of mental illness for years, had been more intrusively engaged by society prior to the attack.

15 I do not know how we can solve the problem of gun violence. A renewed ban on "assault weapons" will do very little to make our society safer. It seems likely to be a *symbolic* step that delays real thinking about the problem of guns for another decade or more. By all means, let us ban these weapons. But when the next lunatic arrives at a school armed with legal pistols and a dozen 10-round magazines, we should be prepared to talk about how an assault weapons ban was a distraction from the real issue of gun violence.

16 I have said nothing here about what might cause a person like Adam Lanza to enter a school for the purpose of slaughtering innocent children. Clearly, we need more resources in the areas of childhood and teenage mental health, and we need protocols for parents, teachers, and fellow students to follow when a young man in their midst begins to worry them. In the majority of cases, someone planning a public assassination or a mass murder will communicate his intentions to others in advance of the crime. People need to feel personally responsible for acting on this information—and the authorities must be able to do something once the information gets passed along. But any law that allows us to commit or imprison people on the basis of a mere perception of risk would guarantee that large numbers of innocent people will be held against their will.

17 More than new laws, I believe we need a general shift in our attitude toward public violence—wherein everyone begins to assume some responsibility for containing it. It is worth noting that this shift has already occurred in one area of our lives, without anyone's having received special training or even agreeing that a change in attitude was necessary: Just imagine how a few men with box cutters would now be greeted by their fellow passengers at 30,000 feet.

18 Perhaps we can find the same resolve on the ground.

—Harris, *The Week*

Checking Your Comprehension

1. What is the main point of this reading?

2. Why might calling 911 not be enough to protect yourself in a dangerous situation?

3. How many guns are there in the United States?

4. What percent of murders are mass shootings?

5. What did the Supreme Court rule about banning guns?

6. Name three types of reforms being called for by gun-control advocates.

7. According to the author, what are the two options available to keep schools safe?

8. What change does the author want when it comes to public violence?

Critical Reading and Thinking

1. What is the author's purpose for writing this article?

2. What types of information does the author use to support the main points of the article?

3. How does the first paragraph relate to the rest of the article?

4. What is the tone of the reading?

Words in Context

Directions: Locate each word in the paragraph indicated and reread that paragraph. Then, based on the way the word is used, write a synonym or brief definition. You may use a dictionary, if necessary.

1. proponents (par. 1)

 ____

2. altercation (par. 3)

 ____

3. prevail (par. 5)

 ____

4. implementing (par. 12)

 ____

5. ludicrous (par. 13)

 ____

Vocabulary Review

Directions: Match each word in Column A with its meaning in Column B.

	Column A	Column B
______	1. zealots	a. believable
______	2. apprehension	b. fanatics
______	3. primacy	c. infer
______	4. psychosis	d. procedures
______	5. onerous	e. horrible acts
______	6. plausible	f. difficult
______	7. stigmatized	g. highest importance
______	8. extrapolate	h. marked as shameful
______	9. atrocities	i. uneasiness
______	10. protocols	j. mental illness

Summarizing the Reading Selection

Directions: Write a summary of the reading "Why I Own Guns" on a separate sheet of paper.

Writing Exercises

1. Do you own a gun? Why or why not? Explain your reasons by writing a paragraph.
2. Do you believe armed police are needed at schools? Write your opinion in paragraph form and offer reasons for your position.
3. Write a paragraph describing what you think it would be like to live in a country where guns are illegal for citizens to own. Would it be safer? Would there be more dangerous people with guns or fewer?

Con: More Guns, More Mass Shootings—Coincidence?

Mark Follman

Additional research contributed by Deanna Pan and Gavin Aronsen.

In this selection from the magazine *Mother Jones*, the author discusses gun ownership in light of recent mass shootings. As you read, identify the writer's position on the issue and evaluate the evidence he offers to support his position. This is a shortened version of the original article. The complete article is on the Mother Jones website.

Vocabulary Preview

plausibility (par. 1) believability
lethal (par. 2) deadly
proliferation (par. 3) rapid increase
arsenal (par. 5) large collection of weapons
vigilante (par. 7) a person who takes the law into his or her own hands
abound (par. 9) exist in large numbers
scrutinized (par. 14) examined carefully

Prereading

1. Do you think the author will present a biased or objective examination of the issue?

   ____

2. Do you predict this reading will be easy or difficult to read? Why?

   ____

"America now has 300 million firearms, a barrage of NRA-backed gun laws—and record casualties from mass killers"

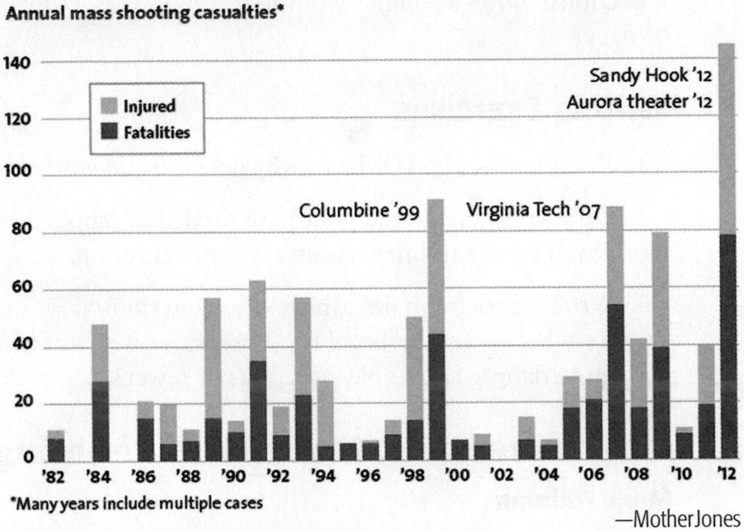

—MotherJones

Figure 1

1 In the fierce debate that always follows the latest mass shooting, it's an argument you hear frequently from gun rights promoters: If only more people were armed, there would be a better chance of stopping these terrible events. This has plausibility problems—what are the odds that, say, a moviegoer with a pack of Twizzlers in one pocket and a Glock in the other would be mentally prepared, properly positioned, and skilled enough to take out a body-armored assailant in a smoke- and panic-filled theater? But whether you believe that would happen is ultimately a matter of theory and speculation. Instead, let's look at some facts gathered in a five-month investigation by *Mother Jones*.

2 In the wake of the massacres this year at a Colorado movie theater, a Sikh temple in Wisconsin, and Sandy Hook Elementary School in Connecticut, we set out to track mass shootings in the United States over the last 30 years. We identified and analyzed 62 of them, and one striking pattern in the data is this: In not a single case was the killing stopped by a civilian using a gun. And in other recent (but less lethal) rampages in which armed civilians attempted to intervene, those civilians not only failed to stop the shooter but also were gravely wounded or killed. Moreover, we found that the rate of mass shootings has increased in recent years—at a time when America has been flooded with millions of additional firearms and a barrage of new laws has made it easier than ever to carry them in public places, including bars, parks, and schools.

3 There is no evidence indicating that arming Americans further will help prevent mass shootings or reduce the carnage, says Dr. Stephen Hargarten, a leading expert on emergency medicine and gun violence at the Medical College of Wisconsin. To the contrary, there appears to be a relationship between the proliferation of firearms and a rise in mass shootings: By our count, there have been

two per year on average since 1982. Yet, 25 of the 62 cases we examined have occurred since 2006. In 2012 alone there have been seven mass shootings, and a record number of casualties, with more than 140 people injured and killed.

4 Armed civilians attempting to intervene are actually more likely to increase the bloodshed, says Hargarten, "given that civilian shooters are less likely to hit their targets than police in these circumstances." A chaotic scene in August at the Empire State Building put this starkly into perspective when New York City police officers trained in counterterrorism confronted a gunman and wounded nine innocent bystanders in the process.

5 The country's vast arsenal of handguns—at least 118 million of them as of 2010—is increasingly mobile, with 69 of 99 new state laws making them easier to carry. A decade ago, seven states and the District of Columbia still prohibited concealed handguns; today, it's down to just Illinois and DC. (And Illinois recently passed an exception cracking the door open to carrying). In the 62 mass shootings we analyzed, 54 of the killers had handguns—including in all 15 of the mass shootings since a surge of pro-gun laws began in 2009. In a certain sense the law was on their side: nearly 80 percent of the killers in our investigation obtained their weapons legally.

6 We used a conservative set of criteria to build a comprehensive rundown of high-profile attacks in public places—at schools, workplaces, government buildings, shopping malls—though they represent only a small fraction of the nation's overall gun violence. The FBI defines a mass murderer as someone who kills four or more people in a single incident, usually in one location. (As opposed to spree or serial killers, who strike multiple times.) We excluded cases involving armed robberies or gang violence; dropping the number of fatalities by just one, or including those motives, would add many, many more cases.

7 There was one case in our data set in which an armed civilian played a role. Back in 1982, a man opened fire at a welding shop in Miami, killing eight and wounding three others before fleeing on a bicycle. A civilian who worked nearby pursued the assailant in a car, shooting and killing him a few blocks away (in addition to ramming him with the car). Florida authorities, led by then-state attorney Janet Reno, concluded that the vigilante had used force justifiably, and speculated that he may have prevented additional killings. But even if we were to count that case as a successful armed intervention by a civilian, it would account for just 1.6 percent of the mass shootings in the last 30 years.

8 More broadly, attempts by armed civilians to stop shooting rampages are rare—and successful ones even rarer. There were two school shootings in the late 1990s, in Mississippi and Pennsylvania, in which bystanders with guns ultimately subdued the teen perpetrators, but in both cases it was after the shooting had subsided. Other cases led to tragic results. In 2005, as a rampage unfolded inside a shopping mall in Tacoma, Washington, a civilian named Brendan McKown confronted the assailant with a licensed handgun he was carrying. The assailant pumped several bullets into McKown and wounded six people before eventually surrendering to police after a hostage standoff. (A comatose McKown eventually recovered after weeks in

the hospital.) In Tyler, Texas, that same year, a civilian named Mark Wilson fired his licensed handgun at a man on a rampage at the county courthouse. Wilson—who was a firearms instructor—was shot dead by the body-armored assailant, who wielded an AK-47. (None of these cases were included in our mass shootings data set because fewer than four victims died in each.)

9 Appeals to heroism on this subject abound. So does misleading information. Gun rights die-hards frequently credit the end of a rampage in 2002 at the Appalachian School of Law in Virginia to armed "students" who intervened—while failing to disclose that those students were also current and former law enforcement officers, and that the killer, according to police investigators, was out of bullets by the time they got to him. It's one of several cases commonly cited as examples of ordinary folks with guns stopping massacres that do not stand up to scrutiny.

10 How do law enforcement authorities view armed civilians getting involved? One week after the slaughter at the *Dark Knight* screening in July, the city of Houston—hardly a hotbed of gun control—released a new Department of Homeland Security-funded video instructing the public on how to react to such events. The six-minute production foremost advises running away or otherwise hiding, and suggests fighting back only as a last resort. It makes no mention of civilians using firearms.

11 Law enforcement officials are the first to say that civilians should not be allowed to obtain particularly lethal weaponry, such as the AR-15 assault rifle and ultra-high-capacity, drum-style magazine used by Holmes to mow down Batman fans. The expiration of the Federal Assault Weapons Ban under President George W. Bush in 2004 has not helped that cause: Seven killers since then have wielded assault weapons in mass shootings.

12 But while access to weapons is a crucial consideration for stemming the violence, stricter gun laws are no silver bullet. Another key factor is mental illness. A major New York Times investigation in 2000 examined 100 shooting rampages and found that at least half of the killers showed signs of serious mental health problems. Our own data reveals that the majority of mass shootings are murder-suicides: In the 62 cases we analyzed, 36 of the shooters killed themselves. Others may have committed "suicide by cop"—seven died in police shootouts. Still others simply waited, as Holmes did in the movie theater parking lot, to be apprehended by authorities.

13 Mental illness among the killers is no surprise, ranging from paranoid schizophrenia to suicidal depression. But while some states have improved their sharing of mental health records with federal authorities, millions of records reportedly are still missing from the FBI's database for criminal background checks.

14 Hargarten of the Medical College of Wisconsin argues that mass shootings need to be scrutinized as a public health emergency so that policy makers can better focus on controlling the epidemic of violence. It would be no different than if there were an outbreak of Ebola virus, he says—we'd be assembling the nation's foremost experts to stop it.

15 But real progress will require transcending hardened politics. For decades gun rights promoters have framed measures aimed at public safety—background checks, waiting periods for purchases, tracking of firearms—as dire attacks on constitutional freedom. They've wielded the gun issue so successfully as a political weapon that Democrats hardly dare to touch it, while Republicans have gone to new extremes in their party platform to enshrine gun rights. Political leaders have failed to advance the discussion "in a credible, thoughtful, evidence-driven way," says Hargarten.

16 In the meantime, the gun violence in malls and schools and religious venues continues apace. As a superintendent told his community in suburban Cleveland this February, after a shooter at Chardon High School snuffed out the lives of three students and injured three others, "We're not just any old place, Chardon. This is every place. As you've seen in the past, this can happen anywhere."

—Follman, *Mother Jones*

Checking Your Comprehension

1. 1.What is the main point of this reading?

2. According to Figure 1, in which year did the highest number of fatalities from mass shootings occur?

3. What pattern did the author find when analyzing mass shootings over the past 30 years?

4. According to Dr. Hargarten, what has the increase in firearms led to?

5. According to the *Mother Jones* investigation, how do most killers obtain their guns?

6. In the video created by the city of Houston, what are civilians first advised to do in a mass shooting?

7. According to the *New York Times* investigation, in addition to access to weapons what is a key factor in mass shootings?

Critical Reading and Thinking

1. 1.What is the author's purpose for writing this selection?

2. What kinds of evidence does the author present?

3. What is the tone of the reading?

4. What connotation does the author's use of words such as massacres (par. 2), carnage (par. 3), chaotic (par. 4), attacks (par. 6) and rampages (par. 8) present?

5. Does the author recognize or refute opposing opinions?

Words in Context

Directions: Locate each word in the paragraph indicated and reread that paragraph. Then, based on the way the word is used, write a synonym or brief definition. You may use a dictionary, if necessary.

1. barrage (par. 2)

2. casualties (par. 3)

3. fatalities (par. 6)

4. perpetrators (par. 8)

5. epidemic (par. 14)

Vocabulary Review

Directions: Match each word in Column A with its meaning in Column B.

	Column A	Column B
______	1. plausibility	a. exist in large numbers
______	2. lethal	b. rapid increase
______	3. proliferation	c. examined carefully
______	4. arsenal	d. large collection of weapons
______	5. vigilante	e. a person who takes the law into his or her own hands
______	6. abound	f. believability
______	7. scrutinized	g. deadly

Summarizing the Reading Selection

Directions: Write a summary of the reading "More Guns, More Mass Shootings—Coincidence?"

Writing Exercises

1. Do you think the rise in mass shootings is related to the rise in gun ownership? Why or why not? Write a paragraph explaining your answer.
2. Did the author persuade you that armed civilians are not the answer to mass shootings? Why or why not? What evidence was compelling about this? Write a paragraph explaining your answer.

Discussing and Thinking Critically about Both Readings

1. Highlight the words in each reading that have strong positive and negative connotations.
2. Compare the tones of the two readings.
3. Does either argument attempt to refute the other? How successful is it?
4. Which reading is more persuasive? Explain your answer.
5. Have these readings changed your opinion about gun ownership? Why or why not?

Issue 6: Pro and Con: Reviving Extinct Species

The following two selections discuss the pros and cons of bringing extinct species back to life. As you read, identify each writer's position on the issue and evaluate the evidence offered in support of the position.

Pro: The Case for Reviving Extinct Species

Stewart Brand

Vocabulary Preview

biodiversity (par. 4) many different types of animals and plants

ecosystems (par. 4) a community of organisms that creates a system in an environment

genomes (par. 9) sets of chromosomes or genes

bottleneck (par. 9) a situation in which no progress can be made

Achilles' heel (par. 10) vulnerable spot

keystones (par. 12) important things that other things depend on

herbivore (par. 13) an animal that eats only plants

boreal forest (par. 13) cold northern forest with pine trees

deciduous forest (par. 14) forest with trees that lose their leaves in the fall

icons (par. 15) symbols

Prereading

1. Identify at least one species the article discusses.

____

____

2. What types of evidence do you anticipate that the author will offer to support his position?

____

1 Many extinct species—from the passenger pigeon to the woolly mammoth—might now be reclassified as "bodily, but not genetically, extinct." They're dead, but their DNA is recoverable from museum specimens and fossils, even those up to 200,000 years old.

2 Thanks to new developments in genetic technology, that DNA may eventually bring the animals back to life. Only species whose DNA is too old to be recovered, such as dinosaurs, are the ones to consider totally extinct, bodily and genetically.

3 But why bring vanished creatures back to life? It will be expensive and difficult. It will take decades. It won't always succeed. Why even try?

4 Why do we take enormous trouble to protect endangered species? The same reasons will apply to species brought back from extinction: to preserve biodiversity, to restore diminished ecosystems, to advance the science of preventing extinctions, and to undo harm that humans have caused in the past.

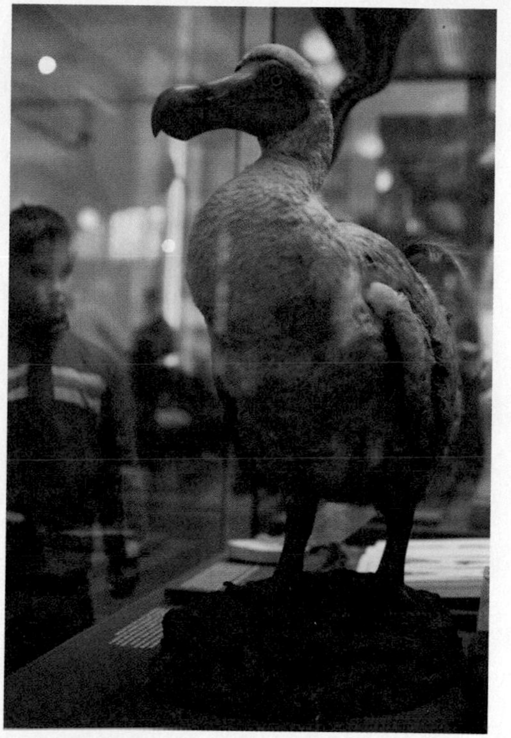

A boy looks at a model of an extinct dodo at the Humboldt Museum in Germany.

5 Furthermore, the prospect of de-extinction is profound news. That something as irreversible and final as extinction might be reversed is a stunning realization. The imagination soars. Just the thought of mammoths and passenger pigeons alive again invokes the awe and wonder that drives all conservation at its deepest level.

6 Then, there's the power of good news. The International Union for Conservation of Nature is adding to its famous "Red List" of endangered species a pair of "Green Lists."

7 One will describe species that are doing fine as well as species that were in trouble and are now doing better, thanks to effective efforts to help them. The other list will describe protected wild lands in the world that are particularly well managed.

8 Conservationists are learning the benefits of building hope and building on hope. Species brought back from extinction will be beacons of hope.

9 Useful science will also emerge. Close examination of the genomes of extinct species can tell us much about what made them vulnerable in the first place. Were they in a bottleneck with too little genetic variability? How were they different from close relatives that survived? Living specimens will reveal even more.

10 Techniques being developed for de-extinction will also be directly applicable to living species that are close to extinction. Tiny populations can have their genetic variability restored. A species with a genetic Achilles' heel might be totally cured with an adjustment introduced through cloning.

11 For instance, the transmissible cancer on the faces of Tasmanian devils is thought to be caused by a single gene. That gene can be silenced in a generation of the animals released to the wild. The cancer would disappear in the wild soon after, because the immune animals won't transmit it, and animals with the immunity will out-reproduce the susceptible until the entire population is immune.

12 Some extinct species were important "keystones" in their region. Restoring them would help restore a great deal of ecological richness.

13 Woolly mammoths, for instance, were the dominant herbivore of the "mammoth steppe" in the far north, once the largest biome on Earth. In their absence, the grasslands they helped sustain were replaced by species-poor tundra and boreal forest. Their return to the north would bring back carbon-fixing grass and reduce greenhouse-gas-releasing tundra. Similarly, the European aurochs (extinct since 1627) helped to keep forests across all of Europe and Asia mixed with biodiverse meadows and grasslands.

14 The passenger pigeon was a keystone species for the whole eastern deciduous forest, from the Mississippi to the Atlantic, from the Deep South clear up into Canada. "Yearly the feathered tempest roared up, down, and across the continent," the pioneer conservationist Aldo Leopold wrote, "sucking up the laden fruits of forest and prairie, burning them in a traveling blast of life."

15 Such animals can also serve as icons, flagship species inspiring the protection of a whole region. The prospect of bringing back the aurochs is helping to boost the vibrant European "rewilding" movement to connect tracts of abandoned farmland into wildlife corridors spanning national boundaries.

16 Similar projects to establish "wildways" joined across American eastern states could benefit from the idea of making the region ready for passenger pigeon flocks and flights of the beautiful Carolina parakeet, once the most colorful bird in the United States.

17 Wilderness in Tasmania is under pressure from loggers and other threats. The return of the marvelous marsupial wolf called the thylacine (or Tasmanian tiger), extinct since 1936, would ensure better protection for its old habitat.

18 The current generation of children will experience the return of some remarkable creatures in their lifetime. It may be part of what defines their generation and their attitude to the natural world. They will drag their parents to zoos to see the woolly mammoth and growing populations of captive-bred passenger pigeons, ivory-billed woodpeckers, Carolina parakeets, Eskimo curlews, great auks, Labrador ducks, and maybe even dodoes. (Entrance fees at zoos provide a good deal of conservation funding, and zoos will be in the thick of extinct species revival and restoration.)

19 Humans killed off a lot of species over the last 10,000 years. Some resurrection is in order. A bit of redemption might come with it.

—Brand, *National Geographic News*

Checking Your Comprehension

1. What is the main point of this reading?

2. Why won't dinosaurs be brought back to life?

3. List three extinct species that could be brought back.

4. How will extinct species that are brought back to life help prevent the extinction of other species?

5. How might restoring extinct animals affect plant growth?

6. How might the possibility of bringing back an extinct species change people's feelings about certain areas of land?

7. Describe how having revived extinct species at zoos could impact conservation.

Critical Reading and Thinking

1. What is the author's purpose for writing this selection?

2. What kinds of evidence does the author present?

3. What purpose does the photograph have?

4. What is the tone of the reading?

____

5. Are the negative effects of species revival discussed or refuted?

____

Words in Context

Directions: Locate each word in the paragraph indicated and reread that paragraph. Then, based on the way the word is used, write a synonym or brief definition. You may use a dictionary, if necessary.

1. extinct (par. 1)

____

2. irreversible (par. 5)

____

3. beacons (par. 8)

____

4. transmissible (par. 11)

____

5. susceptible (par. 11)

____

Vocabulary Review

Directions: Match each word or phrase in Column A with its meaning in Column B.

	Column A	Column B
_______	1. biodiversity	a. many different types of animals and plants
_______	2. ecosystems	b. vulnerable spot
_______	3. genomes	c. sets of chromosomes or genes
_______	4. bottleneck	d. important things that other things depend on
_______	5. Achilles' heel	e. forest with trees that lose their leaves in the fall
_______	6. keystones	f. communities of organisms that create a system in an environment
_______	7. herbivore	g. symbols

_______ 8. boreal forest — h. an animal that eats only plants

_______ 9. deciduous forest — i. cold northern forest with pine trees

_______ 10. icons — j. a situation in which no progress can be made

Summarizing the Reading Selection

Directions: Write a summary of the reading "The Case for Reviving Extinct Species" on a separate sheet of paper.

Writing Exercises

1. Does reviving extinct species give you hope? How would it make you feel if an extinct species were brought back? Write a paragraph explaining your position.
2. Do you think the concept of "rewilding" is important? Why or why not? Discuss your opinion by writing a paragraph.
3. Should it matter whether a species became extinct due to something humans did or due to genetic problems within the species? Does the reason behind the extinction affect whether you think we should revive the species? Write a paragraph to explain your viewpoint.

Con: The Case Against Species Revival

Stuart Pimm

Vocabulary Preview

paleobotanist (par. 1) a scientist specializing in fossil plants
metaphorically (par. 1) not literally, as a figure of speech
pollinators (par. 1) animals that move pollen from one plant to another
symbiotic (par. 1) interdependent
charismatic (par. 2) charming, stand-out
touted (par. 3) praised
cabrito (par. 4) roasted goat
inherent (par. 8) naturally occurring
gimmickry (par. 12) using new or exciting gadgets
rapaciousness (par. 12) greediness

Prereading

1. Do you expect this author to present a reasoned argument or an emotional one? Why?

2. Name several species discussed in this article.

1 In the movie *Jurassic Park*, a tree extinct for millions of years delights the paleobotanist. Then a sauropod eats its leaves. This movie later shows us how to re-create the dinosaur but not how to grow the tree, which at that size would be perhaps a hundred or more years old, or how to do so metaphorically overnight. To sustain even a single dinosaur, one would need thousands of trees, probably of many species, as well as their pollinators and perhaps their essential symbiotic fungi.

2 De-extinction intends to resurrect single, charismatic species, yet millions of species are at risk of extinction. De-extinction can only be an infinitesimal part of solving the crisis that now sees species of animals (some large but most tiny), plants, fungi, and microbes going extinct at a thousand times their natural rates.

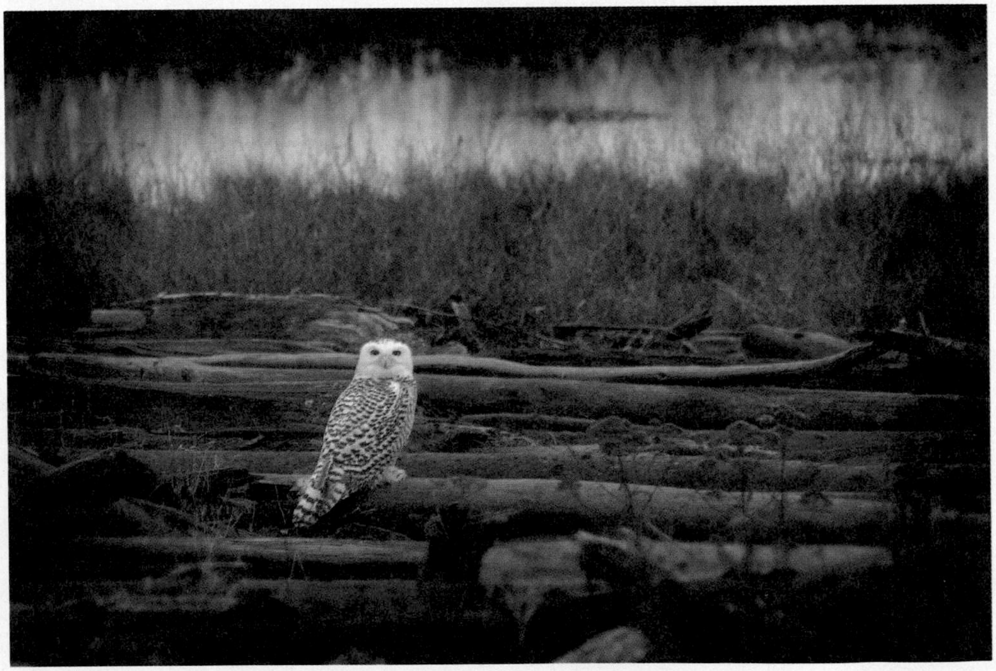

The spotted owl's habitat is threatened by the logging of old-growth forests—an industry that has lawmakers inquiring about more high-tech measures to save the birds in an effort to justify more deforestation.

3 "But wait"—claim de-extinction's proponents. "We want to resurrect passenger pigeons and Pyrenean ibex, not dinosaurs. Surely, the plants on which these animals depend still survive, so there is no need to resurrect them as well!" Indeed, botanic gardens worldwide have living collections of an impressively large fraction of the world's plants, some extinct in the wild, others soon to be so. Their absence from the wild is more easily fixed than the absence of animals, for which de-extinction is usually touted.

4 Perhaps so, but other practical problems abound: A resurrected Pyrenean ibex will need a safe home, not just its food plants. Those of us who attempt to reintroduce zoo-bred species that have gone extinct in the wild have one question at the top of our list: Where do we put them? Hunters ate this wild goat to extinction. Reintroduce a resurrected ibex to the area where it belongs and it will become the most expensive *cabrito* ever eaten. If this seems cynical, then consider the cautionary tale of the Arabian oryx, returned to Oman from a captive breeding program. Their numbers have declined so much that their home, designated as a UNESCO World Heritage site, was summarily removed from the register.

5 Yes, the set of plants alive a century or so ago when the passenger pigeon went extinct are probably still here. Is the pigeon's habitat intact? Surely not: The land use changes since then have been far too extensive.

6 In every case, without an answer to "where do we put them?"—and to the further question, "what changed in their original habitat that may have contributed to their extinction in the first place?"—efforts to bring back species are a colossal waste.

7 De-extinction is much worse than a waste: By setting up the expectation that biotechnology can repair the damage we're doing to the planet's biodiversity, it's extremely harmful for two kinds of political reasons.

8 Fantasies of reclaiming extinct species are always seductive. It is a fantasy that *real* scientists—those wearing white lab coats—are using fancy machines with knobs and digital readouts to save the planet from humanity's excesses. In this fantasy, there is none of the messy interaction with people, politics, and economics that characterizes my world. There is nothing involving the real-world realities of habitat destruction, of the inherent conflict between growing human populations and wildlife survival. Why worry about endangered species? We can simply keep their DNA and put them back in the wild later.

9 When I testify before Congress on endangered species, I'm always asked, "Can't we safely reduce the spotted owl to small numbers, keeping some in captivity as insurance?" The meaning is clear: "Let's log out almost all of western North America's old-growth forests because, if we can save species with high-tech solutions, the forest doesn't matter."

10 Or I'm asked, "Can't we breed in captivity the Cape Sable seaside sparrow?"—an obscure little bird whose survival requires the water in Everglades National Park to be the right amount in the right place at the right time. "Let's

accommodate the sugar growers and damage large areas of the Everglades. Let's tolerate a high risk of extinction because our white-lab-coated science rock stars can save the day!"

11 The second political problem involves research priorities. I work with very poor people in Africa, Brazil, and Madagascar. Rich only in the diversity of life amid which they eke out their living, they generate no money for my university. Too many other universities equate excellence with funds generated, not with societal needs met. Over my career, molecular biologists flourished as university administrators drooled over their large grants and their expensive labs. Field-based biology withered. Many otherwise prominent universities have no schools of the environment, no ecology departments, no professors of conservation. It was all too easy to equate "biology" with molecules and strip faculty positions and facilities from those who worked in the field. De-extinction efforts can only perpetuate that trend.

12 Conservation is about the ecosystems that species define and on which they depend. Conservation is about finding alternative, sustainable futures for peoples, for forests, and for wetlands. Molecular gimmickry simply does not address these core problems. At worst, it seduces granting agencies and university deans into thinking they are saving the world. It gives unscrupulous developers a veil to hide their rapaciousness, with promises to fix things later. It distracts us from guaranteeing our planet's biodiversity for future generations.

—Pimm, *National Geographic News*

Checking Your Comprehension

1. What is the main point of this reading?

 ____

2. What important information does *Jurassic Park* leave out about bringing a dinosaur to life?

 ____

3. If the Pyrenean ibex were resurrected, what would it need in addition to plants in order to survive?

 ____

4. How does the ability to revive extinct species change the way people think about protecting endangered species?

 ____

5. Instead of meeting societal needs, what do many universities see as excellence?

 ____

6. How will reviving extinct species impact the way university biology departments are set up in the future?

____

____

7. According to the last paragraph, what should scientists focus on rather than reviving extinct species?

____

Critical Reading and Thinking

1. What is the author's purpose in writing this selection?

____

2. What is the purpose of the first paragraph?

____

____

3. What kinds of evidence does the author provide?

____

4. Is the author biased or objective?

____

5. What is the purpose of the photograph?

____

____

Words in Context

Directions: Locate each word in the paragraph indicated and reread that paragraph. Then, based on the way the word is used, write a synonym or brief definition. You may use a dictionary, if necessary.

1. sustain (par. 1)

____

2. infinitesimal (par. 2)

____

3. cautionary (par. 4)

____

4. seductive (par. 8)

____

5. perpetuate (par. 11)

____

Vocabulary Review

Directions: Match each word in Column A with its meaning in Column B.

	Column A	Column B
______	1. paleobotanist	a. praised
______	2. metaphorically	b. naturally occurring
______	3. pollinators	c. animals that move pollen from one plant to another
______	4. symbiotic	d. using new or exciting gadgets
______	5. charismatic	e. a scientist specializing in fossil plants
______	6. touted	f. charming, stand-out
______	7. cabrito	g. not literally, as a figure of speech
______	8. inherent	h. greediness
______	9. gimmickry	i. roasted goat
______	10. rapaciousness	j. interdependent

Summarizing the Reading Selection

Directions: Write a summary of the reading "The Case Against Species Revival" on a separate sheet of paper.

Writing Exercises

1. Before you read this selection, what did you think about the movie *Jurassic Park*? How has that changed after reading this selection? Write a paragraph describing this.
2. The author is suggesting that if we can revive extinct animals, we will be less protective of them. Are there things in your own life that are easily replaced? What are they? Are there things that are not so easily replaced? Do you treat these items differently? Why? Describe this difference in one

paragraph. Write a second paragraph describing how this same thinking could apply to animals and the environment.

3. What do you think should be more important: preserving habitats for endangered species or allowing development and commercial use of land? Why? Write a paragraph explaining your answer.

Discussing and Thinking Critically about Both Readings

1. Highlight words in each reading that have strong positive or negative connotations.
2. Compare the tones of the two readings.

   ____

   ____

3. Which argument is more persuasive? Explain your answer.

   ____

4. Are there things that both authors agree on? What are they?

   ____

5. Each selection includes a photograph that illustrates the author's position. Which one did you find to be more compelling? Why?

   ____

6. The authors take very different positions about how reviving extinct species could affect land and plants. Discuss these two different viewpoints. Could both positions be true, or is only one correct?

   ____

Credits

TEXT CREDITS

Chapter 1

17: Jenifer Kunz, *THINK Marriages and Families*, 1st ed., p. 83, © 2011. Printed and electronically reproduced by permission of Pearson Education, Inc., Upper Saddle River, New Jersey.

17: Lawrence G. Gitman, *Principles of Managerial Finance*, 12th ed. Upper Saddle River, NJ: Pearson Prentice Hall, 2009, p. 733.

18: Carl H. Dahlman, William H. Renwick, and Edward Bergman, *Introduction to Geography: People, Places, and Environment*, 5th ed., p. 175, © 2011. Printed and electronically reproduced by permission of Pearson Education, Inc., Upper Saddle River, New Jersey.

22: Leon G. Schiffman, Leslie Lazar Kanuk, and Joseph Wisenblit, *Consumer Behavior*, 10th ed. Upper Saddle River, NJ: Pearson Prentice Hall, 2010, p. 106.

22: Colleen Belk and Virginia Borden Maier, *Biology: Science for Life with Physiology*, 4th ed. San Francisco: Pearson Benjamin Cummings, 2013, p. 277.

22: John W. Hill, Terry W. McCreary, and Doris K. Kolb, *Chemistry for Changing Times*, 13th ed. Upper Saddle River, NJ: Pearson Prentice Hall, 2013, p. 278.

25: John D. Carl, *Think Sociology*, 1st ed., p. 197, © 2010. Printed and electronically reproduced by permission of Pearson Education, Inc., Upper Saddle River, New Jersey. Data source: "Historical Income Tables-People," U.S. Census Bureau, 2006.

27: Patrick Frank, *Prebles' Artforms: An Introduction to the Visual Arts*, 9th ed. Upper Saddle River, NJ: Pearson Prentice Hall, 2009, p. 100.

28: Stephen M. Kosslyn and Robin S. Rosenberg, *Fundamentals of Psychology*, 3rd ed. Boston, MA: Pearson Allyn and Bacon, 2007, pp. 368–369.

34: Eric G. Wilson, "The Allure of Disaster," *Psychology Today* blog, March 13, 2012. © 2012 by Eric G. Wilson. Reprinted by permission of the author. Eric G. Wilson is author of *Everyone Loves a Good Train Wreck: Why We Can't Look Away* and *Against Happiness: In Praise of Melancholy*.

Chapter 2

38: Roger LeRoy Miller, *Economics Today*, 17th ed. Boston: Pearson, 2014, p. 122.

49: James M. Henslin, *Sociology: A Down-to-Earth Approach*, 10th ed., p. G4, © 2010. Printed and electronically reproduced by permission of Pearson Education, Inc., Upper Saddle River, New Jersey.

52: Janice Thompson and Melinda Manore, *Nutrition for Life*, 3rd ed., pp. 106–107, © 2013. Printed and electronically reproduced by permission of Pearson Education, Inc., Upper Saddle River, New Jersey.

62: Janice Thompson and Melinda Manore, *Nutrition for Life*, 1st ed., pp. 109–111, © 2007. Printed and electronically reproduced by permission of Pearson Education, Inc., Upper Saddle River, New Jersey.

68: John Vivian, *The Media of Mass Communication*, 9th ed. Boston, MA: Pearson Allyn and Bacon, 2009, pp. 336–338.

70: Rebecca J. Donatelle, *Health: The Basics*, Green Edition, 9th ed., p. 66, © 2011. Printed and electronically reproduced by permission of Pearson Education, Inc., Upper Saddle River, New Jersey.

73: Jenifer Kunz, *Think Marriages and Families*, 1st ed., pp. 118–120, © 2011. Printed and electronically reproduced by permission of Pearson Education, Inc., Upper Saddle River, New Jersey.

Chapter 3

91: James M. Henslin, *Sociology: A Down-to-Earth Approach*, 10th ed., p. 386, © 2010. Printed and electronically reproduced by permission of Pearson Education, Inc., Upper Saddle River, New Jersey.

91: Michael R. Solomon, *Consumer Behavior: Buying, Having, and Being*, 8th ed. Upper Saddle River, NJ: Pearson Prentice Hall, 2009, p. 19.

92: Rebecca J. Donatelle, *Health: The Basics*, Green Edition, 9th ed., p. 57, © 2011. Printed and electronically reproduced by permission of Pearson Education, Inc., Upper Saddle River, New Jersey.

96: James M. Henslin, *Sociology: A Down-to-Earth Approach*, 10th ed., p. 83, © 2010. Printed and electronically reproduced by permission of Pearson Education, Inc., Upper Saddle River, New Jersey.

97: Rebecca J. Donatelle, *Access to Health*, 11th ed., pp. 355–356, © 2010. Printed and electronically reproduced by permission of Pearson Education, Inc., Upper Saddle River, New Jersey.

Chapter 4

122: James M. Henslin, *Sociology: A Down-to-Earth Approach*, 10th ed., p. 52, © 2010. Printed and electronically reproduced by permission of Pearson Education, Inc., Upper Saddle River, New Jersey.

122: Michael R. Solomon, *Consumer Behavior: Buying, Having, and Being*, 8th ed. Upper Saddle River, NJ: Pearson Prentice Hall, 2009, pp. 62–63.

123: Rebecca J. Donatelle, *Health: The Basics*, Green Edition, 9th ed., p. 34, © 2011. Printed and electronically reproduced by permission of Pearson Education, Inc., Upper Saddle River, New Jersey.

124: James M. Rubenstein, *Contemporary Human Geography*, 2nd ed. Upper Saddle River, NJ: Pearson, 2013, p. 25.

140: Jenifer Kunz, *Think Marriages and Families*, 1st ed., pp. 278–279, © 2011. Printed and electronically reproduced by permission of Pearson Education, Inc., Upper Saddle River, New Jersey.

144: John J. Macionis, *Society: The Basics*, 12th ed., pp. 121–122, © 2013. Adapted and electronically reproduced by permission of Pearson Education, Inc., Upper Saddle River, New Jersey.

Chapter 5

154: Rebecca J. Donatelle, *Health: The Basics*, Green Edition, 9th ed., p. 424, © 2011. Printed and electronically reproduced by permission of Pearson Education, Inc., Upper Saddle River, New Jersey.

155: Frederick K. Lutgens, Edward J. Tarbuck, and Dennis Tasa, *Essentials of Geology*, 10th ed. Upper Saddle River, NJ: Pearson Prentice Hall, 2009, p. 62.

155: Michael R. Solomon, *Consumer Behavior: Buying, Having, and Being*, 8th ed. Upper Saddle River, NJ: Pearson Prentice Hall, 2009, p. 35.

156: Colleen Belk and Virginia Borden Maier, *Biology: Science for Life with Physiology*, 3rd ed. San Francisco: Pearson Benjamin Cummings, 2010, p. 438.

156: James M. Henslin, *Sociology: A Down-to-Earth Approach*, 10th ed., p. 148, © 2010. Printed and electronically reproduced by permission of Pearson Education, Inc., Upper Saddle River, New Jersey.

156: Michael R. Solomon, *Consumer Behavior: Buying, Having, and Being*, 8th ed. Upper Saddle River, NJ: Pearson Prentice Hall, 2009, pp. 392–393.

157: Rebecca J. Donatelle, *Health: The Basics*, Green Edition, 9th ed., p. 282, © 2011. Printed and electronically reproduced by permission of Pearson Education, Inc., Upper Saddle River, New Jersey.

157: Ronald J. Ebert and Ricky W. Griffin, *Business Essentials*, 7th ed. Upper Saddle River, NJ: Pearson Prentice Hall, 2009, p. 12.

157: John D. Carl, *Think Sociology*, 1st ed., p. 51, © 2010. Printed and electronically reproduced by permission of Pearson Education, Inc., Upper Saddle River, New Jersey.

157: Roy A. Cook, Laura J. Yale, and Joseph J. Marqua, *Tourism: The Business of Travel*, 4th ed. Upper Saddle River, NJ: Pearson Prentice Hall, 2010, p. 347.

158: Peter A. Facione, *Think Critically*. Upper Saddle River, NJ: Pearson Prentice Hall, 2011, p. 90.

158: Roy A. Cook, Laura J. Yale, and Joseph J. Marqua, *Tourism: The Business of Travel*, 4th ed. Upper Saddle River, NJ: Pearson Prentice Hall, 2010, p. 52.

160: William E. Thompson and Joseph V. Hickey, *Society in Focus*, 7th ed. Boston: Pearson Allyn & Bacon, 2011, p. 360.

160: Patrick Frank, *Prebles' Artforms: An Introduction to the Visual Arts*, 9th ed. Upper Saddle River, NJ: Pearson Prentice Hall, 2009, p. 5.

161: John D. Carl, *Think Sociology*, 1st ed., p. 128, © 2010. Adapted and electronically reproduced by permission of Pearson Education, Inc., Upper Saddle River, New Jersey.

161: Rebecca J. Donatelle, *Health: The Basics*, Green Edition, 9th ed., p. 18, © 2011. Printed and electronically reproduced by permission of Pearson Education, Inc., Upper Saddle River, New Jersey.

162: John D. Carl, *Think Sociology*, 1st ed., p. 122, © 2010. Adapted and electronically reproduced by permission of Pearson Education, Inc., Upper Saddle River, New Jersey.

162: Ronald J. Ebert and Ricky W. Griffin, *Business Essentials*, 7th ed. Upper Saddle River, NJ: Pearson Prentice Hall, 2009, p. 161.

162: George C. Edwards III, Martin P. Wattenberg, and Robert L. Lineberry, *Government in America: People, Politics, and Policy*, 14th ed. New York: Pearson Longman, 2009, p. 306.

162: Colleen Belk and Virginia Borden Maier, *Biology: Science for Life with Physiology*, 4th ed. San Francisco: Pearson Benjamin Cummings, 2013, p. 208.

163: James M. Henslin, *Sociology: A Down-to-Earth Approach*, 10th ed., p. 6, © 2010. Printed and electronically reproduced by permission of Pearson Education, Inc., Upper Saddle River, New Jersey.

163: Colleen Belk and Virginia Borden Maier, *Biology: Science for Life with Physiology*, 3rd ed. San Francisco: Pearson Benjamin Cummings, 2010, p. 305.

163: Michael R. Solomon, *Consumer Behavior: Buying, Having, and Being*, 8th ed. Upper Saddle River, NJ: Pearson Prentice Hall, 2009, p. 21.

163: Mark Krause and Daniel Corts, *Psychological Science: Modeling Scientific Literacy*. Boston: Pearson, 2012, pp. 273–274.

164: James M. Henslin, *Sociology: A Down-to-Earth Approach*, 10th ed., p. 85, © 2010. Printed and electronically reproduced by permission of Pearson Education, Inc., Upper Saddle River, New Jersey.

164: Frederick K. Lutgens, Edward J. Tarbuck, and Dennis Tasa, *Essentials of Geology*, 10th ed. Upper Saddle River, NJ: Pearson Prentice Hall, 2009, p. 144.

172: Edward F. Bergman and William H. Renwick, *Introduction to Geography: People, Places, and Environment*, 2nd ed. Upper Saddle River, NJ: Pearson Prentice Hall, 2002, p. 365.

172: Hugh D. Barlow, *Criminal Justice in America*. Upper Saddle River, NJ: Pearson Prentice Hall, 2000, p. 271.

173: Rebecca J. Donatelle, *Health: The Basics*, Green Edition, 9th ed., p. 280, © 2011. Printed and electronically reproduced by permission of Pearson Education, Inc., Upper Saddle River, New Jersey.

174: Kathleen German et al., *Principles of Public Speaking*, 14th ed. New York: Longman, 2001, pp. 190–191.

174: Tim Curry, Robert Jiobu, and Kent Schwirian, *Sociology for the Twenty-First Century*, 3rd ed. Upper Saddle River, NJ: Prentice Hall, 2002, p. 138.

175: Michael R. Solomon and Elnora W. Stuart, *The Brave New World of E-Commerce* (Supplement to *Marketing: Real People, Real Choices*). Upper Saddle River, NJ: Prentice Hall, 2001, p. 13.

175: Steven A. Beebe and John T. Masterson, *Communicating in Small Groups*, 6th ed. New York: Longman, 2001, p. 150.

176: Colleen Belk and Virginia Borden Maier, *Biology: Science for Life with Physiology*, 3rd ed. San Francisco: Pearson Benjamin Cummings, 2010, p. 236.

176: Robert A. Divine, et al., *America Past and Present*, Combined Volume, 9th ed. New York: Pearson Longman, 2011, p. 449.

176: Rebecca J. Donatelle and Lorraine G. Davis, *Access to Health*, 6th ed. Boston: Allyn and Bacon, 2000, p. 42.

177: Ronald J. Ebert and Ricky W. Griffin, *Business Essentials*, 7th ed. Upper Saddle River, NJ: Pearson Prentice Hall, 2009, p. 188.

177: George C. Edwards III, Martin P. Wattenberg, and Robert L. Lineberry, *Government in America: People, Politics, and Policy*, 14th ed. New York: Pearson Longman, 2009, p. 9.

177: James M. Henslin, *Sociology: A Down-to-Earth Approach*, 10th ed., p. 46, © 2010. Printed and electronically reproduced by permission of Pearson Education, Inc., Upper Saddle River, New Jersey.

177: Colleen Belk and Virginia Borden Maier, *Biology: Science for Life with Physiology*, 3rd ed. San Francisco: Pearson Benjamin Cummings, 2010, p. 447.

178: Michael R. Solomon, *Consumer Behavior: Buying, Having, and Being*, 8th ed. Upper Saddle River, NJ: Pearson Prentice Hall, 2009, p. 189.

178: Rebecca J. Donatelle, *Health: The Basics*, Green Edition, 9th ed., p. 71, © 2011. Printed and electronically reproduced by permission of Pearson Education, Inc., Upper Saddle River, New Jersey.

178: Rebecca J. Donatelle and Lorraine G. Davis, *Access to Health*, 6th ed. Boston: Allyn and Bacon, 2000, pp. 289–290.

179: Edward F. Bergman and William H. Renwick, *Introduction to Geography: People, Places, and Environment*, 3rd ed., p. 422, © 2005. Printed and electronically reproduced by permission of Pearson Education, Inc., Upper Saddle River, New Jersey.

179: Colleen Belk and Virginia Borden Maier, *Biology: Science for Life with Physiology*, 3rd ed. San Francisco: Pearson Benjamin Cummings, 2010, p. 509.

179: Joseph A. DeVito, *Messages: Building Interpersonal Communication Skills*, 5th ed. Boston: Allyn and Bacon, 2002, pp. 224–225.

182: Michael R. Solomon and Elnora W. Stuart, *The Brave New World of E-Commerce* (Supplement to *Marketing: Real People, Real Choices*). Upper Saddle River, NJ: Prentice Hall, 2001, p. 16.

182: Edward F. Bergman and William H. Renwick, *Introduction to Geography: People, Places, and Environment*, 3rd ed., p. 386, © 2005. Printed and electronically reproduced by permission of Pearson Education, Inc., Upper Saddle River, New Jersey.

182: Jenifer Kunz, *THINK Marriages and Families*, 1st ed., p. 83, © 2011. Printed and electronically reproduced by permission of Pearson Education, Inc., Upper Saddle River, New Jersey.

183: Rebecca J. Donatelle and Lorraine G. Davis, *Access to Health*, 6th ed. Boston: Allyn and Bacon, 2000, p. 78.

183: George C. Edwards III, Martin P. Wattenberg, and Robert L. Lineberry, *Government in America: People, Politics, and Policy*, 14th ed. New York: Pearson Longman, 2009, pp. 205–206.

184: Janice Thompson and Melinda Manore, *Nutrition for Life*, 2nd ed., p. 240, © 2010. Adapted and electronically reproduced by permission of Pearson Education, Inc., Upper Saddle River, New Jersey.

187: Joshua Kors, "War Torn" from *Current Science*, November 28, 2008. Copyright © 2008 by The Weekly Reader Corporation. Reprinted by permission of Scholastic Inc.

189: Drawing of brain: © McClatchy-Tribune Information Services. All Rights Reserved. Reprinted with permission.

Chapter 6

193: "Parent/Teacher Yellow Cake" from *I Like You* by Amy Sedaris. Copyright © 2006 by Amy Sedaris. By permission of Grand Central Publishing. All rights reserved.

194: John V. Thill and Courtland L. Bovée, *Excellence in Business Communication*, 9th ed. Upper Saddle River, NJ: Pearson Prentice Hall, 2011, p. 14.

196: John D. Carl, *Think Sociology*, 1st ed., p. 200, © 2010. Printed and electronically reproduced by permission of Pearson Education, Inc., Upper Saddle River, New Jersey.

197: April Lynch, Barry Elmore, and Tanya Morgan, *Choosing Health*, 1st ed. San Francisco: Pearson Benjamin Cummings, 2012, p. 83.

198: Steve Mariotti and Caroline Glackin, *Entrepreneurship & Small Business Management*. Boston: Pearson, 2012, p. 216.

199: Hugh D. Barlow, *Criminal Justice in America*. Upper Saddle River, NJ: Pearson Prentice Hall, 2000, p. 238.

202: John R. Walker and Josielyn T. Walker, *Tourism: Concepts and Practices*. Upper Saddle River, NJ: Pearson Prentice Hall, 2011, p. 11.

203: George C. Edwards III, Martin P. Wattenberg, and Robert L. Lineberry, *Government in America: People, Politics, and Policy*, 14th ed. New York: Pearson Longman, 2009, p. 239.

203: Thomas F. Goldman and Henry R. Cheeseman, *The Paralegal Professional*, 3rd ed. Upper Saddle River, NJ: Pearson Prentice Hall, 2011, pp. 736–737.

204: Saundra K. Ciccarelli and J. Noland White, *Psychology: An Exploration*, 1st ed. Upper Saddle River, NJ: Pearson Prentice Hall, 2010, p. 249.

204: Thomas F. Goldman and Henry R. Cheeseman, *The Paralegal Professional*, 3rd ed. Upper Saddle River, NJ: Pearson Prentice Hall, 2011, p. 81.

205: Colleen Belk and Virginia Borden Maier, *Biology: Science for Life with Physiology*, 4th ed. San Francisco: Pearson Benjamin Cummings, 2013, pp. 95–96.

205: James M. Henslin, *Sociology: A Down-to-Earth Approach*, 10th ed., p. 383, © 2010. Printed and electronically reproduced by permission of Pearson Education, Inc., Upper Saddle River, New Jersey.

206: Carl H. Dahlman, William H. Renwick, and Edward Bergman, *Introduction to Geography: People, Places, and Environment*, 5th ed., p. 215, © 2011. Printed and electronically reproduced by permission of Pearson Education, Inc., Upper Saddle River, New Jersey.

206: Daniel J. Limmer and Michael F. O'Keefe, *Emergency Care*, 12th ed. Boston: Pearson Brady, 2012, p. 581.

207: Frederick K. Lutgens, Edward J. Tarbuck, and Dennis G. Tasa, *The Atmosphere: An Introduction to Meteorology*, 12th ed. Upper Saddle River, NJ: Pearson Prentice Hall, 2013, pp. 455–456.

207: George C. Edwards III, Martin P. Wattenberg, and Robert L. Lineberry, *Government in America: People, Politics, and Policy*, 14th ed. New York: Pearson Longman, 2009, pp. 458–459.

208: Stephen F. Davis and Joseph J. Palladino, *Psychology*, 3rd ed. Upper Saddle River. NJ: Prentice Hall, 2000, pp. 563, 564, 566.

208: Rebecca J. Donatelle and Lorraine G. Davis, *Access to Health*, 6th ed. Boston: Allyn and Bacon, 2000, pp. 358, 371.

208: John A. Garraty and Mark C. Carnes, *The American Nation: A History of the United States*, 10th ed. New York: Longman, 2000, p. 706.

209: Roy A. Cook, Laura J. Yale, and Joseph J. Marqua, *Tourism: The Business of Travel*, 4th ed. Upper Saddle River, NJ: Pearson Prentice Hall, 2010, p. 209.

209: Palmira Brummett et al., *Civilization: Past & Present*, 9th ed. New York: Longman, 2000, p. 348.

211: H. Edward Reiley and Carroll L. Shry, Jr., *Introductory Horticulture*. Albany, NY: Delmar Publishers, 1979, p. 114.

216: Joan Salge Blake, *Nutrition & You*. San Francisco: Pearson Benjamin Cummings, 2011, p. 24/7.

219: Rebecca J. Donatelle and Lorraine G. Davis, *Access to Health*, 6th ed. Boston: Allyn and Bacon, 2000, pp. 446–447.

219: Palmira Brummett et al., *Civilization: Past & Present*, 9th ed. New York: Longman, 2000, p. 919.

219: Stephen F. Davis and Joseph J. Palladino, *Psychology*, 3rd ed. Upper Saddle River. NJ: Prentice Hall, 2000, p. 609.

220: Roy A. Cook, Laura J. Yale, and Joseph J. Marqua, *Tourism: The Business of Travel*, 4th ed. Upper Saddle River, NJ: Pearson Prentice Hall, 2010, p. 214.

220: Joseph A. DeVito, *Messages: Building Interpersonal Communication Skills*, 5th ed. Boston: Allyn and Bacon, 2002, p. 284.

221: Stephen M. Kosslyn and Robin S. Rosenberg, *Psychology: The Brain, The Person, The World*, 1st ed. Boston: Allyn and Bacon, 2001, pp. 180–181.

223: Paul Bogard, "Let There Be Dark," *Los Angeles Times*, December 21, 2012. © 2012 by Paul Bogard. Reprinted by permission of the author.

Chapter 7

228: Map courtesy of The Weather Channel.

230: Michael R. Solomon, Greg W. Marshall, and Elnora W. Stuart, *Marketing: Real People, Real Choices*, 7th ed. Upper Saddle River, NJ: Pearson Prentice Hall, 2012, p. 85.

231: Gary Armstrong and Philip Kotler, *Marketing: An Introduction*, 11th ed. Upper Saddle River, NJ: Pearson Prentice Hall, 2013, pp. 165–166.

231: John V. Thill and Courtland L. Bovée, *Excellence in Business Communication*, 9th ed. Upper Saddle River, NJ: Pearson Prentice Hall, 2011, p. 473.

231: April Lynch, Barry Elmore, and Tanya Morgan, *Choosing Health*, 1st ed. San Francisco: Pearson Benjamin Cummings, 2012, pp. 75–76.

232: Gary Armstrong and Philip Kotler, *Marketing: An Introduction*, 11th ed. Upper Saddle River, NJ: Pearson Prentice Hall, 2013, p. 181.

234: Excerpt from *The World Book Online Reference Center* © 2010. www.worldbookonline.com. By permission of the publisher. All rights reserved. This content may not be reproduced in whole or in part in any form without prior written permission from the publisher.

235: Robert W. Christopherson, *Elemental Geosystems*, 7th ed. Upper Saddle River, NJ: Pearson Prentice Hall, 2013, p. 40.

235: Stephen M. Kosslyn and Robin S. Rosenberg, *Introducing Psychology*, 4th ed. Boston: Pearson Allyn and Bacon, 2011, p. 166.

235: Michael R. Solomon, *Consumer Behavior: Buying, Having, and Being*, 10th ed. Upper Saddle River, NJ: Pearson Prentice Hall, 2012, p. 508.

240: David Krogh, *Biology: A Guide to the Natural World*, 4th ed., pp. 466–467, 474, © 2009. Printed and electronically reproduced by permission of Pearson Education, Inc., Upper Saddle River, New Jersey.
241: James M. Henslin, *Sociology: A Down-to-Earth Approach*, 10th ed., p. 164, © 2010. Printed and electronically reproduced by permission of Pearson Education, Inc., Upper Saddle River, New Jersey.
242: David Krogh, *Biology: A Guide to the Natural World*, 5th ed. San Francisco: Pearson Benjamin Cummings, 2011, p. 370.
242: Alan Evans, Kendall Martin, and Mary Anne Poatsy, *Technology in Action*, 7th ed. Upper Saddle River, NJ: Pearson Prentice Hall, 2011, p. 271.
245: Roy A. Cook, Laura J. Yale, and Joseph J. Marqua, *Tourism: The Business of Travel*, 4th ed. Upper Saddle River, NJ: Pearson Prentice Hall, 2010, p. 282.
246: Saundra K. Ciccarelli and J. Noland White, *Psychology: An Exploration*, 1st ed. Upper Saddle River, NJ: Pearson Prentice Hall, 2010, p. 280.
247: Colleen Belk and Virginia Borden Maier, *Biology: Science for Life with Physiology*, 3rd ed. San Francisco: Pearson Benjamin Cummings, 2010, p. 372.
247: James M. Henslin, *Sociology: A Down-to-Earth Approach*, 10th ed., p. 37, © 2010. Printed and electronically reproduced by permission of Pearson Education, Inc., Upper Saddle River, New Jersey.
249: David Krogh, *Biology: A Guide to the Natural World*, 4th ed., p. 429, © 2009. Printed and electronically reproduced by permission of Pearson Education, Inc., Upper Saddle River, New Jersey.
250: Michael R. Solomon, *Consumer Behavior: Buying, Having, and Being*, 8th ed. Upper Saddle River, NJ: Pearson Prentice Hall, 2009, pp. 132–133.
250: James M. Henslin, *Sociology: A Down-to-Earth Approach*, 10th ed., pp. 109, 111, © 2010. Printed and electronically reproduced by permission of Pearson Education, Inc., Upper Saddle River, New Jersey.
252: Hugh D. Barlow, *Criminal Justice in America*. Upper Saddle River, NJ: Pearson Prentice Hall, 2000, p. 332.
252: Roy A. Cook, Laura J. Yale, and Joseph J. Marqua, *Tourism: The Business of Travel*, 4th ed. Upper Saddle River, NJ: Pearson Prentice Hall, 2010, p. 170.
253: Thomas F. Goldman and Henry R. Cheeseman, *The Paralegal Professional*, 3rd ed. Upper Saddle River, NJ: Pearson Prentice Hall, 2011, p. 266.
253: Robert A. Divine, et al., *America Past and Present*, Combined Volume, 9th ed. New York: Pearson Longman, 2011, p. 596.
254: Saundra K. Ciccarelli and J. Noland White, *Psychology: An Exploration*, 1st ed. Upper Saddle River, NJ: Pearson Prentice Hall, 2010, p. 321.
254: David Krogh, *Biology: A Guide to the Natural World*, 4th ed., p. 750, © 2009. Printed and electronically reproduced by permission of Pearson Education, Inc., Upper Saddle River, New Jersey.
255: John R. Walker and Josielyn T. Walker, *Tourism: Concepts and Practices*. Upper Saddle River, NJ: Pearson Prentice Hall, 2011, pp. 53–54.
255: Thomas F. Goldman and Henry R. Cheeseman, *The Paralegal Professional*, 3rd ed. Upper Saddle River, NJ: Pearson Prentice Hall, 2011, p. 641.
255: John W. Hill, Terry W. McCreary, and Doris K. Kolb, *Chemistry for Changing Times*, 13th ed. Upper Saddle River, NJ: Pearson Prentice Hall, 2013, p. 682.
256: Rebecca J. Donatelle, *Health: The Basics*, Green Edition, 9th ed., p. 20, © 2011. Reprinted and electronically reproduced by permission of Pearson Education, Inc., Upper Saddle River, New Jersey.
256: David Krogh, *Biology: A Guide to the Natural World*, 4th ed., p. 488, © 2009. Printed and electronically reproduced by permission of Pearson Education, Inc., Upper Saddle River, New Jersey.

256: Colleen Belk and Virginia Borden Maier, *Biology: Science for Life with Physiology*, 3rd ed. San Francisco: Pearson Benjamin Cummings, 2010, p. 451.

256: John R. Walker and Josielyn T. Walker, *Tourism: Concepts and Practices*. Upper Saddle River, NJ: Pearson Prentice Hall, 2011, p. 241.

257: Diane Sukiennik, Lisa Raufman, and William Bendat, *The Career Fitness Program: Exercising Your Options*, 10th ed. Upper Saddle River, NJ: Pearson Prentice Hall, 2013, p. 111.

258: Thomas F. Goldman and Henry R. Cheeseman, *The Paralegal Professional*, 3rd ed. Upper Saddle River, NJ: Pearson Prentice Hall, 2011, p. 183.

259: James M. Henslin, *Sociology: A Down-to-Earth Approach*, 6th ed. Boston: Pearson Allyn & Bacon, 2003, p. 637.

260: Edward F. Bergman and William H. Renwick, *Introduction to Geography: People, Places, and Environment*, 3rd ed., p. 430, © 2005. Printed and electronically reproduced by permission of Pearson Education, Inc., Upper Saddle River, New Jersey.

260: William J. Germann and Cindy L. Stanfield, *Principles of Human Physiology*. San Francisco: Pearson Benjamin Cummings, 2002, pp. 303–304.

266: David Krogh, *Biology: A Guide to the Natural World*, 4th ed., pp. 318–319, © 2009. Printed and electronically reproduced by permission of Pearson Education, Inc., Upper Saddle River, New Jersey.

268: William E. Thompson and Joseph V. Hickey, *Society in Focus*, 7th ed. Boston: Pearson Allyn & Bacon, 2011, p. 493.

268: John W. Hill, Terry W. McCreary, and Doris K. Kolb, *Chemistry for Changing Times*, 13th ed. Upper Saddle River, NJ: Pearson Prentice Hall, 2013, p. 3.

268: Joseph A. DeVito, *The Interpersonal Communication Book*, 9th ed. Boston: Allyn and Bacon, 2001, pp. 219–220.

269: James M. Henslin, *Sociology: A Down-to-Earth Approach*, 10th ed., pp. 389–390, © 2010. Printed and electronically reproduced by permission of Pearson Education, Inc., Upper Saddle River, New Jersey.

269: John R. Walker, *Introduction to Hospitality Management*, 3rd ed. Upper Saddle River, NJ: Pearson Prentice Hall, 2010, p. 361.

269: Jenifer Kunz, *Think Marriages and Families*, 1st ed., p. 16, © 2011. Printed and electronically reproduced by permission of Pearson Education, Inc., Upper Saddle River, New Jersey.

270: Patrick Frank, *Prebles' Artforms: An Introduction to the Visual Arts*, 9th ed. Upper Saddle River, NJ: Pearson Prentice Hall, 2009, p. 127.

270: Frederick K. Lutgens, Edward J. Tarbuck, and Dennis Tasa, *Essentials of Geology*, 10th ed. Upper Saddle River, NJ: Pearson Prentice Hall, 2009, pp. 252–253.

270: David Krogh, *Biology: A Guide to the Natural World*, 4th ed., p. 471, © 2009. Printed and electronically reproduced by permission of Pearson Education, Inc., Upper Saddle River, New Jersey.

271: Michael R. Solomon, *Consumer Behavior: Buying, Having, and Being*, 8th ed. Upper Saddle River, NJ: Pearson Prentice Hall, 2009, p. 13.

272: Alton Fitzgerald White, "Right Place, Wrong Face." Reprinted with permission from the October 11, 1999 issue of *The Nation* (where it was originally titled "Ragtime, My Time"). For subscription information, call 1-800-333-8536. Portions of each week's *Nation* magazine can be accessed at http://www.thenation.com

Chapter 8

278: Elaine N. Marieb, *Essentials of Human Anatomy & Physiology*, 7th ed., pp. 162, 164, © 2003. Printed and electronically reproduced by permission of Pearson Education, Inc., Upper Saddle River, New Jersey.

278: Elaine N. Marieb, *Essentials of Human Anatomy & Physiology*, 7th ed., p. 164, © 2003. Printed and electronically reproduced by permission of Pearson Education, Inc., Upper Saddle River, New Jersey.

283: Richard Fabes and Carol Lynn Martin, *Exploring Child Development*, 2nd ed., p. 454. © 2003 South-Western, a part of Cengage Learning, Inc. Reproduced by permission. www.cengage.com/permissions

285: *Physical Activity for a Healthy Weight: Why is physical activity important?* Atlanta, GA: U.S. Centers for Disease Control and Prevention, September 13, 2011, http://www.cdc.gov/healthyweight/physical_activity/index.html (in Blake, *Nutrition & You*, p. 21/13).

286: Joan Salge Blake, *Nutrition & You*. San Francisco: Pearson Benjamin Cummings, 2011, p. 21/13.

287: Jeffrey Bennett, William L. Briggs, and Mario F. Triola, *Statistical Reasoning for Everyday Life*, 4th ed., Figure 6.14, p. 233, © 2014. Printed and electronically reproduced by permission of Pearson Education, Inc., Upper Saddle River, New Jersey.

288: Richard Fabes and Carol Lynn Martin, *Exploring Child Development*, 2nd ed., p. 281. © 2003 South-Western, a part of Cengage Learning, Inc. Reproduced by permission. www.cengage.com/permissions

290: Richard Fabes and Carol Lynn Martin, *Exploring Child Development*, 2nd ed., p. 196. © 2003 South-Western, a part of Cengage Learning, Inc. Reproduced by permission. www.cengage.com/permissions

290: April Lynch, Barry Elmore, and Tanya Morgan, *Choosing Health*, 1st ed. San Francisco: Pearson Benjamin Cummings, 2012, p. 273.

292: James M. Henslin, *Social Problems*, 6th ed., Figure 11.5, p. 368, © 2003. Printed and electronically reproduced by permission of Pearson Education, Inc., Upper Saddle River, New Jersey.

293: Robert L. Lineberry and George C. Edwards III, *Government in America: People, Politics, and Policy*, 4th ed., p. 253, © 1989. Printed and electronically reproduced by permission of Pearson Education, Inc., Upper Saddle River, New Jersey.

294: Michael R. Solomon, Greg W. Marshall, and Elnora W. Stuart, *Marketing: Real People, Real Choices*, 6th ed., p. 406, © 2009. Printed and electronically reproduced by permission of Pearson Education, Inc., Upper Saddle River, New Jersey.

295: Elaine N. Marieb, *Essentials of Human Anatomy & Physiology*, 7th ed., p. 106, © 2003. Printed and electronically reproduced by permission of Pearson Education, Inc., Upper Saddle River, New Jersey.

295: Elaine N. Marieb, *Essentials of Human Anatomy & Physiology*, 7th ed., Figure 4.9, p. 106, © 2003. Printed and electronically reproduced by permission of Pearson Education, Inc., Upper Saddle River, New Jersey.

297: Edward F. Bergman and William H. Renwick, *Introduction to Geography: People, Places, and Environment*, 3rd ed., p. 69, © 2005. Printed and electronically reproduced by permission of Pearson Education, Inc., Upper Saddle River, New Jersey.

298: Rebecca J. Donatelle, *Health: The Basics*, Green Edition, 9th ed., p. 229, © 2011. Reprinted and electronically reproduced by permission of Pearson Education, Inc., Upper Saddle River, New Jersey.

306: Table A: James M. Henslin, *Sociology: A Down-to-Earth Approach*, 10th ed., p. 483, © 2010. Printed and electronically reproduced by permission of Pearson Education, Inc., Upper Saddle River, New Jersey.

306: James M. Henslin, *Sociology: A Down-to-Earth Approach*, 10th ed., p. 483, © 2010. Printed and electronically reproduced by permission of Pearson Education, Inc., Upper Saddle River, New Jersey.

308: James M. Henslin, *Sociology: A Down-to-Earth Approach*, 6th ed. Boston: Pearson Allyn & Bacon, 2003, p. 489.

311: Mary Ann A. Schwartz and BarBara Marliene Scott, *Marriages and Families*, 7th ed., pp. 237–240, © 2013. Printed and electronically reproduced by permission of Pearson Education, Inc., Upper Saddle River, New Jersey.

313: Table A: From *The Decline of Marriage and Rise of New Families*. Washington, DC: Pew Research Center, Social & Demographic Trends Project, November 18, 2010, p. 8. Reprinted with permission of Pew Research Center, Social & Demographic Trends Project. http://www.pewsocialtrends.org/2010/11/18/the-decline-of-marriage-and-rise-of-new-families/ (In Luscombe, 2010).

Chapter 9

321: John R. Walker, *Introduction to Hospitality Management*, 3rd ed. Upper Saddle River, NJ: Pearson Prentice Hall, 2010, p. 45.
322: Thomas F. Goldman and Henry R. Cheeseman, *The Paralegal Professional*, 3rd ed. Upper Saddle River, NJ: Pearson Prentice Hall, 2011, p. 745.
324: Saundra K. Ciccarelli and J. Noland White, *Psychology: An Exploration*, 1st ed. Upper Saddle River, NJ: Pearson Prentice Hall, 2010, p. 454.
325: George C. Edwards III, Martin P. Wattenberg, and Robert L. Lineberry, *Government in America: People, Politics, and Policy*, 14th ed. New York: Pearson Longman, 2009, p. 285.
326: Norm Christensen, *The Environment and You*. San Francisco: Pearson Benjamin Cummings, 2013, p. 153.
328: Rebecca J. Donatelle, *Health: The Basics*, Green Edition, 9th ed., pp. 94, 96, © 2011. Reprinted and electronically reproduced by permission of Pearson Education, Inc., Upper Saddle River, New Jersey.
329: James A. Fagin, *CJ 2011*. Upper Saddle River, NJ: Pearson Prentice Hall, 2012, p. 31.
340: Kathleen German and Bruce E. Gronbeck, *Principles of Public Speaking*, 14th ed. New York: Longman, 2001, pp. 38–39.
342: Stephen P. Robbins and Mary Coulter, *Management*, 11th ed. Boston: Pearson, 2012, pp. 71–72.
346: Saundra K. Ciccarelli and J. Noland White, *Psychology*, 2nd ed., pp. 169–171, © 2009. Adapted and electronically reproduced by permission of Pearson Education, Inc., Upper Saddle River, New Jersey.

Chapter 10

354: Nancy Clark, *Nancy Clark's Sports Nutrition Guidebook*. Champaign, IL: Human Kinetics, 2008, pp. 21–22.
356: Jenny Lawson, *Let's Pretend This Never Happened: (A Mostly True Memoir)*. New York: Berkley, p. 18.
357: David Batstone, excerpt from "Katja's Story: Human Trafficking Thrives in the New Global Economy," *Sojourners Magazine*, June 2006. © 2006 David Batstone. Reprinted by permission of the author.
359: Susan RoAne, *Face to Face: How to Reclaim the Personal Touch in a Digital World*. New York: Simon & Schuster, 2008, pp. 2–3.
360: Christopher Slobogin, *Privacy at Risk: The New Government Surveillance and the Fourth Amendment*. Chicago: University of Chicago Press, 2007, pp. 3–4.
361: Guy Harrison, *50 Popular Beliefs That People Think Are True*. Amherst, NY: Prometheus Books, 2012, p. 31.
362: John Perkins, Al Ridenhour, and Matt Kovsky, *Attack Proof: The Ultimate Guide to Personal Protection*. Champaign, IL: Human Kinetics, 2009, p. 7.
363: Cathy L. Greenberg and Barrett S. Avigdor, *What Happy Working Mothers Know*. Hoboken, NJ: John Wiley & Sons, 2009, p. 97.
364: Lucinda Holdforth, *Why Manners Matter: The Case for Civilized Behavior in a Barbarous World*. New York: Amy Einhorn Books/G. P. Putnam's Sons, 2009, pp. 16–17.

367: Stephen Crane, *The Red Badge of Courage*. New York: D. Appleton and Company, 1895.
367: Joseph Conrad, *The Arrow of Gold*. London: T. F. Unwin, 1919.
367: Percy Bysshe Shelley, *Adonais: An Elegy on the Death of John Keats* (1821).
368: Martin Luther King, Jr., Acceptance Speech, on the occasion of the award of the Nobel Peace Prize in Oslo, December 10, 1964.
368: Megan Comfort, *Doing Time Together: Love and Family in the Shadow of the Prison*, pp. 1–2. © 2007 by The University of Chicago. Reprinted by permission of The University of Chicago Press.
371: James M. Henslin, *Sociology: A Down-to-Earth Approach*, 10th ed., p. 153, © 2010. Printed and electronically reproduced by permission of Pearson Education, Inc., Upper Saddle River, New Jersey.
375: Ambrose Bierce, *The Devil's Dictionary* (1911).
375: Katrina Montoya, "A Collection for My Mother and Father," *Tribal College Journal of American Indian Higher Education*, vol. 24, no. 1 (Fall 2012), p. 52. © 2012 by Katrina Montoya. Reprinted by permission of the author.
377: Margaret S. Price, *The Special Needs Child and Divorce: A Practical Guide to Evaluating and Handling Cases*. Chicago: American Bar Association, Section of Family Law, 2009, p. 4.
379: Mark Savage, "Inside Yellowstone," *American Snowmobiler*, vol. 27, no. 4 (2013), p. 58.
380: John Steinbeck, *America and Indians*. New York: Viking Press, 1966, pp. 127–128.
380: Karen Olson, "Eat it Raw," *Utne Reader*, March/April 2002, pp. 20–22. Reproduced with permission of Ogden Publications, Inc. via Copyright Clearance Center.
385: Rebecca J. Donatelle and Lorraine G. Davis, *Access to Health*, 6th ed. Boston: Allyn and Bacon, 2000, p. 146.
385: Michael R. Solomon and Elnora W. Stuart, *The Brave New World of E-Commerce* (Supplement to *Marketing: Real People, Real Choices*). Upper Saddle River, NJ: Prentice Hall, 2001, p. 17.
385: Joe E. Kincheloe et al., *Contextualizing Teaching*. Boston: Allyn & Bacon, 2000, pp. 90–91.
386: Michael R. Solomon and Elnora W. Stuart, *Marketing: Real People, Real Choices*, 2nd ed. Upper Saddle River, NJ: Prentice Hall, 2000, p. 59.
386: Palmira Brummett et al., *Civilization: Past & Present*, 9th ed. New York: Longman, 2000, pp. 578–579.
387: Cynthia Audet, "Scar," *The Sun*, Issue 325, January 2003, p. 96. © 2003 by Cynthia Audet. Reprinted by permission of the author.
389: Warren J. Keegan and Mark C. Green, *Global Marketing*, 7th ed., p. 282, © 2013. Printed and electronically reproduced by permission of Pearson Education, Inc., Upper Saddle River, New Jersey.

Chapter 11

394: Michael Smith, "Review: *World War Z*" from *Tulsa World*, June 22, 2013. Courtesy *Tulsa World*.
400: Scott Dobson-Mitchell, "Beat the Clock," *Maclean's*, vol. 122, issue 44 (November 16, 2009), p. 114.
400: Yair Amichai-Hamburger, "Depression Through Technology," *New Scientist* (December 19, 2009), p. 28.
404: Linda Papadopoulos, *What Men Say, What Women Hear*. New York: Simon Spotlight, 2009, p. 22.
409: Carol Dweck, quoted in Andrew Postman, "Raising a Good Loser," *Good Housekeeping*, vol. 250, no. 1 (January 2010), p. 85.
409: Ben S. Bernanke, *Monetary Policy and the Housing Bubble*. Speech at the Annual Meeting of the American Economic Association, Atlanta, Georgia, January 3, 2010.

409: Carol R. Ember and Melvin R. Ember, *Cultural Anthropology*, 13th ed. Upper Saddle River, NJ: Pearson Prentice Hall, 2011, pp. 3–4.

410: William E. Thompson and Joseph V. Hickey, *Society in Focus*, 7th ed. Boston: Pearson Allyn & Bacon, 2011, p. 216.

413: Danny Stone, "Simple Explanations Ease Communication," *Buffalo News*, February 10, 2013. © 2013 by Danny Stone. Reprinted by permission of the author.

415: Michael R. Solomon, *Consumer Behavior: Buying, Having, and Being*, 5th ed. Upper Saddle River, NJ: Pearson Prentice Hall, 2002, p. 19.

420: George C. Edwards III, Martin P. Wattenberg, and Robert L. Lineberry, *Government in America: People, Politics, and Policy*, 9th ed. New York: Pearson Longman, 2000, p. 685.

420: George C. Edwards III, Martin P. Wattenberg, and Robert L. Lineberry, *Government in America: People, Politics, and Policy*, 9th ed. New York: Pearson Longman, 2000, pp. 426–427.

425: Rosie Molinary, "Reality Check: Reality TV Does Not Make You Feel Better," rosiemolinary.com, February 18, 2013. Copyright © 2013 Rosie Molinary. Reprinted by permission of the author.

Part VI

441: Bruce Holland Rogers, "Little Brother™" copyright © Bruce Holland Rogers. From *Strange Horizons*, October 30, 2000. Used by permission of the author.

447: Sara Gruen, excerpted from *Water for Elephants*, copyright © 2006 by Sara Gruen. Reprinted by permission of Algonquin Books of Chapel Hill and HarperCollinsCanada. All rights reserved.

Part VII

455: Will Leitch, "Is Football Wrong?" Originally published in the August 20, 2012 issue of *New York Magazine*. Reprinted by permission of the publisher.

460: Nadia Shahram, "Women Are Subject to Violence and Discrimination by Both the State and Society," *Buffalo News*, February 17, 2013. © 2013 Nadia Shahram. Reprinted by permission of the author.

467: Katherine Bindley, "Teachers Texting Students: Should Schools Ban or Encourage?" From *The Huffington Post*, April 16, 2012. © 2012 by TheHuffingtonPost.com, Inc. All rights reserved. Used by permission and protected by the Copyright Laws of the United States. The printing, copying, redistribution, or retransmission of this Content without express written permission is prohibited. www.huffingtonpost.com

472: Steven Reinberg, "Driving While on the Cell Phone Worse than Driving Drunk," *HealthDay*, June 29, 2006. Copyright © 2006 HealthDay. All rights reserved. Reprinted by permission.

477: Sam Harris, "Why I Own Guns," *The Week*, February 1, 2013. © 2013 by Sam Harris. A longer version of this article appeared originally at SamHarris.org. Reprinted with permission of the author.

484: Mark Follman, "More Guns, More Mass Shootings – Coincidence?" *Mother Jones*, December 15, 2012. © 2012, Foundation for National Progress. Reprinted with permission.

490: Stewart Brand, "The Case for Reviving Extinct Species," *National Geographic News*, March 11, 2013. © 2013 by Stewart Brand. Reprinted by permission of the author.

496: Stuart Pimm, "The Case Against Species Revival," *National Geographic News*, March 12, 2013. © 2013 by Stuart Pimm. Reprinted by permission of the author.

PHOTO CREDITS

Cover: Corey Rich/Getty Images; **Working Together icon:** Andres Rodriguez/Alamy; **1:** Corepics/Fotolia; **34:** Duncan Noakes/Fotolia; **38:** Gerald Herbert/AP Images; **63:** Alex Cao/Getty Images; **65:** Steve Gschmeissner/Science Photo Library/Alamy; **70:** Marili Forastieri/Getty Images; **80:** Lars Borges/Getty Images; **91:** Emily Parrino/Kentucky New Era/AP Images; **96:** Asia Images Group/Getty Images; **97:** Hugo Felix/Shutterstock; **99:** Elke Van de Velde/Getty Images; **103:** Marzky Ragsac Jr./Fotolia; **122:** Bonnie Kamin/PhotoEdit; **144:** Pavel Losevsky/Fotolia; **149:** Will Oliver/AFP/Getty Images; **150 (l):** Zakaz/Fotolia; **(c):** Dorling Kindersley/Getty Images; **(r):** Cedrov/Fotolia; **154:** PerfectMatch/Fotolia; **156:** Eric Thayer/Reuters/Corbis; **164:** Msh Foto/Fotolia; **165:** © The New Yorker Collection 1979 Mischa Richter from cartoonbank.com. All rights reserved.; **176 (t):** Frans Lantus/Corbis; **(b):** Moment/Cultura/Corbis; **182:** Toa555/Fotolia; **184:** Network Productions/The Image Works; **187:** LM Otero/AP Images; **189:** Joshua Kors; **193:** Brent Hofacker/Fotolia; **203 (t):** Carolyn Kaster/AP Images; **(b):** Saul Loeb/AFP/Getty Images; **220:** Sean Gardner/Reuters/Corbis; **223:** Deviantart/Fotolia; **240 (t):** Mgkuijpers/Fotolia; **(b):** Mgkuijpers/Fotolia; **247:** Vrabel Peter1/Fotolia; **250:** Bruce Benedict/Corbis; **254:** Michael Ireland/Fotolia; **256:** Superstock; **266:** Dogs/Fotolia; **270:** Diego Rivera, Mural depicting Detroit Industry, 1932–33. Fresco. The Detroit Institute of Arts. gift of Edsel B. Ford/The Bridgeman Art Library/(c)© 2011 Banco de México Diego Rivera Frida Kahlo Museums Trust, Mexico, D.F./Artists Rights Society (ARS), New York; **273:** Diane Bendareff/AP Images; **277 (t):** Lawrence Manning/Corbis; **(c):** Fotog/Getty Images; **(b):** Tombaky/Fotolia; **280:** Paulo Fridman/Corbis; **281:** David McNew/Getty Images; **282:** Stockbyte/Getty Images; **298:** DigitalVision/Getty Images; **318:** Valerijs Kostreckis/Alamy; **322:** Chris Garrett/Getty Images; **328:** JGI/Jamie Grill/Gettyimages; **347:** Doug Menuez/Getty Images; **352:** © The New Yorker Collection William Haefeli from cartoonbank.com. All rights reserved.; **360:** Scientifica/Visuals Unlimited/Corbis; **364:** Auremar/Fotolia; **369:** Ed Kashi/VII/Corbis; **389:** Iordani/Fotolia; **394:** Pictorial Press Ltd/Alamy; **412:** Ian Shaw/Alamy; **425:** Berc/Fotolia; **430 (tl):** The Granger Collection Ltd.; **(tr):** Portrait Essentials/Alamy; **(bl):** Penguin USA; **(br):** Charles Rex Arbogast/AP Images; **452 (tl):** Arnie Sachs/CNP/Newscom; **(tr):** Hindustan Times/Newscom; **(cl):** Ariel Skelley/Blend Images/Corbis; **(cr):** Benicce/Shutterstock; **(bl):** Timur1970/Fotolia; **(br):** Andrew Nelmerm/Dorling Kindersley, Ltd; **491:** VPC Travel Photo/Alamy; **496:** Edmund Lowe Photography/Getty Images.

Index